The Poverty of Theory & Other Essays

E. P. THOMPSON

The Poverty
of Theory
&
Other Essays

MERLIN·LONDON

Printed in the United States of America

ISBN 085036 232 6

Contents

Foreword i

The Poverty of Theory or
  An Orrery of Errors (1978) 1

Outside the Whale (1960) 211

The Peculiarities of the English (1965) 245

An Open Letter to Leszek Kolakowski (1973) 303

A Note on the Texts 403

Foreword

I commenced to reason in my thirty-third year, and, despite my best efforts, I have never been able to shake the habit off.

I first acquired the habit in 1956, when, with John Saville and others, I was involved in producing a duplicated journal of discussion within the Communist Party, *The Reasoner*. Reasoning was disliked by the leadership of the Party, and the editors were suspended from membership. Since this suspension coincided with the repression of the Hungarian revolution (October/November 1956)—and the exodus of some 10,000 members from the British Communist Party—it was decided that our offensive activities might best be continued outside that structure, and, with the aid of other comrades, *The New Reasoner* was founded in 1957. This quarterly journal continued for 2½ years. It then merged with *Universities & Left Review* to form the *New Left Review*.

The first essay in this book, "Outside the Whale", comes from this moment. By 1963 distinct currents were evident in the first New Left, and the *Review's* founders parted from the *Review*. The second essay, "The Peculiarities of the English", was written two years after this, and offers a definition of certain disagreements. In 1967 some of us came together again, and (under the editorship of Raymond Williams) we published the *May Day Manifesto*. But this analysis and this political initiative were swept brusquely aside, in 1968, by the May events in Paris, by the revival of wages-based (but often a-political) industrial militancy, and by the repression of the Prague "Spring." The first two events appeared to offer to the impatient very much more rapid routes to something called "revolution", while the third event necessarily induced in the minds of those committed to a "Manifesto" perspective an accession of pessimism. In any event, the theatrical and irrational character of some of what went as "the New Left" among the Western intelligentsia in these years tended to place reasoning at a discount.

The mainland of the British Labour movement has never been greatly hospitable towards theoretical exercises; and, when one considers the Theory which has been offered to it, from both "Right" and "Left", this may have saved it from disasters additional to those which it regularly, and in the normal political course, brings upon itself. But at this same time, odd things took place in the archipelago to the "Left" of the Labour Party. Here Theory and practice split into two halves. Theory presented itself in ever more doctrinaire and intellectualised forms, as resurgent "Marxism."

i

But an *anti*-intellectual practice also continued, which sometimes called itself "Marxism" as well. This was not the *ouvrierisme* of a pragmatic working-class movement, but, quite often, the less excusable anti-intellectualism and cult of violence of intellectuals.

I mention this to explain a sense of isolation into which a number of us were thrust in those years. However much the modes changed (and they changed very fast), reasoning was not one of them. It was a time for reason to sulk in its tent—a tactic for which there are historical precedents. We remained identified with the "Left" by common solidarities and common campaigns (as against the Vietnam War). But at the same time much of this Left did not want our arguments and was developing ideas, attitudes and practices inimical to the rational, libertarian and egalitarian principles to which we were committed. If one offered to argue, one was answered, not with argument but with labels ("moralism", "empiricism", "liberal" illusions), or, commonly, with a biological dismissal (the "generation game") which foreclosed further argument.

It was a real sense of isolation and even of alienation from some part of that New Left and from much of that "Marxism" which must explain the personal tone—and even postures—of my "Open Letter to Leszek Kolakowski" (1973). I should perhaps apologise for some of the tone of that letter, and for writing what was in fact a very general argument (in which many others were concerned) in the form of a private meditation. And I do so apologise: I ought not to have reduced so general a case to such personal terms.

But I don't apologise too much. The sense of isolation was real, this was my way of getting out of the tent; and I had to write it in that way. For some years the intellectual "Left" had been in a state of overheated paranoia, and one could not simply signal an uncomplicated adhesion to it. Every pharisee was being more revolutionary than the next; some of them have made such hideous faces that they are likely to be stuck like that for life. That "Left", just then, was not a very comradely place; most of the ushers at the doors were trying to show one out, in order to have proof that one was never serious about being in.

There have been a few signs, in the last year or two, that some part of the intellectual Left has been regaining its reason. It is in this hope that I am publishing this book. It is intended as the first of two volumes. In the second volume, which may be published next year, I will bring together directly-political writings from the past twenty years, and will write a more thorough account of the political context and practical initiatives of the first New Left. This may afford some correction to a certain abstraction and absence of realist texture in the present collection—an absence consequent upon the fragmentation of the first New Left after 1963, and the failure of some of us to maintain an active political presence correlative to our theoretical positions.

I do not suppose that I have gifts as a "political theorist." There is, perhaps, too much sensibility mixed up with my thought—a relapse into an "English idiom" which may confuse international exchanges. Yet the experiences of my lifetime are ones which require a response which cannot be simply negotiated within the stratagems of "Theory." The essays in this book are related to each other by two common themes: the exploration of the crisis within international Communism which became fully declared in 1956, and the critical examination of the Marxist tradition. In the first essay, "The Poverty of Theory", I bring these themes together once more. My hope is that I have argued these positions consistently, and over many years, and that these essays represent some part of the political experience of the past three decades. It is foolish to apologise further. In publishing this work it becomes public property, to be made use of as readers see fit.

There is one further reservation to be made. I find, to my surprise, that over these years I have been carrying a banner inscribed with "populist socialism"; and, in the company of that unlikely "English nationalist", Raymond Williams, I have been developing a "cultural nationalism" marked by "romantic excess and indiscriminate empiricism." (I cull this wisdom from Tom Nairn, *The Break-Up of Britain*, 1977, pp. 303-304).

Since I cannot now anticipate whether I shall have the time and temper to take up Tom Nairn when I put together the second volume of *Reasoning*, I find it necessary to make a plain repudiation. At no time have I ever held up a banner of "populist socialism." If there has been a banner, it has been that of socialist internationalism. My political consciousness cut its teeth on the causes of Spain and of Indian independence, chewed on a World War (in which I played a bit part), and has been offered an international diet ever since—Yugoslavia and Bulgaria, the Peace Movement and the Korean War, and thence to "1956", Suez, Cyprus, Algeria, Cuba, Vietnam, Chile. "1956" was an international confrontation within the Communist movement, and the first New Left developed, for a brief moment, an international presence.

The "banner" of socialist internationalism has become tattered indeed in the last two decades, and on every side. It has not been one to carry proudly aloft. At the most, one has carried a few sheets of paper, and often one has been reduced to muttering to oneself. The commitment has been to an "International" of the imagination, which has had only fleeting embodiment in real movements, detached unequivocally from both Stalinism and from complicity with the reasons of capitalist power. To maintain that commitment has been to be an "alien" not only within this country but within great sections of the purported socialist and Marxist movement itself.

In the last few years it has not always been easy to maintain this position. Some dialogue continues (for example, with Roy Medvedev and Soviet dissidents of his persuasion). What has happened more—partly through a general pressure of the times, partly as a consequence of my own historical writing—has been entry into an increasingly international theoretical discourse. I have gained very much from this, and from increasingly close exchanges with American, Indian, French, German, and other friends.

But internationalism, in this sense, ought not to consist in lying prostrate before the ("Western Marxist") theorists of our choice, or in seeking to imitate their modes of discourse. The reasons why this kind of imitation can never produce more than a sickly native growth are complex. Mimesis, for some reason, can copy but cannot originate or create. The "adoption" of other traditions—that is, adoption which has not been fully worked through, interrogated, and translated into the terms of our own traditions—can very often mean no more than the evacuation of the real places of conflict within our own intellectual culture, as well as the loss of real political relations with our own people.

To articulate the past historically, Walter Benjamin said, "means to seize hold of a memory as it flashes up at a moment of danger." For several decades we have been living through a continuous "moment of danger", so that our history and past culture presents itself to a danger-alerted mind, searching for evidences of democratic endurance and resources of cultural strength and growth. And some part of that cultural inheritance cannot but be "national" in character, with its own particular pressures, resilience and idiom; this must constitute not only some part of what we think and feel about but also some part of what we think and feel with. These resources are unusually large and complex in this island; they are, by no means, always resources of strength, but British historians, of the Marxist tradition, who have sharply interrogated them, have not found them to be as inert and regressive as they appear in Nairn's lampoons. If a future is to be made, it must be made in some part from these. It will not be made out of some Theorist's head.

If I may pass from the ridiculous to the sublime, I do not think that the fact that Gramsci grounded his thought upon an interrogation of Italian history and culture made him into something less than an internationalist. And internationalism ought to consist, not only in listening attentively to an international discourse, but in contributing to it on our own account. We are not truly present in any conversation if we are only silent auditors. So that I would like to suppose that I am not some English "populist socialist" but a socialist internationalist speaking in an English tongue. I was influenced once by Kolakowski, and I have attended to Althusser. And then I have *argued back*. Internationalism should not be like a net-work of television stations, each beaming national programmes to passive viewers in alien lands. It should be a concourse, an exchange. Argument is its true sign.

iv

Acknowledgements, in such a book as this, must either be inadequate or indefinitely prolonged. These arguments have been part of the work of a diffuse movement—part national, part international—and I owe everything to that. In the second volume I will refer more particularly to the comrades who supported *The New Reasoner* and to those who initiated the New Left. Here I will simply thank John Saville and Ralph Miliband, in whose *Socialist Register* two of these essays first appeared; Martin Eve, the publisher of the *Register* and of this volume; Leszek Kolakowski, for receiving my intemperate letter, and then answering back with reasons; and Dorothy Thompson, for reasoning with and against me for twenty and more years—she does not agree with all my reasons, but without her argument they would have been worse. None of these friends, of course, are responsible for my views—and least of all for "The Poverty of Theory."

Worcester   *February, 1978*

"To leave error unrefuted is to encourage intellectual immorality." Karl Marx

The Poverty of Theory or An Orrery of Errors

"Disciples do own unto masters only a temporary belief and a suspension of their own judgement until they be fully instructed, and not an absolute resignation or perpetual captivity. . . So let great authors have their due, as time, which is the author of authors, be not deprived of his due, which is, further and further to discover truth."

Francis Bacon

"Reason, or the ratio of all we have already known, is not the same that it shall be when we know more."

William Blake

i

For some time, for many decades, the materialist conception of history—the first-born intellectual child of Marx and Engels—has been growing in self-confidence. As a mature practice ("historical materialism") it is perhaps the strongest discipline deriving from the Marxist tradition. Even in my own lifetime as a historian—and in the work of my own compatriots—the advances have been considerable, and one had supposed these to be advances in *knowledge*.

This is not to say that this knowledge is finite, or subject to some "proof" of positivistic scientism. Nor is it to suppose that the advance has been unilinear and un-problematic. Sharp disagreements exist, and complex problems remain not only unsolved but scarcely even disclosed. It is possible that the very success of historical materialism as a practice has encouraged a conceptual lethargy which is now bringing down upon our heads its necessary revenge. And this is the more possible in those parts of the English-speaking world where a vigorous practice of historical materialism has been conducted within an inherited "empirical"

1

idiom of discourse which is reproduced by strong educational and cultural traditions.[1]

All this is possible, even probable. Even so, the case should not be over-stated. For what a philosopher, who has only a casual acquaintance with historical practice, may glance at and then dismiss, with a ferocious scowl, as "empiricism", may in fact be the result of arduous confrontations, pursued both in conceptual engagements (the definition of appropriate questions, the elaboration of hypotheses, and the exposure of ideological attributions in pre-existing historiography) and also in the interstices of historical method itself. And the Marxist historiography which now has an international presence has contributed significantly not only to its own self-criticism and maturation (in *theoretical* ways), but also to imposing (by repeated controversies, much arduous intellectual labour, and some polemic) its presence upon orthodox historiography: imposing (in Althusser's sense) its own—or Marx's—"problematic" upon significant areas of historical enquiry.

Engaged in these confrontations we had, I suppose, neglected our lines of theoretical supply. For in the moment when we seemed to be poised for further advances, we have been suddenly struck from the rear—and not from a rear of manifest "bourgeois ideology" but from a rear claiming to be more Marxist than Marx. From the quarter of Louis Althusser and his numerous followers there has been launched an unmeasured assault upon "historicism." The advances of historical materialism, its supposed "knowledge", have rested—it turns out—upon one slender and rotten epistemological pillar ("empiricism"); when Althusser submitted this pillar to a stern interrogation it shuddered and crumbled to dust; and the whole enterprise of historical materialism collapsed in ruins around it. Not only does it turn out that men have never "made their own history" at all (being only *träger* or vectors of ulterior structural determinations) but it is also revealed that the enterprise of historical materialism—the attainment of historical knowledge—has been misbegotten from the start, since "real" history is unknowable and cannot be said to exist. In the words of two post-Althusserians, whose merit it is to have carried Althusserian logic to its own *reductio ad absurdam*, "History is condemned by the nature of its object to empiricism." But empiricism, as we know, is a disreputable manifestation of bourgeois ideology: "Despite the empiricist claims of historical practice the real object of history is inaccessible to knowledge." It follows that:

> Marxism, as a theoretical and a political practice, gains nothing from its association with historical writing and historical research. The study of history is not only scientifically but also politically valueless.[2]

The project to which many lifetimes, in successive generations, have been given is thus exposed as an illusion (if "innocent") and something worse (if not). And yet historical materialists, of my own generation, have been slow to acknowledge their own abject exposure. They go on working in their old, reprobate ways. Some are too busy to have read the indictments entered against them, but those who have appear to have reacted in one of two ways. Many have glanced at the antagonist in a casual way, seeing it as a weird apparition, a freak of intellectual fashion, which, if they close their eyes, will in time go away. They may be right in the first assumption—that Althusserian "Marxism" is an intellectual freak—but it will not for that reason go away. Historians should know that freaks, if tolerated—and even flattered and fed—can show astonishing influence and longevity. (After all, to any rational mind, the greater part of the history of ideas is a history of freaks.) This particular freak (I will argue) has now lodged itself firmly in a particular social *couche*, the bourgeois *lumpen-intelligentsia*[3]: aspirant intellectuals, whose amateurish intellectual preparation disarms them before manifest absurdities and elementary philosophical blunders, and whose innocence in intellectual *practice* leaves them paralysed in the first web of scholastic argument which they encounter; and *bourgeois*, because while many of them would *like* to be "revolutionaries", they are themselves the products of a particular "conjuncture" which has broken the circuits between intellectuality and practical experience (both in real political movements, and in the actual segregation imposed by contemporary institutional structures), and hence they are able to perform *imaginary* revolutionary psycho-dramas (in which each outbids the other in adopting ferocious verbal postures) while in fact falling back upon a very old tradition of bourgeois élitism for which Althusserian theory is exactly tailored. Whereas their forebears were political interventionists, they tend more often to be diversionists (enclosed and imprisoned within their own drama) or "internal emigrées."[4] Their practical importance remains, however considerable, in disorganising the constructive intellectual discourse of the Left, and in reproducing continually the élitist division between theory and practice. Maybe, if we suffer experiences sharp enough, the freak *will* eventually go away, and many of its devotees may be reclaimed for a serious political and intellectual movement. But it is time that we pushed it along the road.

The other reaction commonly found among historical materialists is more reprehensible—that of complicity. They glance at Althusserian Marxism and do not wholly understand it (nor like what they understand), but they accept it, as "a" Marxism. Philosophers cannot be expected to understand history (or anthropology, or literature, or sociology) but Althusser is a philosopher doing his own thing. And some conceptual rigour is no doubt necessary; perhaps even bits can be borrowed ("over-determination", "instances")? After all, we are all Marxists together. In this way, a sort of tacit compromise is negotiated, although most of the negotiation is made up of silence, and *all* the negotiation consists in ceding ground to Althusser. For Althusser has never offered compromise of any kind: and certainly not to "historicism", "humanism" and "empiricism."

This is reprehensible because it is theoretically unprincipled. Althusser and his acolytes challenge, centrally, historical materialism itself. They do not offer to modify it but to displace it. In exchange they offer an a-historical theoreticism which, at the first examination, discloses itself as idealism. How then is it possible for these two to co-exist within one single tradition? Either a very extraordinary mutation has been taking place, in the last few years, in the Marxist tradition: or that tradition is now breaking apart into two—or several—parts. What is being threatened— what is now actively rejected—is the entire tradition of substantive Marxist historical and political analysis, and its accumulating (if provisional) knowledge. And if (as I suppose) Althusserian Marxism is not only an idealism but has many of the attributes of a *theology*, then what is at issue, within the Marxist tradition, is the defence of reason itself.

ii

I will offer at the outset a map of where I mean to go, since there will inevitably be certain detours, and the doubling back upon my own tracks. I shall direct my central attention to Althusser—and to the critical formative texts, *For Marx* and *Reading Capital*—and will not spend time over his numerous progeny. It is true that many of these disown their master, and that others are influenced only in certain areas of their thought. But I hope that some of my general arguments (in particular on "empiricism" and "moralism") may be taken to include them also. I apologise for this neglect; but life is too short to follow (for example) Hindess and Hirst to every one of their theoreticist lairs. Nor shall I take up the lists against a more formidable opponent, Poulantzas, who—with Althusser—repeatedly fails to understand the *historical* categories (of class, ideology, etc.) employed by Marx. Another time, perhaps. Let us stay now with the Aristotle of the new Marxist idealism.

I will argue the following propositions, and examine them in sequence. 1) Althusser's epistemology is derivative from a limited kind of academic learning-process, and has no general validity; 2) As a result he has no category (or way of handling) "experience" (or social being's impingement upon social consciousness); hence he falsifies the "dialogue" with empirical evidence inherent in knowledge-production, and in Marx's own practice, and thereby falls continually into modes of thought designated in the Marxist tradition as "idealist"; 3) In particular he confuses the necessary empirical dialogue with *empiricism*, and consistently mis-represents (in the most naive ways) the practice of historical materialism (including Marx's own practice); 4) The resultant critique of "historicism" is at certain points *identical* to the specifically anti-Marxist critique of historicism (as represented by Popper), although the authors derive from this opposite conclusions.

This argument will take us some way on our road. I will then propose: 5) Althusser's structuralism is a structuralism of *stasis*, departing from Marx's own historical method; 6) Hence Althusser's conceptual universe has no adequate categories to explain contradiction or change—or class struggle; 7) These critical weaknesses explain why Althusser must be silent (or evasive) as to other important categories, among them "economic" and "needs"; 8) From which it follows that Althusser (and his progeny) find themselves unable to handle, except in the most abstract and theoretic way, questions of value, culture—and political theory.

When these elementary propositions have been established (or, as Althusser will have it, "proved") we may then stand back from the whole elaborate and sophistical structure. We may even attempt another kind of "reading" of his words. And, if we are not exhausted, we may propose some questions of a different kind: how has this extraordinary fracture occurred in the Marxist tradition? How are we to understand Althusserian structuralism, not in its self-evaluation as "science", but *as ideology?* What were the specific conditions for the genesis and maturation of this ideology and its rapid replication in the West? And what is the political significance of this unmeasured assault upon historical materialism?

iii

I commence my argument at a manifest disadvantage. Few spectacles would be more ludicrous than that of an English historian—and, moreover, one manifestly self-incriminated of empirical practices—attempting to offer epistemological correction to a rigorous Parisian philosopher.

I can sense, as I stare at the paper before me, the shadowy faces of an expectant audience, scarcely able to conceal their rising mirth. I don't intend to gratify them. I don't understand Althusser's propositions as to the relation between the "real world" and "knowledge", and therefore I can't expose myself in a discussion of them.

It's true that I've *tried* to understand them. Throughout *For Marx* the question as to how these "raw materials" from the real world arrive in the laboratory of theoretical practice (to be processed according to Generalities I, II and III) cries out for some answer. But the opportunity for disclosure is passed by. Turning to *Reading Capital* we learn, with rising excitement, that now, at last, an answer will be given. Instead, we are offered anti-climax. We first endure some tedium and more exasperation, as a ritual commination against "empiricism" is conducted; even a mind without philosophic rigour cannot overlook the fact that Althusser continually confuses and conflates the empirical mode (or techniques) of investigation with the quite different ideological formation, *empiricism*, and, moreover, simplifies his own polemics by caricaturing even this "empiricism", and ascribing to it, indiscriminately and erroneously, "essentialist" procedures of abstraction.[5] But at length, after fifty pages, we arrive at—what?

> We can say, then, that the mechanism of production of the knowledge effect lies in the mechanism which underlies the action of the forms of order in the scientific discourse of the proof. (*R.C.* 67)

Thirty-three words. And then silence.

If I understand these words, then I find them disgraceful. For we have been led all this way only to be offered a re-statement, in new terms, of the original question. Knowledge effects arrive, in the form of "raw materials" (Generalities I, which are already artefacts of culture, with more or less ideological impurity), obediently as "the scientific discourse of the proof" demands. I must explain my objection: and, first, what my objection is *not*.

I don't object to the fact that Althusser offers no "guarantees" as to an identity between the "real" object and its conceptual representation. One would expect any such formal guarantee to be of doubtful efficacy: even a casual acquaintance with philosophy suggests that such guarantees have a short term of validity and contain many clauses in small print which exonerate the guarantor from liability. Nor do I object to the fact that Althusser has abandoned the weary ground of attempting to elucidate a one-to-one correspondence between this "real" material event or object and that perception/intuition/sense-impression/concept. It would, perhaps, have been more honest if he had frankly confessed that, in doing so, he was also abandoning certain of Lenin's propositions in *Materialism and Empirio-Criticism*—but for the least syllable of Lenin he professes a religious awe.[6] And he certainly might have confessed that, in shifting his ground, he was *following* and not setting philosophical fashion.

In the old days (one supposes) when the philosopher, labouring by lamp-light in his study, came to this point in his argument, he set down his pen, and looked around for an object in the real world to interrogate. Very commonly that object was the nearest one to hand: his writing-table. "Table," he said, "how do I know that you exist, and, if you do, how do I know that my concept, table, represents your real existence?" The table would look back without blinking, and interrogate the philosopher in its turn. It was an exacting exchange, and according to which one was the victor in the confrontation, the philosopher would inscribe himself as idealist or a materialist. Or so one must suppose from the frequency with which tables appear. Today the philosopher interrogates instead the word: a pre-given linguistic artefact, with an indistinct social genesis and *with a history.*

And here I begin to find terms for my objection. It is, first, that Althusser interrogates this word (or this "raw material" or this "knowledge effect") too briefly. It exists only to be worked up by theoretical practice (Generality II) to structural conceptualisation or concrete knowledge (Generality III). Althusser is as curt with linguistics and with the sociology of knowledge as he is with history or anthropology. His raw material (object of knowledge) is an inert, pliant kind of stuff, with neither inertia nor energies of its own, awaiting passively its manufacture into knowledge. It may contain gross ideological impurities, to be sure, but these may be purged in the alembic of theoretical practice.

Second, this raw material appears to present itself for processing as discrete mental events ("facts", *idées reçus,* commonplace concepts): and it also presents itself with discretion. Now I don't wish to jest with the very serious difficulties encountered by philosophers in this critical epistemological area. Since every philosopher encounters them I must believe that these difficulties are indeed immense. And, at this level, I can hope to add nothing to their clarification. But a historian in the Marxist tradition is entitled to remind a Marxist philosopher that historians also are concerned, every day, in their practice, with the formation of, and with the tensions within, social consciousness. Our observation is rarely singular: this object of knowledge, this event, this elaborated concept. Our concern, more commonly, is with multiple evidences, whose inter-relationship is, indeed, an object of our enquiry. Or, if we isolate the singular evidence for particular scrutiny, that evidence does not stand compliantly like a table for interrogation: it stirs, in the medium of time, before our eyes. These stirrings, these events, if they are within "social being" seem often to impinge upon, thrust into, break against, existent social consciousness. They propose new problems, and, above all, they continually give rise to *experience*—a category which, however imperfect it may be, is indispensible to the historian, since it comprises the mental and emotional response, whether of an individual or of a social group, to many inter-related events or to many repetitions of the same kind of event.

It may perhaps be argued that experience is a very low level of mentation indeed: that it can produce no more than the grossest "common sense", ideologically-contaminated "raw material", scarcely qualifying to enter the laboratory of Generalities I. I don't think that this is so; on the contrary, I consider that the supposition that this is so is a very characteristic delusion of intellectuals, who suppose that ordinary mortals are stupid. In my own view, the truth is more nuanced: experience is valid and effective but within determined limits: the farmer "knows" his seasons, the sailor "knows" his seas, but both may remain mystified about kingship and cosmology.

But the point immediately before us is not the limits of experience, but the manner of its arrival or production. Experience arises spontaneously within social being, but it does not arise without thought; it arises because men and women (and not only philosophers) are rational, and they think about what is happening to themselves and their world. If we are to employ the (difficult) notion that social being determines social consciousness, how are we to suppose that this is so? It will surely not be supposed that "being" is here, as gross materiality from which all ideality has been abstracted, and that "consciousness" (as abstract ideality) is there?[7] For we cannot conceive of any form of social being independently of its organising concepts and expectations, nor could social being reproduce itself for a day without thought. What we mean is that changes take place within social being, which give rise to changed *experience:* and this experience is *determining,* in the sense that it exerts pressures upon existent social consciousness, proposes new questions, and affords much of the material which the more elaborated intellectual exercises are about.[8] Experience, one supposes, constitutes some part of the raw material which is offered up to the procedures of the scientific discourse of the proof. Indeed, some intellectual practitioners have suffered experiences themselves.

Experience, then, does not arrive obediently in the way that Althusser proposes. One suspects that some very aetiolated notion of knowledge is here. He has offered to us less an epistemology which takes into account the actual formative motions of consciousness than a description of certain procedures of academic life. He has abandoned the lamp-lit study and broken off the dialogue with an exhausted table: he is now within the emplacements of the École Normale Superieur. The data have arrived, obediently processed by graduates and research assistants at a rather low level of conceptual development (G I), they have been interrogated and sorted into categories by a rigorous seminar of aspirant professors (G II), and the G III is about to ascend the rostrum and propound the conclusions of concrete knowledge.

But outside the university precincts another kind of knowledge-production is going on all the time. I will agree that it is not always rigorous. I am not careless of intellectual values nor unaware of the difficulty of their attainment. But I must remind a Marxist philosopher that knowledges have been and still are formed outside the academic procedures. Nor have these been, in the test of practice, negligible. They have assisted men and women to till the fields, to construct houses, to support elaborate social organisations, and even, on occasion, to challenge effectively the conclusions of academic thought.

Nor is this all. Althusser's account also leaves out the thrusting-forth of the ''real world'', spontaneously and not at all decorously, proposing hitherto unarticulated questions to philosophers. Experience does not wait discreetly outside their offices, waiting for the moment at which the discourse of the proof will summon it into attendance. Experience walks in without knocking at the door, and announces deaths, crises of subsistence, trench warfare, unemployment, inflation, genocide. People starve: their survivors think in new ways about the market. People are imprisoned: in prison they meditate in new ways about the law. In the face of such general experiences old conceptual systems may crumble and new problematics insist upon their presence. Such imperative presentation of knowledge effects is not allowed for in Althusser's epistemology, which is that of a recipient—a manufacturer who is not concerned with the genesis of his raw material so long as it arrives to time.

What Althusser overlooks is the *dialogue* between social being and social consciousness. Obviously, this dialogue goes in both directions. If social being is not an inert table which cannot refute a philosopher with its legs, then neither is social consciousness a passive recipient of "reflections" of that table. Obviously, consciousness, whether as unself-conscious culture, or as myth, or as science, or law, or articulated ideology, thrusts back into being in its turn: as being is thought so thought also is lived—people may, within limits, *live* the social or sexual expectations which are imposed upon them by dominant conceptual categories.

It had been habitual among Marxists—indeed, it had once been thought to be a distinguishing methodological priority of Marxism—to stress the determining pressures of being upon consciousness; although in recent years much "Western Marxism" has tilted the dialogue heavily back towards ideological domination. This difficult question, which many of us have often addressed, may be left aside for the moment; it is in any case a question more usefully resolved by historical and cultural analysis than by theoretical pronouncements. If I have stressed the first party in the dialogue rather than the second, it is because Althusser has almost nothing to say about it—and refuses to attend to the accounts of historians or anthropologists who have. His silence here is both a guilty one and one necessary to his purpose. It is a consequence of his prior determination to wall up the least aperture through which "empiricism" might enter.

iv

Let us resume. Althusser's "epistemology" is founded upon an account of theoretical procedures which is at every point derivative not only from academic intellectual disciplines but from *one* (and at the most three) highly-specialised disciplines.[9] The discipline is, of course, his own: philosophy: but of a particular Cartesian tradition of logical exegesis, marked at its origin by the pressures of Catholic theology, modified by the monism of Spinoza (whose influence saturates Althusser's work[10]), and marked at its conclusion by a particular Parisian dialogue between phenomenology, existentialism and Marxism. Thus the procedures from which an "epistemology" is derived are not those of "philosophy" in general, but of one particular moment of its presence. There is no reason why philosophers should necessarily identify their own procedures with those of every other kind of knowledge-production: and many have been at pains to make distinctions. It is an elementary confusion, a function of academic imperialism, and it is a tendency rather easy to correct. And it has been, very often, so corrected.

But not by Althusser. On the contrary, he makes a virtue of his own theoretical imperialism. The peculiarity of certain branches of philosophy and of mathematics is that these are, to an unusual degree, self-enclosed and self-replicating: logic and quantity examine their own materials, their own procedures. This Althusser offers as a paradigm of the very procedures of *Theory*: G II (theoretical practice) works upon G I to produce G III. The potential "truth" of the materials in G I, despite all ideological impurities, is guaranteed by a hidden Spinozan monism *(idea vera debet cum suo ideato convenire)*: a true idea must agree with its original in nature, or, in Althusserian terms, G I would not present itself if it did not correspond to the "real." It is the business of the scientific procedures of G II to purify G I of ideological admixture, and to produce *knowledge* (G III), which, in its own theoretical consistency, contains its own guarantees *(veritas norma sui et falsi—*truth is the criterion both of itself and of falsehood). In a brief aside Althusser allows that G II may, in certain disciplines, follow somewhat different procedures: the discourse of the proof may even be conducted in the form of experiment. This is his only concession: Generality II (he admits) "deserves a much more serious examination than I can embark upon here."[11] And so it does. For such an examination, if scrupulously conducted, would have exposed to view Althusser's continuous, wilful and theoretically-crucial confusion between "empiricism" (that is, philosophical positivism and all its kin) and the empirical mode of intellectual practice.

This question lies close to the question of "historicism" (a matter in which I have my own declared interest), and so I cannot despatch it so quickly. Generalities I include those mental events which are generally called "facts" or "evidence." "Contrary to the ideological illusions. . . of empiricism or sensualism" (Althusser tells us) these "facts" are not singular or concrete: they are already "concepts. . . of an ideological nature." (*F.M.* 183-4) The work of any science[12] consists in "*Elaborating its own scientific facts* through a critique of the *ideological 'facts'* elaborated by an earlier ideological theoretical practice":

> To elaborate its own specific 'facts' is simultaneously to elaborate its own 'theory', since a scientific fact—and not the self-styled pure phenomenon—can only be identified in the field of a theoretical practice. (*F.M.* 184)

This work of *"elaborating its own facts"* out of the raw material of pre-existent ideological concepts is done by Generality II, which is the working body of concepts and procedures of the discipline in question. That there are "difficulties" in the mode of operation of G II is acknowledged, but these difficulties are left unexamined ("we must rest content with these schematic gestures and not enter into the dialectic of this theoretical labour". (*F.M.* 185))

This is wise, since the difficulties are substantial. One of them is this: how does knowledge ever change or advance? If the raw material, or the evidence (G I), which is presented to a science (G II) is already fixed within a given ideological field—and if G I is the *only* route (however shadowy) by which the world of material and social reality can effect an entry (a shame-faced, ideological entry) into the laboratories of Theory, then it is not possible to understand by what means G II can effect any relevant or realistic critique of the ideological impurities presented to it. In short, Althusser's schema either show us how ideological illusions can reproduce themselves endlessly (or may evolve in aberrant or fortuitous ways); or it proposes (with Spinoza) that theoretical procedures *in them-selves* can refine ideological impurities out of their given materials by no other means than the scientific discourse of the proof; or, finally, it proposes some ever-pre-given immanent Marxist Idea outside the material and social world (of which Idea this world is an "effect"). Althusser argues by turns the second and the third proposition, although his work is in fact a demonstration of the first.

But we may leave this difficulty aside, since it would be unkind to interrogate too strictly a Generality which has only been offered to us with "schematic gestures." It is possible that Althusser is describing procedures appropriate to certain kinds of exercise in logic: we examine (let us say) a passage of text from Rousseau (G I): the uses of the words and the consistency of the logic is scrutinised according to rigorous philosophical or critical procedures (G II): and we arrive at a "knowledge" (G III), which may be a useful knowledge (and, within the terms of its own discipline, "true"), but which is critical rather than substantive. To confuse these procedures (appropriate within their own limits) with all procedures of knowledge production is the kind of elementary error which (one would suppose) could be committed only by students early in their careers, habituated to attending seminars in textual criticism of this kind, and apprentices rather than practitioners of their discipline. They have not yet arrived at those other (and equally difficult) procedures of research, experiment, and of the intellectual appropriation of the real world, without which the secondary (but important) critical procedures would have neither meaning nor existence.

In by far the greatest area of knowledge production a very different kind of dialogue is going on. It is untrue that the evidence or "facts" under investigation, always arrive (as G I) already in an ideological form. In the experimental sciences there are extremely elaborate procedures, appropriate to each discipline, intended to ensure that they do not. (This is not, of course, to argue that scientific facts "disclose" their own "meanings" independently of conceptual organisation.) It is central to every other applied discipline (in the "social sciences" and "humanities") that similar procedures are elaborated, although these are necessarily less exact and more subject to ideological determinations. The difference between a mature intellectual discipline and a merely-ideological formation (theology, astrology, some parts of bourgeois sociology and of orthodox Stalinist Marxism—and perhaps Althusserian structuralism) lies exactly in these procedures and controls; for, if the object of knowledge consisted only in ideological "facts" elaborated by that discipline's own procedures, then there would never be any way of validating or of falsifying any proposition: there could be no scientific or disciplinary court of appeal.

The absurdity of Althusser consists in the idealist mode of his theoretical constructions. His thought is the child of economic determinism ravished by theoreticist idealism. It posits (but does not attempt to "prove" or "guarantee") the existence of material reality: we will accept this point. It posits also the existence of a material ("external") world of social reality, whose determinate organisation is always in the last instance "economic": the proof for this lies not in Althusser's work—nor would it be reasonable to ask for such proof in the work of a philosopher—but in the mature work of Marx. This work arrives ready-made at the commencement of Althusser's enquiry, as a concrete knowledge, albeit a knowledge not always aware of its own theoretical practice. It is Althusser's business to enhance its own self-knowledge, as well as to repel various hideous ideological impurities which have grown up within the silences of its interstices. Thus a given knowledge (Marx's work) informs Althusser's procedures at each of the three levels of his hierarchy: Marx's work arrives as "raw material"—however elaborate—at G I; it is interrogated and processed (G II) according to principles of "science" derived from its mature *aperçus*, unstated assumptions, implicit methodologies, etc.; and the outcome is to confirm and reinforce the concrete knowledge (G III) which approved portions of Marx's work already announce.

It scarcely seems necessary to insist that this procedure is wholly self-confirming. It moves within the circle not only of its own problematic but of its own self-perpetuating and self-elaborating procedures. This is (in the eyes of Althusser and his followers) exactly the virtue of this theoretical practice. It is a sealed system within which concepts endlessly circulate, recognise and interrogate each other, and the intensity of its repetitious introversial life is mistaken for a "science." This "science" is then projected back upon Marx's work: it is proposed that his own procedures were of the same order: and that after the miracle of the "epistemological break" (an immaculate conception which required no gross empirical impregnation) all followed in terms of the elaboration of thought and its structural organisation.

> May I sum up all this in one sentence? This sentence describes a circle: a philosophic reading of *Capital* is only possible as the application of that which is the very object of our investigation, Marxist philosophy. This circle is only epistemologically possible because of the existence of Marx's philosophy in the works of Marxism. (*R.C.* 34)

To facilitate the "discourse of the proof" we return to some passages of Marx, but now as raw material (G I): the hand is held over all Marx's "immature" work, nearly all of the work of Engels, those portions of Marx's mature work which exemplify the practice of historical materialism, the correspondence of Marx and Engels (which take us directly into their laboratory and show us their procedures), and the greater part of *Capital* itself ("illustrations"); but between the fingers of the hand one is allowed to peep at de-contexted phrases of Marx, at "silences", and at sub-articulate mediations, which are chastised and disciplined until they confirm the self-sufficiency of theoretical practice. Of course. If the questions are proposed in this way, and if the material is called out—already drilled in its responses, and permitted to answer these questions and no others—then we can expect it to offer to the interrogator a dutiful allegiance.

This mode of thought is *exactly* what has commonly been designated, in the Marxist tradition, as idealism. Such idealism consists, not in the positing or denial of the primacy of an ulterior material world, but in a self-generating conceptual universe which imposes its own ideality upon the phenomena of material and social existence, rather than engaging in continual dialogue with these. If there is a "Marxism" of the contemporary world which Marx or Engels would have recognised instantly as an idealism, Althusserian structuralism is this.[13] The category has attained to a primacy over its material referent; the conceptual structure hangs above and dominates social being.

v

I don't propose to counter Althusser's paradigm of knowledge-production with an alternative, universal, paradigm of my own. But I will follow him a little further into my own discipline. It is not easy to do this with an even temper, since his repeated references to history and to "historicism" display his theoretical imperialism in its most arrogant forms. His comments display throughout no acquaintance with, nor understanding of, historical procedures: that is, procedures which make of "history" a *discipline* and not a babble of alternating ideological assertions: procedures which provide for their own relevant discourse of the proof.

However, let us be cool. Let us approach this problem, not from the suburbs (what historians *think* that they are doing when they consult and argue about "evidence"), but at the citadel itself: Althusser's notion of Theory. If we can storm that aloof, castellated (and preposterous) imperial citadel, then we will save our energies from skirmishes in the surrounding terrain. The land will fall into our hand.

History (Althusser tells us) "hardly exists other than. . . as the 'application' of a theory. . . which does not exist in any real sense." The " 'applications' of the theory of history somehow occur behind this absent theory's back and are naturally mistaken for it." This "absent theory" depends upon "more or less ideological outlines of theories":

> We must take seriously *the fact that the theory of history, in the strong sense, does not exist*, or hardly exists so far as historians are concerned, that the concepts of existing history are therefore nearly always 'empirical' concepts, more or less in search of their theoretical basis—'empirical', i.e. cross-bred with a powerful strain of an ideology concealed behind its 'obviousness'. This is the case with the best historians, who can be distinguished from the rest precisely by their concern for theory, but who seek this theory at a level on which it cannot be found, at the level of historical *methodology*, which cannot be defined without the *theory* on which it is based. (*R.C.* 110)

We will pause for a moment to note one oddity. There has existed for fifty years or more (very much more if we remember Engels and Marx) a Marxist historiography, which, as I have already remarked, now has an international presence. It is curious, then, that all these historians (who might, one supposes, include one or two whom Althusser would nominate as among "the best") have been operating through all these decades without any theory. For they had supposed that their theory was, exactly, derivative in some part from Marx: or from what Althusser would designate as Theory. That is, the critical concepts employed by these historians every day in their practice included those of exploitation, class struggle, class, determinism, ideology, and of feudalism and capitalism as modes of production, etc., etc.,—concepts derived from and validated within a Marxist theoretical tradition.

So this is odd. Historians have no theory. Marxist historians have no theory either. Historical Theory, then, must be something different from Marxist historical theory.

But let us resume our survey of the citadel. We must climb crag after crag before we attain the summit. Theory cannot be found "at the level" of historical practice, whether Marxist or not. *Excelsior!*

The truth of history cannot be read in its manifest discourse, because the text of history is not a text in which a voice (the Logos) speaks, but the inaudible and illegible notation of the effects of a structure of structures. (*R.C.* 17)

Not many historians suppose that the "manifest discourse" of history voluntarily discloses some "truth", nor that the Logos is whispering in their ears. But even so, Althusser's pat antithesis is somehow awry. "Inaudible and illegible"? Not wholly so. "Notation of the effects"? Perhaps: as a metaphor we might let this pass: but is it not a metaphor which leads precisely to that notion of the abstraction of an essence "from the real which contains it and keeps it in hiding" which Althusser, in a different mood, castigates as the hall-mark of "empiricism"? (See *R.C.* 35-37) "Of the effects of a structure of structures"? Where, then, is this "structure of structures" situated, if it is subject to no "empirical" investigation and also (we recall) lies outside the "level" of historical methodology? If we may ask a vulgar question: is this "structure of structures" *there*, immersed in history's happenings, or is it somewhere outside: for example, a Logos, which speaks, not from the text of history, but out of some philosophical head?

The question is irrelevant, says Althusser: worse, it is improper: it is guilty: it arises from a bourgeois and empiricist problematic. To say that structure could be disclosed by procedures of historical investigation is meaningless because all that we can ever know of history are certain conceptual representations: impure Generalities I. Hence historical "truth" can be disclosed only within theory itself, by theoretical procedures ("the process that produces the concrete-knowledge takes place wholly in the theoretical practice") (*F.M.* 186). The formal rigour of these procedures is the only proof of the "truth" of this knowledge, and of its correspondence to "real" phenomena: concrete knowledge, thus established, carries with it all "guarantees" that are necessary—or that can ever be obtained. "History itself is not a temporality, but an epistemological category designating the object of a certain science, historical materialism."[14] "The knowledge of history is no more historical than the knowledge of sugar is sweet." (*R.C.* 106)

This ultimate ascent to the citadel is defended by an idealist netting of assertions so densely-textured as to be almost impenetrable. We may construct our knowledge of history only *within knowledge, in the process of knowledge, not in the development of the real-concrete.*" (*R.C.* 108) And, of course, since everything that we think takes place within thought and its symbols, codes and representations, this is a truism. What occasions surprise is that it was possible for a philosopher, in the late 1960s, to re-iterate such truisms, with such rhetorical fury, with such severe castigation of (always-unidentified) opponents, and with such an assumption of novelty. But the rhetoric and the postures of severity are not "innocent": they are devices to carry the reader from such truisms to the very different proposition that knowledge emerges *wholly* within thought, by means of its own theoretical self-extrapolation. Thus in one elision it is possible to dismiss both the question of *experience* (how G I are presented to theory) and the question of specific procedures of investigation (experimental or other) which constitute that empirical "dialogue" which I will shortly consider. Thus Althusser:

> Once they are truly constituted and developed[15] [the sciences] have no need for verification from *external* practices to declare the knowledges they produce to be 'true', i.e. to be *knowledges*. No mathematician in the world waits until physics has *verified* a theorem to declare it proved... The truth of his theorem is a hundred per cent provided by criteria purely *internal* to the practice of mathematical proof, hence by the *criterion of mathematical practice*, i.e. by the forms required by existing mathematical scientificity. We can say the same for the results of every science... (*R.C.* 59)

Can we indeed? Once again, Althusser falls back upon a discipline which, insofar as it contemplates the logic of its own materials, is a special case: the notion that mathematics could serve as a paradigm, not only for logic, but for the production of knowledge, has haunted the Cartesian tradition, not least in the heretic thought of Spinoza. And Althusser goes on to declare, triumphantly:

> We should say the same of the science which concerns us most particularly: historical materialism. It has been possible to apply Marx's theory with success because it is 'true'; it is not true because it has been applied with success. (*R.C.* 59)

The statement provides its own premise: *because* Marx's theory is true (undemonstrated) it has been applied with success. True theories usually can be so applied. But how are we to determine this success? Within the historical discipline? And what about those occasions when Marx's theories have been applied *without* success? If we were to propose this statement in this form: "It has been possible to apply Marx's theory with success insofar as the theory has been 'true': where the theory has been successful it has confirmed the theory's truth," then we would find ourselves within a different epistemological discourse.

To resume. Althusser allows, in a perfunctory clause (this is evidently a matter at a very low level of theory indeed) that "no doubt there is a relation between *thought*-about-the-real and this *real*, but it is a relation of *knowledge*, a relation of adequacy or inadequacy of knowledge, not a real relation, meaning by this a relation inscribed in *that real* of which the thought is the (adequate or inadequate) knowledge":

> This knowledge relation between knowledge of the real and the real is not a relation *of the real* that is known in the relationship. The distinction between

a relation of knowledge and a relation of the real is a fundamental one: if we did not respect it we should fall irreversibly into either speculative idealism if, with Hegel, we confused thought and the real by reducing the real to thought, by *'conceiving the real as the result of thought. . .';* into empiricist idealism if we confused thought with the real by reducing thought about the real to the real itself. *(R.C.* 87)

I do not pretend to understand this very well. It would not occur to me to define the relation between knowledge and its real object in terms of a "relationship" to which there were two *active* parties—the "real", as it were, attempting actively to disclose itself to the recipient mind. The real, however active in its other manifestations, is epistemologically null or inert: that is, it can become an object of epistemological enquiry only at the point where it enters within the field of perception or knowledge. In Caudwell's words, "object and subject, as exhibited by the mind relation, come into being simultaneously", and "knowing is a mutually determining relation between knowing and being."[16] There can be no means of deciding the "adequacy or inadequacy" of *knowledge* (as against the special cases of logic, mathematics, etc.) unless one supposes procedures (a "dialogue" of practice) devised to establish the correspondence of this knowledge to properties "inscribed in" that real.

Once again, Althusser has jumped from a truism to theoreticist solipsism. He has approached the problem with a commonplace assertion which presents no difficulties:

Thought about the real, the conception of the real, and all the operations of thought by which the real is thought or conceived, belong to the order of thought, the elements of thought, which must not be confused with the order of the real. *(R.C.* 87)

Where else could thought take place? But the "knowledge relation between knowledge of the real and the real" can still perfectly well be a real, and determining, relation: that is, a relation of the active appropriation by one party (thought) of the other party (selective attributes of the real), and this relation may take place *not on any terms which thought prescribes* but in ways which are determined by the properties of the real object: the properties of reality determine both the appropriate procedures of thought (that is, their "adequacy or inadequacy") and its product. Herein consists the dialogue between consciousness and being.

I will give an illustration. . . and, aha! I see my table. To be an object, to be "null or inert", does not remove that object from being a determining party within a subject-object relation. No piece of timber has ever been known to make itself into a table: no joiner has ever been known to make a table out of air, or sawdust. The joiner appropriates that timber, and, in working it up into a table, he is governed both by his skill (theoretical practice, itself arising from a *history*, or "experience", of making tables, as well as a history of the evolution of appropriate tools) and by the qualities (size, grain, seasoning, etc.) of the timber itself. The wood imposes its properties and its "logic" upon the joiner as the joiner imposes his tools, skills and his ideal conception of tables upon the wood.

This illustration may tell us little about the relation between thought and its object, since thought is not a joiner, nor is it engaged in this kind of manufacturing process. But it may serve to emphasise one possible form of relation between an active subject and an "inert" object, wherein the object remains (within limits) determinant: the wood cannot determine *what* is made, nor whether it is made well or badly, but it can certainly determine what can *not* be made, the limits (size, strength, etc.) of what is made, and the skills and tools appropriate to the making. In such an equation "thought" (if it is "true") can only represent what is appropriate to the determined properties of its real object, and must operate within this determined field. If it breaks free, then it becomes engaged in freakish speculative botching, and the self-extrapolation of a "knowledge" of tables out of pre-existent bigotry. Since this "knowledge" does not correspond to the reality of the wood, it will very soon demonstrate its own "adequacy or inadequacy"; as soon as we sit down at it, it is likely to collapse, spilling its whole load of elaborate epistemological sauces to the floor.

The real object (I have said) is epistemologically inert: that is, it cannot impose or disclose itself to knowledge: all that takes place within thought and its procedures. But this does not mean that it is inert in other ways: it need by no means be sociologically or ideologically inert. And, to cap all, the real is not "out there" and thought within the quiet lecture-theatre of our heads, "inside here." Thought and being inhabit a single space, which space is ourselves. Even as we think we also hunger and hate, we sicken or we love, and consciousness is intermixed with being; even as we contemplate the "real" we experience our own palpable reality. So that the problems which the "raw materials" present to thought often consist exactly in their very active, indicative, intrusive qualities. For the dialogue between consciousness and being becomes increasingly complex—indeed, it attains at once to a different *order* of complexity, which presents a different *order* of epistemological problems—when the critical consciousness is acting upon a raw material made up of its own kind of stuff: intellectual artefacts, social relationships, the historical event.

A historian—certainly a Marxist historian—should be well aware of this. That dead, inert text of his evidence is by no means "inaudible"; it has a deafening vitality of its own; voices clamour from the past, asserting their own meanings, appearing to disclose their own self-knowledge as knowledge. If we offer a commonplace "fact"—"King Zed died in 1100

A.D."—we are already offered a concept of kingship: the relations of domination and subordination, the functions and role of the office, the charisma and magical endowments attaching to that role, etc.; and we are presented with these not only as an object of investigation, a concept which performed certain functions in mediating relationships in a given society, with (perhaps) several conflicting notations of this concept endorsed by different social groups (the priests, the serving-girls) within that society—not only this, which the historian has to recover with difficulty, but also this evidence is received by the historian within a theoretical framework (the discipline of history, which itself has a history and a disputed present) which has refined the concept of kingship, from the study of many examples of kingship in very different societies, resulting in concepts of kingship very different from the immediacy, in power, in common-sense, or in myth, of those who actually witnessed King Zed die.

These difficulties are immense. But the difficulties are multiplied many times over when we are considering not one event or concept (kingship) but those events which most historians regard as central to their study: historical "process", the inter-relationship between disparate phenomena (as economies and ideologies), causation. The relationship between thought and its object now becomes so exceedingly complex and mediated; and, moreover, the resulting historical knowledge establishes relations between phenomena which could never be seen, felt or experienced by the actors in these ways at the time, and it organises the findings according to concepts and within categories which were unknown to the women and men whose actions make up the object of study—all these difficulties are so immense that it becomes apparent that "real" history and historical knowledge are things totally distinct. And so of course they are. What else could they be? But does it thereby follow that we must cut down the bridge between them? May not the object (real history) still stand in an "objective" (empirically-verifiable) relationship to its knowledge, and a relationship which is (within limits) determinant?

In the face of the complexities of such a conclusion, a certain kind of rational mind (and, in particular, a rational mind innocent of practical knowledge of historical procedures, and impatient for an easy route to the Absolute) recoils. This recoil can take many forms. It is of interest (and it ought to be of interest to Marxists) that, at the initial stage of the recoil, both empiricism and Althusserian structuralism arrive at an identical repudiation of "historicism." So far from Althusser's positions being original, they signify a capitulation to decades of conventional academic criticism of historiography, whose outcome has sometimes been relativist ("history" as an expression of the pre-occupations of the present), sometimes idealist and theoreticist, and sometimes one of extreme radical scepticism as to history's epistemological credentials. One route may have been through Husserl and Heidegger: another through Hegel and Lukàcs: another through a more "empirical" tradition of "Anglo-Saxon" linguistic philosophy: but all routes have led to a common terminus.

At the end of his working life it was possible for that formidable practitioner of historical materialism, Marc Bloch, to assume with robust confidence the objective and determinant character of his materials: "The past is, by definition, a datum which nothing in the future will change."[17] By the 1960s no such confidence might be expressed in respectable intellectual company; it was possible for a gifted writer within the Marxist tradition to assume historical relativism as a commonplace:

> For the human sciences, the historical individuality is constructed by the choice of what is essential *for us*, i.e. in terms of our value-judgements. Thus, historical reality changes from epoch to epoch with modifications in the hierarchy of values.[18]

The particular reasons proposed for history's epistemological lack of credibility have been different: as have been the preferred solutions: but Oakeshott and Althusser, Lucien Goldmann and Raymond Aron, Popper and Hindess/Hirst have all been loitering in the same area with similar intent.[19]

"History" had perhaps called down this revenge upon itself. I don't mean to deny that the nineteenth and twentieth centuries engendered authentic and sometimes monstrous "historicisms" (evolutionary, teleological, and essentialist notions of "history's" self-motivation); nor to deny that this same historicism permeated some part of the Marxist tradition, in the notion of a *programmed* succession of historical "stages", motored towards a pre-determined end by class struggle. All this merited severe correction. But the correction administered to historical materialism too often assumed its guilt without scrupulous enquiry into its practice; or, if examples of guilt were identified (often in the work of ideologues rather than in the mature practice of historians), it was then assumed that these invalidated the whole exercise, rather than calling in question the practitioner, or the maturity of historical knowledge. And if critics and philosophers (Collingwood apart) were rather generally guilty of this convenient elision, no-one has been more outrageous in his attribution of "historicism" to the practice of historical materialism than Althusser: from start to finish the practice of historians (and of Marxist historians) is assumed by him but not examined.

Let us return the scrutiny of criticism back upon the critics, and see how Althusser and Popper came to a common rejection of "historicism." For Popper there is a very limited sense in which he will allow that certain "facts" of history are empirically verifiable. But once we step across a shadowy (but critical) border from discrete facts or particular evidences to questions of process, social formations and relationships, or causation, we instantly enter a realm in which we must either be guilty of "historicism" (which consists, for him, in part in attributing to history predictive laws, or in propounding "general interpretations", which arise from improper "holistic" categories imposed by the interpreting mind, which are empirically unverifiable, and which we smuggle into history ourselves) or we are avowedly offering an interpretation as a "point of view." The discrete facts are in any case contaminated by their random or pre-selected provenance. Evidence about the past either survives in arbitrary ways or in ways which impose a particular pre-supposition on the historical investigator, and since—

> The so-called 'sources' of history only record such facts as appeared sufficiently interesting to record. . . the sources will, as a rule, contain only facts that fit in with a pre-conceived theory. And since no further facts are available, it will not, as a rule, be possible to test that or any other subsequent theory.

Most interpretations will be "circular in the sense that they must fit in with that interpretation which was used in the original selection of the facts." Hence historical knowledge, in any large or general sense, is its own artefact. While Popper allows that an interpretation may be *dis*proved, because it does not correspond with empirically-ascertainable discrete facts (an allowance which Althusser cannot make), by his criteria of proof—criteria derived from the natural sciences—we can go no further. The experimental proof of any interpretation is impossible: hence interpretation belongs to a category outside of historical knowledge ("point of view"); although each generation has a right, and even a "pressing need", to offer its own interpretation or point of view as a contribution to its own self-understanding and self-evaluation.[20]

Thus Popper: we cannot know "history", or at best we may know only discrete facts (and these ones which happen to have survived through their own or historical self-selection). Interpretation consists in the introduction of a point of view: this may be legitimate (on other grounds) but it does not constitute any true historical knowledge. Althusser sets out from much the same premise:[21] although the suggestion that we can know even discrete facts encounters his scorn, since no fact can attain to epistemological identity (or the significance of any meaning) until it is placed within a theoretical (or ideological) field: and the theoretical act is prior to and informs whatever is pretended as "empirical" investigation.

In Althusser's schema, ideology (or Theory) take on the functions offered by Popper as interpretation or point of view. It is only in their conclusions that we find any marked disagreement. For **Popper** "there is no history of mankind, there is only an indefinite number of histories of all kinds of aspects of human life." These histories are created by historians out of an "infinite subject matter" according to contemporary pre-occupations.[22] The emphasis falls with the monotony of a steam-hammer upon the unknowability of any objective historical process and upon the dangers of "historicist" attribution. We must grope out way backwards in an empiricist dusk, making out the dim facts at our feet, piece-meal and one at a time. But where Popper sees danger Althusser sees a splendid opportunity, a conceptual space, a vacancy inviting his imperial occupation. Historical process is unknowable as a real object: historical knowledge is the product of theory: theory *invents* history, either as ideology or as Theory ("science"). The only trouble is (we remember) that "the theory of history, in the strong sense, does not exist." But Althusser can provide this theory to historians. We have no need to grope in the dusk: we will leap, with one gigantic epistemological bound, from darkness to day.

We have already noted this astounding idealism. To be sure, idealism is something that Althusser is very stern, even prim, about. "Speculative idealism" (he tells us) confuses thought and the real by reducing the real to thought, and by "conceiving the real as the result of thought." Now Althusser does not, in so many words, make this superfluous gesture. (To deny explicitly the prior existence of a material world might even call down upon him some curious looks from the leaders of the P.C.F.) As a dutiful "materialist", Althusser asserts that the real *does* exist, somewhere out there.

> For us, the 'real' is not a *theoretical slogan;* the real is the real object that exists independently of its knowledge—but which can only be defined by its knowledge. In this second, theoretical, relation, the real is identical to the means of knowing it. . . (*F.M.* 246)

And, just so, over 350 years ago, a philosopher arguing from an opposite brief, declared:

> For us, God is not a *theoretical slogan;* God is the First Cause who exists independently of our knowledge, etc.

—or, to be more precise, "Certain it is that God worketh nothing in nature but by second causes." The argument did not prevent Francis Bacon from being accused as a secret atheist, and Althusser should not be surprised at being accused of dissolving reality in an idealist fiction. For this pious and necessary gesture once made (as a kind of genetic *a priori,* an "in the last instance" proviso), the "real" is shuffled quickly off the scene. All that thought can know is thought—and pretty bad artefacts of thought at that, "for the mind of man is. . . like an enchanted glass, full of superstition and imposture, if it be not delivered and reduced."[23] Theory must now set that right.

Althusser does not so much confuse thought and the real as, by asserting the unknowability of the real, he confiscates reality of its determinant properties, thus reducing the real to Theory. This Theory lay immanent, awaiting Marx's epistemological break. And the knowledge then appropriated by Marx (although "revealed" would be a better word) was determined in no way by its object. Historians have entirely misread *Capital*:

> They did not see that history features in *Capital* as an object of theory, not as a real object, as an 'abstract' (conceptual) object and not as a real-concrete object; and that the chapters in which Marx applies the first stages of a historical treatment either to the struggles to shorten the working day, or to primitive capitalist accumulation refer to the theory of history as their principle, to the construction of the concept of history and of its 'developed forms', of which the economic theory of the capitalist mode of production constitutes one determinate 'region'. (*R.C.* 117)

And again:

> Despite appearances, Marx does not analyse any 'concrete society', not even England which he mentions constantly in Volume One, but the CAPITALIST MODE OF PRODUCTION and nothing else. . . We must not imagine that Marx is analysing the concrete situation in England when he discusses it. He only discusses it in order to 'illustrate' his (abstract) theory of the capitalist mode of production. (*L. & P.* 76)

Arrayed in this scarlet and furred gown of Theory, Althusser may now storm into every adjacent lecture-theatre, and, in the name of philosophy, denounce the incumbents and expropriate them of their poor defective disciplines which pretend to be knowledges. Before these disciplines may proceed at all, they must first sit before his rostrum and master his lessons:

> In particular, the specialists who work in the domains of the 'Human Sciences' and of the Social Sciences (a smaller domain), i.e. economists, historians, sociologists, social psychologists, psychologists, historians of art and literature, or religious and other ideologies—and even linguists and psycho-analysts, all these specialists ought to know that they cannot produce truly scientific knowledges in their specializations unless they recognize the indispensability of the theory Marx founded. For it is, in principle, the theory which 'opens up' to scientific knowledge the 'continent' in which they work, in which they have so far only produced a few preliminary knowledges (linguistics, psycho-analysis) or a few elements or rudiments of knowledge (the occasional chapter of history, sociology, or economics) or illusions pure and simple, illegitimately called knowledges. (*L. & P.* 72)

No matter if the vassals in these continents or "smaller domains" had supposed themselves to be Marxists already: they were imposters, and should perhaps now pay a double tribute to the "theory which Marx founded" but which no-one, including (notably) Marx, understood before the annunciation of Althusser. As for my own poor, laborious, discipline of history, the expropriation of our petty principality (no doubt a very small domain indeed) is total:

> We must once again purify our concept of the theory of history, and purify it radically, of any contamination by the obviousness of empirical history, since we know that this 'empirical history' is merely the bare face of the empiricist ideology of history... We must grasp in all its rigour the absolute necessity of liberating the theory of history from any compromise with 'empirical' temporality. (*R.C.* 105)

Above all, we must overthrow the "incredible power" of a prejudice,

> Which is the basis for contemporary historicism and which would have us confuse the object of knowledge with the real object by attributing to the object of knowledge the same 'qualities' as the real object of which it is the knowledge. (*R.C.* 106)

It is clear that Althusser and his regiment of assistants intend to impose punitive taxation on this petty (and now subjugated) domain of history, and to visit our sins upon the heads of our children down to the third generation.

One stands astounded in this inverted world of absurdity. And yet its magic transfixes those minds which stray within, unless they come in under arms and under the discipline of criticism. ("Common sense" will do them no good: every visitor is searched at the frontier and stripped of that.) Enchanted minds move through humourless, visionary fields, negotiate imaginary obstacles, slay mythical monsters ("humanism", "moralism"), perform tribal rites with the rehearsal of approved texts. There is drama: the initiates feel that they have something to do (they are developing a "science") as they discover fresh "silences" in Marx, and extrapolate further from the self-extrapolating reasons of Theory. And there is the greater drama of heretics and heresies, as pupils and disciples fall from the faith, as rival prophets arise, and as sub- and post-Althusserianisms and derivative structuralisms (linguistic and semiotic) multiply. Of course: for it is exactly in conditions when a theory (or *a theology*) is subject to no empirical controls that disputes about the placing of one term lead on to theoretical parturition: the parturition of intellectual parthenogenesis.

So that is where we are. One more astonishing aberrant spectacle is added to the phantasmagoria of our time. It is a bad time for the rational mind to live: for a rational mind in the Marxist tradition it is a time that cannot be endured. For the real world also gesticulates at reason with its own inversions. Obscene contradictions manifest themselves, jest, and then vanish; the known and the unknown change places; even as we examine them, categories dissolve and change into their opposites. In the West a bourgeois soul yearns for a "Marxism" to heal its own alienation; in the

"Communist" world a proclaimed "socialist basis" gives rise to a "superstructure" of orthodox Christian faith, corrupt materialism, Slav nationalism and Solzhenitsyn. In that world "Marxism" performs the function of an "Ideological State Apparatus", and Marxists are alienated, not in their self-identity, but in the contempt of the people. An old and arduous rational tradition breaks down into two parts: an arid academic scholasticism and a brutal pragmatism of power.

All this is not unprecedented. The world has gone through such changes of scene before. Such changes signal the solution (or by-passing) of some problems, the arrival of new problems, the death of old questions, the invisible presence of new and unstated questions all around us. "Experience"—the experience of Fascism, Stalinism, racism, and of the contradictory phenomenon of working-class "affluence" within sectors of capitalist economies—is breaking in and demanding that we reconstruct our categories. Once again we are witnessing "social being" determining "social consciousness", as experience impinges and presses upon thought: but this time it is not bourgeois ideology but the "scientific" consciousness of Marxism which is breaking under the strain.

This is a time for reason to grit its teeth. As the world changes, we must learn to change our language and our terms. But we should never change these *without reason*.

vi

To reply to Althusser. I will deny myself the advantage of fighting this battle upon favourable terrain—that is, the terrain of Marx's and Engels's own writings. While in a contest on these terms almost every skirmish could be won (for, repeatedly, Marx and Engels, in the most specific terms, infer the reality of both process and structure "inscribed in" history, affirm the objectivity of historical knowledge, and pillory "idealist" modes of thought identical to those of Althusser) I refuse to conduct the argument on this terrain for three reasons. First, while each skirmish might be won, the battle would remain undecided: all that the retreating dogma needs to do is to "read" Marx even more selectively, discover new silences, repudiate more texts.[24] Second, I have long ceased to be interested in the defence of Marxism as doctrine in this kind of way.[25] Third, although *I know these texts*, and perhaps even know how to "read" them in a different way to Althusser's readings—that is, I know them as an apprentice and as a practitioner of historical materialism, have employed them in my practice for many years, have tested them, have been indebted to them, and have also, on occasion, discovered different kinds of "silence" or inadequacy in them—although all this is true, I think that the time has gone by for this kind of textual exegesis.

In this point, and in this point only, I may approach to some agreement

with Althusser. For either of us to point to a congruity between our
positions and a particular text of Marx can prove nothing as to the validity
of the proposition in question: it can only confirm a congruity. In one
hundred years the intellectual universe has changed, and even those
propositions of Marx which require neither revision nor elucidation were
defined in a particular context, and very often in antagonism to particular
and now-forgotten opponents; and in our new context, and in the face of
new and, perhaps, more subtle objections, these propositions must be
thought through and stated once again. This is a familiar historical
problem. Everything must be thought through once more: every term
must sit for new examinations.

I must delay a little longer over some practical objections. While these
present themselves instantly to any practising historian, a philosopher will
no doubt find them trivial: they can be spirited off with an epistemological
wand. But the objections should be mentioned. For the descriptions of
historical procedures proposed by Popper or by Althusser do not
correspond to what most historians *think* they are doing, or "find" themselves to be doing in practice. One finds that some philosophers (and
more sociologists) have a theoretic, but uninformed, notion of what
historical "sources" are. Thus one has little sense of self-recognition in the
statement (Popper) that "the so-called 'sources' of history only record
such facts as appeared sufficiently interesting to record"; nor in the statement (Hindess/Hirst), "facts are never *given;* they are always produced."
Popper's statement appears to direct attention to the *intentionality* of the
historical actors: historical evidence comprises only those records which
these actors *intended* to transmit to posterity, and hence imposes their
intentions as a heuristic rule upon the historian. Hindess and Hirst, who
acknowledge themselves to be, in their epistemology, true Althusserians
(although more rigorous then their master), shift attention from the genesis
of evidence to its appropriation (within a particular theoretical field) by
the historian, who "produces" facts, out of something not "given".

Both statements are half-truths: which is to say, they are untrue. By far
the greater part of historical evidence has survived for reasons quite un-
related to any intention of the actors to project an image of themselves
to posterity: the records of administration, taxation, legislation, religious
belief and practice, the accounts of temples or of monasteries, and the
archaeological evidence of their sites. It may be true that the further back
we press into the margins of recorded time, more of the evidence becomes
subject to Popper's attribution of intention. This is not, however, a property
of the evidence which ancient historians and archaeologists have un-
accountably overlooked. Indeed, when they consider the earliest Mayan
glyphs or cuneiform inscriptions of ancient Babylonia, an important object
of study is, precisely, the intentions of the recorders: and, through this,

the recovery of their cosmology, their astrology and calendars, their exorcisms and charms—the "interests" of the recorders.

Intended evidence (evidence intentionally provided to posterity) may be studied, within the historical discipline, as objectively as unintended evidence (that is, the greater part of historical evidence which survives for reasons independent of the actors' intentions). In the first case, the intentions are themselves an object of enquiry; and in both cases historical "facts" are "produced", by appropriate disciplines, from the evidential facts. But does the confession that, in this disciplined sense, historical facts are "produced" warrant the half-truth of Hindess and Hirst, that "facts are never *given*"? If they were *not*, in some sense, given, then historical practice would take place in an empty workshop, manufacturing history (as Althusser and Hindess/Hirst would like to do) out of theoretical air. And the very *given-ness of facts*, the determinate properties which they present to the practitioner, constitutes one half of that dialogue which makes up the discipline of the historian.

Popper seems to see all historical evidence as the Chronicles of Kings. Little historical evidence is "recorded" in this self-conscious sense: and what there is may still be read in Blake's "infernal" sense: that is, held upside-down and shaken, until it discloses what its authors assumed but did not intend to record—implicit assumptions and attributes inscribed within the text. Most written sources are of value with little reference to the "interest" which led to their being recorded. A marriage settlement between a landed scion and the daughter of an East India merchant in the eighteenth century may leave a substantial deposit in a record office, of protracted negotiations, legal deeds, property agreements, even (rarely) an exchange of love letters. The intention of none of the actors was to record interesting facts to some general posterity: it was to unite and to secure property in particular ways, and perhaps also to negotiate a human relationship. The historian will read these materials, and, in the light of the questions which he proposes, he may derive from them evidence as to property transactions, as to legal procedures, as to the mediations between landed and mercantile groups, as to particular familial structures and kinship ties, as to the institution of bourgeois marriage, or as to sexual attitudes—none of which evidence the actors intended to disclose, and some of which (perhaps) they might have been horrified to know would come to light.

It is the same again and again: *all the time.* People were taxed: the hearth-tax lists are appropriated, not by historians of taxation, but by historical demographers. People were tithed: the terriers are appropriated as evidence by agrarian historians. People were customary tenants or copy-holders: their tenures were enrolled and surrendered in the rolls of the manorial court: these essential sources are interrogated by historians again and again, not only in pursuit of new evidence but in a dialogue in which they propose new questions. So that it seems to a mere historian to be rubbish (as a matter of "fact", I know that it *is* rubbish) to assert, with Popper, that "the sources will, as a rule, contain only facts that fit in with pre-conceived theory."

That facts are *there*, inscribed in the historical record, with determinate properties, does not, of course, entail some notion that these facts disclose their meanings and relationships (historical knowledge) of themselves, and independently of theoretical procedures. Few empiricists would argue this: and certainly not Popper. But insofar as this notion survives, it survives at a level of methodology rather than theory: that is, if only the correct *method* can be designed, usually quantitative (positivism armed with a computer), then the facts will disclose their meanings independently of any rigorous conceptual exercise. I have argued with the stasis of this kind of "empiricist" position, for many years, in my own practice,[26] and I do not mean to argue it all again. Some small part of what Althusser has to say about "empiricism" (when conceived as ideology) is just;[27] and it is the instant recognition of the obviousness of this justice—both its "common sense" and its general academic acceptability—which is the usual gate-of-entry for inexperienced readers, and which beckons them into the interior of his absurd syllogistic world.

Instead of rehearsing this old tale once more, let us put it in this way. A historian is entitled in his practice to make a provisional assumption of an epistemological character: that the evidence which he handles has a "real" (determinant) existence independent of its existence within the forms of thought, that this evidence is witness to a real historical process, and that this process (or some approximate understanding of it) is the object of historical knowledge. Without making such assumptions he cannot proceed: he must sit in a waiting-room outside the philosophy department all his life. To assume thus does not entail the assumption of a whole series of intellectually illiterate notions, such as that facts involuntarily disclose their own meanings, that answers are supplied independently of questions, etc. We are not talking about pre-history, even if, in some quarters, pre-history survives and even sits robed in chairs. Any serious historian knows that "facts" are liars, that they carry their own ideological loads, that open-faced, innocent questions may be a mask for exterior attributions, that even the most highly-sophisticated supposedly-neutral and empirical research techniques—techniques which would deliver to us "history" packaged and untouched by the human mind, through the automatic ingestion of the computer—may conceal the most vulgar ideological intrusions.[28] So: this is known: we have been sucking our own eggs for as long as philosophers have been sucking theirs.

The historical evidence is there, in its primary form,[29] not to disclose its own meaning, but to be interrogated by minds trained in a discipline of attentive disbelief. The discrete facts may be interrogated in at least six very different ways: 1) Before any other interrogation can be commenced, their credentials *as* historical facts must be scrutinised: how were they recorded? for what purpose? can they be confirmed from adjacent evidence? And so on. This is the bread-and-butter of the trade; 2) At the level of their own appearance, or apparent self-disclosure, but within terms of a disciplined historical enquiry. Where the facts under interrogation are social or cultural phenomena, we will most often find that the enquiry adduces *value-bearing evidence,* in which those very qualities of self-evaluation inherent in the phenomena (e.g. attitudes towards or within marriage) become the object of study; 3) As more or less inert, "neutral", *value-free evidences* (indices of mortality, wage-series, etc.), which are then subjected to enquiry, in the light of the particular questions (demographic, economic, agrarian) proposed: such enquiries having their own appropriate procedures (e.g. statistical) designed to limit (although by no means always successfully) the intrusion of ideological attributions; 4) As *links in a linear series* of occurrences, or contingent events—that is, history "as it actually happened" (but as it can never be fully known)—in the construction of a narrative account; such a reconstruction (however much it may be despised by philosophers, by sociologists, and by an increasing number of contemporary historians who have been frightened by the first two) being *an essential constituent of the historical discipline,* a pre-requisite and premise of all historical knowledge, the ground of any objective (as distinct from theoretic) notion of causation, and the indispensible preliminary to the construction of an analytic or structured account (which identifies structural and causative relations), even though in the course of such an analysis the primitive sequential narration will itself undergo radical transformation; 5) As *links in a lateral series* of social/ideological/economic/political relations (as, for example—this contract is a special case of the general form of contracts at that time: such contracts were governed by these forms of law: they enforced these forms of obligation and subordination), enabling us thereby to recover or infer, from many instances, at least a provisional "section" of a given society in the past—its characteristic relations of power, domination, kinship, servitude, market relations, and the rest; 6) It may follow from this, if we press the point a little further, that even discrete facts may be interrogated for *"structure-bearing" evidence.*

This suggestion is more controversial. Many (perhaps most) practising historians would assent to my first five points: these ways of interrogating evidence belong to the discipline, and to its own "discourse of the proof." A historical materialist may argue that the structural organisation of given societies may be inferred not only from larger evidences (to which we will, in time, come) but may be inferred, in some part, from certain kinds of seemingly discrete facts themselves. Thus a tenure exists as "fact" as some

Latin formula inscribed upon a court roll: but what that tenure "meant" cannot be understood independently of an entire structure of tenurial occupancy and attendant law: that is, within a tenurial *system:* hence this "fact"—and, very certainly, a series of facts of the same order (for certain philosophers of history isolate "facts" for epistemological scrutiny and lay these on their seminar table for scrutiny one at a time, whereas historians are always handling facts in bunches and in series)—carries within it some "index" towards that system, or, at least, it should propose to the interrogator an indicative question. Similarly, a bill-of-exchange is an "index" towards a particular system of credit within which that bill may be negotiated.

The point has significance, not only in relation to Althusser's notion that "structure" cannot possibly be "inscribed in" the real (that theory "produces" this history), but in relation to Popper's nominalism, and "methodological individualism", which regards all notions of collectivity and of structure as "holistic" fictions or as abstractions imposed by the observer. But, as MacIntyre has shown, "the army" is, in Popper's sense, an abstract concept; "the soldier" is a concrete one, a discrete evidence which he will allow. And yet,

> You cannot characterise an army by referring to the soldiers who belong to it. For to do that you have to identify them as soldiers; and to do that is already to bring in the concept of an army. For a soldier just is an individual who belongs to an army. Thus we see that the characterisation of individuals and of classes has to go together. Essentially these are not two separate tasks.[30]

A nominalist, if he were sufficiently strict, would have to describe the copyhold entry and the bill-of-exchange as passages of writing upon vellum or paper: and he would be at a loss even to describe writing independently of the concept of language. It is the children of yesterday's nominalists who are now the pupils of Althusser.

We will leave it there. I have proposed certain ways of interrogating facts, and no doubt other disciplined and appropriate ways may be proposed. These ways have two common attributes: 1) they assume that the historian is engaged in some kind of encounter with an evidence which is not infinitely malleable or subject to arbitrary manipulation: that there is a real and significant sense in which the facts are "there", and that they are determining, even though the questions which may be proposed are various, and will elucidate various replies; 2) they involve disciplined and thoughtful application, and a discipline developed precisely to detect any attempt at arbitrary manipulation: the facts will disclose nothing of their own accord, the historian must work hard to enable them to find "their own voices." Not the historian's voice, please observe: *their own voices,* even if what they are able to "say" and some part of their vocabulary is determined by the questions which the historian proposes. They cannot "speak" until they have been "asked".

I have proposed in the foregoing argument certain "practical objections", from appearances: i.e. what a historian thinks that he is doing, his self-knowledge of his own procedures. It suggests very different procedures from those gestured at by Popper. And Althusser would find in my account reprehensible capitulations to "empiricist ideology". But I don't intend to prolong this line of defence: it could be greatly extended, greatly elaborated, and we could enter more closely into the historian's workshop. But to offer a defence would be to agree that a serious case has been made out which requires such defence. And this is not so. Neither Popper nor Althusser show any close acquaintance with the historian's procedures: neither understands the nature of historical knowledge. Popper shows the greater curiosity, and therefore his objections deserve the courtesy of some reply;[31] but his repeated confusions between procedures in the experimental sciences and in the historical discipline, and between the different kinds of knowledge which eventuate, defeat his enquiry.[32] Althusser shows no curiosity at all. He does not like the product, historical knowledge, and his distaste is perhaps so great that it prevents any kind of nearer acquaintance. He knows that Theory could write better history.

"The knowledge of history is no more historical than the knowledge of sugar is sweet." Thus Althusser. Let us tease this brave epigram a little. It compels assent in an inattentive mind because of its "obvious" common sense, indeed its banality: no knowledge can be the same thing as its object. How true! And we could set up an epistemological Mint, to coin epigrams of the same order. "The knowledge of the French Communist Party is no more Communist than the knowledge of water is wet." (One could recommend this as a mental distraction during boring railway journeys). Even so, the terms of this banal epigram have been loaded to trick us into a false conclusion. In the first clause ("history. . . historical") we are deliberately pitched into an ambiguity: for "historical" may mean appertaining to real historical events or evidence, or it may mean appertaining to the historical discipline (the knowledge of history). Althusser intends us—for a rigorous philosopher could not commit such a solecism in innocence—to confuse these two meanings. For if he had proposed that "historical knowledge no more appertains to history than sugary knowledge is sweet," we would not at once recognise a revelation of truth. We would suspect (rightly) that we were being "got at." And we would then look more critically at the second clause. Why "sweet"? In what ways do "historical" and "sweet" stand in relation to each other which permits a logical analogy to be drawn? "Historical" is a generic definition: it defines very generally a common property of its object (appertaining to the past and not to the present or the future). "Sweet" isolates one property only, from a number of other properties which might propose themselves. Sugar has chemical properties and constitution, it looks brown or white, it is cubed or in powder, it weighs so much, and the price of it keeps going up. The property singled out by Althusser—sweetness—concerns, not knowledge, but sense-perception. Sugar *tastes* sweet, but no-one has ever tasted history, which would, perhaps, taste bitter. Hence these two clauses stand only in a rhetorical or polemical relation to each other.

An honest balancing of the clauses would have given us this: "The knowledge of history is no more historical than the taste of sugar is sweet." This would not have astounded innocent readers with Theory's wisdom, nor have sent them running to consult Bachelard and Lacan. Or it could have been proposed in another form again: "The knowledge of history is no more historical than the knowledge of sugar is chemical." This would have brought us closer to an analogy; but, then, it would not have served so well the purposes of the Althusserian trick. For we would reflect that the knowledge of history *is* historical (it pertains to the historical discipline) in just the same way as the knowledge of sugar *is* chemical (it finds its definition within chemical science).

What Althusser wishes us to receive from his epigram is this: "The knowledge of history has got no more to do with real history than the knowledge of sugar has got to do with real sugar." We would then see that we have been offered no brave discovery, but either an epistemological truism (thought is not the same thing as its object) or else a proposition both of whose clauses are untrue and whose implications are even a little mad. But we are invited to enter the Althusserian theatre through many little verbal turnstiles of this kind: we "buy" these exalted propositions as our entry fee. All that we need exchange for them is a little of our reason. And once inside the theatre we find that there are no exits.

We might examine other corrupt propositions in the same way, but I will not expose my readers to the tedium. It is time to ask a more serious question: how is it that Althusser, the rational architect, constructed this theatre of the absurd? What problems was Althusser addressing, whose complexities led him into these agonies of self-mystification? An answer might be proposed at two different levels: ideological and theoretical. We leave aside, for the moment, the ideological enquiry. First, we will do him the justice of considering his ideas at their own self-evaluation: we will suppose that he arrived at irrationalism by procedures (however faulty) of reason.

We have seen that the central fracture which runs through Althusser's thought is a confusion between empirical procedures, empirical controls, and something which he calls "empiricism." This fracture invalidates not this or that part of his thought but his thought as a whole. His epistemological stance prevents him from understanding the two "dialogues" out of which our knowledge is formed: first, the dialogue between social being and social consciousness, which gives rise to experience; second, the dialogue between the theoretical organisation (in all its complexity) of evidence, on the one hand, and the determinate character of its object on the other. As a consequence of the second failure, he cannot understand (or must mis-represent) the character of those empirical procedures which are elaborated, within different disciplines, not only to interrogate "facts" but to ensure that they reply, not in the interrogator's voice, but in their own voices. As a consequence of the first failure, he cannot understand either the real, existential genesis of ideology, or the ways in which human *praxis* contests this ideological imposition and presses against its bonds. Since he ignores both dialogues, he cannot understand either how historical knowledge "arrives" (as experience) nor the procedures of investigation and verification of the historical discipline. The "epistemological break", with Althusser, is a break *from* disciplined self-knowledge and a leap into the self-generation of "knowledge" according to its own theoretical procedures: that is, a leap out of knowledge and into theology.

He takes this leap because he cannot see any other way out of the compulsive ideological field of genuine empiricism, with its own intellectual complacency and its own self-confirming positivist techniques. "Positivism, with its narrowed view of rationality, its acceptance of physics as the paradigm of intellectual activity, its nominalism, its atomism, its lack of hospitality to all general views of the world"[33]—this was not invented by Althusser. What he wishes to escape from—the self-enclosed, empiricist prison, whose methodologies patrol with (statistical, linguistic) keys at their belts, locking all doors against the admission of structured process—certainly exists. Althusser has scaled its walls; leapt; and now he constructs his own theatre on an adjacent site. Prison and theatre scowl at each other. But (a curious thing) both prison and theatre are built from much the same materials, even though the rival architects are sworn to enmity. Viewed from the aspect of historical materialism, the two structures exhibit an extraordinary identity. In certain lights the two structures appear to echo each other, merge into each other, exemplify the identity of opposites. For both are the products of conceptual stasis, erected, stone upon stone, from static, a-historical categories.

The critical question concerns less epistemology in its relation to discrete facts (although we have already noted certain similarities here) than the epistemological legitimacy of *historical* knowledge, when considered in its aspect as knowledge of causation, of structure, of the modalities of relationship between social groups or institutions, and of the logic (or "laws") of historical process. It is here that prison and theatre join common forces against historical materialism, for both assert this knowledge (as a knowledge of the real) to be epistemologically illegitimate. Althusser cannot bruise "empiricism" at all, because he starts out from the same premise: he merely "breaks" at a certain point to an idealist conclusion. Both Popper (a) and Althusser (b) affirm the unknowability of history as a process inscribed with its own causation, since (a) any notion of structures and structural mediations entails improper "holistic" attributions, and "historicist" notions of causation and of process are unverifiable by experimental tests; or since (b) the notion that knowledge is "already *really* present in the real object it has to know" is an illusion of "abstractionist" empiricism, mistaking as empirical discoveries its own ideological attributions. What does it matter that Althusser should *then* leap to the conclusion that knowledge does and should manufacture out of its own theoretical stuff a historical "knowledge" which is (in Popper's use of the term) an arrant "historicism"? A real empiricist will be happy with this, for in his eyes Althusser has only confirmed, by his idealist agility, the unverifiable and ideological character of all such pretensions to historical knowledge. Althusser offers a prime example to the seminar discussion: an epilogue to *The Poverty of Historicism*.

The objections to historical materialism which these antagonists hold in common are: "facts" (even if knowable) are discrete: they are as "raw material" impure: therefore (unstated but assumed) multiples of "facts" multiply impurities. Historical facts survive (as texts) in fortuitous or pre-selected ways: they arrive already within an ideological field (of a given society in the past, and in terms of its own self-evaluation); they are therefore in no way "neutral". Historical notions of causation or of structure are highly-elaborated theoretical constructions; as such, they are the properties of theory and not of its object, "real" history. No empirical procedures can identify the category, social class; no experiment can be run through to prove the bourgeois character of bourgeois ideology, nor, indeed, to licence such a holistic notion. The vocabulary may be distinct, but the logics of both parties converge. At this point the philosophers shake hands, kiss each other's cheeks, and part. The true empiricist then says: "The discrete facts are all that can be known. 'History' is an improper holistic concept to cover a sequence of discrete facts as in fact they succeeded upon each other. If we introduce concepts, we introduce these as 'models' which assist us to investigate and organise these facts; but we must be clear that these models exist in our heads and not 'in' the history. And we must develop ever more refined, value-free, and preferably quantitative empirical techniques to enable these facts to disclose themselves as in fact they took place. Whatever happens, I will make sure that no facts escape from their discrete prison cells, enter into relationships, or hold mass meetings." The exalted Marxist structuralist says: "Goodbye! Your procedures bore me. I am going back to my theatre to write the script from some better, revolutionary, history."

But the curious thing is that, walking off in opposite directions, they end up in much the same place. We will see how this occurs. The "sciences" (Althusser proposed), "have no need for verification from *external* practices to declare the knowledge they produce to be 'true'." And (we recall) he explicitly nominates historical materialism as one such science. "Marx's theoretical practice is the criterion of the 'truth' of the knowledges that Marx produced." It is true that he once says, in a rare gesture towards an extra-philosophical world, that the successes and failures of this theoretical knowledge "constitute pertinent 'experiments' for the theory's reflection on itself and its internal development."[34] The gesture is indistinct; the 'experiments' are not identified; the criteria of success or failure go unspecified; the tone suggests that such 'experiments' are pertinent but inessential; and there is no suggestion that they could determine, in any respect, the "internal development" of theory. So that, once again, we find a remarkable congruence between Althusser's idealist structuralism and Popper's "weak empiricism."

Our two philosophers have been walking on distinct, but parallel, paths, nodding to each other across the epistemologically-illiterate flower-beds of the historians. But now the paths converge once again. Popper's radical scepticism has seemed to place us under the guidance of a vigilant logic; Althusser's epistemology directs us to the rigours of theoretical practice; both seem to dignify theory or logic, and to place these above the illusory appearances of "objective reality." But the consequence is that both meet, not at the fountain of thought, but staring with bewilderment into the gold-fish pond of appearances. Both paths of logic lead into the same bondage of things.

Popper disallows what cannot be sensed, tested by experiment, verified: but the inter-connections of social phenomena, causation within historical process—these seem to lie beyond any experimental test: hence a weak empiricism leaves us to stare uncomprehendingly at the world's most immediate manifestations, accepting them as what they are because that is what they seem to be. Althusser, on the contrary, is nothing if not vigilant against "common sense" appearances. He suspects *every* manifestation, *every* "exterior" signal: theoretical practice is equipped with its own criteria and its own discourse of the proof. But what follows from this? Since theory has only internal means for its own self-verification, it could develop, by its own extrapolation, in whichever way it pleases. (And so, in some highly-theoreticist expressions, it does). But we can't in fact get through the business of life in this way, nor can we get through the business of thinking in any substantive manner or about any substantive question. Once we leave epistemology behind, and ask questions about our neighbours, or about the economy, or history, or political practice, then some kind of assumptions (as to what we are thinking *about*) must be made before we can even begin to think.

Since theory disallows any active appropriation of the external world in the only way possible (by active engagement or dialogue with its evidence)

then *this whole world must be assumed.* The "raw materials" (G I) which
arrive are simply taken *as given;* and no amount of purely-internal
processing by G II into G III can make silk purses out of these sows' ears;
they remain (however mocked-up and sophisticated) exactly as they
started off—as assumptions (prejudices, cursory "common sense" surveys
of "what-everyone-knows") which happen to fall conveniently to hand
for the confirmation ("illustration") of the prior propositions of the
theory. It does not really matter that Popper and Althusser, bent in
bewilderment over the same pond, see differently coloured fish: that
bourgeois-empirical and Marxist-structural notions of "what-everyone-
knows" are supported upon differing ulterior presuppositions. Both have
immaculate epistemological reasons for seeing exactly what they came
to see.

There in the pond the appearances swim: to Althusser the fish seem
red, to Popper they are grey: one sees a gorgeous Workers' State swim by,
the other sees, lurking amidst the weeds, a reticent Open Society. They
must both end with appearances since both commenced by denying that
appearances are the inscription of an ulterior reality, of relationship and
practices, whose significance can be disclosed only after arduous
interrogation.

The appearances will not disclose this significance spontaneously and of
themselves: does one need to say this yet again? It is not part of my
intention to deny the seductive "self-evident" mystification of appearance,
or to deny our own self-imprisonment within unexamined categories. If we
suppose that the sun moves around the earth, this will be confirmed to us
by "experience" every day. If we suppose that a ball rolls down a hill
through its own innate energy and will, there is nothing in the appearance
of the thing that will disabuse us. If we suppose that bad harvests and
famine are caused by the visitation of God upon us for our sins, then we
cannot escape from this concept by pointing to drouth and late frosts and
blight, for God could have visited us through these chosen instruments. We
have to fracture old categories and to make new ones before we can
"explain" the evidence that has always been there.

But the making and breaking of concepts, the propounding of, new
hypotheses, the reconstructing of categories, is not a matter of theoretical
invention. Anyone can do this. Perhaps the famine was some frolic of the
devil? The blight in England a consequence of French witch-craft? Or
perhaps it was in fulfilment of some ancient curse, consequent upon the
Queen's adultery? Appearance will confirm each one of these hypotheses
as well: the devil is well known to be abroad, the French well known to be
witches, and most queens to be adulterous. And if we suppose the Soviet
Union to be a Workers' State guided by an enlightened Marxist theory;
or that market forces within capitalist society will always maximise the
common good; then in either case we may stand in one spot all day,

watching the blazing socialist sun move across blue heavens, or the ball of the Gross National Product roll down the affluent hill, gathering new blessings on its way. We need not recite this alphabet once again.

This alphabet, however, is not some special code, understood only by logicians. It is a common alphabet, to be mastered at the entry to all disciplines. Nor is it a severe lesson, to be administered periodically to "empiricists" (and only to them). To be sure, there are such empiricists who require this correction. But the lesson has two edges to its blade. Self-generating hypotheses, subject to no empirical control, will deliver us into the bondage of contingency as swiftly—if not more swiftly—than will surrender to the "obvious" and manifest. Indeed, each error generates and reproduces the other; and both may often be found, contained within the same mind. What has, it seems, to be recited afresh is the arduous nature of the engagement between thought and its objective materials: the "dialogue" (whether as *praxis* or in more self-conscious intellectual disciplines) out of which all knowledge is won.

vii

There will now be a brief intermission. You may suppose that the lights have been turned up and the ushers are advancing with trays of ice-cream. During this intermission I intend to discuss historical logic. Philosophers or sociologists who have a dislike or a profound disbelief in this subject are advised to withdraw to the foyer and the bar. They may rejoin us at section viii.

It is not easy to discuss this theme. Not very long ago, when I was in Cambridge as a guest at a seminar of distinguished anthropologists, when I was asked to justify a proposition, I replied that it was validated by "historical logic." My courteous hosts dissolved into undisguised laughter. I shared in the amusement, of course; but I was also led to reflect upon the "anthropological" significance of the exchange. For it is customary within the rituals of the academy for the practitioners of different disciplines to profess respect, not so much for the findings of each other's discipline, as for the authentic credentials of that discipline itself. And if a seminar of historians were to laugh at a philosopher's or anthropologist's very *credentials*, (that is, the logic or discipline central to their practice) this would be regarded as an occasion for offence. And the significance of this exchange was that it was very generally supposed that "history" was an exception to this rule; that the discipline central to its practice was an occasion for laughter; and that, so far from taking offence, I, as a practitioner, would join in the laughter myself.

It is not difficult to see how this comes about. The modes of historical writing are so diverse; the techniques employed by historians are so various; the themes of historical enquiry are so disparate; and, above all, the conclusions are so controversial and so sharply contested within the profession, that it is difficult to adduce any disciplinary coherence. And I can well see that there are things within the Cambridge School of History which might occasion anthropological, or other, laughter. Nevertheless, the study of history is a very ancient pursuit, and it would be surprising if, alone among the sciences and humanities, it had failed to develop its own discipline over several thousand years: that is, its own proper discourse of the proof. And I cannot see what this proper discourse is unless it takes the form of historical logic.

This is, I will argue, a *distinct* logic, appropriate to the historian's materials. It cannot usefully be brought within the same criteria as those of physics, for the reasons adduced by Popper and many others: thus, "history" affords no laboratory for experimental verification, it affords evidence of necessary causes but never (in my view) of sufficient causes, the "laws" (or, as I prefer it, logic or pressures) of social and economic process are continually being broken into by contingencies in ways which would invalidate any rule in the experimental sciences, and so on. But these reasons are not objections to historical logic, nor do they enforce (as Popper supposes) the imputation of "historicism" upon any notion of history as the record of a unified process with its own "rationality." They simply illustrate (and, on occasion, more helpfully, define) the conclusion that historical logic is not the same as the disciplinary procedures of physics.

Nor can historical logic be subjected to the same criteria as analytic logic, the philosopher's discourse of the proof. The reasons for this lie, not in historians' lack of logic, as in their need for a different *kind* of logic, appropriate to phenomena which are always in movement, which evince— even in a single moment—contradictory manifestations, whose particular evidences can only find definition within particular contexts, and yet whose general terms of analysis (that is, the questions appropriate to the interrogation of the evidence) are rarely constant and are, more often, in transition alongside the motions of the historical event: as the object of enquiry changes so do the appropriate questions. As Sartre has commented: "History is not order. It is disorder: a rational disorder. At the very moment when it maintains order, i.e. structure, history is already on the way to undoing it."[35]

But disorder of this kind is disruptive of any procedure of analytic logic, which must, as a first condition, handle unambiguous terms and hold them steadily in a single place. We have already noted a propensity in philosophers, when scrutinising "history's" epistemological credentials, to place "facts" as isolates upon their table, instead of the historians' customary materials—the evidence of behaviour (including mental, cultural behaviour) eventuating through time. When Althusser and many others accuse historians of having "no theory", they should reflect that what they take to be innocence or lethargy may be explicit and self-conscious *re-fusal:* refusal of static analytic concepts, of logic inappropriate to history.

By "historical logic" I mean a logical method of enquiry appropriate to historical materials, designed as far as possible to test hypotheses as to structure, causation, etc., and to eliminate self-confirming procedures ("instances", "illustrations"). The disciplined historical discourse of the proof consists in a dialogue between concept and evidence, a dialogue conducted by successive hypotheses, on the one hand, and empirical research on the other. The interrogator is historical logic; the interrogative a hypothesis (for example, as to the way in which different phenomena acted upon each other); the respondent is the evidence, with its determinate properties. To name this logic is not, of course, to claim that it is always evidenced in every historian's practice, or in any historian's practice all of the time. (History is not, I think, unique in failing to maintain its own professions.) But it is to say that this logic does not disclose itself involuntarily; that the discipline requires arduous preparation; and that three thousand years of practice have taught us something. And it is to say that it is this logic which constitutes the discipline's ultimate court of appeal: *not*, please note, "the evidence", by itself, but the evidence interrogated thus.

To define this logic fully—and to reply to certain of Popper's objections—would require writing a different, and more academic, essay, with many instances and illustrations. In addressing myself more particularly to the positions of Althusser it may be sufficient to offer, in defence of historical materialism, certain propositions.

1) The immediate object of historical knowledge (that is, the materials from which this knowledge is adduced) is comprised of "facts" or evidences which certainly have a real existence, but which are only knowable in ways which are and ought to be the concern of vigilant historical procedures. This proposition we have already discussed.

2) Historical knowledge is in its nature, a) provisional and incomplete (but not therefore untrue), b) selective (but not therefore untrue), c) limited and defined by the questions proposed to the evidence (and the concepts informing those questions) and hence only "true" within the field so defined. In these respects historical knowledge may depart from other paradigms of knowledge, when subjected to epistemological enquiry. In this sense I am ready to agree that the attempt to designate history as a "science" has always been unhelpful and confusing.[36] If Marx and, even more, Engels sometimes fell into this error, then we may apologise, but we should not confuse the claim with their actual procedures. Marx certainly knew, also, that History was a Muse, and that the "humanities" construct knowledges.

3) Historical evidence has determinate properties. While any number of questions may be put to it, only certain questions will be appropriate.

While any theory of historical process may be proposed, all theories are false which are not in conformity with the evidence's determinations. Herein lies the disciplinary court of appeal. In this sense it is true (we may agree here with Popper) that while historical knowledge must always fall short of positive proof (of the kinds appropriate to experimental science), false historical knowledge is generally subject to *dis*proof.[37]

4) It follows from these propositions that the relation between historical knowledge and its object cannot be understood in any terms which suppose one to be a function (inference from, disclosure, abstraction, attribution or "illustration") of the other. Interrogative and response are mutually determining, and the relation can be understood only *as a dialogue*.

Four further propositions may now be presented at greater length.

5) The object of historical knowledge is "real" history whose evidences must necessarily be incomplete and imperfect. To suppose that a "present", by moving into a "past", thereby changes its ontological status is to misunderstand both the past and the present.[38] The palpable reality of our own (already-passing) present can in no way be changed because it is, *already*, becoming the past for posterity. To be sure, posterity cannot interrogate it in all the same ways; to be sure, you and I, as experiencing instants and actors within our present, will survive only as certain evidences of our acts or thoughts.

While historians may take a decision to select from this evidence, and to write a history of discrete aspects of the whole (a biography, the history of an institution, a history of fox-hunting, etc.), the real object remains unitary. The human past is not an aggregation of discrete histories but a unitary sum of human behaviour, each aspect of which was related in certain ways to others, just as the individual actors were related in certain ways (by the market, by relations of power and subordination, etc.). Insofar as these actions and relations gave rise to changes, which become the object of rational enquiry, we may define this sum as historical *process:* that is, *practices* ordered and structured in rational ways. While this definition arrives in response to the question asked,[39] this does not "invent" process. We must take our stand here, against Goldmann, and with Bloch (see p. 20). The finished processes of historical change, with their intricate causation, actually occurred, and historiography may falsify or misunderstand, but can't in the least degree modify the past's ontological status. The objective of the historical discipline is the attainment of that history's truth.

Each age, or each practitioner, may propose new questions to the historical evidence, or may bring new levels of evidence to light. In this sense "history" (when considered as the products of historical enquiry) will change, and ought to change, with the pre-occupations of each generation, or, as it may be, each sex, each nation, each social class. But this by no means implies that the past events themselves change with each questioner, or that the evidence is indeterminate. Disagreements between historians may be of many kinds, but they remain as mere exchanges of attitude, or exercises of ideology, unless it is agreed that they are conducted within a common discipline whose pursuit is objective knowledge.

To this proposition it is necessary to add a rider. When we speak of the "intelligibility" of history, we may mean the understanding of the rationality (of causation, etc.) of historical process: this is an objective knowledge, disclosed in a dialogue with determinate evidence. But we may also imply the "significance" of that past, its meaning *to us;* this is an evaluative and subjective judgement, and to such interrogatives the evidence can supply no answers. This does not entail the conclusion that any such exercise is improper. We may agree (with Popper) that each generation, each historian, is entitled to express a "point of view", or (with Kolakowski) that we are entitled to attribute such "immanent intelligibility" to history as an "act of faith", provided that we are clear that this rests, not upon scientific procedures, but upon a "choice of values."[40]

We may agree not only that such judgements as to the "meaning" of history are a proper and important activity, a way in which today's actors identify their values and their goals, but that it is also an *inevitable* activity. That is, the pre-occupations of each generation, sex or class must inevitably have a normative content, which will find expression in the questions proposed to the evidence. But this in no way calls in question the objective determinacy of the evidence. It is simply a statement as to the complexity, not just of history, but of ourselves (who are simultaneously valuing and rational beings)—a complexity which enters into all forms of social self-knowledge, and which requires in all disciplines procedural safeguards. It is, exactly, within historical logic that such attributions of meaning, if covert and improper, are exposed; it is in this way that historians find each other out. A feminist historian will say, or ought to say, that this history-book is wrong, not because it was written by a man, but because the historian neglected contiguous evidence or proposed conceptually-inadequate questions: hence a masculine "meaning" or bias was imposed upon the answers. It is the same with the somewhat intemperate arguments which I and my Marxist colleagues often provoke within the academic profession. The appeal is not (or rarely) to a choice of values, but to the logic of the discipline. And if we deny the determinate properties of the object, then no discipline remains.

But I cannot leave this rider while giving the impression that the attribution of "meaning", as valued-significance, is only a matter for regret, a consequence of human fallibility. I think it to. be greatly more important than that. I am not in the least embarrassed by the fact that, when presenting the results of my own historical research, I offer value judgements as to past process, whether openly and strenuously, or in the form of ironies or asides. This is proper, in one part, because the historian is examining individual lives and choices, and not only historical eventuation (process). And while we may not attribute value to process, the same objections do not arise with the same force when we are considering the choices of individuals, whose acts and intentions may certainly be judged (as they were judged by contemporaries) within the due and relevant historical context.

But this is only a special case of a more general question. Only we, who are now living, can give a "meaning" to the past. But that past has always been, among other things, the result of an argument about values. In recovering that process, in showing how causation actually eventuated, we must, insofar as the discipline can enforce, hold our own values in abeyance. But once this history has been recovered, we are at liberty to offer our judgement upon it.

Such judgement must itself be under historical controls. The judgement must be appropriate to the materials. It is pointless to complain that the bourgeoisie have not been communitarians, or that the Levellers did not introduce an anarcho-syndicalist society. What we may do, rather, is identify with certain values which past actors upheld, and reject others. We may give our vote for Winstanley and for Swift; we may vote against Walpole and Sir Edwin Chadwick.

Our vote will change nothing. And yet, in another sense, it may change everything. For we are saying that these values, and not those other values, are the ones which make this history meaningful *to us*, and that these are the values which we intend to enlarge and sustain in our own present. If we succeed, then we reach back into history and endow it with our own meanings: we shake Swift by the hand. We endorse in our present the values of Winstanley, and ensure that the low and ruthless kind of opportunism which distinguished the politics of Walpole is abhorred.

In the end we also will be dead, and our own lives will lie inert within the finished process, our intentions assimilated within a past event which we never intended. What we may hope is that the men and women of the future will reach back to us, will affirm and renew our meanings, and make our history intelligible within their own present tense. They alone will have the power to select from the many meanings offered by our quarrelling present, and to transmute some part of our process into their progress.

For "progress" is a concept either meaningless or worse, when imputed as an attribute *to* the past (and such attributions may properly be denounced as "historicist"), which can only acquire a meaning from a particular position in the present, a position of value in search of its own genealogy. Such genealogies *exist*, within the evidence: there have been men and women of honour, courage, and "foresight", and there have been historical movements informed by these qualities. But in spite of Goldmann's authority, we must argue, not that "historical reality changes from epoch to epoch with modifications in the hierarchy of values," but that the "meaning" which we attribute to that reality changes in this way.

This "rider" to my proposition has taken us a little out of our way. The proposition concerned the objectivity of "real' history. We seem to return, again and again, to the narrowing circuits of this epistemological whirlpool. Let us try to advance.

6) The investigation of history as process, as eventuation or "rational disorder", entails notions of causation, of contradiction, of mediation, and of the systematic organisation (sometimes structuring) of social, political, economic and intellectual life. These elaborate notions[41] "belong" within historical theory, are refined within this theory's procedures, are thought within thought. But it is untrue that they belong *only* within theory. Each notion, or concept, arises out of empirical engagements, and however abstract the procedures of its self-interrogation, it must then be brought back into an engagement with the determinate properties of the evidence, and argue its case before vigilant judges in history's "court of appeal." It is, and in a most critical sense, a question of dialogue once more. In the sense that a thesis (the concept, or hypothesis) is brought into relation with its antithesis (atheoretical objective determinacy) and a synthesis (historical knowledge) results we might call this the dialectics of historical knowledge. Or we might have done so, before "dialectics" was rudely snatched out of our grasp and made into the plaything of scholasticism.

Historical practice is above all engaged in this kind of dialogue; with an argument between received, inadequate, or ideologically-informed concepts or hypotheses[42] on the one hand, and fresh or inconvenient evidence on the other; with the elaboration of new hypotheses; with the testing of these hypotheses against the evidence, which may involve interrogating existing evidence in new ways, or renewed research to confirm or disprove the new notions; with discarding those hypotheses which fail these tests, and refining or revising those which do, in the light of this engagement.

Insofar as a notion finds endorsement from the evidence, then one has every right to say that it *does* exist, "out there," *in* the real history. It does not of course actually exist, like some plasma adhering to the facts, or as some invisible kernel within the shell of appearances. What we are saying is that the notion (concept, hypothesis as to causation) has been brought into a disciplined dialogue with the evidence, and it has been shown to "work"; that is, it has not been *dis*proved by contrary evidence, and that it successfully organises or "explains" hitherto inexplicable evidence; hence it is an adequate (although approximate) representation of the causative sequence, or rationality, of these events, and it conforms (within the logic of the historical discipline) with a process which did in fact eventuate in the past. Hence it exists simultaneously both as a "true" knowledge and as an adequate representation of an actual property of those events.

7) Historical materialism differs from other interpretive orderings of historical evidence not (or not necessarily) in any epistemological premises, but in its categories, its characteristic hypotheses and attendant procedures,[43] and in the avowed conceptual kinship between these and the concepts elaborated by Marxist practitioners in other disciplines. I do not see Marxist historiography as being attendant *on* some general corpus of Marxism-as-theory, located somewhere else (perhaps in philosophy?). On the contrary, if there is a common ground for all Marxist practices then it must be where Marx located it himself, in historical materialism. This is the ground from which all Marxist theory arises, and to which it must return in the end.

In saying this, I am not saying that Marxist historians are not indebted for certain concepts to a general Marxist theory which extends itself towards, and draws upon the findings of, Marxists at work in other fields. This is evidently the case; our work goes on in a continual exchange. I am disputing the notion that this is a Theory, which has some Home, independently of these practices: a self-validating textual Home, or a Home in the wisdom of some Marxist party, or a Home in purified theoretical practice. The homeland of Marxist theory remains where it has always been, the real human object, in all its manifestations (past and present): which object however, cannot be known in one theoretical *coup d'oeil* (as though Theory could swallow reality in one gulp) but only through discrete disciplines, informed by unitary concepts. These disciplines or practices meet at each other's borders, exchange concepts, converse, correct each other's errors. Philosophy may (and must) monitor, refine, and assist the conversation. But let philosophy attempt to *abstract* the concepts from the practices, and build from them a Home for Theory independently of these, and far removed from any dialogue with theory's object, then we will have—the theatre of Althusser!

It follows that if Marxist concepts (that is, concepts developed by Marx and within the Marxist tradition) differ from other interpretive concepts in historical practice, and if they are found to be more "true", or adequate to explanation, than others, this will be because they stand up better to the test of historical logic, and not because they are "derived from" a true Theory outside this discipline. As, in any case, they were not. Insofar as I am myself deeply indebted for certain concepts to Marx's own practice, I refuse to evade responsibility by falling back upon his authority or to escape from criticism by leaping from the court of appeal. For historical knowledge, this court lies within the discipline of history and nowhere else.

Appeal may take two forms: a) evidential, which has been sufficiently discussed, and b) theoretical—to the coherence, adequacy and consistency of the concepts, and to their congruence with the knowledge of adjacent disciplines. But both forms of appeal may be conducted only within the vocabulary of historical logic. The court has been sitting in judgement upon historical materialism for one hundred years, and it is continually being adjourned. The adjournment is in effect a tribute to the robustness of the tradition; in that long interval the cases against a hundred other interpretive systems have been upheld, and the culprits have disappeared "downstairs". That the court has not yet found decisively in favour of historical materialism is not only because of the ideological *parti pris* of certain of the judges (although there is plenty of that) but also because of the provisional nature of the explanatory concepts, the *actual* silences (or absent mediations) within them, the primitive and unreconstructed character of some of the categories, and the inconclusive determinacy of the evidence.

8) My final proposition brings a fundamental reservation to bear upon Althusserian epistemology, and also upon certain structuralisms or functional systems (e.g. Parsonian sociology) which periodically attempt to over-run the historical discipline. Certain critical categories and concepts employed by historical materialism can only be understood *as historical categories:* that is, as categories or concepts appropriate to the investigation of process, the scrutiny of "facts" which, even in the moment of inter-rogation, change their form (or retain their form but change their "meanings"), or dissolve into other facts; concepts appropriate to the handling of evidence not capable of static conceptual representation but only as manifestation or as contradiction.

The construction of historical concepts is not of course a special privilege peculiar to historical materialism. Such concepts arise within the historians' common discourse, or are developed within adjacent disciplines. The classic concept of the crisis of subsistence[44] proposes a rational sequence of events: as, for example, poor harvest → dearth → rising mortality → the consumption of next year's seed → a second poor harvest → extreme dearth → a peak in mortality, accompanied by epidemic → a sharply rising conception-rate. The concept of the familial development cycle proposes a particular three-generational sequence within the same peasant household, modified by the particular conditions of land tenure and inheritance practice. These concepts, which are generalised by logic from many examples, are brought to bear upon the evidence, not so much as "models" but rather as "expectations." They do not impose a rule, but they hasten and facilitate the interrogation of the evidence, even though it is often found that each case departs, in this or that particular, from the rule. The evidence (and the real event) is not rule-governed, and yet it could not be understood without the rule, to which it offers its own irregularities. This provokes impatience in some philosophers (and even sociologists) who consider that a concept with such elasticity is not a true concept, and a rule is not a rule unless the evidence conforms to it, and stands to attention in one place.

Historical concepts and rules are often of this order. They display extreme elasticity and allow for great irregularity; the historian appears to be evading rigour as he disappears into the largest generalisations at one moment, while at the next moment he disappears into the particularities of the qualifications in any special case. This provokes distrust, and even laughter, within other disciplines. Historical materialism employs concepts of equal generality and elasticity—"exploitation", "hegemony", "class struggle"—and as expectations rather than as rules. And even categories which appear to offer less elasticity—"feudalism", "capitalism", "the bourgeoisie"—appear in historical practice, not as ideal types fulfilled in historical evolution, but as whole families of special cases, families which include adopted orphans and the children of typological miscegenation. History knows no regular verbs.

It is the misfortune of Marxist historians (it is certainly our special misfortune today) that certain of our concepts are common currency in a wider intellectual universe, are adopted in other disciplines, which impose their own logic upon them and reduce them to static, a-historical categories. No historical category has been more misunderstood, tormented, transfixed, and de-historicised than the category of social class;[45] a self-defining historical formation, which men and women make out of their own experience of struggle, has been reduced to a static category, or an effect of an ulterior structure, of which men are not the makers but the vectors. Not only have Althusser and Poulantzas done Marxist history this wrong, but they then complain that history (from whose arms they abducted this concept) has no proper theory of class! What they, and many others, of every ideological hue, misunderstand is that it is not, and never has been, the business of history to make up this kind of inelastic theory. And if Marx himself had one supreme methodological priority it was, precisely, to destroy unhistorical theory-mongering of this kind.

History is not a factory for the manufacture of Grand Theory, like some Concorde of the global air; nor is it an assembly-line for the production of midget theories in series. Nor yet is it some gigantic experimental station in which theory of foreign manufacture can be "applied", "tested", and "confirmed." That is not its business at all. Its business is to recover, to "explain", and to "understand" its object: real history. The theories which historians adduce are directed to this objective, within the terms of historical logic, and there is no surgery which can transplant foreign theories, like unchanged organs, into other, static, conceptual logics, or *vice versa.* Our objective is historical knowledge; our hypotheses are advanced to explain this particular social formation in the past, that particular sequence of causation.

Our knowledge (we hope) is not thereby imprisoned within that past. It helps us to know who we are, why we are here, what human possibilities have been disclosed, and as much as we can know of the logic and forms of social process. Some part of that knowledge may be theorised, less as rule than as expectation. And exchanges may and should take place with other knowledges and theories. But the exchange involves vigilance, as the theoretical coin of one discipline is translated into the currency of another. Philosophy ought not to stand on every frontier like a huckster, offering spurious "universal' bank-notes current in all lands. It might, instead, operate a watchful *bureau de change*.

Those propositions of historical materialism which bear upon the relation between social being and social consciousness, upon the relations of production and their determinations, upon modes of exploitation, class struggle, ideology, or upon capitalist social and economic formations, are (at one pole of their "dialogue") derived from the observation of historical eventuation *over time*. This observation is not of discrete facts *seriatim* but of *sets* of facts with their own regularities: of the repetition of certain kinds of event: of the congruence of certain kinds of behaviour within differing contexts: in short, of the evidences of systematic social formations and of a common logic of process. Such historical theories as arise (not of themselves, but, at the other pole of the dialogue, by arduous conceptualisation) can not be tested, as is often supposed, by calling a halt to process, "freezing" history, and taking a static geological section, which will show capitalism or class hierarchies at any given moment of time as an elaborated structure.[46] In investigating history we are not flicking through a series of "stills", each of which shows us a moment of social time transfixed into a single eternal pose: for each one of these "stills" is not only a moment of being but also a moment of becoming: and even within each seemingly-static section there will be found contradictions and liaisons, dominant and subordinate elements, declining or ascending energies. Any historical moment is both a result of prior process and an index towards the direction of its future flow.

There are well-known difficulties, both in explaining historical process and in verifying any explanation. "History" itself is the only possible laboratory for experiment, and our only experimental equipment is historical logic. If we press improper analogies with experimental sciences, we will soon find out that the whole business is unsatisfactory. History never affords the conditions for identical experiments; and while, by comparative procedures, we may observe somewhat similar experiments in different national laboratories (the rise of the nation state, industrialization) we can never reach back into those laboratories, impose our own conditions, and run the experiment through once again.

But such analogies have never been helpful. The fact that the difficulties of historical explanation are immense should surprise no-one. We inhabit the same element ourselves (a present becoming a past), a human element of habit, need, reason, will, illusion and desire, and we should know it to be made up of obstinate stuff. And yet there is one sense in which the past improves upon the present, for "history" remains its own laboratory of process and eventuation. A static section may show us certain elements (A, B, & C) in mutual inter-relationship or contradiction; eventuation over time will show us how these relationships were lived through, fought out, resolved, and how ABC gave rise to D; and this eventuation will, in turn, throw light back upon the ways in which the elements were previously related and the strength of the contradiction.

In this sense the eventuation confirms or disproves, hardens or qualifies, the explanatory hypothesis. This is a bad laboratory in one sense: that the event took place in this way may be the consequence of some contingent element (X) overlooked in the explanation; thus ABC + X may have eventuated in one way (D), but ABC + Y would have eventuated differently (E); and to overlook this is to fall into the familiar error of arguing *post hoc ergo propter hoc*. This is a besetting problem of all historical explanation, and philosophers who have glanced at our procedures have made a hearty meal of it. But they overlook the fact that in another sense "history" is a good laboratory, because process, eventuation, is present within every moment of the evidence, testing every hypothesis in an outcome, providing results for every human experiment that has ever been conducted. Our logic is fallible. But the very multiplicity of experiments, and their congruence to each other, limit the dangers of error. The evidence as to any particular episode may be imperfect: there will be plenty of gaps when we consider eventuation in the form of discrete facts in series: but (at least in less distant history)[47] sufficient evidence survives to disclose the logic of this process, its outcome, the characteristic social formations, and how ABC in fact gave rise to D.

We may make this point more clear if we consider a problem, not from the past, but from the historical present. The Soviet Union is such a problem. In order to explain one aspect of this problem—who holds power and in what direction is political process tending?—a number of explanatory hypotheses are proposed. For example, the Soviet Union is a Workers' State (perhaps with certain "deformities") capable of ascendant self-development, without any severe internal struggle or rupture of continuity: all "short-comings" are capable of self-correction, owing to the guidance of a proletarian party, informed by Marxist Theory, and hence blessed with the "know-how" of history. Or the Soviet Union is a state in which power has fallen into the hands of a new bureaucratic class, whose interest it is to secure its own privileges and continued tenure of power—a class which will only be overthrown by another proletarian revolution. Or the Soviet State is the instrument of a historically-specific form of forced industrialization, which has thrown up an arbitrary and contingent collocation of ruling-groups, which may now be expected to be the agents of the "modernization" of Soviet society, bringing it into tardy and imperfect conformity with that true model of modern man: the United States. Or (which is closer to my own view) the Soviet State can only be understood with the aid of the concept of "parasitism", and whether or not its ruling groups harden into a bureaucratic *class*, or whether episodic reform can be imposed upon them by pressures of various kinds (from the needs and resistances of workers and farmers, from intellectual dissenters, and from the logic arising from their own inner contradictions, factional struggles, and incapacity to perform essential functions, etc.) remains, historically, an unfinished and indeterminate question, which may be precipitated into one or another more fully-determined direction by contingencies.

There is a real and important sense in which these (or other) hypotheses will only find confirmation or refutation in the *praxis* of eventuation. The experiment is still being run through, and (much as Althusser dislikes Engels's Mancunian colloquialism) "the proof of the pudding will be in the eating." The result, when brought within the scrutiny of future historians, may appear to confirm one hypothesis, or may propose a new hypothesis altogether. Any such "confirmation", if it should arise, can never be more than approximate: history is not rule-governed, and it knows no sufficient causes: and if future historians suppose otherwise they would be falling into the error of *post hoc ergo propter hoc*. The hypotheses, or the blend of ideology and of self-knowledge, which we, or the Soviet people, adopt in this present will themselves enter as an element within eventuating process. And if some different "contingency" had impinged upon these elements (for example, if a Third World War had arisen from the Cuba crisis), then all would have eventuated differently, the military and security forces would have been immensely strengthened, and a different hypothesis might then appear to have explanatory force.

But this is not as devastating a qualification as may at first appear. For it will be *as* matters eventuate, *as* the "experiment" works out, which will afford to future historians immense additional insight as to the critical relations structuring Soviet society, which underlie the appearances of our historical present. The "result" will afford to them additional insight into which formidable elements (perhaps the State ideology of Marxism-Leninism) were to prove, in the event, to be fragile and in decline, and which inarticulate, loosely-structured elements pre-figured an emergent opposition. The historians of the future, who will know *how* things turned out will have a powerful aid to understanding, not why they *had* to turn out in that way, but why in fact they did: that is they will observe in the laboratory of events the evidence of determination, not in its sense

as rule-governed law but in its sense of the "setting of limits" and the
"exerting of pressures."[48] And today's historians stand in exactly the same
position in relation to the historical past, which is, simultaneously, the
object of investigation and its own experimental laboratory.

That historical explanation cannot deal in absolutes and cannot adduce
sufficient causes greatly irritates some simple and impatient souls. They
suppose that, since historical explanation cannot be All, it is therefore
Nothing; it is no more than a consecutive phenomenological narration.
This is a silly mistake. For historical explanation discloses not how
history *must* have eventuated but why it eventuated in this way and not
in other ways; that process is not arbitrary but has its own regularity and
rationality; that certain kinds of event (political, economic, cultural) have
been related, not in any way one likes, but in particular ways and within
determinate fields of possibility; that certain social formations are—not
governed by "law" nor are they the "effects" of a static structural
theorem—but are characterised by determinate relations and by a particular
logic of process. And so on. And a great deal more. Our knowledge may
not satisfy some philosophers, but it is enough to keep us occupied.

We have left our eighth proposition behind, and we may now rehearse
it once again. The categories appropriate to the investigation of history are
historical categories. Historical materialism is distinguished from other
interpretive systems by its stubborn consistency (alas, a stubbornness
which has sometimes been doctrinaire) in elaborating such categories, and
by its articulation of these within a conceptual totality. This totality is
not a finished theoretical "truth" (or Theory); but neither is it a make-
believe "model"; it is a developing *knowledge*, albeit a provisional and
approximate knowledge with many silences and impurities. The development of this knowledge takes place both within theory and within
practice: it arises from a dialogue: and its discourse of the proof is
conducted within the terms of historical logic. The actual operations of this
logic do not appear, step by step, on every page of a historian's work; if
they did, history books would exhaust all patience. But this logic should
be implicit in each empirical engagement, and explicit in the way in which
the historian positions himself before the evidence and in the questions
proposed. I do not claim that historical logic is always as rigorous or as
self-conscious as it ought to be; nor that our practice often matches our
professions. I claim only that there is such logic. And that not all of us are
wet behind the ears.

viii

The intermission is now over. Philosophers and sociologists are requested
to cease chatting in the aisles, and to resume their places in the empty
seats around me. The auditorium is darkening. A hush falls in the theatre.

And Althusser resumes the stage.

The great impressario has returned refreshed, and in an uncustomary mood of geniality. He announces that the heavy epistemological drama will be suspended: we have done with history and tragedy for the time. Instead, he will present a burlesque sketch of his own composition, a little influenced by Sade. A superannuated clown with pretensions to epistemological respectability, will be brought in (the audience must please keep straight faces at first), quizzed, exposed, mocked, tormented, and finally booted and hooted off the stage. From the wings he drags on, gouty, dim-eyed, a fool's cap upon his head, that poor old duffer, Frederick Engels.

The sketch starts a little slowly, and with subtlety. Engels is interrogated about "parallelograms of forces", about "individual wills" and historical "resultants"; he is convicted of tautology; he hangs his head; he is forgiven ("I am quite prepared to ignore Engels's reference to *nature*"). He is convicted of worse confusion, of association with bourgeois ideology; he hangs his head again; is sharply reprimanded (a "futile construction"), but then is given a toffee (he has "genial theoretical intuitions"). He smiles and nods to the audience, little expecting what is to follow. The dialogue is a little difficult to follow, especially as the clown is not allowed to respond. We will take the script home and comment on it later.[49]

Now the whip is brought out:

When, in *Anti-Dühring*, Engels writes that 'Political Economy is. . . essentially a historical science', because 'it deals with material which is historical, that is, constantly changing', he touches the exact spot of the ambiguity: the word '*historical*' may either fall towards the Marxist concept or towards the ideological concept of history, according to whether this word designates the *object of knowledge* of a theory of history, or, on the contrary, the real object of which this theory gives the knowledge. We have every right to say that the theory of Marxist political economy derives from the Marxist theory of history, as one of its regions; but we might also think [i.e. Engels's words might allow us to suppose] that the theory of political economy is affected even in its concepts by the peculiar *quality* of real history (its 'material' which is '*changing*').

The clown "rushes us into this latter interpretation in a number of astonishing texts which introduce history (in the empiricist-ideological sense) even into Marx's categories." Absurdity of absurdities! He even says that it is wrong to expect "fixed, cut-to-measure once and for all applicable definitions in Marx's works." And he argues:

It is self-evident that where things and their inter-relations are conceived, not as fixed, but as changing, their mental reflections, *the concepts are likewise subject to change and transformation.*

Worse still, he is caught with his buttocks exposed, in an obscene anti-theoreticist posture:

> To science definitions are worthless because always inadequate. The only real definition is the development of the thing itself, but this is no longer a definition. [50] To know and show all forms of life we must examine all forms of life and present them in their inter-connexion. (R.C. 113. Althusser's exclamatory italics)

Thus the old buffer is exposed in an "astonishing" relapse into empiricist "ideology." He is convicted of supposing that "the necessary concepts of any theory of history are affected in their conceptual substance, by the properties of the real object":

> In this way, Engels applies to the concepts of the theory of history a coefficient of mobility borrowed directly from the concrete empirical sequence (from the ideology of history), transposing the 'real-concrete' into the 'thought-concrete' and the historical as real change into the concept itself. (R.C. 114)

But this time the old clown's abject apologies earn him no remission of punishment. The boot and the whip fall inexorably. For it turns out that he is not a clown at all; he is a cunning fellow, masquerading in clown's motley, hoping to pass off as jests the malice of his true nature. This nature is fully revealed at the very end of the act; for in March 1895, five months before his death, the old man sheds all disguises and is found writing to Conrad Schmidt:

> The objections you raise to the law of value apply to all concepts, regarded from the standpoint of reality. The identity of thinking and being, to express myself in Hegelian fashion, everywhere coincides with your example of the circle and the polygon. Or the two of them, the concept of a thing and its reality, run side by side like two asymptotes, always approaching each other yet never meeting. This difference between the two is the very difference which prevents the concept from being directly and immediately reality and reality from being immediately its own concept. Because a concept has the essential nature of that concept and cannot therefore prima facie directly coincide with reality, from which it must first be abstracted, it is something more than a fiction, unless you are going to declare all the results of thought fictions because reality corresponds to them only very circuitously, and even when only with asymptomic approximation.

Now at last the sketch is brought to a close, the old man is booted whimpering into the wings, the curtain is rung down. Engels's letter "is astounding (despite the banality of its obviousness")." Engels's blunders would mark "Marxist philosophical theory. . . and with what a mark! The mark of the empiricist theory of Knowledge. . ." On every side of me the audience bursts into rapturous applause.

What a clever sketch! It is a pity it was so brief, perhaps, because—now it has been shown to us—one can think of other earlier lines of this same clown which could have been turned to equal account. There was, for example, that malicious (decidedly not innocent) assault on philosophy itself, in *Ludwig Feuerbach*, which Althusser has no doubt not forgiven, and for which he is now taking his revenge. "The proof" of the Marxist conception of history (Engels unashamedly avowed) "is to be found in history itself":

> This conception, however, puts an end to philosophy in the realm of history, just as the dialectical conception of nature made all natural philosophy both un- necessary and impossible. It is no longer a question anywhere of inventing inter- connections from out of our brains, but of discovering them in the facts. For philosophy, which has been expelled from nature and history, there remains only the realm of pure thought (so far as it is left): the theory of the laws of the thought-process itself, logic and dialectics. (*L.F.* 69)

What self-restraint in Althusser not to flagellate these notions ("discovering them in the facts"!!!): but the comedy would have been over-facile. Or there is that other "astonishing" text in *Anti-Dühring:*

> If we deduce world schematism not from our minds, but only *through* our minds from the real world, deducing the basic principles of being from what is, we need no philosophy for this purpose, but positive knowledge of the world and of what happens in it; and what this yields is also not philosophy, but positive science. (*A-D*, 45)

(How does it happen that no record of Marx's explosion before this apostasy has been recorded?) Or we could have browsed more generally through the old clown's later letters. Even that letter to Schmidt, which Althusser has singled out for corrective treatment, does not end there; it *goes on*, and, if anything, gets *worse!* All of Marx's economic concepts— the general rate of profit, the law of wages, rent—indeed, "economic laws in general—none of them has any reality except as approximation, tendency, average, and not as *immediate* reality." It is the same for historical concepts also:

> Did feudalism ever correspond to its concept? Founded in the kingdom of the West Franks, further developed in Normandy by the Norwegian conquerors, its formation continued by the French Norsemen in England and Southern Italy, it came nearest to its concept—in Jerusalem, in the kingdom of a day, which in the *Assises de Jerusalem* left behind it the most classic expression of the feudal order. Was this order therefore a fiction because it only achieved a short-lived existence in full classical form in Palestine, and even that mostly only—on paper?

And the same epistemological irresponsibility is displayed even with reference to the present, and *to the future!* For Engels tells Schmidt that the laws of value and of profit,

> Both only attain their most complete approximate realisation on the pre-supposition that capitalist production has been everywhere completely established, society reduced to the modern classes of landowners, capitalists (industrialists and merchants) and workers—all intermediate stages, however, having been got rid of. This does not exist even in England and never will exist—we shall not let it get so far as that.

What a solecism! To introduce into the discourse of the proof a category, "we" (the agency of an old man and his imaginary friends), derived from a different "region" (and a suspect region, too—does it not smack of "humanism"?) and for which the Theory has made no provision!

But (for we are stern critics) the dramatist might surely have enriched his sketch in other ways? Why only *one* clown? Why not *two* clowns, a thin one stooping with age, and a fatter one, more robust and youthful, as foils to each other? Let us drag from the wings, perspiring, tormented by carbuncles, the super-clown, fatty Marx! He makes his bow, and recites from an early letter (to P.V. Annenkov, December 1846) (and *after* the "epistemological break"), a criticism of Proudhon:

> He has not perceived that *economic categories* are only the *abstract expressions* of these actual relations and only remain true while these relations exist. He therefore falls into the error of the bourgeois economists who regard these economic categories as eternal and not as historic laws which are only laws for a particular historical development. . . Instead, therefore, of regarding the political-economic categories as abstract expressions of the real, transitory, historic social relations, Monsieur Proudhon only sees, thanks to a mystic transposition, the real relations as embodiments of these abstractions. These abstractions therefore are formulae which have been slumbering in the heart of God the Father since the beginning of the world.

Categories, then, "are historic and transitory products," whereas, according to Proudhon, "they, and not men, make history":

> The *abstraction,* the *category taken as such,* i.e. apart from men and their material activities, is of course immortal, unmoved, unchangeable, it is only one form of the being of pure reason; which is only another way of saying that the abstraction as such is abstract. An admirable *tautology!*

And, writing to Schweitzer nearly twenty years later (January 1865), Marx returned to the critique of Proudhon, in exactly the same terms: "he shares the illusions of speculative philosophy in his treatment of the *economic categories;* for instead of conceiving them as *the theoretical expression of historic relations of production, corresponding to a*

particular stage of development in material production, he garbles them
into pre-existing *eternal ideas. . ."*

But let us cease to imagine improvements in the sketch. Let us sit down
and examine it as it has been presented.

ix

What is all this about? It would be simple to dismiss the whole argument
on the grounds that Althusser has proposed a spurious question,
necessitated by his prior epistemological confusions. This is, in fact, a large
part of the answer, and a sufficient answer to Althusser, and it can be
briefly stated. He has proposed a pseudo-opposition. On the one hand, he
presents Theory (and *Capital* itself) as "occurring exclusively in knowledge
and concerning exclusively the necessary order of appearance and
disappearance of concepts in the discourse of the scientific proof." (*R.C.*
114) On the other side, across from this rather grand project, he presents
the petty projects of "empiricism", which constitute "ideology." Engels
is trying to muddle the two, which would be disastrous (the mark of the
empiricist Beast!), since the discourse of the proof must, as a pre-requisite,
demand the fixity and unambiguity of concepts. But we have already seen
that Althusser's notion of "empiricism" is false, and that it imposes the
canons of philosophy upon quite different procedures and disciplines. We
need follow this argument no further.

Even within its own terms, Althusser's argument offers self-contradictions
and evasions. Thus he tells us that "we have every right to say that the
theory of Marxist political economy derives from the Marxist theory of
history, as one of its regions"; but he also tells us (see p. 14) that the
theory of history, even now, 100 years after *Capital,* "does not exist in
any real sense." So that in one of its "regions" Marxist political theory
was derived from "an absent theory." This goes along with the evasion of
the evident fact that in *other* of its regions, this political economy was
derived, very directly, from empirical engagement, either directly (from
the mountain of blue books, etc., etc., to which Marx pays such generous
tribute,[51]) or less directly, by intense and critical scrutiny of the
empirically-based studies of other writers.

So that Althusser set out with a bad argument, and he rigged the terms
to make it look better. Engels would appear to have been arguing two
propositions. First, the inherently "approximate" nature of all our
concepts, and especially of those necessarily "fixed" concepts which arise
from and are brought to the analysis of changing, *un*fixed social development. This may be a "banality" in its "obviousness" to a philosopher, who
supposes that it "is only another way of saying that the abstraction as
such is abstract", an "admirable *tautology*" which rarely leaves Althusser's
lips. But, to a historian or an economist, it is (while "obvious" as theory)

exceptionally complex in fact: it is an obviousness which can only too easily be forgotten in practice, and of which we need reminders.

Moreover, Engels is not just saying that concepts and their "real object" are different. It is true that he overstates his case in a moment of exasperation at the old bourgeois scholastics and the new "Marxist" schematists on every side: "to science definitions are worthless." We understand his exasperation only too well. But the point of his letter to Schmidt is to argue, a) that because all concepts are approximations, this does not make them "fictions", b) that only the concepts can enable us to "make sense of", understand and know, objective reality, c) but that even in the act of knowing we can (and ought to) know that our concepts are more abstract and more logical than the diversity of that reality—and, by empirical observation, *we can know this too.* We cannot understand European medieval society without the concept of feudalism, even though, with the aid of this concept, we can also know that feudalism (in its conceptual logic) was never expressed "in full classical form"; which is another way of saying that feudalism is a heuristic concept which represents (corresponds to) real social formations, but, in the manner of all such concepts, does so in an overly purified and logical way. The definition cannot give us the real event. In any case, Engels's words are clearer than my gloss. What they come back to, as so often in these last letters, is the cry for "dialectics", whose true meaning is to be found less in his attempt to reduce these to a formal code than in his practice. And an important part of this practice is exactly that "dialogue" between concept and evidence which I have already discussed.

Engels's second point concerns the nature of specifically *historical* concepts, concepts adequate to the understanding of materials which are in continuous change. Althusser exclaims against the notion that "the theory of Political Economy is affected even in its concepts by the peculiar *quality* of real history (its 'material' which is 'changing')." The short answer to this is that if the real object of this knowledge is changing, and if the concepts cannot encompass the processes of change, then we will get extremely bad Political Economy. Not only Marxist but orthodox bourgeois Political Economy had an arsenal of such concepts of change (laws of this and that, rising and falling rates of the other, even the mobilities of supply and demand). What Althusser means to exclaim against is an irreverence to the fixity of categories. Engels says not only that the object changes but that the concepts *themselves* must be "subject to change and trans- formation." For Althusser capitalism must be one thing: or another thing: or nothing. It cannot be one thing now, and another thing tomorrow. And if it is one thing, then the essential categories must remain the same, how- ever much "play" there may be inside them. If the categories change as the object changes, according to a "coefficient of mobility", then science or Theory are lost; we drift among the tides of phenomena, the tides themselves moving the rudder; we become (as Marx accused the students of Ranke) the "valets" of history.

But it is not clear that Engels has set us adrift like this. The offensive words (in my view) are not "concepts... are subject to change and transformation" (for that may well indicate, and *does* indicate for Engels, the strenuous theoretical-empirical dialogue entailed in transformation), but the preceding words, "their mental reflections."[52] And Engels may equally be signalling—and, I think, is signalling in his discussion of the concept, feudalism—the particular flexibility of concepts appropriate in historical analysis: that is, the necessary generality and elasticity of historical categories, as expectations rather than as rules. I have had occasion enough to observe in my own practice that if a category as generous as "the working class" is improperly hardened by theoreticians to correspond to a particular historical moment of class presence (and an ideal moment at that), then it very soon gives false and disastrous historical/political results; and yet without the (elastic) category of class— an expectation justified by evidence—I could not have practised at all.

So that I think that Engels is talking good sense, that Althusser has misrepresented him, and is talking no sense at all. But, nevertheless, it is true that a real problem remains. We cannot just say that Engels is right and Althusser wrong. Althusser has mis-stated the problem, but at least we may admit that he has pointed to the area where the problem lies. The problem concerns, from one aspect, the differing modes of analysis of *structure* and of *process*. And, from another aspect, the status of "Political Economy" and, hence, the status of *Capital*. We will take it from the second aspect first.

We must commence, at once, by agreeing that *Capital* is not a work of "history". There is a history of the development of the forms of capital inscribed within it, but this is rarely developed within the historical discipline, or tested by the procedures of historical logic. The historical passages are something more than "instances" and "illustrations", but something less than the real history. We will explain this more fully in a moment. But we must say at once that Marx never pretended, when writing *Capital*, that he was writing the history of capitalism. This is well known, but we will offer reminders. Marx hopes (as is apparent from the *Grundrisse* notebooks) that his work would "also offer the key to the understanding of the past—a work in its own right which, it is to be hoped, we shall be able to undertake as well."[53] This hope was not fulfilled. The work which was completed was that described (to Lassalle in 1858) as "a critique of the economic categories or the system of bourgeois economy, critically presented"; and it dealt (he told Kugelmann) with "capital in general." The first volume "contains what the English call 'the principles of Political Economy'." And its title was: *Capital, a Critique of Political Economy.*[54]

One way of proceeding may be to stand back from the structure for a moment, and enquire what kind of structure it is. First, we must note that some part of the power of the work comes not from its explicit procedures, and from its disclosure of its object, but from choices as to values (and their vigorous and relevant expression) which could not possibly be deduced from the conceptual procedures themselves, and which are not the object of study. That is, Marx does not only lay bare the economic processes of exploitation, but he also expresses (or presents his material so as to evoke) indignation at suffering, poverty, child labour, waste of human potentialities, and contempt for intellectual mystifications and apologetics.

I comment on this, neither to commend it nor to condemn it, although the relevance may appear later. Since Marx's choice of values could be justified only with reference to a "region" which Althusser curtly dismisses as "ideology", we might have to explain (even condone) it as a vestige of bourgeois moralism, even humanism. Certainly, no such vestiges appear with Althusser and Balibar: when they have "read" *Capital* it has been disinfested of all this. We may, or we may not, prefer the first to the second "reading" of *Capital;* the point is that, in this significant respect, they are different books.

Second, it may follow from this, and I think it *does* so follow, that if we disinfest *Capital* in this way of all "moralistic" intrusions, a very considerable part of that work—the major part—could be taken *just as* "what the English call 'the principles of Political Economy' ": an analytic critique of the existing "science", and an exposition of an alternative "science", of economic functions, relations, and laws. That is, if we did not (for exterior "reasons" of value) disapprove of exploitation, waste and suffering, then we would find ourselves presented with an alternative lawed structure of economic relations. To be true, the reader whose interests lay with "capital" would find its conclusions pessimistic; for the system is presented as moving rapidly towards a final crisis (which has not yet eventuated). But this could not afford any "scientific" reasons for disagreement.

These two considerations are not introduced for "moralistic" purposes. They help us to take a sighting of *Capital* within the intellectual context of its moment of genesis. And they remind us that the notions of *structure* and of *system* were not inventions of Marx (although one might suppose so from some contemporary statements). We had, as is well known, in eighteenth-century Britain very marvellous structures, the admiration of the world and the envy of the French. In particular, the constitutional structures were exemplary, and had perhaps been provided to the British by God:

Britain's matchless Constitution, mixt
Of mutual checking and supporting Powers,
Kings, Lords and Commons. . .

Or, in the familiar clockwork analogy, as employed by William Blackstone:
"Thus every branch of our civil polity supports and is supported, regulates
and is regulated, by the rest. . . Like three distinct powers in mechanics,
they jointly impel the machine of government in a direction different from
what either, acting by itself, would have done. . ."

God, as Bacon had pointed out, worked by second causes, and these
causes, whether in nature, in psychology or in the constitution, often
appeared as *sets* of interacting causes (structures). The sets that mechanical
materialism proposed followed the paradigm of the clock, or of the mill.
The constitutional set was governed by the rule of law. But bourgeois
Political Economy (from Adam Smith forward) discovered a different set,
seen now more as a "natural process", whose nexus was the market, where
intersecting self-interests were mediated, under the government of that
market's laws. By the time that Marx confronted it, this Political
Economy had become, by way of Malthus, Ricardo, and the Utilitarians, a
very sophisticated structure indeed, rigorous in its procedures and inclusive
in its claims.

Marx identified this structure as his major antagonist, and he bent the
whole energies of his mind to confounding it.[55] For nearly twenty years
this was his major preoccupation. He had to enter into each one of the
categories of Political Economy, fracture them, and re-structure them. We
can see the evidences of these encounters in the *Grundrisse* notebooks of
1857-8, and it is customary to admire their exhaustive ardour. And I do so
admire them. But I cannot altogether admire them. For they are evidences
also that Marx was *caught in a trap:* the trap baited by "Political
Economy." Or, more accurately, he had been sucked into a theoretical
whirlpool, and, however manfully he beats his arms and swims against the
circulating currents, he slowly revolves around a vortex which threatens to
engulf him. Value, capital, labour, money, value, reappear again and again,
are interrogated, re-categorised, only to come round once more on the
revolving currents in the same old forms, for the same interrogation.[56]
Nor am I even able to agree that it *had* to be like this, that Marx's thought
could only have been developed in this way. When one considers the
philosophical breakthrough of the 1840s, and the propositions which
inform the *German Ideology* and *Communist Manifesto*, there would
appear to be indications of stasis, and even regression, in the next
fifteen years. Despite the significance of the *economic* encounter in the
Grundrisse, and despite the rich hypotheses which appear in its interstices
(as to pre-capitalist formations, etc.), there is something in Marx's
encounter with Political Economy which is obsessive.

For what was this "Political Economy"? It did not offer a total account of society or of its history; or, if it pretended to do so, then its conclusions were entailed in its premises. These premises proposed that it was possible, not only to identify particular activities as "economic", but to isolate these as a special field of study from the other activities (political, religious, legal, "moral"—as the area of norms and values was then defined—cultural, etc.); where such isolation proved to be impossible, as in the impingement of "politics" or "law" *upon* "economic" activity, then such impingement might be seen as improper interference with "natural" economic process, or as second-order problems, or as the fulfilment of economic goals by other means.

It might also be proposed (although not necessarily) that economics, and, with Malthus, demography, were first-order problems, and that these determined (or, in a "free" state, should and would determine) social development as a whole. These "underlay" the elaborate superstructures of civilization, determining the wealth of nations and the pace and direction of "progress." Thus isolated, economic activities became the object of a "science", whose primary postulates were interests and needs: self-interest at a micro-level, the interests of groups ("agriculture" and "industry") or even of classes ("Labour" and "Capital") at a macro-level, the groups and classes being defined according to the economic premises of the science. To develop such a science with rigour demanded accurate definition and fixity of categories, a mathematical logic, and the continuous internal circulation and recognition of its own concepts: its conclusions were acclaimed as "laws".

This is the structure of "Political Economy." From the outside, in the 1840s, it appeared to Marx as ideology, or, worse, apologetics. He entered within it in order to overthrow it. But, once inside, however many of its categories he fractured (and how many times), the structure remained. For the premises supposed that it was possible to isolate economic activities in this way, and to develop these as a first-order science *of society.* It is more accurate to say that Marx, at the time of the *Grundrisse,* did not so much remain within the structure of "Political Economy" as develop an *anti*-structure, but within its same premises. The postulates ceased to be the self-interest of men and became the logic and forms of capital, to which men were subordinated; capital was disclosed, not as the benign donor of benefits, but as the appropriator of surplus labour; factional "interests" were disclosed as antagonistic classes; and contradiction displaced the sum progress. But what we have at the end, is not the overthrow of "Political Economy" but *another* "Political Economy."[57]

Insofar as Marx's categories were anti-categories, Marxism was marked, at a critical stage in its development, by the categories of Political Economy: the chief of which was the notion *of* the "economic", as a first-order activity, capable of isolation in this way, as the object of a science giving rise to laws whose operation would over-ride second-order activities. And there is another mark also, which it is difficult to identify without appearing to be absurd. But the absurdities to which this error has been taken in the work of Althusser and his colleagues—that is, the absurdities of a certain kind of static self-circulating "Marxist" structuralism—enable us to risk the ridicule. There is an important sense in which the movement of Marx's thought, in the *Grundrisse*, is locked inside *a static, anti-historical structure.*

When we recall that Marx and Engels ceaselessly ridiculed the pretensions of bourgeois economy to disclose "fixed and eternal" laws, independent of historical specificity; when we recall the movement *within* the structure, the accumulation of capital, the declining rate of profit; and when we recall that Marx sketched, even in the *Grundrisse*, capital in terms of the development of its historical forms, then the proposition seems absurd. After all, Marx and Engels enabled historical materialism to be born. And yet the proposition has force. For once capital has emerged on the page, its self-development is determined by the innate logic inherent within the category, and the relations so entailed, in much the same way as "the market" operates within bourgeois Political Economy, and still does so within some "modernization theory" today. Capital is an operative category which laws its own development, and capital*ism* is the effect, in social formations, of these laws. This mode of analysis must necessarily be anti-historical, since the actual history can only be seen as the expression of ulterior laws; and historical evidence, or contemporary (empirically-derived) evidence, will then be seen as Althusser sees it, as instances or illustrations confirming these laws. But when capital and its relations are seen as a structure, in a given moment of capital's forms, then this structure has a categorical stasis: that is, it can allow for no impingement of any influence from any other region (any region not allowed for in the terms and discourse of this discipline) which could modify its relations, for this would threaten the integrity and fixity of the categories themselves.

This is an extraordinary mode of thought to find in a materialist, for capital has become Idea, which unfolds itself in history. We remember so well Marx's imprecations against idealism, and his claims to have inverted Hegel, that we do not allow ourselves to see what is patently there. In the *Grundrisse*—and not once or twice, but in the whole mode of presentation—we have examples of *unreconstructed* Hegelianism. Capital posits conditions *"in accordance with its immanent essence"*,[58] reminding us that Marx had studied Hegel's Philosophy of Nature, and had noted of "the Idea as nature" that "reality is posited with immanent determinateness of form."[59] Capital posits this and that, creates this and that, and if we are to conceive of capital*ism* ("the inner construction of modern society") it can only be as "capital in the totality of its relations."[60]

It is true that Marx reminds us (or is he reminding himself?) that "the new forces of production and relations of production" of capital "do not develop out of *nothing*. . . nor from the womb of the self-positing Idea." But he goes on, immediately, to add:

> While in the complicated bourgeois system every economic relation presupposes every other in its bourgeois economic form, and everything posited is thus also a presupposition, this is the case with every organic system. This organic system itself, as a totality, has its presuppositions, and its development to its totality consists precisely in subordinating all elements of society to itself, or in creating out of it the organs which it still lacks. [61]

The "organic system" is then its own subject, and it is this anti-historical stasis or *closure* which I have been indicating. The "it" inside this organism is capital, the soul of the organ, and "it" subordinates all elements of society to itself and creates out of society "its" own organs.

The point is not only that in the light of this kind of lapse Engels's warnings to Schmidt are necessary and salutary: concepts and economic laws have no reality "except as approximation": "Did feudalism ever correspond to its concept?" There is a point of greater importance. For Marx has moved across an invisible conceptual line from *Capital* (an abstraction of Political Economy, which is his proper concern) to *capitalism* ("the complicated bourgeois system"), that is, the whole society, conceived of as an "organic system." But the whole society comprises many activities and relations (of power, of consciousness, sexual, cultural, normative) which are not the concern of Political Economy, which have been *defined out of* Political Economy, and for which it has no terms. Therefore Political Economy cannot show capital*ism* as "capital in the totality of its relations": it has no language or terms to do this. Only a historical materialism which could bring all activities and relations within a coherent view could do this. And, in my view, subsequent historical materialism has *not* found this kind of "organism", working out its own self-fulfilment with inexorable idealist logic, nor has it found any society which can be simply described as "capital in the totality of its relations." "We" have *never* let it get so far as that: even Fascism, which might be offered as "its" most ferocious manifestation, would then have to be glossed as an expression of its irrationality, not of its inherent rational logic. But historical materialism has found that Marx had a most profound intuition, an intuition which in fact *preceded* the *Grundrisse:* that the logic of capitalist process has found expression within all the activities of a society, and exerted a determining pressure upon its development and form: hence entitling us to speak of capitalism, or of capitalist societies. But this is a very different conclusion, a critically different conclusion, which gives us an organicist structuralism on one side (ultimately an Idea of capital unfolding itself) and a real historical process on the other.

This is only a part of the *Grundrisse*, of course. And, of course, Marx conceived of himself, pugnaciously, as a materialist. In his introduction he vindicated his method, of proceeding from abstractions to the concrete in thought; and his method was largely vindicated in the results: only by the fiercest abstraction could he crack those categories apart. But he also discounted, in cavalier fashion, the inherent dangers of the method. Hegel went astray because, proceeding by this method, he "fell into the illusion of conceiving the real as the product of thought unfolding itself out of itself." It seemed so easy to cast this silly illusion aside, but to proceed by much the same method. But if Marx never forgot that thought was not self-generating but was "a product, rather, of the working-up of observation and conception into concepts,"[62] this mode of abstraction could still give him, on occasion, capital as the unfolding of its own idea.

I think that, for ten years, Marx *was* in this trap. His delays, his carbuncles, cannot all be attributed to the bourgeoisie. When he came to write *Capital* the trap had been in some part sprung. I am not expert enough to describe his partial self-deliverance, but I would suggest four considerations. First, the trap was never fully closed. Marx had conceived of capital*ism* in historical terms in the 1840s, continued to do so, by fits and starts, in the *Grundrisse*, and these were also years in which applied and concrete political analysis continued to flow from his pen. Second, and alongside this, he continued to develop, not only in his historical but also in his practical political experience, as a historical actor in his own part, and in observing the growth, flux and recession of working-class struggles in Europe. These two considerations are self-evident.

The other two may be more controversial. For the third, I would emphasize once again the important influence of *The Origin of Species* (1859). I am aware that my admiration for Darwin is regarded as an amiable (or guilty) eccentricity, and that there is a general mind-set among progressive intellectuals which attributes to Darwin the sins of teleological evolutionism, positivism, social Malthusianism, and apologias for exploitation (the "survival of the fittest") and of racism.[63] But I am not convinced of these objections, and, to be honest, I am not even convinced that all these critics have read *The Origin of Species*, nor read informed scientific evaluations of it. I know very well how Darwin's ideas were put to use by others, and I also know of his subsequent (rather few) lapses. But what is remarkable in his work is the way in which he argues through rigorously, and in an empirical mode, the logic of evolution which is *not* a teleology, whose conclusions are *not* entailed in their premises, but which is still subject to rational explanation.[64] In any case, my admiration, whether innocent or not, was certainly shared by Engels and Marx. Marx read the book in December 1860, and at once wrote to Engels: "Although it is developed in the crude English style, this is the book which contains the basis in natural history for our view." To Lassalle he wrote in the next month, the book "is very important and serves me as a basis in natural science for the class struggle in history. . . Despite all deficiencies, not only is *the death-blow dealt here for the first time to 'teleology' in the natural sciences but their rational meaning is empirically explained.*"[65]

There are two important recognitions here: first, Marx recognised, grudgingly, that the empirical method, however "crude", however "English", had educed a substantial contribution to knowledge; second, Marx recognised in the *non-teleological* explication of a rational logic in natural process "a basis. . . for our view", indeed "a basis in natural science for the class struggle in history." There is surely a recognition here that this "basis" had *not* been provided before (in the *Grundrisse*), and even the suggestion that Marx was aware that his abstractionist mode of procedure was not proof against such teleology? It is not that Marx supposed that Darwinian analogies could be taken unreconstructed from the animal to the human world: he very soon reproved a correspondent who, with the aid of Malthus, was supposing that.[66] It is rather a question of method, in which Darwin's work was taken as exemplar of the rational explication of the logic of process, which, in new terms, must be developed in historical practice. And I cannot see that we have any licence to pass this off as some momentary fancy. Still, in 1873, Marx took the trouble to send to Darwin a copy of *Capital*, inscribed by him as a gift from "his sincere admirer."[67]

It is at this time (1860) that the work of fashioning the *Grundrisse* into *Capital* commenced. And this leads me to my fourth consideration. It appears to me that Marx was more self-critical of his earlier work than many commentators allow. I will not delay to puzzle over the various hints that survive as to his own self-dissatisfaction.[68] But in my view the writing of *Capital* involved a radical re-structuring of his materials, in ways partly influenced by *The Origin of Species*. It is argued (for example, by Martin Nicolaus, the editor of the *Grundrisse*) that the changes may be attributed to Marx's desire to make his work more "popular", more "concrete", and hence more widely available to the revolutionary movement; but "the *inner* structure of *Capital* is *identical* in the main lines to the *Grundrisse*." In the first, "the method is visible; in *Capital* it is deliberately, consciously hidden. . ." I do not think so. And I think even less of the attempt to explain away Marx's letter to Engels (15 August 1863), in which he writes of the slow progress of *Capital*, and explains that he has "had to turn everything round", as meaning that "he had to over-throw virtually all of previous Political Economy." The phrase is this: "when I look at this compilation now and see how I have had to turn everything round and how I had to make even the *historical* part out of material of which some was quite unknown": and it cannot bear this construction. The "overthrow" of previous political economy had been done, already, in the notebooks (*Grundrisse*) of 1857-8; what was new was "the historical part" and the "turning around" of the rest.[69]

This turning round, I am arguing, involved not only adding a historical dimension to the work, and much greater concrete exemplification (derived from empirical investigation) but also attempting to bring under control and reduce to the rational explication of process the "idealist" (even self-fulfilling, teleological) formulations derived from the abstractionist mode. What comes into *Capital*, in a new way, is a sense of history, and a concretion of exemplification (accompanied, we recall, by "extraneous" expressions of wrath).

And yet Nicolaus is not wholly wrong; in some part—and that part specifically the anti-structure of "Political Economy"—the structure of *Capital* remains that of the *Grundrisse*.[70] It remains a study of the logic of capital, not of capitalism, and the social and political dimensions of the history, the wrath, and the understanding of the class struggle arise from a region independent of the closed system of economic logic. In that sense *Capital* was—and probably had to be—a product of theoretical miscegenation. But miscegenation of this order is no more possible in theory than in the animal kingdom, for we cannot leap across the fixity of categories or of species. So that we are forced to agree with seven generations of critics: *Capital* is a mountainous inconsistency. As pure Political Economy it may be faulted for introducing external categories; its laws cannot be verified, and its predictions were wrong. As "history" or as "sociology" it is abstracted to a "model", which has heuristic value, but which follows too obsequiously ahistorical economic laws.

Capital was not an exercise of a different order to that of mature bourgeois Political Economy, but a total confrontation *within* that order. As such, it is both the highest achievement of "political economy", and it signals the need for its supersession by historical materialism. To say the former is not to diminish Marx's achievement, for it is only in the light of that achievement that we are able to make this judgement. But the achievement does not *produce* historical materialism, it provides the preconditions for its production. A unitary knowledge of society (which is always in motion, hence a historical knowledge) cannot be won from a "science" which, as a presupposition of its discipline, isolates certain kinds of activity only for study, and provides no categories for others. And the structure of *Capital* remains marked by the categories of his antagonist, notably *economy* itself. In this sense it is true that in *Capital* "history" is introduced to provide exemplification and "illustration" for a structure of theory which is not derived from this discipline. However reluctantly, we must go half-way towards the positions of Althusser and Balibar. But we need not go all the way, for these "illustrations" would have been of no value if they were *wrong*, snatched from "history's" received accounts, and not both researched ("I had to make even the *historical* part out of material of which some was quite unknown") and interrogated in new ways.

It is more true to say that the history in *Capital,* and in attendant writings, is immensely fruitful *as hypothesis,* and yet as hypothesis which calls in question, again and again, the adequacy of the categories of Political Economy. We find here a veritable cornucopia of hypotheses, informed by consistent theoretical propositions (the determining pressures of the mode of production), hypotheses which historical materialism has been setting to work ever since. But setting them to work has not involved only "testing" them or "verifying" them,[71] it has also entailed revising and replacing them. Even Marx's more elaborated historical hypotheses (for example, as to the struggle to lengthen the working day, or as to the enclosure movement in England and its relation to labour supply for industry), as well as his more cryptic or more complex hypotheses (for example, as to the transition from feudalism to capitalism, or as to the British "bourgeois revolution", or as to "oriental despotism" and the "Asiatic mode of production") have always undergone, in historical materialism's own discourse of the proof, either reformation or very much more radical change.[72]

How could it be otherwise? To suppose differently would be to suppose, not only that everything can be said at once, but that immanent Theory (or Knowledge) found its miraculous embodiment in Marx, not fully mature to be sure (it had yet to develop to Althusser's full stature), but already perfectly-formed and justly-proportioned in all its parts. This is a fairy-story, recited to children in Soviet primary classes, and not even believed by them. *Capital,* volume I, is rich in historical hypotheses; volumes II and III are less so; the "anti-structure" of Political Economy narrows once again.[73] Marx's hope of himself developing historical materialism in practice remained, very largely, unfulfilled. It was left to the old clown, Frederick Engels, to make some attempts to remedy that; and his essay in historical anthropology, *The Origin of the Family* (Darwin's influence again!) is generally taken by Marxist anthropologists today to exemplify the infancy rather than the maturity of their knowledge.

In his final years, Engels looked around in alarm and noted the gathering consequences of their great omission. There are "many allusions" to the theory of historical materialism in *Capital* (he wrote to Bloch in 1890), and "Marx hardly wrote anything in which it did not play a part." But he wrote nothing in which it played a leading part, and Bloch was directed to *Anti-Dühring* and *Ludwig Feuerbach* as the places in which might be found "the most detailed account of historical materialism which, so far as I know, exists." And, in the same year, to Conrad Schmidt, "All history must be studied afresh, the conditions of existence of the different formations of society must be individually examined before the attempt is made to deduce from them the political, civil-legal, aesthetic, philosophic, religious, etc., notions corresponding to them. Only a little has been done here up to now. . ."

It is sobering to reflect upon how many human activities (for none of which Political Economy afforded categories) are comprised within this sentence. But Engels was in an increasingly sober mood:

> Too many of the younger Germans simply make use of the phrase, historical materialism (and *everything* can be turned into a phrase), in order to get their own relatively scanty historical knowledge (for economic history is still in its cradle!) fitted together into a neat system as quickly as possible, and then they think themselves something very tremendous.

So that not only historical materialism, but the region of it most immediately proximate to *Capital*, economic history, Engels could see to be "still in its cradle." It now seemed to him, with gathering urgency, that what was wrong with Marx's uncompleted life-work, *Capital*, was that it was not historical *enough*. To Mehring, in 1893:

> There is only one other point lacking, which, however, Marx and I always failed to stress enough in our writings and in regard to which we are all equally guilty. We all, that is to say, laid and were bound to lay the main emphasis at first on the derivation of political, juridical and other ideological notions, and of the actions arising through the medium of these notions, from basic economic facts. But in so doing we neglected the formal side—the way in which these notions come about—for the sake of the content.

"It is the old story," Engels continued: "Form is always neglected at first for content." But this failure had given purchase to the criticisms of "the ideologists", with their—

> Fatuous notion. . . that because we deny an independent historical development to the various ideological spheres which play a part in history we also deny them any effect in history. The basis of this is the common undialectical conception of cause and effect as rigidly opposite poles, the total disregarding of interaction. . .

The letters are familiar, and it may be wondered why I rehearse them. I do this now to emphasise, first, that Engels clearly acknowledged that Marx had *assumed* a theory of historical materialism which he had neither fully posed nor begun to develop. For some part of its proposition we are, indeed, dependent upon Engels's late letters. Althusser ridicules these letters, but we should note a curiosity in the fact that he can, in the same moment, borrow notions ("relative autonomy," "in-the-last-instance determination") of central importance to his thought from passages which lie cheek-by-jowl in the same letters which he lampoons. I will add that these letters were as familiar to me and to fellow practitioners in historical materialism in 1948 as in 1978, and that this was where we started *from*.

We did not have to wait upon Althusser to learn that the *critical* problems lay in the area of "relative autonomy", etc.; these phrases pointed towards the problems which we then set out in our practice to examine. I will come back to this question, since it indicates a very different Marxist tradition from that of Althusser.

The second reason for rehearsing these letters is that we find in them that Engels is (as I think) correctly indicating the area of the largest (and most dangerous and ambiguous) of the real silences left by Marx's death— and shortly to be sealed by his own. But in the same moment, in the very terms in which he discusses this absent theory he reveals the inadequacy of its terms. For "political, juridical and other ideological notions" cannot be derived from "economic facts" within a discourse of Political Economy so exacting that its very definitions of the "economic" affords to these extraneous evidences no entry. And the notion that the concepts of Marxism should be historical categories and "subject to change and transformation" would play havoc with the credentials of Marxism as an exact "science" of the capitalist mode of production. So that Engels is saying, in effect, that historical materialism and Marxist Political Economy have failed to find a common junction and a theoretical vocabulary capable of encompassing both process and structure; that Marxism is in danger of becoming imprisoned within the categories of *Capital;* but that the pressure of incipient historical materialism can be seen within its structure (in its *in*consistencies as much as its hypotheses), which pressure he could authenticate (from Marx's other work and from their long common project). He wished, in these final letters, to give to historical materialism a charter of liberation from the structure of the old *Grundrisse,* but he could not solve the theoretical problems thus entailed nor find the terms to do so. Subsequent historical materialism, in its practice—although in-sufficiently in its theory—has sought to serve under this charter of liberation. Althusser and his colleagues seek to thrust historical materialism back into the prison of the categories of Political Economy.

I think that contemporary Marxist economists are right to note that "in *Capital. . .* Marx repeatedly uses the concept of the circuit of capital to characterise the structure of the capitalist economy"—and, more than that, of capitalist society more generally.[74] But historical materialism (as assumed as hypothesis by Marx, and as subsequently developed in our practice) must be concerned with other "circuits" also: the circuits of power, of the reproduction of ideology, etc., and these belong to a different logic and to other categories. Moreover, historical analysis does not allow for static contemplation of "circuits", but is immersed in moments when all systems go and every circuit sparks across the other. So that Engels is in this sense wrong: it is not true that he and Marx "neglected the formal side—the way in which these notions come about— for the sake of the content." It was, rather, the over-development of the formal side, in the "anti-structure" of Political Economy, which in its genesis and form was derived from a bourgeois construction, and which confined the real historical content into impermissible and unpassable forms.

Our concern must now be to approach this problem from a different aspect: the alternative heuristics of "structure" and of "process." But, first, may we take a brief adieu of our old clown? It is now *de rigueur* to make old Engels into a whipping boy, and to impugn to him any sign that one chooses to impugn to subsequent Marxisms. All this has now been written out, and by many hands, and I need not go over it all again.[75] I am willing to agree that several of the charges stick. Thus I think it is true that in his writings i) Engels gave credibility to epistemological "reflection theory",[76] ii) he introduced a paradigm of "natural process" (a misapplied Darwinism) in his anthropological and historical work, which drifted towards a positivist evolutionism, iii) he certainly introduced—as did, with equal certainty, Marx—historicist notions of lawed and pre-determined development. These are heavy charges, although I cannot accept the pleadings which always find Marx and Lenin innocent and leave Engels alone in the dock. And to these I have added my own, more marginal, charges, as to Engels's unfortunate and ill-considered influence in the formative British socialist movement.[77] But when all this has been said, what an extraordinary, dedicated and versatile man he was! How closely he followed his own times, how far he risked himself—further, often, than Marx—in engagements with his contemporary historical and cultural thought, how deeply and passionately he was engaged in a movement which was spreading to the five continents, how generously he gave himself in his last years to the papers of his old friend and to the incessant correspondence of the movement! If we must learn, on occasion, from his errors, then he would have expected this to be so. And it is, least of all, for the "revisionist" letters of his last decade that he is to be cast as a whipping boy.

It is taken to be a truism by the young that older is worse than younger, but I cannot see that Engels exemplifies that general case. The "General", in his last decade, did not renege upon the propositions of his youth; rather, he dwelt nostalgically upon "the salad days" of the 1840s, and in the wisdom and foreboding of age he noted that there was something in the young movement of the 1880s and 1890s which was turning away from the intuitions of his and Marx's original theses. If he is to be punished, he should be punished for these late letters of qualification and of warning least of all. That the letters proposed, but did not answer, many problems can be agreed; but if the warnings had been fully attended to, then the history of Marxism might have been different. I will not allow Frederick Engels to be cast as a senile clown after all. He should be taken, until his last year, as he would have wished: his great sanity, his errors, his breadth of understanding (but his excessive "family" possessiveness) of the movement, all inter-mixed.

x

We will now discuss structure and process. It is customary at this point to launch into a long disquisition on the diachronic and the synchronic heuristics. But I hope that we may take this as read. However eloquent, the disquisition is likely to leave us with the conclusion that *both* heuristics are valid and necessary. I must make it clear, without equivocation, that in the argument which follows I am not disputing the necessity for synchronic procedures in social, economic and (on occasion) in historical analysis. Such procedures (a general view of a whole society, "frozen" at a certain moment, or a systematic isolation from the whole of certain selected activities) have always been employed by historians, and a glance down the volumes of our "trade" journals (for example, *Past and Present* or *Annales E.S.C.* or the *Economic History Review*) will show that specialist synchronic vocabularies have been brought to interrogate "history" more frequently in the last three decades than at any previous period.

Historical materialism offers to study social process in its totality; that is, it offers to do this when it appears, not as another "sectoral" history—as economic, political, intellectual history, as history of labour, or as "social history" defined as yet another sector[78] —but as a total history of society, in which all other sectoral histories are convened. It offers to show in what determinate ways each activity was related to the other, the logic of this process and the rationality of causation. We need only to state this claim to note two observations which must at once follow upon it. First, historical materialism must, in this sense, be the discipline in which all other human disciplines meet. It is the unitary discipline, which must always keep watch over the isolating premises of other disciplines (and the fictional stasis entailed by the freezing of process in yet others), but whose maturity can only consist in its openness towards and its summation of the findings of those other disciplines. So—"History" must be put back upon her throne as the Queen of the humanities, even if she has sometimes proved to be rather deaf to some of her subjects (notably anthropology), and gullible towards favourite courtiers (such as econometrics). But, second, and to curb her imperialist pretensions, we should also observe that "History", insofar as it is the most unitary and general of all human disciplines, must always be the *least* precise. Her knowledge will never be, in however many thousand years, anything more than proximate. If she makes claims to be a precise science these are wholly spurious. But (as I have sufficiently argued) her knowledge remains knowledge, and it is attained through its own rigorous procedures of historical logic, its own discourse of the proof.

As we have seen, the credentials of historical materialism have, in the last decades, come under sustained and ferocious assault; and this assault has been mounted equally from positions within orthodox "bourgeois" academic disciplines (epistemology, sociology, etc.), from enclaves within the historical profession itself (genuine empiricism, quantitative positivism, etc.), and from a "Marxist" structuralism. And, as with epistemology, what distinguishes all these attacks—and what should be taken note of by Marxist philosophers and sociologists—is the *similarity* of their forms, their modes of argumentation and their conclusions. All commence by questioning the knowability of process, as a total logic of change of sets of inter-related activities, and end up by tilting the vocabularies of knowledge very heavily (even absolutely) towards synchronic rather than diachronic procedures. The diachronic is waived away as mere unstructured "narrative", an unintelligible flow of one thing from another. Only the stasis of structural analysis can disclose knowledge. The flow of events ("historicist time") is an empiricist fable. The logic of process is disallowed.

Before approaching this more closely I will stand back for a moment and take a historical perspective on this problem: for it seems to me that the rise of structuralism has real roots in historical experience, and that this drift of the modern mind must be seen to be, in some part, a drift of *ideology*. Structuralism may indeed be seen as the illusion of this epoch, just as evolutionism ("progress") and voluntarism have characterised earlier moments in this century. Evolutionism was a "natural" ideological confusion within the socialist movement in the decades preceding the First World War. Year by year (with minor "set-backs") the movement was gathering force, new adhesions were announced to the International, trade union and party membership enlarged, more socialist deputies were elected. As Walter Benjamin was to comment:

> Nothing has corrupted the German working class so much as the notion that it was moving with the current. It regarded technological developments as the fall of the stream with which it was moving. From there it was but a step to the illusion that the factory work which was supposed to tend toward technological progress constituted a political achievement.[79]

Marxism was hence infiltrated by the vocabulary (and even premises) of economic and technical "progress"—which in Britain meant the vocabulary of utilitarianism—and of an evolutionism which borrowed improperly from the natural sciences and Darwinism. In bad times and adversity, militants might still uphold their cause by means of an evolutionism which, as Gramsci showed, was compressed into a kind of determinist stamina: "history" was on their side, and they would be vindicated in the end. While the First World War offered to this evolutionism a check, the October revolution gave to it a new and more utopian incarnation. Utopianism (in its customary Marxist denigratory notation[80]) has an astonishing and flourishing reincarnation within Marxism itself, in the form of a prettified and wholly fictional projection of "the Soviet Union": to outsiders this utopia was offered as the emblem of their own future "history", their own glorious and inexorable future.

This evolutionism (and its vocabulary) persisted, of course, and notably in the former colonial world, where "evolution", once again, seemed to be the ally of the militants: I have found the vocabulary (although fiercely disputed) still vigorous among Marxists in India today. But I think that there were ways in which the decade, 1936-46, gave to it a sharp check. Marxism, in the decisive emergencies of Fascist insurgence and of the Second World War, began to acquire the accents of voluntarism. Its vocabulary took on—as in Russia after 1917 it had taken on—more of the active verbs of agency, choice, individual initiative, resistance, heroism and sacrifice. Victory in those emergencies no longer seemed to be in the course of "evolution": far from it. The very conditions of war and repression—the dispersal of militants into armies, concentration camps, partisan detachments, underground organisations, even isolated positions— threw squarely upon them as individuals the necessity for political judgement and active initiation. It seemed, as the partisan detachment blew up the crucial railway bridge, that they were "making history"; it seemed, as the women endured the bombs or as the soldiers stood with their backs to Stalingrad, that "history" depended on their endurance. It was a decade of heroes, and there were Guevaras in every street and in every wood. The vocabulary of Marxism became infiltrated from a new direction: that of authentic liberalism (the choices of the autonomous individual) and perhaps also of Romanticism (the rebellion of spirit against the rules of fact). Poetry, rather than natural science or sociology, was welcomed as a cousin. It was all very disgusting, and, as events were to prove, futile. All that it left were the bones of our more heroic brothers and sisters to bleach on the plains of the past under a hallucinated utopian sun. And, to be sure (although a small matter) a war—a necessary and historic confrontation—that was won. But I cannot disclaim the fact that my own vocabulary and sensibility was marked by this disgraceful formative moment. Even now I must hold myself steady as I feel myself revert to the poetry of voluntarism. It is a sad confession, but I prefer it even today to the "scientific" vocabulary of structuralism.

The vocabulary of voluntarism survived for a little longer. It was done in technicolour in the Soviet epics of the Great Patriotic War. Once again, it survived longest, and with most justice and authenticity, in the colonial and—thence—the "Third World." This or that political or military action against the imperialists could still command heroism, summon up initiatives, demand choices, and be felt as "making history." The poetry arose in a late flaring of intensity in Cuba. And, as with evolutionism, voluntarism could even co-exist with adversity for a little while: for it was only by rebellion against the overwhelming presence of "established fact" that people could assert their humanity.[81] But in the past two decades both evolutionism and voluntarism have lost their nerve and have fallen silent, notably in the West. The vocabulary of structuralism has pushed all else aside.

And is this, now, at last the truth, the true Marxist vocabulary, restored to the original of Marx? We will examine this in its own terms in a moment. But our historical perspective must be continued until we come closer to our own self-knowledge. Voluntarism crashed against the wall of the Cold War. No account can convey the sickening jerk of deceleration between 1945 and 1948. Even in this country the Marxist Left seemed to be moving with "the fall of the stream" in 1945; in 1948 it was struggling to survive amidst an antagonistic current. In Eastern Europe that same sickening jerk stopped the hearts of Masaryk, Kostov and of Rajk. In the West our heads were thrown against the windscreen of capitalist society; and that screen felt like—*a structure*. "History", so pliant to the heroic will in 1943 and 1944, seemed to congeal in an instant into two monstrous antagonistic structures, each of which allowed only the smallest latitude of movement within its operative realm. For more than two decades each impulse towards independent forward movement within either realm (Hungary 1956, Prague 1968, Chile 1973) has been suppressed with a brutality which has confirmed the paradigm of structural stasis. Even in those parts of the Third World, where the rival structures operate only by diplomatic, economic and ideological extension, the same field-of-force has been exerted. Only the immense and enigmatic presence of China has escaped (at the cost of self-isolation) from this structural stasis.

This mutual confrontation of imperial structures is without historical precedent: not even Christendom and Ottoman Empire confronted each other (save at their rubbing edges) so massively, so watchfully, with such all-pervasive ideological refraction. In the West the "natural" flow of social process coagulated to a thin stream of hesitant reformism (each individual reform achieved after immensely disproportionate effort). This at its best; more often, the regenerated capitalist mode of production simply co-opted and assimilated those reforms (the product of earlier struggles), assigned to them new functions, developed them as "organs" of its own. Or this is how it *seemed:* for, please note, in moving towards our present time, I have already, as if involuntarily, fallen into the vocabulary of structuralism, and reified a process which, however confusedly, was still the outcome of human choices and struggles. For this is my point: the vocabulary of structuralism was given by the seeming "common sense", the manifest appearances, of three decades of Cold War stasis. And in its most pervasive accents, this has been a *bourgeois* vocabulary, an apologia for the *status quo* and an invective against "utopian" and "mal-adjusted" heretics. By the 1950s structuralisms—sometimes the product of lonely minds working in prior contexts—were flowing *with* the stream, and replicating themselves on every side as ideology: psychology was preoccupied with "adjustment" to "normality", sociology with "adjustment" to a self-regulating social system, or with defining heretics as "deviants" from "the value-system" of the consensus, political theory with the circuits of psephology.[82] In the end, more ambitious and more sophisticated structuralisms have come into fashion. The vocabularies of structuralism have been borrowed, not from natural science or from poetry, but now from sociology, now from linguistics and anthropology, and now from the anti-structure of Marxist Political Economy—the "*Grundrisse* face" of Marx.

I must guard myself against a misunderstanding. When I speak of vocabularies in this sense, it is, very certainly, in their sense as ideology. That is, I have argued that in each of these periods there has been a pressure of real experience which has seemed to licence the adoption of a particular language of social and political analysis, an ideological pre-disposition towards one vocabulary or another. This ought to put us on our guard. The experiences of the decades before the First World War pre-disposed minds to adopt the premises and terms of evolutionism; the crisis years of 1917 and of 1936-46 were, like all revolutionary moments, propitious for the premises and terms of voluntarism; and the unprecedented stasis and, in the profoundest sense, historical conservatism (the continuous reproduction of material goods and of ideology within a seemingly-closed circuit) markedly dispose contemporary minds towards the premises and terms of structuralism. In this sense, a historian recognises in structuralism an analogy within the circulatory or clock-work-impelled justificatory systems of prior societies, and notes that these were generally *ancien régimes* anxious to validate established power or middle-aged post-revolutionary regimes anxious to consolidate power with an ideological apologia. So—a historian, confronting structuralism, must sniff the air and scent a conservatism.

But this sniffing of the ideological air does not end the question. For, first, the very fact of this ideological predisposition is itself a kind of guarantee that the ideas in question have some partial correspondence to the historical moment: there *was* a "progress" of the labour movement before the First World War, there *were* heroic initiatives and acts of will between 1936 and 1946, there *is* a profound sociological conservatism around us on each side today. So that we must recall that ideology has its own kind of "truth." And, second, an ideological predisposition to accept a particular vocabulary does not, of course, in itself expose that language, its premises and terms, to be invalid. That must be the object of a distinct enquiry. One day a "conjuncture" may arrive when thousands of minds are simultaneously predisposed to believe—the truth! To be sure, historians know no records of such events. But perhaps, with Althusser, this utopian conjuncture has now at last arrived?

But let us first, before returning to Althusser, delay to admire another structuralism of our time, albeit one that is a little faded and un-fashionable today. It falls to my hand because it happens to be a somewhat rare and audacious exercise, an attempt to replace structure within the historical record and to surmount the most difficult theoretical problem of any such system, the analysis of change through time. Let us first of all move directly to its vocabulary:

> From the industrial perspective the cotton-textile revolution appears as a dramatic rearrangement of all the factors of production. The revolution originated with a series of dissatisfactions legitimized by the dominant value-system of the day. In several sequences of differentiation the industry emerged with a structure more adequate to meet the demands of the foreign and domestic markets.[1] Such a revolution naturally did not occur in a vacuum. It was initiated by non-economic elements such as religious values, political arrangements, and social stratification. At the same time, the industrial revolution in cotton created *a source of dissatisfaction*, which, when combined with other elements, initiated several sequences of differentiation in other social sub-systems.[83]

I don't have time here to enter closely into argument with Professor Smelser as to his use of sources, his selection and interpretation of these, nor as to the emptiness of his "boxes." I wish now only to point to the reification of process entailed by the very vocabulary of analysis. Systems and sub-systems, elements and structures, are drilled up and down the pages pretending to be people. Smelser is anxious to show that social process occurred rationally and in an approved Parsonian fashion. There is a self-regulating social system (whose wisdom always appears most apparent if you happen to be at the top of it), "governed" by a value-system (which, again, is enshrined in the institutions and attitudes of the system's governors), directed to goals legitimized by this value-system, which, when any major element within it differentiates structurally is precipitated into disequilibrium, resulting in dissatisfactions (always grossly misunderstood by those at the bottom, who, when they suffer, manifest "negative emotional reactions" and "unjustified disturbance symptoms"), but even these plebeian manifestations of irrationality the system is able to turn to functional account, since various superior non-economic "elements" some-where at the top of the system (such as "political arrangements" or superior religious values or more simply the army and the police) "handle and channel" these disturbance symptoms, and, if the system's organs should flash out a "justified" signal, devise, through several refined "steps", "new ideas" or institutions (which however are always devised in forms more wise than those agitated for by the deluded sources of disturbance)—thereby bringing to the structurally-differentiated "system" a glorious return in "an extraordinary growth of production, capitalization and profits," which, however, in the end falls short of the goals prescribed by the dominative value-system, thereby producing new dissatisfactions which in turn. . . I don't know how to extricate myself from this sentence, since the Parsonian system has indeed unlocked the secret of perpetual motion.

In this system there are no good or evil men; or, rather, all men are of equally neuter will, their wills surrendered into the inexorable will of social process. They are (or should be) the *träger* or supports of that process. The social will is beneficent: "the industry emerged with a structure more adequate to meet the demands of. . . markets." And I have done Smelser an injustice in suggesting that he sees men and women only as inert passengers in this differentiating mechanism of reification. *Left to itself* the system would move us all forward to meet the goal of larger markets. But unfortunately the "disturbance-symptoms" of the majority of those being moved are not only unjustified in minor ways but are often hugely unjustified. They become Luddites, trade unionists, Peterloo and Ten Hour Men, Chartists. They impede the thing-society from proceeding smoothly down its thing-ways to its thing-conclusion. It is fortunate that in contemporary societies we have sociologists who can explain to the disturbed that their symptoms are unjustified, and who can advise "political arrangements" as to the best means of "handling and channelling." We all now know that phenomena which to the uninformed eye (or stomach) might appear as justified cause for disturbance are in fact manifestations of the ulterior working-out of a wisdom-thing. And behind this again one may glimpse an ancient theological form of thought: every phenomenon *must*, as evidence of Divine will, have a function.

Of course the Smelserian system's pretence of transcending the insertion into "history" of intention and of norms is wholly specious. We have in this system, and at every stage, the imposition of exterior value. This is nowhere more clear than in Smelser's handling of the value-system, whether as generalised concept or in relation to particular social groups, such as the handloom weavers. As theory he proposes this:

> Every social system is governed by a value-system which specifies the nature of the system, its goals, and the means of attaining these goals. A social system's first functional requirement is to preserve the integrity of the value-system itself and to assure that individual actors conform to it. This involves socializing and educating individuals, as well as providing tension-control mechanisms for handling and resolving individual disturbances relating to the values.

This snake has, however, already got its tail deeply into its own mouth. For on the same page, Smelser has told us:

> A social system. . . is governed by a value-system which defines and legitimizes the activities of the social system. Second, these values are institutionalized into

regulatory patterns which govern the interaction of the more concrete units. Third, the more concrete units specialize in social sub-systems which cluster around functional imperatives governing the social system.

But also (on another page) the value-system is its own judge and arbitrator: "it specifies the conditions under which members of the system should express dissatisfactions and prepare to undertake change." Values alone lie outside this model of structural differentiation. If they change, they change "more slowly than social structure," and this is "a separate analytical problem."[84]

This is a proper epistemological pudding. The first relation proposed between value-system and social system is symbiotic. The social system is "governed" by the value-system, which, indeed, selects the system's goals; but equally the social system's "first functional requirement is to preserve the integrity of the value-system." Hence value-system and social system are mutually supportive, but of the two the first is prior. The first function of the social system is to reproduce in their integrity the values which govern it. This is where the snake got its tail into its mouth. Now it begins to swallow itself. For the social system is also made up of "concrete units" (not, alas, as yet people!), specialized in "social sub-systems which cluster around functional imperatives governing the social system." But we have already been informed as to what the *first* of these functional imperatives is: to preserve the integrity of the value-system. What is society? It is a value-system whose first function is, through the mediation of empty boxes and an ugly terminology, to reproduce its own value-system.

Who holds these values? If choice appears, who decides which sets of value are the dominant value-system? The snake—or what is left of it, for it is now a wriggling knot—has an answer to this too. The value-system which is dominant is exactly that which dominates. (It is not necessary to go further and say the values of those who hold political, economic and other institutional (e.g. religious, academic) *power*, since power has been tabulated somewhere among "political arrangements" whose function is the attainment of goals selected by "the" value-system). Moreover, the value-system itself "specifies" whether dissatisfactions should or should not arise: that is, it actively inhibits alternative values from arising and provides "tension-control mechanisms" for "resolving individual disturbances relating to values." Plop! The snake has disappeared into total theoretical vacuity.

It is, of course, a highly conservative vacuity: what is governs what is whose first function is to preserve the integrity of is-ness; what dominates has the functional imperative of preserving its own dominance. As presented by Smelser, this structural theory cannot be criticised in terms of alternative theories of process or of class conflict because the terminology of his theory is so fashioned that such concepts may not at any point be allowed to enter. The vocabulary excludes criticism before criticism can commence.

Nevertheless, as I have said, we have in this system, at every stage, the imposition of exterior value. There was not, of course, in the industrial history which Smelser offers to restructure *one* dominant value-system but many competing sets of value, one of which was dominant only because it was professed by men who held power. The values of Poor Law Commissioners and of paupers, of Assistant Hand-Loom Weavers Commissioners and of weavers, can't be subsumed within the same system. And even if we attempt to do so, by gesturing at some vague notions like "independence", we find that the social system is so structured that what makes for the independence of some men makes for the dependence of others. The "social system" had no "goal", no internalised intentionality, since the men and women within that system pursued opposing goals and intentions. Smelser has simply commenced analysis by assuming his own goal, which is the old one of Weberian rationalisation in pursuit of maximum economic growth. Deep within his thing-mechanism, masked but still at the controls, is Sombart's entre-preneur, a man of unimpeachable goodwill whose only motivation is to maximise his own profits and hence the productive resources of man-kind. Here is the *primum mobile* of the capitalist system. And this is why Smelser's system, in its larger pretentions,[85] not only outrages the dis-course of historical logic but is, as sociology, only to be understood as a moment of capitalist ideology.

As ideology it may, perhaps, be seen as the product of that moment of polarised ideological stasis at the height of the Cold War which I have already indicated.[86] It was also at this moment that Stalinism afforded a caricature of Marxism, which offered, in very different terminology but with an equally abstracted vocabulary, an identical reification of process, in which a "superstructure" was reduced to confirming or legitimating a base. This "base" (Stalin wrote in 1950) "is the economic structure of society at a given stage of its development", and "the superstructure consists of the political, legal, religious, artistic, and philosophical views of society and the political, legal, and other institutions corresponding to them:

> The superstructure is a product of the base; but this does not mean that it merely reflects the base, that it is passive, neutral, indifferent to the fate of its base, to the fate of the classes, to the character of the system. On the contrary, no sooner does it arise than it becomes an exceedingly active force, actively assisting its base to take shape and consolidate itself, and doing everything it can to help the new system finish off and eliminate the old base and the old classes.
>
> It cannot be otherwise. The base creates the superstructure precisely in order that it may serve it, that it may actively help it to take shape and consolidate

itself, that it may actively strive for the elimination of the old, moribund base and its old superstructure.

This appears to say: "What is creates what is whose first function is to consolidate its own is-ness—and also to clobber whatever was." This is an approximate description of High Stalinism, in which the State was indeed "an exceedingly active force" doing everything it could to "finish off and eliminate the old base and the old classes," although historians of the Soviet Union nourish a suspicion that at a certain stage the "is" of Stalin's superstructure was artificially (and in a theoretically improper way) creating its own base. This consorts less easily with another of Stalin's remarkable formulations:

> The superstructure is not directly connected with production, with man's productive activity. It is connected with production only indirectly through the economy, through the base. The superstructure therefore does not reflect changes of development of the productive forces immediately and directly, but only after changes in the base, through the prism of changes wrought in the base by the changes in production. This means that the sphere of action of the superstructure is narrow and restricted.[87]

My point is not, in these latter days, to scrutinise Stalin's credentials as a Marxist theoretician. The present point is to note an identical reification of historical process in both Smelser and in Stalin, entailed in the premises and extending into the vocabulary of analysis: both offer (or pretend to offer) history as a "process without a subject", both concur in the eviction from history of human agency (unless as the "supports" or vectors of ulterior structural determinations), both present human consciousness and practices as self-motivated *things*.

There is a further point. The explicit concept of history as "a process without a subject" is a discovery not of Smelser or of Stalin but of Althusser; and, moreover, he proposed that this is "the basis of all the analyses in *Capital*." (*L. & P.*, 117; *P. & A.*, 182-5; *Essays*, 51). But we may surmise that the origin of this remarkable insight lay in Stalin's *Marxism and Linguistics*, a text for which Althusser has always shown unusual respect. We know that Althusser joined the French Communist Party in 1948, and felt himself to be, subjectively, confronting a great difficulty:

> A professional philosopher who joins the Party remains, ideologically, a petty bourgeois. He must revolutionize his thought in order to occupy a proletarian class position in philosophy. (*L. & P.* 17)

In this difficulty, he cut his teeth on Stalin's "original" contribution to theory (1950) which provided the "first shock" which began to dislodge the sectarianism and dogmatism which characterised the Communist movement at his initiation. Or so he presents the event in retrospect—a "period summed up in caricature by a single phrase, a banner flapping in the void: 'bourgeois science, proletarian science'."

> Paradoxically, it was no other than Stalin, whose contagious and implacable system of government and thought had induced this delirium, who reduced the madness to a little more reason. Reading between the lines of the few simple pages in which he reproached the zeal of those who were making strenuous efforts to prove language a superstructure, we could see that there were limits to the use of the class criterion, and that we had been made to treat science, a status claimed by every page of Marx, as merely the first-comer among ideologies. We had to retreat, and, in semi-disarray, return to first principles. (F.M., 22, 27)[88]

It is thus that he presents his own intellectual development: a "petty bourgeois", initiated into Stalinist dogmatism, but rescued from its uttermost delirium—by Stalin. The rescue-operation left him, precisely, with the immanent concept of history as "process without a subject", with a reified structuralist vocabulary, with an inexorable and mechanical metaphor of basis and superstructure—and with a notion of Marxism as a "science" which belonged to neither!

Althusser has, of course, subsequent to *Reading Capital*, denied that his version of Marxism is a structuralism, even though he allows that "the young pup. . . slipped between my legs."[89] The argument, which turns largely upon certain structuralist notions of the "combinatory", is not one which we intend to address. Instead, we will address directly his own text, its vocabulary, its premises and terms.

The critical concept of Althusserian sociological theory is that of a "mode of production." Few Marxists will object to this. We think, if we are historians, of—*production:* and of land, dues, rents, property, technologies, markets, capital, wages, and the like. But Althusser assumes all this and posts forward to the essence of the matter, the concept, the "arrangement" of the "terms":

> On the one hand, the *structure* (the economic base: the forces of production and the relations of production); on the other, the *superstructure* (the State and all the legal, political and ideological forms).

So far, we have been guided by the firm hand of Stalin. But now we may improve upon him. Marx introduced "a *new conception* of the relation between *determinant instances* in the structure-superstructure complex which constitutes the essence of any social formation." (F.M., 111) Althusser then throws himself into the posture of wrestling for the purity of Marxist science against four antagonists—"*economism* and even *technologism*" (F.M., 108), on one side, humanism and historicism on the other. The relation between basis and superstructure must be verbalised and sophisticated in new ways, introducing the concepts of structure-in-dominance, in-the-last-instance determination, and over-determination. Marx gives us "two ends of the chain": "on the one hand, *determination in the last instance by the (economic) mode of production;* on the other, *the relative autonomy of the superstructure and their specific effectivity.*" (*F.M.* 111) (Strictly speaking, these are not two ends of a chain, but two ways of saying the same thing, for what is determinant, but only in the last instance, must allow for the effectivity of other relatively autonomous effects in other instances.) But, Althusser assures us, this determination, while ever-present, is only fictive, since "from the first moment to the last, the lonely hour of the 'last instance' never comes." (*F.M.* 113) The problem, then, which, to a historian, might appear to require further empirical investigation and elaboration, appears to Althusser as one which arises from the deficiency of "*the theory of the specific effectivity of the superstructures. . .*" (*F.M.* 113) This he sets out to repair: "and before the theory of their effectivity or simultaneously (for it is by formulating their effectivity that their *essence* can be attained) there must be elaboration of *the theory of the particular essence of the specific elements of the superstructure.*" (*F.M.* 114)

One feels that "formulations" of this order, which repeatedly attain to the dignity and special clarity of italics, must indeed prepare us for the unveiling of mystery. Nor are we disappointed. For we are introduced to a very great lady, who is not at all to be seen as a slender superstructure sitting on a somewhat large basis, but as a unitary figure, *La Structure à Dominante.* She is a "totality", but not a spurious Hegelian or Sartreian totality: she is infinitely more "definite and rigorous." (*F.M.* 203) What determines her existence and structures her dominant personality is, in the last instance, "economic"; but since the last instance never arrives, it is courteous very often to overlook this material determination. It is impolite to keep on reminding a great lady that she is determined by her tummy. It is more helpful to characterise her by the contradictions in her temperament, and to examine these contradictions in their own right, instead of continually harping on the fact that they originate in a bad digestion.

If every contradiction is a contradiction in a complex whole structured in dominance, this complex whole cannot be envisaged without its contradictions, without their basically uneven relations. In other words, each contradiction, each essential articulation of the structure, and the general relation of the articulations in the structure in dominance, constitute so many conditions of the existence of the complex whole itself. This proposition is of the first importance. For it means that the structure of the whole and therefore the 'difference' of the essential contradictions and their structure in dominance, is the very existence of the whole; that the 'difference' of the contradictions. . . is identical to the conditions of the existence of the complex whole. In plain terms this position implies that the 'secondary' contradictions are not the pure phenomena of the 'principal' contradiction, that the principal is not the essence and the secondaries so many of its phenomena, so much so that the principal contradiction might practically exist *without* the secondary contradictions, or without some of them, or might exist *before* or *after* them. On the contrary, it implies that the secondary contradictions are essential even to the existence of the principal contradiction, that they really constitute its condition of existence, just as the principal contradiction constitutes their condition of existence. As an example, take the complex structured whole that is society. (*F.M.* 204-5)

Ah, yes. Let us take an example, even if a trivial one: "society". For "in plain terms" we had even supposed that Althusser was going a long and windy way around to say that in any complex whole or organism all attributes must be taken together as one set; and if analysis identifies a "principal contradiction" this is (a) inherent to its structure, and (b) does not thereby disallow subordinate contradictions. But "society", it turns out, can be more rapidly despatched:

In it, the 'relations of production' are not the pure phenomena of the forces of production; they are also their condition of existence. The superstructure is not the pure phenomenon of the structure, it is also its condition of existence. . . Please do not misunderstand me: this mutual conditioning of the existence of the 'contradictions' does not nullify the structure in dominance that reigns over the contradictions and in them (in this case, determination in the last instance by the economy). Despite its apparent circularity, this conditioning does not result in the destruction of the structure in domination that constitutes the complexity of the whole, and its unity. Quite the contrary, even within the reality of the conditions of existence of éach contradiction, it is the manifestation of the structure in dominance that unifies the whole. *This reflection of the conditions of existence of the contradiction within itself, this reflection of the structure articulated in dominance that constitutes the unity of the complex whole within each contradiction,* this is the most profound characteristic of the Marxist dialectic, the one I have tried recently to encapsulate in the concept of 'overdetermination'. (*F.M.* 205-6)

It is good to know that we have arrived at length at "the most profound characteristic of the Marxist dialectic"; although we have arrived by Althusser's characteristic idealist methods—from ideal premises we arrive at "society", as an example! This reorganisation of vocabulary has been forced upon Althusser by the deficiencies of "economism", **which sees the** relation between basis and superstructure in an analogy with clockwork mechanism:

It is *'economism'* (mechanism) and not the true Marxist tradition that sets up the hierarchy of instances once and for all, assigns each its essence and role and defines the universal meaning of their relations. . . It is economism that identifies eternally in advance the determinant-contradiction-in-the-last-instance with the *role* of the dominant contradiction, which for ever assimilates such and such an 'aspect' (forces of production, economy, practice) to the principal *role,* **and such** and such another 'aspect' (relations of production, politics, ideology, theory) to the secondary *role*—whereas in real history determination in the last instance by the economy is exercised precisely in the permutations of the principal role between the economy, politics, theory, etc. (*F.M.* 213)

The concession as to "real history" is welcome (and unusual) although practising historians can scarcely find the resolution at the end of that sentence to be enlightening. What Althusser appears to be saying is that "economism" proposed a clockwork analogy which was both crude and disreputable: and he proposes instead to sophisticate the clockwork:

Unevenness is internal to a social formation because the structuration in dominance of the complex whole, this structural invariant, *is itself the precondition for the concrete variation of the contradictions* that constitute it, and therefore for their displacements, condensations and mutations, etc., and inversely because *this variation is the existence of that invariant.*

Uneven development "is not external to contradiction, but constitutes its most intimate essence." (*F.M.* 213) All this certainly sounds more reputable; we have got rid of Stalin's grandfather clock, which was increasingly coming to look like a rather ugly antique. But what we are left with is simply a new-styled, more complicated clock, with many more moving parts, and these parts are not substantial components, derived from historical investigation (monetary systems, constitutions, norms, property-rights), but interpollated neologisms. The reorganisation has taken place, not in substantive analysis (theory interacting with enquiry), but in the vocabulary alone.

The reason why we are still left with clockwork (or philosophical *mechanism*) lies in the theory's character: as a structuralism. Very clearly, Althusser's system is more than a "flirtation" with structuralist terms. It does not matter at all whether or not this system qualifies as a structuralism according to certain recent Parisian notations in linguistics, anthropology or psycho-analysis. What constitutes a structuralism, in a more general sense, is, (i) that however many variables are introduced, and however complex their permutations, these variables maintain their original fixity as categories: with Smelser, the "value-system", the factors of production, "political arrangements", and (the motor) "structural differentiation"; with Althusser, "the economy", "politics", "ideology", and (the motor) "class struggle." Thus the categories are *categories of stasis*, even if they are then set in motion as moving-parts. (ii) Movement can only take place *within the closed field* of the system or structure; that is, however complex and mutually-reciprocating the motions of the parts, this movement is enclosed within the overall limits and determinations of the pre-given structure. For both these reasons, history *as process*, as open-ended and indeterminate eventuation—but not for that reason devoid of rational *logic* or of determining *pressures*—in which categories are defined in particular contexts but are continuously undergoing historical re-definition, and whose structure is not pre-given but protean, continually changing in form and in articulation—all this (which may be said to constitute far more truly "the most profound characteristic of the Marxist dialectic") must be denied.

And we face here a very difficult problem, and a problem insuperable to those philosophers (or sociologists) who suppose that a "formulation" is at a higher level than "empirical" analysis, and that what is requisite is not theoretically-informed *knowledge* but a "theory of history." For it is exceptionally difficult to verbalise as "theory" history as process; and, in particular, no analogies derived from mechanical or organic mechanism, and no static structural reconstitution, can encompass the logic of in-determinate historical process, a process which remains subject to determinate pressures. In the last analysis, the logic of process can only be described in terms of historical analysis; no analogy derived from any other area can have any more than a limited, illustrative, metaphoric value (and often, as with basis and superstructure, a static and damaging one); "history" may only be theorised in terms of its own properties. We may well agree that historical materialism should become more theoretically alert, both as to its procedures and its conclusions. But what requires interrogating and theorising is historical knowledge.

xi

We have by no means finished with the problem of structure and of process, nor with our commentary upon Althusser's propositions. But we may at this point attempt to view this problem in a different perspective, by stepping behind both Althusser and Marx, and situating ourselves in eighteenth-century Naples, with Giambattista Vico.

The concept of history as process raises at once the questions of intelligibility and intention. Each historical event is unique. But many events, widely separated in time and place, reveal, when brought into relation with each other, regularities of process. Vico, confronted with these regularities, struggled to define process in ways which foresaw simultaneously the anthropological discipline and historical materialism:

> He proceeds to discuss the natural law of the peoples, and shows at what certain times and in what determinate ways the customs were born that constitute the entire economy of this law. These are religions, languages, property rights, business transactions, orders, empires, laws, arms, trials, penalties, wars, peaces and alliances. And from the times and ways in which they were born he infers the eternal properties which determine that the nature of each, that is the time and way of its origin, shall be such and not otherwise.[90]

Vico was able, in a remarkable way, to hold in simultaneous suspension, without manifest contradiction, a Hegelian, a Marxist, and a structuralist (Lévi-Straussian variant) heuristic. With Hegel he described "an ideal eternal history traversed in time by the history of every nation." "Uniform ideas originating among entire peoples unknown to each other must have a common ground of truth." From one aspect, this uniformity can be seen as evidence of "divine providence." But this providence works its way out through naturalistic means: "our Science proceeds by a severe analysis of human thoughts about the human necessities or utilities of social life, which are the two perennial springs of the natural law of nations":

> Human choice, by its nature most uncertain, is made certain and determined by the common sense of men with respect to human needs or utilities. . .

And "common sense" is "judgement without reflection, shared by an entire class, an entire people, an entire nation, or the whole human race." Hence from another aspect providence may be seen as necessity, human needs or utilities determining social consciousness in uniform ways. But the uniformity of this "judgement without reflection" implies also a uniformity of mental structure:

> The natural law of nations is coeval with the customs of the nations, conforming one with another in virtue of a common human sense. . .

And:

> There must in the nature of human things be a mental language common to all nations, which uniformly grasps the substance of things feasible in human social life. . .[91]

So that, from a third aspect, we encounter the notion of a "common mental language" and common structure of myth. Since this mental language was given to man by divine providence, the circle of argument is closed.

Thus Vico is offering us history as a process *with* a subject, but this need not necessarily be a historicism. If "divine providence" is taken as the subject (or as the ultimate directive agent) and humanity as vectors of divine will, then of course we are offered a historicist theology. But since this providence is worked out through natural determinations, then men and women can be seen to be the subjects or agents of their own history. And the ambiguity of Vico's term as usually translated as "law" ("the natural law of nations", *diritto naturale delle gente*) has haunted historical materialism from this time forward. If we employ "law" so as to entail pre-determination and prediction, we are open to 700 objections, some 650 of which have been patiently expounded by Sir Karl Popper. It is futile to deny that both Marx and Engels did, on occasion, employ "law" in this sense; and when they do so, the objections may sometimes be upheld.[92] But of course *law, droit, diritto*, are words with many inflexions and ambiguities of meaning, in a set which moves from *rule* by way of *regularity* to *direction*. Historical materialism, from the time of Vico, has been in search for a term which addresses the uniformities of customs, etc., the regularities of social formations, and analyses these not as lawed necessities nor as fortuitous coincidences but as shaping and directive pressures, indicative articulations of human practices. I have already suggested that the argument will be advanced if we discard the concept of "law" and replace it with that of "the logic of process."[93]

It is Vico's insight into this logic which sustains his position as a precursor of historical materialism. He saw clearly that the historical event is something quite distinct from the sum of individual goals and intentions:

> It is true that men have themselves made this world of nations. . ., but this world without doubt has issued from a mind often diverse, at times quite contrary, and always superior to the particular ends that men had proposed to themselves; which narrow ends, made means to serve wider ends, it has always employed to preserve the human race upon this earth. Men mean to gratify their bestial lust and abandon their off-spring, and they inaugurate the chastity of marriage from which the families arise. The fathers mean to exercise without restraint their paternal power over their clients, and they subject them to the civil powers from which the cities arise. The reigning orders of nobles mean to abuse their lordly freedom over the plebeians, and they are obliged to submit to the laws which establish popular liberty. The free peoples mean to shake off the yoke of their laws, and they become subject to monarchs. . . That which did all this was mind, for men did it with intelligence; it was not fate, for they did it by choice; not chance, for the results of their always so acting are perpetually the same.[94]

I am directing attention not to Vico's own attempt to attribute to process a cyclical intelligibility, but to his superb expression of process. This is the point from which all sustained historical thought must start. It is to this point that Engels returned in his famous (perhaps one should say "notorious", in view of Althusser's heavy-handed treatment of it)[95] letter to Bloch of September 1890: "We make our own history, but in the first place under very definite presuppositions and conditions. Among these the economic ones are finally decisive. . ." How, then, can we be said to "make our own history" if "the economic movement finally asserts itself as necessary"? In proposing a solution, Engels quietly exchanges subjects, and replaces "we make" with "history makes itself":

> History makes itself in such a way that the final result always arises from conflicts

between many individual wills, of which each again has been made what it is by a host of particular conditions of life. Thus there are innumerable intersecting forces, an infinite parallelogram of forces which give rise to one resultant—the historical event. This again may itself be viewed as the product of a power which, taken as a whole, works *unconsciously* and without volition. For what each individual wills is obstructed by everyone else, and what emerges is something that no one willed. Thus past history proceeds in the manner of a natural process and is also essentially subject to the same laws of movement.

And in his conclusion, Engels attempts to bring the two alternative subjects into relationship. "Individual wills" (i.e. "we") "do not attain what they want, but are merged into a collective mean, a common resultant," and yet "each contributes to the resultant and is to this degree involved in it."

Althusser has no patience with this "whole futile construction" (*F.M.* 121), which in some part of his critique he patently misreads.[96] But with other parts of his critique I find myself in unfamiliar agreement. I would phrase my objections rather differently, but at points we concur. 1) Engels has not offered a solution to the problem, but re-stated it in new terms. He has commenced with the proposition that economic presuppositions are "finally decisive", and this is where he concludes. 2) On the way he has gathered in an infinitude of "individual wills" whose agency, in the result, is cancelled out ("something that no one willed"). 3) The model of "an infinite parallelogram of forces", derived from physics, obscures what it should clarify. 4) In adopting this model Engels has unconsciously fallen back upon "the presuppositions of classical bourgeois ideology and bourgeois political economy" (*F.M.* 124)—Adam Smith's sum of self-interest, Rousseau's general will.[97] But the historical "resultant" cannot usefully be conceived as the involuntary product of the sum of an infinity of mutually-contradictory individual volitions, since these "individual wills" are not de-structured atoms in collision but act with, upon, and against each other as *grouped* "wills"—as families, communities, interests, and, above all, as classes. In this sense, Vico, who proposes not "individual wills" but fathers/clients, nobles/plebeians, free peoples/monarchs, has stated the problem of process better than Engels. And if Engels, in this hurried letter, had remembered his own thinking and writing on all this, then he would have offered not a re-statement of the problem but some indication of a resolution. For these "individual wills", however "particular" their "conditions of life", have been conditioned in class ways; and if the historical resultant is then seen as the outcome of a collision of contradictory class interests and forces, then we may see how human agency gives rise to an involuntary result—"the economic movement finally asserts itself as necessary"—and how we may say, at one and the same time, that "we make our own history" and "history makes itself."

I have, in these last sentences, departed a very long way from Althusser.

We shall see how far in a moment. One or two of our local criticisms of the text are concurrent. But Althusser sees the whole construction as "futile", because Engels has proposed a non-problem: if the "economic movement" produces the historical result, then we should get on with the analysis of structures and dismiss "individual wills." The very notion of human agency is no more than "the semblance of a problem for *bourgeois ideology*." (*F.M.* 126) I, on the contrary, consider that Engels has proposed a very critical problem (agency and process) and that, despite deficiencies, the general tendency of his meditation is helpful. At least he does not discount the crucial ambivalence of our human presence in our own history, part-subjects, part-objects, the voluntary agents of our own involuntary determinations. Four years before Engels wrote to Bloch, an English Communist had reflected upon the same problem, in his own very different idiom:

> I pondered all these things, and how men fight and lose the battle, and the thing that they fought for comes about in spite of their defeat, and when it comes turns out not to be what they meant, and other men have to fight for what they meant under another name. . .[98]

For William Morris the accent falls even more sharply upon agency; but men are seen as the ever-baffled and ever-resurgent agents of an unmastered history.

Since process ensued in regularities which did not conform to the actors' intentions, Vico saw history as issuing "from a mind. . . always superior to the particular ends that men have proposed to themselves." Engels was reduced to a metaphor which introduced analogies from positivist law: "the historical event. . . may itself be viewed as the product of a power which. . . works unconsciously" (a reminder of Vico's divine providence); but, also, "history makes itself" and "proceeds in the manner of a natural process" (a reminder of Vico's necessity of "human needs or utilities"). It is manifest that, when we say that history is not only process but process with intelligible regularities and forms, the mind finds it difficult to resist the conclusion that history must therefore be *programmed* in some way (whether the programming be divine or "natural"); and, again and again, we notice the attribution of extra-historical or teleological sequences and goals—goals to which process is seen to move *towards:* "issuing from a mind", "the product of a power", the realisation of a *potentia* immanent within the essence or at the origin of the process, which manifests itself in the "development of forms."[99] This attribution can certainly be resisted, and it is *not* entailed in the premises of process and of social formations. But neither Vico nor Engels succeeded always in resisting it; nor did Marx (in his *"Grundrisse* face"); nor, very certainly, does Althusser, despite his repeated polemics against "historicism."

Althusser's proferred solution is in two parts. First, he evicts human agency from history, which then becomes a "process without a subject." Human events *are* the process but human practice (and, still less, intentions, "wills") contributes nothing to this process. So far from being original, this is a very ancient mode of thought: process is fate. But if a human process without a (human) subject appears, nevertheless, to be not wholly fortuitous—a mere outcome of random collisions—but to be shaped and patterned in ways intelligible to humans, then, by an equally ancient mode of thought, it must be seen as being *willed*, being subject to some extra-human compulsion: Providence, the Divine Will, the Idea, evolutionary Destiny, Necessity.

Althusser wishes to expell such teleologies ("historicism"). So, in his second part, he evicts process from history. Rather like a medieval emblem of Death, he leans over history's death-bed, operates on the prone body, and liberates its soul. After this surgical parturition, under the knife of "theoretical practice", history reappears in two forms. Form 1: an infinity (a "bad infinity") of human events and collisions of human wills, which, however, since they are formless, *are not "historical"*. Events turn out to be non-events. For "what makes *such and such* an event *historical* is not the fact that it is an *event*, but precisely its *insertion into forms which are themselves historical...*" (*F.M.* 126) Whatever cannot be inserted into these forms are unhappenings (historically), and very much of the inert body of history turns out to be composed of such. Form 1 can now be dismissed, and hurriedly, for the body is corrupting even before it is interred. Form 2 of history is its soul. But what can this soul be, if it is not events, unless it be those forms which guarantee that an event is truly "historical"? A historical fact is "*a fact which causes a mutation in the existing structural relations.*" (*R.C.* 102) Process turns out to be, not historical process at all (this wretched soul has been incarnated in the wrong body) but the structural articulation of social and economic formations, as Smelser and others had long supposed. Form 2, the soul, must therefore quickly be re-incarnated in a more theoretically-hygienic body. The soul of process must be arrested in its flight and thrust into the marble statue of structural immobilism: and there she sits, the gracious lady whom we have already met, *La Structure à Dominante*.

This is not one of Althusser's more elegant passages of argument. At a first, "common sense" reading it might pass. After all, if I get up from my desk (as I will do shortly), to take the darned dog for a walk, this is scarcely an "historical" event. So that what makes events historical must be defined in some other way. But historical events remain *events* even after we have made a theoretical selection; theory does not reduce events to structures; even when we have defined out innumerable events as of negligible interest to historical analysis, what we must analyse remains as a process of eventuation. Indeed, it is exactly the significance of the event to this process which affords the criterion for selection. Nor is there any guarantee against teleology—as Althusser appears to suppose—in reducing process to stasis. It was the old error of mechanical materialism—and also of analogies from "natural process" brought to bear upon human affairs— to suppose that a clock is a clock is a clock. But on closer inspection, ideological clock-makers have been identified, and goals have been found— not only at the terminus of process—but planted in the automatic motions of clocks. For if a mode of production is proposed to entail a regular and rational form of sequential development, and a complex (but uniform) internal relational structuration, *independent of the rationality and agency of the human actors who in fact produce and relate*, then, very soon, the questions will be asked: whose is the divine will which programmed this automating structure, where is the ulterior "unconscious power"?

Perhaps Althusser was aware of the tawdry texture of this argument in *For Marx*. For in subsequent writings he has returned, with increasing obsessiveness, to these two evictions from history: the eviction of human agency, the eviction of historical time, or process. I have presented these two propositions in sequence, but in fact they arise in his theory simultaneously. We will consider first his elevated disquisition on historical time in *Reading Capital.*

This is difficult for a historian to handle with patience. It is composed, in about equal parts, of banalities, of elaborate verbalisations which offer no purchase whatsoever for actual historical analysis, and of ridiculous errors. The banalities are composed of polemics against antagonists of straw, and pompous observations directed towards historians (to "draw their attention to the empiricist ideology which, with a few exceptions, over- whelmingly dominates every variety of history" (*R.C.* 109)) as to matters which have been the object of advanced historical investigation for decades. The best that we can say of these observations is that they served the purpose of revealing Althusser's ignorance of historiography in his own country (as, Marc Bloch's comparative methods, Braudel's reflections on historical time).[100] The kindest thing that can be said is that one or two of the problems which he gestures towards had been formulated long before in historical practice; how else could British and French historians exchange views on "the bourgeois revolution", British and Indian historians bring into a common discourse "medieval" societies governed by Plantaganets and Moghuls, American and Japanese historians exchange knowledge on the differential developments of industrial revolutions, with- out this being so? The worst that can be said is that, once again, Althusser announces, as original and rigorous Marxist theory, notions disintegrative of the full historical process, notions highly regarded within bourgeois historiography (notably in the United States)—as in certain forms of comparative history, development theory, and modernization theory: theories supported by an elaborated armoury of positivistic methodology.

As so often before, Althusser has been arrested by bourgeois concepts and taken for a bourgeois ride; he seeks, not to transform these concepts, but to convert their vocabulary.

The verbalisations and the errors we can take together.

We must grasp in all its rigour the absolute necessity of liberating the theory of history from any compromise with 'empirical' temporality, with the ideological concept of time which underlies it and overlies it, or with the ideological idea that the theory of history, *as theory*, could be subject to the 'concrete' determinations of 'historical time. . .' (*R.C.* 105)

In what does this "liberation" consist? It consists, precisely, in displacing process by structure. More strictly, structures (modes of production, social formations) do not eventuate and undergo transformations within the larger historical process. Structure, like a whale, opens its jaws, and swallows process up: thereafter, process survives unhappily in structure's stomach. To do this trick of theoretical practice, it is necessary to re-define synchrony and diachrony. Structure cannot be disclosed by synchronic procedures (in their customary sense): for example, by freezing "history" into a momentary pose, taking a "section" at a moment of stasis, analysing the articulation of a "totality". For (swallowed) process is inscribed within structure, and survives as the development of that structure's forms. Not only does structure have a developmental progression (vestigial process) but it is articulated with great complexity and characterised by uneven development.

I have shown[101] that in order to conceive this 'dominance' of a structure over the other structures in the unity of a conjuncture it is necessary to refer to the principle of the determination 'in the last instance' of the non-economic structures by the economic structure; and that this 'determination in the last instance' is an absolute precondition for the necessity and intelligibility of the displacements of structures in the hierarchy of effectivity, or of the displacement of 'dominance' between the structured levels of the whole. . . (*R.C.* 99)

But at any particular "conjuncture", when we might choose to arrest history or take a "section", the "last instance" (which, we remember, never arrives) is not likely to be around. This kind of synchrony, which looks for a simultaneous instant of "totality", will misread the evidence. Moreover, most of the other "instances" or "levels" of the structure will present themselves improperly, since they are all motoring around on different schedules:

We can argue from the specific structure of the Marxist whole that it is no longer possible to think the process of the development of the different levels of the whole *in the same historical time*. Each of these different levels does not have the same type of historical existence. On the contrary, we have to assign to each level a *peculiar time,* relatively autonomous and hence relatively independent, even in its dependence, of the 'times' of the other levels. We can and must say: for each mode of production there is a peculiar time and history, punctuated in a specific way by the development of the productive forces; the relations of production have their peculiar time and history, punctuated in a specific way; the political super-structure has its own history...; philosophy has its own time and history...; aesthetic productions... scientific formations... etc. Each of these peculiar histories is punctuated with peculiar rhythms and can only be known on condition that we have defined the *concept* of the specificity of its historical temporality and its punctuations (continuous development, revolutions, breaks, etc.) The fact that each of these times and each of these histories is *relatively autonomous* does not make them so many domains which are *independent* of the whole: the specificity of each of these times and each of these histories—in other words, their relative autonomy and independence—is based on a certain type of articulation in the whole, and therefore on a certain type of *dependence* with respect to the whole... (*R.C.* 99-100)

And so we drone on, as we may well do, for the possible permutations of "structure", "levels", "instances", "last instances", "relative autonomy", "specificity", "peculiar", and "articulation" are inexhaustible: "the mode and degree of *independence* of each time and history is therefore necessarily determined by the mode and degree of *dependence* of each level within the set of articulations of the whole."

The point is, that the customary ("ideological") notion of synchrony is likely to overlook all this. Nor can we even take a ragged, temporarily-slantwise "section" of the structure, since while this might give us an indication of the hierarchy of "levels" (and in fact Althusser is always giving us vaporous verbal "sections" of this kind), it will not show us the operative principles of dominance and development. We must be enabled to "think, in its peculiar articulation, the *function* of such an element or such a level in the current configuration of the whole." The task is:

To determine the relation of articulation of this element as a function of other elements, of this structure as a function of other structures, it obliges us to define what has been called its *overdetermination* or *underdetermination* as a function of the structure of the determination of the whole, it obliges us to define what might be called, in another language, the *index of determination,* the *index of effectivity* currently attributable to the element or structure in question in the general structure of the whole. By *index of effectivity* we may understand the character of more or less dominant or subordinate and therefore more or less 'paradoxical' determination of a given element or structure in the current mechanism of the whole. And this is nothing but the theory of the conjuncture indispensable to the theory of history.

I do **not** want to go any further with this analysis, although it has still hardly been elaborated at all. (*R.C.* 106-7)

This is wise, because the "theory of the conjuncture", which is "indispensable" but which is nowhere elaborated, would not appear to be a "theory" at all, but an exalted way of saying "Now". But "now" (whether today's "now" or some moment of "now" in the past) may also be seen as synchronic knowledge:

> The synchronic is then nothing but *the conception* of the specific relations that exist between the different elements and the different structures of the structure of the whole, it is the *knowledge* of the relations of dependence and articulation which makes it an organic whole, a system. *The synchronic is eternity in Spinoza's sense,* or the adequate knowledge of a complex object by the adequate knowledge of its complexity. This is exactly what Marx is distinguishing from the concrete-real historical sequence in the words:
>
> > How, indeed, could the single logical formula of movement, of sequence, of time, explain the body of society, in which all economic relations co-exist simultaneously and support one another? *(Poverty of Philosophy).* (*R.C.* 107)

The synchronic, then, is this new usage, is a concept of immense dignity: it is nothing less than the theory of Spinozan eternity, the knowledge of the exceedingly complex character of *La Structure à Dominante.* But there is still a small place left for the diachronic, which (we remember) was swallowed by structure some time ago, but still has an impoverished existence within structure's stomach. "Historical time" is an "ideological" concept derived by "empiricism" from the supposed "obviousness" of the "concrete-real historical sequence." Under theoretical scrutiny, diachrony reveals itself to be "merely the false name for the *process,* or for what Marx called the *development of forms.*" (*R.C.* 108) But this "process" is no longer the whole process of historical eventuation, within which structures and social formations arise and are transformed. This "process" is now an *attribute* of structure, or, more exactly, it is the history of structure's possible permutations, combinations, and forms. This concept of historical time—

> Can only be based on the complex and differentially articulated structure in dominance of the social totality that constitutes the social formation arising from a determinate mode of production, it can only be assigned a content as a function of the structure of that totality, considered either as a whole, or in its different 'levels.' In particular, it is only possible to give a content to the concept of historical time by defining historical time as the specific form of existence of the social totality under consideration, an existence in which different structural levels of temporality interfere, because of the peculiar relations of correspondence, non-correspondence, articulation, dislocation and torsion which obtain, between the different 'levels' of the whole in accordance with its general structure. (*R.C.* 108)

Thus the eviction of process from history, and its subsequent incorporation as a secondary attribute of structure. In all this exposition, I have more than allowed to Althusser his "say"; and I think that I have even improved upon his argument by marking sequential propositions more firmly and by compressing some of his repetitious rhetorical invocations. We will now offer some observations. And, first, it can be seen that this is very much more than a "flirtation" with the vocabulary of structuralism. This is an inexorable structuralism, even though it is, in this or that respect, a different one from those derived from Saussure, Lévi-Strauss or Lacan. It shares fully in that ideological pre-disposition of that moment ("conjuncture"?) of the Cold War stasis, which Sartre has identified: a "dominant tendency" towards "the denial of history." In this moment, structuralism "gives the people what they needed":

> An eclectic synthesis in which Robbe-Grillet, structuralism, linguistics, Lacan, and *Tel Quel* are systematically utilized to demonstrate the impossibility of historical reflection. Behind history, of course, it is Marxism which is attacked.[102]

Second, we should note the apparent "reputability" of the rhetorical acrobatics. If we suppose (as Althusser always does appear to suppose) that the only possible alternative to his version of "Marxism" is the most crude caricature of vulgar "economism", then any aspirant intellectual subjected to the cynical scrutiny of "bourgeois" scholars will clearly opt for Althusser. If we must say *either* (with Stalin) that "the base creates the superstructure precisely in order that it may serve it", *or* (with Althusser) that "between the different 'levels' of the whole" there are "peculiar relations of correspondence, non-correspondence, articulation, dislocation and torsion", then, if we are in a seminar at the Sorbonne, we will find the latter vocabulary more reputable. We may also find that the assignment of different times and histories to different ("relatively autonomous") "levels" (political, aesthetic, scientific, philosophic, etc.) affords to us a "Marxist" legitimation for carrying on with age-old academic procedures of isolation which are abjectly disintegrative of the enterprise of historical materialism: the understanding of the full historical process. Thus Althusser can only pose as a "flexible" theorist by suppressing any recognition of the actual practice, theory, and findings of historians in the Marxist tradition: and in other traditions as well.

Third, we may note, once again, the characteristically idealist mode of discourse. Althusser supposes that we can attain to a theory of structure, of history, by re-arranging and elaborating our vocabulary. Now, clearly, any statement, however "abstract", however "empirical", is constituted of an arrangement of words. And certain crucially-significant conceptual discoveries may at first be formulated in a highly abstract manner. One ought to welcome the informed scrutiny by philosophers of the lax employment by historians of unexamined concepts. But it is difficult to understand how a theory of history can be elaborated which does not, at any point, submit itself to the historical discipline, to historians' own discourse of the proof. And this, as I have sufficiently argued, involves the (empirical) interrogation of evidence, the dialogue of hypothesis and "fact."

Well, then, it might be argued that Althusser, in his generosity, has presented to historians, not one concept, but several volumes of concepts and hypotheses, which should now be tested in historical laboratories. But this will never be possible, unless in such factories as that of Messrs Hindess and Hirst, who have discovered the secret of manufacturing synthetic history and synthetic sociology out of conceptual air. For Althusser's categories have already been de-socialised and de-historicised before we can start. They commence their life as *categories of stasis:* that is, however elaborate the orbits in which they rotate, the permutations between orbits and the distortions as they are presented to the differential fields of gravity of other orbiting categories and the great attractive power of *La Dominante*—however much fussy complexity of motion is simulated by the vocabulary, the categories remain distinct, isolated from each other, the same.

Moreover, we are offered an arbitrary selection of categories—as "economics", "politics", "ideology"—and neither the principle of selection nor the categories themselves are examined. In the crucially-important passages which we set out at length above, we hear nothing about the State and almost nothing about classes. Other categories are absent throughout: we hear nothing about *power*—perhaps this is "politics", although in "real history" it may often also be "economics" or "law" or "religion". We hear nothing about *consciousness* (whether as *mentalité* or as culture or *habitus* or as class consciousness) and nothing about values or value-systems (unless in their dismissal along with "moralism" and "ideology"). Thus we are given an arbitrary (theoretically unjustified) selection of categories, and these are static, unexamined ones, which supposedly maintain their analytic effectivity not only through all the development of forms of a given mode of production but also in differing modes of production (for feudalism also has "politics", "economics", "religion", etc.) But over historical time the real content of these categories has changed so profoundly as to impose upon the historian extreme care in their employment, just as, over the same period, "science" has changed from magic to alchemy to science to technology—and sometimes to ideology.

The reason why Althusser is able to employ static categories in this way is that they are empty of all social and historical content: all that has been tipped away, and his rotating "instances" are like so many hollow tin cans. If we scarcely hear about the State or about class, we can not expect to hear about particular state formations or about *which* classes or about alternative and conflicting beliefs within "ideology". The talismanic concepts are "relative autonomy" and "in the last instance determination." We were given these by Engels, and we learned them in our theoretical cradle. Althusser now polishes them, gives them back to us, and supposes that they illuminate the whole historical landscape. But *determination,* which is at the still centre of his whole revolving gravitational field, does not merit one sentence of theoretical scrutiny.[103] "In the last instance" is not examined: it is merely perpetually postponed. "Relative autonomy", on the contrary, has been lovingly elaborated, over many pages, and re-appears as "instances", "levels", differential temporalities, dislocations and torsions. Yes, yes, and perhaps all this is so. But how might we put such a concept to work? Is law, for example, relatively autonomous, and, if so, autonomous of what, and how relatively?

I have, as it happens, been interested in this myself, in my historical practice: not, of course, in any grand way—for the whole of history, nor for the capitalist mode of production everywhere, but in a very petty conjuncture: in an island on the edge of the Atlantic, very well supplied with lawyers, at a moment in the eighteenth century. So my evidence is highly marginal, as well as being seriously contaminated by empirical content. But what I discovered there would make *La Structure à Dominante* boggle. For I found that law did not keep politely to a "level" but was at *every* bloody level; it was imbricated within the mode of production and productive relations themselves (as property-rights, definitions of agrarian practice) and it was simultaneously present in the philosophy of Locke; it intruded brusquely within alien categories, re-appearing bewigged and gowned in the guise of ideology; it danced a cotillion with religion, moralising over the theatre of Tyburn; it was an arm of politics and politics was one of its arms; it was an academic discipline, subjected to the rigour of its own autonomous logic; it contributed to the definition of the self-identity both of rulers and of ruled; above all, it afforded an arena for class struggle, within which alternative notions of law were fought out.

But how about "in the last instance determination"? Did I observe that? Well, for most of the time when I was watching, law was running quite free of economy, doing its errands, defending its property, preparing the way for it, and so on. . . But. . . I hesitate to whisper the heresy. . . on several occasions, while I was actually watching, the lonely hour of the last instance *actually came.* The last instance like an unholy ghost, actually, grabbed hold of law, throttled it, and forced it to change its language and to will into existence forms appropriate to the mode of production, such as enclosure acts and new case-law excluding customary common rights. But was law "relatively autonomous"? Oh, *yes.* Sometimes. Relatively. *Of course.*[104]

Please do not misunderstand me. I am not only arguing that Althusser has taken his categories unexamined from his own academic surroundings: the departments of politics, law, economics, etc.,—academic isolates which any historian in his apprenticeship learns to disregard. Nor am I only arguing that Althusser's elaborate constructions advance enquiry not one jot: that we commence with "relative autonomy" and, after tedious exercises in sophistication (but without putting the concept to any real work or feeding it with any content), we come out at the end with, exactly, "relative autonomy"—a kind of oratorical sauce with which to season our researches, but for which (since my palate has always approved it) we have to thank not Althusser but Engels. Nor am I only arguing that Althusser's concepts and constructions are futile because they are merely arrangements of words, so lacking in substantive content that they afford no purchase to a historian as analytic tools. All these things are true. But I am also arguing that Althusser's constructions are actively *wrong* and thoroughly misleading. His notion of "levels" motoring around in history at different speeds and on different schedules is an academic fiction. For all these "instances" and "levels" are in fact human activities, institutions, and ideas. We are talking about men and women, in their material life, in their determinate relationships, in their experience of these, and in their self-consciousness of this experience. By "determinate relationships" we indicate relationships structured within particular social formations in class ways—a very different set of "levels", and one generally overlooked by Althusser—and that the class experience will find simultaneous expression in all these "instances", "levels", institutions and activities.

It is true that the effectivity of class experience and conflict will be differently expressed in different activities and institutions, and that we may, by an act of analytic isolation, write distinct "histories" of these. But at least some part of what is expressed—as, fear of the crowd in "politics" reappearing as contempt for manual labour among the genteel reappearing as contempt for *praxis* in the academy reappearing as Black Acts in the "law" reappearing as doctrines of subordination in "religion"— will be *the same unitary experience* or determining pressure, eventuating in the *same* historical time, and moving to the *same* rhythm: a peasant revolt or the Gordon Riots may accentuate the pressure, a *longue durée* of good harvests and demographic equilibrium may allow it to relax. So that all these distinct "histories" must be convened within the same real historical time, the time within which process eventuates. This integral process is the ultimate object of historical knowledge, and it is this which Althusser offers to disintegrate.

Certainly, "relative autonomy" is a helpful talisman against reductionism—against collapsing art or law or religion abjectly back into class or "economics"; but, without substantial addition, and substantive analysis, it remains as nothing more than a warning-notice. Certainly, the hour of the last instance never comes, if, by that hour, one supposes the total collapse of all human activities back into the elementary terms of a mode of production. Such collapses may be detonated on paper (they often are) but they cannot be observed in history. But, in another sense, the "last instance" has *always arrived,* and is ever-present as a pressure within all of Althusser's "instances"; nor is the last instance ever lonely, for it is attended by all the retinue of class.

That was a long observation. Althusser's mode of discourse is idealist: he employs static categories derived from the disciplines of the academy: *La Structure à Dominante* is too well-bred to acknowledge class in her character: and his constructions are disintegrative of process. The fourth observation may be brief. Althusser's constructions of the "theory of history" afford no terms for *experience,* nor for process when it is considered as human *practice.* We have already discussed, long ago, Althusser's epistemological refusals of experience ("empiricism"). That was odd, but a pardonable oddity in a philosopher, who can cite formidable precedents. But it is not pardonable in anyone who offers to think about history, since experience and practice are manifest; nor is it pardonable in a "Marxist", since experience is a necessary middle term between social being and social consciousness: it is experience (often class experience) which gives a coloration to culture, to values, and to thought: it is by means of experience that the mode of production exerts a determining pressure upon other activities: and it is by practice that production is sustained. The reason for these omissions will become clear when we consider the other eviction, the eviction of human agency.

My fifth observation has been argued sufficiently in passing. Althusser's structuralism is, like all structuralisms, a system of *closure* (see p. 83). It fails to effect the distinction between structured process, which, while subject to determinate pressures, remains open-ended and only partially-determined, and a structured whole, within which process is encapsulated. It opts for the latter, and goes on to construct something much more splendid than a clock. We may call it Althusser's orrery, a complex mechanism in which all the bodies in the solar system revolve around the dominant sun. But it remains a mechanism, in which, as in all such structuralisms, human practice is re-ified, and "man is in some way developed by the development of structure."[105] So inexorable is this mechanism, in the relation of parts to the whole within any mode of production, that it is only by means of the most acrobatic formulations that we can envisage the possibility of transition from one mode of production to another.[106]

In all the passages of argument cited above, there is only one argument which I find to be good. This is in Althusser's critique of the synchronic methods of other structuralisms (or sociological theories), which by arresting process and taking a "section" suppose that the articulation of a totality will be revealed (p. 91). But the critique is inadequate, and for good reasons, for an adequate critique would have exploded in Althusser's own face. It is not only that the structuration of process, (or, as I would

Vulgar Marxism, or Economism
H = Basis
A − B − C = Superstructure
The machine is operated by the pulley (K) of class struggle. Note: this model represents the primitive state of Marxism before Althusser.
PLATE I

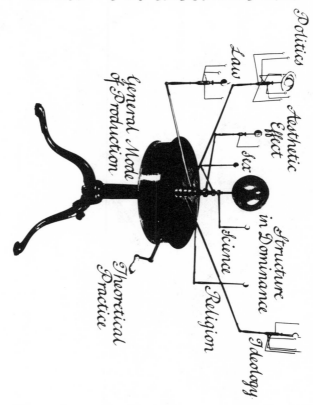

Althusser's Marxist Orrery
Note: While this machine may be simply rotated by turning the handle of theoretical practice, it is possible to replace the handle with a motor: see next plate.

PLATE II

Plates II and III are reproduced by permission of the Trustees of the National Maritime Museum, Greenwich.

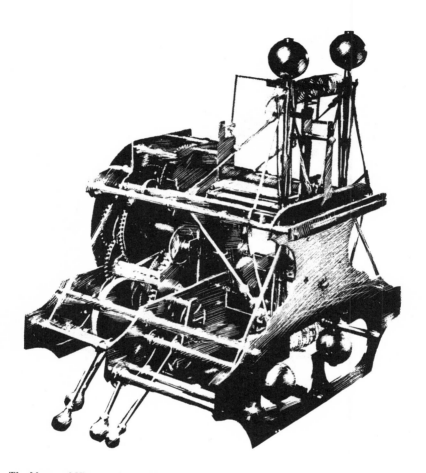

The Motor of History: Class Struggle
The motor, which may be attached to the orrery is operated by four simple levers at the base: these activate respectively the four gears of bourgeoisie, petty bourgeoisie, proletariat, and peasantry. When left to run automatically, the motions are governed by four globes (two above, two at base) of the true and false consciousness of bourgeoisie and proletariat. In both cases the true and false globes are held in tension by a spring (ideology), and the resultant torsion regulates the motor.

PLATE III

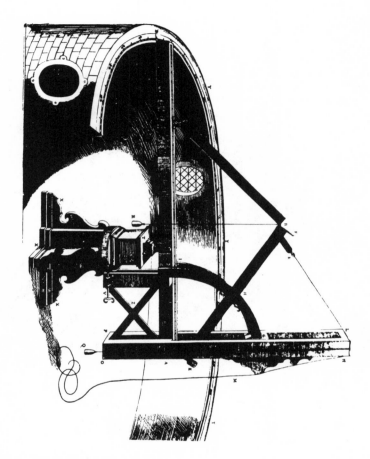

Mode of Production/Social Formation

X = the basis of productive forces. Upon this rest the productive relations (W & T), regulated by the screw (V) of surplus value extraction. The long horizontal arm is the economy, or, more strictly, capital, positing the conditions for its reproduction. This arm inscribes the shape and limits of the social formation (the wall, Y). This high vertical arm is the State, from which are deployed two pulleys: the Repressive State Apparatus (R), and the Ideological State Apparatus (Q). Note: a very much refined model of this, without any necessary correspondence between horizontal arm and wall, has now been patented by Messrs Hindess and Hirst.

PLATE IV

prefer, the congruent logics of process) can only be revealed in the observation of process over time. It is also that each moment, each "now" ("conjuncture"), should not be seen as a frozen moment of the intersection of multiple subordinate and dominant determinations ("overdetermination") but as a moment of *becoming*, of alternative possibilities, of ascendant and descendant forces, of opposing (class) definitions and exertions, of "double-tongued" signs. Between these two notions of the "now" there lies an unbridgeable gulf, which falls between Necessity (or Vico's divine will) and Morris's ever-baffled but ever-resurgent human agents. On the one hand, history as a process without a subject: on the other, history as unmastered human practice. We know which side Althusser is on: process programmed within a structure, an orrery turned by a hidden hand.

xii

And yet—we had almost forgotten—a motive-power is provided. For— "class struggle is the motor of history." We first meet with this "basic Marxist proposition" in *For Marx* (p. 215). We have found the hidden hand. We hear about this less in *Reading Capital:* the class struggle scarcely appears in any of its critical formulations on history, and this may account for my forgetfulness. But it reappears, and with the sternest political countenance, in the wigging which Althusser gave to the good Dr. Lewis. It is now a thesis of Marxism-Leninism: " 'The class struggle is the motor of history' (Thesis of the *Communist Manifesto*, 1847)." (*Essays*, 47)

Now there are certain points to make about this "basic Marxist proposition", unexceptionable as it may be. First (and a trivial point) I can find the proposition nowhere in Marx, nor can my more learned friends. It is certainly not to be found in the *Communist Manifesto*, although the reader might suppose—I did suppose—that we were being offered a direct quotation. What the *Manifesto* does say, in its opening line, as should be too well-known to repeat, is: "The history of all hitherto existing society is the history of class struggles," to which Engels subsequently added a footnote excusing from the formulation primitive societies (which, we must presume, had no "motor"). The two statements, in any case, are not the same. But I do find, on occasion, in Marx and Engels analogies which bring us very close to "motor." For example, in a letter of 1879 to the German Party leaders (Bebel, etc.) over the signatures of both, they write:

> For almost forty years we have stressed the class-struggle as the immediate driving power of history, and in particular the class-struggle between bourgeoisie and proletariat as the great lever of the modern social revolution. . .[107]

So: the point turns out to be a quibble: Althusser may keep his "motor", and we may offer him a "lever" as well.

There was another point, which I cannot now remember... Oh, yes, "motor" is not a "basic proposition" or a concept or a "thesis" at all: it is an *analogy*. This point is a little more difficult. If Marx *had* said (and I think he did not) that "the class struggle is the motor of history" he would not have meant that the class struggle had somehow transmogrified itself into a Boulton & Watt steam-engine driving history's moving-parts. The statement is of the order of "as if": we may envisage the history of society *as if* it were driven forward by the power (engine, motor) of the class struggle. Analogies may be good or bad, but my present point is that they serve the purpose of explication or illustration—they are a condiment to argument often used only once or twice in passing, but they are not the argument itself. They may sometimes be greatly illuminating, and in ways unintended by the author; they merit a "symptomatic" reading; in certain authors (for example, Burke) they may be more illuminating than the argument itself; they are often the sign of thought's vitality. But, and still, analogies, metaphors, images are not the same thing as concepts. They cannot be transfixed with the arrow of theory, plucked from the side of the text which they explicate, and mounted as concepts, on a plinth inscribed "Basic Proposition." It may not matter much in this case. But it does matter, very much, in the case of another analogy, which has more generally been petrified into a concept: that of basis and superstructure. The graveyard of philosophy is cluttered with grand systems which mistook analogies for concepts. A headstone is already being prepared for Marxist structuralism.

Point three: is it a good analogy? Not particularly. The reader who has bothered to accompany me this far can certainly think this out for himself.

I have argued before (p. 84) that there are definite reasons why analogies derived from mechanism or from natural process can *never* be adequate to human process, which includes properties not to be found in either. Given that the attempt must sometimes be made, for purposes of explication, the analogy of "driving-power" is inoffensive. "Driving-power" is not, of course, the same thing as the engine or "motor" itself, which initiates the drive. Marx and Engels, who lived in the pre-history of the internal combustion engine, were perhaps thinking of a Lancashire cotton mill, and not of the engine and its furnace, but of the shafts and transmission belts which directed the same *drive* to different machines and moving parts: this drive, transmitted equally to law and politics and ideology, becomes, by analogy, the class struggle, and all the parts in motion together (the factory) become "history."

The analogy may be helpful in some ways,[108] and unhelpful in others. But what concerns us is the use to which it is put by Althusser. For we remember that for Althusser "history", in its common usage as eventuating human process, is an "ideological" concept, to be rejected along with "historical time." But Althusser also must recognise that Marx himself was not innocent of this "ideological" error. (Indeed, how could he not recognise this, when Marx and Engels's works are full of allusions and invocations to history as process?) Marx offers us a structuralism (a premonition of Althusserianism) but he was insufficiently aware (theoretically) of what he was offering, and of the difference between this and a "historicism." He "did not think the *concept* of this distinction with all the sharpness that could be desired; he did not think theoretically. . . either the concept or the theoretical implications of the theoretically revolutionary step he had taken." (*R.C.* 120-1) Following Vico, Marx blundered into "a remarkable presupposition: that the 'actors' of history are the authors of its text, the subjects of its production." (*R.C.* 139) (One might note, in passing, that this is not one presupposition but two different analogies: actors certainly are not usually authors of their text, but they are subjects of a theatrical production, although in ways partially determined by the producer.) In Marx's discourse there are "lacunae, blanks and failures of rigour", and these occur when we encounter the word "history"—an "apparently full word" but "in fact theoretically an empty word", replete with ideology. However, in Althusser's "epistemological and critical reading. . . we cannot but hear behind the proferred word the silence it conceals, see the blank of suspended rigour, scarcely the time of a lightning-flash in the darkness of the text." It is the business of theoretical practice, like a skilled restorer of old manuscripts, to mend these tears, repair these blanks and silences, and restore the text. (*R.C.* 143)

It must follow that if both Marx and Althusser say that class struggle is the "motor" of history (which Marx does not) they are saying different things: for Marx is thinking absent-mindedly of an (ideological?) process of struggle and eventuation, and Althusser has rigorously thought a structural orrery:

> History is an immense *natural-human* system in movement, and the motor of history is class struggle. History is a process, and a *process without a subject.* (*Essays,* 51)

For Marx the historical process eventuates *as if* it was impelled forward by this generalised drive (of conflicting actors); for Althusser the orrery of system *literally is motored* through all its evolutions and permutations by class struggle.

We are not for a moment allowed to suppose that classes are the *subjects* of history, which might then be seen as the outcome of refracted human agency. Althusser does, in a concession to a supposedly simple-minded English public, once offer the "thesis": "It is the *masses* which make history." (*Essays,* 46) (No-one, it seems, had warned him that, in this empirical island, the category of "masses" had long been scrutinised, and found to be a disreputable—indeed, a "bourgeois" concept.)[109] But the concession is no sooner made than it is withdrawn: for the masses are *made* to make history, they are motored by the class struggle, and the classes also (it turns out) are motored. Class is a category which, in Althusser's major work, goes unexamined. And the classes which do make an entrance from time to time, and march up and down the pages—the bourgeoisie, the proletariat—are exceedingly crude projections of Theory, like primeval urges with iron heads, since "politics", "law", etc., etc., have been taken out of their heads and put at different "levels", and since consciousness, values, and culture have been excluded from the vocabulary. So that, while we are told that class struggle is the "motor" of history, there is a theoretical cut-off beyond which we may not go: we are not informed as to the nature of classes, nor how struggle eventuates, nor how this "motor" works. Althusser's contribution to *Reading Capital* concludes: "The reader will know how Volume Three ends. A title: *Classes*. Forty lines, then silence." (*R.C.* 193) Then silence.

After Althusser, his epigonees: Balibar, Hindess and Hirst, Poulantzas, and a hundred others have been happily filling in that silence, taking advantage of the blank pages in Marx's unfinished notebook. I do not like what they write. For historical materialism has also made, over many decades, its own very substantial investigations into class struggle, and has developed its findings in theoretical ways. There are disagreements among practitioners, of course; but in this area, and within the British tradition of Marxist historiography, there is very substantial agreement. And our findings can not, with any exercise of verbal agility, be compressed into the forms of Althusser's orrery.

I have written about this so often that I bore, not only my audience, but myself. I will not go over it all again. Class formations (I have argued) arise at the intersection of determination and self-activity: the working class "made itself as much as it was made." We cannot put "class" here and "class consciousness" there, as two separate entities, the one sequential upon the other, since both must be taken together—the experience of determination, and the "handling" of this in conscious ways. Nor can we deduce class from a static "section" (since it is a *becoming* over time), nor as a function of a mode of production, since class formations and class consciousness (while subject to determinate pressures) eventuate in an open-ended process of *relationship*—of struggle with other classes—over time.

As it happens, Althusser and I appear to share one common proposition: class struggle is the prior concept to class, class does not precede but arises out of struggle.[110] But the coincidence is only an apparition. For in one view (a view shared by most Marxist historians) classes arise because men and women, in determinate productive relations, identify their antagonistic interests, and come to struggle, to think, and to value in class ways: thus the process of class formation is a process of self-making, although under conditions which are "given." But this view is intolerable to Althusser, since it would give back to process a subject, for the process would then be seen to be one in which men and women (however baffled, and however limited their space for agency) remain agents. Althusser however, while silent on class, has never taken one step along this dangerous "humanist" road. For, prior to the concept of the class struggle is the concept of "contradiction", and the second concept is a function of the first:

> The specific difference of Marxist contradiction is its 'unevenness', or 'over-determination', which reflects in it its condition of existence, that is, the specific structure of unevenness (in dominance) of the ever-pre-given complex whole which is its existence. Thus understood, contradiction is the motor of all development. (*F.M.* 217)

The whole of this monstrous "theoretical expression" (and several lines more) are italicised to emphasise their centrality and their rigour, but I have spared the reader's eyes. I cannot so easily spare his thoughts. For we now find that contradiction is the motor which motors the motor of class struggle. Tracing these motors back in series, Balibar concludes, with estimable logic:

> Classes are *functions of the process of production as a whole.* They are not its subjects, on the contrary, they are determined by its form. (*R.C.* 267)

The subject (or agent) of history disappears once again. Process, for the nth time, is re-ified. And since classes are "functions of the process of production" (a process into which, it seems, no human agency could possibly enter), the way is thrown open once again to all the rubbish of deducing classes, class fractions, class ideologies ("true" and "false") from their imaginary positioning—above, below, interpellatory, vestigial, slant-wise—within a mode of production (or within its multiple contradictions, torsions, dislocations, etc. etc.), and this mode of production is conceived of as *something other than* its eventuation in historical process, and within "the ensemble of social relations", although in fact it exists only as a construction within a metaphysical oration.

We might define the present situation more precisely if we employed a category found frequently in Marx's correspondence with Engels, but a category which evaded Althusser's vigilant symptomatic scrutiny. All this "shit" (*Geschichtenscheissenschlopff*), in which both bourgeois sociology and Marxist structuralism stand up to their chins (Dahrendorf beside Poulantzas, modernization theory beside theoretical practice) has been shat upon us by conceptual paralysis, by the de-historicising of process, and by reducing class, ideology, social formations, and almost everything else, to categorical stasis. The sociological section: the elaborate differential rotations within the closure of the orrery; the self-extrapolating programmed developmental series; the mildly disequilibrated equilibrium models, in which dissensus strays unhappily down strange corridors, searching for a reconciliation with consensus; the systems-analyses and structuralisms, with their torques and their combinatories; the counter-factual fictions; the econometric and cleometric groovers—all of these theories hobble along programmed routes from one static category to the next. And all of them are *Geschichtenscheissenschlopff*, unhistorical shit.

And yet, in these days, we are offered little else. They torture us on the rack of their interminable formulations until we are brought to the limits of endurance. We may not answer in any other language: only this one is rigorous and reputable. Above our heads, in the high academies, the inquisitors dispute; they fiercely disagree, but they recognise each other's complexity and repute. At last they extract from us a denial: a denial of human agency, creativity, a denial even of self. But, as we rise from their theoretical racks, we see, through the window, the process of history going on. *"E per' si mouve!"*—and yet, *it does move!* We know—for in some remote part of our personality we remain determined by reason—that we must, somehow, find the courage to repudiate our own denial.

As our senses return, we remember why we never did much like the analogy of class struggle as the motor of history. For it supposes two distinct entities: "history", which is inert, an intricate composite of parts; and a "motor" (class struggle) which is brought *to* it, and which drives these parts, or sets them in motion. Medieval scholastics would have used a different analogy: class struggle would have been the vital breath or soul that animated history's inert body. But class struggle *is* the process (or some part of it) and struggling classes *are* the body (or some part of it). Seen from this aspect, history is its own motor.

This leads us to a general reflection upon the language of structuralism. Once again, we can observe the pressure of social being upon social consciousness, not only within "bourgeois" ideology but within Marxist thought as well. I have sketched already the political and sociological context: the glaciation of all social process induced by the Cold War. But there have been other, intersecting, reasons. European thinkers, in the nineteenth century, were disposed to grasp at analogies from natural process (often progress), not only for manifest political and sociological reasons, but because this language seemed to be given by the technology and the natural sciences of their time. Today's theorists are very differently situated. In the first place, they are segregated more than ever before from practice; they work within institutions, which are complexly-structured, according to "schedules" and programmes; less of their information arises from observation (unless in forays "into the fields") and more arrives before them as Althusser's G II or G III; their knowledge of the world is composed, increasingly, within their heads or their theories by non-observational means. They are surrounded on every side by "structures." Even their universities (and especially the new ones) are not architectural utterances but structures, with a subterranean basis, visited only by proletarian porters and boiler-men, with economics and the social sciences on the first two floors, and philosophy and literature, which can only be reached by elevator, at much higher levels. Meanwhile technology (or what they know of technology by report) is no longer a matter of driving-shafts and belts and extending railway communications, but a matter of circuits, intricate gearing, automated programmes; the natural sciences report on complex molecular structures and the torque of DNA; institutions are subjected to systems-analysis; and within all this there arrives, with inevitable punctuality, cybernetics and the computer, which sieves, sorts, and organises impartially all languages—of technology, natural science, sociology, economics, history—on one condition only: that the categories which it ingests shall be unambiguous and constant, in conformity with the constancy of its own complex binary programme.[111]

I do not set all this down in order to reject it in a fit of romantic temper. This is where we live now; and this gives us some of our experience. But this experience must inevitably press into our vocabulary, and, in particular, into the vocabulary of analogy. And sometimes we must plainly resist this pressure, when we have reason to suspect that its "common sense" disguises ideology. Just as Marx had to repudiate the "shit" of Political Economy's Malthusian and market analogies, so we must repudiate inappropriate analogies of levels, circuits, and complex closures. Nor can we allow the computer to dictate that our categories stand still for its convenience. The organic analogies of the nineteenth century, derived from the observation of plants, of stock, of growth, were sometimes improperly applied to human occasions, but they were, at least, analogies derived not from structure but from process. But as the observational field of today's theorists becomes more specialised and more segregated from practice, where are they to turn for comparable analogies, for a vocabulary of interaction and eventuation? We might start, I suggest, by observing ourselves.

I have hurled sufficient invective at the head of categorical stasis. And what is the alternative? An intuitive, empirical refusal of theory? A historical relativism which demands fresh categories for every context? We may be helped at this point by Sartre, whose thought I cannot (as a good Englishman) always follow in its subtlety—nor always assent to—but whose understanding of history, and whose relationship to political reality, is altogether superior, at every point, to that of Althusser.

Althusser, like Foucault, sticks to the analysis of structure. From the epistemological point of view, that amounts to returning to siding with the *concept*
against the *notion*. The concept is atemporal. One can study how concepts are
engendered one after the other within determined categories. But neither time
itself nor, consequently, history, can be made the object of a concept. There is
a contradiction in terms. When you introduce temporality, you come to see that
within a temporal development the concept modifies itself. *Notion*, on the
contrary, can be defined as the synthetic effort to produce an idea which develops
itself by contradiction and its successive overcoming, and therefore is homogenous
to the development of things.[112]

I am not sure that I accept this notion of notion. But Sartre's argument
conforms closely to my own earlier argument as to the approximate and
provisional nature of historical concepts, as to their "elasticity" and
generality ("classes", "class struggle"), as to their character as expectations
rather than as rules. (See p. 46) It conforms also to vigilant rejection of
the closed and static concept or analogy in favour of the open and the
shaping, formative one: as, by replacing "law of motion" by "logic of
process", and by understanding determinism, not as pre-determined programming or the implantation of necessity, but in its senses as the "setting
of limits" and the "exerting of pressures."[113] It means retaining the
notion of structure, but as structural actuation (limits and pressures)
within a social formation which remains protean in its forms. It means
the refusal of that trick of thought, discussed by Raymond Williams in
considering "basis" and "superstructure", by which the "metaphorical
terms for a relationship" are extended "into abstract categories or
concrete areas", until these analytic categories—

As so often in idealist thought, have, almost unnoticed, become substantive
descriptions, which then take habitual priority over the whole social process to
which, as analytic categories, they are attempting to speak.[114]

It means that even when we decide, for legitimate reasons, to isolate
certain activities for distinct analysis—as we may do with modes of
production or economic process—we do not allow ourselves to be deluded
by our own procedures into supposing these systems to be distinct. It
means that in such procedures we employ especial care whenever we come
to those "junction-terms", which lie at the point of junction between
analytic disciplines (as, "need" in economics which may be seen as a
"norm" in anthropology) or between structure and process (as, "class"
and "mode of production", which lie forever on those borders).

This is not all. We need, also, more historical *thought;* a greater
theoretical self-consciousness as to our own concepts and procedures; and
more effort, by historians, to communicate their findings to others in
theoretically-cogent forms. (In all the chatter of "theoretical practice"

about modes of production, pre-capitalist formations, ideology, the labour process, class, the State, ISAs and RSAs, FMPs and CMPs, historians who have made these problems the object of sustained investigation have, in general, been ignored, and they have returned the compliment with a disdainful silence.) Communication will flow in both directions of course. But what we do *not* need is "a theory of history", in Althusser's sense. For this theory will be nothing but a thin enigma unless it is fattened on the content of substantive historical analysis. If we want to know *how* "autonomous", and "relative" to *what*, we may think the problem but then we must *find out*, and think again about our findings. We must put theory to work, and we may do this either by interrogating evidence (research) or by interrogating historiography and other theories (critique); and both these methods were the ones most commonly employed by Marx. Theoretical practice, which rejects the first procedure ("empiricism"), and which reduces the second procedure to caricature by measuring all other positions against its own pre-given orthodoxy, is evidence of nothing but the self-esteem of its authors. For the project of Grand Theory—to find a total systematised conceptualisation of all history and human occasions—is the original heresy of metaphysics against knowledge.

It is not only that this is like trying to catch running water in a sieve. It is not only that we can never reproduce with finality within the forms of thought—

> . . . history, that never sleeps or dies,
> And, held one moment, burns the hand.

It is not only that the attempt to do so, in a "science" devoid of substance, ends up very much like Engels's characterisation of the Hegelian inheritance: "a compilation of words and turns of speech which had no other purpose than to be at hand at the right time where thought and positive knowledge were lacking."[115] All this is not all. The project itself is misbegotten; it is *an exercise of closure*, and it stems from a kind of intellectual agoraphobia, an anxiety before the uncertain and the unknown, a yearning for security within the cabin of the Absolute. As such, it reproduces old theological modes of thought, and its constructions are always elaborated from ideological materials. More than this, such total systems have, very generally, been at enmity with reason and censorious of freedom. They seek, not only to dominate all theory—or to expel all other theories as heresies—but also to reproduce themselves within social reality. Since theory is a closure, history must be brought to conform. They seek to lasso process in their categories, bring it down, break its will, and subject it to their command. Within the *last in*stance we find the anagram of Stalin.

Nor is this all. There is also the matter of dialectics. Many critics have noted that Althusser has extruded, along with Hegel, dialectics. This should be apparent without further demonstration. I do not mean his extrusion of this or that "law" of dialectics, as in his commendation of Stalin for his prescience in challenging the credentials of "the negation of the negation." The ontological status of any such "laws" is questionable. I mean that even in the moment that Althusser acclaims *La Dialectique,* and boasts possessively as to his intimacy with her, he strikes her into a statuesque pose; and in that pose we recognise, once again, our old friend, *La Structure à Dominante.* She is modeling a new gown, which superbly expresses her inner contradictory nature:

> *This reflection of the conditions of existence of the contradiction within itself,*
> *this reflection of the structure articulated in dominance that constitutes the*
> *unity of the complex whole within each contradiction,* this is the most profound
> characteristic of the Marxist dialectic. (*F.M.* 205-6; and above p. 82)

This gown is a reflection of contradiction, and the creation is presented to us by its designer under the name, "over-determination". The gown is fitted perfectly to the model's form; but it is so tight that *she cannot move.* In all of Althusser's texts, dialectics, conceived as the logic of the logic of process, never appears.

My readers will eagerly anticipate that a hundred page disquisition on dialectics will now ensue. I am sorry to disappoint them. It is beyond my competence. I wish only to make a few observations, situating myself on the *outside* of an argument into whose complexities I would be foolhardy to enter. First, I am of the opinion that the understanding of dialectics can only be advanced if an absolute embargo is placed upon the mention of Hegel's name. This will appear to be absurd and whimsical. But I mean to argue it through. Manifestly, Engels and Marx "owed" their dialectics to Hegel, often returned to Hegel, and often acknowledged their debt. All this has been examined by others, and with much ability, and I do not dispute the value of the examination. One day it should be resumed. But at this point the discussion is not only exhausted, it has become counter-productive. For its tendency has been to align its protagonists into "Hegelian" Marxists, who, with whatever efforts at inversion, tend to see dialectics as a Hegelian suffusion *within* process; and anti-Hegelians (whether empirical "historicists" or Althusserians) who tend, in effect, to discard dialectics along with Hegel.

But, second, the account which theorists offer of their procedures need not be the same thing as those procedures themselves. We may agree to reject the account which Engels offered in *The Dialectics of Nature,* but the matter cannot be ended there.[116] There still remain the very motions of thought implicit in many passages of Marx and Engels's analysis, their procedures, and their self-consciousness of these procedures. When old

Engels thundered out to Schmidt, "What these gentlemen all lack is dialectic", he went on to adduce, not dialectical "laws", but the mode of apprehension of a fluent and contradictory eventuation:

> They never see anything but here cause and there effect. That this is a hollow abstraction, that such metaphysical polar opposites only exist in the real world during crises, while the whole vast process proceeds in the form of interaction (though of very unequal forces, the economic movement being by far the strongest, most elemental and most decisive) and that here everything is relative and nothing is absolute—this they never begin to see.

It is true that the letter ends: "Hegel never existed for them." Hegel (inverted) "taught" them to see in this way. But let us think more about the seeing and less about the teacher. The great-great-grandchildren of "these gentlemen" have read their *Logic* upside-down and backwards, but they have been taught nothing. "Contradiction" is antagonism, a "motor" of struggle: it is not a moment of co-existent opposed possibilities. "Reformism" must be incorporation within capitalist structures: it cannot *also* be reforms and the modification of those structures to allow a space for incorporation. And so on: and on and on. "They never see anything but here cause and there effect."

Thus it is always possible that (as Marx remarked of Spinoza) "the real inner structure of his system is, after all, wholly different from the form in which he consciously presented it."[117] And, third, even if we set aside Hegel, we will still have to deal with William Blake. I offer Blake, not as a hitherto-unrecognised tutor of Marx, but in order to emphasise that the dialectic was not Hegel's private property. Blake reminds us of a very old, sometimes reputable, sometimes arcane hermetic tradition—often a tradition of poets—which sought to articulate modes of apprehension appropriate to a reality which was always in flux, in conflict, in decay and in becoming. Against the "single vision" of mechanical materialism, Blake sought, and succeeded, to think co-existent "contrary states" and to marry heaven and hell. We must agree that Hegel was the vector through whom this tradition was transmitted to Marx, and we may agree that this transmission was an ambiguous inheritance and that Hegel's attempt to objectify a mode of apprehension as laws was invalid. But this does not invalidate the mode of apprehension.

I am suggesting that Hegel obscures our vision. He gets between us and the light. If we set him aside, we may then more easily look directly at dialectics themselves. I am not certain what we shall see, except that it will certainly not be contradiction caught in a stationary pose. The attempt to see a logic inscribed within "natural" process itself has been disabling and misleading. But from another aspect, we seem to be offering a description, within the terms of logic, of the ways in which we apprehend this process.[118]

I am certain only that this mode of apprehension of "double-edged, double-tongued" process is to be found in Marx and Engels' own practice. And (here I may speak confidently for others within "my" tradition) that in my own work as a historian I have repeatedly observed this kind of process, and have, in consequence, come to bring "dialectics", not as this or that "law" but as a habit of thinking (in co-existing opposites or "contraries") and as an expectation as to the logic of process, into my own analysis. How else are we to be prepared to understand the paradox that the apparent agent of socialist revolution, the CPSU (B), has become the organ which, above all, articulates and imposes upon the self-activating social and intellectual process of Russian society a system of *blockade?*

The eviction of dialectics from the Althusserian system is deplorable, but it flows as a necessary consequence from the inner stasis of structuralism.[119] I am less sure that there is much to be gained from giving to "the dialectic" elaborate logical and formal expression. We have often been told that Marx had a "method", that this method lies somewhere in the region of dialectical reason, and that this constitutes the *essence* of Marxism. It is therefore strange that, despite many allusions, and several expressions of intent, Marx never wrote this essence down. Marx left many notebooks. He was nothing if not a self-conscious and responsible intellectual worker. If he had found the clue to the universe, he would have set a day or two aside to put it down. We may conclude from this that it was not written because *it could not be written,* any more than Shakespeare or Stendhal could have reduced their art to a clue. For it was not a method but a practice, and a practice learned through practising. So that, in this sense, dialectics can never be set down, nor learned by rote. They may be learned only by critical apprenticeship within the same practice.

We will take leave of this section with some different observations. I promised at the outset to eschew the method of swapping quotations from Marx. I am not interested in the defence of Marxism as an orthodoxy. But we cannot dismiss as irrelevant the question as to whether Althusser's reading of Marx is "authorised"—whether indeed Marx's work had been mis-recognised (as a "historicism") when it was always a structuralism, affording premonitions of the Althusserian orrery. A sufficient way of answering this question will be to note several of the devices which Althusser employs to validate his reading, not only as truly orthodox but as *more* orthodox than Marx.

We have noted one device, in the "motor": to *gloss* a text ("thesis of the *Communist Manifesto*") and to *invent* from this gloss a "basic Marxist proposition." We have noted another, in the transmutation of analogies into concepts, and of analytic categories into substantive descriptions. A further essay could follow here on the Althusserian employment of "in the last instance." The "last" instance (*in letzter Instanz*) may be variously rendered into English as "in the last analysis", "in the (court of) last resort", "ultimately", "in the final judgement." That fine Communist scholar, Dona Torr, working ten hundred miles outside of academia, who first translated and edited the *Selected Correspondence,* in 1934, in those incredibly dim days when (as we are assured by Eagleton, Anderson and a dozen others) *soi-disant* British Marxists had nothing in their hands but a few impoverished polemical tracts—Dona Torr first rendered the passage in Engels's letter to Bloch—that passage which becomes the axle of Althusser's oratory, but which, we recall, is abstracted from a letter which also supplies the script in which the old man is made to play as clown— she rendered it thus:

According to the materialist conception of history the determining element* in history is *ultimately* the production and reproduction in real life. More than this neither Marx nor I have ever asserted.

Thus *in letzter Instanz* appears first as "ultimately", and, later in the letter, as "in the last resort." And at the asterisk* Torr allowed herself one of her rare editorial intrusions: "**Moment*—element in the dialectical process of becoming." She was already, it seems, forty years ago, keeping a watchful eye on the horizon for the arrival of Althusser. This is what Althusser gives: "production is the determinant factor"[120] (*F.M.* 111)— "production" itself being another category which he and Balibar are intent to stabilise and re-ify. And how can a last *analysis* then become an "instance" at a "level", a "political instance" or a "legal instance" assigned an operative indicative force by *La Structure à Dominante?* What are we to make of Poulantzas's definition: "By *mode of production* we shall designate... a specific combination of various structures and practices, which, in combination, appears as so many instances and levels..."?[121] How can a mode of production appear as so many *instances* (analyses, judgements, last resorts) unless it has become a metaphysical mode, producing neither goods nor knowledge, but re-producing itself endlessly in differentiating levels and instances, engendering only theoretical famine? "But the truth is, they be not the highest instances that give the securest information"—

As may be well expressed in the tale so common of the philosopher, that while he gazed upwards to the stars fell into the water; for if he had looked down he might have seen the stars in the water, but looking aloft he could not see the water in the stars.

We might describe this last device as "transplantation." An organ of one argument is cut out and put into the side of another. A more familiar device has already been well described as "ventriloquism."[122] Althusser rarely allows Marx to speak: when he does, he throws his own voice into Marx. Or, which is little different, he *produces* Marx; prepares the scene; rehearses the script; presents a cue; and then a few lines, proper to that moment of the scene, are permitted. Let us follow through one example. Althusser has noted, with delight, a *footnote* in *Capital*—and, moreover, a note only to be found in the French edition—defining the word "process":

> The word 'procès' (process) which expresses *a development considered in the totality of its real conditions* has long been part of scientific language throughout Europe. In France it was first introduced slightly shamefacedly in its Latin form—*processus*. Then, stripped of this pedantic disguise, it slipped into books on chemistry, physics, physiology, etc., and into works of metaphysics. In the end it will obtain a certificate of complete naturalization. (*L. &P.* 117; *P. &H.* 185)

The production requires at this point that Marx should speak a few lines to authorise Althusser's thesis of history as a "process without a subject"; moreover, he wishes to catch the word "process" (which the knowledgeable reader will know that Marx used rather freely) and put it under arrest. If historical process can be defined as "a development considered in the totality of its real conditions" then it can be put back *inside* structure, as a mechanism to turn the orrery around. One way (an honest way) of approaching this question might have been through examining Marx's arguments in *Capital* at some central places in the text. But Althusser prefers a footnote limited to the French edition. He offers these lines as his authority. Why, then, did Marx choose such an obscure way to express a point of such importance? A chauvinist reply would be: "Because only the French reader could have the logic to comprehend a point so nice." But Althusser, at this point, is no chauvinist; he has a better argument—it was only the three or four years interval which had elapsed since the publication of *Capital* in German which had permitted Marx to clarify his own thought, "which had allowed him to grasp the importance of this category and to express it to himself." (*L. & P.* 117)

This is the production; it is superb. But the producer gets little assistance from his script; the dramatist has nodded. For the note defines *the word*, "process", as employed indifferently within works of chemistry, physics, physiology and metaphysics. The note says nothing, absolutely nothing, about how Marx sets the word to *work*, about Marx's notion of *historical* process (for this we must refer to his books). And it is self-evident from the note that it has been inserted in the French edition because the word has not yet been allowed "naturalization", is unfamiliar in political and economic theory (or so Marx supposes), possibly because it offended against the fixity of categories in French logic, possibly because French intellectuals scrutinise with care the credentials of alien conceptual intruders before they are permitted familiar access to their discourse. And I do not say this in criticism of the French. British intellectuals, so anxious to "Europeanise" themselves, might learn something here from the caution of the French. There are some recent intruders—"conjuncture", "overdetermination", "instance", "structure-in-dominance"—whose certificates of naturalization should be refused.

We have noted these devices: invention: transmutation of analogies into concepts: improper conceptual transplants: "ventriloquism" or "production". The most general device, however, is the employment of readings which are partial or which are wholly misleading, and in ways which cannot be "innocent". As a final example, we will follow one of these. We have already noted that Althusser, at an important place in his argument, cites the authority of *The Poverty of Philosophy*, Marx's polemic (in 1847) against Proudhon:

> How, indeed, could the single logical formula of movement, of sequence, of time, explain the body of society, in which all economic relations co-exist simultaneously and support one another?

This appears, as we have seen (p. 93), at a critically-important stage of his argument for a structurally-synchronic mode of analysis. I do not think that there is any other text of Marx's which he works harder. This text is his licence to own an orrery. It is employed at at least four significant points in *Reading Capital* (*R.C.* 65, 66, 98, 107); it is "rigorously expressed", and in "those few lucid sentences" Marx "warns us that he is looking not for an understanding of the mechanism of the production of society as a *result* of history, but for an understanding of the mechanism of the production of the *society effect* by this result." (*R.C.* 66) These sentences, in a work which comes directly after the "epistemological break"—one of the first utterances of the "mature" Marx—are indeed of "absolutely decisive scope", they direct us to the essence of his revolution in Theory, his discovery of "science."

It is not clear why this is so, but it is clear that the sentence must be supported by its context. To this we must return. The context is chapter two of *The Poverty of Philosophy*, entitled "The Metaphysics of Political Economy", and commencing with some observations on method. What has most annoyed Marx in *La Philosophie de la Misère* is Proudhon's pretention to a new metaphysical method: "We are not giving a *history according to the order in time*, but *according to the sequence of ideas*." In place of the sequence of actual history, Proudhon proposes to develop economic theories in "their *logical sequence* and their *serial relation in the understanding:* it is this order that we flatter ourselves to have discovered." (Proudhon, cited in *C.W.* VI, 162)

Marx's several observations develop, most emphatically, different aspects of the same objection: the metaphysical and unhistorical character of Proudhon's method. Bourgeois economists have developed "the division

of labour, credit, money, etc., as fixed, immutable, eternal categories",
but "they do not explain... the historical movement that gave them
birth." Proudhon takes these categories (from the economists) as given,
and wishes to put them into a new sequential order, a serial relation in
the understanding:

> The economists' material is the active, energetic life of man; M. Proudhon's
> material is the dogmas of the economists. But the moment we cease to pursue
> the historical movement of production relations, of which the categories are but
> the theoretical expression... we are forced to attribute the origin of these
> thoughts to the movement of pure reason. (Ibid. 162)

This Marx sees as the heresy of metaphysics. Everything is presented, not
in the analysis of social and historical reality, but as a sequence of
abstracted logical categories:

> Thus the metaphysicians who, in making these abstractions, think they are
> making analyses, and who, the more they detach themselves from things,
> imagine themselves to be getting all the nearer to the point of penetrating to their
> core—these metaphysicians in turn are right in saying that things here below are
> embroideries of which the logical categories constitute the canvas.

(We stir uncomfortably, and remember "society effect", and men as
träger: embroideries upon the canvas of structure.) Marx thunders on:

> If all that exists, all that lives on land and under water can be reduced by
> abstraction to a logical category—if the whole real world can be drowned thus
> in a world of abstractions, in the world of logical categories—who need be
> astonished at it?
>   All that exists, all that lives on land and under water, exists and lives only by
> some kind of movement. (Ibid. 163)

Proudhon has at least noticed this. And he seeks to enclose movement
within his categories by means of a crude deployment of the Hegelian
dialectic. But what he has done is to abstract movement itself into a series
of logical categories:

> Apply this method to the categories of political economy, and you have the logic
> and metaphysics of political economy, or, in other words, you have the economic
> categories that everybody knows translated into a little-known language which
> makes them look as if they had newly blossomed forth in an intellect of pure
> reason; so much do these categories seem to engender one another, to be linked
> up and intertwined with one another by the very working of the dialectic
> movement. (Ibid. 165)

We are now beginning to understand why Althusser held his hand so firmly over the text of *The Poverty of Philosophy*, and allowed us only to peep through his fingers at one single sentence. But if we are to understand the context of this sentence, and, therefore, Marx's meaning, we have to turn back for a moment from chapter two ("The Method") to chapter one, where Marx makes an entry directly into the question of Proudhon's concept of value. Proudhon seeks to explain the genesis of exchange value, not in its real historical genesis, but in its genesis within a sequence of logical categories: the "history" is that of the genesis of *ideas* in "serial relation in the understanding." Proudhon presents this sequence in this kind of way:

> Since a very large number of the things I need occur in nature only in moderate quantities, or even not at all, I am forced to assist in the production of what I lack. And as I cannot set my hand to so many things, I shall *propose* to other men, my collaborators in various functions, to cede to me a part of their products in *exchange* for mine. (Proudhon, cited in Ibid. 111)

(As Marx remarks elsewhere, this is a characteristic petit-bourgeois notion of economic relations: the "I" is a little master hatter or brass-founder, who would exchange in this way if the State, taxation, feudal privilege, did not intervene.)[123] From this "logical sequence" (a "history", but a history only in ideas, or ideology) Proudhon derives the division of labour. As Marx remarks, " 'A man' sets out to '*propose* to other men. . .' that they establish exchange," but Proudhon has not explained the genesis of this proposal, "how this single individual, this Robinson, suddenly had the idea of making 'to his collaborators' a proposal, of the type *known* and how these collaborators accepted it without the slightest protest." (Ibid. 112) This is a sample of what Proudhon describes as his "historical and descriptive method" (Ibid. 113). The logical sequence of categories, one engendering the next in series, may then be placed within a small balloon named "I", and this balloon may then be puffed up with rhetoric until it has become "the impersonal reason of humanity", or, at another place, "Prometheus", who, "emerging from the bosom of nature", sets to work, and "on this first day", his product "is equal to ten:

> On the second day, Prometheus divides his labour, and his product becomes equal to a hundred. On the third day. . . Prometheus invents machines, discovers new utilities in bodies, new forces in nature. . . (Proudhon, cited in Ibid. 157)

But (we scarcely need to rehearse Marx's critique) this is to invert the real historical sequence:

> Labour is organised, is divided differently according to the instruments it has at its disposal. The hand-mill presupposes a different division of labour from the

steam-mill. Thus it is slapping history in the face to want to begin with the division of labour in general, in order to arrive subsequently at a specific instrument of production, machinery. (Ibid. 183)

In this sense, it is the machine which (historically) "discovers" the division of labour and determines its particular forms.[124] We cannot usefully discuss the production of wealth "without the historical conditions in which it was produced." Put this "Prometheus" back into history, and what does it turn out to be?

It is society, social relations based on class antagonism. These relations are not relations between individual and individual, but between worker and capitalist, between farmer and landlord, etc. Wipe out these relations and you annihilate all society. . . (Ibid. 159)

Thus the whole of *The Poverty of Philosophy*, a remarkable and cogent polemic, is a set of variations upon the theme of Proudhon's unhistorical metaphysics. This gives us the context, and hence the meaning, of Althusser's one sentence "licence." Economic categories are "the abstractions of the social relations of production." (Ibid. 165) But these relations are continually in movement, and the categories themselves are *"historical and transitory products."* Proudhon seeks to wrest the categories from their context, eternise them, and then re-order them as a serial relation in the understanding. (Ibid. 166) He does not wish to present "history according to the order in time." This "real history" is, in Proudhon's view, only the "historical sequence in which the categories have *manifested* themselves." (Ibid. 169) But we can improve upon real history "by taking the economic categories. . . successively, one by one. . ." (Ibid. 168) As a result, for Proudhon, "everything happened in the *pure ether of reason.*" (Ibid. 169) But we cannot detach economic categories from their context in this way, since "the production relations of every society form a whole." Proudhon's serial relation of categories in the understanding leads him to consider "economic relations as so many social phases, engendering one another, resulting one from the other like the antithesis from the thesis, and realising in their logical sequence the impersonal reason of humanity." But we cannot analyse productive relations, economic relations, as this kind of series, since all the relations (and the categories) coexist and presuppose each other. We must take these together as one set. To arrive at value, Proudhon "could not do without division of labour, competition, etc. Yet in the *series. . .* in the *logical sequence*, these relations did not yet exist":

In constructing the edifice of an ideological system by means of the categories of Political Economy, the limbs of the social system are dislocated. The different limbs of society are converted into so many separate societies, following one upon the other. *How, indeed, could the single logical formula of movement, of sequence, of time, explain the structure of society, in which all relations coexist simultaneously and support one another?* (Ibid. 166-7: my italics)

We have arrived at last at Althusser's talisman, the jewel of "absolutely decisive scope." But Marx has not finished. In the next observations he posts on. Proudhon has dislocated the "limbs" of the social system, and given these as separate "societies"—production, exchange, a monetary system, distribution—following one upon the other in a logical, categorical sequence. We have to reconstitute these limbs, and see them as acting together. But how are we to do this, unless within "real history", the history within which these relations were engendered? When we do this, we return once again to the point of origin of the economists' material, "the active, energetic life of man." And when we do so, the illusion of bourgeois economics—that society is the effect of categories, and that men are the carriers of structures—is at last dispelled:

> We are necessarily forced to examine minutely what men were like in the eleventh century, what they were like in the eighteenth, what were their respective needs, their productive forces, their mode of production, the raw materials of their production—in short, what were the relations between man and man which resulted from all these conditions of existence. To get to the bottom of all these questions—what is this but to draw up the real, profane history of men in every century and to present these men as both the authors and the actors of their own drama? (Ibid. 170)

Does the point need explaining further? Arguments, as well as production relations, form a whole. We cannot sever one limb, and that limb a tiny one (one sentence), the upper joint of a little finger. Marx's argument is at no point an argument against "historicism"; it is an argument for integrative historical analysis against the disintegrative "*single* logical formula" of Proudhon, as a serial relation of categories. Moreover, we can now understand Althusser's silence as to the substantial arguments of *The Poverty of Philosophy*. For the "heresies" which Althusser wishes to unmask—the heresy of "empiricism" ("to examine minutely what men were like"), the heresy of "historicism" ("the real, profane history of men"), and the heresy of "humanism" ("as both the authors and the actors of their own drama")—these heresies do not appear merely as the momentary "blank of suspended rigour, scarcely the time of a lightning-flash in the darkness of the text" (see p. 297)—these are integral to the text, they *are* the argument, they *are* the thunder and the lightning which are hurled against Proudhon's darkness.

Moreover, it is only necessary to perform one small operation upon Marx's text—by changing at every point the name of Proudhon to

Althusser—and it may be read as a sustained premonitary polemic against the latter's "Theory". It is true that Althusser has replaced Proudhon's sequential logic with an inconsequential logic. But the polemic strikes home every time: the fixity of categories; the engenderment of categories from pure reason rather than through historical analysis; the metaphysical heresy, categories engendering society and men as their effects; the mystifying "novelty" of the vocabulary; the re-organisation of real history into a more proper categorical logic, "as the development of forms" (structure swallowing process); the disintegrative method which separates a whole into "limbs" ("levels", "instances"); and the manipulation of these limbs in an ether of pure reason independently of the specificities of historical time and class. In going to the office of authority, and taking out this text, M. Althusser has made a big mistake. What he supposed was a licence to entertain the public with his orrery was in fact a court order to put down his own dog, "theoretical practice." And the order is signed, "Karl Marx." And the order must be executed, instantly, by the public, if Althusser refuses. For the dog has bitten philosophy and sociology already, and made them mad.

A final observation. We will propose it in the form of a question. How does Althusser have the *neck*?

xiii

So many pages! And yet we have only traced two of Althusser's ogres, "historicism" and "empiricism", to their lairs. Somewhere in the forest those even more hideous monsters, "humanism" and "moralism", still lurk. But I do not think that we will need so many pages to find them. As we have seen (p. 36), a ball rolls down the hill through its own innate energy and will. All of Althusser's subsequent propositions roll down in the same way, once he has placed them on this idealist summit.

It should also be clear, by now, that these propositions belong not to reason or to "science" but to ideology; and therefore we can despatch them somewhat more briskly. That men and women are not agents in their own history, but *träger*—carriers of structures, vectors of process—must follow upon the concept of a "process without a subject." To suppose otherwise is to fall into the sin of "humanism." Althusser's first elaborated anathema against this sin appeared in an article, "Marxism and Humanism", in 1964. Why did it appear *then*?

We shall see.

But to see we must make ourselves into historians for a moment. I am sure that my most critical readers will not accuse me of having confused, up to this moment, Theory with the sociology of ideology. Our critique has been "rigorous", "within Theory" and its "discourse of the proof." Well, most of the time. Not a syllable of the partisan or the personal has been allowed to intrude. Not often.

Now, however, we must not only admire Althusser's orrery (which we shall continue to do) but ask also why it was made, and whom it was intended to entertain? But, first, *the text*.

This is how it commences:

> Today, Socialist 'Humanism' is on the agenda.
> As it enters the period which will lead it from socialism. . . to communism. . . the Soviet Union has proclaimed the slogan: All for Man, and introduced new themes: the freedom of the individual, respect for legality, the dignity of the person. (*F.M.* 221)

"This is a historical event", Althusser goes on. It is premonitory of a dialogue between Communists and men of goodwill "who are opposed to war and poverty. Today, even the high-road to Humanism seems to lead to socialism." But this is only a *seeming*. In fact, humanism ("Man") is a very foul bourgeois ideological concept, and one to which Marx himself was victim in his early manuscripts. He liberated himself from this concept in the course of his encounter with Feuerbach—the argument (the argument of Engels's *Ludwig Feuerbach*) is too familiar to rehearse. Beneath the grand phrases of "humanity" was concealed the exploitation by the bourgeoisie of the proletariat. Hence revolutionary proletarian "humanism" could only be a "class humanism": "for more than forty years, in the U.S.S.R., amidst gigantic struggles, 'socialist humanism' was expressed in the terms of class dictatorship rather than in those of personal freedom." (*F.M.* 221) But "the end of the dictatorship of the proletariat in the U.S.S.R. opens up a second historical phase."

> In the U.S.S.R. men are indeed now treated without any class distinction, that is, as *persons*. So, *in ideology,* we see the themes of class humanism give way before the themes of a socialist humanism of the person. (*F.M.* 222)

Very nice. But, before we can order a stock of the same commodity for ourselves, we are sternly reminded that it is a product, not of Theory but of *ideology*. Ideology *"is as such an organic part of every social totality."* Like it or not, even Socialist states must have "ideology." "Human societies secrete ideology as the very element and atmosphere indispensable to their historical respiration and life." (*F.M.* 232, 235) But this particular ideological stock cannot be exported from the U.S.S.R.; indeed, it is a seed carefully prepared only for Siberian conditions. The "world opening up before the Soviets" is one with "infinite vistas of progress, of science, of culture, of bread and freedom, of free development—a world that can do without shadows or tragedies." (*F.M.* 238) But that is their world, not ours: "the themes of socialist humanism (free development of the individual, respect for socialist legality, dignity of the person, etc.) are the way the Soviets and other socialists are *living* the relations between themselves

and these problems, that is, the *conditions* in which they are posed."
(*F.M.* 238-9) If we live in different conditions, we cannot cultivate the
same crops. In "China, etc." only a "class humanism" can as yet be
grown. (*F.M.* 222) And what of the capitalist West? Very clearly the stock
cannot be imported. For it would be transmogrified in the passage, and
would spring up, in these conditions, as a virulent bourgeois crop of anti-
Communism. It would come up, not as socialist at all, but as the old
ideological notion of "Man". For we must not forget for an instant the
difference between ideology and science, and that "the frontier separating
ideology from scientific theory was crossed about one hundred and
twenty years ago by Marx." (*F.M.* 246) "Strictly in respect to theory,
therefore, one can and must speak of *Marx's theoretical anti-humanism. . .*
(*F.M.* 229)

> Simply put, the recourse to ethics so deeply inscribed in every humanist ideology
> may play the part of an imaginary treatment of real problems. Once *known,*
> these problems are posed in precise terms: they are organizational problems of
> the forms of economic life, political life and individual life. (*F.M.* 247)

These problems must be given *"their scientific names."* Thus we see that
in *theory* (while it may do for the Soviet Union as ideology: i.e. rhetoric)
"socialist humanism" is the old enemy; it is the couple, abstract "goodwill"
(moralism) and "Man" (humanism) in partnership against real Communism.

Very nice, again. But who are the *träger* or vectors of these hideous
ideological impurities? Can we envisage bourgeois "socialist humanism"
in corpore vile, and give it a local habitation and a name? *Who* is the ogre?
We shall see.

But, first, we must make two general observations on Althusser's
procedures. (1) There is a method of "theoretical practice" which I will
describe as *The Kangaroo Factor.* We have noted long ago (p. 35) that
this kind of idealism, since it prohibits any actual empirical engagements
with social reality, is delivered, bound and gagged, into the hands of the
most vulgar empiricism. That is, since it cannot know the world, the world
must be assumed in its premises. And what is that world but the most
vulgar manifestations and prejudices of "what everyone knows"? Hence
the theoretical practitioner proceeds in gigantic bounds through the
conceptual elements, with the most gracious curvatures of thought; and
while he is bounding he performs the most elegant acrobatic twirls and he
paws the air with sublime gestures. But every so often (since the law of
gravity cannot be disregarded for ever) he comes down: *bump!* What he
comes down upon is an assumption about the world. But he does not
linger on this assumption, sniff it, taste the grass. *Hop!* He is off into the
air again.

I apologise. The analogy is grossly unfair to kangaroos, which bound forward with a purposive air to an objective, keep their paws tidily in place, and every now and then stop, eat, and survey the world. Theory hops onwards for ever, even through the Stalinist night.

Of course, if the reader shares already all of Althusser's "common sense"—that the Soviet Union in 1964 was a land living the themes of dignity of the person, free development of the individual, respect for legality, etc., with "infinite vistas" of progress, a world "without shadows or tragedies"—then my analogy is wasted upon him. And he had better stop reading this essay, since these pearls are not for him.

We shall notice the *kangaroo factor* again.

(2) The second observation. Althusser's theoretical practice may be defined as a contestation without an opponent. Throughout *For Marx* and *Reading Capital* his antagonists are scarcely ever (unless in an allusion, a footnote) defined. The practice is that of monologue, not dialogue, *within* the corpus of Marxist concepts. But this is not strictly true. At a few points opponents *are* defined, and these are: young Marx, Hegel, mature Marx (his blanknesses and failures of rigour), poor old Engels, and Gramsci. (I will not turn aside now to defend that creative, but ambiguous, thinker; he does not require my defence, and he has defenders enough.) Apart from these moments of argument—an argument which is "produced"—we have, not particular ogres—antagonists who developed particular arguments in definite places—but a generic *ogreism*. We have "empiricism" without any empiricists, "historicism" without any attention to historians, and now we have "humanism" and "moralism" without any faces. But no matter: we cannot see these ogres for a very good reason: they are hidden within the dense undergrowth of the forest of "bourgeois ideology."

But then a very strange thing occurs. Suddenly, in 1972, an ogre does shamble out of the forest, dazzled and confused in the unaccustomed daylight. Hurriedly, an orthodox Communist audience is gathered around. And then, in the arena of Theory, a supreme tournament is staged, with an *actual* antagonist: Dr. John Lewis.

And why should he choose *this* opponent? We shall see.

Who was John Lewis? It is Althusser's whimsy (for even rigour may be allowed its little jokes) to offer him as a youngish philosopher—perhaps a "man of goodwill" who was *trying* to be a Marxist but who had not overcome the influence of Sartre[125]—and not, as he was, the elderly guardian of the tablets of the British Communist Party's ideological law. Between 1945 and 1956, during the era of high Stalinism, Lewis was the editor of the party's intellectual organ, *The Modern Quarterly*. The young are uncharitable, as I am now old enough to know. And no doubt I and my immediate friends in the Communist Party in those days took an uncharitable view of Lewis, in seeing him as a superintendent among "King Street's" ideological police, along with Burns, Dutt, Garman, Klugmann and co. That is, in intellectual and cultural matters, he was two fixed points between which a "correct line" could always be drawn. His own speciality—and he gave himself a generous allowance of the journal's pages—was homiletics on Communism and ethics, morality and humanism.

Now this seems, at first sight, to conform exactly to Althusser's requirements: Lewis is taken as a triple personification of the ogre, "dogmatism", the ogre, "humanism", *and* the ogre, "moralism." These three ogres, of bourgeois origin, had slipped unobserved from their natural habitat, into the forest of *Stalinism*. In unmasking Lewis, Althusser is taking even further his long and rigorous project of unmasking the "Stalinian deviation." And it is the easier for him to do this by selecting an elderly target in the British Communist Party (which the leaders of the P.C.F. have always despised) rather than an ogre in his own party who might always bite back. Moreover, Althusser is able to present himself as being way ahead of his own lagging times, in the *avant-garde* of Theory: "In *For Marx*—that is, in 1965—I was already writing about Stalin, about the Twentieth Congress of the Soviet Communist Party, and about the split in the International Communist Movement. John Lewis, on the other hand, writes as if Stalin had never existed. . . (*Essays*, 36)

But this is in fact not a tourney at all. It is a race, *in the same direction*, between two kangaroos. It is true that, while in the air, the kangaroos make different noises, in different national idioms; but since every other country is now allowed its own "national" Marxism, why should not "Anglo-Marxism" be allowed? If Franco-Marxism is permitted to utter, in Cartesian tones, the *leçons* of *raison*, why should Anglo-Marxism not emit, in the organ-tones of a unitarian or theosophist chapel, the homilies of moral man? But both kangaroos hop to the same rhythm, go the same way, and land from time to time, *bump*, on the same clumps of unexamined "common-sense"—the Party, Marxism-Leninism, and astounding illusions as to Soviet history and contemporary reality.

What Althusser is saying as to bourgeois "humanism" as ideology and as to proletarian "class humanism" (embodied in the dictatorship of the proletariat in the Soviet Union embodied in the Party guided by Marxist science) is, *exactly*, what Lewis was saying in the high Stalinist years, and saying repetitiously to the exclusion of all other themes. This was Lewis's "thing." In 1946 ("The Great Moral Muddle") he started off hopping at the same point at which Althusser commenced in 1964. "The soberest estimate of Soviet achievement", based on the reports of "the most cautious investigators" reveal "a respect for personality, an achievement of freedom from want and insecurity, an equality of opportunity, that has filled the Soviet people with boundless confidence and hope." But Lewis saw all this placed on the agenda as early as the new Soviet Constitution, in 1936, in which Stalin proclaimed the "equality of rights for citizens", secured by legal guarantees. He did not neglect to take us through the same Feuerbach routine. "Ethics can only be understood in terms of the class interests they are called upon to serve"; "to make any ideal effective it must become the ideal of a class, that is to say it must express the actual interest of a class." ("Marxism and Ethics", 1950) Thus we have Althusser's "class humanism."

Hence also the new humanism of socialism realised. This does not arise "from metaphysical principles, or from the acceptance of some utopian ideal or set of abstract moral principles." On the contrary, it must be seen, like Althusser's "ideology", as "the moral aspect of a particular mode of production." This is the basis of "the new morality" in Russia. ("The Moral Complexion of Our People", 1951) But, like Althusser again—for they are both still *way up*, in the air, at the apex of their graceful curve— there is the same stern prohibition upon the import, to the capitalist world, of "the new morality" in the form of abstract principles. "It is against the background of the complete moral collapse of bourgeois society that we have to put the bad conscience which projects all the wickedness of which it is guilty upon the new and nobler world that is coming to birth." "The stalwart champions of eternal principles" must be exposed as wearing "class interests behind the mask of absolute values." But there is no need for the proletariat to wear this mask, for "the realisation of proletarian aims makes possible for the first time a truly human morality. . ." This is achieved "by means of a *class* victory, inspired by a *class* morality. . . There is no other way in which a morality which is above classes can be realised."

It is here that the gestures and tones of Lewis and Althusser (both still *way up*) diverge a little—the accents of *raison* and those of moral plenitude:

> Because the workers know that in fighting for their own emancipation they are fighting for all mankind, the ethical drive behind their movement far exceeds both in purity and intensity that which inspired all preceding systems of class ethics and becomes one of the most potent of those energising and mobilising forces which, as Stalin has pointed out, play such a vital part in the development of society. ("Marxism and Ethics")

Now both our moralists descend to the ground, and not very far from the point they started from. This ground, for Althusser, is a Soviet world "with infinite vistas of progress", a world "that can do without shadows or tragedies." True, they call this utopia by different names: for Althusser it is the world of Theory Realised, of Science Incarnate: for Lewis it is the world of Truly Human Man:

> It is because the leading members of the Soviet Commonwealth are imbued with a morality which leads them *to respect and care for people* that they succeeded in

their great task. They owe much of this finely human attitude to Stalin, whose deep wisdom and broad humanity has long inspired the Party, as it now inspires the state of which he is the leader. His ethics and the whole of moral aim of the Soviet state are well summed up in his own moving declaration of the supreme value of human personality. "Our leaders," he says, "should display the most solicitous attitude towards our workers... We must learn to value people... It is time to realise that of all the valuable capital the world possesses, the most valuable and most decisive is people." ("The Moral Complexion of Our People")

And when did Stalin say this? In his Address to the Graduates from the Red Army Academy in 1935. How unfortunate it was that so many of these graduates turned out, in the next two years, to be, not "people" at all, but "alien elements", the *träger* of capitalist conspiracy, who merited liquidation.[126]

Lewis, then, was a very parfit, gentle kangaroo. The rhetoric was different here and there ("man"/"masses": socialist "ideology"/new morality); but the essential arguments and assumptions of both men were the same. How is it, then, that John Lewis should shamble, in 1972, as the ogre of "humanism" out of the forests of bourgeois ideology? And how is it that Althusser's arguments, first commenced in 1964, may be presented as the initiation of a rigorous critique of the "Stalinian deviation", while Lewis, presenting *the same arguments*, in the years between 1946 and 1956, should be seen as an exemplar of that deviation? And why does the whole tourney, and the ground on which it is fought, seem so unreal?

We shall see.

I am sorry to be so tedious. These last pages bore me inexpressibly. But I am trying to unravel a tangle of wool. And I am trying to do this patiently, for the benefit of a generation which thinks itself to be "post-Stalinist" (but which, very often, *is not*), whose "rigour" has enabled them to repudiate, along with "historicism", the most elementary knowledge of the immediate past of the Communist movement, in Russia, in Britain, in France. This innocence is allowing them to be made, every day, the victim of a gigantic confidence trick, in which resurgent Stalinism presents itself as anti-Stalinism, and in which the long, explicit, and arduous critique of Stalinism sustained in a thousand places and a thousand struggles on the Left is presented as "bourgeois ideology." The tourney between these identical twins, dogmatism and *dogmatisme*, was faked up by Althusser to further this trick.

It is all done by mirrors. We have been drawn into an illusionist's parlour. Let us return again to the 1964 article: why did Althusser then find it necessary to demystify "socialist humanism"? Was it because of some grave error already committed by John Lewis? No: so far as I know, Lewis was not in the habit of coupling those words. But the words stir a faint memory in my mind. For there were other people, a lot of other people in leading positions in the international Communist movement, who were denouncing "socialist humanism" between 1956 and 1964. Thus I recall Arnold Kettle, the token representative of British Culture on the executive of the British Communist Party, denouncing "middle class people... spouting a lot of pious generalisations about socialist humanism."[127] By these middle class people he can scarcely have been referring to himself, nor to John Lewis, nor even to Althusser, who was, in 1964, to give muted approval to the term—but only as *ideology*, and only in the Soviet Union.[128] On every side the mirrors reflect back upon each other; but every one is empty; in none of them is any actual ogre to be seen.

And then, as I screw up my eyes, and gaze intently in the nearest mirror, the terrible realisation comes. There I am staring into the bloated visage and bared fangs of the most hideous of ogres. And it is myself! M. Althusser has done me the incomparable tribute of addressing an article to *me!*

Readers will pardon the egotism of this hyperbole. Of course we cannot suppose that a publication emanating from Yorkshire would have been attended to in Paris. But I was, from 1957, co-editor of a journal, *The New Reasoner*, subtitled "A Quarterly Journal of Socialist Humanism". And in the first number of that journal I was the author of a long, immature, but not, I think, radically mistaken article on "Socialist Humanism", which was, very specifically, a critique of Stalinist ideology and practice.[129] It was part of an international discourse, and, if it did not reach Paris, it certainly reached Moscow. For I received more than one tribute from Soviet theorists. Thus in *Oktober* (1958) I was singled out for special commendation:

> One of these crusaders... is Edgar Thompson, the acknowledged leader of the British revisionists, one-time editor of *The Reasoner*, the journal which fell into oblivion so quickly. [It was ordered to cease by the E.C. of the British C.P. E.P.T.], and now editor of *The New Reasoner* which has its inglorious existence today...

My article on "Socialist Humanism" was particularly noted: "Thompson repeats slanders which... are served up in one form or another by revisionists of all shades."[130] In *Novy Mir* (1958) the tributes were even more touching. The journal of "Socialist Humanism" was noted as being conducted by "a group of renegades": "the venal scribblers writing in the reactionary imperialist press could well sue the author for plagiarism: Thompson assiduously rehashes their fantasies about 'Stalinism', 'Zhdanovism', about the suppression of the individual in the U.S.S.R.; fervently he calls for nothing less than a 'revolt' against Soviet ideology." "Like all traitors... like all renegades and anarchists", E. Thompson uses the term socialist humanism as—

A smoke-screen. . . to proclaim the identity of proletarian class morals with 'an administrative, bureaucratic, despotic attitude to human beings.' Calling for a revolt 'against inhumanity' this philosophizing slanderer in every possible way counterposes the abstract 'man in general' to society, to the collective, to the communist party. Far-reaching claims for some kind of allegedly new 'socialist humanism' are concluded with the following declaration: 'It is *humanism* because it places once again real men and women at the centre of socialist theory and aspiration instead of the resounding abstractions—the Party, Marxism-Leninism—Stalinism, the Two Camps, the Vanguard of the Working Class—so dear to Stalinism.'[131]

Perhaps—since ogres are notorious for their vanity—I may quote also the next sentence (neglected by *Novy Mir*)—which exposes my hideous project even further: "It is *socialist* because it re-affirms the revolutionary perspectives of Communism, faith in the revolutionary potentialities not only of the Human Race or of the Dictatorship of the Proletariat but of real men and women."

There my face is, hideous, contorted with renegade malice, drooling with bourgeois spittle. We might notice also that Mr. Ozerov, the gifted theorist of *Novy Mir*, has anticipated Althusser's method of exposure: "this philosophizing slanderer. . . counterposes the abstract 'man in general' to society. . ."—although, as it happens, I had counterposed "real men and women" to the abstractions so dear to Stalinism. My premises were "men, not in any fantastic isolation or definition, but in their actual, empirically perceptible process of development under definite conditions."[132] And quite a lot of those men, under the abstract draperies of Marxist orthodoxy, were already dead.

So let us stop fooling and picking: the wool has come free. I do not know who first revived "socialist humanism" as the motto of the Communist libertarian opposition in 1956, although certainly *The New Reasoner* carried it to some parts of the English-speaking world. But it arose simultaneously in a hundred places, and on ten thousand lips. It was voiced by poets in Poland, Russia, Hungary, Czechoslovakia; by factory delegates in Budapest; by Communist militants at the eighth plenum of the Polish Party; by a Communist premier (Imre Nagy), who was murdered for his pains. It was on the lips of women and men coming out of gaol and of the relatives and friends of those who never came out.

After November 4th, 1956, when Soviet forces blasted into Budapest, there was initiated a general disciplinary action through the international Communist movement: to re-impose the disciplinary controls of State or Party, to re-establish ideological orthodoxy—in effect, to reconstruct, within changed conditions, Stalinism without Stalin. This proceeded, in differing circumstances and different countries, at a different pace and in different forms; in one place, a palpable police action (Nagy shot, Tibor Dery gaoled, anti-Stalinist militants of the Budapest Workers Councils one or the other); in another place, the expulsion of "revisionists", the closure of dissident journals, the re-establishment of the most rigid Stalinist norms of democratic centralism. Alongside this, of course, there was an ideological police action. The "main enemy" was seen to be, not Trotskyism (which was a subordinate tendency within the opposition), but "revisionism", "renegades", "petty bourgeois elements", and their ideological virus was identified as "moralism" and as—"socialist humanism."

Thus we can see the emergence of Althusserianism as a manifestation of a general police action within ideology, as the attempt to reconstruct Stalinism at the level of theory. This is not to say (things are never as simple as that) that the leaders of the French Communist Party immediately appointed Althusser as chief of ideological police. They distrusted *all* philosophy, as an infected area; Althusser's language was difficult, and his "rigour" ("theoretical anti-humanism") deprived them of some antique rhetoric—for the special virtuosity of the older kangaroo consisted in demonstrating (with apt quotations from Stalin) that *whatever* happened in the Communist world constituted a Victory for Man. John Lewis has shown us that. It was only after *Reading Capital* (1965)—and after a sharp dispute—that an understanding was come to, and that Waldeck Rochet, the Secretary-General of the P.C.F., spent a long day (June, 1966) with Althusser, "talking about Spinoza." (*Essays*, 104) This understanding reproduced an old project of the Enlightenment. The absolute monarch (the Party) agreed to be enlightened by the *philosophe* (Theory).[133] The price of the pact, for Althusser, may be seen in a little subsequent tinkering with his orrery (ambiguous confessions of "theoreticism"), in the increasing brutality of his formulations (RSAs and ISAs, "philosophy as class struggle"), and in his posturings as a veteran militant of true class war, smelling of the cordite of innumerable arduous contestations with bourgeois heresy.[134] And also—here is the parlour of mirrors—with "dogmatism" and Stalinism.

I am concerned, in this essay, with theory. I will comment further on the actual history in another place.[135] But I am entitled, as I think, to locate this particular theoretical problem in this way. In terms of chronological time (which, as we know, is "ideological") M. Althusser is some six years older than me. But in true, structural, theoretical time, I am (by the same number of years) his political senior. I joined the Communist Party in 1942, at the age of eighteen. Althusser joined the P.C.F. in 1948, at the age of thirty. I know nothing about his prior history (which is irrelevant to Theory), except that he was "active" as a member of the Jeunes Étudiants Catholiques. His initiation into the Communist movement came at a time when the voluntarism of the anti-fascist war and the Resistance was receding, and the rival structures (political and ideological) of the Cold War had congealed. The whiff of cordite which is brought to us in his reminiscent allusions is not that of men "making history" but that of "the Stockholm Appeal and of the Peace Movement" (*F.M.* 22)—that is, of a period in which the necessary struggle for peace was fought by the blind on a ground of falsehood and under the banner of illusion. When the illusions were finally dispelled, in 1956, it was Althusser's business to sew up people's eyes and block their ears, to put the whole corrupt structure of falsehood back in a more sophisticated form.

I was never deceived by this structure for an instant. Nor were my comrades and friends. We knew it of old, we knew it *all too well.* Althusser was (for us) the ancient enemy, the reasons of Stalinist power. But to a "post-Stalinist generation" the trick is passed. This rigorous critic of "dogmatism", "economism" (supply as required), almost on his own (*Essays,* 84), set himself the arduous task of restoring Marxist science; *"already"*, in 1965, he was "writing about Stalin" (Ibid. 36). By 1972 he was able, at "personal risk", to advance a "hypothesis" as to a "Stalinian deviation" (Ibid. 89, etc.).

"Already", in 1965! *So where was Althusser in 1956?* We know the answer. In truth, this "already" should make me uncomfortable as well, as it should all penitent kangaroos: if 1956, why not 1953, 1948, etc.? But how was Althusser's "critique" so unaccountably postponed? In 1956 it was, at length, officially "revealed" that Stalinism had, for decades, been swatting down men like flies—Communists and non-Communists alike—and, after a further nine years, Althusser coughed, came out of his rigorous meditation, and muttered "dogmatism"; after a further seven years, he coughed again, and risked the hypothesis of a "deviation" ("the posthumous revenge of the Second International"!!) (*Essays,* 89); two or three years later, and he had a few severe words to say about Zhdanov and Lysenko.[136] But, on the other side of his face, he has been altogether more voluble and incomparably more severe. The main enemy has been—socialist humanism.

And yet, socialist humanism was, above all, the voice of a Communist opposition, of a total critique of Stalinist practice and theory. How on earth could the Althusserian illusion have been passed, even for an instant? It had to be supported by other illusions, each of them mirrors of the first. We have time now to admire only three. First, there was the ancient trick (itself a circle of mirrors) which identified all opposition as, by definition, "objectively", the voice of reactionary imperialism. Proposition 1: these critics attack the Party, Marxism, etc. Proposition 2: but the Party *is* the ultimate good, the guarantee of Theory, etc. Proposition 3: therefore these critics are enemies of all that is good, and objectively they are imperialist swine. Thus the high theory of *Novy Mir:* thus Althusser—criticism of Stalinism, unless in terms prescribed by *his* theory, stems from "the most violent bourgeois anti-Communism and Trotskyist anti-Stalinism" (*Essays,* 82-3) Q.E.D.

Second, reflected across the parlour, the criticism is "bourgeois"—

"middle class people" spouting about socialist humanism. This criticism is most commonly found on the spouting lips of middle class people (Althusser, Kettle). As a characterisation of the social complexion of the Communist opposition in 1956 it is a direct lie. It was no more true of the workers of Poznan, of the spontaneous councils of Budapest, than it was to be of the initiatives for "socialism with a human face" in Czechoslovakia in 1968.[137] Nor was it true for those who composed the "party" of socialist humanism in Britain in 1956. For the veteran leader of the Derbyshire miners, Bert Wynn, solidarity with our critique meant (as for many others) severing connections within his own heart; for the full-time organiser of the Leeds Communist Party, Jim Roche, formulating the positions of socialist humanism meant getting out his tools and returning to the cutter's bench; for the pit delegate from Ballingry, Lawrence Daly, it involved a critique not only in theory but in political practice, as he initiated the Fife Socialist League, and carried the highly-politically-conscious miners of West Fife along in its own "discourse" of agitation; for the shop stewards' convenor at Briggs Motor Bodies (Dagenham), Johnny McLoughlin, it involved calling for an "organized movement of the Marxist anti-Stalinist Left." So that illusion is not only a lie, it is an insolent and élitist lie. And it stems from an ulterior intellectual contempt for the intelligence and moral sensibility of the working class.

Third, this lie is reflected in ormulu and gilt mirrors across the parlour. Socialist humanism (being, as we know, bourgeois) must of course be no more than a supine relapse into "bourgeois ideology"—humanism, moralism, u.s.w. This illusion is the more interesting, in a theoretical consideration, since it is the one commonly passed on intellectuals. Stalinism blocks all exits from its system by defining in advance any possible exit as "bourgeois." And, alas, in this respect Trotskyism actually reinforced the Stalinist intellectual system, by rehearsing the same legends and setting up identical blocks. Thus, when I offered, in 1957, a critique of epistemological "reflection theory", with reference to Lenin's *Materialism and Empirio-Criticism,* Peter Fryer (a recent convert to Trotskyism) declared that I was waging "an all-out assault on the philosophy of dialectical materialism", and taking a road "which leads inevitably into the swamp of subjectivism and solipsism."[138] Althusser, in a condescending little foreword ("To my English Readers") to *For Marx,* patiently explains it thus:

> The critique of Stalinist 'dogmatism' was generally 'lived' by Communist intellectuals as a 'liberation'. This 'liberation' gave birth to a profound ideological reaction, 'liberal' and 'ethical' in tendency, which spontaneously rediscovered the old philosophical themes of 'freedom', 'man', the 'human person' and 'alienation'. (*F.M.* 10)

(It must be difficult to "speak" a theory like this, when at every second word, one must "contort" one's features into a knowing "leer", to "signify" to the reader that one "knows" *the true meaning* of these words behind their apparent "meaning".) In 1972 he had become more blunt; he had only one recourse to inverted commas; "after the Twentieth Congress an openly rightist wave carried off (to speak only of them) many Marxist and Communist 'intellectuals', not only in the capitalist countries, but also in the socialist countries." (*Essays*, 83)[139]

So that is what we all were—"an openly rightist wave". Almost alone, Althusser confronted the danger. He wrote *For Marx* "to combat the contagion which was 'menacing' us." It is strange that this "rightist wave", this "contagion", although it swept in men and women of all occupations and ages, should have swept most strongly through the generation of the anti-fascist struggle and the Resistance, through the generation most possessed still by the illusions of voluntarism (that they were "makers of history"), the generation which Althusser appears to have missed.

This, then, is the missing protagonist with whom Althusser wrestles in *For Marx* and *Reading Capital:* the anti-Stalinist revolt, the total intellectual critique, which converged for a time under the motto: "socialist humanism." Please don't misunderstand me: I am not offering "socialist humanism" as an alternative orthodoxy, nor as an adequate definition of all that this critique entailed, nor yet as a motto endorsed on every side. The term has had its own ambiguous history and I am not so tender at the passing of time as to wish to preserve it in theoretical amber. But this, if anywhere, is where all these critiques and actions converged.

This is the object of Althusser's police action, the unnamed ghost at whom his arguments are directed. But the ghost is allowed no lines of his own. The reader of the "post-Stalinist generation" is encouraged to suppose him to be some timid intellectual, remote from any political action, "shocked" in his bourgeois moral sensibility, putting on his glasses, peering at Marx's 1844 manuscripts, and collapsing back into a "rightist" Feuerbachian complacency. This also is a direct lie. The actual themes of the critique: the structure and organisation of the Party: the control of the membership by the full-time apparatus: the Moscow orientation (and training) of that apparatus: the self-perpetuating modes of control ("democratic centralism", the "panel" system, the outlawing of "factions")—and from thence to the wider political and intellectual themes: none of these themes appear.

Of course, if one defines oneself as being in the middle of a sea, then any other waves *must* be on the "right" or on the "left". The other waves will see it differently. From my own position, I cannot conceive of any wave in the working-class movement being further to the "right" than Stalinism. From any consideration of working-class self-activity, of socialist liberty, how is it possible to be further to the "right" than the anti-historicism and anti-humanism of Althusser?

But there is a final, an ultimate, illusion still to be performed. "Socialist humanism" may be the ghost with which Althusser was arguing. But, it turns out, this was only the *alias* for an even greater ghost, the unnamed ogre whose shadow falls across his lines. In 1972 this ogre is finally named: socialist humanism is the mask of Joseph Stalin! Not Stalin himself, please be clear: for behind the mask, Stalin's visage is unclouded, proletarian, and theoretically unblemished: his thought "continues to hold itself comfortably above the uproar, in its bases, its 'line' and certain of its practices" (*Essays*, 83). But in certain *other* of its practices we may detect the "Stalinian deviation", and this is the twin, "economism/ humanism", which must always be taken as "an ideological pair." Stalin's "economism" was "hidden by declarations which were, in their own way, cruelly 'humanist'." (*Essays*, 85, 91) We are to suppose that the "deviation" arose from a certain absent-mindedness, a relapse into the rhetoric of bourgeois ideology. Excessively preoccupied with building a productive "base" ("economism") he slipped into exalted reveries about the "New Soviet Man", and did not notice what was happening to "productive relations" (i.e. men and women) in between. Hence "socialist humanism"—an "imaginary treatment of real problems"—is only a new projection of the "Stalinian deviation."

And now a contortionist is brought on to illustrate the trick. A certain Grahame Lock, who has felt himself called upon to introduce the latest writings of Althusser and Balibar to a British public, takes up the centre of the parlour and glosses the texts. Economism is "to forget about class struggle, and to forget about class struggle is *humanism.*" Stalin was forgetful in this way, and "fell into both economism and humanism." Hence he fell (just as we were to do in 1956) into certain traps prepared by the cunning of the bourgeoisie. The *gulags*, faked trials, and all that "were *bourgeois methods* used against the bourgeoisie, and they backfired disastrously."

> The trials and purges played a role *determined in the last instance by the class struggle inside the USSR*, even if in practice their victims were the 'wrong' ones. (*Essays*, 14-15)

We will leave Mr Lock there, wriggling on the floor, one foot behind his neck, the other in his mouth. We have only introduced him for the purposes of light relief.

This whole section has been awful. Theory is so much clearer than history. I have written it only out of compassion for the innocence of a "post-Stalinist generation." One day or the other they would have to be told. I have tried to unravel a tangled skein, to explain the function of Althusserianism as an ideological police action *against* any fundamental socialist critique of Stalinism, but a police action which presents itself (through a series of distorting mirrors) as exactly such a critique. I hope that I may have dispelled these illusions in two or three minds.

But even if doubtfully convinced, these minds will still propose further questions. As they should. They may ask: "Why do you drag us back into all this old stuff? The sins were committed long ago, in another country, and, anyway, the wench is dead. They have all been confessed. And Euro-Communism is a thoroughly reformed character. Why should we, of a post-Stalinist generation, be haunted by your memories?"

My answer may be brief or extended. The brief answer is this. You are *not* a "post-Stalinist generation." You are a generation amongst whom the reasons and legitimations of Stalinism are, by means of "theoretical practice", being reproduced every day.

We may now extend this answer. The agenda presented to each generation is *always*, in good part, presented to it by the past. "My" socialist generation was not "responsible" for Fascism or for Stalinism. We found these already there when we came of age. We dealt with the first, and we neglected, for too long, the second. Hence it was transmitted, as perhaps the largest of all problems, to socialists today.

We must distinguish—as with all such phenomena—between Stalinism as a particular historical/political/sociological eventuation, and the ideology, institutions, and practices which arose within that particular moment of eventuation. Stalinism, in the first sense, certainly belongs to the past. It was not cunningly planned, nor—as Althusser and Lock appear to suppose—was it the outcome of some "deviation" *in theory*, some momentary lapse in Stalin's theoretical rigour. It was the product of baffled human agency, within a desperate succession of contingencies, and subject to the severe determinations of Soviet history. This very difficult examination must be pursued in its own right. At a certain point, Stalinism may be seen as a systematic social formation, with a consonant ideological logic and legitimation—Marxism-Leninism-Stalinism.

Thus from this historical matrix there emerged Stalinism, in a second sense. Stalinism was not just certain "errors" or unsatisfactory practices, which, after some twenty years, even Althusser is able to call "crimes." We are not only (please remember) just talking about some millions of people (and most of these the "wrong" people) being killed or *gulaged*. We are talking about the deliberate manipulation of the law, the means of communication, the police and propaganda organs of a state, to blockade knowledge, to disseminate lies, to slander individuals; about institutional procedures which confiscated from the Soviet people all self-activating means (whether in democratic modes or in forms of workers' control), which substituted the Party for the working class, the Party's leaders (or leader) for the Party, and the security organs for all; about the confiscation and centralisation of all intellectual and moral expression, into an ideological state orthodoxy—that is, not only the suppression of the democratic and cultural freedoms of "individuals": this even Euro-Communism has come to regret (and we are glad that this is so) although, even in the moment of regretting, it is sometimes implied that these freedoms of individual dissent are "extras", additions to the menu of socialist construction, which, after sixty years, the Soviet State should be able to afford: it is not only this, but within the confiscation of individual "rights" to knowledge and expression, we have the ulterior confiscation of the processes of communication and knowledge-formation of a whole people, without which neither Soviet workers nor collective farmers can know what is true nor what each other thinks.

From this historical matrix, then, there emerged Stalinism as a set of institutions and practices. And along with these there emerged the apologia, the theoretical legitimation of the practice. Spreading outwards from the Soviet Union, through the Comintern, this permeated the entire international Communist movement. The practices and the ideology were replicated, and the agents of this replication (the inner and trusted bureaucracies of national Communist parties) became, by a very exact analogy, the priesthood of a universal Church, adept at theological apologetics and "humanistic" homiletics, directly and knowingly deceiving their own memberships, agile in casuistry, and reinforcing their control by distinctively Stalinist procedures and forms—"democratic centralism", the suppression of faction and discussion, the exclusive control of the Party's political, theoretical and (as far as possible) intellectual organs, the slander of critics and opponents, and the covert manipulation of fellow travellers and front organisations. It is not true that international Communism "did not know" about Stalinism, prior to the Twentieth Congress of the CPSU; it both knew a great deal, and endorsed it, and it did not *wish* to know about the rest, and denounced this as slander; what it "did not know" was that it was now "correct" to denounce as the crimes of *one man* what it had previously exalted and apologised for, in the language of Marxist theory.

It will be seen that I am—as *Novy Mir* and Althusser predicted of socialist humanism—falling back upon "the most violent bourgeois anti-Communism and Trotskyist anti-Stalinism." But at least I am not hopping like a kangaroo. Every single point in the last two paragraphs is abundantly documented, and not only in the works of scholars who may conveniently be ruled out of court as "bourgeois hacks", but by Soviet and socialist authors (Victor Serge, Deutscher, Lewin, Claudin, Medvedev). Some part of it I can confirm by direct experience. Members of a "post-Stalinist generation" who have agonised over Balibar and Lacan but who have not acquainted themselves with the elementary history of socialism in this century might postpone their theoretical practice until they have dried themselves behind the ears.

But, if I may speak for "my" generation, for the moment of total contestation *within* Stalinism—that is, between Stalinism and alternative Communist traditions and forms—which was most manifest in "1956", then two important reservations must be entered. First, we never, for one moment, said or supposed that this was *all* that international Communism was, or is, or was doing in those decades. Communists can never be reduced to agents of a Stalinist conspiracy; they were doing a hundred other things, many were important and within an alternative, authentic socialist tradition, some were heroic, and some of them no-one else would do. This is one reason why the contestations *within* Communism have been so sharp. Second, in our contestation with Stalinism we never allowed to lapse, for one moment, our contestation with capitalism and with Western imperialism. Not only this, but we never relapsed into the dishonest attempt to divorce Stalinism from its historical genesis in emergency and contingency, emergencies and contingencies supplied in good part by the furious hostility of international capitalism at the emergence of *any* socialist society. We never supposed that Stalinism was to be attributed in its origin to this or that theoretical "error", nor to the innate evil will of Marxism, nor that analysis was ended by clucking our tongues in moral disapproval. We always saw international capitalism as a co-parcener in socialist degeneration.

But that it was a profound degeneration, in actuality, in thought, and in organisational forms, we had no doubt. To combat this degeneration was the agenda which "history" passed down to us. The generation of "1956" did not say that God had failed; we said that *we* had failed, and that we meant to clear that failure up. And so? Is not that moment still far in the past? And perhaps we *succeeded?* For many of that old Stalinist priest-hood have died or been pensioned off. Contingencies and contexts have changed; in what we had supposed to be the corpse of international Communism, movement can be seen once again. It breathes and stirs its limbs. Perhaps the critique of "1956" was too precipitate, too passionate, too purist: but it was not altogether wrong? In mysterious ways, and through the basic instincts of the proletarian organism, Communism is proving capable of self-reform. Euro-Communism has left Stalinism long behind; it has passed resolutions against it; Althusser is pursuing a theoretical critique.

Some part of this is so. And that part is welcome. We have never supposed that Stalinism penetrated equally to all parts of the international movement. Nor have we ever proposed that Communism (in which "we" also invested so many of our thoughts and acts) was an insanitary area. There *is* movement. There is even genuine self-questioning, real discussion, dialogue. It moves at different paces, here and there. With Italian Communism, which contained, in Gramsci, a moment of theoretical honour, it has moved in interesting ways. It has even moved in France. And M. Marchais, as we know, has promised that when he comes to power he will be kind to animals. My cat, who read this over my shoulder, laughed. But I did not laugh. I think that, in certain favourable contingencies, and, recalling, above all, the libertarian traditions of the French and Italian peoples, expressing themselves within the membership of these mass parties, and imposing their will upon the leaderships—given all this, the outcome of Communist participation in governments of the Left might be one which opened new and more democratic socialist possibilities. All this is possible, as historical eventuation.

But this does not mean that the project of "1956" has been fulfilled. For, even if we take the most generous view of these changes and the most optimistic view of future tendencies, this project can only be fulfilled on one condition: that the agenda of 1956 is carried through to the bitter end. Of course, Stalinism as historical eventuation belongs to the past; it will not come back in that form; the future will eventuate in other ways. And, of course, there are plenty of opportunistic reasons why Western Communist Parties wish that the smell of the past would go away. It is an electoral inconvenience that Solzhenitsyn should appear in the capitalist press every other day. No-one *wanted gulags* to happen, and no-one— certainly not M. Marchais—wants them to happen in France. Stalinism belongs to the past. We are already moving on.

And yet, *does it* belong to the past? For it was, not only a particular historical eventuation, but also one of the ultimate disasters of the human mind and conscience, a terminus of the spirit, a disaster area in which every socialist profession of "good faith" was blasted and burned up. And if one was bred in *that* area, hopping about and proclaiming it to be utopia, does one get out of it by only a few more opportunist hops?

So let us stop playing the "generation game." If we consider Stalinism in its second sense, as a set of institutional forms, practices, abstracted theories, and dominative attitudes, then the "post-Stalinist generation" has not yet been born. Stalinism, in this sense, gave to us the agenda of the present, and its forms and modes "weigh like an alp" on the brains of the living. And the living (never mind which generation) need their combined strength to shift that alp. If you have had an alp on your mind, you will know that it is not removed by a theoretical shrug of the shoulders ("economism", "humanism").

I do not only mean that the Soviet Union, the largest alp of all, is governed by practices and legitimated by a State ideology ("Marxism") which is directly derivative from Stalinism. (I may safely predict that, over the next twenty years, we will have sufficient lurid reminders of that; that the multiform self-assertions of the Soviet people will, more often than not, appear as a nausea with the Party and with its ideology; and that M. Marchais will meet with repeated electoral disappointments.) I do not only mean that enigmatic China revives, year by year, more disturbing memories; that when the country's most respected leaders and Marxist *clairvoyants* become overnight a "gang of four", we do not understand what is happening but we do know that neither we nor the Chinese people will be told, and we remember, uneasily, previous exposures of "traitors" at the peaks of power. Nor do I only mean that there are certain *continuities* in the personnel, forms, procedures, vocabulary, strategies and methods of "reformed" Euro-Communist parties—continuities which may be modified by opportunist measures but which, very often, may not be subjected to a sustained and principled critique (unless by an "enemy of the Party"). I have asked my cat, and he has explained that it is all this which made him laugh. But there is still something more than all these. It has been, throughout, the subject of this essay.

Stalinism, in its second sense, and considered as theory, was not one "error", nor even two "errors", which may be identified, "corrected", and Theory thus reformed. Stalinism was not absent-minded about crimes: it *bred* crimes. In the same moment that Stalinism emitted "humanist" rhetoric, it occluded the human faculties as part of its necessary mode of respiration. Its very breath stank (and still stinks) of inhumanity, because it has found a way of regarding people as the bearers of structures *(kulaks)* and history as a process without a subject. It is not an admirable theory, flawed by errors; it is a heresy against reason, which proposes that all knowledge can be summated in a single Theory, of which it is the sole arbiter and guardian. It is not an imperfect "science", but an ideology suborning the good name of science in order to deny all independent rights and authenticity to the moral and imaginative faculties. It is not only a compendium of errors, it is a cornucopia out of which new errors ceaselessly flow ("mistakes", "incorrect lines"). Stalinism is a distinct, ideological mode of thought, a systematic theoretical organisation of "error" for the reproduction of more "error."

All this I could see, even if unclearly, as the smoke was rising above Budapest. Thousands of others, in a thousand different places, could see the same. I itemised the "errors" of Stalinist theory, one by one: the "dictatorship of the proletariat" (in its Stalinist version): the "military vocabulary": the theory of the Party—

> And the mechanical theory of human consciousness is wrong: the theory that historical science 'can become as precise a science as, let us say, biology': the subordination of the imaginative and moral faculties to political and administrative authority is wrong... the fear of independent thought... the mechanical personification of unconscious class forces... all this is wrong.[140]

And I identified also the reproductive organs of all this teeming "error": "the Stalinist mode of thought is... that of mechanical idealism", and "we must view Stalinism as an ideology—a constellation of partisan attitudes and false, or partially false, ideas", "establishing a *system* of false concepts within a mode of thought which—in the Marxist sense—is idealist."[141] Finally, I identified Stalin's own claim to pre-eminence as practitioner of this system. He was not only, as had recently been discovered at his birthday, the Greatest Marxist, Greatest Philosopher, Greatest Linguist, etc., but he was also the Greatest Kangaroo. For an idealist mode of this kind, must, of necessity, through its imperviousness to "empirical" discourse, repeatedly reproduce "mistakes" and "wrong results." "The Stalinist oscillates between the axiom and *realpolitik*, dogmatism and opportunism. When the axioms cease to produce results a 'mistake' is recognised. But the cornucopia from which 'mistakes' flow in such abundance is never recognised."[142] *Hop!*—(dialectical materialism)—*hop!*—(theoretical practice)—*bump!* At the end of that high theoretical exercise: Khruschev's secret speech.

Yes, all of this thousands of us could see. But we could not, finally, identify the organisation of Stalin's theoretical structure. This was not only owing to our own incompetence. It was also because that structure, in its pure theoretic beauty and conceptual coherence, had not yet been made. For Stalin was a mixture of Marxist theorist, pragmatist, and hypocrite. Some bits of the system he had time to attend to (the "super-structure is created by the basis precisely in order to serve it"), but it was full of rents and holes, which he patched up with humanist rhetoric, rule-of-thumb decisions, and security decrees. It is only in our own time that Stalinism has been given its true, rigorous and totally coherent theoretical expression. This is the Althusserian orrery.

I do not wish to be ungenerous to a "post-Stalinist generation", but it is necessary to be plain. Theoretical practitioners are familiar with a central concept of Marx: that a given productive system not only produces commodities, it also reproduces itself, its productive relations and its ideological forms and legitimations. These, in their turn, become a necessary condition for the process of reproduction. Stalinism as ideology has continued to reproduce itself long after the particular historical moment of high Stalinism has passed. And so long as it does so in theory, it will tend to reproduce itself in fact—not in exactly the same form, of course, but in a form sufficiently uncomfortable for its human objects, and even for some of the intellectuals who serve as its priests. So far from being a "post-Stalinist generation", the Althusserians, and those who share their premises and idealist modes, are working hard, every day, on the theoretical production-line of Stalinist ideology. In terms of theory, they are the Stalinists. They are the carriers of those "reasons" of irrationality and inhumanity against which we drew up the agenda of 1956. . .

> But this is passion over-near ourselves,
> Reality too close and too intense,
> And mingled up with something, in my mind,
> Of scorn and condemnation personal. . .

And the patient, "post-Stalinist" reader, who has followed me this far, will still have other questions on his mind: "Well? And did you people, with your 'agenda', correctly identify the theoretical sources of Stalinism? What came of it all? Did you construct a better Theory?"

I will answer these questions. And conclude.

xiv

First, let us return from the vulgar sociology of ideas to theory and its pure discourse of the truth. Let us revisit the orrery for a last time. Let us not only admire its parts but also notice the parts with which it is *not* supplied.

Althusser's eviction of "humanism" and "moralism", in *For Marx*, was somewhat brutal. So he returned to the theme, with renewed sophistication, in *Reading Capital*. The "real" world, the gross manifestations of the "obvious", the unpurified concepts of Generalities I, these epiphenomena would lead us (unless guided by Theory) into a world of *maya*, illusion. The text of history (we remember) is "the inaudible and illegible notation of the effects of a structure of structures." (*R.C.* 17) Beneath all, we will find *La Structure à Dominante*. The theory of *Capital* is "the theory of a mode of production." And "what Marx studies in *Capital* is the mechanism which makes the result of a history's production exist *as a society*", hence "producing the '*society effect*' which makes this result exist *as a society...*" (*R.C.* 65):

> We are beginning to suspect, even if it is only because of the works of contemporary ethnology and history, that this *society effect* differs with different modes of production.

Moreover, this society effect is made up of other, lesser effects: "the knowledge effect for theoretical practice, the aesthetic effect for aesthetic practice, the ethical effect for ethical practice, etc." "The search for each of these specific 'effects' demands the elucidation of the *mechanism* that produces it..." (*R.C.* 66) This "mechanism" will be found within the structure of the mode of production. On two occasions, on these two crucial pages, Althusser proudly flourishes what he supposes to be his licence of authority—that sentence from *The Poverty of Philosophy* which we have found out to be in fact a court order to put his dog down.

Thus society, social formations, are *effects* of the structure of a mode of production. *Capital* also enables us to understand the particles of which this structure is composed:

> It defines for the capitalist mode of production the different forms of individuality required and produced by that mode according to functions, of

which the individuals are 'supports' (*Träger*), in the division of labour, in the different 'levels' of the structure. Of course, even here, the mode of historical existence of individuality in a given mode of production is not legible to the naked eye in 'history'; its concept, too, must therefore be *constructed*, and like every concept it contains a number of surprises, the most striking of which is the fact that it is nothing like the false obviousness of the 'given'—which is merely the mask of current ideology. (*R.C.* 112)

Even if we allow ourselves to suppose, for a moment, that we are offered here an astounding insight, which de-mystifies "the false obviousness of the 'given' " and takes us directly to essential truths illegible to the "naked eye in 'history' ", it is difficult to know how our devastating insight can be, as it were, "spoken." Let us suppose that, at a certain conjuncture, there is a moment within the society effect which "gives" itself to "history's" naked eye with the false obviousness of a shop steward saying to his fellow-workers: "Hey, lads! The production manager is coming to the canteen today to give us a pep talk on measured day work. Let's give him a hot reception!" In order to de-mystify these sentences, and *construct* them, within theory, as rigorous concepts, we must verbalise them thus: "O *träger* of proletarian productive relations! The *träger* alloted a dominant function within bourgeois productive relations will manifest itself in the 'canteen' at this overdetermined conjuncture through the mechanism of a relatively autonomous ethical effect determined in the last instance by the law of motion of capitalist production relations at the level of the intensified extraction of surplus-value from the labour-power of the proletarian *träger*. It is determined that this conjuncture shall manifest itself in the form of a 'hot' contradiction!"

It will be seen that we have successfully reduced the shop-steward's ideology to *science*, with the exception of two words. "Canteen" is irredeemably polluted with the obviousness of "fact", and "hot" is an irreducibly moralistic invasion, so that these words must be contained within inverted commas lest they should contaminate the adjacent scientificity of the text. It will also be seen that de-mystification has necessitated the use of 84 words in place of 27. This is, very generally, the case. But it is a small inconvenience to accompany the attainment of revolutionary rigour. No doubt at all, de-mystification of such devastating clarity, if practised within the heart of the productive structures as a political *praxis* (philosophy as class struggle) will detonate the whole capitalist order. I cannot understand why the Althusserians are waiting. Why don't they hurry down to Dagenham or Longbridge and try?

But no reports of such *praxis* have yet come back to me. And for this there must be some *theoretical* reason. And an even more rigorous post-Althusserian—let us say, a Hindessian-Hirstian—will detect this by a scrupulous symptomatic reading of Althusser's decidedly-not-innocent "text". For, under this scrutiny, the shop steward—and indeed *the whole sentence*—can be exposed as a pseudo-problem, as an abjectly ideological intrusion. This is given away *in the very first word*, the vocative, "O". For this is to smuggle back into theory both historicism and moralism, by allowing us to suppose that the workers are *subjects*, that they can "intervene" as "men" in "history". But the situation alluded to in these sentences is in fact a *society effect* of contradiction within the mode of production. This effect is already inscribed within productive relations and requires no imaginary interpellation of vocatives and subjects. We may relax in our chairs. We may even doze, since contradiction will continue to manifest its effects as shop stewards. There is no need to go down to Dagenham after all.

This has been a vulgar, even empiricist, response. Let us resume our exposition. Humanism, Althusser argues, is the heresy which introduces "men" as agents or subjects in their own history by an "underhand reduction", "by treating the *relations of production* as mere *human relations*." (*R.C.* 139)

> History then becomes the transformation of a human nature, which remains the real subject of the history which transforms it. As a result, history has been introduced into human nature, making men the contemporaries of the historical effects whose subjects they are, but—and this is absolutely decisive—the relations of production, political and ideological social relations, have been reduced to historicized '*human relations*', i.e. to inter-human, inter-subjective relations. This is the favourite terrain of historicist humanism. (*R.C.* 140)

Althusser entertains for anthropology a malice even fiercer than that which he entertains for "history".[143] The notion of man making his own nature is one which "a horde of cultural anthropologists have adopted." (*R.C.* 140) Even Marx is convicted of relapsing from time to time into a "latent anthropology", a " 'naive' anthropology" given in the hidden assumptions of Political Economy. Balibar is honest enough to allow that, again and again, Marx and Engels afford support for "the idea that *it is men who make history on the basis of previous conditions*." "But who are these 'men'?" "The concept of 'men'. . . constitutes a real point where the utterance *slips away* towards the regions of philosophical or common-place ideology." "The 'obviousness', the 'transparency' of the word 'men' (here charged with every carnal opacity) and its anodyne appearance are the most dangerous of the traps I am trying to avoid. I shall not be satisfied until I have. . . *eliminated* it as a foreign body. . ." (*R.C.* 207-8)

One trouble with this mode of theoretical practice is that an un-tutored and protestant mind keeps "slipping away" into wholly irrelevant reflections. For example, at "carnal opacity" I fall into a reverie, and wonder whether M. Balibar also came to intellectual maturation within the Jeunes Étudiants Catholiques? And then, by random association, I recall that Stalin served his own intellectual apprenticeship in a seminary of the Greek Orthodox priesthood... And then, since I am a fussy stylist, I wonder whether *"eliminated* as a foreign body" might not be improved, when we consider the "anodyne" concept of "men", by the verb, "to *liquidate"*? For, if we think about persons in a certain way, it becomes more easy to enact our thoughts. If we think about women as "dolls" or "pieces" or "chicks" or whatever, it may be more easy to behave to them in this way. (Some women may even think themselves so.) If we think about men as the *träger* of structures—or of their actions as "unjustified disturbance symptoms"—then the thought will guide the act. As those lofty theoretical practitioners, the *daleks,* used to say, when confronted by "men": *"Exterminate!"*

This reminds me, once again, of anthropology. For Althusser became involved, for a moment, in chapter seven of *Reading Capital,* in an interesting argument. He stood back and confronted (as I have earlier done (p. 59)) Political Economy as an object, as a structure. And he found, as I think correctly, that Political Economy is based upon a prior definition and delimitation of a given field of activities. But to generalise from these activities, and to assert claims for itself as a universal or fundamental science of society, there must be, within Political Economy, an ulterior assumption; and this can be located in the concept of "need". For "need" is what I have called a "junction-concept", in this case between economics and anthropology. (It will be seen that I am not following Althusser's words, but clarifying them and putting them into some order.) He then discovers that classical economics is founded on the presupposition of "a *'naive' anthropology* which founds all the acts involved in the production, distribution, reception and consumption of economic objects on the economic subjects and their needs." *(R.C.* 162) Thus "need" is defined in such a way (self-interest) that its conclusions are entailed in its premises. All basic human needs are economic ones, as defined by Political Economy; therefore Political Economy is the basic science of society.

What then would seem to follow? It might seem that Marx, in shattering bourgeois Political Economy, would liberate anthropology—or at least provide a precondition for its liberation, in freeing "need" from definitions imposed by bourgeois and utilitarian convenience, and permitting anthropology to investigate "need's" larger resonance. But not at all! As we enter chapter eight, we find that the "theoretical pretensions", not of bourgeois Political Economy, but of *anthropology* "have been shattered by Marx's analysis." *(R.C.* 166) Marx is now offered to us as a *dalek,* rushing down upon anthropology, and crying out: *"Exterminate!"* But if we exterminate the very presupposition upon which Political Economy is founded—if we take away from economics its support in "need"—then it would seem to rest on a vacancy. Did Marx find a better concept of need, a better anthropological basis? Not at all: "an anthropological basis becomes therefore purely mythical." *(R.C.* 167)

Needs are not economic, they are *defined by* the economic, they are "subject to a double *structural*. . . determination." Needs are *assigned* their content and meaning by "the structure of the relations between the productive forces and the relations of production." (*R.C.* 167) They are not only assigned their content, but also their meaning *as economic.* For to be *economic* is not to be "economic", in a vulgar, "common-sense" way of being concerned with "economic" needs. It means occupying a certain space, a certain function, to which *La Structure à Dominante assigns* a meaning, according to the modulation and flux of her mode of production. "To construct the concept of the economic is to define it rigorously as a level, instance or region of the structure of a mode of production." (*R.C.* 178)

> The economic cannot have the qualities of a *given* (of the immediately visible and observable, etc.) because its identification requires the concept of the structure of the economic, which in turn requires the concepts of the structure of the mode of production. . . because its identification therefore presupposes the construction of its *concept.* The concept of the economic must be constructed *for each mode of production*. . . (*R.C.* 183)

This manoeuvre solves (or should we say dissolves?) a number of difficult problems which have bothered historians and anthropologists for decades into a single wet theoretical pabulum. Kinship in primitive societies is the "level, instance or region" to which the structure has assigned the "economic"; military and political dominance is the economic "instance" in feudal society. And so on. "Need" in one case may appear as the need for seven wives and in another case as the need to behead a traitor to his oath of fealty, but both are "economic", and we certainly have no need of any anthropology to decipher either. Moreover, what could be more abject than the ideological illusion that men and women might participate subjectively, at any "level" whatsoever, in the definition of need? For they are *träger*—supports of structures within which needs are assigned.

I am becoming tired, and my mind has slipped off once again. For all that Althusser has done, in exterminating anthropology, is to throw "need" back upon the bosom of *La Structure à Dominante,* so that not one part or "region" of her "totality" but her whole person is subjected to the gross utilitarian embraces of the "economic." And I recall a critique of the utilitarian concept of "need", presented at the annunciation of the capitalist mentality, in the words of one great proto-Marxist, King Lear:

> O, reason not the need: our basest beggars
> Are in the poorest things superfluous:
> Allow not nature more than nature needs,
> Man's life is cheap as beast's. . .
>   But for true need—
> You heavens, give me that patience, patience I need!

Patience is, very certainly, our first "need" if we are to reason with Althusser.

I will be patient, but for a last time. I will look once more at the concept of *träger*, I will argue it through, and then this scrutiny of the orrery is done. The fullest statement is thus:

> The structure of the relations of production determines the *places* and *functions* occupied and adopted by the agents of production, who are never anything more than the occupants of these places, insofar as they are the 'supports' *(Träger)* of these functions. The true 'subjects' (in the sense of constitutive subjects of the process) are therefore not these occupants or functionaries, are not, despite all appearances, the 'obviousness' of the 'given' of naive anthropology, 'concrete individuals', 'real men'—but *the definition and distribution of these places and functions. The true 'subjects' are these definers and distributors: the relations of production* (and political and ideological relations). But since these are 'relations', they cannot be thought within the category *subject. (R.C.* 180)

The errors with which this argument is littered are so elementary that we need only indicate them one by one. First, there is the confusion of the notion of structure with structural*ism.* Structures (social, economic, conceptual) are not a discovery of the last two decades, with a lonely fore-runner in Karl Marx. As soon as we talk about "organisation" (or "organism"), about "system", about the "laws" of supply and demand, or about "institutions" (and about "functionaries"), we are talking about structure: and we are likely also to be talking about the ways in which human behaviour is ruled, shaped, ordered, limited and determined. This notion, and the theoretical and empirical exploration of these structures, have been with us for many generations. So far from being a revolutionary notion, it has been quite often—when pursued by practitioners to the ultimate of theoretical "rigour"—a profoundly conservative one, since it tends to see men and women as fixed in "stations", on ladders of "rank", subject to "laws" (of Smith or of Malthus), allocated "roles", or as moments of conformity or deviance within an ulterior consensus.

This is in no sense to argue that the notion is untrue or reactionary in itself, although when pushed illegitimately from structure to structural*ism* it always is both. It is simply a reminder that Althusser here, as elsewhere, is simply reproducing in "Marxist" terminology notions long sanctified within orthodox ("bourgeois") disciplines. Although some of his followers do not yet seem to have found this out,[144] the notion of men as *träger,* or carriers of functions allocated to them by the market—"laws" of supply and demand which were even moralised as "divine"—was at the very heart of vulgarised bourgeois Political Economy. During Marx's lifetime this ideology sought exactly to *impose* this structure upon the working class, and, at the same time, to convince them that they were powerless to resist these "immutable" laws; and much of the history of the British working class, in these decades, can only be understood as a heroic (even "moralistic") *refusal* to be reduced to being supports of the reasons and necessities of capital. When Marx refers, at one point, to the labourer as "the bearer of living labour" it is in the context of exactly such a discussion of the alienation of "the productive powers of social labour" as the property of a stranger, and as subject to the (anti-humanist) requirements of capitalist production: "It is entirely different in the factories owned by the labourers themselves, for instance, in Rochdale."[145] When Marx, in his well-known comment in the first Preface to *Capital*, disclaimed making any judgement on individual capitalists, it was because from "my *stand-point*, from which the *economic formation* of society *is viewed* as a process of natural history" individuals could be seen, not as malevolent and responsible agents, but as "the personifications of economic categories, embodiments of particular class-relations and class-interests." But this was to view persons as they appear *"in the domain of Political Economy"*:[146] i.e. as they were continually being *"viewed"* within the orthodox apologetics of the age. So that Marx was writing, with his tongue firmly in his cheek, and striking a pre-emptive blow against his critics by borrowing the rhetoric closest to the hearts of every exploiter who could exonerate himself as being the *träger* of economic "laws."

Thus, as always with Althusser, we are offered an ideological penny, greasy with bourgeois use, and told it is Marxist gold. That penny's twin is still being passed every day in Parsonian and structuralist-functional systems: behind Althusser's *"definition and distribution of. . . places and functions"*, with all its italicised "rigour", we find the Smelserian "social system",[147] behind *träger* we find "roles", and behind Althusser's grotesque notion of ideological "interpellation" or "hailing" we find even more *chic* notions of men and women (*except*, of course, select intellectuals), not thinking or acting, but being *thought* and being *performed*.[148] All these exalted thinkers, "bourgeois" or "Marxist", proceed from the same "latent anthropology", the same ulterior assumption about "Man"—that all men and women (except themselves) *are bloody silly*.

Second, there are two trivial and furtive sleights of hand in Althusser's argument which could only deceive an audience hand-picked from the *lumpen-intelligentsia*.[149] a) Althusser tries to take out another licence of authority by gesturing at Marx's theoretical rupture with Feuerbachian "Man", the "human essence." Of course, as any first-year student finds out, in rejecting abstracted and generic "Man", Marx rediscovered men and women, within "the ensemble of social relations", within societies structured in class ways, and within "empirically observable" conditions.[150] As a matter of fact, it is a question, and a very difficult one, how far Marx and Engels ever did fully reject the concept, "man", which reappears in the concept of alienation, in the notion of a "truly human morality", and in what some scholars detect as an historical teleology of human immanence. I mention this question, which I cannot turn aside for now and which has been exhaustively discussed by others, only to note that Althusser blocks and dismisses (as lapses, immaturities surviving after the "epistemological break") theoretical problems manifestly present in Marx's writing, which other critics have found to be either fertile or severely disabling.[151] My immediate concern is only to notice that Marx and Engels, in their major investigations, dislodged the concept, "man", in order to return to empirically-observable *real men*.

b) The other sleight of hand is the same trick performed backwards. "Humanists"—and all "anthropologists"—return to the concept, "man", "by treating the *relations of production* as mere *human relations*", i.e. reducing these to "historicized" relations, "to inter-human, inter-subjective relations." This trick could only be passed upon an audience innocent of all knowledge of both history and anthropology, and it is disturbing that a "practice" of this kind could attain to academic reputability. I am by no means endorsing all sociology, all historiography, nor all that has been produced by the "horde of cultural anthropologists." In fact, some practitioners within these disciplines are reducing men and women to *träger* of structures as happily as Althusser. But scarcely a soul among them will be found to be commencing with the proposition of a "human essence" nor making their object of study "individual men", in "inter-subjective relations", as against "society." Their objects of study may include kinship systems, inheritance practices, demographic norms, value-systems, social structures, political institutions, class relations, ideological forms, symbolic modes, consensual rules. The "social sciences" today are the products of a methodological revolution, one of whose initiators was Marx. It is precisely their structural preoccupations which place their feet upon the *glissade* which leads to structuralism, and which prepare their novices for Althusser's embrace.

The third elementary error is to confuse the findings of particular analytical disciplines with the "truth" about the total phenomenon from which the procedures of that discipline have selected only relevant evidences. I have argued this already, and with particular reference to Political Economy (pp. 59-60); this discipline defines its own field of enquiry, and selects its evidence in accordance with these definitions, and its findings are relevant within the terms of this discipline. Everyone knows this; we do not turn to Ricardo for an explanation of Socinianism. In a certain kinship system, a wife's brother's second cousin may be understood (within the discipline of anthropology) as a certain point within a structured set of relations, and thus as (metaphorically) a "bearer" *(träger)* of those relations; and in exactly the same way, a capitalist may be "viewed" as a "bearer" of capitalist productive relations.[152] The discipline has already decided that we define this person so. That this second cousin or this capitalist may be defined quite differently within other disciplines, may be viewed (by a wife or by his own workers) in quite different lights, does not—or *need* not—invalidate the findings in question.

Theoretical practitioners are often to be observed, in small intense groups, interrogating categories. But, because of their empirical blockages, they are incapable of interrogating the point (in society or history) where these categories intersect. Instead of interrogating a category, we will interrogate a woman. It will at least be more agreeable. We will suppose this woman to be the "wife" of one man, the "mistress" of another man, the "mother" of three children of school age. She is a clothing worker and a "shop steward", she is "treasurer" of her local ward Labour Party, and on Thursday evenings she is a "second violin" in an amateur orchestra. She has a strong constitution (as she must have) but she has a mildly neurotic depressive disposition. She is also (I nearly forgot) a member of the Church of England, and an occasional "communicant."

As you will see, she is kept very busy. Viewed in a certain light, she is a point at which a number of "structures" intersect. When these get on top of her, her depression sometimes takes the form of staying in bed, so that she cannot fulfil her other roles. The psychiatrist sees her as being determined in her behaviour by a structured neurosis. But she is not "over-determined", her constitution (material basis) is sound, and she soon bounces back. As a "wife" she is seen by a sociologist as being within "the institution" of marriage, and performing the "roles" of housewife and of mother; she is indeed the carrier of these roles. According to his variant of sociological theory, he will try to construe her behaviour as a mistress; he has difficulty in deciding whether to list it within the category "deviance" or whether to exclude it from the computer-programme as irrelevant. For the woman herself, one part of this "role" (the sexual act) is objectively much the same with husband or lover; what defines the difference is nothing in the act (well, perhaps a little in that) but the expectations and rules which the society imposes upon her. She ought to be a better carrier of these expectations, and the parson (who has heard about her affair) is censorious.

Meanwhile, the local branch of the Labour Party, of which she is a "functionary", gets into debt. Her husband keeps making scenes, and her lover is becoming bored. And at work, where she is a *träger* of proletarian productive relations, the boss (the *träger* etc., etc.,) decides to screw down piece-rates. She gets headaches, and stops playing in the orchestra. Beset with the contradictory exhortations of psychiatrist, priest, husband, lover, society, conductor, boss, fellow workers, party officials, all of whom see her as a carrier of this and that, as well as the shopping, she goes back to bed. In bed she reads an article by a demographer, which shows the number of her children diverges from the norm, and one by an ecologist which shows that three children are too many. Her depression deepens. . .

We will leave her in this sad state in order to note that none of the disciplines or categories have done her any wrong. The demographer has correctly described her deviation from the norm, and he has not the least interest in her lover, even if she should conceive by him, since the question of paternity is irrelevant to this norm. The party official who is seeking to collect the branch dues is not in the least concerned with her household affairs; he sees her, correctly, as an inefficient functionary. She is in no sense the subject of the expectations and sexual norms of "society" or of the Church, she is the object of their scrutiny. And at work, she may certainly be seen as the carrier of productive relations. But not one of these definitions affect the fact that she remains a woman. Is the woman then no more than a point at which all these relations, structures, roles, expectations, norms and functions *intersect;* is she the carrier of all of them, simultaneously, and is she *acted* by them, and absolutely determined at their intersection? It is not by any means an easy question, for many of these roles are not only imposed, they are internalised, and they have gathered up like a knot inside her head. To answer this question we would have to *observe her history.*

I don't know how her history eventuates. I have two alternative scripts. One of them is obvious. She is carried off to a mental home, after a suicide attempt, and kept going on vallium. In the other, she goes back to work, because, *in the last instance,* the mortgage has to be paid and the children fed. At work things are blowing up to a crisis. A militant workmate (this bit is unlikely) gives her Althusser to read. She turns the pages. Enlightenment breaks through. She shouts out: "I'm not a bloody THING!" She throws the book at the foreman. She calls out the workshop on strike. She leaves her husband and she sacks her lover. She joins women's lib. She leaves the Church of England. She rejoins the orchestra, and greatly enjoys performing within that structure, a process with fifty subjects determined by conductor and score. But, alas! She fancies the conductor, and all her muddles are, once again, about to begin. . .

As it happens, I do not know this woman, although I have known several like her, who have been good comrades, and men like her as well. I have introduced her only as the "bearer" *(Träger)* of an analogy. The analogy may not be pressed too far, because the procedures required to observe the behaviour of an individual are not the same as those required to observe historical eventuation. We cannot construct our historical or economic knowledge by first positing "individuals" as isolates. But the analogy will serve if it reminds us that, in the people we observe and know, we find intersecting determinations, which they are always trying to handle and reconcile; that "over-determination" can manifest itself as illness or immobility; that it is legitimate to view a person as a carrier of structures, but that we can arrive at that person only through a sum of many views; that whatever we conclude, in the endlessly receding argument of pre-determination and free will—for our friend may have been determined by her protestant upbringing to cry out, "I am not a bloody THING!"—it is profoundly important that our protestant prejudice should be renewed, that we should *think* ourselves to be "free" (which Althusser will not allow us to think); and that, finally, neither a person nor a society may be viewed as a sum of intersecting determinations, but can be known only in observation over time.

We may offer another analogy, which evades the difficulties of positing an "individual". We are familiar with analogies drawn from the rules of a game. Any complex game is unintelligible until we understand the rules. People appear to run around, to start and stop, in arbitrary and confused ways. A careful observer (who already has some notion of games) can infer the rules; once this has been done, everything becomes clear, and continued observation will confirm or refine the rules which he has inferred. The anthropologist or historian is in much the same position as the observer. Societies (and a "society" itself is a concept describing people within an imaginary boundary and actuated by common rules) may be seen as very complex "games", which sometimes afford very material evidences as to their character (the pitch, the goals, the teams), sometimes are governed by visible rules (rule-books of law and constitution), and are sometimes governed by invisible rules, which the players know so deeply that they are never spoken, and which must be inferred by the observer. For example, the players rarely kill the referee.

The whole of life goes forward within "structures" of such visible and invisible rules, which prohibit this action and assign a special symbolic significance to that. Marx's most extraordinary accomplishment was to infer—"read"—"de-code"—the only-partly visible structure of rules by which human relations were mediated by money: capital. He often glimpsed, sometimes grasped, other invisible rules which we, after one hundred years, are—or ought to be—able to read more plainly. There were other, and significant, symbolic and normative rules which (in my view) he overlooked. Some of these were not within the view of his contemporary knowledge, and for such rules Political Economy had no terms.

When the rules of a game have been read or inferred, we can then assign to each player his role or function in the game. He is (in terms of those rules) the game's carrier, an element within its structure—a half-back or a goal-keeper. In exactly this sense we can say that a "worker" is the bearer of productive relations; indeed, we have already defined her in this way when we called her a "worker", rather than a "second violin". But we must take the analogy further. For we do not go on to say that the goal-keeper is *being gamed,* or the capitalist is *being capitaled.* This is what Althusser, and, also, some structuralist anthropologists and socio-logists, would wish us to say. Althusser offers us a pseudo-choice: either we must say that there are no rules but only a swarm of "individuals", or we must say that the rules *game* the players.

The difference between "playing" a game and being gamed illustrates the difference between rule-governed structuration of historical eventuation (within which men and women remain as subjects of their own history) and structural*ism*. As always, Althusser has simply taken over a reigning fashion of bourgeois ideology and named it "Marxism". In the old days, vulgar Political Economy saw men's economic behaviour as being *lawed* (although workers were obtuse and refractory in obeying these laws), but allowed to the autonomous individual an area of freedom, in his intellectual, aesthetic or moral choices. Today, structuralisms engross this area from every side; we are *structured* by social relations, *spoken* by pre-given linguistic structures, *thought* by ideologies, *dreamed* by myths, *gendered* by patriarchal sexual norms, *bonded* by affective obligations, *cultured* by *mentalités*, and *acted* by history's script. None of these ideas is, in origin, absurd, and some rest upon substantial additions to knowledge. But all slip, at a certain point, from sense to absurdity, and, in their sum, all arrive at a common terminus of unfreedom. Structuralism (this terminus of the absurd) is the ultimate product of self-alienated reason—"reflecting" the common-sense of the times—in which all human projects, endeavours, institutions, and even culture itself, appear to stand *outside* of men, to stand *against* men, as objective things, as the "Other" which, in its own turn, moves men around as things. In the old days, the Other was then named "God" or Fate. Today it has been christened anew as Structure.

I have said that Marx made visible the "rules" of capital. To do this, it was necessary to proceed by way of a "Critique of Political Economy." In this way he was able to construct the concept of a capitalist "mode" of production, both as the circuit of capital and as a mode of self-reproduction, by which capital reproduced the productive relations which enabled its own reproduction. This mode of production could then be conceptualised as an integral structure, in which all relations must be taken together as one set, and in which each rule is assigned its definition within that totality. From this he adduced (although sometimes wrongly) the forms of development through which such a mode might pass, and, further (and more rashly) he projected its "law of motion" into the future. That these "laws" or "tendencies" did not (as he once truculently asserted) work "with iron necessity towards inevitable results" may be explained, in part, by the fact that he understated the countervailing tendencies at work. Contrary to the view of some theoretical practitioners, no worker known to historians ever had surplus-value taken out of his hide without finding some way of fighting back (there are plenty of ways of going slow); and, paradoxically, *by* his fighting back the tendencies were diverted and the "forms of development" were themselves developed in unexpected ways. In another part, this was due to the fact that other countervailing tendencies arrived unbidden out of "regions" for which Political Economy had no terms.

But these reservations do not in any way go to show that Marx's project was not legitimate. It was an epoch-making advance in knowledge to construct, by arduous theoretical engagement, by hypothesis and by equally arduous empirical investigation, the concept of a structured mode of production in this way.

"Aha!", I am asked: "Is this not to give back to Althusser with my left hand all that I have taken away with my right? And is not Althusser licensed to envisage capitalism as structure?" The answer is "no". And whoever asked that question may go to the back of the class. A capitalist mode of production is not capital*ism*. We pass on the exchange of one letter from the adjectival characterisation of a mode of production (a concept within Political Economy, albeit within Marxist "anti" Political Economy) to a noun descriptive of a social formation in the totality of its relations. We will leave our interrogator on the back bench for a few pages, to meditate upon his folly, and return to the mode of production.

After all the rancour of my previous critique, this should at last be the occasion for a happy reunion. For historians within the Marxist tradition have for many decades employed the concept of a mode of production, have examined the labour process and the relations of production. I can recall a time, in this country, when there were not many of us, when this was our distinctive preoccupation, and one which was decidedly disreputable. And now—not only among Althusserians, but among theoretical practitioners very generally—the "mode of production" has become the focus of a truly obsessional preoccupation. This, decidedly, is their "thing". They are always undoing it and doing it up again. They are always examining its "mechanism"; rearranging its components; inserting a new pinion here, a balance-wheel there, and oiling the moving parts with purified abstractions. The "mode of production" has become like a base camp in the Arctic of Theory, which the explorers may not depart from for more than a hundred yards for fear of being lost in an ideological blizzard.

What is odd about this "mode of production" is that it can be constructed and reconstructed within Theory without any recourse to the knowledge of historians, anthropologists and others. Althusser and Balibar are too rigorous even to acknowledge the findings of these disciplines; Hindess and Hirst show a casual acquaintance with some secondary work, and employ themselves in demonstrating that this work (being ideological in origin) is unnecessary to Theory; and historians repay these tributes, not with anger, but with boredom. They do not reply, or argue, simply because the whole project of theoretical practice is idealist and irrelevant. For theoretical practice engenders these modes of production, not within theory or society, but within metaphysics; and a metaphysical mode of production, in its turn, will produce, not commodities, but metaphysical concepts and categories, while at the same time reproducing endlessly its own conditions for metaphysical self-reproduction. Like all cooks of the Absolute, these practitioners have found the instant theoretical recipe, the handful of wholesome ingredients out of which all history and every society is baked.

So that this is not, after all, a place of happy reunion but a place of total disassociation between incompatible methods and traditions. It is as if a conference were to be held, with, on the one hand, all those concerned with sexual relations, gender roles, the forms and history of the family, kinship structures, child nurture, homosexuality, sexual psychology, the literature of profane and romantic love; and, on the other hand, a party of theoretical practitioners who had reduced all this to the metaphysical contemplation of the reproductive organs, which produce all these "manifestations" and which, at the same time, reproduce themselves. One party would attain to knowledge through the investigation of a multiplicity of evidence in its own authentic expression; the other would be locked into a metaphysical circuit of ovulation and sperm. The participants would be baffled. They would decide to disengage, and continue their proceedings in separate rooms. As theoretical practice and historical materialism have done.

It is not a question of disagreement about this or that, but one of total incompatibility in the way in which a historian and such a "theorist" situates himself before a mode of production. We have authorities on "productive relations" who have never looked inside a feudal tenure, or a bill of exchange, or a woollen Piece Hall, or a struggle around piece-rates; and we have authorities on "the labour process" who have never found relevant to their exalted theory Christopher Hill's work on "the uses of sabbatarianism", nor mine on "time and work-discipline", nor Eric Hobsbawm's on "the tramping artisan", nor that of a generation of (American, French, British) "labour historians" (a group often dismissed with scorn[153]) on time-and-motion study, Taylorism, and Fordism.

It is not only that this kind of theoretical idealism is actively unhelpful: that, for example, in the immense area of study recently opened up, the study of peasant societies (in which so much turns on subsistence economy, taxation and marketing, traditional norms and needs, inheritance practices, familial modes, particularist customary law), theoretical practitioners are left fiddling with their model, trying to take into account the rural millions who are somehow "marginal" to the proper circuits of capital. It is not only that gross historical materiality stubbornly refuses to "correspond" to the purity of its concept; that, whatever theoretical allowance is made for "contradiction" it is never allowance enough, for in every historical "now" (conjuncture) the circuit of capital is being obstructed and resisted at every point—as men and women refuse to be reduced to its *träger*—so that the "forms" are "developed" and diverted in theoretically improper ways by the class struggle itself. It is also that this idealism is *actively* misleading and diversionary, giving us false historical results at every turn, imposing its own presuppositions upon the evidence, blockading all the "empirical" canals of the senses of knowledge, and, as contemporary political theory, leading only to bizarre kangaroo strategies (in which conclusions are already pre-empted by the arbitrary premises of this party or that sect) or else to the security of an arm-chair.

But is not this dismissal unfair? Is not theoretical practice, with its "relative autonomy" and its intricate gearing, greatly more subtle and rigorous than the "vulgar economism" which it displaced? The answer, in brief, is that this is a "yes-type" question: to which we must reply "no". It is a "yes-type" question because it reduces to a faceless and unidentifiable caricature all precedent theory and practice, and seeks to erase any evidence as to the vigorous alternative tradition on behalf of which I speak. And the reply must be "no", because, despite all its abstraction and saving clauses, the theoretical product is an idealist reductionism as vulgar in its economism as anything that has gone before.

We will, however, allow a more leisurely answer. And in this we may first offer an apology to Marxist economists. The theory of a mode of production belongs, very properly, within their own conceptual system. It is proper that it should be interrogated and refined. The continuing debates among economists may well be significant, and historians hope to be helped by their findings. More generally, the employment of the concept of a mode of production is an improvement upon a certain slipshod use of the terms "material base" and "productive forces"—or it *could* be an improvement, in minds open to any empirical conversation. As Williams has noted:

> It was not Marxism, but the systems with which it contended and continues to contend, which had separated and abstracted various parts of this whole social process. It was the assertion and explanation of political forms and philosophical and general ideas as independent of, 'above', the material social process that produced a necessary kind of counter-assertion. In the flow of polemic this was often overstated, until it came to repeat, in a simple reversal of terms, the kind of error it attacked.

Hence Marxism "often took the colouring of a specifically bourgeois and capitalist kind of materialism."[154] This is certainly true. But, then, it is also—and for the same reasons—true that to reduce all social and intellectual phenomena to "effects" of an essentialist, metaphysical "mode of production"—by whatever elaboration of "mechanisms"—is to do no more than enclose that old bourgeois materialism within idealist amber.

There is also, we will allow, a great difference in the quality of theoretical practice. It is possible to practice upon a mode of production badly or well. Balibar practices so badly that he allows no purchase for a historian's interrogation. But Simon Clarke, practising on Althusser and Balibar, is able to illuminate their inconsistencies and absurdities in the clearest ways, and hence to emerge, by way of critique, with a lucid restatement of the concept of a mode of production. I find this helpful, and, at the same time, I am relieved of the labour of going over the same task. Clarke has evidently come to the very verge of the kangaroo reserve. But he is not yet quite over that verge. For he is able, when discussing "different forms of society", to write:

> The relations of production on which these various modes of production are based will provide the basis for different forms of exploitation, and correspondingly different relations of distribution. They will also be expressed in specific economic, ideological and political forms, which must be analysed as *developed* forms of the fundamental relation of production.[155]

This is the same kind of circular act which we noted in Smelser, where the snake ate its own tail; instead of a "value-system", the "fundamental relation of production" is swallowing its own effects. And the critical problem lies in the last few lines—"economic, ideological and political forms... must be analysed as *developed* forms of the fundamental relation of production." The essentialist notion of "immanance", the ultimate platonism, lies there.

Should we return to Marx? Or should we argue the point, independent of any authority? Let us try to do both together. It is certainly true—and it is generally held to be a fundamental "Marxist" proposition—that there is some correspondence between a given mode of production and a social formation (including political and ideological forms). This is hardly surprising, since production, social relations, political modes, and ideological constructions are all human activities. The Marxist proposition goes further, and asserts not only "some correspondence", but a correspondence in which the mode of production is determinate. Marx and Engels expressed this correspondence and this determination in a number of different ways; by the elaborate (but, ultimately, mechanical and unsatisfactory) spatial analogy of "basis" and "superstructure"; by means of blunt propositions, such as "social being determines social consciousness" (itself a polemical "counter-assertion" of the kind indicated by Williams); by enigmatic but suggestive analogies from natural science ("a general illumination in which all other colours are plunged"); and by swift metaphorical gestures—the hand-mill *gives you* society with the feudal lord", religious ideologies are a *"reflection"* of productive relations, which *"appear as"* categories within Political Economy, and these relations reveal "the innermost secret, the hidden basis of the entire social structure, and. . . the corresponding specific form of the State."[156] When we recall that some reciprocal interaction is also proposed (e.g. as between "superstructure" and "basis") there is "play" enough in these propositions to allow for many adjustments and interpretations.

Presented with these indecisive propositions, the practitioner who works within a "Marxist" tradition might take one of two courses. He might decide to select among them for the "correct" and "scientific" formulation; screw it down more tightly; tinker with the "mechanism"; eliminate all "play"; theorise about the "society effect" and the "ideological effect"; and perfect an orrery. I suppose that one may condone this course in a certain kind of philosopher or theologian, who has never engaged in the difficult labour of reconstituting from historical materials an actualised mode of production, who does not understand the historian's necessary recourse to analogies and metaphorical suggestions as an indication of the connections and directions of the social process, and mistakes these for literal statements as to some "mechanism." He has never heard a stick break in the forest as a commoner disputes his rights with the King, nor listened to the anguished silence and then the hysterical saturnalia as a heretic is burned. He thinks it can all be plotted in a map in his head: this basis, that terrain, this region, level and instance. In the end he thinks that his thinking makes it so: "the process that produces the concrete-knowledge takes place wholly in the theoretical practice." (*F.M.* 186)

There is, however, another possible course. We may commence with these various propositions as hypotheses, and then we may *find out.* This will lead us at once into a very different set of questions. Are these propositions true? Did Marx show them to be true, or did he assume them without further testing? If they are true, are they significant and suggestive, or are they truisms which still leave everything to be found out? And, again, if they are true, *why* are they true? In what ways, and through which means, does this correspondence assert itself? And, finally, does our new knowledge (gained in response to such questions) enable us to return again to Marx, not to adjust and tighten up one formulation, but to modify and re-organise his concepts?

The alternative Marxist tradition has been asking these kinds of questions for some decades. I don't hold power of attorney to speak for "history", so that I can only report my own understanding of historical knowledge. The first question—"are these propositions true?"—is, alas, an "empirical" one. In my own view, they *have* been shown to be true, but in terms even more lax, and equivocal, than those of Marx. In diverse historical circumstances, research has shown that "the economic movement finally asserts itself as necessary"; the comparative study of feudal societies, or of industrial revolutions, has demonstrated the ways in which a generic mode of production has found roughly analogous expression within different societies and state institutions; and Marx's most fertile hypothesis (as stated in his well-known letter to Weydemeyer of 1852) that "the *existence of classes* is only bound up with *particular, historic phases in the development of production*", seems to me to have been demonstrated beyond doubt, and with many consequent riders as to analogous forms of class expression within intellectual and social life.

But the findings, while positive, have been equivocal. They suggest not only a greater complexity and reciprocity of relations than Marx proposed, but also they raise the question of what significance we can place upon the correspondence. The complexity, as I have sufficiently argued, is not in the least illuminated by giving to it a reputable new name, like "relative autonomy" (see p. 97). The critical concept (unexamined by Althusser) is that of "determination" itself; hence the importance—as Williams and I and others have been insisting for years (and to the deaf) of defining "determine" in its senses of "setting limits" and "exerting pressures" and of defining "law of motion" as "logic of process." This helps us, at once, to break out of the idealist circuit; we can no longer offer social formations as "society effects" or as "developed forms" of an immanent mode.

The question as to the significance to be placed upon the correspondence is even more difficult. For the idealist notion commences with the proposition that "the economic" is (in the last instance, etc.) determining, and then leaps, hand-in-hand with its twin, vulgar "economism", to the good old utilitarian assumption that it is therefore somehow more "real" in all ways. Once landed here, theoretical practice can deploy a number of arguments. Thus if, in a given society, the decisive region appears to be non-economic (kinship, military power), then this can simply be re-defined as the area to which the "economic instance" has been "assigned" (see p. 146). More commonly, other areas are simply regarded as being *less* real—as second or third-order problems, as the concern of another "region" of theory (as yet immature and undeveloped), or simply as non-problems, which may be spirited away with the wand of "relative autonomy."

But it is of little consolation to a prisoner, languishing in 1976 in the foetid and overcrowded compound of a Calcutta gaol, to be told that his is a third-order problem, and that he is the victim of a relatively autonomous society effect. Worse than this: the half-hidden assumption, that what is "relatively autonomous" is therefore less "real" (and less deserving of theoretical or historical attention) than the mode of production, can afford to the theoretical practitioner, if whim or ideology should strike him, a stupefying laxity in analysis. Indeed, religions, ideologies, and the State itself, with all its armoury of repressive apparatuses, being "relatively autonomous", may develop, over half-centuries or centuries, *in any way they like,* and the theorists of the "mode of production", in the security of their self-confirming propositions, need not turn a theoretical hair. For they have already defined this mode as being essential and truly real, and the effects, or regions, or levels, may go on their autonomous way. In exactly this way, in 1963, Althusser waves his wand, and Stalinism (unless as a third-order problem) was made to disappear:

> Everything that has been said of the 'cult of the personality' refers exactly to the domain of the *superstructure* and therefore of State organization and ideologies; further it refers largely to *this domain alone,* which we know from Marxist theory possesses a 'relative autonomy' (which explains very simply, in theory, how the socialist *infrastructure* has been able to develop without essential damage during this period of errors affecting the superstructure). (*F.M.* 240)

Very simple. But this arbitrary separation of a "mode of production" from everything that actually goes on in history (so characteristic of the idealist/economist twin) ends up by telling us nothing and apologising for everything. Such Theory is rather like a doctor who, when his patient is in agony with a disease, consults for an hour, and then pronounces that, while the disease is determined in the last instance by the body, it is a relatively autonomous body-effect. As indeed it is; the disease is not a projection of the patient's soul; but medicine learned this many centuries ago. And for a long time this spurious dissociation of "production"/ "consciousness"—itself only the old dichotomy matter/mind or body/soul reappearing in Marxist form—has been challenged, in the Marxist tradition, on one side by historians and anthropologists, who have insisted that ideas, norms and rules be replaced *within* the mode of production, without which it could not be carried on for a day;[157] and on the other side by cultural materialists who have insisted that the notion of a "superstructure" "was never materialist enough."[158]

"Determination" is a large, self-important word, which appears to pronounce on each case with finality. But when it has driven away in its Bentley, we are left to discover that everything is still to be found out. To revert to our earlier analogy, there may be a true sense in which a man's neurotic state may be determined in the last instance by his sexual nature, which, in its turn, is determined by his male reproductive organs. But this does not make his neurosis any less "real", nor are we likely to understand it or cure it by prolonged scrutiny of his penis. And, moreover, to complicate the matter further, one symptom of his neurosis may be, precisely, to render him impotent. It is a simplistic analogy, since societies are as complex as persons but in different ways. But these two reservations—as to the complexity of the "correspondence" and as to its significance—are so severe as to call in question the effectivity of Marx's general notions. Very few of the critically-significant (the most "real") problems which we confront in our actual lives appear to be *directly* and causally implicated in this field of correspondence: nationalism, racism, sexual oppression, Fascism, and Stalinism itself are certainly not removed from this field (for the pressure of class antagonisms and class-based ideologies can be felt in all), but equally certainly they cannot be seen as "developed forms of the fundamental relation of production"; they are forms in their own right, and for their analysis we require (just as the psychiatrist requires) a new set of terms, not entailed within the premises of Political Economy.

This is not to say that Marx's propositions were wrong, although they were sometimes expressed so over-confidently that they licensed wrong conclusions. It was important to learn that neurosis was not caused by Satanic possession, and important to learn that human affairs did not express the mind of divine providence, or of great men, or of unfolding Ideas, or of a benevolent class-neutered market. Marx took knowledge across a threshold, pointed her towards the world, and told her to go and *find out*. And in that outer world, beyond the secure "base" of the mode of production, many of the most cherished of human concerns are sited.

Moreover, this raises in a new way the whole problem of the effectivity of human agency, of men and women as subjects of their own history. Within the secure circuits of a mode of production, it is easy enough for Althusser to envisage men as *träger*, and to relapse into exactly the same mode of thought as that which Marx identified in Proudhon: "From his point of view man is only the instrument of which the Idea or the eternal reason makes use in order to unfold itself."[159] But in the world outside that door, it might possibly be shown that agency had larger scope to exercise its effects. To be sure, this agency will not be set free from ulterior determinate pressures nor escape determinate limits. It is unlikely to hasten on the resolution of the extraordinary complexity and contradictions of India's overlapping modes of production. But it might be able to open the gate to the Calcutta gaol and set our prisoner free. Indeed, it has done exactly that. It might even be able to resist or to legitimate the dominant ideological pressures of our time. It might collapse into complicity with Stalinist pre-destinarianism, or it might reason with Althusser and help to liberate from his influence another mind.

Moreover, if we look towards any future described as "socialist", there is no error more disabling and actively dangerous to the practice of any human freedom than the notion that there is some "socialist" mode of production (as public or State ownership of the means of production) within which some "socialist" relations of production are *given*, which will afford a categorical guarantee that some immanent socialist society (values, ideas, institutions, etc.) will *unfold itself*: not, perhaps, instantaneously (for there is "relative autonomy", etc. etc.), but in good time, out of the womb of the mode of production itself. This is wholly untrue: every choice and every institution is still to be made, and to suppose otherwise is to fall into an error as astonishing in its mystical crudity as Althusser's notion that under Stalin the "socialist *infrastructure*" was able "to develop without essential damage." (p. 160) So far from Theory affording to us such comforting guarantees, the appearance, within parties and ideologies which claim themselves to be in the "vanguard" of socialist endeavour, of metaphysical theologies so monstrous (within which will, choice, value, and men and women themselves disappear) is a most ominous premonition. We must liberate our minds *now;* if that ideology should ever claim a share in power it will be too late.

xv

We may now attempt to bring this argument together. I proposed, in an earlier section, that the hypotheses of historical materialism and the "anti" Political Economy of *Capital* were, however, closely related, distinct. This was clearly stated by Marx in his preface to the "Paris Manuscripts" (1844), when he outlined his impossibly ambitious life-project:

> I will therefore, present one after another a critique of law, of morality, politics, etc., in different independent brochures and then finally in a separate work try to show the connection of the whole and the relationship of the parts to each other and end with a criticism of the elaboration of the material by speculative philosophy. Therefore, in the present work the connection of the Political Economy with the state, law, morality, civil life, etc. *is only dealt with in so far as Political Economy itself professes to deal with these subjects.* [160]

Meanwhile, the hypotheses of historical materialism ("the relationship of the parts to each other") were rapidly presented, between 1845 and 1848, in *The German Ideology, The Poverty of Philosophy*, and *The Communist Manifesto*. Frederick Engels played a major part in the development of these hypotheses, and, behind Engels, we find the direct influence of the class organisations and class consciousness of the British working-class movement; as Stedman Jones has shown, in a helpful study, Engels was too modest as to his own part in this joint production, [161] and there is thus the greater reason to attend with respect to the *caveats* in his late letters.

Thus the hypotheses of historical materialism were already presented by 1848. These hypotheses Engels resumed in several of his subsequent prefaces to editions of the *Manifesto*. Thus (to the German edition of 1883):

> The basic thought running through the Manifesto—that economic production and the structure of society of every historical epoch necessarily arising therefrom constitute the foundation for the political and intellectual history of that

epoch; that consequently... all history has been a history of class struggles... this basic thought belongs solely and exclusively to Marx.[162]

These propositions, Engels claimed in his preface to the English edition of 1888, were "destined to do for history what Darwin's theory has done for biology." Nevertheless, as we have seen (pp. 66-7), these hypotheses remained largely undeveloped over the next forty years; they were elaborated more by Engels than by Marx, and at the end of his life Engels could clearly see that "only a little has been done."

Meanwhile, and for at least twenty years, Marx had turned aside to wrestle with his antagonist, Political Economy, and in this contest to elaborate what I have argued (pp. 60-1) may be seen as itself an "anti-structure" to that structure. I have argued that Marx was himself, for a time, trapped within the circuits of capital—an immanence manifesting itself in "forms"—and that he only partly sprung that trap in *Capital.* It is to this trap (the *Grundrisse* face of Marx) that theoretical practice so eagerly returns;[163] it is from the heart of this trap that Althusser extracts his textual licences of authority, and he wishes to return us to the conceptual prison (mode of production = social formation) that had been imposed upon Marx by his bourgeois antagonist. How far Marx himself ever became fully aware of his imprisonment is a complex question, and not one which (in my view) is of much importance to the present advance of knowledge. We are interested in advancing history, and the understanding of history, and not in Marxology. But at least we should note, that Marx, in his increasing preoccupation in his last years with anthropology, was resuming the projects of his Paris youth.[164]

The problem, as we have sufficiently argued, is to move from the circuits of capital to capital*ism;* from a highly-conceptualised and abstracted mode of production, within which determinism appears as absolute, to historical determinations as the exerting of pressures, as a logic of process within a larger (and sometimes countervailing) process. It would, of course, be ridiculous to suggest that Marx, in *Capital,* did not repeatedly come to the margin between Political Economy and history, structure and process, and repeatedly gesture—often in greatly enlightening ways—as to the pressure of the first upon the forms and logic of the second. But the gestures *remain hypotheses;* they are assumed rather than shown to be so; and, moreover, the assumptions are supported by the prior hypotheses of historical materialism, which long precede *Capital,* but which have been left both undeveloped and unexamined. And the problems arise, repeatedly, at what I have called the "junction-concepts" (p. 110): "need", which may reappear within anthropology as "norm" and within history as "wants" or "values"; "mode of production" which may reappear as a determining pressure within a complex historical process; "class", as posited as the structuring of a mode of production, or as eventuating in ways which may never be pre-determined (as historians have sufficiently shown); "determinism" itself, as closure or as pressure.

Moreover, Political Economy, including Marx's "anti" structure, had no terms—had deliberately, and for the purposes of its analytical science, *excluded* the terms—which become, immediately, essential if we are to comprehend societies and histories. Political Economy has terms for use-value, for exchange-value, for monetary value, and for surplus-value, but not for normative value. It has no terms for other areas of consciousness: how does one do the symbolic rituals of Tyburn or of Lenin's (or, now, Mao's) mausoleum into terms of value, price and profit? We may hypothesise that one "vocabulary" will "reappear" within the other, but we still do not know how, by what means or mediations. And it is here that we find that Engels's analogy between Darwin and Marx was, in one respect, even closer than he intended. For just as Darwin proposed and demonstrated an evolutionary process which proceeded by means of a hypothetical transmutation of the species—species which had hitherto been hypostasised as immutable and fixed—and yet remained wholly in the dark as to the actual genetic means of this transmission and trans-mutation—so, in an analogous way, historical materialism, as a hypothesis, was left unprovided with its own "genetics." If a correspondence could be proposed—and, in some part, demonstrated—between a mode of pro-duction and historical process, how, and in what ways, did this come about? It is an important question: because one answer will be simply to set aside the problem unanswered. And theology will then say that evolution manifests the peculiar working-out of the divine will, while theoretical practice will then say that history manifests the "development of the forms" of capital. The other answer (the tradition of Mendel, and of historical and cultural materialism) will be to *find out*.

What we have found out (in my view) lies within a missing term: "human experience." This is, exactly, the term which Althusser and his followers wish to blackguard out of the club of thought under the name of "empiricism." Men and women also return as subjects, within this term— not as autonomous subjects, "free individuals", but as persons experiencing their determinate productive situations and relationships, as needs and interests and as antagonisms, and then "handling" this experience within their *consciousness* and their *culture* (two other terms excluded by theoretical practice) in the most complex (yes, "relatively autonomous") ways, and then (often but not always through the ensuing structures of class) acting upon their determinate situation in their turn.

It must be emphasised that, while this is not incompatible with the hypotheses of Engels and Marx, it is not exactly the same as their propositions. For we have introduced one term, "culture", which in its "anthropological" derivation, Althusser would deplore, and which in its subsequent definition and elaboration within historical knowledge was not available to Marx. It is a term which I am wholly committed to defend, and to defend, if Marxologists insist that it is necessary, *against* Marx. For it is not true that Marx passed over in innocence the need to provide his theory with some "genetics". He attempted such a provision, first, in his writings on alienation, commodity fetishism, and reification; and, second, in his notion of man, in his history, continuously making over his own nature. (We will only note in passing, since other critics have examined this question, that Althusser excludes all exploration of either set of suggestive notions from his canon). Of the first set of concepts I wish only to say this: they propose to supply a "genetics"—to explain how history is determined in ways which conflict with the conscious intentions of its subjects—in terms of mystified *rationality*. Men imprison themselves within structures of their own creation because they are *self-mystified*. While historians may find these notions suggestive in certain areas (as in the study of ideologies), they would argue—I certainly will argue—that, in more general application, they are the product of an overly-rational mind; they offer an explanation in terms of mystified rationality for *non*-rational or *ir*rational behaviour and belief, whose sources may not be educed from reason. As to the second set of concepts (man making over his own nature), while they are important and point the right way, they remain so undeveloped that, in effect, they do little more than restate the prior question in new terms: we are still left to *find out* "how"?

Thus we return to the missing term, "experience", and at once we enter into the real silences of Marx. This is not only a point of junction between "structure" and "process", but a point of *dis*-junction between alternative and incompatible traditions. For one tradition, that of idealist dogma, these "silences" are blanknesses or absences of "rigour" in Marx (failures fully to theorise his own concepts), and they must be sewn together by bridging concepts, conceptually generated from the same conceptual matrix. But, as we have seen (p. 111), this pursuit of the security of a perfect totalised theory is the original heresy against knowledge. Such perfect idealist creations, each seam superbly joined by invisible conceptual stitching, always end up in the jumble sale. If Marx had really designed a Theory like that, it would be down in the bargain basement already, along with Spencer, Dühring, and Comte, to be snapped up by some graduate student looking for a bizarre patch of material to sew onto her doctoral jeans.

In its present incarnation as "theoretical practice", this notion of Theory is like a blight that has settled on the mind. The empirical senses are occluded, the moral and aesthetic organs are repressed, the curiosity is sedated, all the "manifest" evidence of life or of art is distrusted as "ideology", the theoretical ego enlarges (for everyone else is mystified by "appearances"), and the devotees gather intensely around the Mode of Production. Like the approaches to the altar of Lakshmi in an ancient

Hindu temple, the passages are long, slippery, and ornate, but there at length she is, the goddess of material wealth, encrusted with gold and jewels, roped with garlands, and with nothing visible but her huge enigmatic eyes. They do her obeisance, and incant her several names, *La Structure à Dominante*, The Mode, the CMP. The rites which they perform are sometimes pitiful, sometimes comic. Critics struggle to decode poems as the re-enactment of theory or of ideology in opaque terms. And behind these terms lies The Mode, the CMP. Just as, in the inert platonism of their theory, all culture and all social life has been reduced to the Mode, so their vocabulary is stewed down until it is reduced to the same de-natured glue.

> A double-articulation GMP/GI-GI/AI/LMP is, for example, possible, whereby a GI category, when transformed by AI into an ideological component of an LMP, may then enter into conflict with the GMP social relations it exists to reproduce.[165]

It is kind of this literary critic to provide us with an "example". But to suppose this to advance a "science" of materialist aesthetics is to calumniate both science and materialism.

Not all the rites are so whole-hearted. The pilgrims are sometimes critical and querulous. But since, in some part of their hearts, they still wish to worship the Absolute, they do not repudiate but seek only to amend the rites. Hence the problems (which they can really see) are reduced to pseudo-problems within a conceptual system designed to repel their solution. Even excellent historians, who ought to know better (and who perhaps do), ponder the lack of a "precise structural *mechanism*" to "connect" the base and the superstructure, and meditate on the ways in which this omission can be conceptually repaired.[166] But what is wrong, and was always wrong, is the analogy we start with (body/soul), and the notion that the joint can be mended with a "mechanism." Socialist feminists, who have a genuine grudge against the "silences" of Marxism, attempt by arduous exercises of theory to insert a new flywheel (reproduction of the labour force) into the orrery, hoping that its inertia will somehow miraculously motor all the variegated "developed forms" of sexual repression and expression, familial modes and gender roles. But what is wrong is not that they have proposed the problem, but that they have reduced it to a pseudo-problem by attempting to insert it into a machine designed for its exclusion. And, at the same time, they have been tricked into dismantling their problem's whole challenge and identity, and have subdued it to the same general blight.

A cloud no bigger than a man's hand crosses the English Channel from Paris, and then, in an instant, the trees, the orchard, the hedgerows, the field of wheat, are black with locusts. When at length they rise to fly on to the next parish, the boughs are bared of all culture, the fields have been stripped of every green blade of human aspiration: and in those skeletal forms and that blackened landscape, theoretical practice announces its "discovery": the mode of production. Not only substantive knowledge, but also the very vocabularies of the human project—compassion, greed, love, pride, self-sacrifice, loyalty, treason, calumny—have been eaten down to the circuits of capital. These locusts are very learned platonists: if they settled on *The Republic* they would leave it picked clean of all but the idea of a contradiction between a philosopher and a slave. However elaborated the inner mechanisms, torsions, and autonomies, theoretical practice constitutes the ultimate in reductionism: a reduction, not of "religion" or "politics" to "economics", but of the disciplines of knowledge to one kind of "basic" Theory only. Theory is for ever collapsing back into ulterior theory. In disallowing empirical enquiry, the mind is confined for ever within the compound of the mind. It cannot walk abroad. It is struck down with theoretical cramp, and the pain is tolerable on condition that it does not move its limbs.

That, then, is the system of *closure*. It is the place where all Marxisms, conceived of as self-sufficient, self-validating, self-extrapolating theoretical systems, must end. At its worst (and this is where it is usually at) theoretical practice *is* this end, and we may thank Althusser for demonstrating this with such "rigour." But if we return to "experience" we can move, from that point, once again into an *open* exploration of the world and of ourselves. This exploration makes demands of equal theoretical rigour, but within that dialogue of conceptualisation and empirical engagement which we have already examined (pp. 39-40). This exploration may still be within the Marxist tradition, in the sense that we are taking Marx's hypotheses and some of his central concepts, and setting these to work. But the end of this exploration is not to discover a (reformed) finite conceptual system, Marxism. There is and can never be such a finite system.

I am sorry to disappoint those practitioners who suppose that all that it is necessary to know about history can be constructed from a conceptual meccano set. One can only return, in the end, from these explorations with better methods and a better map; with a certain sense of the whole social process; with expectations as to process and as to structured relationships; with a certain way of situating oneself before the materials; with certain key concepts (themselves to be employed and tested and reformed) of historical materialism: class, ideology, mode of production. On the margins of the map we will always meet the boundaries of the unknown. What remains to be done is to interrogate the real silences, through the dialogue of knowledge; and as these silences are penetrated, we do not just sew up one new concept to the old fabric, we find it is necessary to re-order the whole *set* of concepts. There is no innermost altar that is sacrosanct against interrogation and revision.

Here lies the difference between Marx*ism* and the Marxist tradition. It is possible to practise as a Marxist but to regard Marx*isms* to be obscurantic-isms—as, manifestly, in a dozen forms, they have become. This has nothing to do with one's admiration for Marx and his work. On the contrary, to admire that work is to place oneself as apprentice to it, to employ its terms, to learn to work in a dialogue of the same kind. But emulation should never rest upon literal-minded reverence—not even (as with Althusser) pretended reverence for what Marx intended to say but, un-accountably, forgot. It must arise from an understanding of the provisional and exploratory nature of all theory, and the openness with which one must approach all knowledge. This must also entail a respect for the continuity of intellectual culture, which is not to be seen as fractured into two halves, between the B.C. and A.D. of Marx's "epistemological break", and in which all other minds and knowledges are to be measured against the rule of Marxist Science.

It is in the very notion of Marx*ism* as "Science" that we find the authentic trade-mark of obscuranticism, and of an obscuranticism borrowed, like so much else, from a bourgeois ideology of great longevity. Utilitarians, Malthusians, Positivists, Fabians, and structural-functionalists, all suppose(d) themselves to be practising a "science", and the most unabashed academic centre of brutalised capitalist ideology in contemporary England acclaims itself as a School of Economics and Political *Science*. When Marx and Engels claimed that they were applying scientific methods to the study of society, the claim may, on occasion, be upheld; when they supposed that they were founding a Science (Marx*ism*) they were locking prison-gates upon their own knowledge.

The matter is now more grave than that. Marx*ism* has for decades been suffering from a wasting disease of vulgar economism. Its motions have been enfeebled, its memory failing, its vision obscured. Now it has swiftly passed into a last delirium of idealism, and the illness must prove terminal. Theoretical practice, is already, the *rigor mortis* of Marx*ism* setting in. Marx*ism* no longer has anything to tell us of the world, nor any way of finding out.

The impulse is to fly for our reason from this scene of devastation. Honourable men, like Cornelius Castoriadis, who have not abandoned for an instant their engagement with capitalism, have left the Marxist tradition in this way: they see it as irreparable, inherently élitist, dominative and anti-democratic (the "scientists" and the vulgar rest), and condemned by its orthodox and Stalinist fruits.[167] And I go with their critique a good part of the way (a salute, old comrades of *Socialisme ou Barbarie!*): some part I have stated in my own terms. But even in their bitter polemic with

"Marxism" we see that they are employing—and putting to better use— concepts which they first learned from Marx. For Marx*isms* and the tradition of open, empirical enquiry, originating in the work of Marx, and employing, developing, and revising his concepts, have never been the same thing.

So, then, why fight over a name? For a Marx*ism* I would not fight, for I would fight with a guilty conscience. Marx was often wrong, and sometimes wrong in damaging ways. Not all of Althusser's licences of authority are as spurious as his sentence from *The Poverty of Philosophy*. Some part of Marx points towards system and "science" in ways which afford uncomfortable continuities to the isms and State ideologies of our time. The *"Grundrisse* face" of Marx, the notion of capital's "immanence", affords a premonition of Althusser, although these premonitions are plainly contradicted in a hundred other places. Marx shares with other great and fertile thinkers (Hobbes, Machiavelli, Milton, Pascal, Vico, Rousseau) an ambiguity inherent in the very vigour and openness of their thought. In taking us across a threshold, he leaves us at a door; we leave old problems behind, and we gain, exactly, a perspective upon the further range of problems ahead, some of which he could see, but few of which he could (in anticipation) solve. He places us in a new theoretical space, from which alternative developments lead forward. One name for this space is ambiguity, another is possibility. The very diversity of schools of thought which all claim a common Marxist inheritance (and all of which can produce different licences of authority) is proof of that.

Marx*ism* has been one possible development, although one with only an attenuated relationship to Marx. But the open, exploratory, self-critical Marxist tradition has been another development altogether. Its presence can be found in every discipline, in many political practices, and in every part of the world.

I had intended, at this point, to insert some comments upon a Marxist tradition which I know well—that of historiography. But I will reserve these notes for another place.[168] I don't wish to personalise what is a very severe and general intellectual crisis, nor to allow it to be supposed that I am placing some "Anglo-Marxist tradition" against the "Franco-Marxism" of Althusser. The first tradition is not Anglo-Saxon: it is vigorous, not only in Scotland and Wales, but in France and in India, in Italy and (as, for example, in the tenacious tradition of *Monthly Review*) in the United States: nor is it, in any sense, confined to historiography. The second ism is not representative of the best French socialist thought, and is only one extreme systematisation of systems which are found also as state ideologies or within "Western Marxism." Nor do I have any authority to speak for my fellow historians in the British Marxist tradition.

I will therefore simply indicate this as one location for an alternative tradition. And make one comment. Those who suppose (and these include half the *lumpen-intelligentsia* of Oxbridge) that Althusser and his colleagues were making some novel and "flexible" reappraisals of the Marxist "problematic" when they gestured at "relative autonomy" and "in the last instance"—and that before this "revolution" all practising Marxists were subdued to vulgar dogma or dumb "empiricism"—these people are simply disclosing their ignorance of historical and cultural materialism. In particular, their knowledge of history can only have been gathered from travellers' tales; and from such travellers as "Sir John Mandeville", the good burgher of Liège, who never left his notary's office.

"Relative autonomy" was where we started from, and we started with the aid of others who had started there before us. It would, after all, have been somewhat difficult for us to have examined the drama of Aeschylus, ancient Greek science, the origins of Buddhism, the city-state, Cistercian monasteries, utopian thought, Puritan doctrines, feudal tenures, the poetry of Marvell, Methodist revivalism, the symbolism of Tyburn, *grandes peurs* and riots, Behmenist sects, primitive rebels, economic and imperialist ideologies, and every type of class confrontation, negotiation and refraction, without, somewhere along the line, stumbling upon a difficulty. I do not claim that "we" have done all this expertly, definitively, or even well. My concern is a different one. It is to emphasise that we entered, through historical experience, directly into the real silences of Marx.

What did we find? Not, I fear, a better Theory (historical materialism as a new closed *ism*). We found some new knowledge, we developed our own methods and the discourse of our discipline, and we advanced towards a common understanding of the full historical process. What else we discovered is more controversial, and I can only report my own sense of this. We confirmed all of those late warnings of Engels: it is impossible to move, by the change of a letter, from the capitalist mode of production to capitalism as a social formation. We explored, both in theory and in practice, those junction-concepts (such as "need", "class", and "determine") by which, through the missing term, "experience", structure is transmuted into process, and the subject re-enters into history. We greatly enlarged the concept of class, which historians in the Marxist tradition commonly employ—deliberately and not out of some theoretical "innocence"—with a flexibility and indeterminacy disallowed both by Marx*ism* and by orthodox sociology. And at "experience" we were led on to re-examine all those dense, complex and elaborated systems by which familial and social life is structured and social consciousness finds realisation and expression (systems which the very rigour of the discipline in Ricardo or in the Marx of *Capital* is designed to exclude): kinship, custom, the invisible and visible rules of social regulation, hegemony and deference, symbolic forms of domination and of resistance, religious faith and millenarial impulses, manners, law, institutions and ideologies—all of which, in their sum, comprise the "genetics" of the whole historical process, all of them joined, at a certain point, in common human experience, which itself (as distinctive *class* experiences) exerts its pressure on the sum.

When I say that "we" explored outwards in this way, I don't mean that we were the first-comers, or that we were unaided by historians, anthropologists and others in different traditions. Our debts are manifold. But, in my view, we did not discover other, and co-existent, *systems*, of equal status and coherence to the system of (anti) Political Economy, exerting co-equal determining pressures: a Kinship Mode, a Symbolic Mode, an Ideological Mode, etc. "Experience" (we have found) has, in the last instance, been generated in "material life", has been structured in class ways, and hence "social being" has determined "social consciousness." *La Structure* still dominates experience but from that point her determinate influence is weak. For any living generation, in any "now", the ways in which they "handle" experience defies prediction and escapes from any narrow definition of determination.

I think that we have found out something else, of even greater significance for the whole project of socialism. For I introduced, a few pages back, another necessary middle term: "culture." And we find that, with "experience" and "culture" we are at a junction-point of another kind. For people do not only experience their own experience as ideas, within thought and its procedures, or (as some theoretical practitioners suppose) as proletarian instinct, etc. They also experience their own experience as *feeling*, and they handle their feelings within their culture, as norms, familial and kinship obligations and reciprocities, as values or (through more elaborated forms) within art or religious beliefs. This half of culture (and it is a full one-half) may be described as affective and moral consciousness.

This is, exactly, *not* to argue that "morality" is some "autonomous region" of human choice and will, arising independently of the historical process. Such a view of morality has never been materialist enough, and hence it has often reduced that formidable inertia—and sometimes formidable revolutionary force—into a wishful idealist fiction. It is to say, on the contrary, that every contradiction is a conflict of value as well as a conflict of interest; that inside every "need" there is an affect, or "want", on its way to becoming an "ought" (and *vice versa*); that every class struggle is at the same time a struggle over values; and that the project of Socialism is guaranteed *BY NOTHING*—certainly not by "Science", or by Marxism-Leninism—but can find its own guarantees only by *reason* and through an open *choice of values*.

And it is here that the silence of Marx, and of most Marx*isms*, is so loud as to be deafening. It is an odd silence, to be sure, since as we have already noted (p. 58), Marx, in his wrath and compassion, was a moralist in every stroke of his pen. Besieged by the triumphant moralism of Victorian capitalism, whose rhetoric concealed the actualities of exploitation and imperialism, his polemical device was to expose all moralism as a sick deceit: "the English Established Church will more readily pardon an attack on 38 of its 39 articles than on 1/39th of its income." His stance became that of an anti-moralist. This was true, in equal degree, of Engels, whose inadequate arguments in *Anti-Dühring* I do not mean to examine. By the 1880s, Engels's overt distaste for moralism was such that he looked straight through the extraordinary genius of Morris, and failed even to notice what was there.

To the end of his life, when confronting, in his anthropological researches, problems manifestly demanding analysis in terms not derivative from Political Economy, Marx—while acknowledging the problems—was always trying to shove them back into an economic frame of reference. When Maine referred to "the mass of influences, which we may call for shortness moral", Marx impatiently annotated the text: "This 'moral' shows how little Maine understands of the matter; as far as these influences (economical before everything else) possess a 'moral' modus of existence, this is always a derived, secondary modus and never the prius."[169] But this is not any analysis: it is simply a refusal to break a silence. If the "moral" influences exist as a moral "modus" then they exist and must be analysed in a vocabulary of norms, values, obligations, expectations, taboos, etc. That they are "economical before everything else" and are "derived, secondary" is a pre-judgement, or, more politely, an hypothesis, which nowhere in Marx's work is fully examined, which his major project excludes from consideration, and which, in its turn, is derived from a particular and limited definition of the "economic." In this whole area Morris was immensely more perceptive than Engels or Marx.

This silence was transmitted to the subsequent Marxist tradition in the form of a repression. This repression, in its turn, made it more easy for the major tradition to turn its back upon Morris (and many other voices) and to capitulate to an economism which, in fact, simply took over a bourgeois utilitarian notion of "need"; and, as a necessary complement to this, to foster a paltry philistinism towards the arts. It was only necessary for Marxist Science to enter into the kingdom of Socialism, and all else would be added thereunto. And Marxism-Leninism-Stalinism did. And we know with what results.

That is a crassly over-simplified account of a more complex, and more contested, development. But we have now tracked the last of Althusser's ogres, "moralism", to its lair. Its lair is found to be, less in the forest of bourgeois ideology, than deep in the heart of the international working-class movement itself. This ogre has given to that movement a utopian nerve of aspiration, the muscles of solidarity, and, on occasion, the courage of revolutionary self-sacrifice. It has also, on repeated occasions, impelled revolts and defections within Communist Parties, and a running polemic against the practices of those Parties and the moral vacancy of the Marxist vocabulary. In 1956 it assumed the proportions of a mass revulsion within the international Communist movement against Stalinist practices and apologetics; its most articulate spokesmen (the ogres incarnate) were very often poets and novelists: Tuwim, Wazyk, Pasternak, Dery, Illyes, Solzhenitsyn. Once again, so far from Althusser advancing a critique of Stalinism, he is engaged in an ideological police-action against that critique, by attempting to disallow the most important terms in which that critique has been made.

In this case, and in this case only, the license of authority which Althusser produces is authentic. It is, indeed, signed by Marx and counter-signed (with a caveat as to "truly human morality") by Engels. This is, perhaps, why Althusser never bothers to argue the case, but can simply assume that all Marxists must agree that "moralism" is a hideous enormity. What he has to say about "moralism" is rarely specific. In *For Marx* and *Reading Capital* the problem's presence is to be noted mainly in the careful strategies employed to ensure its absence from the text. On the one hand, all questions of norms, affective relationships and rules, are dismissed in the same gesture that dismisses "anthropology" (p. 145). This enables him (and all theoretical practitioners) to set aside unread fifty years of work in social history, anthropology, and adjacent disciplines, some of it by Marxist practitioners, and all of it enlightening the problem of "relative autonomy" which is supposedly an object of Althusser's rigorous labours.

On the other hand, "morality" is simply equated to "bourgeois morality": i.e. ideology. This is a "world of alibis, sublimations and lies", or, with "politics and religion", a world of "myths and drugs" (*F.M.* 140, 145), and Marxists can have no interest in it except to demystify it. "Moralism", or "the recourse to ethics", is the shadow of "humanism", whose function (we remember) is to offer "an imaginary treatment of real problems." Old comrades will certainly recognise this invincible Stalinist formula—pronounced on every uncomfortable occasion by every Party hack: true morality equals whatever furthers the best interests of the working class: the Party, guided by Marxist "science", is best able to decide what those best interests are (and how lucky the working class is to have Daddy to do that!): and since what are at issue are *interests*, which can be determined with the precision of science, no choice of values (or of means) can be involved. When it was decided, after his death, by the Party, that Stalin was in some points wrong, no question of Stalinism's moral stench was involved—an investigation of *that* might have brought even Marxism and the Party under suspicion. The vocabulary permitted only "errors" and "mistakes" (misjudgement of best interests) to be allowed. That, after some years, the decidedly-unscientific term, "crimes", has now been allowed may be attributed, not to revisionism, but to an opportunist reflex in the face of the accusing moral sensibility of the millions.

There is something more in Althusser's subsequent essay on "Ideology and Ideological State Apparatuses" (*L. & P.* **pp.** 123-173). This is, perhaps, the ugliest thing he has ever done, the crisis of the idealist delirium. I will spare myself the tedium of criticism, since in its naivety, its refusal of all relevant evidence, and its absurd idealist inventions, it exposes itself. "Ethics", etc., are offered as an ideological State apparatus (and only as that), imposed upon the innocent and utterly passive, recipient, man, by means of "the family State apparatus" and "the educational State apparatus." This ideology imposes upon individuals "the imaginary relationship. . . to their real conditions of existence." And to explain how it does this, Althusser invents a (wholly imaginary) device of "interpellation" or "hailing", by which the State via its ideological apparatus ("religious, ethical, legal, political aesthetic, etc ") cries out to individuals: "Ahoy, there!" It is only necessary for the State to hail them, and they are "recruited" instantly to whatever "imaginary relationship" the State requires. Hailing has always gone on, and it always will, in any society. This is so, not because people cannot live and sustain relationships without values and norms, but because "ideology. . . is indispensable in any society if men are to *be formed,* transformed and equipped to respond to the demands of their conditions of existence." (*F.M.* 235) (Notice, once again, the passive, transitive form, the reification of agency by the Other.) By means of "interpellation", or hailing, men and women are constituted (within ideology) as (imaginary) subjects: for example, as Jeunes Etudiants Catholiques or as Ulster Protestants.

It is a touching scenario, and one which could only have been written by a gentleman who has lived a retired life. It suggests a future for its author as a script-writer for "Watch with Mother." The wicked witch of State appears! The wand of ideology is flourished! And, hey presto! Not only has the prince become a frog, but the entire coach-and-six of the reformist trade union movement (another "ideological State apparatus") has become a match-box drawn by six white mice. But if any readers in this country have been imposed upon (or "interpellated") by the loud-hailing of the several British import agencies for "Western Marxism" (including, *hélas,* one heavy import agency which, some years ago, I had a part in founding) to suppose that this is the best that the Marxist tradition in France can do with sociology, communications and educational theory, etc., then I beg them to be disabused. They might commence their re-education by attending to Pierre Bourdieu.

What is obvious about these tormented constructions is that they are the desperate devices employed by a naive rationalism in an attempt to trick up a new rationalist explanation for non-rational behaviour: that is, the affective and moral consciousness must somehow be construed as displaced rationality ("ideology") and not as *lived experience* "handled" in distinctive ways. (Althusser might at least have learned from Merleau-Ponty that consciousness is *lived* as much as it is *known*.)[170] These devices can, as always, boast formidable credentials within bourgeois ideology. The "value"/"fact" antimony, in which "value" or "morality" is supposedly an autonomous area of choice resting upon the de-socialised individual, has continually reappeared as its *alter ego:* the eviction of value from social and economic "science", the segregation of "morality" within the pallisades of "the personal"—a socially-ineffectual space of private preferences. (We are permitted, today, to have "moral" preferences about sexual conduct, but the questions of economic "growth" are scientific matters in which no choices of value are entailed.) The good old utilitarian notion that all facts are quantifiable and measurable (and hence can be ingested by a computer), and that whatever is not measurable is not a fact, is alive and kicking and in possession of a large part of the Marxist tradition. And yet, what cannot be measured has had some very measurable material consequences.

This may explain why theoretical practitioners refuse to admit historical evidence to their seminars on "moralism" and "ideology". Historians would very soon have to point out that all that was being done was to invent for utilitarianism a new set of idealist credentials. Values are neither "thought" nor "hailed"; they are lived, and they arise within the same nexus of material life and material relations as do our ideas. They are the necessary norms, rules, expectations, &c, learned (and "learned" within feeling) within the *"habitus"* of living; and learned, in the first place, within the family, at work, and within the immediate community. Without this learning social life could not be sustained, and all production would cease.

This is not to say that values are independent of the colouration of ideology; manifestly this is not the case, nor how, when experience itself is structured in class ways, could this be so? But to suppose from this that they are "imposed" (by a State!) as "ideology" is to mistake the whole social and cultural process. This imposition will always be attempted, with greater or less success, but it cannot succeed at all unless there is some *congruence* between the imposed rules and view-of-life and the necessary business of living a given mode of production. Moreover, values no less than material needs will always be a locus of *contradiction*, of struggle between alternative values and views-of-life. If we say that values are learned within lived experience and are subject to its determinations, we need not therefore surrender to a moral or cultural relativism. Nor need we suppose some uncrossable barrier between value and reason. Men and women argue about values, they choose between values, and in their choosing they adduce rational evidence and interrogate their own values by rational means. This is to say that they are *as much but no more* determined in their values as in their ideas and actions, they are *as much but no more* "subjects" of their own affective and moral consciousness as of their general history. Conflicts of value, and choices of value, always take place. When a person joins or crosses a picket-line, that person is making a choice of values, even if the terms of the choice and some part of what that person chooses *with* are socially and culturally determined.

Historical and cultural materialism cannot explain "morality" away as class interests in fancy dress, since the notion that all "interests" can be subsumed in scientifically-determinable material objectives is nothing more than utilitarianism's bad breath. Interests are what interest people, including what interests them nearest to the heart. A materialist examination of values must situate itself, not by idealist propositions, but in the face of culture's material abode: the people's way of life, and, above all, their productive and familial relationships. And this is what "we" have been doing, and over many decades.

Althusserian notions of "ideology" have the quaintness of an antique, a piece of ornate rationalist Victoriana. We have examined the value-systems of peasantries, of the patriarchal household, the acquisitive values of insurgent capitalism (and the intense struggles around these), the values of foresters, yeomen, artisans, handloom-weavers, factory workers. We have examined these as a locus of conflict, at inarticulate, sub-articulate, sublimated, and at complex and arduously-contested levels of articulacy (what else is *The Country and the City* about?). For the affective and moral consciousness discloses itself within history, and within class struggles, sometimes as a scarcely-articulate inertia (custom, superstition), sometimes as an articulate conflict between alternative, class-based value-systems (the "moral economy" of the crowd, the confrontation around the 1834 Poor Law), sometimes as a displaced, confused, but none-the-less "real" and passionate encounter within religious forms (Methodism, millenarianism), sometimes as the brutal imposition by Church or State of a "moralism" (the sanctified burning of heretics, sanctified Stalinist State "trials"), and sometimes as one of the most rigorous and complex disciplines known within intellectual culture—the full disclosure of values, and the rational argument between values, exemplified in literature and in a certain kind of disciplined moral critique.

All this will not go away because it is defined out of our Theory. I can only suppose, from certain references of theoretical practitioners to "moralism", that these imagine a moral choice, or a choice between values, to be a kind of grunt, and a grunt which is the reflex of "ideology"; and that they suppose that one grunt is as good as any other, and have never noticed that it may take the form of a discipline with its own arduous and relevant "discourse of the proof." There are, of course, rotten "moralisms" just as there are rotten ideologies and philosophies (we have been examining one). And in so far as the full disclosure of choices between values is inhibited, in so far as the articulate "discourse of the proof" is actively suppressed, so any value-informed view of life will rot away into rhetoric and hypocritical moralistic oratory. This is, exactly, the case with Stalinism; this is, exactly, why Stalinism has always most

distrusted poets; this is, exactly, why the intellectual apologists for
Stalinism have always sought to block off any possible moral critique; and
this is, exactly, why one form of the protest against Stalinist ideology and
forms has very often been "moralistic", but, since it has been denied
every opportunity for open articulation, it often appears as a kind of
displaced, illusory, and, of necessity, "utopian" moralism—as a reversion to
Greek Orthodox faith, as nationalist self-exclusion, as personalist self-
isolation, or as Solzhenitsyn—as the agonised heartbeat within a heartless
world. And so, we may confidently predict, the Soviet Union will continue
to astonish us; ever more bizarre and immaterial forms of moral
consciousness will arise as "superstructure" upon that severely-scientific
material "base". The Soviet repressive and ideological State apparatuses, in
inhibiting any open argument about values, have not only denied to
"individuals" the right of "self-expression", they have denied to Soviet
society the means to express, and to examine, itself.

Thus the moral critique of Stalinism has never been some grunt of moral
autonomy. It has been a very specific and practical political critique. It has
concerned particular forms and practices within the international Communist movement; the subordination of the imagination (and of
the artist) to the wisdom of the Party; the imposition of a notion of
"political realism", which refuses any debate over values, at every level of
the Party organisation; the economistic strategies and the narrow
propaganda of material need, which is blind to whole areas of (sexual,
cultural) need, which despises the people's own cultural resources, and
which assumes, but does not permit people to choose, what they really
"want". As a result, in its inhibition of all "utopianism", and in its
repression of the "education of desire", it reproduces, within capitalism,
the very reasons of capital—the utilitarian definition of "need"—and hence,
in the very moment that it offers to struggle against its power, it
inculcates obedience to its rules.[171] Theoretical practice, in its spurious
pretentions to be Science, is seeking to validate the bad faith of the
Marxist tradition, and is reproducing as ideology the central vacancy
of Stalinism.

It was the oldest error of rationalism to suppose that by defining the
non-rational out of its vocabulary it had in some way defined it out of life.
I rediscovered this, with a happy sense of recognition, in a recent debate
on "moralism" in the pages of *Radical Philosophy.* The practitioners, who
as yet are only apprentices to Theory, should not be scolded too much.
But we move here, with solemnity, through three propositions. (1) All
morality = ideology. Thus: for Marx, "morality was an historically specific
ideological institution functioning to mystify and discipline people in
accordance with the oppressive and exploitive needs of class society."[172]
(Marx certainly never said *that;* insofar as he afforded licence for some
of that to be said, one can only say "alas!", and recall how far his

contemporary thought was saturated with the same rationalist illusions.)
But the equation is derived, not only from Marx, but from "Historical
Materialism" (whose products these authors have evidently found it unnecessary to consult). Marxist history, it seems, has demonstrated that
"moral ideology has a socially repressive function."

Proposition (2). In contradistinction to "moral ideology" (which the
ruling class inculcates for its own convenience) we are to suppose that "a
form of practical reason is possible which is in no sense moral or socially
repressive." Moral ideology "must be antagonistic to natural values
(happiness, the satisfaction of wants)." Thus there are "naturalistic"
imperatives (simple ones, like "happiness") and these can be instantly
deduced by "reason." "The removal of moral motives would leave
man. . . to rationally pursue his naturalistic ends." This, apart from leaving
the reason inside a split infinitive, would leave no other problems:

> Practical reason of a non-moral kind involves understanding one's own needs,
> developing them in such a way that their most satisfying form of satisfaction is
> possible, gaining knowledge and therefore power over the world, selecting the
> best means for the satisfaction of needs, etc.

But—a shadow passes across this sunlit field at the recollection of the
possible egotism of *other* people which might interfere with "one"
satisfying one's needs satisfactorily—this "practical reason" must "often be
in the collective mode, i.e. the question will be not 'what shall I do' but
'what shall we do', collective naturalistic self-interest being the ground
for choice."

Our learned Theban, having disposed of this problem to his satisfaction,
passes forward to proposition (3). A classless society will see the
withering away of all morality. "The elimination of moral ideology
is. . . taken as a rational desideratum."

> The classical position of Marxism on this subject is that morality as an autonomous
> form of practical reason would disappear with the abolition of class antagonisms.

Moreover, we can hasten that about by living naturalistically now:

> There is no moral basis for socialism, no such thing as 'living as a socialist' within
> capitalist society, and no imperatives incumbent upon socialists as such other
> than that of working for socialism. How a socialist gets his money or his kicks is
> politically irrelevant.[173]

Proposition (1): Morality = Ideology. (2) But there are "naturalistic
ends", a "collective naturalistic self-interest", which can be determined by
reason. (3) Classless society will ensure the withering away of morality,

with a rider as to present-day money and kicks which (it is fair to note) one or two fellow practitioners disputed.[174] The rest, it seems, could be taken as the "classical position of Marxism"! Morality is a repressive mechanism for inhibiting the naturalistic libido.

"O, reason not the need. . ."! One might be pardoned for supposing that some apprentice practitioners have no more notion of the social formation (and clash) of values than might be afforded by recollections of nasty school rules and even nastier family quarrels. The "ideological State apparatus" *(sic!)* of the only family that ever appears in their writing is, indeed, hideously repressive:

> In the monogamous nuclear family, however liberal, the child is at the mercy of her family, deprived of responsibility (determining agency) or choice of friends, and denied the opportunity for full, wide and many-sided relationships with peers and older people. Thus are reinforced the isolated, anxiety-ridden, competitive character structures of the bourgeoisie and as well, the tamed law-aspiring proletarian.[175]

The description is, perhaps, a touch moralistic (even priggish)—and, since "Marxism" (or Althusser) has demonstrated that the notion of "responsibility" (determining agency) in *adults* is a noxious humanist illusion, how is it that children do not come within the same theoretical provision?

Never mind. The quarrels (one might hazard) have been about such "naturalistic ends" as sex, money and pot. And this reminds us that the repudiation of all "moralism" has been very much the mode for some time. The revolting young bourgeoisie have long been into doing their own thing, and, if they are moralists at all, this comes out in their disapproval of all "heavy" speeches from their elders about "oughts." The more sensitive among them have not only been *into* doing their own thing, they are already coming *out*, chastened, at the thing's other side. They have discovered that to have "the most satisfying form of satisfaction" sometimes leaves the source of satisfaction as a heart-broken wreck; that egos must be socialised and humanised (or sat upon) if they are not to make each others' lives into a hell; that "happiness" does not come, like a dog, to the whistle of reason; that "socialists" who get their money and kicks in certain ways will also be somewhere else in any political emergency; and that even those monstrous apparatuses, the family and the school, have one or two functions subsidiary to that of repression.

So—some of these revolting young bourgeois are doing O.K. They may yet take their parts in the socialist movement, while the others— the egotists who posture as "revolutionaries" as one of their "kicks"— will no doubt graduate as vigilant headmasters and tyrannical papas. (I've seen all this, not only in my own empiricist "experience", but also, repeatedly, in historical research.) Very soon the best of them will turn away from exclusive moral scrutiny of their own inter-personal affairs, and take a larger view of society. And there they will discover the same logic writ out at large. "Gaining knowledge and therefore power over the world" will, for the unconstrained egotist, mean getting other people within his power. The reasons of Reason, unencumbered by the moral consciousness, become, very soon, the reasons of interest, and then the reasons of State, and thence, in an uncontested progression, the rationalisations of opportunism, brutality, and crime.

There is not, nor can there ever be, any "naturalistic" morality, any "naturalistic ends." Certainly, historical and cultural materialism have never found them. Ends are chosen by our culture, which affords us, at the same time, our own medium of choosing and of influencing that choice. To suppose otherwise is to suppose that our "needs" are *there*, somewhere outside of ourselves and our culture, and that, if only ideology would go away, the reason would identify these needs at once.

And this, of course, is the moment of recognition. For we have gone back, in one swift step, to one of the dottiest moments in the Enlightenment. The "naturalistic ends" were given, in a rational way, as self-interest by Adam Smith; but it was left to Bentham to invent a means of determining these needs "in such a way that their most satisfying form of satisfaction is possible"—the Felicific Calculus. And the notion of "the collective naturalistic self-interest" was proposed, in a rational way, by Rousseau and others (the general will, the common good); but it was left to William Godwin to ascend, by the spiral of Hartleyan associationist psychology, from self-interest to "benevolence"—from which lofty height the enthroned Reason could see through all the spurious ideological bonds of sentiment—gratitude, love of kin, the family, the servitude of the irrational crowd:

> This was the time, when all things tending fast
> To depravation, the Philosophy
> That promised to abstract the hopes of man
> Out of his feelings, to be fix'd thenceforth
> For ever in a purer element
> Found ready welcome. Tempting region that
> For Zeal to enter and refresh herself,
> Where passions had the privilege to work
> And never hear the sound of their own names;
> But, speaking more in charity, the dream
> Was flattering to the young ingenuous mind
> Pleas'd with extremes, and not the least with that
> Which makes the human Reason's naked self
> The object of its fervour. What delight!
> How glorious! in self-knowledge and self-rule,
> To look through all the frailties of the world,
> And, with resolute mastery shaking off
> The accidents of nature, time, and place,

> That make up the weak being of the past,
> Build social freedom on its only basis,
> The freedom of the individual mind,
> Which, to the blind restraints of general laws
> Superior, magisterially adopts
> One guide, the light of circumstances, flash'd
> Upon an independent intellect.

This great passage from a great work, *The Prelude*, reminds us that the mind has walked these cliffs before. It is itself—when taken in its full context—exemplary of that argument of values, that disciplined "discourse of the proof" to which I have referred. Marxism also has offered often to "abstract the hopes of man/Out of his feelings", and to fix them in the purer element of "science." And Stalinism was the empire, and theoretical practice is the vocabulary (with "moralism", "humanism", and human agency expelled from it in ignominy)—

> Where passions had the privilege to work
> And never hear the sound of their own names.

And Godwinism itself, which freaked out half the young intelligentsia in England between 1794 and 1798, was exactly such a moment of intellectual extremism, divorced from correlative action or actual social commitment, as we have seen in the last decade.

So, if we shift a digit around (1798/1978), we are in the same synchronic moment of structured time. But. . . the second time as farce. For those Godwinians, in the only moment when the English intelligentsia adopted, in their theory, an ultra-Jacobin posture, had some spirit about them. They questioned everything. They questioned Reason itself. Seconded by Wollstonecraft (who came less from a rationalist than from a Dissenting and Romantic tradition) they made the institution of marriage spin. They frightened everyone. They frightened their own culture into a premature Victorianism, before Victoria herself was born. They frightened, above all, themselves. Theoretical practice, however, can lay claim to only one achievement in this country. It has frightened Mr Julius Gould, who, in such matters, is well known to be an uncommonly nervous fellow. For the rest, it has been a diversion, a retreat into the privacy of a complacent internal discourse, a *dis*engagement from the actual political and intellectual contests of our time.

As for the Godwinian moment, and its tragic aftermath, I hope to tell that story another time.

xvi

We left our "post-Stalinist" reader, many pages back, enquiring: "Well? Did you identify the sources of Stalinism? Did you construct a better Theory?"

I hope that the answer to both questions has now become clear. Stalinism appeared to us, in those old days, less as a coherent theoretical system than as a mish-mash of repressive practices, dominative modes, hypocritical rhetoric, "wrong theories", Leninist forms and tactics derived from the necessities of illegal agitation and turned into universalist axioms, and all this bound together within the short-sighted opportunism of the reasons of Soviet State power. Stalinism as high Theory did not precede but followed after the fact.

If we wished to translate its practices into a consistent theoretical system, then we would design a Theory in which close empirical analysis of its practices was, as a matter of epistemological principle, disallowed ("empiricism"); in which any moral critique was utterly prohibited ("moralism"); in which the universal validity of Leninist forms (but of forms in an advanced state of bureaucratic degeneration) was assumed without examination (the characteristic theoretical short-circuit, the proletariat = the Party); in which a structuralist reductionism both guaranteed the fundamental health of the Soviet system in its supposedly socialist economic "basis" (thereby displacing all political, legal and cultural questions into secondary or tertiary areas) and disallowed any materialist historical analysis of this system ("historicism"); in which men and women were seen as the bearers of ineluctable structural determinations, in which their responsibility and historical agency was denied ("humanism"), and in which it was, hence, more easy to view them as "rotten elements" or things; and all this united within a notion of Theory both as enclosure and as "science", which Theory could be grasped in its essentials by the rigorous contemplation of texts written over one hundred years before the major historical experiences which it seeks to explain took place. In short, Althusserianism *is* Stalinism reduced to the paradigm of Theory. It is Stalinism at last, theorised as ideology.

Thus there is a sense in which we failed fully to identify Stalinism as Theory, because we were waiting upon Althusser for this theory to be invented. But we did, at least, identify essential components of this theory, in its characteristic idealist mode of thought (p. 140), and we never comforted ourselves with the apology that Stalinism represented only some unaccountable "rupture of theory and practice."[176] Moreover, we saw, very clearly, that from its particular matrix in Soviet history, Stalinism had entered deeply within the theory, practices, strategies and forms of the international Communist movement; and, further, that the complicity of orthodox Marxism in funding Stalinism with its vocabulary of apologetics—in proving itself to be pliant enough to provide the elements for the State

Ideology of the Soviet bureaucracy—entailed the strong probability that Marxism itself stood in need of radical scrutiny, and that it would never be adequate to ravel it up again into a better *system*.

This gave us an agenda, and it is hardly surprising that this agenda could not be completed in six or seven years—years of heightened political activity. This also gives an answer to the second question. It was exactly the notion of Marxism as a self-sufficient theoretical Sum which constituted the essence of the metaphysical heresy against reason, and which inhibited the active investigation of the world within the developing, provisional, and self-critical tradition of historical materialism. I have argued this sufficiently.

Althusserianism is only one, sophisticated, form of a number of "Marxisms" which pushed our unfinished agenda aside, and crowded into the minds of a section of the Western intelligentsia from the 1960s onwards. The case of Althusserianism is one of the simplest, since, as we have seen, it is a straightforward ideological police action. It constructs a theory which ensures not only that radical questions about Stalinism, Communist forms, and "Marxism" itself are not asked, but that they *cannot be asked*. If we take Althusser at his own self-evaluation—if we suppose him to be "innocent"—then we can only say that he has lost himself so far inside his own head that when he looks at the world he sees only the projection of his own concepts: the P.C.F. is embodied proletarian ideology, Stalinism in decomposition is "socialist humanism", the murder of a revolution's cadres is the dictatorship of the proletariat, the substantial gains over decades of the Western working classes are an index of their more intense exploitation. In a certain sense we can be charitable; there is a logic in all this; mechanical materialism ("economism") *must*, when every evidence from the real world disproves its theories, when every socialist expectation is abjectly falsified, stop up its ears and eyes, and pass abruptly into the delirium of idealism.

Not all the "Marxisms" have been of this wholly reactionary order. There have also been various Maoisms, Trotskyisms,[177] and innumerable Marxist academicisms. Most of these share, however, the same religious cast of thought, in which a Marxism is proposed as an ultimate system of truth: that is, a theology. All seek to put Marx back into the prison of Marx*ism*. Why there should have been this "epistemological break" from rationality to idealism, this rejection of the beginnings made in the 1950s and early 1960s, this reversion to an inner world of magical incantation and exalted theoretical illusion, this sealing off of the empirical senses, this self-closure of a tradition. . . this is a different problem, a problem of ideology and of the sociology of ideas which would require a distinct and extended treatment. I can now offer a few suggestions only.

Althusserianism is only one extreme form—and perhaps a passing form—of a general malaise, not of theory only, but of the political presence of today's Socialist movement. In marking off its characteristics *as ideology*, I intend to mark also certain features which it shares with other Marxisms of closure.

The ideology has arisen, and been replicated, not in the Soviet Union, but within an advanced intellectual culture in the West. Its characteristic location has been in universities and other educational institutes. The intellectual culture which it inhabits is itself marked, through the structuration of educational institutions and for other reasons, by a sharp division between "theory" and "practice." The radicalisation of intellectuals within these institutions is often a somewhat enclosed and autonomous process, with no direct correlation with other sectors of society. So far from all Communist Parties providing this missing correlation, certain of these (for example, the PCF) directly express, in their organisational forms, another kind of severance of "theory" from "practice"—the higher echelons of the Party apparatus are possessed of the "science" which guides the "militants" of the "base." The Party intellectuals are often further segregated, both within Paris (the intelligentsia's provincial ghetto) and within their own university branches.

Thus we commence with a *de facto* sociological and intellectual segregation of theory and practice. And, for larger political reasons, the kind of experience of mass political activity, in which intellectuals have played a minority and a subordinate (sometimes overly subordinate) part alongside comrades of diverse experience—and, in particular, alongside comrades with practical positions of leadership within their own communities and places of work—this kind of experience has largely passed them by. There has been no experience of anti-Fascist struggle, war and Resistance; not even any consistent and hard-fought programmatic or electoral struggle which intellectuals could bear to support; May, 1968 was over in a matter of days; such industrial struggles as the British miners' strike, which brought a government down, were accomplished without the necessity of any intellectual participation. Of course, here and there real struggles have flared up; and some comrades have gained authentic experience in the intense inner life of this or that sect. But in general it may be said that there has never been a generation of socialist intellectuals in the West with *less* experience of practical struggle, with less sense of the initiatives thrown up in mass movements, with less sense of what the intellectual can learn from men and women of practical experience, and of the proper dues of humility which the intellect must owe to this.

This is to say that today's Western Leftist intelligentsia is distinguished by its lack of political experience and judgement. But this is not offered in any sense as an accusation of sin. It is a necessary consequence of the determinations of our time. We cannot remedy it by wishing it was otherwise. But it provides, nevertheless, the necessary ground within which the ideological deformations of our time are nurtured. Isolated within intellectual enclaves, the drama of "theoretical practice" may become a *substitute* for more difficult practical engagements. Moreover, this drama can assume increasingly theatrical forms, a matter of grimaces and attitudinising, a game of "chicken", in which each theorist strives to be "more revolutionary than thou." Since no political *relations* are involved, and no steady, enduring struggle to communicate with and learn from a public which judges, cautiously, by actions rather than professions, the presses may reek with ideological terror and blood.

Moreover, this is precisely the ground which can nurture an *élitism* for which intellectuals, by a multitude of precedents, are only too well prepared. A generation indoctrinated by selective educational procedures to believe that their own specialised talents are a guarantee of superior worth and wisdom, are only too willing to accept the role offered to them by Althusser. It is easy for them to posture as "a very specific type of militant intellectual, a type unprecedented in many respects":

> These are real initiates, armed with the most authentic scientific and theoretical culture, forewarned of the crushing reality and manifold mechanisms of all forms of the ruling ideology and constantly on the watch for them, and able in their theoretical practice to borrow—against the stream of all 'accepted truths'—the fertile paths opened up by Marx and barred by all the reigning prejudices. (*F.M.* 24)

That Althusser should also predicate "an unshakeable and lucid confidence in the working class and direct participation in its struggles" can be easily met, either by taking out a Party card, or by hypothesising an ideal working class (for the present one is mystified into a false consciousness) which will be engendered in the image of Theory. For, as Althusser insists, "Marxist theory is produced by a specific theoretical practice, *outside* the proletariat", and "Marxist theory must be *'imported'* into the proletariat". (*R.C.* 141) Indeed, his whole account of Marx's "epistemological break" proposes that Theory was prior to and independent of the working-class movement's own self-discovery, and that, ever since, that movement has been acting out, however ineffectually, Theory's script.

What is so obvious is that this new *élitism* stands as direct successor in the old lineage: Benthamism, Coleridgean "clerisy", Fabianism, and Leavisism of the more arrogant variety. Once again, the intellectuals—a chosen band of these—have been given the task of enlightening the people. There is no mark more distinctive of Western Marxisms, nor more revealing as to their profoundly anti-democratic premises. Whether Frankfurt School or Althusser, they are marked by their very heavy emphasis upon the ineluctable weight of ideological modes of domination—domination which destroys every space for the initiative or creativity of the mass of the people—a domination from which only the enlightened minority of intellectuals can struggle free.[178] No doubt this ideological predisposition was itself nurtured within the terrible experiences of Fascism, of mass indoctrination by the media, and of Stalinism itself. But it is a sad premise from which Socialist theory should start (all men and women, except for us, are originally stupid) and one which is bound to lead on to pessimistic or authoritarian conclusions. Moreover, it is likely to reinforce the intellectual's disinclination to extend himself in practical political activity. To be sure, the (ideal) proletariat may, in this or that critical conjuncture, suddenly shift itself, like a geological fault, into a revolutionary posture, when it will be ready to receive the ministrations of Theory. Meanwhile, why bother to try to communicate—to educate, agitate, and organise—since the reason is powerless to penetrate the mists of "ideology"?

In this way, a "revolutionary" and "Marxist" critique, which despairs of communication and which has only a fictional political correlative, and which, moreover, reveals that all social evils are insoluble within capitalism, ends up as "the ideological husk of passivity", in which the proclaimed need for "revolution" becomes a licence for intellectual withdrawal. In this way, as Enzensberger has warned,

> Marxist theory. . . can become a false consciousness if, instead of being used for the methodical investigation of reality through theory and practice, it is misused as a defence against that very reality. . . Those who wish to deprive Marxism of its critical, subversive power and turn it into an affirmative doctrine, generally dig in behind a series of stereotyped statements which, in their abstraction, are as irrefutable as they are devoid of results.[179]

Althusserian theory has been perfectly adapted to this function, and designed for exactly this élitist intellectual *couche*. In particular, it allows the aspirant academic to engage in a harmless revolutionary psycho-drama, while at the same time pursuing a reputable and conventional intellectual career. As we have seen, every central theoretical position of Althusser is heavily derivative from orthodox bourgeois positions, in epistemology, structuralist sociology, &c. The dwarfing of human initiatives by ideologies and things is entirely consonant with the dominant common-sense of conservative disciplines. Moreover, as political theory—because of the denial of experience and the repudiation of empirical controls—the practice can lead to *anything*, and justify *everything;* in any "conjuncture" a political or ideological "instance" can be hypothesised as "dominant", and the "kangaroo factor" will carry it blithely from one prejudice to the next.

If this is all that Althusserianism is, as ideology—if it is no more than one of the successive fashions by which the revolting Western intelligentsia can do their thing without practical pain—then we have been wasting our time. But it is more serious than that. It is actively reinforcing and reproducing the effective passivity before "structure" which holds us all prisoners. It is enforcing the rupture between theory and practice. It is diverting good minds from active theoretical engagement. And, at a level of more vulgar political discourse, it affords theoretical legitimations for all the stupidest and most dangerous half-truths which, one had supposed, had at last gone away: that "morality = the interests of the working class", that "philosophy = class struggle", that "democratic rights and practices = 'liberal' ideology", and so on. Such a theory, if ever afforded any power, so far from "liberating" the working class would, in its insufferable arrogance and pretentions to "science", deliver them into the hands of a bureaucratic clerisy: the *next* ruling-class, waiting on the line.

This outcome seems unlikely. Most of those who have fallen under Althusserian influence are not cut out to be Stalinist priests. They are simply young men and women, who would *like* to be socialist revolutionaries, who have not found a medium of practical engagement, and hence have been taken for a ride. The terminus of that ride is outside the city of human endeavour and outside the domain of knowledge. So we can expect them to be absent from both. And yet, at the same time, we should not forget that this Theory is affording comfort and arguments to the most conservative elements within the most conservative Communist apparatuses. Like all ideologies, this one confirms the situation out of which it arose. In strengthening the extreme right-wing of the "Left", it reproduces that inertia and that paralysis of the socialist will which was its own precondition of existence.

I cannot say whether theoretical practice is being taken up within the State orthodoxies of the Soviet Union and of Eastern Europe. It is, I suspect, both too sophisticated and too undisguisedly Stalinist for that; after all, if Stalin were alive today, he would be the first to recognise that Stalin committed. . . errors. The ultimate dream of theoretical practice is the resuscitation of the duality of temporal and spiritual powers in medieval Christendom: the Holy Proletarian Emperor will make his pilgrimage to Theory's abode, where, after due interrogation in the doctrine, he will be crowned. This is not likely to come about. But a more sombre, and more conceivable, scenario comes to mind when one contemplates the situation in certain countries in the Third World. For Althusserianism is rather exactly tailored to the ideological requirements of an aspirant ruling-class— the *next* ruling-class to be—in societies where a section of the intelligentsia, greatly distanced from the masses, adopts policies which demand ruthless "modernization", Marxist and anti-imperialist rhetoric, contempt for democratic practices, and effective reliance on the economic and military protection of the Soviet State. If one considers for a moment the possible consequences if the Communist Party of India (one of the most unreconstructed Stalinist parties in the world) were to reinforce its existing anti-libertarian tendencies and contempt for the "petit-bourgeois" masses—tendencies amply displayed in its partnership in the recent

Emergency—with a dose of Althusserian arrogance; and if its largely bourgeois and intellectual upper cadres were to become theoretical practitioners; and if the opportunity to practice, not only in theory, but upon the body of India, should return—then we could expect nothing less than the re-enactment of the full repertoire of high Stalinism within the raging inferno of Indian "scarcity."[180]

But we may leave this to the good sense of our comrades in India or Latin America, who face, every day, problems more palpable and more exacting than our own, who cannot pretend to draw the blinds upon experience or to place their theory here and their practice over there. All the same, it would be good to talk about it, and to exchange experiences on the political problems which we have in common. It would be good if the authentic international dialogue of libertarian Communism could be resumed.

xvii

I will conclude, as is now obligatory, with an *auto-critique*.

Five years ago, in my "Open Letter to Leszek Kolakowski", I discussed several meanings of contemporary Marxisms, and concluded with a general notion of Marxism as Tradition. Within this "tradition" I saw an immense variety of discourse, and quite incompatible sub-traditions; but, nevertheless, I argued that (uncomfortable as such co-habitation may be) all were united in the sense of employing a common vocabulary of concepts, many of which derived from Engels and from Marx. I suggested that one must be resigned to the strenuous activity of continually defining one's position within this "tradition"; and that the only alternative was that of evacuating this tradition altogether—a choice which I refused. I preferred to remain within that tradition, even if some few of us remained only as "outlaws."

I can now see that this was an inadequate and evasive resolution. Politically, it has long been impossible for the Stalinist and anti-Stalinist positions to cohabit with each other. It is clear to me now, from my examination of Althusserianism—and my implicit critique of other related Marxisms—that we can no longer attach any theoretical meaning to the notion of a common tradition. For the gulf that has opened has not been between different accentuations to the vocabulary of concepts, between this analogy and that category, but between idealist and materialist modes of thought, between Marxism as closure and a tradition, derivative from Marx, of open investigation and critique. The first is a tradition of theology. The second is a tradition of active reason. Both can derive some licence from Marx, although the second has immeasurably the better credentials as to its lineage.

I must therefore state without equivocation that I can no longer speak of a single, common Marxist tradition. There are *two* traditions, whose bifurcation and disengagement from each other has been slow, and whose final declaration of irreconcilable antagonism was delayed—as an historical event—until 1956. From this point forward, it has been necessary, both within politics and within theory, to declare one's allegiance to one or the other. Between theology and reason there can be no room left for negotiation. Libertarian Communism, and the socialist and Labour movement in general, can have no business with theoretical practice except to expose it and drive it out.

If I thought that Althusserianism was the logical terminus of Marx's thought, then I could never be a Marxist. I would rather be a Christian (or hope to have the courage of a certain kind of Christian radical). At least I would then be given back a vocabulary within which value choices are allowed, and which permits the defence of the human personality against the invasions of the Unholy Capitalist or Holy Proletarian State. And if my disbelief, as well as my distaste for churches, disallowed this course, then I would have to settle for being an empirical, liberal, moralistic humanist.

But I refuse these spurious choices which theoretical practice (and allied Marxisms) seek to impose. And, instead, I declare unrelenting intellectual war against such Marxisms: and I do so from within a tradition one of whose major founders was Marx. There is a certain cant, which has long been about, which seeks to avoid this engagement under the slogan: "No enemies to the Left!" That slogan had a necessary and honourable origin, in the emergencies of anti-Fascist resistance; and, in political terms, such emergencies will often recur. But how is it possible to say that there are no such enemies, after the experience of high Stalinism, after Budapest 1956, after Prague 1968? And, within theory, what possible meaning is attached to "the Left" when it teaches lessons of anti-moralism, anti-humanism, and the closure of all the empirical apertures of reason? Could Marx, or Morris, or Mann, have recognised any of the theory or practice of Stalinism, and acknowledged these as having even a notional relation to "the Left"? Does the suppression of reason, and the obliteration of the imagination, have any place on "the Left"? Does the confiscation by an all-knowing, substitutionist Party or vanguard of the self-activity and means of self-expression and self-organisation of the working people, constitute the practice of a "Left"?

What the cant slogan does is simply erect a moralistic defence around orthodox Communist organisation and practices—defences supplemented by the "ideological terrorism" of Althusser—intended to impress any socialist critic with a sense of guilt, a breach of solidarity. Hence the *status quo* is inviolable; any socialist critique is illicit (or is evidence of malicious "bourgeois or Trotskyite slander"); and the only licit criticism must be within the slow and opportunistic procedures of the apparatus itself. Hence the fight against Stalinism as theory and as practice must be left for ever unresolved. And as a consequence we are constricted into a space within which we commit daily breaches of solidarity with our comrades who are striving to dismantle Stalinism and who suffer under the reasons of Communist power.

In declaring "war" in this way—and in asking that others declare themselves less equivocally—I do not make a simple equation: Stalinism = all Communist organisations and forms. I do not declare all Communism to be infected, and suffering a terminal illness. I do not reject necessary, and clear-eyed, political alliances with Communist movements. I do not ignore the honourable (and, indeed, democratic) elements in the record of Communist struggle, in the West and in the Third World. I do not doubt the courage and commitment of Communist cadres, in a hundred anti-imperialist and anti-capitalist struggles. I do not confuse Stalinism as theory, and as particular forms and practices, with the historical and sociological existence of Communist mass movements. I do not deny that, within the turn towards "Euro-Communism", genuine struggles over principle are involved, as well as opportunist adjustments to an electorate. I do not refuse to note the genuine concern—and the public registration of this concern—at aspects of Soviet reality which have been increasingly evident within "Euro-Communism" since the time of Prague, 1968. I do not dismiss all this as hypocrisy; it is a welcome and important indication of an ulterior shift, often imposed upon the leadership by their own militant "base". Above all, I expect, in the coming decades, fresh reinforcements for the war against Stalinism to arise—whether East or West—from within the Communist movements themselves. How these struggles will eventuate—and with what differences in Poland, Spain or Bengal—is a historical question, as to which theory would be foolish to predict.

What I mean is, rather, this. First, libertarian Communism, or a Socialism which is both democratic and revolutionary in its means, its strategy and objectives, must stand firmly, on an independent base, on its own feet, developing its own theoretical critique and, increasingly, its own political forms and practices. Only on these presuppositions can any "alliance" be negotiated; and if emergencies demand such an alliance, then it cannot be on orthodox Communism's usual imperative terms: that ulterior theoretical and strategic differences be obscured or silenced, in the interests of a "Broad Left" (whose interests are, in turn, ultimately those of the Party).

Second, the conditions for any common action must be a continuing and unequivocal critique of every aspect of the Stalinist legacy. Until the "agenda" of 1956 is completed, down to the last item of Any Other Business, any pretences as to the self-reform of Euro-Communism can rest only on the insecure pledges of electoral opportunism. The struggle must irradiate every level of theory and of practice—leading to radical changes in the forms of Communist Party organisation, and in the practical relations of Communists with other socialist bodies and with their own "constituencies"—and only on these preconditions, that common action *accelerates* such changes and *discloses* ulterior differences, can our purposes be served.

In Britain, with its small and declining Communist Party, these questions are of secondary importance. But, equally, the failure of the alternative, libertarian tradition, to enter that vacuum and establish itself as a political presence alongside the Labour movement—this failure is the more serious and less explicable. In the much-publicised "revival of Marxism" in Britain in the last two decades, a mountain of thought has not yet given birth to one political mouse. Enclosed within the intelligentsia's habitual élitism, the theorists disdain to enter into any kind of relation with a Labour movement which they know (on *a priori* grounds) to be "reformist" and "corporative", whose struggles created the institutions in which they are employed, whose labour made the chairs in which they sit, which manages to exist and to reproduce itself without them, and whose defensive pressures are all that stand between them and the reasons of capitalist power. Nor have these theorists created any independent agencies of political communication and education; the only agencies created are journals in which they can converse with each other. But this is to raise a new range of political questions, to be discussed on some other day.

I may sound more bitter than I am. I think there is, indeed, much energy and ability inside those barrels of enclosed Marxisms which stand, row upon row, in the corridors of Polytechnics and Universities. By striking a sharp and bitter blow at the Althusserian bungs, I hope I may let a little of that energy get out. If it should do so, then the problems of creating in this country an independent Left, engaged in a continual and fraternal dialogue of practice with the larger Labour movement, might not prove to be insuperable after all. Those massive and impassive "structures" of our time might prove to be more vulnerable to human agencies than the Marxisms suppose.

And if any minds should get out, I hope they will bring Marx with them. I hope they will not bring *only* Marx; and they must certainly rid themselves of the truly scholastic notion that the problems of our time (and the experiences of our century) will become understood by the rigorous scrutiny of a text published one hundred and twenty years ago. To return, in every motion of analysis, to propositions of Marx is like going on a cross-country run in leaden boots. William Morris expressed the matter with unerring sanity. "Tough as the job is you ought to read Marx", he advised a correspondent: "up to date he is the only completely scientific Economist on our side."[181]

As the assembled ranks of Marxists express their sense of scandal, or dissolve into laughter, I will continue my argument. It is not on the question of whether or not it is adequate to describe Marx as an "Economist." This was the Marx available to Morris; and, one might add, it is the Marx to which the man is reduced, in effect, by "mode of production" manipulators and by *Capital* navel-scrutinising groups. The point is, that *Marx is on our side; we are not on the side of Marx.* His is a voice whose power will never be silenced, but it has never been the only voice, and its discourse does not have limitless range. He did not invent the socialist movement, nor did socialist thought in some way fall into his sole possession or that of his legitimate heirs. He had little to say (by choice) as to socialist objectives, as to which Morris and others said more—and more that is pertinent today. In saying this little he forgot (and at times appeared to deny) that not only Socialism but *any* future made by men and women rests not only upon "science", or upon the determinations of necessity, but also upon choices of values, and the struggles to give these choices effect.

The choice which faces the Marxist tradition today, and which has long faced it, is that between idealist irrationalism and the operative and active reason. As for the Althusserians, they have long made that choice, and retired to the rituals of their own secluded observatory:

> As if an astronomical observatory should be made without any windows, and the astronomer within should arrange the starry universe solely by pen, ink and paper, so M. Althusser, in *his* Observatory (and there are many like it) had no need to cast an eye upon the teeming myriads of human beings around him, but could settle all their destinies on a slate, and wipe out all their tears with one dirty little bit of sponge.[182]

Maybe this observatory is already collapsing upon its rotten foundations. But other, more fashionable, more *avant-garde* observatories will be erected around its ruins. Before they are enclosed within some even more well-appointed "Marxism", I ask my readers also to choose.

I have now, on three occasions, beaten the bounds of "1956". No doubt my critics are right; the return to that moment in the past has been, with me, obsessional; "there have been few confessions of fossilization as sad as this."[183] At each defeat one should pick oneself up, brush the dust off one's knees, and march cheerily on with one's head in the air. But what if the defeat be total and abject, and call in question the rationality and good faith of the socialist project itself? And what if the protagonists within the socialist movement finally disengage at that point, and their absolute antagonism becomes declared? Can one then go on, head even higher in the air, just as before? I do not think so. But I promise not to mention the matter again. My dues to "1956" have now been paid in full. I may now, with a better conscience, return to my proper work and to my own garden. I will watch how things grow.

NOTES

This essay is a polemical political intervention and not an academic exercise, and I have not thought it necessary to document every assertion. The editions of Althusser's works which I cite in the text are: *Essays—Essays in Self-Criticism* (New Left Books, 1976); *F.M.—For Marx* (Vintage Books, 1970); *L. & P.—Lenin and Philosophy* (New Left Books, 1971); *P. & H.—Politics and History* (New Left Books, 1977); *R.C.—Reading Capital* (New Left Books, 1970); *C.W.—*Karl Marx, Frederick Engels, *Collected Works* (Lawrence & Wishart, in progress); *Grundrisse* (Pelican, 1973).

1. I tried to distinguish "empiricism" and an empirical "idiom" in "The Peculiarities of the English", *Socialist Register*, 1965, pp. 336-7. See below p. 273.
2. B. Hindess and P.Q. Hirst, *Pre-Capitalist Modes of Production* (London, 1975), pp. 310, 312.
3. I am indebted for this category to my friend, Rodney Hilton, although he is not responsible for the ways in which I use it.
4. See Hans Magnus Enzensberger, *Raids and Reconstructions* (Pluto Press, 1976), p. 296; and (discussing "a very dangerous form of internal exile") Raymond Williams, "Notes on Marxism in Britain since 1945", *New Left Review*, 100, November 1976—January 1977, p. 92.
5. See Leszek Kolakowski, "Althusser's Marx", *Socialist Register*, 1971, pp. 124-5; "The reader with an elementary knowledge of the history of philosophy will notice at once that what Althusser means by 'empiricism', could well be considered as the Aristotelian or Thomist theory of abstraction but that modern empiricism—beginning not with Locke but at least with fourteenth century nominalists—means exactly the opposite of this idea."
6. Only later (*L. & P.* 53) did Althusser make a *sotto voce* acknowledgement that Lenin's categories "may" have been "contaminated by his empiricist references (e.g. the category of reflection)."
7. It has of course since been so supposed, and in some quarters it still is: the opening chapters of Raymond Williams, *Marxism and Literature* (Oxford, 1977), are in one sense a sustained polemic against this supposition.
8. For the purposes of exposition in these pages, I leave aside the question of differential class experiences (and consequent ideological predispositions) which I discuss elsewhere.
9. The other two are mathematics—acclaimed, but not drawn upon—and psychoanalysis, from which certain concepts are confiscated in a most arbitrary way.
10. The influence, scarcely acknowledged in *F.M.* (although see p. 78, note 40), is more pronounced in *R.C.* (p. 102: "Spinoza's philosophy introduced probably the greatest philosophical revolution of all time"), and fully declared in *Essays*, pp. 104, 132-141, 187, 190. See the helpful comments of Perry Anderson, *Considerations on Western Marxism* (New Left Books, 1976) pp. 64-65, 85.
11. See the opaque footnote in *F.M.* pp. 184-185.
12. Althusser follows Bachelard's notion of a science which is constituted by an "epistemological break" with its "ideological" prehistory. Both *F.M.* (see pp. 167-8) and *R.C.* see post-1846 Marxism as constituting a Science ("Theory") in this way. In his subsequent self-criticism, Althusser takes away this notion with his left hand and then returns it (by way of the Party) with his right: *Essays*, pp. 107-125.

13. For an excellent demonstration of the incompatibility of Althusser's method with that of Marx, see Derek Sayer, "Science as Critique: Marx versus Althusser", in J. Mepham and D. Rubin (eds.), *Essays in Marxist Philosophy* (Harvester, 1978). I have found this essay helpful throughout, and also the lucid and thorough study by Simon Clarke, "Althusserian Marxism", an important study as yet unpublished (copies obtainable from the author, Dept. of Sociology, University of Warwick).

14. As defined in the Glossary to *R.C.* (p. 322) prepared by Ben Brewster and approved by Althusser.

15. See note 12 above. The emphasis in *R.C.* (pp. 59-60 and other passages) is such as to suggest that experiment and "other practices" (while perhaps permissible in the natural sciences) are evidence as to a science's prehistory.

16. See my essay on "Caudwell", *Socialist Register,* 1977, p. 241.

17. Marc Bloch, *The Historian's Craft* (Manchester, 1954), p. 58.

18. Lucien Goldmann, *The Human Sciences and Philosophy* (London, 1969), pp. 42-43.

19. The reasons for this congruence lie in the ulterior congruence of Althusserian and positivist epistemology. This was argued long ago, in a forcible polemic by Paul Piccone, "Structuralist Marxism?", *Radical America,* III, no. 5, September, 1969, which concluded: "Althusser is not aware of the history of recent positivism so that he does not realize that he has unwittingly appropriated their entire discarded problematic" (pp. 27-28). For an exact correspondence with Althusser's propositions, see M. Oakeshott, *Experience and its Modes* (Cambridge, 1933), p. 168. For a resumé of the congruence, see H. Gilliam, "The Dialectics of Realism and Idealism in Modern Historiographic Theory", *History and Theory,* XV, 3, 1976.

20. K.R. Popper, *The Open Society and its Enemies* (1962 edn.) II, pp. 265-8.

21. Hindess and Hirst follow the same positivist premises even more slavishly: see pp. 2-3, 310, 311.

22. Popper, op. cit., II, p. 270. Compare Hindess and Hirst, p. 311.

23. Francis Bacon, *Of the Advancement of Learning* (Everyman edition), p. 132.

24. By 1969 Althusser had narrowed the fully-approved texts to two: the *Critique of the Gotha Programme* (1875) and the *Marginal Notes on Wagner's 'Lehrbuch der politischen Okonomie'* (1880): these alone "are *totally and definitively exempt* from *any* trace of Hegelian influence" (*L. & P.* 90). See also François George, "Lire Althusser", *Les temps modernes* (May, 1969).

25. See my "Open Letter to Leszek Kolakowski", *Socialist Register,* 1973, pp. 18-33.

26. As for example, the chapter, "Exploitation", in *The Making of the English Working Class.*

27. But this is too generous, since Althusser's "definition" of empiricism is so slovenly and unlocated, on one hand, and so all-embracing ("rationalist", "sensualist", and "Hegelian thought") on the other, as to leave us with only an epithet to attach to any views which he dislikes. See *R.C.* pp. 35-36.

28. One may take heart from the principled criticism which (after a little delay) American historians visited upon Fogel and Engerman's *Time on the Cross.* The French historical profession (to judge by *Annales E.S.C.* in recent years) has not always offered the same principled defence against the universalist claims of the computer.

29. In its secondary form it is the accepted "findings" or accumulating knowledge of historians, which is (or ought to be) passed under continuous critical review.

30. Alasdair MacIntyre, "Breaking the Chains of Reason", in *Out of Apathy* (London, 1960), pp. 219-220.

31. Popper's objections to the "predictive" character of certain notions of historical "laws" have force, and are stubbornly argued. Althusser would benefit from reading them.

32. In a blistering chapter ("The Need for a Philosophy of History") in his *Autobiography*, R.G. Collingwood exposed exactly these confusions. "It was clear to me that any philosopher who offered a theory of 'scientific method', without being in a position to offer a theory of historical method, was defrauding his public by supporting his world on an elephant and hoping that nobody would ask what kept the elephant up" (Pelican, 1944; p. 61).

33. MacIntyre, op. cit., p. 234.

34. See note 15. The argument is little more than a gesture towards a particular French tradition of epistemology and idealist structuralism: Bachelard, Cavaillès, Canguilhem and Foucault. See Simon Clarke, "Althusserian Marxism", Part III, section 1, and *R.C.* 43-46. It is significant that the only historian commended by Althusser is Foucault, his former pupil, who in his earlier work (work dominated by the concept of the "episteme"), also gives us history as a subject-less structure, and one in which men and women are obliterated by ideologies.

35. "Sartre Aujourd'hui", *l'Arc*, no. 30, translated in *Telos*, 9 (1971), pp. 110-116.

36. One part of this claim has come from authentic efforts to establish "scientific" procedures of investigation (quantitative, demographic, &c.); the other part has stemmed from academic humbug, as "social scientists" have sought to maintain parity with scientific colleagues within educational structures (and in the face of grant-awarding bodies) dominated by utilitarian criteria. The older, "amateurish", notion of History as a disciplined "Humanity" was always more exact.

37. J.H. Hexter's "reality rule"—"the most likely story that can be sustained by the relevant existing evidence"—is, in itself, a helpful one. Unfortunately it has been put to work by its author in increasingly unhelpful ways, in support of a prior assumption that *any* "Marxist" story *must* be unlikely.

38. For a prime example of this misunderstanding, see Hindess and Hirst, op. cit., p. 312.

39. This does not mean that "history" may be seen *only* as process. In our time historians—and certainly Marxist historians—have selected process (and attendant questions of relationship and causation) as the supreme object of enquiry. There are other legitimate ways of interrogating the evidence.

40. Leszek Kolakowski, "Historical Understanding and the Intelligibility of History", *Tri-Quarterly*, 22, Fall 1971, pp. 103-117. I have offered a qualification to this argument in my "Open Letter to Kolakowski."

41. See Sartre's interesting distinction between the "notion" and the "concept", cited above, p. 110. But, notwithstanding this, I will continue to use both.

42. By "concepts" (or notions) I mean general categories—of class, ideology, the nation-state, feudalism, &c., or specific historical forms and sequences, as crisis of subsistence, familial development cycle, &c.—and by "hypotheses" I mean the conceptual organisation of the evidence to explain particular episodes of causation and relationship.

43. One helpful elucidation of these procedures is in E.J. Hobsbawm, "Karl Marx's Contribution to Historiography", in R. Blackburn (ed.), *Ideology in Social Science* (1972).

44. For which we are particularly indebted to French historical demography.

45. I have recently re-stated my position in "Eighteenth-Century English Society: Class Struggle without Class?", *Social History,* III, no. 2 (May, 1978). See also E.J. Hobsbawm, "Class Consciousness in History", in I. Meszaros (ed.), *Aspects of History and Class Consciousness* (1971), and C. Castoriadis,"On the History of the Workers' Movement", *Telos,* 30, Winter 1976-77.

46. Such static "models" may of course play a useful part in certain kinds of investigation.

47. The problem of "gaps" in the evidence as to ancient societies is discussed in M.I. Finley, *The Use and Abuse of History* (1971), pp. 69-71.

48. See Raymond Williams, *Marxism and Literature,* and the important chapter on "Determination".

49. *F.M.,* pp. 117-28, discussed above, pp. 86-8.

50. Cf. Anon., *The Making of the English Working Class,* p. 11: "Class is defined by men as they live their own history, and, in the end, this is its only definition."

51. *Capital* (1938), p. xviii.

52. It is significant that Althusser passes over the most serious epistemological error of Engels ("reflection theory") without any critique. For critique would have involved him in (a) a consideration of the whole problem of "dialogue", (b) in a consequent critique of Lenin (see note 6), and (c) in a self-critique which must have led on to a self-destruct, since his own epistemology (with Generalities I arising unbidden and unexamined) is a kind of "theoreticist" reflection-theory, reproduced in idealist form.

53. *Grundrisse,* p. 461.

54. Book I of *Capital* ("Capitalist Production") of course appeared in advance of Books II and III, and was sub-titled, in the English edition edited by Engels, "A Critical Analysis of Capitalist Production."

55. When I made this self-evident point in 1965 I was sternly rebuked for my "incredibly impoverished vision of Marx's work": Perry Anderson, "Socialism and Pseudo-Empiricism", *New Left Review,* 35 (January-February 1966), p. 21. I had not then read the *Grundrisse.* The point is surely now established beyond any reach of argument?

56. Marx to Lassalle, 22 February 1858: "The thing makes very slow progress because as soon as one tries to come to a final reckoning with questions which one has made the chief object of one's studies for years, they are always revealing new aspects and demanding fresh consideration." (*Selected Correspondence,* p. 224). But seven years before Marx had assured Engels that "in five weeks I will be through with the whole economic shit." He would then throw himself "into a new science. . . I am beginning to be tired of it." Cited in David McLellan, *Karl Marx, His Life and Thought* (1973), p. 283.

57. I am of course aware that this is a contentious area in which a hundred books and theses have been deployed. I am only reporting my own considered conclusion. Althusser also sees *Capital* as a work of Political Economy (Marxist Science), although he sees this as a merit: "the theory of Political Economy, of which *Capital* is an example. . . considers one relatively autonomous component of the social totality" (*R.C.* 109). He also allows that, if chapter one of *Capital* is not read in *his* sense, it would be "an essentially Hegelian work" (*R.C.* 125-126). He repeatedly insists that the object of *Capital* is neither theory nor social formations, but the capitalist mode of production (e.g. *L. & P.* 76, cited above p. 23; *P. & H.,* p. 186). Colletti sees the problem (Is Marx making a critique of *bourgeois* Political Economy, or is he criticising Political Economy as such?) as remaining un-

resolved: "Interview", *New Left Review*, 86 (July-August 1974), pp. 17-18; Castoriadis, examining much the same problem, flatly concludes that Marxist economic theory is untenable: "Interview", *Telos*, 23 (1975) esp. pp. 143-149.

58. *Grundrisse*, p. 459. My italics.

59. *C.W.* I, p. 510.

60. *Grundrisse*, p. 276. Roman Rosdolsky, *The Making of Marx's 'Capital'* (London, 1977) has made a definitive analysis of the Hegelian structure of the *Grundrisse* and of the central status of the concept of "capital in general", a status which remains central in *Capital*. The question arises throughout, but see especially pp. 41-52, 367-8, and his correct emphasis (p. 493) that "the model of a pure capitalist society in Marx's work. . . represented a heuristic device, intended to help in the illustration of the developmental tendencies of the capitalist mode of production, free from 'all disturbing accompanying circumstances.'" See also I.I. Rubin, *Essays on Marx's Theory of Value* (Detroit, 1972), p. 117.

61. *Ibid.*, p. 278. Such passages are licences for Althusser's view of history as a "process without a subject."

62. *Ibid.*, p. 101. There is of course now an immense literature on the Hegel-Marx relationship. Althusser's attempt to deny the Hegelian influence upon *Capital* has not survived it. For my purposes I wish to stress the strong and continuing Hegelian influence in these critical years: for 1857-8, see McLellan, op. cit., p. 304; for circa 1861-2 see "Marx's Précis of Hegel's Doctrine of Being in the Minor Logic", *International Review of Social History*, XXII, 3, 1977; and also T. Carver, "Marx and Hegel's *Logic*", *Political Studies*, XXII, 1976, and Rosdolsky, op. cit., passim.

63. See e.g. Anderson, "Socialism and Pseudo-Empiricism", pp. 19-21.

64. When Gareth Stedman Jones, "Engels and the End of Classical German Philosophy", *New Left Review*, 79, (May-June 1973), refers (p. 25) to "the Darwinist laws of evolution", it is not clear to me which *laws* are being referred to; although it is true that Engels, in *Dialectics of Nature*, saw evolutionary process as exemplifying dialectical laws: as Darwin did not.

65. *Selected Correspondence*, pp. 125-126. My italics. Engels had previously written to Marx that Darwin had "finished off" teleology, and spoke of his "magnificent attempt. . . to demonstrate historical development in nature."

66. *Ibid.*, p. 198. McLellan, for some reason, renders Marx's "death-blow" to teleology as a blow to "*religious* teleology" (which Marx does *not* say). But he also usefully documents Marx's subsequent criticisms of Darwin, pp. 423-24. These vary from comments on the ideological intrusion of notions of competition ("Hobbes's 'bellum omnium contra omnes'") to the (very different) complaint that "in Darwin progress is merely accidental." Lawrence Krader is the only authority known to me who has made a scholarly and exact definition of the point at issue: "The opposite of a teleological, directed law of nature and man attracted Marx to the conceptions of Darwin": see *The Ethnological Notebooks of Karl Marx* (Assen, 1974), esp. pp. 82-85, also pp. 2, 354-355, 392-393. While Engels certainly employed more un-considered analogies between natural evolution and historical process than did Marx, the attempt of many recent Marxologists to dissociate Marx from their common admiration of Darwin is absurd.

67. See Gerratana's helpful (but over-reverent) essay, "Marx and Darwin", *New Left Review*, 82 (November-December 1973), pp. 79-80. However, the supposition that Marx had wished to dedicate a volume of *Capital* to Darwin has now been shown to be in error. (Darwin's correspondent, on that occasion,

was Edward Aveling.) See Margaret A. Fay, "Did Marx offer to dedicate *Capital* to Darwin?", *Journal of History of Ideas*, XXXIX, January-March, 1978; and *Annals of Science*, XXXIII, 1976.

68.   Thus Marx's reminder to himself, at one point in the *Grundrisse*, "to correct the idealist manner of this analysis."

69.   Nicolaus (*Grundrisse*, p. 60) follows Rosdolsky here. Since Rosdolsky's work has been acclaimed in some quarters as definitive, it is necessary to make a critical comment on his very serious and scrupulous study. His discussion of the whole question of the historical dimension of *Capital* is confined to one footnote (p. 25, note 56), dismissive of the phrase "turn everything round", and to brief discussions of primitive accumulation in which Marx's historical and empirical analyses are commended for "liveliness and persuasiveness" (p. 61) but scarcely considered further. In short, Rosdolsky shows little interest in historical materialism, sees the Hegelian structure ("capital in general") of *Capital* as always a merit, and hence does less than justice to critics (including Marxist critics): notably to Rosa Luxembourg. I am not competent to comment on Rosdolsky's status as an economic theorist; but one must regret that he can see *Capital* only as a heuristic academic exercise in economic theory, that his study contains *no* discussion of Darwin or of the intellectual and political context more generally. In short, it is a serious but profoundly ahistorical work.

70.   As Rosa Luxembourg wrote in a private letter from prison: "the famed Volume I of *Capital* with its Hegelian Rococo ornamentation is quite abhorrent to me": *Briefe an Freunde*, p. 85, cited Rosdolsky, pp. 492-3. As Althusser exalts exactly these "Rococo" elements into "Science" I find myself coming to share Luxembourg's abhorrence of them.

71.   Thus Balibar (*R.C.*, p. 202) declares that *Capital* sets the "hypothesis" of historical materialism to work "and *verifies* it against the example of the capitalist social formation." A good example of Balibar's general nonsense. A historical hypothesis could only be "verified" in historical investigation: and (as he and Althusser repeat *ad nauseam*) *Capital's* object is the capitalist mode of production and not "the capitalist social formation."

72.   The "historical" chapters of *Capital* have inevitably had a stronger formative influence upon the British tradition of Marxist historiography than that of any other country; and for the same reason, a slavish adoption of Marx's hypotheses was replaced fairly early by a critical apprenticeship to them. An interesting case is the suggestive final chapter of Volume One on "Primitive Accumulation", which raised questions which were re-examined by M.H. Dobb, *Studies in the Development of Capitalism* (1946), which in turn gave rise to controversies which are resumed and discussed by John Saville, *Socialist Register*, 1969. But Saville's discussion leaves open areas (accumulation through "colonial plunder") which are being re-opened from several directions (Wallerstein, Perry Anderson, and Indian Marxist historians such as Irfan Habib), who demand renewed attention to Britain's imperial and colonial role. The point is that they are those hypotheses of Marx which are most alive which continue to undergo interrogation and revision.

73.   Marx was himself, on occasion, careful to indicate the limits of this structure. Thus *Capital*, Volume Three (Chicago, 1909), p. 37, commences by speaking of "the life circle of capital", and characterises Volume One as an analysis of the capitalist productive process "without regard to any secondary influences of conditions outside it." On p. 968: ". . . the actual movements of competition belong outside of our plan. . . because we have to present only the internal organization of the capitalist mode of production, as it were, in its ideal average." And so on. On other occasions he was less careful.

74. Ben Fine and Laurence Harris, "Controversial Issues in Marxist Economic Theory", *Socialist Register*, 1976, p. 141.

75. One must also note Sebastiano Timpanaro's defence of Engels, *On Materialism* (New Left Books, 1976).

76. In any case, the positivist credentials of the natural sciences have themselves long been at the centre of controversy—a controversy which Caudwell anticipated in *The Crisis in Physics* and in *Further Studies in a Dying Culture.*

77. In my *William Morris, Romantic to Revolutionary* (Merlin Books, revised edition, 1977).

78. See E.J. Hobsbawm, "From Social History to the History of Society", *Daedalus*, 100 (1971), esp. pp. 31-32.

79. Walter Benjamin, *Illuminations* (Fontana, 1973), p. 260.

80. I have challenged this notation in the Postscript to my revised *William Morris.* It is also challenged, in even wider terms, by M.-H. Abensour, "Les Formes de L'Utopie Socialiste-Communiste" (thèse pour le Doctorat d'Etat en Science politique, Paris, 1973).

81. One characteristic of "1956" was the resurgence among Communist "revisionists" of a voluntarist vocabulary—notably Poland, Hungary, but also throughout the world movement. The various oppositions of 1956 were often led by militants whose sensibility had been formed in the decade 1936-46. A similar expression of "rebellion against fact" was evinced in the British Campaign for Nuclear Disarmament. It is obligatory today to deplore the supposed "moralism" of this movement, although that "moralism" did more to exert a presence and to shift the terms of politics in this country than has anything in the fifteen subsequent years of Marxist "revival."

82. I have discussed this phenomenon in "Outside the Whale", *Out of Apathy* (1960): see below, pp. 211-43.

83. Neil J. Smelser, *Social Change in the Industrial Revolution* (1959), p. 180.

84. Ibid., pp. 11, 16, et passim.

85. In its less pretentious chapters, Smelser's book did raise interesting questions as to the changing inter-relations between the organisation of work in the cotton industry and the family structure of the operatives.

86. In view of Alvin Gouldner's analysis of the genesis of Parsonian structuralism (*The Coming Crisis in Western Sociology*) I should make it clear that I do not mean that this thought was genetically the product of Cold War stasis: Gouldner is clearly right to place the critical experiential matrix in an earlier context. I mean that the ascendancy of Parsonianism as *ideology*, with massive academic and institutional support, was so.

87. J.V. Stalin, *Marxism and Linguistics* (1950), reprinted in Bruce Franklin (ed.), *The Essential Stalin*, (1973), pp. 407-409, 411.

88. There is another reverent reference to Stalin on linguistics in *R.C.* 133.

89. *Essays*, 125 et passim. See also the Preface to the Italian edition of *R.C.* Ardent theoretical practitioners suppose that Althusser's "self-criticisms" remove all possible difficulties in *F.M.* and *R.C.* While I have noted these criticisms, they are either (a) marginal and so qualified as to constitute rhetorical (rather than intellectual) negotiations, or (b) so large that, if taken seriously, they call in question the earlier work *in toto*. We are thus entitled to take *F.M.* and *R.C.* as the most elaborated and most influential part of the Althusserian corpus. The subsequent writings are, generally, brutalised versions of the earlier, and are largely to be distinguished by the "militant" and "revolutionary" posturing demanded by his Office as the leading philosopher of the P.C.F.

90. M.H. Fisch and T.G. Bergin (eds.), *The Autobiography of Giambattista Vico* (New York, 1944), p. 171.

91. G. Vico, *The New Science* (New York, 1948), passim, esp. paras 141, 347, 161, 349.

92. I say the objections may be upheld only "sometimes", since on some occasions, when the isolates of economic theory are in question, the notion is valid, and on other occasions it can be seen that "law" is being used metaphorically, as "logic", direction, or tendency. But this cannot excuse Marx's references, as in his first Preface to *Capital*, to "the natural laws of capitalist production... tendencies working with iron necessity towards inevitable results." How is it possible for Marxist "scholars" to *then* accuse Engels of "positivism" and to exonerate Marx of all blame?

93. "An Open Letter to Leszek Kolakowski", below, p. 330.

94. *The New Science*, p. 382 (para. 1108).

95. *F.M.*, pp. 117-128.

96. Thus he commences his "reading" (*F.M.* 117-118) by making a wholly unwarranted translation of Engels's *"accidents"* into "superstructures"!! (See *Selected Correspondence*, p. 475.)

97. Engels uses the same paradigm of individuals/history in the analogous passage of *Ludwig Feuerbach* (Martin Lawrence, n.d.), p. 58.

98. William Morris, *The Dream of John Ball* (1886).

99. See my "Letter to Kolakowski", below, pp. 341-65.

100. This was dealt with by P. Vilar, "Histoire marxiste, histoire en construction. Essai de dialogue avec Althusser", *Annales E.S.C.*, 1973, englished in *New Left Review*, 80 (July-August 1973). I must say that (these comments apart) I found Vilar's rejoinder to be altogether too deferential.

101. See Kolakowski, "Althusser's Marx", p. 127: "Althusser often formulates a general statement and then quotes it later and then refers to it by saying 'we showed' or 'it was proved.' "

102. *Telos*, 9 (1971), p. 110.

103. "Determination" does not even appear in the "Glossary" to *F.M.* and *R.C.* although "overdetermination" does!

104. See my *Whigs and Hunters* (1976), esp. the final section.

105. Sartre, op. cit., p. 112.

106. Hindess and Hirst at least notice this (*Pre-Capitalist Modes of Production*, chapter 6), and offer alternative verbal arrangements. But since their productions are manufactured from an even more rarefied air—a scholasticism parasitic upon a scholasticism—we need follow them no further.

107. See McLellan, op. cit., p. 437.

108. I notice that I use it myself in "Peculiarities of the English", below, p. 295.

109. See Raymond Williams, *Culture and Society*, Conclusion, and *Keywords* (1976): "In most of its uses *masses* is a cant word..." This is certainly true of Althusser's use in his polemic with Lewis.

110. *Essays*, pp. 49-50. For a restatement of my own views, see note 45 above.

111. See the pertinent comments of Raoul Makarius on Lévi-Strauss in "Structuralism—Science or Ideology?", *Socialist Register*, 1974.

112. Sartre, op. cit., p. 114.

113. Raymond Williams, *Marxism and Literature* ("Determination") and also *Keywords*, pp. 87-91.

114. *Marxism and Literature*, pp. 80-81.

115. Engels, review of Marx's *Critique of Political Economy*, in *Selected Works*, I, pp. 370-1.

116. As far as I am concerned, Jeff Coulter's excellent study, "Marxism and the Engels Paradox", *Socialist Register*, 1971, settles that question. The logical critique of Engels's *Naturdialektik* is, as far as it goes, sound; and it has been resumed, in somewhat similar ways, by K. Popper, "What is Dialectic?",

Conjectures and Refutations (1963), by Colletti in *Marxism and Hegel,* and by G. Stedman Jones, "Engels and the End of Classical German Philosophy", *New Left Review* (May-June 1973)—which follows Colletti. But all then throw out the baby ("the conscious interception of the object in its process of development") along with the Hegelian bathwater: see Coulter, pp. 129-132, 137-141.

117. Cited in *Grundrisse,* p. 60.

118. I am not competent to say whether Zeeman's "catastrophe theory" in mathematics (the first cousin to logic) affords a new point of entry into the problem.

119. Althusser's distrust of dialectics follows, once again, contemporary fashion; as Coulter remarks (p. 143, citing G. Pask, *An Approach to Cybernetics* 1963), cybernetic considerations have prevailed over notions of "dialectical leap", especially in those disciplines concerned with "structures with finite variables entering into definable states of internal organization": i.e. structuralisms.

120. *Selected Correspondence,* p. 475. I don't know how Althusser gets *factor* out of *element ("Moment")* (since I haven't checked back on French translations), but it consorts well with his antique factoral notion of history: *F.M.* 111-2; Althusser, *Pour Marx* (Paris, 1966), p. 111: "La production est le facteur déterminant, &c."

121. N. Poulantzas, *Political Power and Social Classes* (New Left Books, 1973), pp. 13-15.

122. A. Glucksmann, "A Ventriloquist Structuralism", *New Left Review,* 72 (March-April 1972), originally published in *Les temps modernes,* 1967.

123. I have discussed the experiential basis of these beliefs in *The Making of the English Working Class,* chapter 16, sections 3 & 4.

124. But only *in this sense.* It is in the context of this polemic that Marx's famous epigram arises ("The hand-mill gives you society with the feudal lord; the steam-mill, society with the industrial capitalist": *C.W.* VI, 166)—an aphorism which has been taken as licence for technological determinism: the productive forces "give you" society (Stalin—but also, in the last instance, Althusser, Balibar, Poulantzas). But the proposition can only be understood as a counter-proposition to Proudhon, for whom the division of labour proceeds from the idea ("I propose") in a rational serial to the workshop and thence to the machines: see esp. *C.W.* VI, pp. 178-190 and *Selected Correspondence,* p. 10 (this whole letter to Annenkov in 1846 is a superb summary of *The Poverty of Philosophy*).

125. See *Essays,* p. 124 note 8: where Althusser bets on Lewis's "weakness for Jean-Paul Sartre." But maybe this was not a joke: perhaps Althusser is one of those who believes that no Englishman could get *any* ideas, however bad, unless from a French philosopher.

126. "The Great Moral Muddle", *Modern Quarterly,* I, 4 (Autumn, 1946); "Marxism and Ethics", ibid., V, 3 (Summer 1950); "The Moral Complexion of Our People", VI, 1 (Winter, 1950-1); "Science and Religion", VIII, 4 (Autumn, 1953).

127. Arnold Kettle, "Rebels and Causes", *Marxism Today,* March 1958.

128. In the Glossary to the English edition of *R.C.,* which suggests that "the *ideology* of a socialist society may be... a proletarian 'class humanism'," Althusser condescends to interpolate a proviso: "an expression I obviously use in a provisional, half-critical sense." p. 314.

129. I shall republish a revised and shortened version of this in *Reasoning,* Vol. II.

130. *New Reasoner,* 7 (Winter 1958-9), pp. 143-148.

131. V. Ozerov, "About Proletarian Humanism and Abstract Moralizing", *Novy Mir,* 6, 1958, extracted in *New Reasoner,* 9, (Summer 1959), pp. 147-8.

132. Anon., *The German Ideology*.

133. In return, the Central Committee of the P.C.F. passed in 1966, a special proviso permitting Party philosophers to publish their work without Party supervision.

134. I have not attempted to sketch the full and complex history. An early consequence of Althusserian influence was expressed in a Maoist freak-out among his student following; then Althusser's conservative posture during the May events, 1968, led to secessions and Althusserian heresies. And so on. These bits of theatre were predictable. Some part of the story is to be found in the lively apostasies of Jacques Rancière, *La leçon d'Althusser* (Gallimard, 1974); Rancière, "On the theory of Ideology", *Radical Philosophy*, 7 (Spring 1974); and in Simon Clarke, "Althusserian Marxism."

135. In the Introduction to *Reasoning*, Volume II.

136. See Althusser's introduction to Dominique Lecourt, *The Case of Lysenko*, (New Left Books, 1977).

137. In *Essays*, p. 77, Althusser went so far as to write that "the national mass movement of the Czech people. . . merits the respect and support of all Communists", exactly as "the 'humanist' philosophies of western intellectuals (at ease in their academic chairs or wherever)" merited their criticism. Where, then, has Althusser been sitting, these last few years? And why should the same phenomenon merit the respect of Communists, but (if "Marxist humanists" should respect it) it must call for criticism?

138. Peter Fryer, "Lenin as Philosopher", *Labour Review*, September-October, 1957.

139. By 1975, when, in a curious piece of theatre, Althusser defended his doctoral "thesis" at Amiens, his language, as reported in *Le Monde*, had become even uglier: "I would never have written anything were it not for the 20th Congress and Khruschev's critique of Stalinism and the subsequent liberalisation. . . My target was therefore clear: these humanist ravings, these feeble dissertations on liberty, labour or alienation which were the effects of all this among French Party intellectuals": *Radical Philosophy*, 12 (Winter 1975).

140. "Through the Smoke of Budapest", *The Reasoner*, 3 (November 1956), reprinted in part in David Widgery, *The Left in Britain* (Penguin, 1976), pp. 66-72.

141. "Socialist Humanism", *New Reasoner*, 1 (Summer 1957), p. 107.

142. Ibid., p. 137.

143. It is the more surprising that anthropological work of vitality and originality has emerged from within the sphere of Althusserian influence. Possibly Althusser's ambiguous redefinition of the "economic" (see p. 146) gave back to French Marxist anthropologists a little space for movement. It must also be remembered that anthropology finds it easier to co-habit with a structuralism than does history. In any event, Godelier at least has fought his way stubbornly out of the orrery; and he *knows why*.

144. Thus John Mepham, "Who Makes History?", *Radical Philosophy*, 6 (Winter 1973) declares that, if you suppose that "men make history", then "you would need to know their subjective states, beliefs, attitudes, prejudices, etc. This is how Political Economy thought about men. And also empiricist philosophy, utilitarianism etc." So why did Dickens create Mr. Gradgrind?

145. *Capital*, III (1909), pp. 102-103.

146. *Capital*, I (1938), p. xix. My italics.

147. Among others who have drawn attention to the coincidence between Althusserian thought and structural-functionalism are Dale Tomich in

Radical America, III, 5 (1969) and IV, 6 (1970); Simon Clarke, "Marxism, Sociology and Poulantzas' Theory of the State", Capital and Class (Summer 1977).

148. These (Lacanian) notions are found, in their most ridiculous version, in L. & P., pp. 160-170, in the theory of ideological interpellation. More recently, Ernesto Laclau (Politics and Ideology in Marxist Theory, New Left Books, 1977, chapters 3 & 4), has sought to put this fairy-story to use. That Laclau occasionally appears to be more sensible than Althusser does not arise from any improvement in "theory" but from the fact that he starts off with rather more information about the real world. No doubt he will be embarrassed by this accusation—since he tells us that "modern epistemology asserts" (!!!) that "the 'concrete facts' are produced by the theory or problematic itself" (p. 59)—but in fact he does know a little about Fascism, Populism, &c. He remains a kangaroo, but one who settles for longer periods and sniffs the real grass before he bounds off into the theoretical elements.

149. In case it should be supposed that this term has élitist connotations, I must note that it is a social category to be found thickest on the ground in Oxford, Cambridge, Paris, London, &c.

150. Marx's sixth thesis on Feuerbach declared that "the human essence is no abstraction inherent in each single individual. In its reality it is the ensemble of the social relations." Mepham (see note 144) reports that "Marx's formulation" was that "men are 'ensembles of social relations' "! How is one to keep up with mis-readings of this order?

151. This is discussed by (among others) Norman Geras, "Althusserian Marxism", New Left Review, 71 (January-February, 1971); Geras, "Marx and the Critique of Political Economy", in Ideology and Social Science.

152. It is true that Marx sometimes appears to gesture towards a larger claim, notably in chapter XLVIII of Capital, III ("The Trinitarian Formula"). This chapter, which is especially beloved by theoretical practitioners, was composed of three different fragments (in fact, three different unfinished attempts to write the same thing) which Engels found among Marx's papers. We may leave to Marxologists the question as to the status to be afforded to such fragments. I find them suggestive, but they also provide renewed evidence as to Marx's entrapment within the anti-structure of Political Economy: capital is seen as "a perennial pumping machine of surplus labour" (p. 957) which (if we forget that the resistance of labour is continually gumming up the pump) gives us another motor for an orrery.

153. See e.g. Gareth Stedman Jones, "History: the Poverty of Empiricism", in Ideology and Social Science, p. 107.

154. Marxism and Literature, pp. 91-92.

155. Simon Clarke, "Althusserian Marxism", p. 54. See note 13.

156. This is another of Althusser's special licences for structuralism (Capital, III, p. 919), arising in a highly-condensed discussion of feudal "labour rent". See the discussion in Clarke, op. cit.

157. See Maurice Godelier's significant re-statement, "La Part Idéelle du Réel", forthcoming.

158. Raymond Williams, op. cit., p. 92.

159. Marx to Annenkov, 28 December 1846, Selected Correspondence, p. 9.

160. Cited in D. McLellan, Marx before Marxism (Penguin, 1972), p. 280. My italics. Korsch long ago argued that Marxist Political Economy and "the 'subjective' description of history as a class struggle" were "two independent forms of Marxist thought, equally original and not derived one from the other...": Karl Korsch, Karl Marx (London, 1938), pp. 228-9.

161. Gareth Stedman Jones: "Engels and the Genesis of Marxism", *New Left Review*, 106 (November-December 1977).

162. As Jones shows (above), Engels was very much too modest. One may hazard that his extreme generosity to his friend was prompted by the fact that Marx had died only three months previously. In a subsequent note (to the new German edition of 1890) he was more just to himself.

163. Althusser returns constantly to this moment of Marx's theoretical (and Hegelian) immobilism: in an index to Marx's works in *R. C.* the longest entry is to the "1857" Introduction, the next longest to the Preface to the *Critique*.

164. See L. Krader, op. cit.

165. Terry Eagleton, *Criticism and Ideology* (New Left Books, 1976), p. 61.

166. Gareth Stedman Jones, "Engels and the End of Classical German Philosophy", op. cit., p. 31. One must add that the author has increasingly overcome this idealist legacy in his subsequent work.

167. Cornelius Castoriadis, *L'éxperience du mouvement ouvrier* (Paris, 1974); *La societé bureaucratique* (Paris, 1973); *L'institution imaginaire de la societé* (Paris, 1975); *Les Carrefours du labyrinthe* (Paris, 1978). In recent years the journal *Telos* has presented some of the work of Castoriadis and of Claude Lefort to an English-speaking public. Unfortunately I am unable to recommend the account of their work by an American enthusiast, Dick Howard, *The Marxian Legacy* (London, 1977). Howard's study is an extraordinary essay in ahistorical and apolitical weightlessness, which reduces everything to an interminable North American post-New-Left academic seminar in something which he calls (inaccurately) "ontology". Castoriadis has never been engaged in academicisms of this kind. The English "Solidarity" group has published some pertinent extracts from Castoriadis ("Paul Cardan") in pamphlet form: "Solidarity", c/o 123 Lathom Road, London E.6. Notably *Modern Capitalism and Revolution* (75p) and *History and Revolution* (20p). The latter pamphlet is twenty pennyworth of the best emetic to prescribe to Marxist theologians and theoretical practitioners—a sectarian emetic to be administered only to sectarians.

168. I find helpful James Henretta, "Social History as Lived and Written" (Newberry Library, Chicago, 1977). I find actively unhelpful recent attempts to suggest a rupture in British Marxist historiography between the work of Maurice Dobb, and the historiography of the 1960s (including the work of myself and Eugene Genovese). I see on *both* sides of this supposed "break" a *common* tradition of Marxist historiography submitted to an empirical discourse (albeit with differing emphases); and "culturalism" is a term which I refuse: see R. Johnson, G. McLennan, B. Schwarz, *Economy, Culture and Concept* (Centre for Contemporary Cultural Studies, Birmingham University, 1978).

169. Krader, op. cit., pp. 39, 329.

170. "La conscience est plutôt un reseau d'intentions significatives, tantot claires pour elles-même, tantôt au contraire vécues plutôt que connues": *La structure du comportement* (Paris, 1942). See also James Miller, "Merleau-Ponty's Marxism", *History and Theory*, XV (1976).

171. I have argued this again recently in my Postscript to *William Morris*. It has long been a theme of Castoriadis's flanking attacks on Marxist theory and organisation: see e.g. "On the History of the Workers' Movement", *Telos*, 30, Winter 1976-77. Agnes Heller, *The Theory of Need in Marx* (1976) deploys some of the materials for the necessary argument, but see also the thoughtful criticisms by Kate Soper, *Radical Philosophy*, 17, Summer 1977, pp. 37-42.

172. Tony Skillen, "Marxism and Morality", *Radical Philosophy*, 8, Summer 1974.

173. Andrew Collier, "The Production of Moral Ideology", *Radical Philosophy*, 9, 1974.

174. A very much more serious critique was commenced by Philip Corrigan and Derek Sayer, "Moral Relations, Political Economy and Class Struggle", *Radical Philosophy*, 12, Winter 1975, which starts excellently but then becomes dispersed, perhaps because the authors were unwilling to press their critique so far as to recognise the "silence" in Marx.

175. Skillen, op. cit.

176. An empty phrase which Anderson can still fall back upon in his self-critical *Considerations on Western Marxism*, p. 103.

177. But the Trotskyisms have rarely offered "Theory" in such pretentious and mystifying ways. More often they represent a more old-fashioned return to a notional purified Leninism, which, while usually "economistic", often inept, and always stridently self-righteous, is at least redeemed by some political activity, in the course of which the "cadres" learn a good deal, and often learn enough to carry them out of their own self-enclosed sects.

178. In certain hands, the Gramscian concept of "hegemony" can induce the same pessimistic determinism, as can Marcusian notions of the co-optation of the working class and of its organisations; so also can certain theoreticised notions of patriarchal and male domination, which—although sometimes presented by feminist writers—end up by depreciating women's presence, and by confiscating their historical identity.

179. Enzensberger, op. cit., pp. 276-7.

180. One recalls, with anxiety, that some of the leading cadres of the Khmer Rouge in Cambodia received their training in "Marxism" in Paris in the 1960s.

181. See my *William Morris* (1977 edn.), p. 761.

182. I apologise. In copying this extract from *Hard Times* I mistook the name of Mr Gradgrind for M. Althusser.

183. Anderson, "Socialism and Pseudo-Empiricism", p. 39.

Afterword

The text of *The Poverty of Theory* was completed in February 1978. In March the Union of the Left was defeated in the French elections. At the end of April Althusser published four articles in *Le Monde*, polemicising against the leadership of the French Communist Party. These have subsequently been republished by Maspero *(Ce qui ne peut durer dans le parti communiste francais)*, and englished in *New Left Review*, 109, May-June 1978.

These articles have been variously presented, in different organs of the British Left, as a "dramatic and eloquent intervention", and as the "devastating" pronouncements of a "non-dogmatic" and "supple" Marxist. Althusser has become a new "anti-Stalinist" culture-hero of the francophile British intelligentsia, and I have shown my usual ineptitude in choosing this moment to publish my critique.

Unfortunately I have not been able to obtain these "eloquent" and "devastating" articles. They have not yet reached me at Worcester. The articles which I have read were given up to the kind of political in-fighting predictable in the aftermath of a lamentable political defeat—a defeat ensured by the double-talk, double-tactics, and unabashed opportunism of the PCF. One is given the impression that, if the Union of the Left had won 2% more of the poll, M. Althusser would have denied the world the benefit of his views. But defeat, repeating the experience of promise deferred which has become perpetual to generations of the French Left, has unloosed a squall of dismay, in which Althusser must either raise his voice above the others, or be consigned to nullity.

It would have been more impressive if Althusser's critique (and in particular, his recommendation of joint action of the Left at the "base") had been issued *before* the defeat, and in time to have influenced the campaign. It is, after all, rather familiar for unsuccessful politicians to find themselves exposed to retribution in the aftermath of defeat—and Althusser and his friends are playing the part of Mrs Thatcher to the Edward Heath of Marchais.

What distinguishes Althusser's polemics is not their eloquence but their self-righteous tone and their utter lack of self-criticism. The Political Committee of the PCF is held responsible for all—for the Party's history, its strategies, and its ideology. The polemic is sharp, and sometimes caustic, in its exposure of the Party's bureaucratic organisation and quasi-military control. But this is, after all, a very old story, and one profoundly familiar to anyone with a practical (as opposed to theoretic) knowledge of the French Left. It has been written out, over several decades, by many hands: by Trotskyists and syndicalists, by the Communist oppositions of 1956 and subsequently, by Sartre at large in the late 1950s, by our comrades of the first Nouvelle Gauche, of *France-Observateur* and the U.G.S., by *Socialisme ou Barbarie*, by the activists of May 1968, and by many others. Throughout these decades, Althusser has refused any permissibility to this critique, and, as we have seen, has denounced it as "the most violent bourgeois anti-Communism and Trotskyist anti-Stalinism."

No doubt we should admire his "supple", even agile, Marxism. He has been able to move from "the cult of the personality" (1965) to "a Stalinian deviation" (1973) to a quite explicit dissent from Stalinist theory and forms—and all this in less than twenty years! We should perhaps welcome Althusser as a late developer, a philosopher innocent of practical political knowledge who has at length been enlightened by an electoral *débacle* in the classic arena of bourgeois democracy. But to what practical conclusions does this polemic lead? With much courting of the "militants of the base", he calls for "a thorough critique and reform of the Party's internal organisation." Very good. And in what should such a reform consist? Rather little, perhaps, for Althusser insists that "democratic centralism" must be sacrosanct: the "militants" and the "masses" need no advice from "experts in bourgeois democracy—be they Communist or not." This is a pre-emptive strike: Communist critics are forewarned that if they propose reforms which are not to Althusser's taste, he will enter their names in the Black Book of Bourgeois Democracy. For the rest, we are offered a delphic inscrutability. My friend Douglas Johnson, who is rumoured to have private information, tells us *(New Statesman,* 7 July 1978) that Althusser's proposed reforms would be of extensive reach: "Discussion should be possible within the cells. A militant should be able to write to the Central Committee and have the right to a reply." I must remember to propose such devastating reforms in the cell of my local Labour Party.

What gives more pause for thought is Althusser's third article *(Le Monde,* 26 April) on "Ideology." Here he demands "a Marxist theory brought back to life: one that is not hardened and deformed by consecrated formulae, but lucid, critical and rigorous." And he carefully explains that such a theory must be accompanied by *concrete analysis!* And, more than this, by *concrete analysis of class relations!* How very remarkable! And how remarkable, also, that he can intone these platitudes without a single tremor of self-criticism! For two decades Althusser and his immediate circle have had more influence upon the ideology of French Communist intellectuals than any other group. And this influence can be seen, precisely, in the reduction of Marxism to elaborate consecrated formulae, in the abject divorce (under the blanket attack of "empiricism") between "theory" and concrete analysis, and in the reduction of the analysis of class relations to metaphysical permutations. So that the first requisite of a critique of the ideology of the PCF must be a rigorous and unforgiving critique of Althusser's works themselves.

I borrow the term "unforgiving" from Althusser. He tells us that concrete analysis, and also theory, "do not forgive." But the necessary critique of the theory and practices of the PCF will turn out to be very much less forgiving than he supposes. For the PCF was, for many years, the major bastion of Stalinism in the non-Communist world, and its leaders had unusual positions of influence within the counsels of the Comintern.

It is true that Althusser takes a step towards honesty, when he admits that ("between 1948 and 1965") the PCF held its own faked "trials" of critics and intimidated and blackballed independent sections of the French Left with campaigns of calumny. But, cheek by jowl with this, he twice invokes the memory of Maurice Thorez, and a supposed Golden Age of vital theory and honest practice. This is a useful demogogic trick to pass on the "militants", in whose memory Thorez is indelibly identified with the great mass anti-fascist struggles of the 1930s. But does not Althusser also know that Thorez (the Moscow exile of the Resistance) was a major engineer of Stalinism within the Comintern, the architect of that subordination of the International to Soviet interests, and of those structures, practices and ideology which *now* (in 1978) Althusser can at last identify as Stalinist? Does he not know that, according to the testimony of two members of the Central Committee of the PCF of that time (*Politique Hebdo*, Spring 1976; *Socialist Register*, 1976), in 1956 Thorez attempted to suppress from his own members any knowledge of Khrushchev's secret report to the 20th Congress, and was associated with Molotov, Malenkov and Kaganovitch in their attempt to overthrow Khrushchev in a *coup?* Althusser is a signatory to the appeal for the clearing of the name of Bukharin, and this does him credit. No doubt he will be interested to learn that, when Khrushchev and his colleagues signified their intention to "rehabilitate" Bukharin, Rykov and Zinoviev, it was Thorez who flew to Moscow to beseech them to maintain silence (Ken Coates, *The Case of Bukharin*, Postscript).

If Althusser wishes to revive the tradition of Thorez, then new Althusser is but old Thorez writ large. With Althusser, the critique of Stalinism has not even begun, nor can it begin, since his own thought is both the consequence of Stalinism and its continuance. But I do not wish to trespass further into French affairs: we can safely leave this unforgiving accounting to our French comrades.

What concerned me in *The Poverty of Theory* was not the particular situation of Althusser in France—the signs, and the complexities, of that situation I may not always have correctly read—but the influence of transposed Althusserian thought outside of France. And it is necessary to note the consistent misinformation as to French political realities, and mystification as to French intellectual affairs, which has been passed upon the English-speaking Left by the British francophiles who have, for some fifteen years, been promoting a purported "revival of Marxism" in this country.

I make no objection to francophilia. There is very much in French intellectual and political life to learn from and to admire. But our own agencies, who have taken out their franchises to import Althusser, Balibar, Poulantzas, Lacan, &c., have consistently presented images of French life and politics which are little more than fairy-tales derived from Parisian café gossip. *New Left Review* (and New Left Books) hold a particular responsibility for this, since over the past fifteen years they have issued, to the accompaniment of ecstatic "presentations" and theoretical heavy breathing, every product, however banal, of the Althusserian *fabrik;* and, from France or about France, they have *issued nothing else.* So that, whatever esoteric reservations the *Review's* editors may hold as to Althusser, the imposition has been passed upon an innocent public that the French proletariat = the PCF, a Party supposedly composed of a heroic, uncomplicated, militant "base", adjoined to which are rigorous and lucid Marxist theorists, imbricated in the concrete life of the Party.

One distasteful aspect of this fairy-story is that it has contributed, over the same period, to an actual breach of solidarity between ourselves and the very vigorous libertarian and anti-Stalinist Left in France, with which the first New Left had the closest fraternal associations, but whose activities are now neither examined nor even reported. So that, in the name of francophilia, exchanges have actually become more difficult with those independent French intellectuals and activists whom the PCF has chosen to blackball or calumniate. And an equally distasteful consequence is that the *soi-disant* Marxist Left in Britain is wholly unprepared to understand the long-delayed disaster that has now, at length, overtaken the Communist intellectual tradition in France.

For the drama of the last two decades has been wholly misreported in this country. It has never been the arduous intellectual epic that British promoters supposed. A number of episodes have been—and have been *seen,* by an increasing number of French intellectuals, to be—farce. One does not have to be as old as Methuselah to recall the years when Roger Garaudy (the Dr John Lewis of France) held the Office of Corrector of Bourgeois Heresies throughout the Western World—an office from which he was deposed as preliminary to his reconciliation with the Catholic Church! More than in any other Western country, the PCF succeeded in intimidating their intellectuals and in neutralising them with bourgeois guilt. The intellectuals were segregated in their ghettos, and subordinated to the discipline of the Party's clerisy. The consequent rupture between theory and practice found a classical expression in Althusserian thought. More resistant to the education of experience than any other Western Communist Party, the PCF met the demise of Stalinism and the re-invigoration of capitalism with the rigorous response of an ostrich. This meant, for the Party leadership, a collapse into pragmatism and opportunism; and, for the intellectuals, a swift passage into idealism—a theoretically-justified *refusal* of evidence, of history, of "empiricism." Now, after many decades of battering at the door, social being is finally making a late forced entry upon social consciousness. Suddenly, the Party intellectuals in their breached fortress are making "eloquent" and "devastating" signals of recognition of. . . what everyone outside that fortress has long known.

I will not predict Althusser's future evolution. He is unlikely to follow the path of Garaudy. What I will predict is that all that high and rigorous theory will collapse, for a decade, into a shambles, and that the tenacious posthumous Stalinism of the French Communist intelligentsia will vanish in a year or two amidst cries of *sauve qui peut!* I cannot say that this prospect displeases me. I found the cruel and largely-unmerited *débacle* of an honourable French Communist tradition of the Thirties and of the Resistance to be tragic; but in the last two decades I have seen less honour and more bad faith in that quarter. The work of rebuilding a libertarian revolutionary tradition in France has long been going on elsewhere.

In certain of these judgements I may be ill-informed. It is possible, even, that Althusser may prove to be more serious in his new-found anti-Stalinism than I suppose. Let us hope that this is so. But if he is to be so, then he must revoke the greater part of his own published theory. And this is what *The Poverty of Theory* is about. For the theory remains *as* theory, is replicated as theory, and is transplanted as theory, whatever personal or public contingencies arise. In this, at least, I am glad to be confirmed by Althusser. For, as he remarked rather grandly in an inter-view to *Les Nouvelles Littéraires* (8 June 1978): "Philosophe, je ne suis pas piégé par les effets de la politique publique quotidienne. . ." Historian, je ne suis pas either. There is not one sentence in *The Poverty of Theory* which I wish to retract.

6 August, 1978.

Outside the Whale*

> "You know, I have connections—even in California."
>
> T.S. Eliot, *The Cocktail Party*

"The Vision that Eludes us All"

In the General Election of 1955 the British people elected the government which was to see them through the crises of Quemoy, Suez, Hungary, hydrogen bomb tests, Jordan and other critical incidents of the twentieth century. The three major parties ensured that the election was conducted entirely within the political and strategic premises of NATO. And it was an election in which the great majority of British intellectuals were silent.

There was a notable exception. Lord Russell, the 83-year-old philosopher, intervened—upon a Labour candidate's platform—to remind the electorate that "the only alternative to living together is dying together." It was, appropriately, Mr. Alistair Cooke, the New York correspondent of the *Manchester Guardian*, who was employed to reduce this intervention to the proper scale of electoral trivia. Mr. Cooke cocked an ironic eyebrow at "Lord Russell's Modern Apocalypse":

> A midget suspended against a huge CinemaScope screen, the last of the Whigs snapped his eaglet eyes under the white thatch of hair and flexed his arms at the elbow in a "hey presto" motion, like a charming puppet straining for a miracle and in the act wobbling the tiny wire frame of his body.

After some more of this, Mr. Cooke permitted the "charming puppet" to speak:

> "It is," he said in his high nasal voice, "the most important question that men have ever had to decide in the whole history of the human race."

Even Pasternak's more vulgar traducers made some pretence of attacking him for his ideas. They did not whinny at his "nasal voice" nor mock the infirmities of an elderly man ("the frail figure," Mr. Cooke went on to tell us, "pattered to the middle of the stage.") But the conclusion to the report must be quoted at greater length. Lord Russell was speaking of

---

*From *Out of Apathy,* ed. E.P. Thompson (1960). For the status of this text, see A Note on the Texts, p. 403.

the dangers of chemical, bacteriological, and nuclear warfare: "There is no end to what science can do by way of destruction, and also no end to what it can do the opposite way":

> There was a great surge of applause for this sentiment, and the stolid house-keepers pounded their hands in the hope that belief would create its object. The noble and ageing lord himself was seized with the same emotion, and what practical steps we could take to... bully the great protagonists into loving each other, were forgotten in a long and poignant passage about the shining alternative to the world we know...
>
> Poverty was wholly unnecessary. "China, India and Africa could all be raised up to a standard of living that would equal that of the most prosperous countries... the things by which we stand together are infinitely more important than the things which divide us." Again another wave of wishful applause.
>
> "The brotherhood of man is an old idea and it has been propounded by very many wise men. Now it is the alternative to death."
>
> He clenched his bony hands again, to grasp the vision that eludes us all, not least our legislators, and begged them to go away and bring about an era of "happiness such as has never existed before... If we would, we could make life splendid and beautiful."
>
> He had done. The decent crowd clapped him all the way out on his careful legs...

Since that time the old philosopher has found others to stand on platforms beside him. But the questions raised by Lord Russell's intervention and Mr. Cooke's handling of it still remain. And they are very many. Why, in 1955, was Lord Russell's action an exception to the rule of intellectual passivity? (A fair number of "cultural workmen" shared his opinions, but in the world's "oldest democracy" they felt that there was "nothing they could do." Why?) What had become, in 1955, of the socialist generation of the 1934-45 decade? And what of those whom Mr. Cooke patronised as the "stolid housekeepers", the "decent crowd"? These survivors of the victory of 1945 do not seem to have contracted out of political citizenship. How was it that Mr. Cooke could assume, when writing for the favourite newspaper of British intellectuals, that the very picture of this "decent crowd" listening to Lord Russell's "Apocalypse" would raise a sophisticated laugh? Could assume, moreover, a conditioned sensibility upon which he could play for known responses—which would endorse the ideas of the brotherhood of man and of human happiness as *vieux jeux*, and would find the spectacle of an old humanist offering the prospect (the faint prospect) of progress to mankind as quaint and ineffectual?

The questions are related. They are the proper concern of this essay. What is argued here is that in the fifties there has been a polarisation of human consciousness which has corresponded to the polarisation of world power. The world orthodoxies have been constructed in mutual antagonism. In the Soviet Union the ideology is clearly defined, since it is enclosed by censorship, reinforced by repressive institutions and periodically confirmed or revised by Authority. In the "free world" (or Natopolis) the centres of ideological orthodoxy are rarely defined. The diversity of intellectual trends within the orthodoxy, the indeterminate and shifting character of its boundaries, the existence of real centres of dissent (and the licence given to even Stalinist opposition)—all these conspire to create the central illusion of "Natopolitan" culture, that there is in fact *no* orthodoxy but only an infinite variety of opinions among which each man is free to choose. But beneath this illusion there are both outer and inner compulsions which give to Natopolitan ideology its peculiar power.

Running across Europe there has been not only the frontier of power but also a cultural fault. And this fault has opened up within the minds of individual men on either side of the divide. Its location will be found among those assumptions about the nature of man, and about the way in which men make, or cannot make, their own history which underlie most disciplines. And while the pressures inducing conformity have at times appeared overwhelming on both sides, it has never been inevitable that individual minds should submit. In fact, the pure "Stalinist," the pure "Natopolitan," has been rare; there have been many intermediate positions within each pattern of default, and many stubborn centres of resistance. We do not introduce the term "Natopolitan" as one more label for indiscriminate abuse, but to indicate the existence of an active ideological pattern.

This ideology is the *active* component of apathy, just as prevailing circumstances have provoked apathy as a passive response. It is an intellectual and cultural fact in its own right—a certain *stance* in relation to circumstances, a capitulation of the centres of agency. While the prevalence of this ideology of apathy endangers the world, it was not thought up by some master of deceit in a conscious plot to destroy the world. Rather, it grew by its own logic within a social context conducive to its growth. In its growth it went through two stages. In the first stage, responsible minds recoiled from a social reality which they found inexplicable or unbearable. The characteristic form of recoil was disillusion in Communism, so that by the mid-forties this disenchantment had become a central *motif* within Western culture. The resultant withdrawal has been reminiscent of the disillusion among the radical intelligentsia in Britain in the aftermath of the French Revolution, when, upon Napoleon's ascendency:

> . . . all was quieted by iron bonds
> Of military sway. The shifting aims,
> The moral interests, the creative might,
> The varied functions and high attributes
> Of civil action, yielded to a power

> Formal, and odious, and contemptible.
> —In Britain, ruled a panic dread of change;
> The weak were praised, rewarded and advanced;
> And, from the impulse of a just disdain,
> Once more did I retire into myself.
>   (Wordsworth, *Excursion* III, 821 *et seq.*)

In the second stage, withdrawal leads on to capitulation to the *status quo;* it is proper to speak of a cultural *default.* Disenchantment ceases to be a recoil of the responsible in the face of difficult social experience; it becomes an abdication of intellectual responsibility in the face of all social experience. And, in the context of the Cold War, and of exhausted imperialism, the withdrawal or despair of the disenchanted was twisted—often by lesser men—into an apologia for complicity with reaction. This apologia was more than a cultural "norm"—those loose assumptions and received ideas which the mind exposed in the fifties tended to take as "given." It was an active cultural pattern, a *logic* which carried the mind down established grooves from one premise to the next, a *drift* of the sensibility. It remains the dominant ideology as we enter the sixties, and it tends towards the negation of man.

If history has repeated itself, it has most certainly done so as farce. Half a century, and years of self-examination, divide Wordsworth, the ardent revolutionary, from Wordsworth, the Laureate of Queen Victoria. In our time the reversion took place in a decade. Napoleonic disenchantment and Victorian conformity have been telescoped into one. Wordsworth's Solitary and Dickens' Mr. Podsnap have inhabited a single skin.

"The Menacing Shapes Of Our Fever. . ."

To understand the first stage of this regress, we may turn to Auden's *Spain,* which was published in pamphlet form in 1937. It was re-published in the volume *Another Time* in 1940, with significant omissions and revisions. The poem is constructed in four movements. First, a series of stanzas whose cumulative historical impressionism brings the struggle of "today" within the perspective of the evolution of civilisation. Second, a passage in which poet, scientist and poor invoke an amoral life-force to rescue them from their predicament; and the life-force responds by placing the responsibility for moral choice and action upon them ("I am whatever you do. . . I am your choice, your decision. Yes, I am Spain.") The third, and central, movement of the poem follows immediately upon this reply:

> Many have heard it on remote peninsulas,
> Or sleepy plains, in the aberrant fisherman's islands
>   Or the corrupt heart of the city,
> Have heard and migrated like birds or the seeds of a flower.

They clung like birds to the long expresses that lurch
Through the unjust lands, through the night, through the alpine tunnel;
   They floated over the oceans;
They walked the passes. All presented their lives.

On that arid square, that fragment nipped off from hot
Africa, soldered so crudely to inventive Europe;
   On that tableland scored by rivers,
Our thoughts have bodies; the menacing shapes of our fever

Are precise and alive. For the fears which made us respond
To the medicine ad. and the brochure of winter cruises
   Have become invading battalions;
And our faces, the institute-face, the chain-store, the ruin

Are projecting their greed as the firing squad and the bomb.
Madrid is the heart. Our moments of tenderness blossom
   As the ambulance and the sandbag;
Our hours of friendship into a people's army.

To-morrow, perhaps the future. . .

In the fourth movement we pass away, once again, from the Spanish war,
into a passage of inventive impressionism (balancing the first movement)
suggestive of an imagined socialist future; and this leads to the coda, which
picks up once again the theme of the third movement, and which places
"today" in a critical poise of action and choice between yesterday and
tomorrow:

To-day the deliberate increase in the chances of death,
The conscious acceptance of guilt in the necessary murder;
   To-day the expending of powers
On the flat ephemeral pamphlet and the boring meeting.

To-day the makeshift consolations: the shared cigarette,
The cards in the candlelit barn, and the scraping concert,
   The masculine jokes; to-day the
Fumbled and unsatisfactory embrace before hurting.

The stars are dead. The animals will not look.
We are left alone with our day, and the time is short, and
   History to the defeated
May say Alas but cannot help nor pardon.

The poem is commonly underestimated today. And readers of the
amended version, as presented in *Another Time* (1940) and in the
Collected Shorter Poems (1950), may be forgiven for overlooking its
strengths. The crucial section of the third movement now reads:

> On that arid square, that fragment nipped off from hot
> Africa, soldered so crudely to inventive Europe;
>   On that tableland scored by rivers,
> Our fever's menacing shapes are precise and alive.
>
> To-morrow, perhaps the future. . .

Two verses have been cut out, thereby excising in a single operation the fulcrum of the poem's formal organisation and the focus of the preceding and succeeding imagery. Auden cannot be exonerated from a calculated act of mutilation upon his own poem.

His motives are not our immediate concern, although it should be noted that all his early poems were submitted to a similar process of political bowdlerisation. The important point is that the stanzas were excised because they indicated an affirmation which, by 1940, Auden had abjured. In his earlier poems there is a fruitful ambiguity in his diagnosis of the human malaise. There is a running argument between the "change of heart" invoked in "Sir, no man's enemy. . ." and the concept of man who "is changed by his living" in the Chorus to *The Dog Beneath the Skin:*

> Do not speak of a change of heart, meaning five hundred
>   a year and a room of one's own,
> As if that were all that is necessary. . .

The guilts and anxieties, the deformities of "love", are seen within the context of a diseased society, which may only be healed by political revolution; and yet fascism and reaction are seen as the projection of neuroses, and revolution is envisaged as the product of an affirmation of love, both of which must originate from the individual heart. The ambiguity is productive of tensions in thought and feeling, and gives to some poems their probing, undoctrinaire, diagnostic tone; but insofar as it is the expression of irresolute thought and unresolved conflict it can also be felt as a limitation, the source of a slurring of definitions, abrupt shifts of focus, and evasions covered up by passages of hectoring or clever pastiche. The importance of *Spain* is that Auden found in the Spanish Civil War a theme capable of bearing the full weight of this ambiguity and demanding a resolution.

This resolution was offered in the two verses excised. It was in Spain that the heart must be changed, and upon the outcome might depend the answer to the questions of poet, scientist and poor. The "meaning" of history remains undefined because it has yet to find its definition in its outcome; and this outcome is not inevitable, but will be the product of human actions and choices which the Spanish War symbolises. The war is the objectification of the human malaise; but it is a malaise capable of cure, since men may remake their own nature in action. "Out thoughts have bodies", and the guilts, neuroses and anxieties are objectified in the "invading battalions" of fascism, while "love" ("our moments of tenderness") and the affirmative social values are objectified in the "people's army." If the source of the conflict may still be traced to the individual human heart, the issue must be decided in the Spanish theatre of war. And the decision, if favourable, may prove to be a watershed for human nature alike. "Tomorrow" ("The walks by the lake. . . the bicycle races/Through the suburbs on summer evenings. . .") may be an epoch of unheroic, but affirmative and untormented, social intercourse. There is no ambiguity. And seen within this context the refrain to the poem ("But to-day the struggle") seems no more inappropriate than the refrain to Yeats's *Easter 1916*. If the issue was indeed so pregnant with historical consequence, then the generation of "to-day" might with reason feel called to endure sacrifice in the interests of "to-morrow", and (but there are quicksands here) not feel too many scruples on the way:

> Not caring if the wind did now and then
> Blow keen upon an eminence that gave
> Prospect so large into futurity.
> (Wordsworth, *The Prelude* (1805), X, 750)

Auden cannot have been unaware of the significance of such a resolution—shedding light backwards upon his earlier work. And, in 1940, he had come to feel that this light was darkness. The reasons for this change lay in the international events of 1937 to 1939; among them, the Soviet purges and their repercussions throughout the international Communist movement, the debacle of Munich, the struggle for power within the Spanish Republican forces, the increasing ideological orthodoxy of the Popular Front, and the Russo-German pact of 1939. And, in the knowledge that world war was imminent, Auden wrote his poem, *September 1, 1939*.

This is a poem which expertly expresses the tensions of a mind in recoil from experiences too difficult and painful to admit of any easy resolution. But the shedding of the illusions of the thirties ("As the clever hopes expire/Of a low dishonest decade") is perhaps too facile. (Which hopes? Were all the hopes dishonest? And can the poet's personal responsibility be shuffled off so easily?) And from this there follows a rejection of the "meaning" of history, which he had offered in *Spain*. If a meaning can be found, it is at best irrelevant, since beneath the sequence of cause and effect can be found an extra-historical cause in human nature:

> Accurate scholarship can
> Unearth the whole offence
> From Luther until now
> That has driven a culture mad,

> Find what occurred at Linz,
> What huge imago made
> A psychopathic god:
> I and the public know
> What all schoolchildren learn,
> Those to whom evil is done
> Do evil in return.

The madness of European culture is no longer seen as the function of an acquisitive society; it is in the last analysis the function of man's capacity for evil. Whence comes this evil? It is "the error bred in the bone/Of each woman and each man": self-love. Self-love may be rooted in the biological, psychological or moral nature of man—but we are recognisably entering within the pattern of traditional Christian doctrine and the *locus* of original sin. The remedy, if there is any remedy, must be in a change of heart: "We must love one another or die." But whence is this change to come, since both rulers and ruled (the "dense commuters" and the "helpless governors") are in common victims within the reciprocal circuit of evil? It can only come from outside the circuit—from healer, prophet or priest, or from the handful of disenchanted intellectuals who have seen through the lie:

> Defenceless under the night
> Our world in stupor lies;
> Yet, dotted everywhere
> Ironic points of light
> Flash out wherever the Just
> Exchange their messages:
> May I, composed like them
> Of Eros and of dust,
> Beleaguered by the same
> Negation and despair,
> Show an affirming flame.

For a second time, the ambiguity of Auden's earlier work is resolved. But the resolution contradicts at every point the resolution of *Spain*.

Let us look at the revision of that poem again:

> On that tableland scored by rivers,
> Our fever's menacing shapes are precise and alive.

Nothing more: no Madrid, no invading battalions, no hours of friendship, no people's army; no historic conflict between good and evil, neurosis and health, objectified in an actual political conflict. Although the structure of the poem is made irrelevant, and the preceding and succeeding imagery are deprived of their nexus, Auden felt it to be necessary to excise the notions of purposive historical commitment and of the redemption of man through political action. "Our fever" is now undiagnosed; it might, indeed, be "the error bred in the bone." Spain is now the symbol not of a particular and critical predicament of men in history but of "the human predicament."

"And, from the impulse of a just disdain,/Once more did I retire within myself": in *September 1, 1939*, Auden has reached this point of withdrawal. Nor is there dishonour here. The extent of the European disaster in 1939 could not be medicated with some cheap intellectual balm. But if it is true that "We must love one another or die," this is still only to state the problem; the problem itself—*how* this "love" is to be expressed in human relations and embodied in history—remains. The central place of cultural conflict is the place where the arguments of "love" and the arguments of necessity contend. But if it is part of the "human predicament" that love will always be overruled by power, then the affirmation of "love" may appear only as a personal resolution: "love" appears as a state of personal experience, but no longer as an effective and active social attitude. And it is here that the *second* stage of regress begins, where recoil can lead on to capitulation. Already we can detect elements which were later twisted into the discrete ideology of intellectual alienation and of quietism, the apologia for apathy. In the "dense commuters" we have already a suggestion of Mr. Cooke's "stolid housekeepers" and "decent crowd." In the "helpless governors" we have "the vision that eludes us all, not least our legislators." In the ironic "Just" who see through the "lie of Authority" but who are powerless to offer any challenge we have foreshadowed the attitude which informed the "Natopolitan" intellectual of the fifties.

It is not the authenticity of Auden's experience which we are disputing, but the default implicit in his response. There is, after all, some difference between confronting a problem and giving it up. The giving up of the problem was punctuated by his emigration to America. In the interval between 1939 and 1945, when many of the housekeepers and commuters were showing an affirming flame on the seven fronts of fire and oppression unleashed by the Spanish defeat, Auden's own flame had been dowsed: he had surrendered to "negation and despair." He emerged in 1945 as a sort of unauthorised literary amanuensis of a Kierkegaardian Mr. Eliot. Mr. Cooke's smile at Lord Russell's vision (*any* vision) of human brotherhood finds its sanction in this—or a dozen other equally derivative passages:

> In our bath, or the subway, or the middle of the night,
> We know very well we are not unlucky but evil,
> That the dream of a Perfect State or No State at all,
> To which we fly for refuge, is a part of our punishment.
>   Let us therefore be contrite but without anxiety,
> For Powers and Times are not gods but mortal gifts from God;

> Let us acknowledge our defeats but without despair,
> For all societies and epochs are transient details,
> Transmitting an everlasting opportunity
> That the Kingdom of Heaven may come, not in our Present
> And not in our Future, but in the Fullness of Time.
> Let us Pray.

The courageous individual flame, burning in despite of a seemingly incomprehensible and evil world, has become an acquiescent prayer; and a prayer for something whose topography in Time and chronology in Space is portentously evasive.

And here we must effect a transition from Auden's personal regression, and the way in which, within a particular social context, the regression exemplified in his case has been twisted into the pattern of Natopolitan ideology. For this most materialist of civilisations, characterised by conspicuous consumption within and nuclear power strategy without, has secreted a protective ideology so metaphysical in form and so purged of social referents that it must make the Yogi ashamed of depending upon a bed of nails. The most marvellous thing about a strict adherence to the doctrine of original sin (in its Manichaean connotations) is that there is nothing to be done about it. The sin is *there;* and to attempt any large-scale demolition project would be blasphemy. The quietist knows that "all societies and epochs are transient details": he has attained through meditation and spiritual exercise to the great Natopolitan truth first stumbled on by Henry Ford: "History is bunk."

And this truth leads on to a moral determinism no less rigid than in orthodox Stalinism. If, in the one, evil may be justified in the name of "historical necessity," then in the other it is accepted as a necessary part of the "human condition." It is not a question of the "loss of vision"; granted the premises, *any* affirmative social vision is suspect (Auden's Herod was, of course, a liberal humanist). At a certain point in the declension, the blaring moral loudspeakers ("progress," "humanism," "history" and the rest) were simply switched off with a tired gesture, since if evil is a *necessary* part of the human condition there is not much point in bursting one's moral boilers about it.

Within this regression, we can understand why Auden deleted from *Collected Shorter Poems* the stanza of *September 1, 1939,* which embodied its strongest affirmation:

> All I have is a voice
> To undo the folded lie
> The romantic lie in the brain
> Of the sensual man-in-the-street
> And the lie of Authority
> Whose buildings grope the sky:
> There is no such thing as the State

And no one exists alone;
Hunger allows no choice
To the citizen or the police:
We must love one another or die.

It was futile (perhaps dangerous) to try to "undo the folded lie,"
futile to try to speak to the "sensual man-in-the-street." Art and social
reality had divided into two worlds, between which communication was
impossible or purposeless:

No more movements. No more manifestoes. Every poet stands alone. . . The ideal
audience the poet imagines consists of the beautiful who go to bed with him, the
powerful who invite him to dinner and tell him secrets of state, and his fellow
poets.

(W.H. Auden in *Poets at Work* (1948).)

It was also futile to affirm "love" in its active social connotations; hence
that retreat, in Auden's subsequent verse, into an abstract capitalised
"Love", undefined by any context of human obligation. And in this, once
again, Auden exemplifies a more general pattern of regression.

Among the middle-aged disenchanted, only one manifestation of "evil"
really provokes a sharp, engaged response. Since disillusion in Communism
stands at the very origin of the pattern of default, it becomes a psychological necessity for this disillusion to be continually renewed. As in
Christian ritual the God must be crucified anew each year, so in
Natopolitan ritual the Communist God must be seen each year to have
"failed." But the nature of the requisite failure becomes, with every year,
more complex. On one level, the Soviet Union, the nation of moon
rockets and gargantuan industrial growth, is all too successful. On another
level, the failure of Stalinist ideology—its reduction to a perfunctory state
orthodoxy, riddled with contradictions and in imminent expectation of
general disintegration—is so manifest that any critique appears superfluous.
But it is not Stalin, nor Khrushchev, nor even Gomulka who must be seen
to have failed, so much as the entire historic struggle to attain a classless
society with which the particular, and more or less ephemeral, systems of
Communist Party organisation and doctrine have been associated. What
must be seen to have "failed" is the aspiration itself: the revolutionary
potential—not within Russian society alone—but within *any* society,
within man himself.

Some years ago the occasion for the Cold War became forgotten. It
now commands the lives of mankind through its own inertia. The
permanent war economy is one reason for its existence; the rivalry of
military and political strategies has its own developing logic. And,
increasingly, within Natopolitan culture it is the idea and not the actuality
of Communism which is the point of origin for a permanent defensive

ideology. The ritual demolitions of Marxism perform necessary theological functions. They would remain a necessity to Natopolis, as a Satanic Idea, even if the Soviet Union were to vanish from the earth. And the remaining intellectual apologists for Stalinism are as necessary to the functioning of the cultural life of the Free World as was the odd atheist, witch, or Saracen within mediaeval Christendom.

For the most part, the characteristic tone of the Natopolitan ideology is one of tired disenchantment. It is not necessary to follow the logic to its end: the Christian doctrine of original sin is not obligatory—some rationalist surrogate can make do, such as the doctrine of original acquisitiveness, or of original sexual repression, or the original gullibility of mass man. It is sufficient that the broad prospects of social aspiration be barred, and a notice in Gothic script—NO THROUGH ROAD—be nailed across. Its tone is that of a generation which has "had" all the large optimistic abstractions, and has stopped its ears to the booming "rhetoric of time." This tone has permeated the arts and such social sciences as it recognises. But the utilitarian sciences, which make the Bomb and the conspicuously-consumed goods, are dismissed as irrelevant. Herod (the liberal) is never more boring than when he appears in the guise of the ameliorative man of science, offering automation or improved methods of birth control as remedies for "the human condition." Did not Mr. Eliot see through all this in *The Rock?*

> O weariness of men who turn from GOD
> To the grandeur of your mind and the glory of your action,
> To arts and inventions and daring enterprises,
> To schemes of human greatness thoroughly discredited. . .
> Binding the earth and the water to your service,
> Exploiting the seas and developing the mountains,
> Dividing the stars into common and preferred,
> Engaged in devising the perfect refrigerator,
> Engaged in working out a rational morality,
> Engaged in printing as many books as possible,
> Plotting of happiness and flinging empty bottles,
> Turning from your vacancy to fevered enthusiasm
> For nation or race or what you call humanity. . .

And hence that schizophrenic feature of Natopolitan ideology, the "two cultures": the one a vast Cain armed with the Bomb, the other an acquiescent, pietistic Abel baring his genteel hair-shirt for the blow:

> O do not falter at the last request
> But, as the huge deformed head rears to kill,
> Answer its craving with a clear I Will.

This tone of disenchantment has, finally, permeated the "liberal imagination" and such vestigial intellectual activities are as associated with the orthodox Labour movement. It has cohabited with Herod for a long time in the *New Statesman*. And (through one of those historical jokes which it is usual for Marxists to announce with the preface: "It is no accident that. . .") it has fitted itself out with a permanent establishment in *Encounter*. And *Encounter* is subsidised by the Congress for Cultural Freedom. And the Congress for Cultural Freedom is subsidised by the Ford Foundation. So that Stephen Spender, co-editor of *Encounter* and one-time author of "oh young men oh comrades," is now a gaffer on the great international pipeline which pumps out to the remotest province of Natopolis the message of the Founder of the Brave New World: "History is Bunk."

Inside Which *Whale?*

There are no good causes left, not because of any lack of causes, but because within Natopolitan culture the very notion of a good cause is a source of embarrassment. "The passive attitude will come back," Orwell predicted in *Inside the Whale* (which was published in 1940—the same year in which Auden revised *Spain*):

> The passive attitude will come back, and it will be more consciously passive than before. Progress and reaction have both turned out to be swindles. Seemingly there is nothing left but quietism—robbing reality of its terrors by simply submitting to it. Get inside the whale—or rather, admit that you are inside the whale (for you *are*, of course). Give yourself over to the world-process, stop fighting against it or pretending that you control it; simply accept it, endure it, record it.

But, as Orwell reminded, the yearning for the Jonah myth is not heroic; "the whale's belly is simply a womb big enough for an adult."

> There you are. . . with yards of blubber between yourself and reality, able to keep up an attitude of the completest indifference, no matter *what* happens. . . Short of being dead, it is the final, unsurpassable stage of irresponsibility.

And yet *Inside the Whale* must itself be read as an apology for quietism. It is true that the attitude which Orwell commended in Henry Miller—"fiddling with his face towards the flames"—may be seen as a gesture of personal dissociation from the "world-process," even as an act of protest. But the fiddling of Henry Miller is close to the exchange of ironic points of light between the Just. And in this essay we can observe the way in which Orwell's mind, exposed to the same European disasters as was Auden's, entered into a similar pattern of default. Orwell's profound political pessimism tended in the same direction as Auden's spiritual pessimism, and like his it was later twisted (*1984* helped to give the twist) into the pattern of Natopolitan ideology. This does not mean that Orwell was wrong to state the problem: in 1940 it was surely more honourable to state it than to evade it with Communist apologetics. But, once again, at a certain point the problem was simply given up.

We do not mean that this pessimism was without adequate cause. *Homage to Catalonia* gives a part of the background; the collapse of the Popular Front gives the rest. 1940 was a nadir of hope which may be compared with 1948-51. And in Orwell's personal experience this meant also broken friendships, the failure of years of endeavour, daily exposure to fraudulent propaganda from the Left as well as from the Right. We must give credit to the stubborn criticism, the assertion of the value of intellectual integrity, which Orwell presented throughout the 1936-46 decade. But since the *form* of Orwell's pessimism has contributed a good deal to the form of a generalised pessimism which has outlasted the context in which it arose, and which has become dominant within Natopolitan ideology, it is necessary to examine the premises. The presumption of a determined pattern of institutional change for the worse turns out, at bottom, to be uncommonly like the assumption of original sin. The premise is found in the phrase—"Progress and reaction have both turned out to be swindles"—so reminiscent of Auden's dismissal of a "low, dishonest decade." "Swindle" is an imprecise tool of analysis, a noise of disgust. Orwell had first used the notion that "progress is a swindle" in *The Road to Wigan Pier,* in the context of his polemic against the euphoric scientific utopianism of Wells; now the notion is attached to "progress" at large, and, in particular, to all manifestations of Communism.

It is true, of course, that Orwell was offering an essay in individual interpretation: his style is aggressively idiosyncratic and avowedly tendentious. Such an essay is an attempt at instant contemporary diagnosis of the kind which is performed in an emergency ward where there is no time for strict clinical (or in this case historical) discipline. But how many of its historical judgements can be taken seriously? "In 1930 the English Communist Party was a tiny, barely legal organisation, whose main activity was libelling the Labour Party." How many readers, carried forward by Orwell's gruff assertiveness, notice the Establishment odour of that "tiny, barely legal"? And how about "libelling the Labour Party"? How many readers hesitate for long enough to put that into context, to recall that in 1930 the Labour Party was officered by MacDonald, Snowden, Jimmy Thomas, and that Oswald Mosley was in the Cabinet—a party rather difficult for a socialist to "libel"?

Throughout *Inside the Whale* the same tone of wholesale, indiscriminate rejection can be heard whenever Communist ideas or organisation come under discussion:

The years 1935-39 were the period of anti-Fascism and the Popular Front, the heyday of the Left Book Club, when red duchesses and "broad-minded" deans toured the battlefields of the Spanish war and Winston Churchill was the blue-eyed boy of the *Daily Worker.*

Yes? True, there *was* one duchess and one dean, and the *Daily Worker* on occasion found Churchill a useful stick to beat Chamberlain with. But was this *all* that anti-Fascism, the Popular Front, and the Left Book Club movement added up to? Of course, Orwell himself did not think so, although the reader could scarcely guess from this that *The Road to Wigan Pier* was one of the most successful and widely discussed of Left Books.

What was, in 1940, a provocation, is accepted by many, in 1960, as a sober historical evaluation. Indeed, one wonders what on earth the post-war generation can make of the "history" presented, out of context and out of chronological sequence, in the Penguin *Selected Essays;* it must appear like an endless football game in which one side (Fascism, Reaction) is invisible, while the other side (Anti-Fascism, Communism, Progress) spend their whole time fouling each other or driving the ball into their own goal. Orwell is like a man who is raw all down one side and numb on the other. He is sensitive—sometimes obsessionally so—to the least insincerity upon his left, but the inhumanity of the right rarely provoked him to a paragraph of polemic. To the right ("decent people," "average thinking person"), every allowance; to the left ("bearded fruit-juice drinkers who come flocking towards the smell of 'progress' like bluebottles to a dead cat"), no quarter. What is noticeable about Orwell's characterisation of Communism in *Inside the Whale* is that time after time his prejudices are angry, antagonistic responses to the ruling Left orthodoxy, so laying the basis for a new orthodoxy-by-opposition. He assumes Communism to be a Bad Thing, driven forward by the mainspring of its own bad will—the powerdrives of the Russian State and the deracinated romanticism of Western intellectuals. A sentence such as this:

> The Communist movement in Western Europe began as a movement for the violent overthrow of capitalism, and degenerated within a few years into an instrument of Russian foreign policy

contains a half-truth which, at a certain level of policy and of ideology, is an aid to the interpretation of the evolution of the Third International. But at another level none of the historical questions are asked. How far was this "degeneration" caused by (or accelerated by?) the European counter-revolution which culminated in Fascism? How far was it fostered by the active anti-Soviet policies of Nazi Germany, Conservative Britain? How far, within this context, did the Communist argument—that the "heartland" of Socialism must be defended—have validity? How far did the foreign policy of Litvinov *deserve* to command the support of Western socialists, as against that of Ribbentrop, Laval or Sir Samuel Hoare? How far, anyway, is it a statement about the *deformities* of the movement, but not about the nature and function of the movement itself?

But to all such questions the tone of disgust ("swindle") was sufficient reply. In consequence, the complex and contradictory character of the Communist movement, the inner tensions, were never seen. Who would suppose, from Orwell's indiscriminate rejection, that there were many Communists from Tom Wintringham to Ralph Fox who shared his criticisms of orthodoxy? That all Communist intellectuals were not public school boys with a "taste for violence," that they were not all "squashily pacifist" and "the kind of person who is always somewhere else when the trigger is pulled"? That, within the rigid organisation and orthodoxy, the Communist movement in the thirties (and forties) retained (in differing degrees in different contexts) a profoundly democratic content, in the innumerable voluntary initiatives and the deep sense of political responsibility of the rank and file? But Orwell was blind to all such discriminations; and in this he anticipated the wholesale rejection of Communism which became a central feature of Natopolitan ideology. And this failure was important, not only because it helped to blind a later generation to the forces within Communism making for its transformation, but because it denied the possibility of *hope* within the pattern of social change wherever Communist influence could be detected. This denial of hope had the force of an irrational taboo; and, as Orwell himself noted, "even a single taboo can have an all-round crippling effect upon the mind" *(The Prevention of Literature)*. In this case the taboo contaminated all confidence in social man and imprisoned Orwell in the negations of *1984*.

We should also note another characteristic device of Orwell's polemic. He continually replaced the examination of objective situations by the imputation of motive. If it is assumed that Communism was a Bad Thing ("Why did these young men turn towards anything so alien as Russian Communism?"), the problem is to discover the motivations which made intellectuals turn towards it. The motives to which they themselves pretended are, of course, suspect. Intellectuals in the thirties (Orwell discovered) were in revolt because of the "softness and security of life in England" of the "soft-boiled emancipated middle class" (notice the anti-intellectual tone of *soft-boiled*, and that *emancipated* has become a sneer-word). Internationalism was really the patriotism of the deracinated, the appeal to collective security was really "warmongering," and the Left was Reaction. Ironically, Orwell was providing arguments which later became prominent in Natopolitan double-think.

In support of this interpretation, Orwell offered a stanza from the concluding section of Auden's *Spain* and a gloss upon it:

> Today the deliberate increase in the chances of death,
> The conscious acceptance of guilt in the necessary murder;

Today the expending of powers
On the flat ephemeral pamphlet and the boring meeting.

The. . . stanza is intended as a sort of thumbnail sketch of a day in the life of a
'good Party man.' In the morning a couple of political murders, a ten-minutes'
interlude to stifle 'bourgeois' remorse, and then a hurried luncheon and a busy
afternoon and evening chalking walls and distributing leaflets. All very edifying.
But notice the phrase 'necessary murder.' It could only be written by a person
to whom murder is at most a *word.* Personally I would not speak so lightly of
murder. It so happens that I have seen the bodies of numbers of murdered men. . .
To me, murder is something to be avoided. So it is to any ordinary person. . .
Mr. Auden's brand of amoralism is only possible if you are the kind of person
who is always somewhere else when the trigger is pulled.

This is, of course, sheer caricature; but since Auden had himself
renounced his earlier political allegiance at the time when this essay was
printed he doesn't appear to have bothered to reply. (He did, however,
alter the second line to "the fact of murder".) Hence Orwell's judgement
passed into Natopolitan folklore: Kingsley Amis made some use of it in a
Fabian pamphlet on "Socialism and the Intellectuals" in 1957. In the
context of the poem, which is about Spain and the volunteers who went
there, the first two lines have got little to do with the life of "a good party
man" (which Auden never pretended to be) and nothing to do with
"political murders." The volunteers who joined the Spanish Republican
cause (of whom Orwell himself was one) were committed, as soldiers, to
the activity of "murder"; Auden no doubt chose the word with care to
emphasise, exactly, that soldiering, in whatever cause, is *not* "all very
edifying" and that killing entails an "acceptance of guilt"; but this
"murder" Auden then believed was "necessary" because—as the entire
structure of the poem in its first version worked to establish—he believed
that the Spanish War was a confrontation of critical historical importance.

It is true that specious apologetics and romantic attitudes were to be
found amongst the Left intelligentsia in the thirties. Orwell succeeds in
pinpointing those which most irritated him. What he does *not* do is suggest
that any other, more honourable, motivations might have coexisted with
the trivia. And in this he falsifies the record. Nor does he tell us anything
of the actual choices with which the intellectuals of his generation were
faced within an objective context of European crisis. Popular Front, Left
Book Club and the rest are seen, not as a political response within a
definite political context, but as the projection of the neuroses and petty
motives of a section of the English middle class.

It was in this essay, more than any other, that the aspirations of a
generation were buried; not only was a political movement, which
embodied much that was honourable, buried, but so also was the notion
of disinterested dedication to a political cause. Orwell, by indicting the
cause as a swindle *and* by ridiculing the motives of those who supported it,

unbent the very "springs of action." He sowed within the disenchanted generation the seeds of a profound self-distrust. Socialist idealism was not only discounted, it was also *explained away*, as the function of middle-class guilt, frustration or ennui. "A 'change of heart' "—as Orwell reminded us in his earlier essay on Dickens—"is in fact *the* alibi of people who do not wish to endanger the status quo." But so also can be a pessimistic view of a *determined* pattern of institutional change for the worse (a "world-process")—which at bottom reveals itself as an assumption of original sin, or of the original malleability, stupidity, and capacity for self-delusion of men in the mass.

The final consequence of disenchantment was delayed. Europe itself was beleaguered by the forces of negation. The post-war generation, while indoctrinated thoroughly with the legend of the "swindle" of the thirties, has only a hazy understanding of the forties. Perhaps it is necessary to recall that at one time nearly all Europe was lost to Fascism, and that Jewish people, trade unionists (people), liberal intellectuals (people), and Communists (people) were—well, *suffering*. The war was nearly lost. If it had been lost it would probably have made a difference—even though "all. . . epochs are transient details," we would have had to die in *that* epoch. It was not won by quietism, but by people who still held, in less articulate form, to Auden's "illusion" that they were, willy-nilly, actors in a critical contest in history, and who consciously accepted their part in the guilt of "necessary murder." Few of those who fought had any "taste for violence." Communists (intellectuals or others) were not somewhere else when the trigger was pulled—and the greatest influx of intellectuals into Europe's Communist Parties was in this period and not in the thirties. Between 1941 and 1945 *Inside the Whale* got lost. People thought that they were *making* the "world-process"—not as they would wish to do, but in an extremity of necessity. And the voices of personal motive tended to get drowned (dangerously so, as subsequent Communist history shows) in the winds of the historical imperative.

It was after the war and after Hiroshima, as the Four Freedoms fell apart and the Cold War commenced, that people turned back to *Inside the Whale*. Once again, disillusion in the power politics of Communism was felt more keenly (and seen more clearly) than in the power politics of the West. Prompted by Orwell and by Koestler, the disenchanted fastened on the problem of motive. All the obstinate questions of actual context—Had they *really* been wrong to regard the Spanish War as a critical prelude to world war? Could Western liberals (and quietists) so *wholly* absolve themselves from responsibility for the post-war evolution of Stalinism?—these could be set on one side. It was assumed that whatever happened necessarily happened in this way; that because the democratic elements in the Communist tradition were submerged by the authoritarian, this was inevitably so, and revealed the "true" character of

Communism; and that whatever could be observed in Communist history or practice which could not be assimilated to an essential diabolism must—by definition—have been attached to the movement by accident or deceit. And the disenchanted turned to rend the Stalinist apologist as the author of their betrayal. He had asked for it, it is true, and was sometimes the immediate agent. But the real author was inextricably involved in the context of European revolution and counter-revolution, in the backward Russian villages, in the jails of Horthy, in the despair of the oppressed and the unemployed. But the disenchanted failed to distinguish between their own perfectionist illusions and the aspirations which had fed them. It was a long job to "unearth the whole offence" by "accurate scholarship." Easier to dismiss the whole episode as a "swindle" and the motives which had led to their involvement as corrupt.

It was easier, also, for the disenchanted intellectual to see himself as the helpless victim of a "world-process." It was hopeless to attempt any rally of the disenchanted—

> For by superior energies; more strict
> Affiance in each other; faith more firm
> In their unhallowed principles, the bad
> Have fairly earned a victory o'er the weak,
> The vacillating, inconsistent good.
>
> (Wordsworth, *Excursion*, IV, 304 *et seq.*)

Disillusion, reason, self-interest—all seemed to lead to passivity. A "world-process" plus corrupt motives equals original sin. "All societies and epochs are transient details. . ." turns out to be much the same as ' progress and reaction" are "swindles." Auden and Orwell had converged at a common point. Whether you are inside a whale or regard all whales as transient details you will not bother much about navigation.

Somewhere around 1948 the *real* whale of Natopolis swam along this way through the seas of the Cold War. After watching the splashings about of the disenchanted, with mean speculation in its small eyes, it opened its jaws and gulped—not, indeed, so that the intellectuals could sit in a distinguished posture in its belly, but in order to add nourishment to its digestive system. The reduction of political idealism to suspect motive was a welcome titbit. By the fifties, literature from Dostoievsky to Conrad had been ransacked for confirmation. Psychologists were called in to testify. Novels, plays and theses were written, displaying not only Communism but also radicalism as projections of the neuroses of mal-adjusted intellectuals. The theme entered the repertoire of Hollywood spy dramas. The intellectual stood appalled before the seduction of his own more generous impulses. The least chirrup of his undernourished social conscience was silenced lest it should turn out to be a "taste for violence" or a vestige of guilt. "And behind that again"—warned

Kingsley Amis—"lies perhaps your relations with your parents." The Natopolitan intellectual was disabled by self-distrust no less than the Stalinist intellectual was disabled by fear of reverting to bourgeois modes of thought. The very fact of an intellectual espousing any public cause (unless as a career politician) was enough to touch off suspicion. The Western disenchanted delivered themselves over, by their own hand and in confessional mood, to McCarthyism, just as an earlier generation of Communist intellectuals had, by their capitulation before the "infallible" party, delivered themselves over to Zhdanov and to Beria. In Natopolitan culture today, no swearword is more devastating than "romantic", just as the "utopian" or "idealist" is the butt of Stalinist abuse. It was left to Mr. Amis to make the ultimate definition of political romanticism: "an irrational capacity to become inflamed by interests and causes that are not one's own, that are outside oneself" (*Socialism and the Intellectuals*, 1957). Self-interest is not only comfortable: it is also wholesome and sane and does not make revolutions. The aspirations of two decades were put out of their misery without so much as a whimper.

It was a repudiation of responsibility, a *trahison des clercs*, as abject as any that had gone before: not the repudiation of Stalinism, but the inert surrender to the established facts of Natopolis: not the discovery that the motives of some men were wrong, but the capitulation to Eliot's sophistry in which human motives, in an affirmative social context, must always be wrong. And yet it was from the lampoons of the disenchanted that the post-war generation picked up bits of "history." The revolt of Oxford intellectuals in the thirties, one young socialist tells us, "(though quite sincere) was safe, like the tantrums of a spoilt child":

> You could yell and scream in the nursery—because you knew the nursery walls were built to last. You could even kick and scratch old Nanny—because you knew she would never desert you and would even forgive you in the end. (David Marquand in the *Manchester Guardian*, August 18, 1958.)

The self-emasculated had perhaps received the shabby epitaph which they deserved. They had passed on to the next generation only the negative of impotence.

But it is not the epitaph which the historical thirties deserved, any more than the self-flagellation of Wordsworth's Solitary is a true comment upon the men of the Corresponding Societies. It may be years before an objective judgement upon the period can be made. It will not be made until speculations upon motive are placed firmly back onto the whole context of the time. Men were not placed in some pure climate of choice, but in a context of savage counter-revolution and military politics which none had chosen. If their choices had been wiser, world war might conceivably have been averted or limited. If their actions had been more self-centred, then the war would certainly have been lost. And it is difficult to see how the evidence of the thirties and forties (taken together) can be read as an irrevocable verdict upon the darkness of the human heart. The worst evil was defeated. And if every form of evil—power-lust, sadism and the corrosion of humanism into abstractions of power—were displayed on the side of the victor, so also was self-sacrifice, heroism and every generous quality in superabundance. The annals of Communism alone contain enough martyrs to furnish a cycle of religions. More than a sound of mockery should come down to us from Jarama Ridge and the concentration camps. In our recoil from the oppressors we forget the integrity of the oppressed. If good, wise and great went to the wall—some to face the firing squads of their own side—we forget that this death was also an affirmation:

> Mock mockers after that
> That would not lift a hand maybe
> To help good, wise or great
> To bar that foul storm out, for we
> Traffic in mockery.

The Teeth of the Children

From small change, large supplies. Only a minority of the intellectuals of the thirties were actively associated with Communism. Only a minority of these followed through the whole declension from disenchantment to acquiescent quietism. But it is true that the shape of cultural history is decided by minorities. And it was the default of the disenchanted which gave to Natopolitan ideology its form. Their flight from humanism did not take place in some vacant plot but inside the whale of Western capitalism. And upon it the old whale grew fat.

It has happened before that the revolutionary, disenchanted or tamed in youth, has become in middle age the apologist of reaction. His arguments are the more persuasive, since they arise not from self-interest but from despair. They pollute the forces of change at their very source, casting a blight upon hope. The disenchanted revolutionary has seen the Gorgon's head and been visited by the ultimate horror. His negation falls like a chill upon the rebel and absolves the oppressor from his guilt. Lest the children of the next generation be visited with a like horror the penitent goes among them with ashes on his head. At length he is pardoned and appointed tutor to the children of the King.

The disenchanted did not *choose* this function, nor were they consciously chosen. Their despair was authentic and the reasons for it were confirmed in the era of the Rajk trial and of Stalin's Birthday. Because Communism had "failed" it was the more easy to deny all notions of social progress. Central to all was the motif of revolutionary disillusion.

A complex pattern of interaction can be seen—as one mind abandoned one position, another mind was already preparing the evacuation of the next. John Dos Passos' young man found that his adventures ended in a squalid betrayal in Spain; Hemmingway's bell tolled his knell. Orwell found confirmation of his "world-process" in the *Managerial Revolution* of the ex-Trotskyist, James Burnham; and in the writing of the ex-Communist, Arthur Koestler, he found confirmation of the corruption of human motive. By 1946 politics appeared to him as "a mass of lies, evasions, folly, hatred and schizophrenia" (*Politics and the English Language*). *1984* was the product not of one mind, but of a culture.

After the Solitary, Mr. Podsnap. The mind, deprived of faith, sinks back exhausted upon the well-sprung sophisms of the past. In some it was a simple reversion to an older pattern of response which had co-existed with the new. Just as Orwell had noted in Auden the persistence of the Boy Scout, so Gollancz had noted, in his Preface to *The Road to Wigan Pier*, the "compulsion" within Orwell to "conform to the mental habits of his class." It is present in all his early writing, not only in his honest recognition of his own class prejudices, but also in unspoken attitudes which inform more active judgments. The genuine working-class intellectual (he wrote, in *Wigan Pier*):

> ... is one of the finest types of man we have. I can think of some I have met whom not even the most hidebound Tory could help liking and admiring.

And, implied in this, the supreme commendation: *Good man!—make him an N.C.O.!* By 1941, in *England Your England,* he was writing in a manner ("left-wingers... chipping away at English morale," "anti-British," "intellectual sabotage," "a modern nation cannot afford... them") which it is difficult to forgive. This was not *all* that he was writing. But it is important to note the drift which, even where it had positive aspects, made easier an accommodation with traditional ideas and institutions.

The ways in which Natopolitan accommodation took place were various; reversion to nationalism was only one. In some minds, accommodation was only partial—various permutations of vestigial faith and new traditionalism were scattered through our culture. In some places the forms of liberalism were contained within overall defeatism; in others important radical campaigns were fought (often on "personal", "non-political," causes, such as the abolition of capital punishment) within the margin of the general retreat. As we entered the fifties the retreat began to look like a rout. The arts, the Press, the B.B.C., the universities, the Labour benches—each had their quota of Southeys.

It became difficult to distinguish between old disenchanted (whose capitulation had been accompanied with pain and hesitation) and new Natopolitan (who had absorbed the arguments of despair by rote). Both were united in scorn of "those darling dodos" who were stuck fast in the humanist illusions of the thirties.

Custom, Law, the Monarchy, the Church, the State, the Family—all came flooding back. All were indices of the supreme good—stability. A new sociology of adjustment was born. That mercurial quality, human passion, must somehow be "fixed" in a solution of social stasis; even personal relations came to be seen as "behaviour patterns" within "institutions." The relapse of Sue Bridehead into a tormented orthodoxy (in the final part of *Jude the Obscure*) pre-figured the regression of our time. Sociologists, psychologists and husbands discovered that women are "different"; and, under cover of talk about "equality in difference ", the claim of women to full human equality was denied. But if old traditions were revived, they were worn with a new sophistication—like junk jewellery, which everyone knows is worthless, but which matches the contemporary mode. No one believed in the divine right of kings, *of course;* but the state ritual of monarchy might "fix" or sublimate uglier irrational drives among the vulgar. It contributed to stability. Perhaps the supreme essay in the new socio-theology was provided, in 1953, by two former Leftists, Michael Young and an American, Professor Edward Shils. They acclaimed "the assimilation of the working class into the moral consensus of British society" (where was it before?) as "the great collective achievement of modern times":

Moreover, many British intellectuals who in the 1920s and 1930s had been as alienated and cantankerous as any, returned to the national fold during the War.

(Chamberlain and Godfrey Winn had been *in*side the "national fold"; the Orwell of *Wigan Pier*—and the working class—had been *without*.) As a result of this happy gathering of the strayed sheep, "Britain came into the Coronation period with a degree of moral consensus such as few large societies have ever manifested." Hence the Coronation of the Queen was a "great act of national communion," a celebration of the supreme value, the Family: "one family was knit together with another in one great national family through identification with the monarchy":

Devotion to the Royal Family. . . does mean in a very direct way devotion to one's own family, because the values embodied in each are the same.
(*Sociological Review*, December 1953)

Each one of these withdrawals commenced with an attempt to correct a balance which the thirties had set awry—a just sense of real traditions and strengths which the iconoclasts had ignored, a healthy rejection of utilitarian attitudes. But because they were contained within no affirmative framework, the balance simply slumped into worse disequilibrium at the other side. In every field the same withdrawal. When Raymond Williams, in 1958, opened some windows to let out the fug, the reviewer of *Culture and Society* in the *Manchester Guardian* (Anthony Hartley) advised "both Mr. Williams and anyone else whose profession, roughly speaking, is thinking" to "stop lying awake at nights worrying about themselves, society and democracy and try to work a little harder at their job." Solemn historians and social scientists assured us that Chinese peasants and Russian sailors would never have revolted if intellectuals had not dropped the seed of maladjustment in underprivileged soil. Revolutionary ideas were middle-class "constructs"; they could never be engendered of their own accord within the soil of working-class culture, where all ideas and relations are dense, local, particular, and inarticulate. Middle-class intellectuals, alarmed at their own innate tendencies to deracination, pressed their noses against the windows of Working-Men's Institutes and rotting housing estates, seeking to gain vicarious participation in the rituals of the dense and the concrete. Every Marxist term was driven from polite conversation except one: alienation. And alienation was divorced from Marx's context of ownership and class, and posed as a contagious disease of modern man, whose carrier was the intellectual. The intellectual had no duty to society more important than restraining himself. He must sit on his own head.

All this, also, the whale regarded with approval. For almost a decade it was able to swallow and digest most things which came its way. Only when the intellectuals had fled to the institutional security of its stomach did they notice that in the darkness there was concealed a fellow traveller: the hydrogen bomb. Every time the whale lurched, intellectual and bomb rolled on the floor together. Only then did some of them start the long climb out.

But it is not true that all of them were unwitting fellow-travellers. Some knew about the passenger, and had arranged to travel that way. "Unacted desire breeds pestilence," warned Blake; and as the standard aspirations at the source of the romantic movement gave rise to more than one morbid growth within Victorian culture, so this can also be seen in our own time. Quietism is only one step removed from misanthropy. If "all epochs. . . are transient details" it can (although it need not) follow that human compassion in any active form is a waste of energy. No traffic need take place between the world of inner experience and that of outer conformity. However pretentious the spiritual drama, no action need result. We end as we began, with the same people drinking cocktails in the same room in the same way. (They have learned, perhaps, to put up with their dislike of each other, especially within marriage; but only the very rare individual need actually go somewhere and get eaten by ants.) "Detachment/From self and from things and from persons" can afford to regard with disinterest the preparations for a nuclear holocaust. And this, if it comes, will come—not in some great act of passion—but because men (West and East) have lost their sense of their real being in a void of abstract words. The affirmatives will corrode: the negatives remain. The bomb will be sent on its way in the name of the Dictatorship of the Proletariat or of the Love that Passeth All Understanding.

The inner meaning of our time might be disclosed in a critical history of the word "love", in its social connotations; from the unqualified affirmation of Blake ("To Mercy, Pity, Peace and Love") to the active moral energies of Wordsworth ("For mighty were the auxiliars which then stood/Upon our side, we who were strong in love!"), to the self-conscious, ambiguous apostrophes of the early Auden ("O love, the interest itself in thoughtless Heaven"), the guilt and morbid undertones of Graham Greene ("Why, he wondered, swerving the car to avoid a dead pye-dog, do I love this place so much?"), the prevarications and negations of Eliot ("Wait without love/For love would be love of the wrong thing"), and the abstract capitalised "Love" of later Auden. In its latest context the word is so purged of human associations and social referents that it can be taken as no more than a vague acquiescence in the will of God. The central affirmative of our culture has crumbled to dust.

It was from such components that the Natopolitan ideology was formed. It was invented by no-one; rather it *grew*. We have noted the inner compulsions which made possible the twisting into a common strand of the arguments of disenchantment and those of tradition. But an ideology is not constructed out of inner responses alone, but only as these are selected and endorsed within a particular context of power and of social relations. And there were outer compulsions also. This ideology grew inside "the whale"—in the context of Cold War, exhausted imperialism and capitalist "affluence." And an accommodation between the disenchanted intellectuals and the establishment of power offered no difficulty. If you write off all causes as swindles and mutilate your own generous impulses, then there is nothing (except the ever more ghostly voice of personal integrity) to inhibit the fullest indulgence in material success. An ideology is constructed not only by those who work with ideas; but as those ideas are passed through the screens of economic interest and class power. Ideas are transmitted by educational institutions, inextricably involved in the context of power; they are fed through mass media owned by millionaires interested in maintaining the *status quo*. Intellectuals may be employed, promoted, neglected, in ratio to their acceptability to ruling interests. Few are silenced by force and few are bought outright; but fewer still can resist the "natural" economic processes and pressures to conform. And in this way Natopolitan ideology is made not weaker but stronger; its apologists are "inner directed." The intellectual wants his lolly, in cash, esteem or moral credit, just as much as the tired worker switches on with his own hand (and therefore "wants") the programme which depreciates his values. No unseemly rattle of bayonets or sliding of bolts is required. And this is the more so, since the apparent isolation in Natopolis of the intellectual from the consequences of his theory makes it possible for him to effect some partial accommodation or retreat into academicism without loss of self-respect. None are so detached "from self and from things and from persons" that they do not hear the voice of the tempter within:

> Is it not passing brave to be a king
> And ride in triumph through Natopolis?

In such ways as these an ideology acquires its strength and social energies. Viewed from outside (as we view Soviet ideology and *vice versa*) the individual mind seems almost powerless to resist objective pressures to conform; and social consciousness appears to defer to the imperatives of power in a mechanical manner. But viewed from within, as we view Natopolitan ideology, it appears as if we have a multitude of autonomous minds making free choices among a diversity of opinions. It is only when the mind comes into conflict with one of the key "strategic" assumptions of the ideology that it is subjected to severe social and psychological pressures; and then it turns out to be more difficult to think as "a free, autonomous individual" than Orwell supposed.

The assimilation of quietism by the establishment of power took place with the ease of a "natural" process. It had not always been so. *Prufrock* and *The Waste Land* had been a protest against the world of trench warfare and Horatio Bottomley. In 1940 *Inside the Whale* still kicked against the "world-process." But by 1950 the context had changed. The Natopolitan ideology is the ideology of imperialism *in the defensive era of the Cold War*. Gone is the optimistic progressivism of industrial expansion. Gone is the brash assertiveness of imperialism militant. The Business Society is uncomfortable with any philosophy more searching than that of material success. It does not offer any civilising mission, any moral utopia; it offers consumer goods. It does not wish the customer to ask questions about the formulae behind the brand. It requires only that it shall hold what it has, and that its enemies be kept at bay. It asks nothing better than it should be thought of as "the whale."

And the whale's enemies are also those of the disenchanted intellectual. In confronting Communism, business man, general and poet found that they had a common language—however their interpretation of its terms might differ. We have encountered the parts of this ideology on the way, and we may now bring them together. Its political *raison d'être* is the containment of Communism, not in order that we may build the good society but so that we may preserve a philosophical tradition which teaches that no society can ever be good. Its moral principle is the containment of evil, not in order that good may prosper but in order that the spiritual conflict between good and evil may be perpetually resumed. Politics is a swindle, history is bunk. Art must not be polluted by anything from the world of swindles. Only a handful of "the Just"—Matthew Arnold's "aliens"—can see through the swindle; but they are powerless to act because the "stolid housekeepers" are too gullible, and because swindle is endemic to the human predicament (world-process). But the Just must preserve their freedom to exchange "ironic points of light." Intellectuals may travel inside NATO and roll on the floor with the bomb in order to defend their freedom to see through swindles. Apathy is faith. Faith is apathy. Passify ith ape. Two One ZERO...

And what has this transcendental count-down got to do with reigning orthodoxies in economic and political theory? Are we not told three times a day that "politics is the art of the possible"? Is not the orthodoxy which unites Mr. Macmillan and Mr. Gaitskell a belief in cautious, "piecemeal social engineering"? Is not the Labour Movement hedged in by a narrow empiricism, far from all thought of such Natopolitan absolutes? It is here that we come upon a final irony. For quietism and moderate policies of social reform are not at opposite poles; they are the two faces of the Natopolitan coin. More accurately, political empiricism is the "inscape" of the doctrine of original sin. It is the confined space within which you can still move when you are inside a whale. "The possible" is that small space for adjustments which is all that "human nature" allows. In practical politics the *terms* only are shuffled. Sin is now that "pressure of circumstances" (or "mood of the electorate") before which the politicians do obeisance. The Cold War is thought of as an endless condition of international life, because the conflict between good and evil (even if only "peaceful competition") must always endure.

Despite its abstract and universal vocabulary, the inner characteristics of Natopolitan ideology are philistinism and imaginative atrophy. The philistinism which is incapable of really accepting the diminishing influence of the "Western" world is matched by a temporal provincialism. Natopolitan culture has adopted as motto the words of Lord Keynes: "in the long run we are all dead." Economists are forever "priming pumps", politicians "meeting contingencies", trade union leaders keeping up with the cost of living index. The most challenging issue is reduced to a nice choice of expediencies. At the heart of a disintegrating imperial system, with the weapons of annihilation poised over the earth, the Natopolitan walks carefully down well-known streets, putting his faith in his securities in the bank, and speculating on the "aid" which he might give (some day, next week) to his underdeveloped nephews (who, in the meantime, will have come of age). He would feel naked without the "circumstances", like familiar shops and offices, which shelter him on every side.

The circumstances are there, true enough, though most of them are of

Natopolitan making. What is so signally lacking is the will to change them. How far they can be changed we cannot tell until the attempt has been made. But we can be sure that if *we* do not change circumstances, circumstances will change nonetheless; and they are likely to change for the worse. It is not change, but social stasis, which is the illusion. Apathy is a morbid condition of the will; if we do not shake it off, Blake's "pestilence" will strike.

"Pig's Head on a Stick"

There was occasion enough for this despair. The seemingly compulsive logic of feeling derived from the evidence of two decades from which we now avert our eyes. The generation of the thirties had (like Lawrence before them) toiled up Pisgah: the post-war generation was born on the top: both looked down and saw through clouds of "talk of brotherhood, universal love, sacrifice and so on... the graveyard of humanity." Hiroshima ridiculed all protestations of human brotherhood. Perhaps the talk was "just noble phrases to cover up self-assertion, self-importance and malevolent bullying... just activities of the ugly, self-willed ego?" "Pfui!" they said with Lawrence: "The very words *human, humanity, humanism* make one sick." ("Climbing Down Pisgah," "Nobody Loves Me.")

It was not silly to ask questions about the nature of man. It was sillier to pretend that evil did not exist; that it belonged, not to men, but to some beast in the thicket of circumstances which, once overcome, would leave man's original innocence freedom to walk the world without constraint—that, as Soviet ideologues still insinuate, but as the Soviet people have long since ceased to believe, all evil is "alien" to the system, all evil men are agents of the West, all sin is a bourgeois survival. With this evasion, all problems of value and choice could be reduced to problems of power, all moral precepts be derived from the imperatives of "history" and the necessities of the Soviet state. Communist orthodoxy was thus reduced to the single problem of the conquest of working-class power, and all morality was subservient to this *realpolitik*.

But it was equally silly to take only the evidence of evil and ignore the witnesses of good; or to seek to detach the good individual from the evil state (or "history" or "world-process") to which all evil propensities are assimilated. If the Natopolitan detached the "ought" of morality from the "is" of circumstance, in Stalinism the "is" towered above the "ought." Morality, East and West, gave rise to two opposing absolutes: the Absolute of Working-Class Power and the Absolute of Personal Integrity. And yet each absolute, within its own system, served the *status quo;* it was utopian to challenge either the objective laws of history or the subjective limitations of human nature. Man was chained down by necessity, without or within, and above him towered a single absolute: the Established Fact.

But beneath this absolute, men had abandoned their agency. They could not hold back change; but change went with the shuffling gait of circumstance. Events seemed to will men, not men events. For meaning can be given to history only in the quarrel between "ought" and "is"— we must thrust the "ought" of choice into the "is" of circumstance which in its turn defines the human nature with which we choose. Human nature is neither originally evil nor originally good; it is, in origin, potential. If human nature is what men make history *with*, then at the same time it is human nature which they make. And human nature is potentially revolutionary; man's will is not a passive reflection of events, but contains the power to rebel against "circumstances" (or the hitherto prevailing limitations of "human nature") and on that spark to leap the gap to a new field of possibility. It is the aim of socialism, not to abolish "evil" (which would be a fatuous aim), nor to sublimate the contest between "evil" and "good" into an all-perfect paternal state (whether "Marxist" or Fabian in design), but to end the condition of all previous history whereby the contest has always been rigged *against* the "good" in the context of an authoritarian or acquisitive society. Socialism is not only one way of organising production; it is also a way of producing "human nature." Nor is there only one, prescribed and determined, way of making socialist human nature; in building socialism we must discover the way, and discriminate between many alternatives, deriving the authority for our choices not from absolute historicist laws nor from reference to biblical texts but from real human needs and possibilities, disclosed in open, never-ceasing intellectual and moral debate. The aim is not to create a socialist State, towering above man and upon which his socialist nature *depends,* but to create an *"human* society or socialised humanity" where (to adapt the words of More) man, and not money, "beareth all the stroke."

"The job of the thinking person," wrote Orwell in *Wigan Pier,* "is not to reject Socialism but to make up his mind to humanise it." "We must love one another or die." But how are we to thrust that "love" into the context of politics and power? To this point the socialist, West and East, continually returns. It was here that Orwell stood (in his essay on Dickens) before he fell into despair: "The moralist and the revolutionary are constantly undermining one another. . . The central problem—how to prevent power from being abused—remains unsolved." It is to this point that Communist "revisionists" first retraced their steps, to the Marx of the Theses on Feuerbach and the moralist of the 1844 manuscripts, in the attempt to root out from Marxism the luxuriating weed of pre-determinism:

Between obedience to the world of reality and obedience to the moral imperative, an abyss gapes on whose brink the great historical tragedies have been played. . . On both these brinks, the moral history of the revolutionary movement of recent years has also been staged. (Leszek Kolakowski, "Responsibility and History")

But we can be content no longer with a never-ending cyclical argument. We know that power is now too deadly for us to tolerate its abuse. And here we encounter a paradox. For the power of the bomb is also an expression of our own human nature: it is our apathy which hangs above us. For the history of political power and the history of human nature have always been interdependent. Professor Popper has argued the other way:

> There is no history of mankind, there is only an indefinite number of histories of all kinds of aspects of human life. And one of these is the history of political power. But *the history of power politics is nothing but the history of international crime and mass murder...* (*The Open Society,* II, p. 270. Professor Popper's italics.)

To the sentiment we respond. The history of power politics *has* been like this, it ought not to be so. But the fact is that all histories hinge on power. The power of some men has repressed the potential nature of other men. These other men have discovered their own nature only in resisting this power. Not only their economic being, but their intellectual being—their ideas, knowledge, values—have been coloured by the possession of or the resistance to power; at this point all "histories" have found a common nexus. Today we can doubt no longer that we must humanise power and that every other history depends upon the issue. The victims of power politics must enter the arena of power.

But how are we to humanise our own paralysis of will? Will "love" come running up to an apathetic whistle? It is here, amidst the desolate negations of the waste land, that the first peal of thunder is heard. Or, if we must use the imagery of battle, in the extremity of the day—there, pouring over the nearest brow, are history's reserves. And among the first to run up are many who are far removed from the veterans—the militant class warriors—whom we had been led to expect. They jeer at the whole battle even as they throw themselves into its heart. The disciples of Lawrence are coming back to climb Pisgah, and the disciples of Orwell mean, at last, to hunt the whale.

For, beneath the polarisation of power and ideology in the Cold War world, a new, rebellious human nature was being formed, just as the new grass springs up beneath the snow. These abstract ideologies contended for people's minds; but people, educated by circumstances, changed by a logic which challenged these abstractions:

> Change in the whole social system is inevitable not merely because conditions change—though partly for that reason—but because people themselves change... New feelings arise in us, old values depreciate, new values arise... The things we built our lives on crumble and disappear... (D.H. Lawrence, "The State of Funk.")

Moreover, it is always the *truth* of an ideology which is its point of greatest weakness, for when reality is viewed in the light of this truth the ideology may stand condemned. Just as the rituals and resounding absolutes of orthodox Stalinism have induced a nausea in the younger Soviet generation, giving rise to the critique of the "revisionists," the positive rebellion of '56, the negative resistance of the *stilyagi;* so Natopolitan ideology has engendered within itself its own negation—a new critical temper, the positives of Aldermaston, the negatives of "hip" and "beats."

Out of the truth of quietism there stems a new rebellious humanism: the politics of anti-politics. The post-war generation grew to consciousness amidst the stench of the dead, the stench of the politics of power. They opted instead for the absolute of personal integrity. It seemed that on one side there was progress, historical necessity, humanism, totalitarianism, Zhdanov, concentration camps, *1984;* on the other there was integrity, the Christian tradition, empiricism, personal relations and piecemeal social reform. The old Left, because it refused to look evil in the face, because it fudged the truth about Communism or suggested that human nature could be set right by some stroke of administration, appeared mechanical, "bullying", de-humanised: it could only speak in the language of power, not of socialised humanity. It seemed as though it was within traditional institutions and Christian doctrine that the true values of love and of community had been conserved. And, to a certain degree, this was true. For man's yearning for community found solace in the rituals of tradition and it was within Christian myth that symbols could be found unpolluted by the language of power. For a second time religion was felt to be the "heart of a heartless world."

The post-war generation remained in the waste land. It was the cock-crow of the Hungarian rising which—by denying the horror of *1984*—lifted the spell of impotence. It was the threat of nuclear annihilation which made the quietists rebel. They had sought to retire from the world of politics, but in their personal lives they found, on every side, the "cruel steel traps" which the outer world had placed within. They had embraced an ideology which boasted its spirituality, but which, in its art, could give birth to images of evil but not one image of affirmative love, to characters diseased with guilt but not one authentic image of good. Like Jo in *A Taste of Honey*, surrounded in her adolescence with the spurious talk of love, they had opted for honesty: "I don't know much about love. I've never been too familiar with it." But when the last illusion has been shed, feeling arises from a logic beyond either illusion or belief. Pity stirs without intellectual prompting, as the hand rises to protect the threatened child.

And so this rebellious humanism stems outwards from the offence which power gives to the personal—the offence of power against people with different pigment in their skins, the offence of power against people of different social class, the offence of the bomb against human personality itself. The anti-political find themselves once again in the arena of political choice. Because "love" must be thrust into the context of power, the moralist finds that he must become a revolutionary.

It is not a junction that can ever be whole. It is more like a constant quarrel, between morality and circumstance, which is perpetually resumed. But it is a fruitful quarrel, which must not cease, or between the pull of "integrity" and the pull of "necessity", the drift of circumstances will have its way. And it is a quarrel which must engage the conscious mind and the whole will. From the intellectual today a particular dedication is required. It is in his capacity for utopian vision that men's will to change may be contained. If men are paralysed by the horror of their recent history, then it will do no good either to nourish horror or to turn aside and pretend that no horror is there. It is in William Golding's myth of our time, *The Lord of the Flies*, that amidst the pessimism we can find at last a moving image of good:

> The Lord of the Flies hung in space before him.
> "What are you doing out here all alone? Aren't you afraid of me?"
> Simon shook.
> "There isn't anyone to help you. Only me. And I'm the Beast."
> Simon's mouth laboured, brought forth audible words.
> "Pig's head on a stick."

The Beast is real; but its reality exists within our own conformity and fear. We must acknowledge ourselves in the Beast of history, for only so can we break the spell of fear and reduce it to our own size. And then we must meet it as it is. As Simon said, "What else is there to do?"

"The Valley to the Waterers"

We must get outside of the whale. Both whales. How will the historian describe our times? The age of which? Of the Strident Stalinist or of the Quiet Natopolitan? The Age of Apathy? Or the age in which the rebellion of socialist humanism began?

To each its shibboleths: from each its taboos. Stalin has been denounced, Dulles disavowed; but the show continues. Soviet hegemony within the people's democratic camp glares at the Free World defended by the American alliance. Original sin glowers at the New Communist Man. The Positive Hero makes hectoring speeches against the Creature of Guilt. The free, autonomous individual derides collective man. Young people are slipping out of the auditorium and making their own music in the streets, but the Show must go on. . .

Can the new human nature which has formed beneath the orthodox snows express itself in positive rebellion? Can a new generation, East and West, break simultaneously with the pessimism of the old world and the authoritarianism of the new, and knit together human consciousness into a single socialist humanism?

It is to this possibility that our actions should be dedicated; and it must be our work to define this "socialist humanism." If the default of the disenchanted led them on to a place of negation where even the springs of human feeling are dry, this does not mean that we should retrace their steps and re-endorse all the facile notions against which they were in recoil. Another name for the Beast of history is experience; even the swindles have something to teach. A socialist humanism which does not take into account *September 1, 1939*, and *Inside the Whale* will be poor in texture and exposed to error at the point where valid experiences have been denied.

"Terrible is the temptation of Goodness," wrote Brecht. We have learnt what Wordsworth learnt before us: the good life is "no mechanic structure built by rule." Socialism, even at the point of revolutionary transition—perhaps at this point most of all—must grow from existing strengths. No one—neither Marxist vanguard nor enlightened administrator nor bullying humanitarian—can impose a socialised humanity from above. A socialist state can do little more than provide "circumstances" which encourage societal and discourage acquisitive man; which help people to build their own egalitarian community, in their own way, because the temptation of Goodness becomes too great to resist. Socialism can bring water to the valley; but it must give "the valley to the waterers, that it bring forth fruit."

The Peculiarities of the English*

> "One has to put up with the crude English method of development, of course."
>
> Marx on Darwin

Early in 1962, when the affairs of *New Left Review* were in some confusion, the New Left Board invited an able contributor, Perry Anderson, to take over the editorship. We found (as we had hoped) in Comrade Anderson the decision and the intellectual coherence necessary to ensure the review's continuance. More than that, we discovered that we had appointed a veritable Dr. Beeching of the socialist intelligentsia. All the uneconomic branch-lines and socio-cultural sidings of the New Left which were, in any case, carrying less and less traffic, were abruptly closed down. The main lines of the review underwent an equally ruthless modernisation. Old Left steam-engines were swept off the tracks; wayside halts ("Commitment," "What Next for C.N.D.?", "Women in Love") were boarded up; and the lines were electrified for the speedy traffic from the marxistentialist Left Bank. In less than a year the founders of the review discovered, to their chagrin, that the Board lived on a branch-line which, after rigorous intellectual costing, had been found uneconomic. Finding ourselves redundant we submitted to dissolution.

Three years have elapsed since the new direction was taken, and it now seems possible to examine the general tendency of the "new" New Left. For simplicity this may be located in three major areas: analysis of the "Third World": definitions (mainly oblique) of Marxist theory: and the ambitious work of analysis of British history and social structure commenced in a series of articles by Anderson and Tom Nairn.[1] The first area—the Third World—lies beyond the scope of this article. It is undoubtedly the area in which some of the most original and well-informed work of the new editors has been carried out. I shall confine myself here to the other two.

These articles, taken together, represent a sustained attempt to develop a coherent historical account of British society. Undoubtedly the seminal article is Anderson's *Origins of the Present Crisis*. But, if Nairn's work is less inspired, nevertheless both writers clearly inhabit the same mental

---

*From *The Socialist Register*, ed. Ralph Miliband and John Saville, No. 2, 1965. See A Note on the Texts, p. 403.

245

universe. Both feel themselves to be exiles from an "English ideology" which "in its drooling old age... gives rise to a kind of twilight, where 'empiricism' has become myopia and 'liberalism' a sort of blinking uncertainty."[2] Nairn extends the indictment:

> "English separateness and provincialism; English backwardness and traditionalism; English religiosity and moralistic vapouring, paltry English 'empiricism', or instinctive distrust of reason..."[3]

There is "the nullity of native intellectual traditions," the "secular, insular stultification" of British culture, "the impenetrable blanket of complacency" of British social life, "the stony recesses of British trade union conservatism," and "the centuries of stale constipation and sedimentary ancestor-worship" of British society. The English ideology has—

> "embraced a dilettante literary culture descended from the aristocracy and the crudest of lumpen-bourgeois utilitarian philosophies, and held them together in a bizarre Jekyll-and-Hyde union of attraction and repulsion."[4]

"The very urban world" of England "is the image of this archaic, bastard conservatism—an urban world which has nothing to do with urban *civilization,* as this is conceived in other countries with an old and unified bourgeois culture."[5] These judgements are resumed in Anderson's *Origins:*

> "The two great chemical elements of this blanketing English fog are 'traditionalism' and 'empiricism': in it, visibility—of any social or historical reality—is always zero... A comprehensive, coagulated conservatism is the result, covering the whole of society with a thick pall of simultaneous philistinism (towards ideas) and mystagogy (towards institutions), for which England has justly won an international reputation."

And the essence of both authors' analysis of Labourism may be found in Anderson's phrase—"in England, a supine bourgeoisie produced a subordinate proletariat."[6]

No doubt in particular contexts certain of these judgments might be sustained. But what is evident, wherever such judgments obtrude, is the loosening of emotional control and the displacement of analysis by commination. There is, about them, the air of an inverted Podsnappery. "We Englishmen are Very Proud of our Constitution, Sir," Mr. Podsnap explained with a sense of meritorious proprietorship:

> " 'It was Bestowed Upon Us By Providence. No Other Country is so Favoured as This Country...'
> " 'And *other* countries,' said the foreign gentleman. 'They do how?'
> " 'They do, Sir,' returned Mr. Podsnap, gravely shaking his head; 'they do— I am sorry to be obliged to say it—*as* they do.' "

But now the rôles are reversed. Mr. Podsnap (who has swelled to engross all British culture over the past 400 years) is being arraigned in his turn.

> " 'And *other* countries,' said Mr. Podsnap remorsefully. 'They do how?'
> " 'They do,' returned Messrs. Anderson and Nairn severely: 'They do—we are sorry to be obliged to say it—in Every Respect Better. Their Bourgeois Revolutions have been Mature. Their Class Struggles have been Sanguinary and Unequivocal. Their Intelligentsia has been Autonomous and Integrated Vertically. Their Morphology has been Typologically Concrete. Their Proletariat has been Hegemonic.' "

There is, indeed, throughout their analysis an undisclosed model of Other Countries, whose typological symmetry offers a reproach to British exceptionalism. Set against this model, the English working class is "one of the enigmas of modern history,"[7] the historical experience of the English bourgeoisie has been "fragmented, incomplete,"[8] English intellectuals have not constituted "a true intelligentsia."[9]

Every historical experience is of course in a certain sense unique. Too much protestation about this calls into question, not the experience (which remains there to be explained) but the relevance of the model against which it is judged. (We may leave aside the point that Other Countries, if we survey advanced industrial nations over the past fifty years, have not always and in every respect done Better than the British, despite their vertical intelligentsia and their hegemonic proletariat.) The Anderson-Nairn model clearly approximates most closely to the French experience, or to a particular interpretation of that experience; and in this they follow the major, pre-1917 Marxist tradition. When set beside this, English experience fails in three important respects: (1) in the premature, unfulfilled character of the seventeenth-century revolution. In the ensuing compromises of 1688 and 1832, the industrial bourgeoisie failed to attain to an undisputed hegemony, and to remake the ruling institutions of society in its own image. Rather, a "deliberate, systematized symbiosis" took place between the landed aristocracy and the industrial bourgeoisie, in which, however, the aristocracy remained as senior partner; (2) Because the seventeenth-century revolution was "impure," and the struggle was conducted in religious terms, the bourgeoisie never developed any coherent world-view or self-knowledge, and made do with an "ideology" of "empiricism" which has apparently characterized English intellectual culture until the present day:

> "... the ideological legacy of the Revolution was almost nil... Because of its 'primitive', pre-Enlightenment character, the ideology of the Revolution founded no significant tradition, and left no major after-effects..."

(3) A premature bourgeois revolution gave rise to a premature working-class movement, whose heroic struggles during the Industrial Revolution

were nullified by the absence of any commensurate theoretical growth: "its maximum ardour and insurgency coincided with the minimum availability of socialism as a structured ideology." When this movement fell apart after Chartism (through "exhaustion") there followed a "profound caesura" in English working-class history, and the "most insurgent working class in Europe became the most numbed and docile." "Marxism came too late," whereas in Other Countries "Marxism swept the working class." Thereafter, the post-1880 Labour movement has nullified its entire existence by expressing only corporative (and not hegemonic) virtues, and by becoming subject (with Fabianism) to an ideology which mimics, with impoverished equipment, the banal empiricism of the bourgeoisie.

Our authors bring to this analysis the zest of explorers. They set out on their circumnavigation by discarding, with derision, the old speculative charts. Anderson notes "the complete lack of any serious global history of British society," and "nervelessness of our historiography," "no attempt has ever been made at even the outline of a 'totalizing' history of modern British society." Nairn finds that there is not even "a rudimentary historical debate regarding the total development of British society." But our explorers are heroic and missionary. We hold our breath in suspense as the first Marxist landfall is made upon this uncharted Northland. Amidst the tundra and sphagnum moss of English empiricism they are willing to build true conventicles to convert the poor trade unionist aborigines from their corporative myths to the hegemonic light:

> Enmeshed in the dense web of archaic superstructure grafted on to British capitalism. . . the working class could not distance itself aggressively from society and constitute its own autonomous movement towards social hegemony. The cutting instrument needed for this task was lacking. That is, an intellectual stratum torn adrift from the social consensus with sufficient force and capable of functioning as catalyst to the new force striving for expression against the consensus.[10]

The problem is "to create theory in an environment rendered impervious to rationality as such," to create "the intense rational consciousness and activity" which are "the necessary pre-requisites of revolution in this society of totemized and emasculated consciousness."[11] Pulling their snowcaps over their ears, they disembark and struggle onwards to bring the intense rational consciousness of their cutting instruments to the "traditional intelligentsia once buried entirely in the tribal rites of Oxford or literary London."[12] There is a sense of rising suspense as they—the First White Marxists—approach the astonished aborigines.

II

This is ungenerous, for Anderson's *Origins* is a stimulating study—indeed, as a provocation, it is a *tour de force*. If it cannot be accepted as an historical statement in its own right, it is nevertheless an incitement to study and at an uncommon pitch of conceptual intensity. If it is untrue that Britain is Marxist *terra incognita*, it is also true that such attempts at historical self-knowledge must be made again and again, with each advance in knowledge and each refinement of our analytic equipment.

A question which troubles me, however, is whether the equipment which these authors bring to their task has been refined, or merely sophisticated. We may turn to the first proposition as to English exceptionalism, i.e. the seventeenth-century revolution and its outcome:

"What kind of a Revolution was it? It can, perhaps, be said that it was a clash between two segments of a land-owning class, neither of which were *direct* crystallizations of opposed economic interests, but rather were *partially* contingent but *predominantly* intelligible lenses into which wider, more radically antagonistic social forces came into temporary and distorted focus."

"Because it was primarily fought *within* and not *between* classes, while it could and did destroy the numerous institutional and juridical obstacles of feudalism to economic development, it could not alter the basic property statute in England." The outcome was to transform "the body of land-owners into a basically capitalist class," and "it achieved this by profoundly transforming the *rôles* but not the *personnel* of the ruling class."

"In this sense it was a supremely successful *capitalist* revolution. At the same time, however, it left almost the entire social structure intact."

This is on page 30 of *Origins*. But on page 39 we are told that this "bitter, cathartic revolution. . . transformed the structure but not the superstructure of English society."

Which is it to be? And which model are we using? If it is a simple basis-superstructure model, then it is difficult to conceive "a supremely successful capitalist revolution" which nevertheless did not alter "the basic property statute in England." I am not clear as to the meaning of "statute" in this context; but if we were to examine the decomposition of feudal property tenure and relations we would have to commence an analysis of "the Revolution" several centuries earlier than Anderson authorizes. If the primary achievement of the Revolution was to "destroy the numerous institutional and juridical obstacles of feudalism to economic develop-ment," then how is it possible to say that it "transformed the structure but not the superstructure of English society"? In any case, taking 1640 and

1688 together, it is commonly supposed that the function of one very important institution was considerably modified: that is, the monarchy; and that here we have a transformation both in rôle and in personnel.

In fact, the sense of Anderson's analysis appears to be that the Revolution effected *certain* changes in the institutional superstructure, removing crucial obstacles to capitalist development at home and in the colonies; but that the confrontation between social forces was in other respects indecisive, leaving parts of the feudal (or post-feudal, transitional-paternalist?) superstructure intact. This is—as a description—evidently true, although scarcely original.

There is, however, a further ambiguity which grows in importance as their analysis moves from the seventeenth to the nineteenth century. Despite disclaimers, neither Anderson nor Nairn appear to be able to accept, *au fond*, the notion of an agrarian class, whether rentiers or entrepreneurs, as a true bourgeoisie.[13] While the landowners are accredited as a "basically capitalist class" in *Origins,* and we are told, further, that "there was. . . from the start no fundamental, antagonistic contradiction between the old aristocracy and the new bourgeoisie," yet in the analysis of nineteenth-century developments the aristocracy and industrial middle class are described as "distinct social classes" which after 1832 underwent "symbiosis," in which process the bourgeoisie effectively capitulated to the aristocracy ("its courage had gone," "it won two modest victories, lost its nerve and ended by losing its identity"). With Nairn the contrast is even more pointed: the landowners are "protagonists of a distinctive civilization, half-way between the feudal and the modern. . . a civilization. . . in spite of its bourgeois traits qualitatively distinct from the new social order": the aristocratic political elite, its institutions and ethos, were "the emanation of a distinct social class, independent of and separate from the main conflicts and concerns of urban, capitalist society."[14] Moreover, each distinct "class" projected a distinctive ideology: "traditionalism. . . was the natural ideological idiom of the landed class, emerging with Burke;[15] "empiricism," on the other hand, "faithfully transcribes the fragmented, incomplete character of the English bourgeoisie's historical experience." In the nineteenth century both congealed into the same suffocating fog.

The problems involved here certainly are not easy. It is a strain on one's semantic patience to imagine a class of *bourgeois* scattered across a countryside and dwelling on their estates, and it is easier to see in mercantile capital "the only truly bourgeois kernel of the revolution." But if we forget the associations with the French model which the term introduces, and think rather of the capitalist mode of production, then clearly we must follow Marx in seeing the landowners and farmers as a very powerful and authentic capitalist nexus. It is Sir Giles Overreach who prefigures the English Revolution; and it is his kinsman, Edmund the

Bastard, who overthrows Legitimacy, obtaining title to the land not by birth but by wit, and replacing the sanctions of an older order by those of natural law:

> Thou Nature art my Goddess, to thy Law
> My services are bound, wherefore should I
> Stand in the plague of custom, and permit
> The curiosity of Nations, to deprive me?

It is this same natural law ("Nature that hateth emptiness") whose ruthless energy in over-riding "the ancient rights" ("but those do hold or break, as men are strong or weak") both fascinated and repelled the Elizabethan dramatists, and of which Marvell saw in Cromwell the personification. We cannot say that the revolution "made possible the transformation of the body of landowners into a basically capitalist class" because, where wool or the production of commodities for London and urban markets predominated, this process was already very well advanced. But, equally, we cannot say that the revolution effected a dramatic acceleration in this process: the equilibrium of social forces was such that the full consequences of revolution were delayed for nearly 100 years.

What was at issue, from one aspect, was exactly a capitalist redefinition of "the basic property statute," from "ancient right" to "natural law" and purchase; of the mode and rationale of production, from quasi-self-sufficiency to the marketing of commodities for profit; and of productive relations, from the organic compulsions of the manor and guild to the atomized compulsions of a free labour market. And this entailed a comprehensive conflict and redefinition at every level, as organic and magical views of society gave way before natural law, and as the acquisitive ethic encroached upon an authoritarian moral economy. And, from another aspect, the real movement was enormously complex and protracted, commencing (for historical convenience) with the great monastic wool farmers of Domesday, and passing through the enfeeblement of the barons in the wars, the growth of "free labour," the enclosure of the sheep-walks, the seizure and redistribution of Church lands, the pillaging of the New World, the drainage of fens, and, thence, through revolution, to the eventual acceleration of enclosure and the reclamation of wastes.

The movement which so often appears to reproduce itself is that upon which Eileen Power commented, with reference to the financial crisis of the fourteenth century, which "depressed the apex, while it broadened the foundations, of the English middle classes." Already, three centuries before the revolution, she notes an "organic tendency" within this middle class: "though it was continually recruited from the land, it tended always to go back to the land, taking its fortune with it."[16] It is impossible to understand even the beginnings of English capitalism if one peers out, through Parisian eyes, at the backward "provinces", seeing in the landowners only a feudal aristocracy "with bourgeois traits." The Cotswold wool hamlets, the rural rebuilding of the sixteenth century, have left evidence to this day of a style, a solidity, a dispersal of opulence.

The Revolution confirmed a title not to new property but to property which already existed—a title which was menaced by the unregulated exactions of the monarchy, and which had no secure sanction in the authoritarian and magical ideology which had outlived its feudal host. But, once revolution commenced, a quite different threat to property appeared from the Leveller Left. Ireton's famous outburst ("All the main thing I speak for, is because I would have an eye to property") prefigures the settlement of 1688. And this settlement registers not some half-way house between "feudalism" and "capitalism", not some adjustment of interests between a tenacious feudal superstructure and an embryonic capitalist base, but an arrangement exquisitely adjusted to the equilibrium of social forces at that time—so delicately designed, and yet, in its ambiguities, so flexible, that it was to endure not only through a hundred years of comparative social stasis but also through the next fifty years of the dual revolutions.

The beneficiaries of the settlement were exactly those people who were represented in Parliament: that is, the men of substantial property, and especially landed property.[17] Title to the enjoyment of their property was secured by the constitutional impedimenta with which the Crown was surrounded, and by the rule of a Law which was both dispassionate in its adjudication of substantial property-rights and passionately vengeful against those who transgressed against them. At the same time a limited and manipulated franchise, and such restrictive measures as the Test and Corporation Acts, hedged out the petty manufacturers, artisans, etc. The diminished charisma of crown and aristocratic rank helped to hold together the social order, without (thanks to the Jacobite distraction) affording a base for the re-assertion of the old authority. The limp magic of a sordidly-Erastian church (itself under the local control of the gentry) supplemented the authority of the propertied over the people. In Locke the gentry found an apologist for the settlement, with his naturalistic theory of the delegation of powers to the chief magistrate in the interests of possessive individualism.

In the eighteenth century agrarian capitalism came fully into its inheritance. Around the gentry were grouped (as Anderson reminds us) those "affinal groups"—not only mercantile capitalism proper but also that widely dispersed manufacturing industry which still sought protective shelter from the State. Ascendant agrarian capitalism involved not only rent-rolls, improvement, enclosures, but also far-reaching changes in marketing, milling, transport, and in the merchanting of exports and imports; while the gentry were able to employ a professional servant-class, in the lesser clergy, country lawyers, surgeons, surveyors, tutors, etc. The "complex interpenetration" of landed, mercantile, and industrial wealth, to which Anderson draws attention, has long been a concern of our "nerveless historiography," and the delicate mechanisms—economic (credit and banking, the landowners' interest in coal, transport, timber, etc.), social (marriage settlements), and political (purchase of political influence, or of land as a step towards this)—by which this was regulated have not gone unexamined. The comedy of manners attendant upon this process of adjustment between styles was in fact a central preoccupation of eighteenth-century literary culture:

Every upstart of fortune, harnessed in the trappings of the mode, presents himself at Bath. . . Clerks and factors from the East Indies, loaded with the spoil of plundered provinces; planters, negro drivers, and hucksters, from our American plantations, enriched they know not how; agents, commissaries, and contractors, who have fattened, in two successive wars, on the blood of the nation; usurers, brokers, and jobbers of every kind; men of low birth, and no breeding, have found themselves suddenly translated into a state of affluence, unknown to former ages; and no wonder that their brains should be intoxicated with pride, vanity, and presumption. . . All of them hurry to Bath, because here, without any further qualification, they can mingle with the princes and nobles of the land. Even the wives and daughters of low tradesmen, who, like shovel-nosed sharks, prey upon the blubber of those uncouth whales of fortune, are infected with the same rage of displaying their importance; and the slightest indisposition serves them for a pretext to insist upon being conveyed to Bath, where they may hobble country-dances and cotillions among lordings, 'squires, counsellors, and clergy. . . Such is the composition of what is called the fashionable company at Bath; where a very inconsiderable proportion of genteel people are lost in a mob of impudent plebeians. . . (Smollett, *Humphrey Clinker.*)

Even a cursory acquaintance with the sources must dispel all doubts as to the fact that the 18th century gentry made up a superbly successful and self-confident capitalist class. They combined, in their style of life, features of an agrarian and urban culture. In their well-stocked libraries, month by month, "Mr. Urban" of the *Gentleman's Magazine* kept them informed of the affairs of the Town; their elegant provincial capitals and solid market-towns afforded some society in the unfashionable months; their sons were urbanised at Oxford and Cambridge, at the London Inns of Court, and on the tour of Europe, their daughters and wives were urbanised in the London season. To compensate for the isolation of the countryside, their great houses were expanded to accommodate those extended social exchanges (like select urban samples) which provide matter for the novel of fashion. In Bath, Harrogate, Scarborough, etc., they produced peculiar monuments to a civilization in which a sophisticated urbanization was a periodic rite of passage, for the adolescent, for the marriageable, the matronly, and the gout-ridden. A bourgeoisie which had not yet learned hypocrisy, they valued each other, not in the scales of breed and antiquity but in round annual sums.

Nor was this the limit of economic reckoning. There is, perhaps, an important moment of transition around the mid-century when more and more of the gentry (including the great aristocratic magnates) ceased to conceive of their function in *passive* terms (as rent-collectors and as park-keepers, with a more or less stable revenue), but took up, instead, a far more *aggressive* agrarian posture, both in their capacity as substantial farmers in their own right and in the stimulation of those improvements among their tenants upon which their hopes of an expanding income must be founded. A glance at that most remarkable of trade journals, the *Annals of Agriculture*, in whose pages noblemen, clergy, and commoners engage in discussion of the merits of marling, enclosure costs, and stock-breeding, serves to impress upon one the profoundly capitalist style of thought of the class—zestfully acquisitive and meticulous in attention to accountancy.

Moreover, the penetration of the capitalist ethos had an outcome of more far-reaching importance. It is commonly supposed (this is over-looked by Anderson and Nairn but not, as it happens, by K. Marx) that the distinctive contribution of English ideology in the late eighteenth century was neither traditionalism nor empiricism but a naturalistic political economy, most notably with Adam Smith. But—because of the events of 1832 and the subsequent conflict between the agricultural and manufacturing interests over the Corn Laws—we persistently forget that *laissez faire* emerged, not as the ideology of some manufacturing lobby, not as the intellectual yarn turned out by the cotton mills, but in the great agricultural corn-belt. Smith's argument is derived, very largely, from agriculture; a main opponent was the paternalist regulation of the corn trade which—while in an advanced stage of real decomposition—was nevertheless supported by a substantial body of paternalist economic theory and an enormous force of popular (and urban) feeling. The abrogation of the old moral economy of "provision" was not the work of an industrial bourgeoisie but of capitalist farmers, improving landlords, and great millers and corn-merchants. While Arkwright was disciplining his first refractory labour force, and while the woollen and hosiery industries were captive to traditionalism, the agricultural interest embraced an anti-political economy whose harsh profit-and-loss purgatives voided the body politic of old notions of duty, mutuality, and paternal care. And it was exactly this ideology which provided a bridge, during the Napoleonic wars, spanning the interests of cotton and of land; the first administrations profoundly imbued with the outlook of *laissez faire* were—not those formed after 1832—but those of Pitt, Perceval and Lord Liverpool.

It is difficult to see how the experience of this class, which enjoyed this long ascendancy and gave birth to this ideology, can be described as "fragmentary" or "incomplete." It would appear to be unusually fulfilled. True enough, the English agrarian-capitalist mix was, if not unique, highly unusual. It arose, like *every* real historical situation, from a particular equilibrium of forces; it was only one of the seemingly infinite number of social mutations (in which each, nevertheless, maintains a generic affinity to others arising from a comparable conjunction) which actual history provides in such profusion. If there is no place for it in the model, it is the model which must be scrapped or refined.

What appears to present our authors with difficulties is the translation of the agrarian and mercantile capitalism of the eighteenth century into the industrial capitalism of the nineteenth. Were agrarian and industrial capitalists differing interest groups within the same broad social class, or were they distinct social classes? If mutual interpenetration was already rather fluent in the eighteenth century, how are we to account for the very considerable conflict which arose in 1832? What, in any case, *was* "Old Corruption"? What irks them particularly is the failure of the industrial bourgeoisie to undergo an advanced "Jacobin" experience, as any well-brought-up bourgeoisie ought to do.

The solution for which they opt is already implicit in their failure to take seriously the bourgeois revolution of the fifteenth to eighteenth centuries. Agrarian and industrial capitalists *were* distinct social classes, although not so hermetically sealed against each other that antagonisms were irreconcilable. But since the term "agrarian capitalism" is increasingly replaced by "aristocracy" (with its feudal associations) something portentous can be made of secondary antagonisms in institutional forms and in ideology. The fear inspired by the French Revolution, and the challenge of an insurgent proletariat at home, projected these two classes into each other's arms:

"... no 'compromise' or 'alliance'—the usual terms employed—was, in fact, possible as between contrasting civilizations. No conscious tactical arrangement, no deal lasting for a season, was conceivable between social forces of this complexity and magnitude. Amalgamation was the only real possibility, a fusion of different classes and their diverse cultures into one social order capable of guaranteeing social stability and keeping the proletariat in its place."

This is not a genuine dialectical paradox, it is a dialectical trick: two forces (we are told) were so incompatible in interests and outlook that no compromise was possible between them; but, when we have turned our head we find they have *fused*. The logical deception is covered over by an implication that this was not a genuine fusion, since "the aristocracy survived, in the face of the inevitable political and ideological feebleness of the emergent bourgeoisie, as the governors of the most dynamic capitalist system in the world:

"And landowning civilization survived with them, as a mode of living, a culture and language, a type of personality and psychology, a whole dominant ethos."[18]

In this "symbiosis" of two classes the aristocracy emerged as the *"master"*, keeping "control of the State and its main organs," and remaining as "the vanguard of the bourgeoisie." The failure of the bourgeoisie (which at this stage of Anderson's argument becomes a "middle-class" subordinate to an aristocratic "ruling-class"[19]) to achieve an unchallenged hegemony and to rationalize State institutions is the main historical occasion for the "profound, pervasive but cryptic crisis" which afflicts British society: "the living palimpsest which is the ruling bloc in Britain is now decaying from its immemorial accretions."[20]

It is of course possible to see Britain in this way after watching Sir Alec Douglas-Home on television. And if this analysis relates to the perpetuation of a certain aristocratic *style*, and certain archaic institutional continuities, then it is both true and important. But far more than this is suggested: "a whole dominant ethos," "governors", "control of the State", "vanguard", or (at another point in *Origins*) "hegemonic class" which was "faced with the rise of the bourgeoisie."[21] Thus this is not offered as an analysis of styles but of the real movement and equilibrium of social forces. And as such it will not do. I will not labour the point that Marx saw "this most bourgeois of nations" in a very different way. What is objectionable—apart from the elision of whole historical clauses—is the way we slide around in a shifting terminology whose treacherous instability is disguised by a certain metaphorical virtuosity.

It is true that anyone who attempts this kind of class analysis of modern British history becomes involved in terminological confusion;[22] the ambiguities force their way into the analysis because they are there in the history. But one way of approaching this is to play, for a moment, a history-game in which we suppose that A did not happen and B (which did not happen) did. I have suggested, in *The Making of the English Working Class*, that in 1832 a revolutionary outbreak was averted only at the eleventh hour. There were reasons, but not overwhelming ones, why this was averted. If it had not been, then it is reasonable to suppose that revolution would have precipitated a very rapid process of radicalization, passing through and beyond a Jacobin experience; and whatever form a counter-revolution and eventual stabilization might have taken it is unlikely that many eighteenth-century institutions could have survived—the House of Lords, the Established Church, the monarchy, and the juridical and military elite, would probably have been swept away, at least temporarily. Now if it had happened in this way the model-builders at least would now be satisfied; 1832 would be *the* English bourgeois revolution, and 1640 would have fallen into neglect, as a "premature" outbreak, a sort of amalgam of Huguenot wars and Fronde. The tendency to imply that some kind of "feudal" society existed in Britain until the eve of 1832 (as witness the quaint notion that peeps from the edges of some Marxist interpretations of the French Revolution, that "feudalism" prevailed in France in 1788) would have been reinforced.

Let us now put the pieces back and start the game with a different move. In this case we will suppose that 1832 happened as it did, but (less plausibly) 1640 did not—that the Laudian reaction was less provocative, that Charles capitulated before the Grand Remonstrance, and that a circumscribed constitutional monarchy was established, bloodlessly, in 1640, without Marston Moor, the Leveller ferment, the execution of the King, and the Glorious Revolution. In this event the model-builders would be wholly at a loss for *the* Revolution; and, paradoxically, might perforce be better historians, for they would have to construct, from the Wars of the Roses, the Tudor Monarchy (is there a premature Robespierre in Henry VIII, a dictatorship of the bourgeoisie?), the attainder of royal ministers, the religious conflicts of the sixteenth and seventeenth centuries, and from 1832, pieces of that great arch which in fact, in the epochal sense, make up the bourgeois revolution.

I am objecting to a model which concentrates attention upon one dramatic episode—*the* Revolution—to which all that goes before and after must be related; and which insists upon an ideal type of this Revolution against which all others may be judged.[23] Minds which thirst for a tidy platonism very soon become impatient with actual history. The French Revolution was a fundamental moment in the history of the West, and in its rapid passage through a gamut of experiences it afforded incomparable insights and prefigurements of subsequent conflicts. But because it was a gigantic experience it was not necessarily a typical one. So far from an advanced, egalitarian, left-Jacobin phase being an intrinsic part of any fulfilled bourgeois revolution, recent research into the role of the Parisian crowd, the actual social composition of the sections and of the institutions of the Terror and of the revolutionary armies,[24] as well as into the national emergency of war dictatorship, calls into question how far it is meaningful to characterize the Jacobinism of the Year II as an authentic "bourgeois" experience at all. And certainly the *industrial* bourgeoisie cannot be credited with being either the "vanguard" of Jacobinism or the major social force upholding this profoundly ambiguous political moment.

It happened in one way in France, in another way in England. I am not disputing the importance of the difference—and of the different traditions which ensued—but the notion of typicality. When taken to England the model surreptitiously nudges one towards an attempt to explain 1832 and the fracas about the Corn Laws, taken together, as a kind of pusillanimous, low-pressure reproduction of the conflict in France. The term "aristocracy" affords the bridge: both were conflicts between aristocrats and bourgeois, but how petty and inconclusive does the one appear beside the other! The profound difference in the life-situations of an aristocratic *order* and a capitalist *gentry* (as well as of the disaffected groupings) blurs into an acceptable schematic *mélange*.

One may offer a different explanation as to what the conflict of 1832 was about. Despite all that has been observed since Marx's time, as to the operation of élites, bureaucracies, etc., Marxists generally seek to reduce political phenomena to their "real" class significance, and often fail, in analysis, to allow sufficient distance between the one and the other. But in fact those moments in which governing institutions appear as the direct, emphatic, and unmediated organs of a "ruling-class" are exceedingly rare, as well as transient. More often these institutions operate with a good deal of autonomy, and sometimes with distinct interests of their own, within a general context of class power which prescribes the limits beyond which this autonomy cannot with safety be stretched, and which, very generally, discloses the questions which arise for executive decision. Attempts to short-circuit analysis end up by explaining nothing.[25]

Analysis of the governing élite in England before 1832 must surely proceed at this level. The settlement of 1688 inaugurated a hundred years of comparative social stasis, so far as overt class conflict or the maturation of class consciousness was concerned. The main beneficiaries were those vigorous agrarian capitalists, the gentry. But this does not mean that the governing institutions represented, in an unqualified manner, the gentry as a "ruling-class". At a local level (the magistracy) they did so in an astonishingly naked manner. At a national level (desuetude of the old restrictions on marketing, the facilitation of enclosures, the expansion of empire) they furthered their interests. But at the same time a prolonged period of social stasis is commonly one in which ruling institutions degenerate, corruptions enter, channels of influence silt up, an élite entrenches itself in positions of power. A distance opened up between the majority of the middle and lesser gentry (and associated groups) and certain great agrarian magnates, privileged merchant capitalists, and their hangers-on, who manipulated the organs of the State in their own private interest. Nor was this a simple "class" tension between an aristocracy of great magnates and the lesser gentry. Certain magnates only were on the "inside", and influence swung according to factional politics, the diplomacy of great family connections, control of boroughs, and the rest.

This is to say that the exercise of power in the second half of the eighteenth century was very much as that inverted-Marxist, Sir Lewis Namier, described in *The Structure of Politics*—although he unaccountably neglected to go on and characterize it as a sophisticated system of brigandage. It should be seen less as government by an aristocracy (a distinct estate with a common style of life and outlook, and with institutional legitimation) than as a *parasitism*—a racket, which the King himself could not break into except by becoming the croupier. It was not wholly a parasitism: the business of the nation had to be carried on, from time to time the "independent" gentry—and their representatives in parliament— had to be appeased, there were even occasions (although one after another these are called in question as the disciples of Namier break into the archives of the last of the great *mafiosi*) when the interests of the nation or the class, rather than the family or faction, were consulted. Nor was it *only* a parasitism: being conducted upon so gigantic a scale, from bases in private and public wealth of such magnitude, and commanding influence which reached, by the most direct means, into the army, the navy, the chartered companies, the Church, the Law, it was bound to congeal into something that looks almost like an estate; to surround itself in a cocoon of ideological apologetics; and to nourish a style of life, of conspicuous— indeed, spectacular—consumption which is associated with a true aristocracy. Indeed, these great constitutional brigands came, not without reason, to confuse themselves with their French, Prussian, and even Russian cousins—a confusion which was to cost Europe dear during the wars.

Nevertheless, all this does not quite make up an aristocracy, conceived of as a ruling class. It was... nothing but itself. A unique formation. Old Corruption. It could scarcely have seen the eighteenth century out if the French Revolution had not occurred, providentially, to save it. If it commanded immense influence, it raised also immense resentments. It alienated the sisters and the cousins and the aunts of those who had not obtained preferment, the officers who had not been promoted, the clergy who had not found patrons, the contractors who had not obtained orders, the talented who had been passed over, the wives who had been snubbed. Something of this can be seen in the irresponsible zest with which many of the propertied supported Wilkes. Nor was it only elements in the City of London and the nascent industrial bourgeoisie which regarded Old Corruption with a baleful eye. The distance which had opened up, after the American secession, between the brigandage and the gentry from whom, in the last analysis, they derived their power, can be seen in the strength of Wyvill's Association movement in the counties—those county meetings for reform which were one of the only occasions, in the eighteenth century, when the gentry assembled and expressed themselves as a class.

The French Revolution saved Old Corruption, for evident reasons. (Here at least I am in agreement with Anderson and Nairn.) The disaffection of gentry and farmers evaporated in the high noon of enclosures and of corn prices. Pitt (who had once been a Chosen Son of the Associationists) effected some rationalization in the State. The industrial bourgeoisie were kept in good humour—their machinery protected, trade unions repressed, protective labour legislation dismantled.[26] The "symbiosis" of land and commercial and manufacturing wealth continued at political, social and economic levels. But Old Corruption emerged from the wars, despite all modifications, very much as it went into them. In certain respects, through its involvement with European reaction, its repression of democratic impulses (and their auto-suppression among the gentry and middle classes), its spawning of fund-holders in the National Debt, and the accession of mysticism to the ideology of constitutionalism, it emerged in a more parasitic form than it had taken before. And Cobbett, in characterizing it as Old Corruption or "the Thing", may have been a better Marxist than the Marxists who have tried to put him right.

Thus one must observe caution in characterizing the conflict of 1832. The enemy of the reformers was not an aristocratic estate, nor the entire agrarian capitalist class, but a secondary complex of predatory interests. While the industrial bourgeoisie had particular grievances and played a far more active part than it had done, as a group, in previous reform agitations, a considerable part of the gentry were disaffected also. From the 1770s onwards the reform movement had always found support among the gentry; and from this milieu many of its leaders were derived—Cartwright, Wyvill, Burdett, Hunt—while Cobbett always had an audience among the farmers. In the crucial general elections which preceded 1832 Old Corruption held on to most of its own rotten boroughs, but the counties (where, admittedly, there were many urban votes) were carried for reform. And reform was enacted in parliament by one faction of gentry and great magnates against another.

When it came to the push, Old Corruption found that it had little behind it, beyond what its own largesse could buy—and the institutions of State itself. If there had really been a direct confrontation between agrarian and industrial bourgeoisie, then revolution must have occurred. But in fact, as the crisis disclosed itself it appeared increasingly that "the Thing" and the people were "at issue." And this also explains why it is so tempting to say that "the middle classes" were the beneficiaries of the 1832 settlement. If the industrial bourgeoisie had been excluded from the political game in 1688 it was not because their property was industrial but because it was petty. As their property became more substantial they felt a corresponding accession of resentment; but this resentment was shared by many of their cousins (and sometimes literally cousins) in the country and the City. 1832 changed, not one game for another but the rules of the game, restoring the flexibility of 1688 in a greatly altered class context. It provided a framework within which new and old bourgeois could adjust their conflicts of interest without resort to force. These conflicts, not only of direct interest but of outlook, style of life, religion, were considerable; but so also were the attractive forces. We may set the conflict surrounding the Corn Laws on one side; but on the other (and simultaneously) we must set the existence of a common enemy, in Chartism, and the railway boom to which a parliament still overstocked with gentry gave tardy blessings and in the rewards of which the gentry shared.

It is true that the rôle in all this of the industrial bourgeoisie was not especially heroic. They left the longest and hardest part of the agitation to the plebeian Radicals; the parliamentary conduct was in the hands of a section of the gentry and lawyers, and they slipped in through the breach which these contestants made. In this they were not wholly untypical of other industrial bourgeois: mill-owners, accountants, company-promoters, provincial bankers, are not historically notorious for their desperate propensity to rush, bandoliers on their shoulders, to the barricades. More generally they arrive on the scene when the climactic battles of the bourgeois revolution have already been fought.

Thereafter they enlarged their influence pretty much in step with their advancement in real socio-economic power. To examine this statement would require, not an exercise in theoretical virtuosity, but a close, scrupulous, and, alas, empirical examination of the actual history, of the kind which has been offered, for one important moment (1867), by Royden Harrison.[27] It would require a sociological anatomy of the components of the "middle classes"—small gentry, farmers, industrial entrepreneurs with diverse interests, high and low finance, professional groups (independent and salaried), civil service, institutions of imperialism—their conflicts and accommodations, differing outlooks and styles. It would require also examination in strictly political terms, as the surviving positions of the old privilege were eroded, as different interests selected one or the other of the two formative parties as their protagonist, as the mediations of the party system became more complex, and as the appeal to (and the manufacture of) a middle-class public opinion became an important part of the game. One might find, in the political trajectory of Joseph Chamberlain, from the individualist radicalism of the competitive family business, through municipal and eventually State rationalization, and, thence (as the armaments industry, with its State contracts and its imbrication with finance-capital, grew in importance) to imperialism, and, finally, with the hardening of world competition, to protectionism and imperial rationalization, a figurement—which is almost too pat—of the process.

Anderson will have it that the "courage" of the industrial bourgeoisie had gone after 1832. But what need did these bourgeois have of courage when money served them better? Why should they take up arms against primogeniture when, with increasing rapidity, land was becoming only one interest beside cotton, railways, iron and steel, coal, shipping, and finance? Classes do not exist as abstract, platonic categories, but only as men come to *act* in rôles determined by class objectives, to feel themselves to *belong* to classes, to define their interests as between themselves and as against other classes. In the case of the conflicts between 1760 and 1832 there are certainly moments when the gentry and the manufacturers appear to offer the poles around which antagonistic class institutions can indeed be seen, in the magistracy and Church on the one hand, and in Unitarian or Quaker meetings and in the growth of a middle-class press on the other. The Priestley Riots in Birmingham in 1791 show to what extremes this class antagonism might have grown. Given this or that, all might have happened in a different way. But in fact it did not. After the French Revolution evangelicalism blurred some of the differences between the Establishment and Nonconformity (the common preoccupation with disciplining the lower orders facilitated the movement).[28] Some of the manufacturers took their places on the Bench. Coal and canals brought the two together, as did commissions in the Volunteers, common service against Luddism, common resentment against income tax. They shared, although with varying degrees of intensity, a common resentment against Old Corruption. Hence all happened as it did. Given the most perfect model of relations to the means of production ("basis"), no one, in 1760 or 1790, could have been certain as to how the cultural and institutional formations would in fact take place. But, happening as it did, it registered the fact that these were not to take the field of history as class antagonists, and that the "symbiosis" of the two social groups was already well advanced.

In what sense, then, can we accept the Nairn-Anderson thesis that the aristocracy emerged from all this as the "master", the "vanguard", in "control of the State"? It is evident that the 1832 settlement permitted the perpetuation of certain "aristocratic" institutions, areas of privilege, an aristocratic style of life. It also afforded some contribution to the "ethos" of the ruling group (although not the "dominant ethos") and to norms of leadership which (as Anderson notes) was to prove valuable in the government of empire. But when we move closer a judgment must be more qualified. At the level of local government (except in the countryside) aristocratic influence was largely displaced: the Lord Lieutenancy effectually disappeared; the magistracy was partly taken over; the Board of Guardians and the organs of municipal government were satisfactorily urban bourgeois institutions; the police force (one of the first-fruits of 1832) was on an acceptable bourgeois-bureaucratic model. At a national level the record has been ambiguous. If aristocratic modes have been perpetuated in the City, they have been very much less evident in the great institutions of industrial capitalism. If Old Corruption still presides over Oxford and Cambridge, yet London, the civic universities, the technical colleges, etc., have long developed upon a different pattern. If aristocratic privilege held on to the armed forces, it had begun to lose control, even before 1832, of the press, and it has never gained control of more recent media of communication.

Thus on the briefest survey of commonly observed evidence the picture appears very different from the over-strident portrait of our authors. This aristocratic master would appear to govern from the monarchy, the House of Lords, the armed services, Oxford and Cambridge, the City, and the institutions of Empire; and to have had an excessive influence in the two older political parties. This is without doubt an impressive list; but it becomes less overwhelming if we recall that the armed services (for reasons which are well resumed by Anderson)[29] have never exercised an influence within the British power elite comparable to that in German or contemporary American history; and that the influence of the House of Lords has progressively diminished. Moreover, the case of the ancient universities and of the old political parties is exceedingly complex and (in the latter case) very much more complex than the quantitative methods of analysis of post-Namierite historians might lead us to suppose. In a phrase, the politicians whom the public remember are Peel, Bright, Gladstone, Disraeli, the Chamberlains, Lloyd George, and Baldwin, and not Lord Derby or Lord Salisbury, or even, unjustly, Lord Palmerston.

Even so, aristocratic influence is formidable. But to show the aristocracy as a "vanguard" one would have to show a series of significant historical moments when aristocratic influence was directly and effectively opposed to important interests of the newer bourgeoisie. Such moments can be found (Old Corruption transplanted its flag, after 1832, to Dublin Castle), but they are not common and are generally ambiguous or nugatory in their outcome. The *locus classicus* which Anderson and Nairn appear to have overlooked is Bagehot's *English Constitution* (1867). For the devastating cynicism with which Bagehot justified the prominence given in the Constitution to "a retired widow and an unemployed youth" is a very different matter from the "suffocating traditionalism" which they suppose to have endured from the time of Burke.[30] The point is not whether Bagehot's account is accurate, but that the kind of cynicism, and also self-confidence, which his account exemplifies, emasculated bourgeois republicanism in England. Locke had given to the gentry an acceptable naturalistic justification of the institution of monarchy. In the crisis of the French Revolution, Burke inflated naturalism into that traditionalism in which the wisdom of past ages appeared as a vast National Debt whose interest charges it was perpetually the business of the living generation to pay. Bagehot restored the naturalism of Locke, but in a nakedly utilitarian manner. The monarchy and aristocratic institutions (the "dignified part" of the Constitution) were found to be *useful*, in distracting attention from the real operation of power in the "efficient part" (which Bagehot had no doubt was under the "despotic" control of the middle classes). The "theatrical show" of the dignified part held the masses in awe, and it became more, rather than less, necessary after 1867 since (as he noted in his introduction to the second edition (1872)) "in all cases it must be remembered that a political combination of the lower classes, as such and

for their own objects, is an evil of the first magnitude." Bagehot even
found a justification for the perpetuation of some aristocratic influence
within the effective part:

> "As long as we keep up a double set of institutions. . . we should take care that
> the two match nicely, and hide where the one begins and where the other ends.
> This is in part effected by conceding some subordinate power to the august part
> of our polity, but it is equally aided by keeping an aristocratic element in the
> useful part of our polity."

And history has confirmed Bagehot's thesis neatly. In 1688 a bourgeois
parliament exiled a King because he threatened to encroach too far upon
the Constitution's efficient parts. In 1937 it needed only a bourgeois
Prime Minister to give another King his cards, because he was unsuited to
play a sufficiently august part in the "theatrical show."

I offer Bagehot, however, not as a social scientist but as an interesting
moment in bourgeois ideology. He gave to the middle classes an apologia
for the aristocratic parts of the Constitution in the best of bourgeois
terms: (1) they afforded security; (2) they helped to keep the working
class in order. Bagehot, and Gilbert-and-Sullivan, taken together, remind us
of the superb confidence of the Victorian middle class in the face of
Anderson's "vanguard." They give us the reasons why the middle class
tolerated the abominable Empress Brown and failed to give their support
to Dilke. But in fact, as even Marxists are coming to discover, history does
not work with the well-oiled cynicism which Bagehot proposed. The
aristocratic ethos still had a life of its own, and some real bases for
continued growth; and one of the best passages in Anderson's *Origins* is
that in which he discusses the blood-transfusion which the imperialist
climax, after 1880, gave to this influence.[31] But even here one may
suggest a certain dialectic—a limit of tolerance beyond which aristocratic
influence has not been allowed to grow. It may be detected as early as the
French Revolution: the rhetoric of Burke called forth the caustic response
of Byron. The swelling pomp of the theatrical show at the imperialist
climax was swiftly followed by the counter-swell, when even Churchill
could threaten the Lords with the memory of "ironclad pikemen" and
Lloyd George (as Chancellor of the Exchequer) could address cheering
audiences in tones unmistakably borrowed from Tom Paine:

> "[The Peers] need no credentials. They do not even need a medical certificate.
> They need not be sound either in body, or in mind. They only require a
> certificate of birth—just to prove that they are the first of the litter. You would
> not choose a spaniel on these principles. . ."[32]

And, in the pathetic coda of our own time, the enervated conservative
relapse which led up to the accession of Lord Home was a windfall gain

for Labour, provoking, by a long-conditioned reflex, the technocratic face and the Northern burr of Harold Wilson, and the falsetto Gilbert-and-Sullivan of *That Was The Week That Was.*

The British aristocracy has certainly proved itself to be, as Beatrice Webb described it, "a curiously tough substance." But if we are to understand the real balance of forces, instead of importing Sartre's schema of "detotalized totality"[33] we could do worse than refer to her fuller account of "London Society" at the climax of imperialism. This aristocracy, in her observation, certainly surrounded and solidified "Society" and no doubt influenced its style of life. But—

"... it did not surround or isolate the Court; it was already a minor element in the Cabinet; and... it was barely represented in the ever-changing group of international financiers who ruled the money market. The bulk of the shifting mass of wealthy persons who were conscious of belonging to London Society... were, in the last quarter of the nineteenth century, professional profit-makers: the old-established families of bankers and brewers, often of Quaker descent, coming easily in social precedence; then one or two great publishers, and, at a distance, shipowners, the chairmen of railways and some other great corporations, the largest of the merchant bankers—but as yet no retailers."

There were "no fixed caste barriers" of any kind:

"But deep down in the unconscious herd instinct of the British governing class there *was* a test of fitness for membership of this most gigantic of social clubs, but a test which was seldom recognized by those who applied it, still less by those to whom it was applied, *the possession of some form of power over other people.*"[34]

Admission to the élite was not, in fact, within the gift of the aristocracy: the aristocracy, rather, registered those shifts and fluctuations of power which occurred elsewhere, and graced a "Society" which came into existence independently of its influence. They were like the staff at an elaborate and prestigious hotel, who could in no way influence the comings and goings of clientele, who or at what time or with whom, but who could arrange the ball and appoint a Master of Ceremonies.

Beatrice Webb's account precedes the notorious "lowering of tone" of the Court and aristocracy after the accession of Edward VII: the admission of the newspaper barons (who hoisted the aristocracy's chief enemy into the premiership during the war)—not to mention more recent vulgarizations. It is true that each national bourgeoisie has its own peculiar nastiness which it has often inherited from the class which went before; with the Germans, militarism and Statism; with the French, chauvinism and intellectual metropolitomania; with the Italians, corruption; and with the Americans, the ruthless celebration of a human nature red in tooth and law. It is true also that the peculiar nastiness of the British bourgeoisie is in shameless observances of status and obsession with a spurious gentility. It is true, finally, that the "dignified" parts of the Constitution have been in this century an effective source of mystification and that—as Ralph Miliband has documented in *Parliamentary Socialism*—the parliamentary Labour Party has been the first, and most eager, subject of hypnosis. All this is important. But in suggesting that capitalist rationalization today is crippled by this aristocratic inheritance, and that this is the most substantial element of our current crisis (Anderson's *Origins* concludes: "The unfinished work of 1640 and 1832 must be taken up where it was left off"), I think our authors misread our history, and mistake the true character of our ruling class.

Moreover, they have an uncomfortable affinity of tone with those journalistic diagnosticians of the British malaise whom they profess to despise. All this, the anti-Establishment fury, the complaints about British salesmanship, the poor amenities at London airport or the restrictive practices of British trade unions, backward English empiricism and aristocratic suffocation, is very much the mode just now. Mr. David Frost, Mr. Shanks, and Comrade Anderson are saying different things, but there is the same edge to each voice. A great deal of what they say is true, but what alarms me is the things that none of them say—that there are at the same time certain strengths and humane traditions in British life which Other Countries, including those whose airports are superb, whose Marxism is mature, and whose salesmanship is high-powered, do not always display.

More than this, I am not at all sure that they have located the real antagonist. Old Corruption has passed away, but a new, and entirely different, predatory complex occupies the State. It is surely to this new complex, with its interpenetration of private industry and the State (Government contracts, especially for war materials, of an unprecedented size, subsidies, municipal indebtedness to private finance, etc.), its control over major media of communication, its blackmail by the City, its reduction of the public sector to subordinate rôles, and its capacity to dictate the conditions within which a Labour Government must operate— it is surely to this new Thing, with its vast influence reaching into the Civil Service, the professions, and into the trade union and labour movement itself, rather than to the hunting of an aristocratic Snark, that an analysis of the political formations of our time should be addressed?

III

What is extraordinary, in our authors' discussion of the "English ideology," is the degree to which they are themselves imprisoned within the myopic vision for which they express such contempt. They have never imagined the great arch of bourgeois culture. They can see, in bourgeois ideology, only two significant moments: the Enlightenment, and the moment at which Marxism arrived. In both moments (they suggest) the British bourgeoisie had no part. Of 1640:

"Because of its 'primitive', pre-Enlightenment character, the ideology of the Revolution founded no significant tradition, and left no major after-effects. Never was a major revolutionary ideology neutralized and absorbed so completely. Politically, Puritanism was a useless passion."[35]

Thereafter the English bourgeoisie accomplished its destiny by "blind empiricism," and became "estranged from the central current of later bourgeois evolution." It sat out the French Revolution and missed Jacobinism ("the apex of bourgeois progress"). "The English bourgeoisie. . . could afford to dispense with the dangerous tool of reason and stock the national mind with historical garbage."[36] It handed on to the working class "no impulse of liberation, no revolutionary values, no universal language. Instead it transmitted the deadly germs of utilitarianism"—the "one authentic, articulated ideology" which it was able to produce.[37] As for Marxism, no traffic has been known between it and these barbarous shores.

The misunderstandings are so large that it is tempting to capitulate before them. They assume, in any case, hermetic divisions between national cultures which are quite unreal (one thinks of Hobbes and Descartes, Hume and Rousseau, Coleridge and German philosophy).[38] But what our authors have done, *inter alia*, is (after skipping over the entire phase of the heroic annunciation of bourgeois individualism, in which the English contribution, if somewhat late, was by no possible account negligible): (1) to ignore the importance of the Protestant and bourgeois-democratic inheritance; (2) to overlook the importance of capitalist political economy as "authentic, articulated ideology"; (3) to forget the contribution, over more than three centuries, of British natural scientists; (4) to confuse an empirical idiom with an ideology.

It should be sufficient to mention these points for them to become self-evident. And more might be added. One might offer a discussion of the realist novel, or of romanticism, if one had not already been warned off by Nairn's reference to "a dilettante literary culture descended from the aristocracy"—the thought of a *professional* and truly-bourgeois literary culture which would win the approval of *that* tone is enough to make one blench. The point is not to rush in to the defence of British intellectual traditions, or to minimize their characteristic limitations. It is to call for a more collected and informed analysis, and one which takes some account of their historic strengths. Spleen is not a particularly effective cutting instrument.

Britain is, after all, a *protestant* country. Catholicism (as a centre of spiritual or intellectual authority) was smashed in this country more thoroughly than in all but two or three other parts of Christendom. Moreover, it was smashed, not by one rival religious ideology with its own authority, discipline, and well-structured theology, but by the comparative decomposition of any centre of authority. All those sermons and pamphlets, all that prayer before battle, all that wrangling about oaths and altars and bishops, all that sectarian fragmentation, which Anderson finds so unenlightened, so sadly distanced from real economic motives, was in fact part of an epochal cultural confrontation. The English Revolution was fought out in religious terms, not because the participants were confused as to their real interests but because religion *mattered*. The wars were, in good measure, about religious authority. A man's right of property in his own conscience and religious allegiances had become just as real, and momentarily *more* real, than economic property rights. At this point of history, the psychic crisis between old modes and new was exactly here.

Our authors would prefer it if it had been, not about religion, but against religion altogether. An historian cannot bother with this kind of objection. It is more important to note the consequences of what actually happened. To suggest that the "ideological legacy of the Revolution was almost nil" is to confuse formal with real attributes. By destroying the established magic of the Church, triumphant Protestantism made possible the multiplication of rationality, and the dispersal of rational initiatives, throughout the country and in different social milieus. Even before it had taken possession of the market economy, private enterprise and a qualified *laissez faire* had taken over the cultural economy. It was not necessary in Britain for a radical intelligentsia to mobilize under its chieftains to attack clericalism and obscurantism because the enemy, although it persisted, had no power to blockade intellectual life. And since the eighteenth-century Church can scarcely be said to have had an articulated ideology, it was unnecessary for its critics, in that area at least, to develop a systematic opposition. In France the armies of Orthodoxy and Enlightenment faced each other. But Britain was more like a weakly occupied country, in which—whenever orthodoxy had repelled a small frontal attack, it found itself harassed on its flanks, at its rear, or even within its own midst. The Enlightenment proceeded in Britain, not like one of those flood-tides massing against a crumbling dyke, but like the tide which seeps into the eroded shores, mudflats and creeks of an estuary whose declivities are ready to receive it.

Other countries may have produced a "true intelligentsia", an "internally unified intellectual community"; but it is rubbish to suggest that there is some crippling disablement in the failure of British intellectuals to form "an independent intellectual enclave" within the body politic. Rather, there were formed in the eighteenth century *scores* of intellectual enclaves, dispersed over England, Wales and Scotland, which made up for what they lost in cohesion by the multiplicity of initiatives afforded by these many bases and (as the entire record of scientific and technical advance witnesses) by the opportunities afforded for the interpenetration of theory and *praxis*. Much of the best in our intellectual culture has always come, not from the Ancient Universities nor from the self-conscious metropolitan coteries, but from indistinct nether regions. What our authors overlook is the enormous importance of that part of the revolutionary inheritance which may be described, in a secular sense, as the tradition of *dissent*.

At one end of the scale, the gentry (Newton, Fielding, Gibbon) made one contribution; and at the other end the artisans (with their scores of inventors) made another. Oxford and Cambridge, with their attempt to instate an irrelevant theocratic platonism, contributed little, except by a repulsion which accentuated the sceptical tone of those who were repelled. Edinburgh and Glasgow contributed far more (Hume, Smith, the Scottish physiocrats, and on to—*hélas*—James Mill and the *Edinburgh Review*), and redressed the insularity of English thought by their more fluent intercourse with France. In the midst of all this, as the major carrier for these traditions, was that mixed middle-class society, both metropolitan and provincial, somewhat Unitarian in tone—the colleges of Hoxton, Hackney and Warrington, the Birmingham Lunar Society, the Manchester Literary and Philosophical Society, and those circles at Norwich, Derby, Nottingham, or Sheffield whose conversation Coleridge found—when canvassing for *The Watchman* in Birmingham—to be "sustained with such animation [and] enriched with such a variety of information."

These English bourgeois were not, all of them, the bloody fools that Nairn and Anderson take them to be. It is not an argument between them and those of Other Countries. It happened one way in France, and another way here. The French experience was marked by a clarity of confrontation, a *levée en masse* of the intelligentsia, a disposition towards systematizing and towards intellectual hierarchy—the staff officers, attachés, and so on, who grouped round the great radical *chefs de bataille*. The English experience certainly did not encourage sustained efforts of synthesis: since few intellectuals were thrown into prominence in a conflict with authority, few felt the need to develop a systematic critique. They thought of themselves, rather, as exchanging specialized products in a market which was tolerably free, and the sum of whose intellectual commodities made up the sum of "knowledge." This encouraged, in some areas, laxness and irresponsibility. But the number of specialized producers was very large; and the historian of British intellectual culture in the later eighteenth and in much of the nineteenth centuries is impressed with the vigour of the tradition of dissent, the manifold collisions and mutations—not the distinction of this or that mind, but the number of lesser talents, each with some particular but limited distinction.

One may agree that such a tradition was incapable of nurturing a Marx, although without it *Capital* could not have been written. It was, however, capable of nurturing Darwin, and the significance with which that moment illuminates the strengths of certain intellectual traditions illuminates also the fatal blindness of the Anderson-Nairn critique of "empiricism." With the usual pig-headed refusal to conform to schematic proprieties of most British phenomena, English science was given a charter, not by insurgent encyclopaedists, but by a royalist Lord Chancellor. The terms of the charter are worth recalling:

> "For the wit and mind of man, if it work upon matter, which is the contemplation of the creatures of God, worketh according to the stuff, and is limited thereby; but if it work upon itself, as the spider worketh his web, then it is endless, and brings forth indeed cobwebs of learning, admirable for the fineness of thread and work, but of no substance or profit."[39]

And upon the heels of this there followed the astonishing injunction:

> "The end of our foundation is the knowledge of the causes and secret motions of things and the enlarging of the bounds of human empire, to the effecting of all things possible."[40]

The exact nature of the relationship between the bourgeois and the scientific revolutions in England is undecided. But they were clearly a good deal more than just good friends. In a matter of a few decades great territories of natural phenomena which had been shut against the intellectual public were thrown open. Bacon's casuistry of first and second causes ("the contemplation of the creatures of God") neatly dissociated manifest phenomena, whose exploration was fully authorized, from ulterior ideological causes, towards which a formal ritual obeisance was expected but which as effective influences were allowed to lapse. And this suited very well the mood of those intellectuals in the eighteenth century who, finding themselves to be very little opposed by theological authority, were quite content to leave it alone and get on with the exploration of nature. Many of the clergy themselves, from the security of their rectories, were able to further the Enlightenment; even the atrocious Bishop of Llandaff first founded his reputation upon his contributions, not to theology but to chemistry. The Unitarians pushed God so far back into his Baconian heaven of first causes that he became, except for purposes of moral incantation, quite ineffectual. He was left alone (alas! to be fetched out later against the people as a furious Papa) while the bourgeoisie entered into their true inheritance—the exploitation of nature.

It should not have happened this way. Heaven should have been stormed, *molte con brio*, and the fruits of knowledge should have been wrested from the clutches of priests. But happen this way it did. (The contrast between let us say, Zola on the one hand, and Hardy and George Moore on the other, or between Anatole France and E.M. Forster, points to a continuing difference in literary modes.) It was a happening so epoch-making that we can excuse our authors for not noticing it: we often see the houses but ignore the landscape. But it was an advance, however spectacular, that was contained within its own ideological limitations. On the one hand, the framework given by Newton to the physical and natural sciences tended to share the same naturalistic, mechanical bias as English constitutional theory. On the other hand, the licence to explore nature was not extended with the same liberality to the exploration of *human* nature, society.

It is this which makes the moment of *The Origin of Species* so moving, and, in its own terms, a vindication of the empirical mode. For from their base in "second causes" the natural sciences were massing against the First Cause itself; or, if not against God (who as events proved was willing to be shuffled off to an even more remote empyrean), then against magical notations of the origin of the natural world and of man. Biology, geology, natural history, astronomy, after decades of empirical accumulation—all were pressing matters to a decision. And the break-through, the moment of synthesis, came, not with some English Voltaire immersed in metro-politan tumult, but with a neurotic, secluded, intellectually evasive man, once destined for a clerical career, who nevertheless was the protagonist of an inherited empirical habit, which was raised in him to a pitch of intensity until it became a breath-taking intellectual courage, as he laboriously restructured whole sciences and effected a new synthesis. We cannot come away from any account of Darwin without the conviction that a respect for fact is not only a *technique*, it can also be an intellectual force in its own right. When the work was done the fracas could begin. Huxley could storm heaven. Darwin, wiser than him, took evasive action and offered a comment on the fertilization of orchids.[41] He knew that no one in Heaven had the patience to study barnacles long enough to give him any answer. We remember Huxley as the ideologue, Darwin as the scientist.

This indicates one place where the English intellectual tradition offered something more than "nullity." In one sense, Darwinism appears as the natural and inevitable outcome of a culture of agrarian capitalists, who had spent decades in empirical horticulture and stock-breeding. Most revolutions in thought have this "natural" appearance, so that some scholars ask, not how Darwinism happened, but why it took so long to happen. In another sense, nothing was natural about a transmutation of scientific thought which overthrew fixed categories which had stood for centuries and which effected a new view of human nature. There should have been more crisis than there was, more of a parting of the ideological heavens. The intellectuals should have signalled their commitments; signed manifestos; identified their allegiances in the reviews. The fact that there was comparatively little of this may be accounted for by the fact that Darwin addressed a protestant and post-Baconian public, which had long assumed that if God was at issue with a respectable Fact (or if a dogma was at odds with a man's conscience) it was the former which must give way. The intelligentsia of Other Countries have been more fortunate. They have been able to fight their battles with more *panache* and more appeal to Universals because they have managed to preserve Holy Church as a foil to this day.

Two other ideological inheritances of the Revolution (both of them unnoticed by our authors) have this same "natural" appearance. I cannot examine here the bourgeois democratic tradition beyond insisting that, for good or ill, it contributed vastly more to the intellectual universe of the English working class than the utilitarianism of which they make so much. This contribution was made not only at an articulate and institutional level but also to the sub-political consensus of a people who (as two rather perceptive English Marxists once noted) "have always resented harsh mechanical organization of any kind."[42] (It was surely this resistance—greatly re-inforced by the Stalinist experience—which has afforded a great objection to the wide acceptance of "Marxism"? I have often noted the glassy look coming over a working-class audience when being addressed by a strident advocate of this or that brand of orthodox Marxism, as if the *tone*, far more than the argument, stirred in the collective unconscious some memory of the apparitor, the summoner, and the arch-deacon's courts.)

I have commented already upon the genesis of capitalist political economy. This was a far more systematic, highly-structured ideology than is to be found in purely political or philosophical areas. It was so, in part, because the more advanced agriculturalists, as well as some of the manufacturers, found themselves to be impeded by the fairly systematic (although disintegrating) system of mercantilist and paternalist theory, as well as statutory restrictions. One system called into existence a contrary, and superior, system.

Bacon had expelled God from the natural sciences. Adam Smith expelled him from economic theory. Tawney and Hill have examined the preparatory phases, the changing moral notations of men in their economic relations, which led up to this sudden, swift demoralising of them all. Smith brought to the economic functions of the State the same jealousy which Locke had shown to its political functions; like Locke he wished power and initiative to be dispersed among the propertied.

No incitement to the attention of the sovereign can ever counter-balance the smallest discouragement to that of the landlord. The attention of the sovereign can at best be but a very general and vague consideration of what is likely to contribute to the better cultivation of the greater part of his dominions. The attention of the landlord is a particular and minute consideration of what is likely to be the most advantageous application of every inch of ground upon his estate. The principal attention of the sovereign ought to be to encourage, by every means in his power, the attention both of the landlord and of the farmer; by allowing both to pursue their own interest in their own way. . .

The economic protestantism—the "political" (but more truthfully anti-political) economy—which Smith founded did not threaten to overthrow the State: it simply turned its back upon it, leaving to it only vestigial functions—the maintenance of security, facilitation of transport, removal of restrictions upon trade. The triumph of these theories, and the satisfactory manner of their working, explain the comparative indifference of the industrial bourgeoisie to political theory as such: it didn't matter. When placed in relation to this immensely coherent ideology, with its compelling analogies with "natural" process, utilitarianism does not appear as the "one authentic" ideology of the bourgeoisie but simply as a subordinate tradition within it—a reminder (which the complexities of industrialism made daily more pressing) that the State had important functions, and an attempt to rationalise its institutions.

Nor was the theoretical construction of Smith and of his successors in any sense at all the product of "blind empiricism." It was a systematic framework of thought so comprehensive and yet so flexible that it formed the structure within which the social sciences and political thought of Victorian England were still framed; it underwrote commercial imperialism; it conquered the intelligence of the bourgeoisie throughout the world; and after a sharp-fought and impressive resistance (Hodgskin, Owen, O'Brien) the English working-class movement capitulated before it and regrouped in order to maximize its rewards within the framework which it dictated. Finally, it has survived, less in sophisticated theory than in popular myth, until this day. It is in the name of some "natural" law of a free economy that the public tolerates its unfreedom in the face of the monopolists, the land-speculators, the controllers of the media of communication.

How is it possible for Marxists to overlook this when Marx himself saw at a glance that this was his most formidable ideological opponent, and devoted his life's work to overthrowing it? But in all this I cannot see empiricism as an *ideology* at all. Anderson and Nairn have confused an intellectual *idiom*, which for various historical reasons has become a national habit, with an ideology. Bacon and Hazlitt, Darwin and Orwell, may all have employed this idiom, but they can scarcely be said to have been attached to the same ulterior ideological assumptions. There has recently been an attempt, it is true, to erect empiricism *into* an ideology, or an end-of-ideology. But while this has no doubt been flattering to the British, it has not been convincing, and the fashion is very nearly over.

No doubt our authors suffered a painful exposure to this phase of the intellectual Cold War, and their rebellion against those English ideologists, Popper, Hayek, Beloff, Elton, etc., does them credit. My complaint is against carrying a moment of rebellion into an interpretation of history. Something of what they say is true. Idiom is not unimportant. The empirical idiom can favour insular resistances and conceptual opportunism. But it may also conceal acute intelligence and a conceptual toughness which is immanent rather than explicit; at best it has carried the realism of the English novel, and has served—notably in the natural sciences—as an idiom superbly adapted to the interpenetration of theory and *praxis*.

Darwin wrote in an early letter, after a meeting with a friend, "he has a grand fact of some large molar tooth in the Trias."[43] Marx also had this respect for "grand facts", and in both men we can see that exciting dialectic of making-and-breaking, the formation of conceptual hypotheses and the bringing of empirical evidence to enforce or to break down these hypotheses, that friction between "molecular" research and "macro-scopic" generalization to which Wright Mills often referred. In any vital intellectual tradition this dialectic, this abrasion between models and particulars, is always evident. What is so profoundly depressing about so much in the various variants of Marxism since the death of Engels is their stubborn resistance to all the "grand facts" which the twentieth century has thrown into our faces, and their equally stubborn defence (or only trivial modifications) of the inherited model. We may agree as to the mediocrity, sloth, and parochialism of much contemporary British thought. And we must agree that the British working-class movement *"needs* theory like no other."[44] I can myself agree that this theory should be derived from the Marxist tradition, although this is by no means self-evident. But Anderson and Nairn are very sadly mistaken if they think that, in these latter days, they are going to overthrow "empiricism" in the name of a self-sufficient Marxist system, even if this system has been tarted-up with some neologisms. Nor should they be allowed to impoverish the creative impulse of the Marxist tradition in this way. For what their schema lack is the control of "grand facts", and England is unlikely to capitulate before a Marxism which cannot at least engage in a dialogue in the English idiom.

IV

The accounts which Anderson and Nairn offer us of the history of the British working class scarcely encourage enquiry. As we slide down the slopes of Nairn's prose (in his *Anatomy of the Labour Party*) there is no foothold, no growth of historical fact, however stunted and shallowly rooted, to which we may catch hold. Fabians appear, of astonishing influence and longevity, to whom—apart from the Webbs—no name is given; a "Left" is rebuked, which remains, from 1900 to 1960, almost faceless and without a voice; trade unions are moved around the rhetorical board, but *which* trade unions are not identified. History is flattened, stretched, condensed; awkward facts are not mentioned; awkward decades (e.g. 1920 to 1940) are simply elided. As one proceeds, the pharisaism of tone becomes (to borrow a phrase) suffocating. It is not only that no one has ever been right; no one has ever been wrong in an interesting or reputable way. It is "doubtful... if any other working-class movement has produced as many 'traitors'... as has Labourism"; but the thesis must be balanced by an antithetical sneer at "the angry denunciation of leaders in which sectarians and the Labour Left have always indulged." This "Left", which is never identified, is scourged for its "characteristic moralism", "painful and shameful impotence", "mindless passion which is only the obverse of its ideological subjection", and for its "total ignorance about how the Party works and ought to work." Labourism's "dominant ethos" has been "timorous curmudgeonry and funereal moralism", "sunk in hopelessly dusty routines and indescribably boring rhetoric", "its proper place in the British firmament midway between the House of Lords and the Boy Scouts."

We all of us make this kind of face at times, but we do not mistake a grimace for high theory. We may select four critical areas of weakness which both authors display. First, they have an inability to comprehend the *political context* of ideas and choices. Second, there is an absence of any serious sociological dimension to their analysis. Third, there is a crucial vulgarization of Gramsci's notion of "hegemony." And fourth they display not the least insight into the impact upon the British Labour movement of Communism.

The first point—the political innocence of our authors—is the most difficult to discuss, since it could be pursued satisfactorily only in the close examination of particulars. It is the opacity of their argument whenever we come to particular historical contexts which both inhibits discussion and gives to their thesis a certain compulsive plausibility. Every now and then Nairn suspends his commination service momentarily to indicate, in the sketchiest way, some actual historical event, but we are soon hustled past upon some such phrases as "the particular episodes and personalities of the period" are of "little importance", and the hectoring drone of the Marxist kirk elder is resumed.

History, however, is made up of episodes, and if we cannot get inside these, we cannot get inside history at all. This has always been inconvenient to the schematists, as Engels noted in 1890: "the materialist conception of history... has a lot of friends nowadays to whom it serves as an excuse for *not* studying history":

> Our conception of history is above all a guide to study, not a lever for construction after the manner of the Hegelians... Only too many of the younger Germans

simply make use of the phrase, historical materialism. . . in order to get their own
relatively scanty historical knowledge. . . fitted together into a neat system as
quickly as possible, and they then think themselves something very tremendous.[45]

The burden of our authors' argument is that it is the tragedy of our
history that Marxism passed the British working class by. This is blamed
upon the insularity and sociological conservatism of the British trade
unions, and upon the default of British intellectuals. A simple objectivity-
subjectivity model is employed, in which the trade unionists are seen as
blind, instinctive *praxis*, and the intellectuals as the embodiment of
articulate political consciousness. Since the Marxist intelligentsia did not
appear, the workers became subject to a tributary stream of capitalist
ideology, Fabianism. There is more than a hint of a new élitist voluntarism—
if only our First White Marxists had been born earlier, the course of
history would have been changed.

If, however, we place this model in a particular political context, it
does not do so well. At any time between 1890 and the present day we
will find a very substantial minority tradition, influencing major trade
unions, which belongs to the articulate Left. We will find systematic
grass-roots Marxist education—S.D.F., N.C.L.C., Communist Party—
which, while no doubt doctrinaire, has been no more doctrinaire than
the Marxism which (until recently) has been offered to the proletariat
of Other Countries. At the same time an examination of the actual
record would show that our authors have greatly exaggerated the
influence of the "Fabians", and, if we leave aside the direct influence of
Communism, most of the intellectuals who had an important influence
upon the British Labour Movement between 1920 and 1945 were either
social reformers within a Liberal tradition (J.A. Hobson, Beveridge, Boyd
Orr), or *marxisant* independents (Brailsford, Laski, Strachey, Cole), or
ethical socialists (Tawney, Orwell) whose contribution was somewhat
more than "sentimental moralizing." Not one of these loosely defined
groups conforms with Anderson's characterization of Fabianism—
"complacent confusion of influence with power, bovine admiration for
bureaucracy, ill-concealed contempt for equality, bottomless philistinism."
The influence of the "true" Webbian Fabianism over these years was slight,
and was largely confined to certain career politicians of Labour. It became
vastly more important after 1945; but here we should examine the
political context which favoured this tendency, rather than other
tendencies which were on offer and which appeared more influential in
1945. What our authors have done is to pick up a casual impression of the
trade union conservatism and the intellectual inertia of the past fifteen
years, and offer it as an interpretation of a hundred years of history.

The real history will only disclose itself after much hard research; it will
not appear at the snap of schematic fingers. But if we are to begin to

comprehend the British Left since 1880 we must take very much more seriously the international and imperialist context. One of the "grand facts" of the twentieth century which the orthodox Marxist model finds it difficult to accommodate is the resurgent nationalism of the imperialist climax. This foul politico-cultural climate, deeply contaminating the masses in the metropolitan countries, has presented quite exceptional problems to the Left. It is sheer moonshine to present the last eighty years in a way which suggests that the Left has been offered, throughout that time, the clear alternatives of developing a "hegemonic" strategy, aimed at the conquest of class power, or of capitulation to capitalist forms. There have been fleeting moments—the early 1890s, 1911-14, 1945-47—when, in real political terms, a vigorous socialist strategy was practicable. The movement of the 1890s crashed into the Boer War; the syndicalist surge of 1911-14 was smothered in the first great war; while the potentialities of 1945-47 were abolished by the Cold War. It was the night of Mafeking, in which the most sacred class distinctions dissolved in nationalist hysteria, which signalled the entry into this terrible epoch. In the action of the dockers on the Victoria and Albert docks, who threatened to refuse to service all ships which were not decorated in honour of Mafeking's relief—those same dockers upon whose support Tom Mann had sought to found a proletarian internationalism—we can already see the overwhelming defeats ahead.[46]

Thereafter the common experience of the British Left has been to find itself in a context which afforded very little opportunity for strategic advance, but which at the same time imposed exceptional duties of solidarity with other peoples. The "oppositional" mentality of the British Left is certainly a limiting outlook; but it has grown up simply because our Left has had so bloody much to *oppose*. Anyone who has more than a bookish knowledge of the Left knows this to be so.

This Left, both working-class and intellectual, with its crude and no doubt "moralistic" refusal to compromise with imperialism, does not appear in the Nairn-Anderson canon. Indeed, at points the record is plainly falsified:

> "All political groups—Conservatives, Liberals, and Fabians—were militantly imperialist in aims. . . The nascent socialist movement shared in the general jingoism, Webb, Hyndman, and Blatchford—Fabian, 'Marxist' and ILP-supporter—respectively the most influential, the most 'advanced' and the most popular spokesmen of the Left, were all in their different ways vocal imperialists."[47]

This is to cut history to fit a model with a vengeance. Anderson can do this only by ignoring the acute tensions within Liberalism (the Irish conflict, Lloyd George emerging as "pro-Boer", etc.); by confusing the socialist tradition with the small élitist Fabian group;[48] and by trimming his examples—William Morris, Tom Mann and Keir Hardie would have offered a different interpretation. (Similarly, Nairn offers Tillett's notorious outburst of chauvinism at the first annual conference of the I.L.P. as if it were the authentic I.L.P. article; he does not mention that Tillett was immediately rebuked.[49]) It is certainly true that imperialism penetrated deeply into the labour movement and even into the socialist groups; this is the tragedy of European socialism in this century. But an examination of the very examples which Anderson cites—the suspicion which the suppressed jingoism of Hyndman and Blatchford was regarded by a substantial part of their own following, and the rapidity with which they lost this following when it became fully exposed—would reveal a very much more complex picture.

The British Left, in the past eighty years, has never been offered abstract theoretical choices, but has been immersed in ineluctable political contexts characteristic of the metropolitan imperialist power. If we glance across the past *fifty years* at those issues around which the Left-Right conflict was most sharply engaged, we will find that most of them arise from this context: opposition to war, the response to the Russian Revolution, the independence of India, the rise of Fascism, the Spanish War, the Second Front, the Cold War, German Rearmament, the Kenya and Cyprus wars, the Campaign for Nuclear Disarmament. And this is the recurrent life-cycle of a Left upon which our authors never cease to heap scorn for its insularity; the parish within which they suppose the British Left to have been confined is in reality that of their own imperfect historical understanding. Increasingly compromised by, as well as confused by, its responses to Communism, it is a tradition which has lost much of its coherence and self-confidence since the last war. Nevertheless it is still there; and the temporary triumph of C.N.D. at Labour's Annual Conference in 1960 appears not (as Nairn has it) as a "miracle" but as the authentic expression of a tradition, deeply rooted, not only in an intelligentsia but in the trade unions and constituency parties.

Triumphs, of course, have been rare. They have been, in any final form, rare also in Other Countries. But only the platonist supposes that politics is an arena in which the enlightened can pursue, in a single-minded way, only teleological ends, such as "the conquest of class power." They are those who are living today who are oppressed and who are suffering, and politics is about them as much as about the future. A politics which ignores immediate solidarities will become peculiarly theoretic, ruthless, and self-defeating. There is even a sense (but not a Fabian sense) in which in a metropolitan imperialist country even the politics of the Left must be, on occasion, that damnable art of the possible. Have our authors really begun to comprehend the scale of human suffering in this century, and how *many* burning particular issues our Left has had thrust upon it where the obligations of solidarity left no choice—now the Meerut prisoners, now

Munich, now Suez; now Ibadan, now Rhodesia; now Abyssinia, now Kenya; now Spain and now Viet-Nam.

The overthrow of imperialism has generally been, not the first item on the agenda, but a little lower down—among the other business—when we have tried to save these lives, or, perhaps, avert the annihilation of all historical agendas. Meanwhile it has been possible to protest, to alert public opinion, to mobilize pressure-groups in order to mitigate the rigour of imperialist rule, or to express solidarity with Other Countries. British democratic structures, with their innumerable defences against any ultimate confrontation of class forces, have nevertheless exceptional opportunities for registering partial, oppositional pressures. Nairn tells us that the Left and Right in the Labour Party have been engaged, for about sixty years, in pseudo-conflict; but he scarcely ever bothers to tell us what this conflict was *about*. Whose blood was it, then, that flowed beneath those bridges which have carried history to the present day? We are in no position to pass judgment upon its failures unless we can assess whether or not the Left did succeed in influencing events in this actual situation or that. If it could be shown that the Left had contributed effectively to the defeat of Nazism, or to the detachment of India from imperial rule without an Indo-Chinese or Algerian blood-bath, then might we persuade Nairn to restrain for a moment his gestures of disgust? It would, of course, have been better if the Left had seized State power; every sectarian tyro knows that.

So let us look at history *as* history—men placed in actual contexts which they have not chosen, and confronted by indivertible forces, with an overwhelming immediacy of relations and duties and with only a scanty opportunity for inserting their own agency—and not as a text for hectoring might-have-beens. An interpretation of British Labourism which attributes all to Fabianism and intellectual default is as valueless as an account of Russia between 1924 and 1953 which attributes all to the vices of Marxism, or of Stalin himself. And one thing which it lacks (our second point) is any sociological dimension.

This can be seen in our authors' schematic handling of the concept of *class*. In their extraordinarily intellectualized presentation of history, class is clothed throughout in anthropomorphic imagery. Classes have the attributes of personal identity, with volition, conscious goals, and moral qualities. Even when overt conflict is quiescent we are to suppose a class with an unbroken ideal identity, which is slumbering or has instincts and the rest.

This is in part a matter of metaphor; and—as we see in the hands of Marx—it sometimes offers a superbly swift comprehension of some historical pattern. But one must never forget that it remains a metaphorical description of a more complex process, which happens *without* volition or identity. If the metaphor, in the hands of Marx, sometimes misleads, in the hands of Anderson and Nairn it becomes a substitute for history. "It"—the bourgeoisie or working class—is supposed to remain the same undivided personality, albeit at different stages of maturity, throughout whole epochs; and the fact that we are discussing different people, with changing traditions, in changing relationships both as between each other and as between themselves and other social groups, becomes forgotten.

An example may be taken from their handling of the decline of Chartism. Chartism (Anderson finds) was "wrecked by its pitifully weak leadership and strategy"; the working class then suffered "extreme exhaustion", and with the decline of Chartism "disappeared for thirty years the élan and combativity of the class. A profound cæsura in English working-class history supervened." "Henceforward it evolved, separate but subordinate, within the apparently unshakeable structure of British capitalism."[50] As a description this is partly true. The end of Chartism marks a very significant turning-point in the direction of working-class agitation—a turning-point which can be found (usually later, and not always in so decisive a form) in the history of other advanced industrial capitalisms. But if Anderson had taken some account of our "nerveless historiography" he would have found that the turn can already be detected some years before 1848, and that what was going on is a far-reaching change within the working class itself.[51] A part of this change, in sociological terms, was the pulling-apart of different occupational groups, newer and older, skilled and unskilled, organized and unorganized, metropolitan and provincial, which had been momentarily united in the great agitations leading up to the Chartist climax in 1839.

The change can be registered in various ways—the introduction of the "no politics" rule into certain trade unions (e.g. Miners' Association, 1842) is one, the new model consumers' co-operative movement (Rochdale, 1844) is another. What one observes is the formation of the extraordinarily deep sociological roots of reformism. What impressed one shrewd observer, when visiting Lancashire in the depths of the depression of 1842, was not the impermanence of the "factory system" but its durability:

> "Suffering here has not loosened the bands of confidence; millions of property remain at the mercy of a rusty nail or the ashes of a tobacco-pipe, and yet no one feels alarm for the safety of his stock or machinery, though in case of an operative *Jacquerie* they could not be defended by all the military force of England."

On the contrary, the distress "has brought the masters and the men closer together, and exhibited demonstratively their mutuality of interests." The workers had come to fear, above all, not the machine but the *loss* of the machine—the loss of employment.[52]

The psychological adjustment to the "factory system" entailed further adjustments. A "profound cæsura" exists, not in the history but in Anderson's analysis; or, rather, in the kind of history of which he approves. For the workers, having failed to overthrow capitalist society, proceeded to warren it from end to end. This "cæsura" is exactly the period in which the characteristic class institutions of the Labour Movement were built up—trade unions, trades councils, T.U C., co-ops, and the rest—which have endured to this day. It was part of the logic of this new direction that each advance within the framework of capitalism simultaneously involved the working class far more deeply in the *status quo*. As they improved their position by organization within the workshop, so they became more reluctant to engage in quixotic outbreaks which might jeopardize gains accumulated at such cost. Each assertion of working-class influence within the bourgeois-democratic state machinery, simultaneously involved them as partners (even if antagonistic partners) in the running of the machine. Even the indices of working-class strength—the financial reserves of trade unions and co-ops—were secure only within the custodianship of capitalist stability.[53]

One cannot rehearse the whole story. This is the direction that was taken, and, beneath all differences in ideological expression, much the same kind of imbrication of working-class organizations in the *status quo* will be found in all advanced capitalist nations. We need not necessarily agree with Wright Mills that this indicates that the working class can be a revolutionary class only in its formative years;[54] but we must, I think, recognize that once a certain climactic moment is passed, the opportunity for a certain *kind* of revolutionary movement passes irrevocably—not so much because of "exhaustion" but because more limited, reformist pressures, from secure organizational bases, bring evident returns. Far too often in his account of twentieth-century developments, Nairn, in his attention to parliamentary epiphenomena, mistakes these for the real movement, and underestimates both the intensity of actual conflicts on the ground, and the truly astronomic sum of human capital which has been invested in the strategy of piece-meal reform. It is this sociological and institutional basis of reformism which has made it so secure, and no amount of denunciation—by Hyndman of its "palliatives" or by Nairn of its "corporative ideology"—will trouble it at all.

From these sociological formations it is possible to envisage three kinds of socialist transition, none of which have in fact ever been successfully carried through. First, the syndicalist revolution in which the class institutions displace the existing State machine; I suspect that the moment for such a revolution, if it was ever practicable, has now passed in the West. Second, through a more or less constitutional political party, based on the class institutions, with a very clearly articulated socialist strategy, whose cumulative reforms bring the country to a critical point of class equilibrium, from which a rapid revolutionary transition is pressed through. Third, through further far-reaching changes in the sociological composition of the groups making up the historical class, which entail the break-up of the old class institutions and value-system, and the creation of new ones.

It is the second possibility which has been most generally debated in the British Left, although, in my view, the third—or some mixture of the second and third—should still be kept in mind. It is abundantly evident that working people have, within capitalist society, thrown up positions of "countervailing power." Of *course*, "the final balance of forces," the "permanent net superiority of the hegemonic class," is not in dispute.[55] Of *course*, a task of the Left has long been to form what Nairn describes as "an ideological and practical synthesis uniting the immediacy of reforms with the remoter ideal of a socialist society."[56] This is exactly the perspective which the former New Left set itself, although we termed it, somewhat more succinctly, "reformist tactics within a revolutionary strategy." It is nice to see all this heavy theoretical artillery is at last coming down in the same target area. But in any case, whichever method of analysis is pursued, a good deal of this is only warm air: we have stated a problem, but are no nearer its solution. The real work of analysis remains: the sociological analysis of changing groups within the wage-earning and salaried strata: the points of potential antagonism and alliance: the economic analysis, the cultural analysis, the political analysis, not only of forms of State power, but also of the bureaucracies of the Labour Movement. However unsystematic and open-ended our approach may have been, I consider that we were in fact getting ahead with exactly this work better than the new New Left, with its hostility to "empiricism" (i.e. attention to inconvenient facts) and its haste to sew up history into off-the-peg suitings, is likely to do.

An example of our authors' schematizing will be found in the adoption of Gramsci's notion of "hegemony." "Hegemony", Anderson tells us

"was defined by Gramsci as the dominance of one social bloc over another, not simply by means of force or wealth, but by a total social authority whose ultimate sanction and expression is a profound cultural supremacy. . . The hegemonic class is the primary determinant of consciousness, character and customs throughout the society."

To this Anderson adds the antithesis of a "corporate class." The English proletariat emerged in the nineteenth century as a class "distinguished by *an immovable corporate class-consciousness and almost no hegemonic ideology*":

"This paradox is the most important single fact about the English working class. If a hegemonic class can be defined as one *which imposes its own ends and its own vision on society as a whole,* a corporate class is conversely one which *pursues its own ends within a social totality whose global determination lies outside it.*"

The short answer to this is that, by this definition, only a ruling-class *can* be a hegemonic class, and, by the same definition, a subordinate class *must* be "corporate." But Anderson translates this to the ground of ideological aspiration:

> "A hegemonic class seeks to transform society in its own image, inventing afresh its economic system, its political institutions, its cultural values, its whole 'mode of insertion' into the world. A corporate class seeks to defend and improve its own position within a social order accepted as given."[57]

From this point forwards it is possible for Anderson and Nairn to employ these terms, "hegemonic" and "corporate", in *exactly* the same way as socialists have customarily employed the terms "revolutionary" and "reformist." We do not have a new tool of analysis here but a sophistication of the old.[58]

The new terms might be an improvement upon the old; or it may not matter. But it would be unfortunate if this man-handling of the concept were to distract attention from Gramsci's deeply cultured and original (if frequently ambiguous) insights. Gramsci wrote, not about hegemonic classes but the hegemony of a class—"the hegemony of a social group over the entire national society exercised through so-called private organizations, such as the Church, the municipalities, the schools, etc." In the words of a sensitive expositor:

> "By 'hegemony' Gramsci seems to mean a socio-political situation, in his terminology a 'moment', in which the philosophy and practice of a society fuse or are in equilibrium; an order in which a certain way of life and thought is dominant, in which one concept of reality is diffused throughout society in all its institutional and private manifestations, informing with its spirit all taste, morality, customs, religious and political principles, and all social relations, particularly in their intellectual and moral connotation. An element of direction and control, not necessarily conscious, is implied. This hegemony corresponds to a state power conceived in stock Marxist terms as the dictatorship of a class."[59]

Gramsci was breaking out of the schematic model to which Lenin had reduced the theory of the State in *State and Revolution,* and restoring to it a far greater flexibility and cultural resonance. Class power might now be seen, not merely as scarcely disguised dictatorship but in far more subtle, pervasive, and therefore compulsive forms.

I cannot say whether Gramsci's concepts fully surmount the difficulties inherent in the Marxist model of class power. But they certainly contain no warrant for their employment in the manner of Anderson and Nairn: *a state of hegemony* cannot be reduced to an adjectival propensity attached to a class. The antithesis to the hegemony of a class would appear to be, not the corporateness of a class but a state of naked dictatorship by a class which does not have the cultural resources and the intellectual maturity, to hold power in any other way (i.e. what Gramsci termed the "State-as-force" or "statolatry", a condition which he implied followed upon the Russian Revolution). Strictly, the concept can only be related to that of State power, and is inapplicable to a subordinate class which by the nature of its situation cannot dominate the ethos of a society. There may be a sense in which a subordinate class could *prepare* for hegemony, could reach outwards towards it, by exerting increasing influence in the intellectual and moral life of the nation, within its educational institutions, through its control of organs of local government, etc.; but clearly this is most likely to be attempted through the mediation of a political party (such as the P.C.I.) substituting *for* a class, and at once we enter into a very different context from the kind of assured class dominance suggested by *egemonia*. The most that we are entitled to say is that a subordinate class may display an embryonic hegemony, or a hegemony within limited areas of social life.

The danger inherent in accepting the new terms is that we are led to suppose that some radically new explanation has been offered, whereas these are simply new ways of describing a long familiar set of facts. And the new account fails to give adequate weight not only to the sociological strengths of British reformism but also to its real achievements. It is strong because, within very serious limits, it has worked. Though we must never forget the overhanging shadow of imperialism, Britain has remained a comparatively humane society; certain democratic values have been consolidated which are far from evident in the socialist world; the bargaining power of the workers is strong, not only in the matter of wages but over a wide range of further demands. The British working class has dug itself into a dense network of defensive positions. And if it has refused to move out of them and to take up an offensive posture over so many decades, this is not just because of some "corporate" conservatism but also because of an active rejection of what appeared as the only alternative ideology and strategy—Communism.

This is the most astounding lacuna in the Nairn-Anderson thesis. Nairn has accomplished the impossible, an anatomy of Labourism over the past fifty years, in 25,000 words, in which Communism as an effective influence, whether internal or external, never appears.[60] This is to write *Wuthering Heights* without Heathcliffe. Our authors have declaimed against the insularity of the British for so long that a wilful blindness has clouded their vision. They should look at a map. Here is this island, and there, across a few wet miles, are Other Countries. Those waters have, on occasion, been crossed. That city, London, is not in the Antarctic but has been, alongside Paris, Vienna and Prague, a great *European* capital. In its East End there have been deposit after deposit of refugee and immigrant workers. In the universities there have been deposit after deposit of emigré intellectuals. Across that water there came, in the 1930s, wave after wave of refugees from Fascism; across that water there went, in the early 1940s, wave after wave of troops to assist in the liberation of Southern and Western Europe; and across that water there came, in the later 1940s and 1950s, a further wave of refugees from Eastern Europe.

Communism is inextricably part of the history of British Labourism for close on fifty years. I cannot hope to indicate here the extent of its irradiation, into intellectual life and into the "stony recesses" of British trade unionism alike. Nor do I think that this influence, in its full ambiguity, has yet found an interpreter. Those of us who have lived the experience will never be able to hold it at the distance requisite for analysis. In one sense, Communism has been present, since 1917, as the opposite pole to orthodox right-wing Labourism. Anti-Communism has provided an apologia for paralysis, an ideological cover for accommodations, the main means by which orthodox social-democracy (sometimes in active liaison with employers, the popular press, or the State) has sought to isolate the Left. The great betrayals and retreats—and most particularly those after 1945 (Bevin, Deakin, Gaitskell)—have been accompanied by a crescendo of anti-communist propaganda and measures.

In another sense, Communism has been throughout the *alter ego* of the Labour and trade union Left. It is, first of all, an elementary error to suppose that the political and industrial influence of the British Communist Party—or its intellectual influence—can be estimated from a count of party cards. A major clue to the broken circuit between theory and *praxis* will be found somewhere in this history, when the militants of 1920, following the advice of Lenin, formed themselves into this isolated detachment, with its intense inner life, and entered into a pattern of self-isolation already set by the S.D.F. This history is itself of great importance, most of all in the 1930s and 1940s, and not least in intellectual consequences. And, in the second place, Nairn's incomprehension at the strategic vacillation and theoretical ambiguities of the Labour Left would have been less if he had examined the peculiarly close—although not always cordial—relations between this Left and the Communist Party. The great traumatic crises of the Left over thirty years have been somewhere here—the Soviet purges, Spain, the Russo-German pact, Prague, Zhdanovism, the Hungarian Revolution—but despite this the Labour and more especially the trade union Left has over long periods operated from ideological and, to some extent, organizational bases outside the Labour Party altogether. These bases have been maintained by the Communist Party: in its press; in its trade union and shop-floor militants; and from time to time in very much broader popular-front organizations.

The compelling nature of this relationship has arisen, not from some peculiar national weakness, but from the compulsive historical context, and from the British immersion within it. Similar compulsions, taking different forms, can be observed in Other Countries. And, if we except Italy, the Left in Other Countries has found it to be no easier to break out of this ideological field-of-force, and to build authentic independent bases, freed not only from Communist permeation but also from the obsessional recriminations and self-dramatising vanguardism too often found in the Trotskyist tradition. There was some hope, at one time, that our New Left might, in an embryonic way, do exactly this. And the "miracle" of C.N.D. was a related phenomenon, when the moral bankruptcy of the CP after 1956 actually gave rise to the resurgence of an *independent* Left. It was a precious historical moment, and, insofar as we have lost it, it is an unqualified defeat.

Defeats happen. The old ideological compulsions grow weaker year by year, and the chance may return. However, the notion of our First White Marxists that they have only to proclaim an undefined "Marxism" and the native intelligentsia will abandon their primitive empirical rites and flock to them for baptism, arises from peculiarly obtuse misunderstandings. There has been a Marxist traffic with these shores for some time—say, 100 years. It has taken many forms. As a pattern of attraction and repulsion, Marxism and anti-Marxism permeates our culture. It permeates our Labour Movement also, very much more extensively than our authors suppose. We need not labour the deficiencies of the Marxisms offered by the S.D.F. and the C.P. The characteristic movement has been one in which hundreds of thousands in the labour movement have passed through some kind of Marxist educational experience, to emerge after a few years—disillusioned by its irrelevance or doctrinaire tone—with some eclectic *marxisant* variant, articulate or inarticulate, and subdued to the empirical idiom. Perhaps 100,000 passed through the S.D.F.: several times this number must have passed along the great transmission-belt of the C.P. and its auxiliaries: the Trotskyist sects of today repeat, with more factional intensity, the same experience. If our authors will leave their Parisian journals for a moment and encounter the actual personnel of the labour movement they will find very many of them to be a good deal more sophisticated than the conservative *semplici* of their imagination.

They will also find that in their role as self-appointed *illuminati* they must encounter tedious obstacles. When Anderson affirms that "Marxism is the only thought which has rigorously united developmental and structural analysis, it is at once pure historicity (denial of all supra-historical essences) and radical functionalism (societies are significant totalities)"[61] he provokes, even amongst the well-disposed, a tendency to become a little hard of hearing. When Nairn acclaims Marxism as "at once the natural doctrine of the working class, and the summing-up of the Enlightenment and all the highest stages of bourgeois thought into a new synthesis,"[62] the audience begins to shuffle and cough. *This is an old European country.* We have seen not only the rain which the new God brought to Other Countries but also the thunder and lightning—the bloody *deluge.* For more than a generation British intellectuals have done little else than offer blue-prints of the Ark.

V

Our intellectual culture is sensitised to Marxist concepts in a hundred ways. Some of the most formidable positions of established reaction have been thrown up in polemics with Marxism. The crisis of commitment with Communism threw a substantial part of the Left intelligentsia of the Thirties back into the old pattern of cultural retreat established at the time of the French Revolution. But by no means all of that intellectual generation—and very many fewer of the 1956 disenchantment—entered the pattern of default. On the contrary, our intellectual life displays, towards the Left, a strange *marxisant* eclecticism—an unsystematic and sometimes poorly-articulated submission of a vestigial Marxism to the empirical idiom. Any new Marxist *nuncios* arriving on these shores must expect to encounter, not only a very well-informed opposition, but also a searching examination from those who are disposed to give them a hearing. And questioners have, in particular, the right to demand at which points this new Marxism distinguishes itself from that of the Stalinist and post-Stalinist ideologues.

It may be useful, in conclusion, to draw together certain theoretical problems relating to Marxism and history which have arisen in this article. The main problems which we have encountered concern a model of the historical process which is undoubtedly derived from Marx. While our authors have created some difficulties on their own account, by their imperfect historical preparation or their over-schematic approach, other weaknesses appear to be inherent in the model itself. Of these we may examine the following: (1) there is the question as to the proper mode of employment of *any* model; (2) there is the metaphor of basis and superstructure; (3) there is some difficulty in the customary notation of an "economic" process; (4) there is the concept of class; (5) and there are problems arising from a teleological model which is preoccupied with matters of power. Since each of these problems has arisen along the way, we can proceed with the minimum of exemplification.

(1) A model is a metaphor of historical process. It indicates not only the significant parts of this process but the way in which they are inter-related and the way in which they change. In one sense, history remains

irreducible; it remains *all* that happened. In another sense, history does not become history until there is a model: at the moment at which the most elementary notion of causation, process, or cultural patterning, intrudes, then some model is assumed. It may well be better that this should be made explicit. But the moment at which a model is made explicit it begins to petrify into axioms. Nothing is more easy than to take a model *to* the proliferating growth of actuality, and to select from it only such evidence as is in conformity with the principles of selection. This is (I have suggested) what Anderson has done with the English Revolution. One can almost hear the stretching of historical textures as the garment of English events (*"partially* contingent but *predominantly* intelligible lenses") is strained to cover the buxom model of *La Révolution Française.* In the end, with some splitting at the seams, the job is done: it always can be. And yet if earlier Marxists had been less obsessed with the French, and more preoccupied with the English, Revolution, the model itself might have been different. Instead of one climactic moment, *the* Revolution, we might have had a more cumulative, epochal model, with more than one critical transition.

A further danger is that a model, even when flexibly employed, disposes one to look only at *certain* phenomena, to examine history for *conformities,* whereas it may be that the discarded evidence conceals new significances.

Must we dispense with any model? If we do so, we cease to be historians, or we become the slaves of some model scarcely known to ourselves in some inaccessible area of prejudice. The question is, rather, how is it proper to employ a model? There is no simple answer. Even in the moment of employing it the historian must be able to regard his model with a radical scepticism, and to maintain an openness of response to evidence for which it has no categories. At the best—which we can see at times in the letters of Darwin or Marx—we must expect a delicate equilibrium between the synthesizing and the empiric modes, a quarrel between the model and actuality. This is the creative quarrel at the heart of cognition. Without this dialectic, intellectual growth cannot take place.

This dialectic is always passing into a disequilibrium. We cannot get on with anything unless we accept an approximate model as a framework of our work. And the *habit* of the model becomes so strong, and is very often supplemented by ideological determinations, that it becomes impervious to empirical criticism. Or, under the impact of one "grand fact" after another, it disintegrates altogether and we sail through seas of inexplicable phenomena. The Marxist tradition has today fractured in both directions—on the one hand, varieties of competing orthodoxies, all of them schematic, on the other hand, the flotsam and jetsam of a system which tosses in empiric seas. It is generally true that very few, in this country, have examined with sufficient boldness and persistence, how far it may be valuable—not to revise or re-vamp—but to attempt a radical restructuring of the model.

(2) I suggested in 1957 that one crux of the question is to be found in the inadequacy of the model of basis and superstructure.[63] I have not the least illusion that my excursions into theory have been either skillful or original. I claim only a certain doggedness: thousands of us have travelled this intellectual road, but too few of us have left clear maps or marked the false turnings.

The dialectical intercourse between social being and social consciousness—or between "culture" and "not culture"[64]—is at the heart of any comprehension of the historical process within the Marxist tradition. If this is displaced, then we evacuate that tradition altogether. When they have reached this point on the road, my colleagues have usually either evacuated the tradition (but I can see no other that comprehends this dialectic) or have attempted to sophisticate the model (but however one emphasizes complexities, etc., the model continues to give wrong results). So we are stuck.

This may be because we have been dealing with a pseudo-problem. The tradition inherits a dialectic that is right, but the particular mechanical metaphor through which it is expressed is wrong. This metaphor from constructional engineering (similar to the boxes and building terms beloved by some sociologists) must in any case be inadequate to describe the flux of conflict, the dialectic of a changing social process. A vegetation metaphor—"this idea is rooted in this social context" or "flourished in this climate"—very often serves better, since it entails the notion of organic growth, just as biological metaphors (Anderson's "symbiosis", "sclerosed", etc.) can sometimes do. And yet these still exclude the *human* dimension, the agencies of human culture—the difficulty (if we follow the vegetation metaphor through) is not that a tree cannot think but that, if it could think, its thinking could not change—however imperceptibly—the soil in which it is rooted. In the end the dialectic of social change cannot be fixed in any metaphor that excludes human attributes. We can only describe the social process—as Marx showed in *The Eighteenth Brumaire*—by writing history. And even so, we shall end with only an account of a *particular* process, and a selective account of this.

All the metaphors which are commonly offered have a tendency to lead the mind into schematic modes and away from the interaction of being-consciousness. In any case, how useful has the basis-superstructure model proved to be in examining all those "grand facts" of the twentieth century—resurgent Western nationalism, Nazism, Stalinism, racialism? While it offers a point of departure, the *real* analysis of these phenomena must take quite different forms, in which the "superstructure" generally turns out to be interfering in quite improper ways with its "base." The model, in fact, has an in-built tendency to *reductionism,* which is rather evident in Anderson:

> "... the ideological terms in which the struggle was conducted were largely religious, and hence still more dissociated from economic aspirations than political idioms normally are."[65]

and which is all-too-evident in Nairn:

> "... actual consciousness is mediated through the complex of superstructures, and apprehends what underlies them only partially and indirectly."[66]

Reductionism is a lapse in historical logic by which political or cultural events are "explained" in terms of the class affiliations of the actors. When a connection, or causal relationship, has been established between these events (in the "superstructure") and a certain configuration of class interests (in the "base"), then it is thought that the demands of historical explanation—still worse, of evaluation—have been met by characterizing these ideas or events as bourgeois, petit-bourgeois, proletarian, etc. The error of reductionism consists not in establishing these connections but in the suggestion that the ideas or events are, in essence, *the same things* as the causative context—that ideas, religious beliefs, or works of art, may be reduced (as one reduces a complex equation) to the "real" class interests which they express.

But because we know the causative context within which an historical event arose, it does not follow that the event can therefore be explained or evaluated in terms of the cause. Attention must be paid to the autonomy of political or cultural events which, none the less, are causally conditioned by "economic" events. A psychology which reduces the infinite variety of sexual expression, from platonic love to a rape in the Romney marshes, to "sex" tells us everything and nothing. And a history or sociology which is continually reducing a superstructure to a base is either false or tedious. Old Corruption remains Old Corruption. The religious conflicts of the English Revolution were not "economic aspirations" diluted with illusions but conflicts about Church authority and doctrine. We will not understand the intensity of the conflict, the tenacity of the authoritarians nor the energy of the Puritans, unless we understand the kind of people they were, and, hence, the socio-economic context. But the mediation between "interest" and "belief" was not through Nairn's "complex of superstructures" but *through the people themselves.* The Puritans did not relish the authority of the Church because they were people who had come to dispense with (or to resent) the authority of the State in their practical lives; and the authoritarians defended the State Church with such tenacity because they were people who felt that their status and power—a whole way of ordering life—was slipping from them and must at some point be defended. If we wish to understand this mediation, we require, not an incredibly cumbersome and inapposite metaphor but a subtle, responsive social psychology.

(3) The problem is to find a model for the social process which allows an autonomy to social consciousness within a context which, in the final analysis, has always been determined by social being. Can any model encompass the distinctively human dialectic, by which history appears as neither willed nor as fortuitous; as neither *lawed* (in the sense of being determined by involuntary laws of motion) nor illogical (in the sense that one can observe a *logic* in the social process)?

"That which did all this was mind, because men did it with intelligence; it was not fate, because they did it by choice; not chance, because the results of their always so acting are perpetually the same."

But equally, as Vico also knew, it was not *will*, because the outcome has been "quite contrary. . . to the particular ends that men have proposed to themselves."[67] "What these gentlemen all lack is dialectic," Engels exploded when, in his last years, he attempted to revise the schematic model which he, more than Marx, had been responsible for setting up:

"They never see anything but here cause and there effect. That this is a hollow abstraction, that such metaphysical polar opposites only exist in the real world during crises, while the whole vast process proceeds in the form of inter-action (though of very unequal forces, the economic movement being by far the strongest, most elemental and most decisive) and that here everything is relative and nothing is absolute—this they never begin to see."[68]

The trouble here is of two kinds. The first concerns not so much the validity of the model as its usefulness. If the "economic movement" is thrust back to an area of ultimate causation, then, like Bacon's first cause, it can be forgotten in its empyrean. If we relegate it to in-the-last-analysis epochal determination (and then only in the sense that productive relations entail certain characteristic and ineradicable sources of conflict, as well as certain limits which social evolution cannot transcend), then it may be asked how far—except at moments of transition between historical epochs—this model has any real relevance?

We can suppose an epochal context—feudal, capitalist, socialist—within each of which an endless variety of forms of State power, modifications of social relations, etc., may be possible. We can never guess at their range and diversity because, rich as history is, it can never exhaust possibility. But while the number of variants may be infinite, nevertheless it is infinite only within the categories of social "species." Just as, while there may be any number of permutations of breeds of dogs, and of mongrel cross-breeds, all dogs are doggy (they smell, bark, fawn on humans), so all capitalisms remain capitalist (foster acquisitive values, must by their nature leech the proletariat, etc.). The transmutation from one species to another is what we mean by revolution.[69] But when we are (as historians) in the midst of an epoch, the epochal characteristics may, for us and for the generations then living, recede into unimportance beside the local particularities. What mattered to people was, not whether it was a capitalism but whether it was a ruthless or a tolerable capitalism— whether men were hurled into wars, subject to inquisitions and arbitrary arrest, or allowed some freedom of person and of organization.

In order to follow this thought through I have gone further than is warranted. For I do not suppose (any more than Engels did) that this "economic movement" is operative only in an epochal sense. It is there all the time, not only giving definition to an epoch but in the characteristic pattern of conflict and social disequilibrium in the heart of the epoch. But a second difficulty arises in respect to the customary Marxist notation of the term "economic." One part of this, sufficiently understood, is the crude assimilation of productive forces and productive relations, which reached its apogee with Stalin. But even if we effect a clear distinction the notion of economic (as opposed to social, moral, cultural) relations turns out to be an analytic category and not a distinction which can be confirmed by empirical observation:

> "Production, distribution and consumption are not only digging, carrying and eating, but are also planning, organizing and enjoying. Imaginative and intellectual faculties are not confined to a 'superstructure' and erected upon a 'base' of things (including men-things); they are implicit in the creative act of labour which makes man man."[70]

Anthropologists and sociologists have sufficiently demonstrated the inextricable interlacing of economic and non-economic relations in most societies, and the intersection of economic and cultural satisfactions. Those historians who have escaped from the toils of the *Economic History Review* (or of *Marxism Today*) are beginning to take the point. Until the late eighteenth century the common people of France and England adhered to a deeply felt "moral economy" in which the very notion of an "economic price" for corn (that is, a dissociation between economic values on the one hand and social and moral obligations on the other) was an outrage to their culture; and something of the same moral economy endures in parts of Asia and of Africa today. Or, again, in Britain it took two hundred years of conflict to subdue the working people to the discipline of direct economic stimuli, and the subjugation has never been more than partial.

The very category of economics—the notion that it is possible to isolate economic from non-economic social relations, that all human obligations can be dissolved except the cash-nexus—was the product of a particular phase of capitalist evolution. Caudwell has described the movement in one aspect:

"... whereas in earlier civilizations [the] relation between men is conscious and clear, in bourgeois culture it is disguised as a system free from obligatory dominating relations between men and containing only innocent relations between men and a thing... In throwing off all social restraint the bourgeois seemed to himself justified in retaining this one restraint of private property, for it did not seem to him a restraint at all, but an inalienable right of man, the fundamental natural right."

And further:

"In all the distinctive bourgeois relations, it is characteristic that tenderness is completely expelled, because tenderness can only exist between men, and in capitalism all relations appear to be between a man and a commodity... Man is completely free except for the payment of money. That is the overt character of bourgeois relations."[71]

From this movement we can deduce a counter-movement, which in fact came to full expression in the great romantic critique of capitalism which is a theme in Williams' *Culture and Society*, as men who found themselves within the actual and mental universe of "political economy", from which there seemed to be no escape, nevertheless rebelled against the consequences of this dehumanized rationality in the name of ulterior values and sacred human obligations.

Marx and Engels, however, took this political economy as their direct antagonist, and entered into its own categories of analysis in order to overthrow it. Inevitably they were marked by the encounter. Not in Marx's early philosophical manuscripts (which share many romantic positions) but in his mature thought, revolutionary *economic* man is offered as the antithesis to exploited *economic* man. But, first, this was to deduce too far from a particular phase of capitalist evolution. Modes of exploitation have varied enormously, not only as between epochs but at different times within the same epoch. We cannot read Marc Bloch, and emerge with the view that feudal exploitation was in any contemporary meaning primarily economic, as opposed to military, political, etc. In eighteenth-century England the manufacturing workers, miners, and others, were far more conscious of being exploited by the agrarian capitalists and middle-men, as consumers, than by their petty employers through wage-labour; and in this country today consumer and cultural exploitation are quite as evident as is exploitation "at the point of production" and perhaps are more likely to explode into political consciousness. Second, one must be cautious about thinking of an "economic" movement as opposed to cultural, moral, etc. When William Morris brought the romantic and the Marxist critique together, and wrote of the "innate moral baseness" of the capitalist system he did not indicate a moral superstructure derivative from an economic base. He meant—and he abundantly demonstrated his meaning—that capitalist society was founded upon forms of exploitation which are *simultaneously* economic, moral and cultural. Take up the essential defining productive relationship (private ownership of the means of production, and production for profit) and turn it round, and it reveals itself now in one aspect (wage-labour), now in another (an acquisitive ethos), and now in another (the alienation of such intellectual faculties as are not required by the worker in his productive rôle).

Even if "base" were not a bad metaphor we would have to add that, whatever it is, it is not just economic but human—a characteristic human relationship entered into involuntarily in the productive process. I am not disputing that this process may be broadly described as economic, and that we may thus agree that the "economic movement" has proved to be the "most elemental and decisive." But my excursion into definitions may have more than semantic interest if two points are borne in mind. First, in the actual course of historical or sociological (as well as political) analysis it is of great importance to remember that social and cultural phenomena do not trail after the economic at some remote remove; they are, at their source, immersed in the same nexus of relationship. Second, while one form which opposition to capitalism takes is in direct economic antagonism—resistance to exploitation whether as producer or consumer—another form is, exactly, resistance to capitalism's innate tendency to reduce all human relationships to economic definitions. The two are inter-related, of course; but it is by no means certain which may prove to be, in the end, more revolutionary. I have suggested that one way of reading the working-class movement during the Industrial Revolution is as a movement of resistance to the annunciation of economic man. The romantic critique is another kind of resistance, with revolutionary implications. The more recent long struggle to attain humane welfare services is a part of the same profoundly anti-capitalist impulse, even if advanced capitalisms have exhibited a great flexibility in assimilating its pressures. [72] "The misery of the world is economic," Caudwell wrote, "but that does not mean that it is cash. That is a bourgeois error." It is an error which Marxists are rather too prone to fall into. And in the conclusion to his study of "Love" he wrote with an insight which is perhaps too symmetrical:

> "It is as if love and economic relations have gathered at two opposite poles. All the unused tenderness of man's instincts gather at one pole and at the other are economic relations, reduced to bare coercive rights to commodities. This polar segregation is the source of a terrific tension, and will give rise to a vast transformation of bourgeois society." [73]

For men desire, fitfully, not only direct economic satisfactions, but also to throw off this grotesque "economic" disguise which capitalism imposes upon them, and to resume a human shape.

(4) No doubt Anderson might, upon reflection, accept some of these suggestions. The fact that he is aware of the inadequacies of the model can be seen in an emphasis upon complexities, as well as in real insights and subtleties in his handling of political phenomena. Where he and Nairn are at their most schematic is in the handling of the concept of *class*. These classes which are marshalled, sent on manoeuvres, and marched up and down whole centuries bear so little relation to the actual people disclosed in the archives—or, for that matter, in the streets around us. It is a history-game which is infectious: in discussing their work I have found myself hypostasizing class identities—great personalized attributions of class aspirations or volition—which one knows are at best the metaphorical expression of most complex, and generally involuntary, processes.

One cannot object to the employment, upon apt occasions, of this kind of personalized metaphor. It is the *cumulative* attribution, in their writing, of identity, volition, and even notions of inner destiny, which evoke suspicion. When, in discussing class, one finds oneself too frequently commencing sentences with "it", it is time to place oneself under some historical control, or one is in danger of becoming the slave of one's own categories. Sociologists who have stopped the time-machine and, with a good deal of conceptual huffing and puffing, have gone down to the engine-room to look, tell us that nowhere at all have they been able to locate and classify a class. They can only find a multitude of people with different occupations, incomes, status-hierarchies, and the rest. Of course they are right, since class is not this or that part of the machine, but *the way the machine works* once it is set in motion—not this interest and that interest, but the *friction* of interests—the movement itself, the heat, the thundering noise. Class is a social and cultural formation (often finding institutional expression) which cannot be defined abstractly, or in isolation, but only in terms of relationship with other classes; and, ultimately, the definition can only be made in the medium of *time*—that is, action and reaction, change and conflict. When we speak of *a* class we are thinking of a very loosely defined body of people who share the same categories of interests, social experiences, traditions and value-system, who have a *disposition* to *behave* as a class, to define themselves in their actions and in their consciousness in relation to other groups of people in class ways. But class itself is not a thing, it is a happening.[74]

If we use this control—if we keep on remembering that class-as-identity is metaphor, helpful at times in describing a flux of relationship—then a very useful dialogue can be opened up between historians and those sociologists who are willing to throw across the time-switch again. If we do not use this control, we have a very blunt cutting instrument indeed. For

while we may imagine a certain internal logic, a bourgeois arch, which
stretches from the twelfth century to our own time, it is rarely helpful
to think of the bourgeoisie in terms so epochal that they include William
de la Pole, Oliver Cromwell, and Mr. Edward Heath. But the Nairn-
Anderson employment of "working class" does exactly this; we are
carried along by the impersonal pronoun, from 1790 to 1960, supposing a
class with more or less unchanged sociological composition, with (after
1832) the same hermetically sealed "corporate" culture. There *are*
continuities and family likenesses; but for most purposes they are not the
epochal resemblances but the discontinuities which demand the closest
analysis. It is generally a fairly easy matter to locate opposing social poles
around which class allegiances congregate: the *rentier* here, the industrial
worker there. But in size and strength these groups are always on the
ascendant or the wane, their consciousness of class identity is incandescent
or scarcely visible, their institutions are aggressive or merely kept up out of
habit; while in between there are those amorphous, ever-changing social
groups amongst whom the line of class is constantly drawn and re-drawn
with respect to their polarization this way or that, and which fitfully
become conscious of interests and identity of their own. Politics is often
about exactly this—how will class happen, where will the line be drawn?
And the drawing of it is not (as the impersonal pronoun nudges the mind
into accepting) a matter of the conscious—or even unconscious—volition
of "it" (the class), but the outcome of political and cultural skills. To
reduce class to an identity is to forget exactly where *agency* lies, not in
class but in men.

   (5) A final reservation, which has grown more rather than less strong
while reading these authors, concerns not what the model purports to
explain but what it does not take into account at all. The preoccupation
is with power, and with political analysts this is proper. But all human
phenomena cannot be assimilated to the categories of power, nor of class;
and yet there appears to be some tendency among Marxists to assume
that they can, or ought to be. This arises from the teleological characteristics
of the model, as it is commonly employed. The goal—working-class
power—is always there, somewhere ahead, and history—and especially the
history of the working class—is evaluated solely in terms of attainment
towards the goal.

   This is a very large question, but three comments may be made. First,
history cannot be compared to a tunnel through which an express races
until it brings its freight of passengers out into sunlit plains. Or, if it can
be, then generation upon generation of passengers are born, live in the dark,
and die while the train is still within the tunnel. An historian must surely
be more interested than the teleologists allow him to be in the quality of
life, the sufferings and satisfactions, of those who live and die in un-
redeemed time. The abolition of factory labour for children under the age

of 11, or the institution of divorce, or the penny-post, may affect the power-model scarcely at all; but for those who were then living these may have affected them inexpressibly or quite perceptibly. In Nairn's schema social reforms have scarcely any place, unless as distractions from "hegemonic" aspirations; those more subtle inflexions in the quality of life have no place at all. But surely any mature view of history (or of contemporary actuality) must in some way combine evaluations of both kinds—of men as consumers of their own mortal existence and as producers of a future, of men as individuals and as historical agents, of men being and becoming?[75]

Second, there are other things left out. The model appears to brush impatiently aside experiences and social problems which appear to be very little affected by the context of class power. For example, the work-discipline entailed in industrialization appears to have affinities in quite different contexts, whether it is imposed by a Wesleyan or Stalinist ideology. Again, the scale of advanced industrial societies—the massive investment and the scope of centralized control—appear to dwarf certain kinds of individual initiatives, and to distance the individual from power, whatever the nature of this power. Problems of this kind—and there are very many of them—appear to produce only smoke and angry whirring in a power-model which, like a computer, can only answer these questions fed into it which its circuits are already constructed to answer. What goes wrong, in the examples I have cited, is not a model which insists upon the dialectic of social being and social consciousness but one which insists that this dialectic can only be mediated by, and take its significance from, social class.

And, at last, it has not escaped all notice, even in this empirical island, that the Marxist tradition has not offered very effective defences against a rather unwholesome obsession with power—whether in intellectual terms, in the assimilation of all phenomena to crude adjuncts of class, or in more "objective" ways. There is a stridency in the way our authors hammer at class and tidy up cultural phenomena into class categories, as well as a ruthlessness in their dismissal of the English experience, which stirs uneasy memories. It is encountered most often in Nairn:

> ". . . they tended towards an impossible and Utopian rejection of capitalism and industrialism (as with Ruskin and William Morris) or retreated into obscurity and eccentricity (like the novelists Meredith and Samuel Butler.)"[76]

There are men who have heard *that* tone, in the past half century, and who retreated into an obscurity which was profound indeed. It was against that tone—that sound of bolts being shot against experience and enquiry (and the remoter sound of more objective bolts)—that a few of us manned our duplicators in 1956. If this is where we are in 1965, then the locust has eaten nine years. But if it should be so, and if there should be any danger that that tone will be mistaken for the voice of socialist humanism, then, if it comes to that, there are some of us who will man the stations of 1956 once again.

NOTES

1. Perry Anderson, "Origins of the Present Crisis", *New Left Review*, 23 (hereafter *Origins*); Tom Nairn, "The English Working Class", *NLR*, 24; "The British Political Elite", *NLR*, 23; "The Anatomy of the Labour Party—1", *NLR*, 27, and "The Anatomy of the Labour Party—2", *NLR*, 28 (hereafter Nairn 1 and 2).
2. Nairn, "Crowds and Critics," *NLR*, 17, p. 31.
3. "The English Working Class," *NLR*, 24, p. 48.
4. Nairn—2, p. 61, and 1 and 2, *passim*.
5. "The British Political Elite", *NLR*, 23, p. 22.
6. *Origins*, pp. 40, 43.
7. "The English Working Class", p. 43.
8. *Origins*, p. 40.
9. *Ibid.*, p. 42.
10. Nairn—2, p. 49, *[sic.]*
11. "The English Working Class", p. 57.
12. Nairn—2, p. 60.
13. In this they differ from Marx whose abbreviated analysis of the genesis of capitalism, in *Capital*, deals largely with agrarian capitalism, and who declares unequivocally: "in the 'categoric' sense the farmer is an industrial capitalist as much as the manufacturer": *Capital*, ed. Dona Torr (1939), i, p. 774, n. 2.
14. "The British Political Elite", pp. 20-1.
15. This is presumably not the editor of Burke's *Peerage* but the same E. Burke whom Marx characterized curtly as "an out and out vulgar bourgeois": *Capital*, p. 786 n.
16. Eileen Power, *The Wool Trade in English Medieval History* (1941), pp. 122-3. Dobb has reminded us that there had *already* been an almost complete turnover of landed property—a change in personnel—between the reigns of Henry VII and James I: *Studies in the Development of Capitalism* (1946), pp. 181-9, esp. 187. This recalls Harrington's famous analysis in *Oceana*, which concludes: "a monarchy, divested of its nobility, has no refuge under heaven but an army. *Wherefore the dissolution of this government caused the war, not the war the dissolution of this government.*" The general problems have been discussed by Sweezy, Dobb, Hilton and others, in *The Transition from Feudalism to Capitalism* (1954).
17. See Christopher Hill's discussion of "Republicanism After the Restoration", in *NLR*, 3, pp. 46-51.
18. "The British Political Elite", pp. 21-2.
19. See e.g. note to *Origins*, p. 33.
20. Nairn, *op. cit.*, pp. 20-1; *Origins*, pp. 26, 33, 51.
21. *Ibid.*, p. 49.
22. I have no doubt that I am often guilty of this in *The Making of the English Working Class.*
23. My objection applies with equal force to ideal types of *the* proletarian revolution; see my "Revolution" in *Out of Apathy* (1960).
24. See especially R. Cobb, *Les Armées Révolutionaires, Instrument de la Terreur dans les Départements* (1961), i, ch. 3 and 5.
25. Anderson makes very much the same point in *Origins*, p. 47, with illustrations

from Honduras, Confucian China, etc. In his actual analysis, however, he has not sufficiently taken his own point.

26. See *The Making of the English Working Class* (1963), pp. 544-5.

27. See Royden Harrison, *Before the Socialists, Studies in Labour and Politics* (1965), ch. iii.

28. See V. Kiernan, "Evangelicalism and the French Revolution", *Past and Present,* i, February 1952; *The Making of the English Working Class,* ch. xi.

29. *Origins,* pp. 47-8.

30. It is amusing to see that Bagehot is rebuked by Mr. R.H.S. Crossman for sharing the naiveties of Marx: "both succumbed to the temptation to 'explain' politics in terms of the class struggle," *The English Constitution* (1964 edn.) pp. 30-2.

31. *Origins,* pp. 34-5, 41.

32. Frank Owen, *Tempestuous Journey* (1954), p. 187. See also Lloyd George's warning to the peers (November 1909): "The Peers may decree a Revolution, but the People will direct it. If they begin, issues will be raised that they little dream of," p. 183.

33. *Origins,* p. 32.

34. *My Apprenticeship* (Pelican, 1938), i, pp. 64-9.

35. *Origins,* pp. 28, 30.

36. "The English Working Class", p. 45, 48.

37. *Origins,* pp. 40-3.

38. They involve also, I suspect, an even larger confusion between ideology and ideas, between intellectual culture and the mental universe, value-system, and characteristic illusions of particular social groups, which has penetrated so deeply into the Marxist tradition that it would require a distinct examination.

39. Bacon, *Advancement of Learning* (Everyman edn.), p. 26.

40. *The New Atlantis.*

41. When Darwin commenced work on *The Descent of Man,* Emma Darwin wrote resignedly: "I think it will be very interesting, but that I shall dislike it very much as again putting God farther off."

42. William Morris and E.B. Bax, *Socialism, its Growth and Outcome* (1893), p. 116.

43. *Life and Letters of Charles Darwin* (New York, 1896), i, p. 495.

44. "The English Working Class", p. 57.

45. Marx and Engels, *Selected Correspondence* (1943), pp. 472-3.

46. See F. Bealey, "Les Travaillistes et la Guerre des Boers", *Le Mouvement Social,* 45, October-December 1963, pp. 69-70; J.A. Hobson, *The Psychology of Jingoism* (1901).

47. *Origins,* p. 35.

48. See especially B. Semmel, *Imperialism and Social Reform* (1960), ch. iii, for the incredible story of the Coefficients. E.J. Hobsbawm, *Labouring Men* (1964), ch. xiv, emphasizes (in terms which may be too emphatic) that "the actual policies of the Society, up to just before the first world war, were almost always at variance with those of most other sections of the political left, radical or socialist" (p. 264).

49. *Independent Labour Party, Report of First Annual Conference* (1893), pp. 3, 5. Cf. Nairn—1, p. 50, and his comment: "here was the authentic spirit of Labourism; proudly anti-theoretical, vulgarly chauvinist, etc." In fact Hardie called upon Edouard Bernstein, the German fraternal delegate, to reply from the platform to Tillet's attack.

50. *Origins,* pp. 33, 39.

51. See, for example, Asa Briggs, "Chartism Reconsidered", *Historical Studies* ed M. Roberts, ii, (1959), pp. 42-59.

52. W. Cooke Taylor, *Notes of a Tour in the Manufacturing Districts of Lancashire*

(1842), esp. pp. 7, 43, 64, 115. Compare Marx: "The advance of capitalist production, develops a working class, which by education, tradition, habit, looks upon the conditions of that mode of production as self-evident laws of nature. The organization of the capitalist process of production, once fully developed, breaks down all resistance... The dull compulsion of economic relations completes the subjection of the labourer to the capitalist." (*Capital,* p. 761).

53. By one estimate there were in the early 1860s in the cotton towns of South-East Lancashire, 118 co-op stores with a capital of £270,267 and an annual turnover of £1,171,066; 50 manufacturing co-ops, with a nominal capital of £2 million; mortgages to building societies of £220,000 ("the bulk of this sum consists of deposits by the lower middle, and the upper stratum of the working classes"); about £500,000 in 250 friendly societies, and "probably half as much more owned by trades' societies"; and £3,800,498 held by 14,068 depositors (many of them skilled workers) in the savings banks (all Lancashire). J. Watts, *The Facts of the Cotton Famine* (1866), pp. 88-9.

54. C. Wright Mills, "The New Left", *Power, Politics and People* (1963), esp. p. 256; "generally it would seem that only at certain (earlier) stages of industrialization, and in a political context of autocracy, etc., do wage-workers tend to become a class-for-themselves..."; see also my "Revolution Again", *NLR*, 6, esp. pp. 24-30.

55. *Origins,* pp. 49-50.

56. Nairn—1, p. 64.

57. *Origins,* pp. 39, 41.

58. See Gwyn Williams' strictures *(ubi infra)* upon Togliatti's "crude vulgarization, with rival classes wearing their ideologies like uniforms, a gross mutilation of Gramsci's thesis."

59. See especially A. Gramsci, *Il materialismo storico* (Turin, 1955). My Italian is too weak to offer translations and I follow here the admirable account of Gwyn A. Williams, "The Concept of 'Egemonia' in the Thought of Antonio Gramsci", *Journal of the History of Ideas,* xxi, 4, October-December 1960, pp. 586-99. See also H. Stuart Hughes, *Consciousness and Society* (1959), p. 101 *et. seq.*

60. I find one mention only of an internal influence: "after 1941, with the Soviet alliance, communism became fashionable," Nairn—2, p. 37.

61. "Portugal and the End of Ultra-Colonialism", *NLR,* 17, p. 113. I do not intend any general criticism of this very able study.

62. Nairn—1, p. 43.

63. See "Socialist Humanism", *New Reasoner,* 1, 1957.

64. See my discussion of Raymond Williams' "The Long Revolution", *NLR,* 9 and 10.

65. *Origins,* p. 28.

66. Nairn—1, p. 44.

67. *Autobiography of Giambattista Vico* (Cornell, 1944), p. 55.

68. *Selected Correspondence,* p. 484.

69. I use this only for purposes of analogy. Clearly the metaphor of species introduces new rigidities and dangers.

70. "Socialist Humanism", *loc. cit.,* pp. 130-1.

71. C. Caudwell, *Studies in a Dying Culture* (1938), pp. 101, 151.

72. Two ways of regarding this impulse will be seen in J. Saville, "The Welfare State: an Historical Approach", *New Reasoner,* 3, and Dorothy Thompson, "The Welfare State: Discussion", *New Reasoner,* 4, pp. 125-30. See also of course the recent writings of Professor Richard Titmuss.

73. Caudwell, *op. cit.,* p. 157.

74. I am repeating the suggestions I made in the Preface to *The Making of the English Working Class,* pp. 9-11.

75. This involves also the question of ulterior and contingent historical judgments (what does one judge *with*? can one discover an emergent "truly human" standpoint?), which reveals itself sometimes in the muddle about historical forces which appear to Marxists as "objectively progressive" but subjectively very nasty, or vice versa. Thus Anderson (*Origins*, p. 29) finds the "immense, rationalizing 'charge' of the Revolution was detonated overseas" in accelerating mercantile imperialism, the slave-economy of the Caribbean, etc. Other Marxists have found difficulty in deciding whether Levellers, *sansculottes*, and others were an "objectively" reactionary force. The problem is too large to enter into here.

76. Nairn—1, p. 41.

An Open Letter to
Leszek Kolakowski

Dear Leszek Kolakowski,

First, I must introduce myself, since this is an unusual kind of letter. You don't know me, but I know you well.

This must be familiar enough to a man with an international reputation. He must often be beset with the importunities of strangers.

But my claim is more insistent and vulgar than that. I am the stranger who walks into the house, slaps you on the back, sits down at your table, and jests about your youthful escapades, on the pretext of a claim to distant relationship of which you know nothing. I am, in political terms, your mother's brother's stepson. I am an impossible and presumptuous guest, and an uninvited one—you may even suspect that I am an impostor—but the courtesies of kinship disallow you from throwing me from your house.

We were both voices of the Communist revisionism of 1956. Not much can be made of that. The intellectual particles produced in that moment of ideological fission have now fallen out over most parts of the political globe.

But there was a closer and more continuing identity in our preoccupations. We both passed from a frontal critique of Stalinism to a stance of Marxist revisionism; we both sought to rehabilitate the utopian energies within the socialist tradition; we both stood in an ambiguous position, critical and affirmative, to the Marxist tradition. We both were centrally concerned with the radiating problems of historical determinism on the one hand, and of agency, moral choice, and individual responsibility on the other.

When I say that "we both" initiated similar enquiries, I don't, of course, suggest that we both did so with equal success. The inadequacy of my own writings is testified by the silence into which they have fallen. Your own writing, on the other hand, still seems to me to be among the few constructive and enduring consequences of that experience. Your sustained polemic, "Responsibility and History", first published in *Nowa Kultura* in 1957,[1] remains without equal.

In 1956 we lived through a common experience, but we experienced it in different ways. In Britain the small number of Communist intellectuals belonged to a defeated and discredited tradition—or so it was the business of every orthodoxy in our culture to assure us. We were not heretics but barbarians, who desecrated with our presence the altars of the liberal Gods. There are many personal histories and each one is accented differently. But one may say that, in general, our allegiance to Communism was political: it arose from inexorable choices in a partisan world in which neutrality seemed impossible. You are familiar enough with this, and I won't go over all the elisions of truth and the self-deceptions that were involved.

But our intellectual allegiance was to Marxism. It was, at least in some part, pre-Stalinist, or Stalinist in a hang-dog, shame-faced sort of way. We might, from a sense of solidarity, act as apologists for Stalinism. We might even engage in some casuistry to explain away Zhdanovism (a consequence of the tragic sufferings of the war); but few of us, in the depth of our hearts, did not wish for the siege mentality of Communism to fall away. Thus there is a sense in which, even before 1956, our solidarity was given not to Communist states in their existence, but in their potential—not for what they were but for what—given a diminution in the Cold War—they might become.

Hence, whether consciously or unconsciously, we were expectant of exactly what occurred in 1956. These "revelations" represented less a rupture in our understanding than a fulfilment of our half-conscious hopes. From that preposterous military orthodoxy we had hoped for controversy, acknowledgement of human frailty, a moral vocabulary. And for this reason, in spite of its agony, in spite even of the Hungarian tragedy, 1956 was a year of hope. We had seen, not the potential (for this was soon crushed) but the living, indomitable agents of that potential at work within those societies. Behind the posters, novels and films of Stakhanovites we saw (to our relief) workers who were absentees, pilferers, time-servers, as well as workers who were learning to defend themselves, organize, and take common cause with intellectuals. And behind the nonsense of self-validating "correct formulations" we saw the old Adam of a critical, sceptical intelligence. The undefeated old man of the mind still survived, it seemed, among the copybook abstractions of the New Man of History.

You Poles were the worst old Adamists of all! Your poets—Tuwim and Wazyk—your film-makers and sociologists, and, worst of all, your Leszek Kolakowski. In our journals, *The Reasoner* and *The New Reasoner*, we dissident British communists did something to make public your work. A member of our editorial board, Alfred Dressler, followed closely the discussions in *Nowa Kultura* and *Po Prostu*, and visited Poland more than once for exchanges with our friends.

Your voice was the clearest voice out of Eastern Europe in those years, although you didn't offer the easiest answers. You offered not a parcel of solutions, each ready for unwrapping ("freedom", "democracy", "workers control"—although each of these you indicated as objectives, complex in their nature, awaiting attainment), but the resumption of old modes of intellectual and moral aspiration and discourse. And in this, too, we showed what solidarity we could with you.

What we dissident Communists did in Britain—and for this small achievement I still feel a stubborn pride—was to refuse to enter the well-worn paths of apostasy. After the suppression of the Hungarian revolution up to 10,000 people, or one-third of its total membership, walked out of the British Communist Party; and of that 10,000 I can think of not one who took on the accepted role, in liberal capitalist society, of Public Confessor and Renegade. No-one ran to the press with his revelations about Communist "conspiracy" and no-one wrote elegant essays, in the organs published by the Congress for Cultural Freedom, complaining that God had failed. We had had, after all, our experiential political reasons for being opposed to capitalist society, independent of any evolution in Eastern Europe whatsoever. We had had, after all, our intellectual reasons for associating with the Marxist tradition, independent of any follies or self-delusions of Stalinism. So in the face of liberal applause, which was short-lived, and intellectual ridicule, which we were used to, we took up what work we could. Some, no doubt, fell back exhausted into private trajectories. Others continued their work in the working-class organizations to which they already belonged. Others took a part in initiating the New Left and in the Campaign for Nuclear Disarmament. Some of us, in trade unions or in intellectual life, are still not quite dead.

But none of us, I think, are classical renegades. And I claim this as a debt upon you, as a solidarity we paid to you, although you may not see it in the same way at all. Nor do I claim this out of hindsight. Expressly and repeatedly, between 1956 and the early 1960s, I and several of my comrades affirmed our general allegiance, not to the Communist Party as institution or as ideology, but to the Communist movement in its humanist potential. And we did this for two reasons.

First, you and your comrades, striving in the most complex and sometimes threatening circumstances to influence your own societies, were present at every moment in our political consciousness. If such men as you were content to remain Communists (and you will recall that your own membership of the Polish Party was not severed until 1966, and then by expulsion and not by resignation), if such men and women as the Czech insurgents of 1968 were to emerge directly from the Communist tradition, who were we to deny the claims of solidarity? We rejected—as I still reject—any description of Communism or of Communist-governed societies which defines these in terms of their ruling ideologies and the institutions of their ruling élites, and which excludes by the very terms of its definition any appraisal of the conflicts characteristic to them, of the alternative meanings, values, traditions and potentials which they may contain. And I make this point the more strongly, since I have recently noted with astonishment that you yourself, in the last year or two, appear to have been falling back on such conditioned liberal definitions.

The second reason is closely related to this. It is, perhaps, a rephrasing of the first. Nothing distinguished the zenith of Stalinism more than the absolute polarization of two worlds. As you wrote in 1957, "because of the absence of a major social focus that would retain their criticism within the orbit of socialist thought, dissidents from Stalinist communism were easily transformed into renegades". And you continued:

> There is no greater danger to the development of the socialist movement in its present phase than to permit a renewed intensification of the political polarization that tends towards a single alternative . . . The result would be to force legitimate criticism into the position of the counter-revolution.[2]

In 1958 I was writing about very much the same dilemma:

> We can assert with Pasternak that the Revolution's 'indirect results have begun to make themselves felt—the fruits of fruits, the consequences of consequences.' In doing this we must not in any way limit our critique of Stalinism, which must be dismantled in fact and in the human mind, if the fruit is to ripen; but we must not fall in behind the old trek which started in the 1930s, when a romantic espousal of Communism was followed by a purist retreat from life. This, in effect, is only to abandon the pass to Stalinism or to anti-Communism, and to strengthen the advocates of 'no-middle-way'. I think we must be tougher than that, and for this reason I still prefer to call myself a dissident Communist . . . Moreover, we still have a 'Communist' duty to fulfil: to express our solidarity with fellow dissidents in the Communist world, to assert our confidence in the humanist strand within the Communist tradition, to assist the Western labour movement to an understanding of the kind of society immanent within the late-Stalinist forms, and thereby to re-awaken an appreciation of the community of aspiration among the working people East and West . . .[3]

The world has changed a good deal in fifteen years, and neither of us need be accused of inconsistency if we have changed with it. The estrangement of the Russian and Chinese states, the survival of the Yugoslav state, the cautious diversification of Communist orthodoxies (for example, in Italy), and the growth of movements throughout the world which style themselves of the Left, which sometimes actually are of the Left,[4] and which certainly are not subordinated to Stalinist institutions (indeed, the increasing anachronism of the very term "Stalinism")—all these real events mean that neither you nor I would feel the need to define matters as we then did.

But I was explaining a point of history, why I feel that I have some petty claim of relationship to you. (I owe also, of course, for your writings and for your courage, in 1956 and again in 1966, a much greater debt.) My claim is a trivial and abstract one. At a certain moment, partly out of a sense of solidarity with you and your comrades, I and others like me took up certain intellectual and political positions. We refused to disavow "Communism" because Communism was a complex noun which included Leszek Kolakowski. I am sure that the solidarity expressed in little, academically-unreputable journals in England did you no good whatsoever. We brought you neither tanks nor tank-traps; not even an audience among a "reputable" British public.

So the claim turns out to be nonsense. We fought in the same battle once; it was by accident, and anyway the battle was lost. I am, it turns out, an impostor after all—a reader, an admirer, but no kin.

And even as a reader I am sadly behind the fashion. For those editors who present your writings to "Western" readers are inclined to pass over indulgently your writings of 1956-7 and to go posting on to later and better things. Thus Leopold Labedz:

> While in his earlier writings there was little from which a Westerner could learn anything of universal significance, now he has moved from a stage of rediscovery of intellectual landmarks well known in the West to a stage where his search is more original . . . [5]

At least—and perhaps this is our only claim—we "Easterners" in the heart of the enlightened "West" read your earlier work without that kind of self-congratulation and patronage. And even now, having re-read your "Responsibility and History", I am at a loss to know what "intellectual landmarks well-known in the West" you had there rediscovered. Continuities, extensions of prior enquiries—yes; but as to landmarks "well-known in the West", I had overlooked the familiarity of your enterprise. It seemed and it still seems to me that this study, for all its tentative character, remains the most substantial examination of its universally-significant themes since the mid-century. To keep it by me I would trade in ten volumes by Sir Karl Popper: and this, because your thought plays upon the actual stuff of choices in actual contexts and not upon some etiolated arrangement of academic concepts; and because you leave, at the end, victimhood and agency, realism and utopia, arguing with each other down the corridors of history, as they have always done and may always do.

After 1957 censorship and a renewed (but more opportunist and less lethal) conformism closed around you. You pursued your researches in the history of thought[6] and also in more academic fields of philosophy. You maintained and extended your positions as a Marxist revisionist, although you were forced to speak less frequently (or to speak in riddles) to a non-specialist audience. In 1966 you broke your enforced silence, at the request of the students at Warsaw University: your plain account of the deformities and unfreedom of intellectual and cultural life, of the betrayal of the Polish "October", ensured your expulsion from the Party. In 1968, at the onset of a new nationalist and anti-intellectual night, you were dismissed from your Professorship. Since then you have been in West Germany, Montreal, California and are now at All Souls' in Oxford.

That is a bare biography. From what is available of your work in English translation one can detect other themes. You have entered into philosophical dialogue in many areas of contemporary (no doubt Mr. Labedz would call it "western") thought, handling critically but with respect ideas of positivist, phenomenological, existentialist, and Catholic thinkers. In these matters I am a layman, but I can see no fractures, no sharp discontinuities, in your preoccupations. In 1966 you returned with vigour to the themes of historical explanation, determinism and moral choice: I find in these studies a greater philosophical precision, but perhaps also a greater impatience with arguments which to a historian maintain validity (they existed and exist) even if, to a philosopher, they are flawed in logic. [7]

From the time of your enforced exile, in 1968, to the "West", I feel less certain of your identity. Your published statements are few. I must reconstruct what I can from fragments—an article in the *Socialist Register*, an article in *Daedalus*, an interview in *Encounter*, the proceedings of a conference—and these fragments intersect in negatives. For each isolated negative—this expression of contempt for Communist orthodoxy, that outright "no" to Althusser, this frank objection to unexamined socialist slogans—I may feel partial or complete assent. But for the intersection of particular negatives into a general sense of defeat and negation: for the absence of qualifications, for the absence (most of all) of an awareness—contained, as it must be, in the same moment of thought—as to the reasons of capitalist power and ideology: for the absence of expressions from you of intellectual fellowship with your political analogues and former comrades in this "West", the absence of an awareness that we had already (in our very different context) sought to examine some of those objections to revolutionary socialism which you are now propounding in *Daedalus* or at Reading University—and that we had proposed, if not answers, then at least ways of acting in relation to these problems: for all of these I feel concern.

My feelings have even a more personal tone. I feel, when I turn over your pages in *Encounter*, a sense of injury and betrayal. My feelings are no affair of yours: you must do what you think is right. But they explain why I write, not an article or polemic, but this open letter.

It would be impertinent in me to speculate too far upon the experiences which have led you to this point of negation. It may not be as nice as "Westerners" assume for a Pole or a Czech to leave his friends and colleagues, and his context of engagement, and come to "the West". Your arrival in West Berlin coincided with the ascendance of a peculiarly impulsive and intransigent German revolutionary youth movement. Your arrival in California coincided with a culture of "radicalism", which had serious and courageous components, but which was surrounded by a halo of hysteria which—caught up and magnified in the lenses of the sensationalist media—reproduced itself across half the world as a "youth culture" of self-indulgent emotionalism and of exhibitionist style. From Paris to Berkeley, from Munich to Oxford, the "West" offered a supermarket of *avant garde* products, some branded as "Marxism", each cutting the price against the other. But how many of these products, when unpackaged, contained only old and discredited arguments under a new label, or a horrific make-up kit for the revolting young bourgeoisie (a fast sports-car, a villa in the Appenines, and the Thoughts of Mao-Tse-Tung) to act out their transient, fashionable pantomime? Posters of Che Guevara, juxtaposed against mini-skirts, "Mao tunics", and military leather jackets, decorated the most modish, swinging boutiques, in the King's Road and in Royal Leamington Spa; for a year or two, intoxicated by "May 1968" in Paris—or, rather, by this event as assimilated in instant myth —cohorts of leftist students imagined that, by some act of occupation of a few administrators' offices, they could announce in the heart of repressive capitalist society a "red base" which would bring an instant voluntaristic proletarian revolution looming out of the streets.. That was the year of the *gauchistes*, the year when the tragedy of Joanna Southcott's annunciation of the impending birth of the Shiloh was re-enacted, but this time as a rich kid's revolutionary farce; and in both cases the pregnancy of the millenium was diagnosed, at last, as dropsy.

I grant the irrationalisms of that year. It was a bad year for one with your exacting intellectual temper to come to the "West". From your later references to "the blind enthusiasm for the meaningless idea of global revolution" (see p. 335) one can detect how these experiences seemed to you. And yet there are other, and more hopeful, ways of seeing that experience: the challenge to Gaullism, the great strikes in the French motor industry, the first large cracks in the massive, ritualized traditionalism both of French academic institutions and of the routinized politics and routinized ideology of the P.C.F.

And then, again, I must ask against what *perspective* you observed these phenomena? Did you consider that what was remarkable in the German youth movement was not its impulsive form and its lack of bearings, but that these children of Hitler's legionaries had taken to the streets, and in this affirmative way, *at all*? Did you remember, while shrugging off the hysteric harmonics within Californian culture, that these were resonances only from a profound and healthy human chord— a chord which signalled the decomposition of that state-endorsed ideological conformism (chauvinism, hysteric anti-communism—with its rituals of denunciation and of exorcism—and mindless technological consumerism) which had dominated American college culture during the high years of the Cold War? It is from *that* matrix of crew-cut, clean-limbed playboys, of mother-pampered, "christian scientific", systems-conditioned, ambitious, morally-adaptive and intellectually-null college boys of 1946–60 that, one after another, the astonishing cast of Watergate has come. You found the enthusiasms of West Coast revolutionaries in 1968 to be "blind". And perhaps, at this point and at that, I would share your judgement. But what of that? It has always been your work, in Berkeley as in Warsaw, to help the blind to see. Enthusiasm—and an enthusiasm generous enough to act against racialism, to declare against war, to submit to the ministrations of Mayor Daly's helmeted (christian scientific?) state priests—is a better starting-point, one would have thought, than that earlier campus culture which generated men and women who, like propositions from a page of Talcott Parsons, have no vocabulary in which lies, bribery, espionage upon citizens, corruption, can be encompassed at all.

Forewarned by an experience sufficient for any life-time, you need only glance at some of the "Marxisms" currently on offer to identify them as manias. And to this I assent. I would criticize you only for this: that you have assumed that the loudest, the most strident, the most modish or the most "reputable" voices are those that are most significant. You were perhaps unaware of the great "law of development" of intellectual life in "the West", in this stage of competitive consumer society, that cultural modes must change, like sartorial fashions, with dizzy speed from one year to the next; that in ideas as in suburban villas it is style and self-exhibition and not structure that determines acceptance, and that, moreover, very many intellectual workers—even men and women whose work is to teach youth, to write, to present television—literally do not remember positions which they adopted ardently and with vituperation against all opponents two or three years before.

Indeed, this law seems to me to apply most particularly to the intellectual Left. From voluntarism to determinism, from "red bases" on campuses to exclusive dependence upon proletarian revolt, from non-violence to aggression, from apologetics—in the name of supra-nationalist universals—for the Common Market to glorification of the Provisional I.R.A.: between all these positions people oscillate, adopting each with equal fervour, never dropping their voices for reflection in between. Indeed, these contradictions coexist in the same minds. Consistency is a vice of the square and out-of-date. It can't be reconciled with the "contradictions of reality", nor with the imperative to "do one's own thing". Consistency is an old bore.[8]

The voice of the bore is doomed in the end to tail off into silence. And that, in a nutshell, is my own history as any kind of political voice. For a year or two some of us continued to explore old themes from 1956, in *The New Reasoner* and *New Left Review*. The exigencies of our activist concerns, in the attempt to give the word flesh in an actual New Left independent of the old polarities (and the British New Left, unimportant as it may have been, was one of the first of this particular generation of movements) altered perceptibly our former preoccupations. Renewed Cold War, renewed conformism and censorship in the "East", diminished our expectations of any early resolution of the knots tied by history and ideology in Communist societies. We addressed ourselves to the task of encouraging into being in Britain a movement of socialist thought and practice, purged of the old religious anti-Communism, founded experientially upon British conditions, which was revolutionary, rational, democratic: which accentuated self-activity, which was sensitive to cultural forms of exploitation, which affirmed the values of *égalité*.

> O what fine thought we had because we thought
> That the worst rogues and rascals had died out.

In this we left aside the arduous tasks of a more philosophical self-examination—a task for which most of us were, anyway, ill-equipped, and unlikely to find time to equip ourselves amidst the demands of Aldermaston marching, speaking at Left Clubs, fund-raising for our journal (which did not, *mirabile dictu*, receive funds from the Ford Foundation), and attempting to improvise movements out of attitudes. Indeed, one's responsibilities as an intellectual workman became forgotten in one's tasks as an impressario.

Well, I could talk about that. But not now. Our unresolved intellectual debates remained unresolved (although in certain fields—in economic and industrial theory, in historical and cultural analysis—much more than that was done). And for the irresolute, "history" has little patience. We reached a point of personal, financial and organizational exhaustion; and at this moment, the agent of history appeared, in the form of Perry Anderson. We were exhausted: he was intellectually fertile, immensely self-concentrated, decisive. We saw, in a partnership with him and his colleagues, an opportunity to regenerate the review and to recuperate our own squandered intellectual resources. We did not, as it happens, anticipate that the first expression of his decisiveness would be to dismiss the review's founders from its board.

We were, it turned out, insufficiently "rigorous": which was true. We were confined within a narrow nationalist culture and unaware of the truly internationalist Marxist discourse: which meant, in fact, that we had attended most to the voices of Kolakowski, Hochfeld and Wazyk, of Tibor Dery and Illyes, of Basso and of Djilas, of C. Wright Mills and of Isaac Deutscher, and had attended insufficiently to a particular dialogue between Parisian Marxists and Parisian existentialists. And we were not intellectually "reputable": which meant that our work was not well-regarded in Oxford.

This is not the place to attempt a definition of the transition from one tradition to another. But this debate was never raised to any theoretical articulation; it was resolved by an administrative decision. The old New Left could either destroy both old and new in a quarrel over the control of the review; or it could elect for its own administrative dissolution, could withdraw from a signal-house of defined commitments and enter the wilderness of individual intellectual enterprise. This *Register* is the last survivor in the direct line of continuity from the old New Left, and its editors and publisher have done much to keep alive a tradition of undoctrinaire, œcumenical, substantive Marxist analysis. But I think that they would agree that the *Register* has not included all the tendencies which co-existed fruitfully in the older movement.

I explain this because I find even now (outside of Britain) some confusion as to the intellectual relationship between the first and the second *New Left Review*. Since taking on editorial control in 1963 Perry Anderson and his colleagues have conducted the review with system, conviction and decision. There was, however, a fracture in the passage from one tradition to another, which was never exposed to principled discussion. It was a very English transition: that is (according to one's viewpoint) gentlemanly and tolerant, or otiose and manipulative. It was not until 1965 that I raised, in the pages of this *Register*, objections to certain interpretations in the (mutated) *New Left Review*: these pointed to ulterior questions of some significance, although I was inhibited both by my own sense of the shared fellowship of the Left and by editorial advice, from pressing every objection home. In due course, and perhaps with less sense of either inhibition, Anderson replied. His reply, in my view, neither answered my objections nor opened up new problems of significance.[9]

That is where matters remain. My colleagues and I turned back to work in our own specialist, professional, or practical fields. We no longer represented a coherent and identifiable position. Some of us regrouped, in 1967—8, under the initiative of Raymond Williams, to offer such a position and perspective, with the *May Day Manifesto*. This arose, I believe, from theoretical assumptions substantially distinct from those of the present *New Left Review*; but what these ulterior differences are has (unless in some parts of Williams' own work) gone unargued.

To argue for possession of the term "new left" is not worth breath. And even to argue for possession of the term "Marxism" may not be worth the breath that is spent upon it. I am persuaded that it is not. There are arguments of greater substance to be conducted. But to argue them at all requires a certain morale, a certain sense of audience.

If, after a breathy euphoric overture, I have fallen into a moody political silence, it may have arisen from the absence of the last two requisites:

> My mind, because the minds that I have loved,
> The sort of beauty that I have approved,
> Prosper but little, has dried up of late . . .

One cause of this, to which I will soon return, is, paradoxically, the revival in Britain of Marxisms: but of Marxisms with which I cannot associate myself. Another is even deeper: it penetrates to the very language of political discourse, the idiom of thought.

To be a British Communist, on this empirical island anchored off Europe, was never a matter of great international relevance. British Communists did something to assist struggles for colonial independence, and something more than is now remembered to assist in the defeat of Fascism between 1942–5. But to be a Communist dissident or revisionist, or a relict of that tradition, in 1973, is to be a null quantity like a foreign postage-stamp twice cancelled, unusable and not worth a collector's attention.

The language itself provokes smothered ridicule. But when the language comes over in a strong provincial accent, like Aristotle's *Politics* declaimed in scouse, then the joke is so good that it might draw an audience after all. For I belong to a nation which has lost self-confidence, and whose people certainly lay claim to something less in the scale of human rights (such as self-determination) than do the Norwegians. Our intellectual culture has for so long been insular, amateurish, crassly empirical, self-enclosed and resistant to international discourse that the damage done is probably irreparable. But we still have a chance. We are going "into" Europe, and Tom Nairn and other contributors to the *New Left Review* are attempting to teach us the vocabulary which real intellectuals use over there.

This is what we are assured, from many sides, and by many voices other than Tom Nairn's. I am compelled to believe it is so. After all, if our rate-of-growth lags behind that of "Europe", if the pound falls against the mark, if English apples can't stand up to French competition, then it follows, as the night the day, that English intellectuality has no chance of survival unless—exposed to the bracing competition of Paris and Milan—it learns a new vocabulary and efficiency. The process, of course, may be painful. Certain backward, uncompetitive sectors (English empiricism, romanticism, traditionalism) will have to be closed down. One cannot expect M. Sartre and M. Althusser to subsidize these antique survivals. There will necessarily be, in the transition phase, unemployment. Even some executives may (with adequate compensation) be made redundant.

It was in the name of this logic that the founders of the *New Left Review* were some of the first to be laid off. And it is because I sense a justice in my own redundancy that I have been, for some years, silent on the larger issues of political argument. It is not, of course, a matter of an argument only with Tom Nairn. Among younger intellectual workers in Britain there have been, for a decade, indications of a significant mutation in idiom. As Raymond Williams has written:

> British thinkers and writers are continually pulled back towards ordinary language not only in certain rhythms and in choices of words, but also in a manner of expression which can be called unsystematic but which also represents an unusual consciousness of an immediate audience.

This "manner of expression", which I have described as "idiom", and in which Williams can see both negative and positive qualities, appeared to many students in England since the early 1960s as an obstacle to being "intellectuals of a different kind":

> A sense of certain absolute restrictions in English thought, restrictions which seemed to link very closely with certain restrictions and deadlocks in the larger society, made the search for alternative traditions, alternative methods, imperative.

"Everybody except the English, it suddenly seemed, thought or at least wrote" in a more highly-specialized and systematic manner. And in the search for a more rigorous theory, many in the new generation sought to acquire "the highly specialized and internal vocabulary" of an intellectual caste, sometimes acquiring at the same time—

> A language and a manner of the monograph and the rostrum: a blackboard numbering, a dictated emphasis, a pedagogic insistence upon repeatable definitions: habits which interacted strangely with the genuine rigour of new and bold inquiries and terms. [10]

This is well stated. And it relates in specific ways to the mutation in the *New Left Review* tradition. I cannot here attempt a considered assessment of the achievements of this review in its conduct since 1964, and if I indicate only certain points at which I and other founders and contributors of the earlier review have been excluded from its discourse it will suggest a partial, and ungenerous, assessment. But I must make these indications, very briefly, if I am to explain to you the position from which I am now writing. And, first, there has been an exclusion in fact: not only has the review turned away from its founders, but it has passed over their thought without examination and has strenuously denied that any serious Marxist traditions existed in this country before some moment in 1963. Second, while the review has undoubtedly enlarged certain international dimensions it has severely limited others, and, in particular, the interest in (and sometimes dialogue with) Communist "revisionism" and "dissent" which marked the tradition of *The New Reasoner*. (As an example, the review, in the past decade, has not noted your work but has paid respectful and continuing attention to that of Althusser.) Third, the review's intention of deepening and clarifying Marxist exegesis has been accompanied by a distinct narrowing of intellectual referents and a closing down of certain open areas of examination; that is, there has been an insistent pressure to reassert Marxism as doctrine—albeit highly-sophisticated doctrine—of a kind which I will soon discuss. Fourth, this has been further accompanied by an obligatory rejection of the empirical mode of investigation, in which empirical controls (which are very evident in Marx's own procedures) are dismissed along with the proper resistance to empiricism or positivism. Hence heuristic and structural organization of concepts are given priority (even Hegelian priority, albeit expressed in severely anti-Hegelian terms) over substantive analysis. We are always—and not only in the pages of *New Left Review*—arranging ourselves to make analysis, being told *how* analysis may be conducted and (more frequently) how it may *not* be conducted, but the substantive outcome of these arrangements is less clear. And fifth and, for the time being, finally, one may doubt (you and I would certainly doubt) how far the mutant tradition has ever absorbed or worked through the full historical experience of Stalinism. Indeed, I find in the very vocabulary of this new Marxism, with its obligatory face-making at "humanism", "moralism", etc.—its inability to discuss the arts except by translating them into cerebration—and its lack of terms with which to handle moral or value-making process, a suggestion that that experience has passed the new tradition by.

These qualifications may have force. But, even so, it seems that I and some of my colleagues cannot break into that discourse. We do not command the appropriate terms. And I meet, when I confront your own writing of the 1960s, an analogous difficulty. In the view of one of your editors, in your "post-revisionist writings", you—

Show the influence, in about equal measure, of the philosophical ideas of Spinoza, Kant, Hegel, Marx, Dilthey, Mannheim, Husserl, Sartre, Heidegger, and Camus. [11]

To this pantheon (which I must emphasize is not of your own nomination) my first instinctive, but irrepressible, comment would be: "Humph!"—a term too inexact to introduce into philosophical discourse.

If I may borrow your own image of the Priest and the Jester, English intellectuals have played the role of jesters to the universalist priests (Catholic or Anti-Catholic) of Western Europe for several hundred years.[12] Our best idiom has been protestant, individualist, empirical, disintegrative of universals; our best moralism has been contextual. Our poets have, on occasion, advanced philosophy further than our philosophers. If I who have been formed in this idiom think about problems of determinism and free-will, of social process and individual agency, I move not from Spinoza through Marx to Heidegger and Sartre but I fall into a different kind of meditation, conditioned by a literary culture, among instances, objections, qualifications, ambiguous metaphors.

When you are reported to say, as you are in *Encounter* (although you have said it more elegantly elsewhere) that you, as an "inconsistent atheist" find, nevertheless, that "men have no fuller means of self-identification than through religious symbolism", and that "religious consciousness . . . is an irreplaceable part of human culture, man's only attempt to see himself as a whole", then not only the atheist but also some primal Lollard or Anabaptist within me rebels. You may say this in Poland: you may say this, if you wish, in Italy or France. But by what right, what study of its traditions and sensibility, may you assume this as a universal in the heart of an ancient Protestant island, doggedly resistant to the magics of religious symbolism even when they remained believers, cultivating like so many urban gardeners the individual conscience as against some priest-given "religious consciousness"?

I fear that you will not understand me. You will think that your casual reflection has touched off some atheist fury. It is not this at all. I share and accept, in my work as an historian, your imaginative sympathy and intellectual respect for Christian forms, movements and ideas, which as you insist (and as Christopher Hill in this country has long insisted) must be studied in their own reality and autonomy, and not as figments of "false consciousness" in which other more real and material interests were masked. If I devised my own pantheon I would without hesitation place within it the Christian antinomian, William Blake, and I would place him beside Marx.

What you touch off in me—and this is why I introduced the point— is simply the old Adam of the English idiom. You interrupt me in my work. I don't wish to be dragged back into all *that*, I don't wish to be drawn into an argument whose form and even whose philosophical terms arise from a culture in which the old ding-a-dong between Catholic and atheist universalists goes on and on and on; in which, generation after generation, the Catholic theologians and philosophers, like cunning groundsmen, prepare new pitches and dictate to their opponents that they must, once again, play over every inch of this novel pitch or they will have lost the series; in which, to stand somewhere between Catholic and anti-Catholic philosophy, is to give one a unique status as a Referee.

If "going into Europe" entails going back into all that then we might just as well go into Eire. Meanwhile there may be a little time left to get on with our work. I am not clear what you mean by "self-identification" nor by what means we judge how one kind of self-indentification is "fuller" than another, unless the conclusion is entailed in the premise —that only self-identification "through religious symbolism" can be full. In this case, if you are an atheist, your self-proclaimed "inconsistency" must reside in the fact that you find a mystified self-identification to be fuller than a naked and de-mystified one. This does not assort well with your vindication (and your personal example) of the values of rationality, wherever these may lead, nor with your reminders of the tragic side of human culture.

Self-identification through religious symbolism may certainly be more comforting: that is true. But neither your business nor mine has been to provide comforts. I cannot see you in the ward of mortality, like a tea-lady with a philosophical trolley. But your other proposition touches more closely on history: "religious consciousness . . . is an irreplaceable part of human culture, man's only attempt to see himself as a whole—that is to say, as both object and subject."

If religious consciousness is "irreplaceable", this is a statement not only about the past (how man has seen himself) but about the future. I find this surprising, since elsewhere you have written so acidly across the pages of those visionaries who knew what the future must hold. In this case, you must affirm this because from your observation of the past and of the present, you have deduced a constant, an intrinsic component of man's nature, which can only find expression in a "religious consciousness".

There are many statements, of fact and of value, and of value disguised as fact, in that short statement. One may readily grant that the religious consciousness has been a part of past human culture. How far it has been present in *all* past cultures is a highly technical question, in answering which we would not only have to consult anthropologists but would also have to define the term "religious" and decide how far any myth (whether supported or not by a doctrine, by priests or holy men, whether entailing or not notions of an after-life, rewards and punishments, etc.) may be defined as religion. The definition of "religious" would clearly influence very largely our conclusions: if (for the sake of argument) we defined "religious" in such a way as to include all attempts by man to see himself as a whole, then your argument will, like a well-built canoe, ride triumphantly through all succeeding rapids.

Point Two: If we accept that religious consciousness has been part of past human culture, then it follows that it has been irreplaceable, since we cannot replace any part of what is already past. But, and Three. If "irreplaceable" is a statement not of fact but an imputation of value then it is a very different order of statement. If you imply that the religious consciousness was, is, and by implication may always be "irreplaceable", because it fulfils some intrinsic human need—and a profoundly significant and valued need (since who would deny that men should "self-identify" and be allowed to see themselves whole?)— then we are directed to an argument far too large to pursue, an argument, moreover, which entails so many insertions of normative judgements that it could not be pursued by logical means alone. One arm of the compass is fixed upon that single word, "irreplaceable": the other has swung through 180 degrees, from a banal statement of fact to the largest assertion of value: as to the approved function of religious consciousness in the past, as to man's essential nature, and as to future social evolution. As you know, many men could readily assent to Point Two, but find (at Point Three) only a matter for regret: would show that religious consciousness had constricted and confused cultural advance, or had inhibited man's self-knowledge—perhaps even his self-identification. I will not myself be drawn, at this moment, to either side of this argument.

Point Four. When you say this unexamined quantum is "man's only attempt to see himself as a whole" it is a statement which is either—as history—patently and outrageously inexact, or else, once again, the conclusion is entailed in the premise. I don't refer only to those thinkers who have consciously set themselves in the face of religious forms and ideas to see man as a whole, but to an artistic and literary culture (to which I happen myself to owe greater debts) which has been throughout history enlisted in the same attempt. If you tell me that *King Lear* and *Le Rouge et le Noir*, *War and Peace* and *The Prelude* are, at root, manifestations of the religious consciousness, then I can only throw my hand in, and ask that we may play through the game again, more slowly, and without marked cards.

And if (my Fifth Point) you insist upon marking each card of thought or art or secular social ritual as "religion", because of the derivation of its symbols or its forms, we are still in the youth of man's secular self-knowledge. How can you predict, or I contradict, what forms man's self-knowledge, in its fullest affective and symbolic forms, may take? At least (Point Six) one might hope that atheist culture can transcend the aridities of negating religious consciousness, and move to a more positive and unselfconscious appropriation and expression of the (still imperfectly-defined) needs which it fulfilled. As a matter of fact, I had thought that this was what was happening—and had been happening for some two hundred years. It is not because I wish to close the doors to imaginative sympathy towards forms of religious consciousness, whether past or present, but because I resent being drawn back into a fruitless argument upon terms which I reject, that I offer these objections.

The point, however, was my allegiance to an outworn English idiom. I proceed by digressions, and that is an idiom also—an essayist's contrivance. Never mind, we proceed, if circuitously, and there is perhaps more logic in the progress than I mean, as yet, to show. I have been jesting with you, you indomitable and seasoned jester, because I am the product, perhaps the prisoner, of a jesting culture. If you come before us to ask us questions, I will ask questions of your questions.

But I cannot fly. When you spread your wings and soar into the firmament where Kierkegaard and Husserl, Heidegger, Jaspers and Sartre and the other great eagles soar, I remain on the ground like one of the last of the great bustards, awaiting the extinction of my species on the diminishing soil of an eroding idiom, craning my neck into the air, flapping my paltry wings.[13] All around me my younger feathered cousins are managing mutations; they are turning into little eagles, and whirrr! with a rush of wind they are off to Paris, to Rome, to California. I had thought of trying to join them (I have been practising the words "essence", "syntagm", "conjuncture", "problematic", "sign") but my wings grow no bigger. If I were to try I know very well that with my great bulk of romantic moralisms, my short-sighted empirical vision, and my stumpy idiomatic wings, I would fall—plop!— into the middle of the Channel.

I belong to an emaciated political tradition, encapsulated within a hostile national culture which is itself both smug and resistant to intellectuality and failing in self-confidence; and yet I share the same idiom as that of the culture which is my reluctant host; and I share it not only through the habits of a writer but out of preference. This, if I am honest, is my self, my sensibility. Take Marx and Vico and a few European novelists away, and my most intimate pantheon would be a provincial tea-party: a gathering of the English and the Anglo–Irish. Talk of free-will and determinism, and I think first of Milton. Talk of man's inhumanity, I think of Swift. Talk of morality and revolution, and my mind is off with Wordsworth's Solitary. Talk of the problems of self-activity and creative labour in socialist society, and I am in an instant back with William Morris—a great bustard like myself, who has never been allowed into the company of such antiquated (but

"reputable") eagles as Kautsky or Plekhanov, Bernstein or Labriola—
although he could, if given the chance, have given them a peck or two
about their gizzards.

Well, that is what I am, and it is a ludicrous predicament. It is an
excuse for any amount of silence. Holding for too long, and with too
few companions, to an unregarded position breeds—as this letter has
already shown—symptoms identical to those of egotism. I have become
too much aware, in my silence, of the motions of my own mind; too
detached from the thought around me into which my own argument
can never be inserted; too stubborn in resistance to assimilation.

*   *   *

And then, abruptly, out of that unassimilated past there comes a
familiar voice: Leszek Kolakowski! There was something in the élan
of our small detachment which, many years ago, was caught between
two withering ideological fires, which makes me catch my breath, and
resume that past: to question where we are going, what I have become.
It is no fault of yours that all these sheets of paper fall upon your head.

Of course, we have both changed. Let us examine a little how we have
changed and why.

We both adopt (as I understand it) a common stance in relation to
the Marxist tradition. We might classify the ideas which are offered as
Marxisms in several ways. There is, (1) Marxism conceived of as a
self-sufficient body of doctrine, complete, internally-consistent, and
fully realized in a particular set of written texts: of Marx (early or late):
of Marx and Engels: or with some hyphenated addition, as—Lenin,
—Trotsky, —Mao-tse-tung. While here or there an individual may be
found who claims to "know" the true set of texts better than anyone
else, this Marxism is normally found in some institutionalized form:
since no-one can prevent reality from changing in ways which the
texts did not (without some pushing and pulling) anticipate, there must
be not only approved texts, but approved interpretations of those
texts (or opinions outside them); and this entails an Office, or a Priest,
or (with an intellectual sect) at least a priestly editorial board, which
can signify approval and changes in the body of textual truth.

This is very familiar to both of us, and poignantly so. Reality changes,
but the texts do not change: they are interpreted in new ways. Interpretation may be the work of men of great cunning, but I would accept
your definition, of many years ago, that "a Marxist" in sense (1)
"refers to a man with a mental attitude characterized by his willingness
to accept institutionally-approved opinions".[14] One may detect very
quickly the tricks of this mode of thought: when anyone commences a
sentence with "Marxism teaches that . . ." or "Let us apply Marxism
to . . .", one knows that the text is being brought *to* the object of

examination. It is difficult, if one steps out in this way with the right foot, not to ensure that the left foot of self-confirmation follows. But all true intellectual work requires a more dialectical image than that: thought wrestles with its object, and in the encounter both are changed.

We need not be reminded of the disgraces entailed by this mode of thought during the zenith of its most notorious institutional embodiment, under the priestly care of the "Greatest Philologist of the World". You described these in your article on "Permanent and Transitory Aspects of Marxism" (1957):

> The 1950 Marxist knows that Lysenko's theory of heredity is correct, that Hegel represented an aristocratic reaction to the French Revolution, that Dostoevsky was nothing but decadence and . . . also that the resonance theory in chemistry is reactionary nonsense. Every 1950 Marxist *knows* these things, even if he has never learned what chromosomes are, has no idea in which century Hegel lived, never read one of Dostoevsky's books, or studied a high school chemistry book. To a Marxist all this is absolutely unnecessary so long as the content of Marxism is determined by the Office.

In its worst institutional expressions, this Marxism has done man's culture injury enough. It is sufficiently discredited. We may pass it over without further comment.

Or we might suppose that we *should* be able to do so. In fact, "Marxisms" of precisely this order have shown an astonishing vitality. Wherever, in 1956, we could find one such Marxism, we can find now three in its place. At the end of 1960, when our New Left Clubs (which were intended both as open local forums of socialist theory, and as local points of socialist initiatives) were already disintegrating under the attentions of the emissaries of various "fraternal" (and often vituperative) Marxist sects, I made this comment:

> I am getting bored with some of the members of 'Marxist' sects who pop up at Left Club meetings . . . to demand in a your-money-or-your-life tone of voice whether the speaker is a Marxist, whether he 'believes in' the class struggle, and whether he is willing to give instant adhesion to this or that version of the Creed.

Such interlocutors would have achieved much the same effect "if they had simply cribbed the lines of Ancient Pistol: 'Under which king, Besonian? Speak, or die!'"

> Most Clubs have suffered from one or more of these prophets, heterodox or orthodox, of diabolical and hysterical mysterialism. The connections are seen, but they are seen to be everything; and everything can be reduced to a few basic texts . . . Marxism is conceived of, not as a living tradition, but as a self-enclosed doctrine, a means of flattening and simplifying whatever phenomena are under investigation so that certain plausible facts may be selected (and all others discounted) in order to ornament or 'prove' pre-existing assumptions. A great deal of what is today most stridently acclaimed as 'Marxism' is no more than thinking of this order,

whether it commences with the assumption that Soviet leaders are all-sinning or all-knowing. This accounts for the scholastic style in which so many 'Marxist' statements are couched—theses and counter-theses so neatly sewn at every seam that reality cannot break in at any point. [15]

I wrote this in 1960, and since that time such Marxisms have reproduced, have held and added to their adherents, while I and many of my old comrades have, outside of our more professional roles, fallen into silence. The priests have multiplied, the jesters have been laughed down. These Marxisms may be nonsense: but they certainly fulfil some human need.

They are not, of course, altogether nonsense. Their selection of texts may be better than the old ones; an argument among many sects is immensely more fruitful than the apologetics of one orthodoxy; and even where the mode of thought is wrong, subtle and perceptive minds can be found at work within it. And yet, if this is where "Marxism" necessarily leads, then neither of us are of that company.

Let us pass (2) to another mode of thought which is identified as Marxism. In this, Marxism is upheld less as doctrine than as "method". It is a definition which offers difficulties, but difficulties do not make it invalid. Clearly we mean something more than that Marx was a scholar; that (as you reminded us) his work was distinguished by "a relentlessly rationalist attitude, a sense of radical criticism, a distaste for sentimentality in social research, a deterministic method". Such qualities (as you observed) were "not characteristic only of him and his followers", they "do not suffice to distinguish a separate school of thought".

The method must be more exactly defined than that. But if we try to do so (and this argument could be—and has been—immensely prolonged) we encounter, in the end, an irresolvable difficulty in distinguishing between Marx's method and some of his premises and, indeed, some of his conclusions. If we say that his method was dialectical, we are saying something: I believe that we are saying a good deal. But we encounter impossible problems when we attempt to distinguish Marx's dialectics conceived of as pure method from the dialectics of other thinkers. And what is worse, these problems beckon us away from matters of substance to disputations which I can only describe as scholastic. We must therefore go on to say that Marx's method was dialectical and it was also that of historical materialism. I think that this also means something. But in defining that meaning, we must define further historical materialism: that it entails certain proposals as to the relations between social being and social consciousness: indeed, it would be an etiolated definition of Marx's method which did not point us towards his way of examining capital and class-conflict.

I am not jibing at those who associate themselves with Marxism as method. Many of those whose work commands my respect would define their position in this way. But I am not persuaded as to the adequacy of the definition. If by "method" we are using the word in a loose and metaphorical sense—that I associate myself, very generally, with Marx's way of working, with some of his premises, his terms of historical analysis, and with certain conclusions—then we are really saying that we are associated with a "tradition" or school of thought: this is a different position, and one which I will soon discuss. But if by "method" we mean something more exact we will find, in the end, that method inextricable from the work:

> O chestnut-tree, great-rooted blossomer,
> Are you the leaf, the blossom or the bole?
> O body swayed to music, O brightening glance,
> How can we know the dancer from the dance?

The proof of this is to be found in experience. For those who espouse the notion of Marxism as method with the most intellectual rigour are exactly those who are caught insensibly in the undertow which drags them back to Marxism (1) as doctrine. In attempts to define what is "essential" or "basic" to Marx's method they must define the essential texts. As revisionists, they may point to later corruptions or deformities in the Marxist tradition; they dig under the shale and slag which has accumulated over the pure and original load of ore; they discard Lenin, or Engels; they uncover the early Marx. From "method" they pass to "model"; there is an essential model to be uncovered, before or after 1844; fertilized by semiotics or structuralism, their researches break into regions of epistemology undreamed of by Marx; they spin a miracle-world of gossamer threads, "admirable for the fineness of thread and work, but of no substance or profit". Through this filigree fairy-world Marx, whose concrete historical imagination "worketh according to the stuff, and is limited thereby", would have walked with astonishment.

You must forgive, again, the English idiom. I had supposed that Bacon had long voiced a serious objection to both Marxisms (1) and (2), when he had objected (in *The Advancement of Learning*) of the schoolmen—

> For as water will not ascend higher than the level of the first springhead from whence it descendeth, so knowledge derived from Aristotle, and exempted from liberty of examination, will not rise again higher than the knowledge of Aristotle.

But this was before the advance of modern phenomenological technology, and the discovery, by certain projectors on the Left Bank of the Seine, of the Cartesian Well.

Let us say again that the coexistence of many Marxisms (2) is a situation enormously more conflict-fraught, and hence more charged with intellectual vitality, than the dogmatic conformisms or anti-conformisms which passed so widely as Marxisms in 1950. And let us add that—as you argued in your essay "In Praise of Inconsistency"— there are virtues to be found in the fact that all men are not rigorous thinkers.[16] For "Marxism as method", when pursued with less rigour, has served as a kind of permission for a critical eclecticism. Men could use the notion, perhaps with the aid of a little evasion or opportunism, in order to set aside some difficult enquiries for which they were poorly equipped, while pursuing and advancing knowledge in their own more specialist fields.

There is, however, an opportunism rather grander and more evasive than this: I will describe it as Marxism as Heritage (3). All human culture is a super-market in which we may shop around as we choose, although some products are more gorgeous and more heavy than others. Karl Marx was a great man, and so was Jesus Christ; so too were Hegel, Husserl, Tolstoy and Blake. The producer of ideas may be forgotten, it is the customer who must be pleased. If on any day we feel like doing a Marxist or an existentialist or a Hegelian intellectual thing, we can pop into the glittering culture-market and pick up an appropriate product of that brand. We pay our money in a footnote and all debts are met. Why should we concern ourselves further with the ardour and skill of the workman in his ill-lit workshop who first turned this product in his hands?

You are familiar with this argument. Indeed, in a more serious sense you once proposed it (but with a limiting clause to the natural and social sciences) yourself:

> The greatest triumph of an eminent scholar comes precisely when his achievements cease to be a separate school of thought; when they melt into the very tissue of scientific life and become an elemental part of it, losing in their process their separate existence.

"We can assume", you proposed,

> that with the gradual refinement of research techniques in the social sciences and humanities, the concept of Marxism as a separate school of thought will gradually become blurred and ultimately disappear entirely. (There is no 'Newtonism' in physics, no 'Linneism' in botany, no 'Harveyism' in physiology, and no 'Gaussism' in mathematics.) This implies that what is permanent in Marx's work will be assimilated in the natural course of scientific development. In the process some of his theses will be restricted in scope, others will be more precisely formulated, still others will be discarded.

In the social sciences and humanities (you allowed) this process of assimilation would be much slower than in the analogy from natural science. In philosophy you foresaw a rather different evolution: Marxism, like Platonism, would remain as a distinct school of thought.

I was, and remain, uneasy at this presentation, with which you yourself may no longer be in agreement. You were not of course forecasting an instant assimilation: but your metaphor of "gradual blurring" suggested an assimilation already well-advanced, and with little accent upon the ideological conflicts which might be met with on the way.

Your statement arose from your particular experience in Poland and in 1956. You were far more aware (it could not but be so) of the deformities and constrictions of the Stalinist ideology masquerading as Marxism than you were of the deformities of capitalist ideology. It may even have seemed, at times, as if Marx's influence was being held prisoner within the forbidding institution which had been given his name; that he need only be set free to walk at will through intellectual culture; that Stalinism's ill will alone prevented his ideas from meeting with their due acceptance among those men of good-will who made up the social sciences of the rest of the world.

You were proposing a fluency of exchange between Marxist and non-Marxist thinkers, a removal of false suspicions and fictitious polarities between scholars. And your proposition met with an instant assent from one scholar of outstanding courage and of true goodwill in the "West". I am thinking of C. Wright Mills, who at once accepted your extended hand; who proposed, in turn, that this "assimilation" was well-advanced, and that Marx stood with Weber, Mannheim and Veblen in the "classical tradition" of sociology.

And yet I am not persuaded that too much can be made of this assimilation. The influence of certain ideas which perhaps originated from the Marxist tradition is certainly enormous. This influence is sometimes creative, and it can sometimes be found in vulgarized, dwarfish forms within the work of men (one thinks of the paltry economic reductionism in the work of W. W. Rostow) who are ardent anti-Marxists and apologists for capitalism. But in the social sciences, at least, I think you greatly under-estimated the capacity for capitalist society to generate and regenerate its own defensive ideological formations. (That "historicist" metaphor, which elides a more complex process, is offensive to you, I know. I will try to clarify the point of ideological formation later.) Social science, as fostered by many of the institutions of capitalist society, is not always a beast of good-will nor one with which any kind of Marxist finds it easy to assimilate. (Wright Mills wrote more than one eloquent testimony to this point.) Stalinism may have accentuated but certainly did not invent nor determine its intellectual evolution. There have been, after all, other insurgents (such as a native working class) to keep in order.

These arguments belong not to epistemology but to the sociology of knowledge. But my objection could be sustained at other levels. At least you may agree that a loose assertion of Marxism as (3) could, if not further examined, encourage that opportunism of the super-market in which any product is as good as any other and all is consumer's choice —an opportunism of which you are personally so incapable that its seduction for others may not even be imaginable. If you think of assimilation, you think of a strenuous encounter: but others think of a row of miscellaneous paperbacks. If you think of heritage, you think of the active process of intellectual self-reproduction: cleansing thought of inexact concepts and fashioning ones more exact. But in Britain, when we think of heritage (and for all my jests, *some* of what Tom Nairn says is true) we surrender to inertia; we lie upon our heritage like a Dunlopillo mattress and hope that, in our slumbers, those good, dead men of history will move us forward. We are dosed with eclecticism (or with opportunism given the brave name of empiricism) as regularly as we are dosed with librium; the public health service pays for one and the University Grants Committee pays for the other; it scarcely matters which pays for which, since the Government pays for all. Someone will make huge profits one day from the public dispensation of Marxism as Heritage.

We are back within the sociology of knowledge once more. I cannot help it: I am trained as an historian, I must always shuttle to-and-fro, since history itself has always been a weaver. But if we propose a fourth position, Marxism as Tradition (4), then we might escape the objections that I find in (3) and which we both find in (1) and (2).

In choosing the term tradition I chose it with a sense of the meanings established for it within English literary criticism. You might prefer, as a philosopher, the term "school". But it is easier, to my mind, to think of a plurality of conflicting voices which, nevertheless, argue within a common tradition than to think of this plurality within a school.

The notion of tradition entails some of the advantages but avoids certain difficulties of Marxism (2). It allows a large measure of eclecticism—and Marxists (1) and (2) will assert that it allows too much— without the unprincipled invitation to self-dissolution of (3). One difficulty in (2) was that it tended to exclude (at a certain point) all modes of self-criticism which were not self-validating. That is, Marxism as method must insist that *some* method can be defined: and this, I tried to show, entailed endorsing certain premises, certain texts, and indeed certain conclusions as the inviolable essence of Marxism. This may allow for flexible and creative thought. But what remains disallowed is the criticism of that method itself by criteria external to the method: we may criticise one text in the light of another text, or a prior text in the light of a later one, but if we are consistent about a Marxism as some essence of method or doctrine, we are confined, in the end, to criticism of it within its own terms, in terms of itself.

When the intelligent editor of the Pelican edition of *Grundrisse* can write, without irony, that "the manuscript contains enough material to fuel perhaps several generations of additional philosophical treatises", then he demonstrates rather accurately the kind of scholasticism entailed in such exegesis, as well as indicating the socio-intellectual *couche* into whose hands Marxism (2) is increasingly falling. What are lost are, precisely, the empirical controls and the empirical transfusions—leading on to the breaking and making anew of concepts—intrinsic to the method of historical materialism. The recent emphasis given in several Marxist quarters to the structural organization of Marx's concepts, and to their function in revealing "hidden" as opposed to manifest social relations, is valid, and, indeed, familiar; what is invalid is the supposition that such hidden relations are beyond reach of empirical criticism and verification, or the inference that a competence in some kind of "structural" philosophy provides entrance to some higher Marxist academy, aloof from the collisions of evidence and the awkward confrontations of experience.

If, on the other hand, we are willing to bring any and every part of Marxist thought under scrutiny—and to employ any instrument of criticism which seems legitimate (whether historical evidence, or the examination of its inner consistency, or the well-founded objections of intellectual opponents)—then we can only describe ourselves as Marxists in the fourth sense. Nor need this be as airy and indefinite a position as many who have been conditioned by the existence and claims of other Marxisms will suppose.

This is so, in part, because of the very stature, universality, originality and power of Marx's work; the disciplines he commanded and reshaped; his characteristic methods and preoccupations; the many voices added to the tradition since his death; and the extent of contemporary Marxist discourse. This tradition exists; it has defined itself in Marx's work and in the evolution (contradictory as that is) of his ideas. The point is (if one affirms this tradition as one's own) less to define the tradition than to define where one stands within it.

In doing this we are still, in a way, defining that part of the tradition which we most value, and which commands—in spite of inquisitors and impostors—our allegiance. When you did this, for yourself, in 1957, you selected exactly those parts which also command me:

> Typical for Marx is . . . the tendency to emphasize those primary social divisions which are most influential in determining historical development . . . Typical of Marx is a certain kind of historicism which not only does away with evaluating historical phenomena from the standpoint of a moralizer who stands guard over eternal values; which not only is based on a general principle as to the historical

relativity of the subjects under study, but also on the conviction that human nature is the product of man's social history and that our entire conception of the world is 'socially subjective'.

And again; when you are defining Marxism's continuance, as a school, in very much the same sense as my "tradition":

> Marxism in this meaning of the term does not refer to a doctrine which can either be accepted as a whole or rejected as a whole. It does not mean a universal system but a vibrant philosophical inspiration, affecting our whole way of looking at the world; a stimulus forever active in the social intelligence and social memory of mankind. Its permanent validity is a consequence of the new and ever important perspectives which it opened to us: enabling us to look at human affairs through the prism of universal history; to see, on the one hand, how man in society is formed in the struggle against nature, and, on the other hand, the simultaneous process of humanizing nature by man's work; to consider thinking as a product of practical activity; to unmask myths of consciousness as being the result of ever-recurring alienations in social existence and to trace them back to their proper sources . . .

To this (in my own allegiance to the Marxist tradition) I would add little, and, I think, subtract nothing, unless a use of the term "historicism" which I would reject. I would add more explicitly than you do that as an historian I find the dialectical method of analysis—not as reduced to terms of formal logic but as evidenced repeatedly in the fluency of both Marx's and Engel's own analysis—to be the clue to a thousand hidden meanings: this intuition into the double-sidedness of things, the potential within the form, the contradictions of process, the consequences of consequences. And I would add, as you would do, my tribute to Marx's great-hearted commitment to the practical movement of the proletariat.

If one apprentices oneself to a master, one does not do so to become a copyist, but to become a craftsman in one's own right. Apprenticeship may even involve (as Gerard Manley Hopkins once advised) the precept: "Admire and do otherwise." And another problem is involved when thought passes from a master to his disciples: what was a whole way of thinking becomes instantly codified, reduced to system: a metaphor is made into a rule. Indeed, the master himself, solicited by disciples made anxious by the grey in his hair, or impelled by the need to give laws or write programmes, may be an accomplice in reducing his own thought to code. We know well how this turned out in the case of Marx and of Engels.

And so one may give allegiance to a tradition, in which one learned one's own craft, while holding that its codified expression is largely wrong, and not only that some of the master's ideas were wrong (which must go without saying unless we are servants of God) but—and this can be more significant—that certain ideas that were profoundly right were (when set out as system) given an expression that falsified them in perceptible ways. In this, I have no doubt, you and I are in agreement. But our professional preoccupations are different, and we are likely to accent the problems in different ways. So, once again, I must ask you to accompany me on a detour, which may serve to clarify some points which will arise at the end of this letter.

You are concerned to examine Marx's language within an epistemological discipline: you explain the obscure, repair imperfect and hasty passages of logic, and where the logic is too fractured for repair (or involves a hidden and unsuspected assumption) you point this out. I am also concerned with Marx's language, but in the sense in which it sometimes masks or rigidifies his ulterior meaning. To a philosopher such an exercise may seem improper: how can we examine a meaning apart from the words in which it is expressed—or if we can intuit one, what tools are available to carry intuition further?

To this a historian may, I think, give a legitimate answer. If in the process of historical analysis a writer can demonstrate the interconnectedness of disparate phenomena and regularities (within similar causal contexts) of cultural formations—if he can show "the very age and body of the time his form and pressure"—this is an achievement which may properly be distinguished from any formal description which that same writer gives of his own procedures, or, indeed, from any systematic exposition which he may generalize from his findings as to the historical process. We often encounter evidence of this distinction. The further we move from the stricter branches of philosophy the more it becomes true that any account which a cultural producer may offer as to his own mode of working may (important as it will be) be a thing distinct from the way in which he actually works.

Marx's work (and some of the best of the work of Engels) was informed by a fluent and sensitive apprehension of the dialectical interrelations of social being and social consciousness. When they attempted to explain this mode of apprehension and its object (to reduce process to system) they could offer approximate definitions only. And such definitions, if examined with care, may be seen to be ambiguous, in that they may either be read as statements of fact (this structure in society or this historical law may be said to exist) or as a metaphor of the social process (the process may best be understood if we suppose that it happened in this kind of way). I am unskilled in this kind of language: you have expressed arguments of a similar kind more clearly.[17] At least I know that the thinker who mistakes metaphor for fact is in for trouble.

I have already indicated (eight years ago) objections to one such theoretical reification of metaphor: the lamentable image of "basis and superstructure". The Marxist tradition has included too few poets who risked their hand at philosophy. For any poet could tell, in an instant,

that any human existential process *must* be constricted and deformed
which is contained within a metaphor out of the text-book of a constructional engineer. The point was far from original, although the
particular way in which I proposed it—that we must say that the sign-
post was pointing in the wrong direction, while, at the same time, we
must accept the existence of the place towards which it was mis-pointing
—was less familiar.[18]

But such comments as this, proposed too bluntly and in the English
idiom, do not rise to the level of sophistication requisite to merit notice
in the current Marxist discourse. When hundreds of thousands of
brilliant words—and *on this very theme* of infra-structure and supra-
structure—flow from the Euromarxist presses—when there is such a
concatenation of eagles in flight around the loftiest mountains—why
should these interrupt their concourse because one of the last of the
great bustards goes—hop, flap, plonk!—from one dwarfish tussock to
another? Meanwhile in serious intellectual circles the argument about
basis/superstructure goes *on and on and on* . . . The argument is vitiated
at root by this error: and this error, in turn, radiates error into discussions of ideology, aesthetics, social class. A whole continent of discourse is being developed, with its metropolitan centres and its villas in
the mountains, which rests, not upon the solid globe of historical evidence, but on the precarious point of a strained metaphor.

When I deride this metaphor I do so because it offends that very
sense of process, of the inter-action of social being and social consciousness, which I gained from Marx. And also because I have found any
such metaphor (or model derived from it) actively unhelpful in my
own work as historian. I do not propose another model. The closest I
have come to doing so was, many years ago, in a discussion arising from
Raymond Williams's *The Long Revolution*:

> If Mr Williams will abandon his vocabulary of 'systems' and 'elements' and his
> diffuse pluralism, and if Marxists will abandon the mechanical metaphor of base/
> superstructure and the determinist notion of 'law', then both might look once more
> at a phrase of Alasdair MacIntyre: 'what . . . the mode of production does is to
> provide . . . a kernel of human relationship from which all else grows.' Both might
> then accept that the mode of production and productive relationships determine
> cultural processes in an *epochal* sense; that when we speak of the capitalist mode of
> production for profit we are indicating at the same time a 'kernel' of characteristic
> human relationships—of exploitation, domination, and acquisitiveness—which are
> inseparable from this mode, and which find simultaneous expression in all of Mr
> Williams's 'systems'. Within the limits of the epoch there are characteristic tensions
> and contradictions, which cannot be transcended unless we transcend the epoch
> itself: there is an economic logic *and* a moral logic and it is futile to argue as to which
> we give priority since they are different expressions of the same 'kernel of human
> relationship'. We may then rehabilitate the notion of capitalist or bourgeois culture
> . . . (with) its characteristic patterns of acquisitiveness, competitiveness, and
> individualism.[19]

That is expressed more loosely than I might express it now. We remain dependent upon a metaphor, although 'kernel' has the merit of being a vitalist and generative metaphor, and not one which must lead on inevitably to 'concrete' formulations and to 'ivory towers'. It has the more considerable merit of evicting from our very mode of historical apprehension a schizoid notion of man, whose body/soul duality leaves him, in the end, edged towards antinomies in which food is exchanged for morals or for thought. The difficulty with the metaphor of 'kernel' is that it still suggests that all the possibilities of growth and of evolution are implicit, nucleated within the original nut, so that it still fails to comprehend the full dialectical process which entails qualities (consciousness and intentions) not to be expressed in any vegetative, organic analogy.[20] It may well be that no metaphor can be devised which is not in specifically human terms.

I mentioned also the determinist notion of 'law', and we can employ exactly the same method of criticism to examine this. In the course of historical analysis one may identify recurrent patterns of behaviour and sequences of events which may only be described (in a retrospective rather than a predictive sense) as being causally related. Since such events ensue in a manner independent of conscious human volition, it is easy to make this process intelligible by saying it is subject to certain 'laws'. But 'law', once again, may be intended as metaphor or fact. There is a difference between saying that a process works itself out in a known and expected way—that it conforms to laws—and saying that it arises as a consequence of law, is *lawed*.

When we speak metaphorically of "a law of nature" or of "the laws of love" or even (as Marx did) of "the economic law of motion of capitalist society", we may mean something quite different from predictive, scientific law. Law, in the second sense, entails at once a determinism—we cannot be voluntary agents if we are subject to law. In the first sense we can mean (although I do not suggest that I can show that Marx always intended this meaning) something closer to the phrase: "this is the way it works". And in this case an alternative term lies ready to hand. For if we replace the notion of the *laws* of social change by that of *logic*—a metaphor which may include the idea of causal relationships while excluding its determinist, predictive connotations—then certain "historicist" features of Marx's thought fall away and Marxists appear as honest men. "Every honest man is a Prophet", wrote William Blake:

> He utters his opinion both of private and public matters. Thus: If you go on So, the result is So. He never says, such a thing shall happen let you do what you will. A Prophet is a Seer, not an Arbitrary Dictator.

It was through this semantic confusion (to which, certainly, both

Marx and Engels were accomplice) that the notion of the laws of historical change, having a metaphysical (and hence extra-historical) existence independent of man's agency, took root in the Marxist tradition. But if these laws held predictive force, then men's ultimate freedom declined to the recognition of necessity: submission to, or at the most acceleration of, the general historic process; a submission which echoed a submission far older than this in man's thought: "nel sua voluntade è la nostra pace". And in the most corrupt, as also the most influential, sub-tradition of Marxism—the Marxism (1) which, nonetheless, remains historically one part within the Marxism (4)—the notion of agency declined to that of planning: to the manipulation of the economy, or of people, from above by an élite with the scientific know-how of history, the Marxist vanguard. The kingdom of freedom became the kingdom where only one party, and then one man, was free, and where his whim was other men's necessity.

This detour arose from a consideration of Marxism (4). I suggested that the Marxist tradition defined itself historically and existentially, and hence it contains, whether we like it or not, all those sub-traditions (the Marxisms (1) and (2)) which can claim some relevant descent from Marx's ideas—his errors and ambiguities as well as his discoveries. It may also include sub-traditions or individual thinkers who affirm allegiance to the tradition, because they own that Marx, more than any other man, saw to the heart of the matter; but who nevertheless hold themselves free to examine and reject any part of his thought. So far from this being a position of opportunism or eclecticism (as in Marxism (3)), I argued that for any thinker pretending to system it may be—and is at the present time—a comfortless and strenuous one, since it must entail a definition (and definitions continually renewed) as to where he stands within it. And I then entered into this detour, on metaphor and social process, to indicate ways in which I myself attempt this self-definition.

The question arises: if a great part of Marxism (1) is politically damaging and a caricature of rational thought, and if some part of Marxism (2) is intellectually-limiting and resistant to development, why should one maintain allegiance to the tradition at all? One part of the answer, which is intellectual, I hope I have already shown: one cannot be true to one's own thought in any other way. Another part is political: for strong political commitments remain in most Marxisms, and it can happen—I find that it happens sometimes in the case of my own relations with Marxists (1) of Trotskyist derivation—that one can share strong political commitments with Marxists with whom one's greatest source of disagreement is nevertheless about Marxism. It is not a case of hoping to "rescue" Marxism from these Marxists. That, I think, is hopeless. But there are many men with minds inside those

Marxisms, with whom one is engaged in common political struggles, with whom one may continue a dialogue, and who, in the end, may rescue themselves.

Another part of the answer is circumstantial. It depends upon where one is placed, and, for intellectual producers, it may depend even upon what discipline one works within. In my own case the choice presents no difficulty. Marxist historiography was never, in Britain, deformed beyond recovery, even when failing to make a clear intellectual disengagement from Stalinism. We had, after all, the living line of Marx's analysis of British history—in Capital, in Marx and Engels' correspondence—continually present to us. To work as a Marxist historian in Britain means to work within a tradition founded by Marx, enriched by independent and complementary insights by William Morris, enlarged in recent times in specialist ways by such men and women as V. Gordon Childe, Maurice Dobb, Dona Torr and George Thomson, and to have as colleagues such scholars as Christopher Hill, Rodney Hilton, Eric Hobsbawm, V. G. Kiernan and (with others whom one might mention) the editors of this Register. I could find no possible cause for dishonour in claiming a place in this tradition.

Indeed, it is the creative strength of this tradition behind and alongside me which gives me the audacity to flap from tussock to tussock of thought. I think it even possible that the English tradition of Marxist historiography may be able to stand comparison with that of any other country. And (to cease jesting) I am not finally convinced that the English intellectual idiom must necessarily become extinct, or become so archaic that it will debar men from the conversation of the world, under the pressure towards some eurocentric or universal intellectual style. I know of no clause in the Treaty of Rome by which I am obliged to cede my intellectual identity into the hands of some supra-national commission of universalists. Indeed, I have looked at this new euro-marxism, and I doubt its claims to be a more advanced, more rigorous language: one may detect within it, not universalism, but that old brother-and-antagonist of ours, the idiom of Paris—an idiom one of whose historically-constant features has always been its claim to be, not an idiom, but universal thought.

In saying so, one adds that it has, on occasion, almost sustained that claim. And more so than the English, some of whose best thought, embedded in the contexts of drama and verse, in wise saws and instances, in idiomatic moralisms, defies translation. The dialectic of those idioms has long gone on, and each idiom needs the other, as the knife needs the whetstone; and to each knife the whetstone of the other, system ground upon substance, moralism ground upon logic. I will even agree that in many (although not all) areas of culture the French idiom is prior: they propose and we object. If there is another difference it may be that many of the French, and most of all those English intellectuals who adopt a French idiom, assume (as the possessors of an idiom disguised as a universal must) that they could do perfectly well without the English. Whereas any English intellectual who advances to a certain point in his thought knows that he must both learn from and quarrel with the idiom of the French. One must attend to and admire M. Sartre and M. Lévi-Strauss, but in the heart of one's admiration there remains a watchful and quizzical eye.

If this is so, there might, at an outside chance, be a stay of execution for the bustard after all. One attends to what is said and to what one can understand. But it is not yet certain that one must change altogether one's mental vocabulary. Decimalization may have led us on towards a common European culture: towards the "supra-nationalism" of joining a European bourgeoisie with the same washing-powders, the same motels, the same pop stars, the same kinds of anxious marriages, the same cultural antibodies of drop-outs and hash, and the same rebellious students with the same Marxist brands. But even this reminds the traveller that it is *another* country that he goes abroad to see. It is not by our identities but by our differences that we can learn from each other.

It may yet prove to be the same in the itineraries of thought. The English idiom has travelled far, sometimes, it is true, protected by the navies of imperialism. As any historian of ideas has observed, a tradition may be carried by the most unlikely vector, and then by some twist of things, emerge as a creative art or voice. And, in the end, one may only act and write as one is; hoping, like all sad jesters, that some day someone may turn—as Kent turns to King Lear—and say: "This is not altogether fool, my lord."

I have explained why I affirm my allegiance to the Marxist tradition: in my discipline and in my idiom I have fellow workers who sustain me, and I can even (although with difficulty) sustain the quixotic notion that at some time, by some unforeseen twist of events (by conveying some new accent of thought to some emergent Marxist school in Calcutta or in Nairobi or in many-idiomed America) some element of this quaintly-empirical tradition of English Marxism could re-enter an international discourse. Agreed: a time could come when for political reasons, one could no longer choose to affirm oneself a Marxist. If institutional Marxisms, endorsed with power, proliferated and justified new crimes against the intellect and worse crimes against men; if all Marxists except a last grey company were either priests of established power or self-deluded chiliastic sectaries; then we would be bound by a duty beyond intellectual consistency to say, "I dissent!" And we would be compelled to accept the evidence: that there is some cause in Marxist nature that breeds these hard hearts.

But that moment has not come. It has not yet come by any means.

And that we should contest, up to and beyond the last reason for hope, this nightmare becoming true is a reason why one should remain—as a combatant or even as an outlaw—within the Marxist tradition.

*   *   *

I do not know whether you accept these arguments, or where you would place yourself now within the Marxist tradition. You have not, so far as I know, come to the point of saying "I dissent". I imagine that you feel yourself to be a Marxist outlaw. You may even (from your experiences in Poland, West Germany, California—and, if you will forgive me, your lack of *other* experiences and your inattention to other voices) feel that you are more of an outlaw than you are, that (save for a few friends) every Marxist's hand is against you.

Here are three comments of yours in your interview in *Encounter* (October, 1971):[21]

> When, in the West, I hear socialism interpreted in such a variety of obscurantist and even barbaric terms—for instance, the romantic nostalgia for a pre-industrial society, or a Bakuninian faith in the revolutionary potential of the *lumpen proletariat*— that I am reminded of the notion of Hegel and Marx that progress is only brought about through its worst manifestations.

> *   *   *

> The blind enthusiasm for the meaningless idea of global revolution, which I met with particularly in America, was especially repugnant to me. I can't deny the possibility that this irrational revolt may be symptomatic of a genuine sickness of civilisation. But to be the symptom of a disease is not to be its remedy.

And (in reply to the question: "Is there much common ground between the New Left in the West and the Polish Left?"):

> I think the differences are more marked than the similarities. The Polish students who demonstrated in March 1968 were simply claiming the traditional liberties— freedom of speech, of Press, of learning and assembly—which to some elements of the New Left are nothing but 'treacherous bourgeois snares'. A Polish friend . . . recently wrote to me from Sweden saying that whenever he had dealings with the New Left he seemed to be watching a film of which he already knew the end. That is exactly how I feel. The kind of language that was used in the past to justify the most brutal oppression is now being repeated as though nothing had ever happened.

Now, this is difficult. These passages provoke me to a temper in which no kind of letter could be continued. I might simply tear these pages up, and scribble "apostate!" on the wall. I don't think I could ever hope to make you understand the sense of pain with which some of us read that final paragraph, *from you*, and *in that particular place*.

It is true that you point only to "some elements" of the New Left. But if there are other "elements", you have nothing to say of them or to them. And in any case, an acquaintance with us or with our thought would have been superfluous, since we are, precisely, at the end of that film whose end you already "know".

When one is assured in advance that one's end is known, that one's thought can be anticipated and that it is a theorem already disproved (moreover a malevolent theorem which justifies "brutal oppression") it is difficult to go on. You intend no personal offence, I know. As you say in the same interview: "I simply try to answer the questions that seem to me important without giving any special thought to the effect my answers may produce." The effect in this case was to give interior injury to those who had thought themselves your allies and your friends.

But I wish to continue a discussion, although you give me no reason for any expectation that you wish to enter a dialogue. And at this point I must turn back to the offending passages, and acknowledge that *in some part* the objections that you make to "elements" within the miscellaneous Western "Left" are identical with ones which I have already made myself, earlier in this letter, and with equal vehemence. Why, then, should I object? What a curious predicament—a nexus of crossed lines, old brooding grievances and old attachments, the counter-communication of plain anger—we have got into now!

One part of my objection belongs not to your arguments but to the sociology of their presentation: that is, to their consequences in a particular context. I will return to this in my conclusion. Here, let me say only this. In the East the critic of orthodox institutional Marxism must be courageous and intransigent, as you have been. He confronts an orthodoxy buttressed by the organs of the State, by reasons of power, by the inertia of an approved ideology. In the West a critic whose intellectual premises are identical may yet have to learn a different kind of wisdom. The reasons of State, the inertia of approved ideology— all these tilt to the other side.

We have had to learn, in this country where the intellectual components of all the Marxisms put together are small, certain reticencies and courtesies. If you criticize, with stridency, any section of the Left in certain places—and *Encounter* is, by intention and by subsidy, the first of these places—your criticism is not attended to for the sake of any particular discrimination which it may contain. It is absorbed, instantly, into ideology; that is, it is simply assimilated as one more *noise* against the Left, one more evidence that *all* the Left has failed, is brutal, *all* Marxism is incoherent, etc.; and if this evidence comes from Leszek Kolakowski then (not through your cogency but for your high repute) it is a veritable trophy to be hung at the cloudy altar of the established gods.

If a public statement of dissociation from some section (authentic or self-styled) of the Left must be made—as sometimes happens—then it must be as specific as possible, or it will immediately be turned against itself. Such language as "some elements" will not do. Indeed, it reminds me of another vocabulary of commination: have you not often been defined as "certain elements" yourself? I don't of course ask you to inhibit your criticisms, but first to ensure that they are seriously *informed* (and not founded upon a casual impression of an aberrant and utterly transient student exhibition), and second to consider where you *place* them.

The other part of my objection is less contingent. In the last two years you have been passing from the criticism of irony to criticism by means of caricature. This is present in the passages I have cited: "romantic nostalgia for a pre-industrial society", "treacherous bourgeois snares". It is present in another gem dropped before *Encounter* readers: you disclaim belief "in a so-called total or global revolution, or in the *final* elimination of *all* alienation and a *wholly* peaceful state of society without conflicts and contradictions". These are my italics, and I italicize also the words which carry the same dismissive, caricaturing function in a passage from another recent article. In an essay on "Intellectuals against Intellect" published in *Daedalus* (a journal which is also, incidentally, subsidized, like *Encounter*, by the Ford Foundation, although it does not pursue ideological goals with equal zest)[22] you write of—

> *The ideals* of anarchism and *all those other* social utopias that have had envy rather than a striving for justice as their underlying motivation, and that put forward as their aim the pulling down of *the whole of mankind* to the level of its *most ignorant* strata, thereby *glorifying illiteracy* as a proper road to the liberation of humanity.

This is not in criticism of any Marxism and I have no special loyalty to any anarchist thinkers. But it involves the same undiscriminating commination against a section of the Left, and employs the same method of caricature. Can you show, for example, that "the ideals of anarchism", as represented in the actual social aspirations of the most significant European anarchist movement of this century—the anarchists of Spain —conforms to your description? Orwell, Brennan, and other observers have given us a different account. But (you will say) you intended the criticism at a different level: as a criticism of ideas of particular thinkers —or of one thinker: let us say Bakunin. Why, then, is your criticism (in the journal of the American Academy of Arts and Sciences) made in so imprecise a form? And is it, indeed, a criticism in terms of ideas? It would seem to belong (in a distinction which you have often made) to "genetic" rather than epistemological criticism:[23] that is, you are criticizing less the ideas than the psychological or social condition ("envy") out of which the thought arose. By such methods of philosophical criticism one may gain very quick results; and, moreover, results which confirm to the very echo the assumptions with which one started. And what of that other small phrase, dropped in so quietly, as

to "all those other social utopias", similarly grounded upon "envy"?
Surely we have here once again our old acquaintance: "certain elements who . . ."? Since no precisions are offered, the noise which
remains in the head after the voice has stopped is simply this: *all social
utopias . . . envy.*

There is a small point here. In the East you formed a habit of making
precise criticisms but with imprecise identifications of the actual
persons/dogmas/legislation criticized. This was a habit apt to your
context, the arcane wisdom imposed by censors and bureaucrats.
Every reader knew instantly the corruptions, the irrationalisms, the
approved Party spokespeople at which the criticisms were aimed—
every reader except, perhaps, a puzzled censor. A general criticism
might survive and take wing: a particular and poised criticism would
incur administrative erasure. But a good habit in the East may be a
bad habit in the West. So many varieties of doctrine are on offer that
no-one will identify at which a general commination is directed: the
category as a whole—"Marxists", "anarchists", "the New Left",
"utopians"—will receive the attack. And why should this not be so?
If you were to proclaim that you knew that certain leather articles
(such as hand-bags) were infected with anthrax, and also warned
against "all those other leather goods" which were equally infected,
then the whole leather industry—jackets and belts, saddles, upholstery
and shoes—must be regarded with anxiety as a locus of infection.

There are too many passages of this order in this article. Thus you
refer to—

> the conversions of intellectuals to Hitlerism or Stalinism, which were conscious
> conversions to barbarism, known and accepted . . . Stalinism also attracted some
> people as an embodiment of Marxist universalism, and tempted others as a march
> of the 'splendid Asiatics' called to destroy decaying European civilization.

The context suggests that you are referring to "Western" intellectuals
in the 1930s and 1940s. Your criticism is once again "genetic": you
impute certain motivations (and you offer no others): but at the same
time you do not *examine* either motive or context. Any competent
academic historian would explain to his students why one may not
approach either ideas or social history in this kind of way. Nor do I
think that your judgement is well-informed; nor that it contains any
sense of the *politics* of those years, and the way in which choices arose.
Thus I think it might be shown that many Western intellectuals who
could properly be described as deluded or self-deluded by Stalinism
were less interested in the Soviet Union (how much do you or I know
about China today, although events demand that we take up some
attitude?) than in the manifest crisis of the capitalist economy (and
the class conflicts in their own countries), or in events in Spain or in

Germany or, later, in the resistance movements of France, Italy, Yugoslavia and Greece—events in which they were themselves participant and as to which they were very much better informed. They were "converts" to an existent Communist movement, in an actual social context whose ferocity of commitments were not of their intellectual invention, and it was from this that they were led on into other "Stalinist" deformities of thought.

Your premise is that intellectuals (who are distinct from other citizens with a social conscience and responsibilities) always move head-first. And their heads always move towards a system of thought (they are "converted" to Stalinism or anarchism); although, genetically, it may be shown that they only think that their heads are moving, while in reality it is their evil will or some passion ("envy") that invades the head. In a world of pure rationality or pure malevolence this might be so. But the world is not so pure: you cannot "hang it, as the country fellow speakes, by geometry."[24] It is not a question of whether one prefers impurities, an admixture of mind with more fallible human stuff. Whether or no, we must understand this world as it is; the mind's capacity for inconsistency, which you once praised,[25] must be apparent to us at every moment when we seek to analyse, not the logical ordering, but the historical imbrication of ideas in social movements.

Western intellectuals were not converted to Stalinism (or, in the first case, "to Hitlerism or Stalinism"—and why "Hitlerism" rather than the more analytic terms "Nazism" or "Fascism"?) only because they were either (1) conscious converts to barbarism, or (2) attracted by Marxist universalism, or (3)—and finally—tempted by the vision of Splendid Asiatics destroying European decadence. There were many, and more potent, motivations, both intellectual and in actual experience. I am unclear as to the distinction between two of the motivations you have selected: is it that in (1) the love is a love of barbarism *tout court* whereas in (3) we have a finer precision: the barbarism must be "Asiatic"? The discrimination, nice as it is, need not detain us, since while you might find, here or there, individual men, or statements by other men taken out of wider contexts, which supported your argument that such motivations were present, I defy you to show that these motivations were sufficiently widely distributed to be generalized in this way, or could be given anything like the priority among other motivations which you assert. I hold the unfashionable view—a view which is today most unfashionable of all among the non- or anti-Communist Left—that, in terms of the choices presented to them, the Communists of the 1930s and 1940s were not altogether wrong, intellectually or politically; certainly, that they were not wrong all of the time. I *know* that the Western Communist intellectuals with whom I associated did not sustain themselves with visions of splendid Asiatics marching upon the West; their visions were of Panzers or of Sherman tanks rolling into the East, breathing racial purity or the freedom of capital down the barrels of their guns.

This is not a page of apologetics. I am simply asking for analysis and not caricature. One of the first casualties of Stalinist "realist" thought, I know, was Poland. And you, a Pole, cannot lightly forgive such an error. In saying that your thought comes from that tragic context—and I say it with humility—I am also saying that you cannot but think about this in a Polish idiom.

The point which I was offering to illustrate is that you have been passing from irony to caricature: or to mere abuse. Irony may be directed both against a friend and an antagonist. If used with effect, it is a small, accurate, fine-tempered weapon. It may wound, but it can wound only the particular point—the idea, the characteristic—at which it is directed. It is no blunt, belligerent instrument, as is abuse. Irony must succeed in striking exactly where it is aimed. If the aim misses, then it is not the victim but the ironist who is caught off-balance. And if the aim is good, the victim's ideas are not thereby "exploded", utterly exposed: they are questioned or corrected at one particular point. The wound may smart for a moment, but it will heal. Life evidences daily that friendship and indeed marriage can survive the mutual exchange of ironies.

They will not survive abuse nor repeated caricature. For caricature—when it is applied to thought or social movements—signals exactly that dialogue can no longer be sustained. What is caricatured is first set at a distance, then pointed at as "other", then falsified in such a way as to confirm our sense of antagonism, to make it all the easier for us to point out to strangers its deformities—its heavy jowl, its paunch, its shifty eyes. It means that all hope of rational argument has been given up.

Well, then, Leszek Kolakowski, old comrade of another time, where have we got to now? Others on the Left will say that you have "gone too far": all hope of dialogue is at an end. And this I *will* not say. I honour too highly your past, I owe too many debts to your work. Moreover, you write like a man still in a state of shock, whose subjective despair has engulfed, but only for a time, his workman's morale:

> One cannot completely exclude the possibility that contemporary admirers of barbarism represent a real tendency in the historical process and that all the technological and spiritual achievements of modern times will be destroyed in an unprecedented cataclysm, compared to which the fall of the Roman Empire will seem a trivial stumble . . .

I agree: the possibility cannot be excluded.[26] It came very close to us indeed, through the agency of nuclear war, more than once in the two past decades, although the human agents were not exactly those to whom you point. One excludes nothing: and Marx (we should not forget) did not exclude "the mutual ruin of the contending classes."

We do not exclude. Nor do we, without apparent and overwhelming reason, despair. For, if we do, we add in that instant one more particle to the reasons of despair. But with you one feels that despair has already made a deeper entry. It has broken into reason's gates.

*　　*　　*

To despair is to suffer, and we may not accuse a man for his suffering. Least of all may we do so when we have not shared his sequence of tragic experience. All we can do, and all that you would wish us to do, is to reason.

There are three areas of thought which appear among your present preoccupations: (1) the active danger of a messianic element, which you see as intrinsic to the Marxist tradition; (2) a distrust, not of intellect, but of intellectuals; (3) what I must propose as an imperfect assimilation of some parts of Western experience, which leaves you a prey to sociological nightmares of a familiar kind. I will attempt a comment on each of these.

In pursuing the first theme you have shown great consistency. In "Responsibility and History" (1957) you showed the consequences that have followed when "one messianic hope becomes the unique governor of life, the sole source of moral precepts and the only measure of virtue."[27] I did not have the language then to dissect these problems. But (I show this to illustrate that we share more than a formal premise: even "Western" Marxists and former "Stalinists" have had moments of moral suffering) I will cite the crude lines of a poem which I find among my own notes of 1956. The poem is "In Praise of Hangmen":

> How can we other than
> Honour that man
> Who undertakes this social trust
> Since someone must?
>
> How much more honour then
> To all those dedicated men
> Who saved society
> By rope and calumny!
>
> So giving honour, we
> Who moralise necessity,
> With slats of sophistry erect
> A gibbet of the intellect,
>
> And from its foul and abstract rope
> Suspend all social hope,
> Until with swollen tongue
> Morality herself is hung

In whose distended dedicated eyes
All honour dies.

You have worried at that problem (and I worry at it) ever since. In
"The Priest and the Jester" (1959) you suggested:

> The most common hope of historiosophy is to identify or adjust the essence of man
> with his existence; that is, to assure that the unalterable aspirations of human nature
> will be fulfilled in reality.

This "secular eschatology", you implied, had become imbricated in
the Marxist tradition: "current history can be characterized by its striving towards a lasting goal that can be defined and that will irrevocably
end all existing conflicts." Every man is influenced, even in his "daily
endeavours", by his eschatological assumptions: convinced that
"history" is moving towards some final goal, we may consider our own
acts and choices as "a kind of scraping together of pennies toward a
pension fund for ourselves or mankind, and thus run the risk of scorning
current facts and momentary values."

You did not, in this place, pursue the argument in its relation to
Marx's thought: although you did imply (in a very general reference)
that all systems of thought "which are supposed to give us certainty as
the end result of their search, always give it at the very beginning",
and in this sense commence with the revelation which they disclose.
You returned in 1966 to a related problem in a brief study of "Historical
Understanding and the Intelligibility of History".[28]

This gem-like study, whose brevity rebukes my verbosity, glints with
light from each of its facets. You commence with philosophical precisions as to the meanings of "understanding". You show the fallacy of
expressive or behaviouristic notations of "understanding" which proceed by means of improper analogies from the behaviour of individuals
to social process, or historical events. You insist that if history is to be
intelligible—that is, can be "understood" as valued significance and
not as natural process—these values must be inserted by the observer.
As you have observed, "the human species enjoys no one's protection."[29]
Any interpretation which offers a universal significance to man's
history "must presuppose a non-empirical *potentia* which actualizes
itself, thanks to history, but which places itself outside of history and
therefore cannot be inferred or deducted from historical knowledge".

> It is in relation to this *potentia* or 'essence'—that history becomes endowed with
> significance, that it is henceforth not only the sequence of cause and effect, but above
> all the succession of approaches to the actualized essence. It is difficult to imagine a
> theoretical construction of the idea of progress without it.

And just above this you had written:

I want to stress the fundamental coincidence of the three different theoretical constructions of Hegel, Marx, and Husserl. This coincidence is found again (and I say it conscious of the blasphemy) in their anti-historical viewpoint, in the conviction, therefore, that a non-actualized essence of man (or even a non-human essence of which humanity constitutes a stage or 'moment') is *given* in such a manner that it imposes on history, so to speak, the necessity of its actualization.

Your argument clarifies much, although I hold it to be open at one point to question. But, before offering this enquiry, let us pursue your own argument further. You deny that "history" itself has "immanent intelligibility". But if we know that men insert into it an attribution of significance—by an "act of faith"—then the problem appears differently. This act of faith is "creative and fertile": it is a projection which "gives the past its meaning":

This project must contain . . . the hope that it is *really possible* and the faith that its possibilities rest on the pre-historical *eidos* of a *humanitas* whose painful course of incarnation is furnished to us by history. But the project is a decision about the choice of values. It is therefore not a scientific procedure.

You did not, in that study, examine in any particular way Marx's own act of faith, or assumption of a "non-actualized essence of man". You came closest when you asserted:

Hegel, Marx, and Husserl were perfectly aware that, at the moment when they wrote about history, they were not truly writing about history. They were writing the autobiography of spirit. In writing, they continued that about which they were writing. Their project, so to speak, inscribed itself directly in history, giving it intelligibility.

What constitutes the clue to Marx's "autobiography of spirit"? In a recent paper, "The Myth of Human Self-Identity", you argue the case further.[30] You point to a "soteriological myth"[31] hidden in the traditional Marxist anticipation of socialism as based on the "identity of civil and political society." This myth concerns the historical division between "civil" and "political" society, which Marx supposed would come to an end and be transcended in the unity of communist society. You detect a source of this "primordial hope" as to the future "kingdom of freedom" in a passage of *On the Jewish Question* (1843), albeit the idea is expressed there "still in philosophical and embryonic form and not yet in class terms". In the passage which you cite[32]—

the concept of 'human emancipation' lacks any mention of class struggle and of the mission of the proletariat. And yet, the same vision of man returning to perfect unity, experiencing directly his personal life as a social force, makes up the philosophical background of the Marxian socialism. In all later writings . . . the same eschatological concept of the unified man remains.

"What is wrong with this hope?" you ask. "Is there any connection between the Marxian vision of the unified man and the fact that real communism appears only in the totalitarian shape, i.e. as the tendency to *replace* all crystallizations of the civil society by coercive organs of the state?" One way of approaching this problem might have been through a consideration of the actual history by which what you refer to as "real communism" appeared in totalitarian shape. But this way of approach you turn from with an abrupt, dismissive gesture:[33]

> To those who think about the prospects of socialist development the real question is: does the very inquiry into the Marxian idea of the unity of civil and political society allow us to presume that any attempt to set up such a unit will be likely to produce an order with strongly pronounced totalitarian traits?

To this question you offer an unqualified affirmative. You do so partly on experiential or empirical grounds. The distinction between the administering of things and the governing of people is too indefinite to be sustained. "Management of the economy involves command over people", and one cannot usefully distinguish between "political" and "economic" command. The withering-away of the state would presuppose that among the working people material incentives or physical coercion gave way to moral motivations: but "experience of socialist countries" declares firmly against any such "formidable moral revolution in men's minds". Moreover, once production is no longer motivated by private profit, the State must become "the only remaining source of economic initiative": hence socialism must instantly inaugurate "a tremendous growth in the tasks of the state and its bureaucracy." These arguments in your view,

> may justify the suspicion that, far from promising the fusion of civil with political society, the Marxian perspective of unified man is more likely to engender, if put to practical test, a cancerous growth of the quasi-omnipotent bureaucracy, trying to shatter and paralyse civil society and leading the (rightly blamed) anonymity of public life to its extreme consequences.

To these arguments you add considerations of a similar order. There is no reason to suppose that once social classes, in Marx's sense, have been abolished, the struggle of private interests will stop. (Your arguments on this I will leave for later discussion (pp. 368–70).) The "restoration of the perfect unity of the personal and communal life" is myth: it "presupposes an unprecedented moral revolution running against the whole course of the past history of culture."

> The dream of perfect unity may come true only in the form of a caricature which denies its original intention: as an artificial unity imposed by coercion from above, in that the political body prevents real conflicts and real segmentation of the civil society from expressing themselves.

This is not, of course, a conclusion that may be found in Marx's own "primordial intention": his intentions were quite otherwise. But this "primordial intention is not innocent . . . It could scarcely be brought to life in a basically different form, and this not because of contingent historical circumstances but because of its very content . . . There are no reasons to expect that this dream can ever become real except in the cruel form of despotism. The despotism is a desperate simulation of paradise".

I have tried to trace a long sequence of intricate argument fairly. But now I must re-trace my steps and follow your thought in a more argumentative manner. Let us return, first, to "Historical Understanding and the Intelligibility of History".

I found this essay to be open to question at one critical point. This point may be approached by three steps. First, I am not convinced with your conclusion that "from the point of view of historicism which takes into consideration only what is actually given in the historical material, history is inexorably unintelligible and totally opaque"; and hence that "understanding" (when considered as valued significance rather than as reconstruction of a natural process) "must impose itself on knowledge as a hermeneutic rule": i.e. as a rule of interpretation already imposed by the interpreter.

This is a difficult and technical question which concerns what we mean by a social or historical *process*, in which sequences of cause and effect may be observed in the actual work of empirical investigation, and in which regularities of behaviour, of institutional formation, and of cultural expression can be shown to have occurred in social life. This question of course raises further questions as to process, causation, and as to the categories which the researcher brings to his materials. I will take it from several references of your own—for example, to "a real tendency in the historical process" (p. 340 above)—that we are in sufficient agreement as to the objective existence of "process" to set aside this particular matter of definition.

However, you refuse to dignify the description of process with the name of "understanding". Without the attribution of significance by the observer, you argue, "history is *a natural process* [my italics] similar to the evolution of stellar systems and equally incapable of being understood". But, as you well know, it is as hazardous to draw analogies between a historical process and a natural process as it is between an historical event and the motivations or actions of an individual. The stars are not conscious creatures; they do not attain towards the attributes of moral agents or of rational beings. If they did so, a coherent description of the evolution of the stellar system could not be undertaken without the evidence itself imposing upon the most neutral observer problems of explanation of an order distinct from that commonly assumed by the term "natural process". Thus the observer would have to note that the intentions of certain stellar actors were negated by the intentions of others, that certain meanings gained ascendancy and other meanings were lost in inter-stellar space. Hence the observer's "explanation" could not avoid taking in some explanation of the significancies attributed to their own evolution by the actors. And the "explanation" will approach towards "understanding" (in a common usage of the word) in the sense that not only "natural process" but also valued significance will be described.

We are supposing, up to this point, a stellar system, composed of stars with moral and rational attributes, under investigation by a detached, non-stellar observer. It is true that this observer need share at no point the significancies attributed to themselves by the stars. His explanation of the evolution of meaning may be undertaken entirely in terms of the system's own self-attributions. If he becomes partisan, if he adopts the meanings of this sun and rejects the intentions of that planet, then he is projecting *upon* that history his own criteria of intelligibility. But of course the supposition indicates another fracture in the analogy between the explanation of historical and natural process. For we must now see that our stellar investigator (if he is to be akin to an historian) must have a mind and sensibility which is itself a product of that very process of evolution which he is investigating: he is himself a consequence of process, and his nature is exactly one of the possibilities which have evolved. Hence the very meanings which he may attribute to this evolution are themselves a selection from the products of that evolution, and if he succeeds in contorting his consciousness into an extra-stellar state—from which standpoint all stellar meanings can be seen as transient phenomena devalued of significance: i.e. as "natural process" —then he still deludes himself, for he only demonstrates that one of the possibilities within the process of which his consciousness is an outcome is precisely that his own historical evolution may be seen in this way.

I will add at this point—although I am clear that the addendum is by no means entailed by the previous argument—that to one who stands in an affirmative relation to the Marxist tradition, the fact that many thinkers around the mid-20th century have independently come to the view that man's history may be seen as de-valued of significance, might have not only a logical but also a genetic occasion: that is, while treating the argument with respect, I would also wish to examine its situation within the sociology of ideas. If in the 19th century it became rather easy, against a background of accelerating technological innovation and ascendant bourgeois democracy, for thinkers in Western Europe to assume the idea of progress, so it may today, against a background of war, terror, Fascism, and their aftermath (in statist *realpolitik*, a nuclear balance of terror, and the near-universal defeat of socialist utopianism) to assume the idea of devalued process.

In both cases, the observer is projecting backwards upon history an attribution of significance. It is not a case of the former doing so and the latter stoically refusing to himself that consolation, since the latter's stoicism (and indeed the very categories of significance) are themselves derived from an experiential matrix at a certain point in this evolution. Thus in both cases what the observer projects *upon* history is a notation of value which is among the possibilities given to him *by* that history.

If we observe natural process, the question of valued significance does not even arise; if we observe history, it arises compulsively, not only because of its subject-matter (valuing and conscious beings) but also because the observer is by his own moral and intellectual nature a creature of these compulsions. To deny significance to history is not to adopt a "neutral" or scientific, extra-historical posture: it is to make a particular kind of declaration of value.[34]

I hope we may agree that the analogy between natural and historical process is unhappy; and, even more, that a metaphor, so seductive to the academic mind, of an extrahistorical observer examining history as if it were non-human phenomena, is misleading. We may attain towards objectivity; what we cannot attain towards is an inter-stellar, extra-human objectivity, which would thereby be extra-sensory, extra-moral and extra-rational. The historian may choose between values but he may not choose to be without values, because he cannot choose to sit somewhere outside the gates of his own historically-given human nature.

This, then, is the first step of my argument: a philosopher may imagine a value-free history, but he deludes himself and no historian can offer one. But now to the second step. Is it true, as you have argued, that any interpretation which offers a universal significance to man's history "must pre-suppose a non-empirical *potentia* which actualizes itself, but which places itself outside of history and therefore *cannot be inferred or deduced from historical knowledge*"? [my italics].

Let us turn this assertion around, and approach it from a point in your conclusion. You stressed the "fundamental coincidence" of the three different theoretical constructions of Marx, Hegel and Husserl. All adopt an "anti-historical viewpoint"; all themselves endow history with significance, as "the succession of approaches to the actualized essence"; all "were perfectly aware that, at the moment when they wrote about history, they were not truly writing about history. They were writing the autobiography of spirit." You propose this—perhaps savouring your metaphysical insolence a little too indulgently—"conscious of the blasphemy".

Well, we don't mind, in these latter days, about blasphemy. But a historian—and not only a historian in the Marxist tradition—must be a little worried about a philosophical conclusion, so cogent in presentation, which nevertheless conflates the work of three men whose known and demonstrable procedures of historical research—that is, their very stance in relation to the object of research, historical evidence—are so starkly opposed.

Let us pause for a moment with the name of Husserl. I doubt whether the most ardent disciple of Husserl can ever have proposed that his master had more than a casual, eclectic and secondary acquaintance with historical materials. A recent interpreter explains that his arduous project "of laying the groundwork of a strictly scientific philosophy" imposed upon him "a choice which demanded of him great asceticism and which precluded his acquiring the large historical background whose absence is so conspicuous in his writings".[35]

It is without doubt true that Husserl knew perfectly well that he was writing, not about history, but the autobiography of spirit:

> The spiritual *telos* of European Man, in which is included the particular *telos* of separate nations and of individual human beings, lies in infinity, it is an infinite idea, toward which in secret the collective spiritual becoming, so to speak, strives.

It may be admirable to have the innocence so to speak, although it is a difficult question to know how it was possible, in *Prague* and in *1935* for Husserl to speak so:

> No matter how inimical the European nations may be toward each other, still they have a special inner affinity of spirit that permeates all of them and transcends their national differences. It is a sort of fraternal relationship that gives us the consciousness of being at home in this circle.

And Husserl "proves" his assertion by contrasting Europeans with "Indians": "all other human groups" are motivated by a desire "constantly to Europeanize themselves, whereas we, if we understand ourselves properly, will never, for example, Indianize ourselves." Perish indeed, the thought! "In our European humanity there is an innate entelechy that thoroughly controls the changes in the European image and gives to it the sense of a development in the direction of an ideal image of life and of being, as moving toward an eternal pole."[36]

We may agree that Husserl was not writing history: he was concerned with a certain, culturally-embodied, concept of the spirit of rationality—and he was consciously attributing this significance *to* history. I agree that one may attend with sympathy to such concepts. I do *not* agree that such attention can be seen as "prior" to or independent of attention to fact, to evidence; nor that any concept which any philosopher cares to think up and attribute as significance to history is as good as any other. A philosopher who wishes to propound large views as to history and human destiny, but who is "ascetic" in his acquisition of historical knowledge, cannot expect to detain a historian's attention.

If concept be brought *to* history it must equip itself at every point to argue with the facts; it must immerse itself in the acidity of historical evidence and see if then it survives; and if it purports to generalize as to the nature of "Man" it might do well to try first to "Indianize" itself. If we throw our own significance back upon history—if we acclaim these men as progenitors of an outcome which we endorse, if we uphold those values as the ones which we, in our own present, wish to perpetuate and enlarge—we must still wrestle with these historical men and those historical values within the strictest terms (contextual definition, recovery of forgotten meanings and inflexions) of the historical discipline: otherwise we are simply using history as a mirror and glimpsing within it projections of ourselves.

It is preposterous—I will agree after all that we may call it blasphemy —to find a "fundamental coincidence" in a common "anti-historical viewpoint" in both Marx and Husserl. And it is scarcely less preposterous to bring the name of Hegel into the same conjunction. I am not competent to pursue the difficult question as to Hegel's historical method, a method which sometimes—as in the *Phenomenology*—commands the historian's respect, and at other times—as in the *Logic*—provokes his indignation. For Hegel is capable of saying in one and the same moment that history "has constituted the rational necessary course of the World-Spirit", whose unchanging identity unfolds itself "in the phenomena of the world's existence" and appears "as the ultimate *result* of history"; and that "we have to take the latter [i.e. this result] as it is. We must proceed historically—empirically".[37] It is the tension between these two methods which provides much of Hegel's excitement and historical insight, and the over-dominance of the first method over the second which provokes the historian—and which provoked Marx—to exasperation.

But we need not settle this difficult point. It is evident that the historical method proposed and employed by these three men cannot be subsumed into a single viewpoint. Husserl dispensed with empirical controls altogether, and hence his "history" is truly anti-historical. In Hegel there is a complex (but diminishing) tension between the attribution of the ideal and the investigation of the actual, in which, nevertheless, the ideal always maintains a primacy over the actual and can never be thoroughly reformed by empirical self-criticism. In Marx, who was no "ascetic" in his historical studies and whose engagement with the evidence was heroic and lifelong, a historical method is employed in which there is a continual dialectical interaction between concept and actuality—the conceptual selection of evidence, the structural organization of the data, and then the breaking and refashioning of concepts and structures in the light of that criticism which further empirical investigation must bring. So that your argument appears as too neat in its philosophical proportions: for the sake of the delicious savour of "blasphemy" you have inserted within it its own *reductio ad absurdum*. These three men could not all "know" in the same way that they "were not truly writing about history"; there is scarcely a passage in the mature Marx which is not drenched with the sense that it was, exactly, history and its exfoliating meanings that he was writing about. What most remains, after the vibrations of Marx's local investigations die away, is the lasting impression of his historical method.

Your argument was that he, like Husserl and Hegel, interpreted history by attributing "a non-empirical *potentia*" which "cannot be inferred or deduced from historical knowledge". This remains possible, although it is manifest that Marx, in his mature work, thought that he could make such deductions. It is intrinsic to his historical method that the historian may not bring concepts to the materials of history, and select from them only those evidences which conform with the concepts: the concepts must in the same moment of investigation be exposed to the whole available and relevant evidence, to the inconvenient as much as—indeed, more than—to the convenient facts. Husserl's "spiritual *telos* of European Man" is merely silly, because it will not survive the scrutiny of the evidence at all. Hegel's "World-Spirit" is more interesting, because it effects a conjunction with evidence—and, indeed, organizes evidence and gives to it significance—but often in fortuitous and inverted ways. Marx's "fully human" man—a man who was held under firm controls in his mature writings, and as to whom he was perhaps over-reticent—was indeed exposed to some empirical investigation; although he was not exposed (as he has been subsequently) to the investigation of Fascism, of a seemingly-compliant working-class in a consumer capitalist society, nor, above all, of Stalinism. Hence the question as to whether this man can "be inferred or deduced from historical knowledge" is not, as you suppose, a question which permits of a swift philosophical solution—or a question which may be discussed at the level of Marx's intention—but one which demands historical investigation.

Any investigation of man's entire history and destiny must of course require superhuman knowledge. But because no man can ever undertake it—and because its results can never be more than approximate as well as relative to that point in history in which the observer is situated—this does not mean that it is factitious. The attempt to attain a collective accretion of such self-knowledge is one of the justifications for situating oneself within the Marxist tradition of historiography. Moreover, this investigation may be somewhat more strenuous, and more active in the making and breaking of concepts, than some philosophers—in their rather casual references to historiography—appear to suppose. The historical discipline is not a fairground in which different interpreters set up their stalls and solicit the preference of their customers. Historical argument concerns always the exposure. of concept to evidence, or the organizing of evidence by concept. Its common forms of dispute are thus: "this concept, or this ordering of the facts, explains phenomenon A but ignores B and is at variance with phenomenon C"; or thus: "this description of A, B and C is conceptually vacuous and empty of structural organization: it neither shows us how A, B and C are related, nor prepares us for the fact that ABC gave rise to D". Hence, if Marx's partially-concealed notion of the "fully human" attaining towards realization in his history proves to be an inadequate, insufficiently-defined concept (as I think we must now agree), then the historian cannot simply dismiss it from service and leave a de-structured conceptual vacancy: he must set about fashioning a concept which will stand a better chance of standing up to the scrutiny of our sad, 20th-century evidence.

I will resume the second step in my argument. If we agree (for the purpose of argument) that valued significance arises not from the historical evidence itself but from an attribution made by the observer, it is not true that any kind of significance that anyone chooses to attribute is as "good" as any other. There is a crucial distinction to be made between the attributions of the neophyte (and in matters of historical discipline the most worthy philosopher may be a neophyte: it is time that historians defended the integrity of their own discipline) and the sustained submission of that attribution to historical criticism. I offer Husserl as an example of the first, and Marx as exemplar of the second. Therefore the question of any "projection" which Marx made "upon" history is a question which must be discussed with reference to the historical evidence.

The third step is this: you are somewhat cavalier in your attention to the central subject matter with which Marx wrestled—that is, capitalist society and, to a less degree, feudal society and pre-capitalist formations. But if we locate (as we should) Marx's notion of human potential within the actual context of pre-existent social formations—and, in particular, bring it into relation to his concepts of class and of contradiction—we find that we are dealing with a problem that is more real than your essay proposed and which cannot be dismissed by such dexterous philosophical means.

At this stage, while still keeping your first essay in view, I wish to take in points also from your subsequent essay, "The Myth of Human Self-Identity". And here I must cover my own deficiencies in philosophical argument by a kind of short-hand. For we approach the difficult and much-fought-over territory of the relation between the "early" and the "mature" Marx. I don't wish to reproduce in intellectual terms a very material event of my youth, when I was detected crossing an open hillside, with no cover, and subjected to the personal attention of a battery of mortars. Since I don't wish to lie pressing my face into the earth while Messrs Marcuse, Althusser, and their numerous progeny bracket my trembling body with Hegelian and anti-Hegelian shrapnel, I will say this. I reject a great part of Marcuse's work, and for the reasons which Alasdair MacIntyre has expressed with lucidity in his critical study: in particular, I accept those arguments by which he shows that Marcuse's characteristic thought is derived not from the mature Marx but from the Young Hegelians.[38] At the same time I reject in form all, and in content most, of the work of Althusser, for reasons which you have expressed with lucidity in a recent study.[39] I not only reject, but I object, in both writers, to their lack of sincerely-offered, open empirical controls—to their evacuation of the method of historical materialism.

This clears some ground, I hope. But Althusser is of course right that Marx's thought came together into a new kind of totality in the late 1840s; and that those seminal concepts present in earlier writings, of essence and existence, of alienation, of civil and political society, are afforded new meanings within the newly-discovered context of historical materialism. His emphasis is not of course new: the first "education class" which I attended after joining the Communist Party in 1942 consisted of a rather vulgar demonstration as to how Marx turned Hegel "upon his head".[40] Nor was he the only one to note that the renewal of interest in the concept of alienation after 1956 tended to isolate certain ideas from the organization, by Marx in his maturity, of these ideas into a whole.[41] Nor is it useful to spend any further time upon Althusser's particular vocabulary of structure, conjuncture and over-determination. I will prefer, at this point, to borrow a rehearsal of the familiar argument in the crisper terms of MacIntyre:

> . . . the knowledge of man himself depends on grasping the individual as part of a totality. Yet we cannot grasp the totality except insofar as we understand the individuals who comprise it. Marx wrote:
>
>> A loom is a machine for weaving. It is only under certain conditions that it becomes *capital*; isolated from these conditions it is as far from being capital as gold, in its natural state, is from being coin of the realm.
>
> What are these conditions? They include both the existence of a whole system of economic activity and the informing of human activities and intentions by concepts which express the relationships characteristic of the system. We identify a loom as capital or gold as coin only when we have grasped a whole system of activities as a capitalist or monetary system. The individual object or action is identifiable only in the context of the totality; the totality is only identifiable as a set of relationships between individuals. Hence we must move from parts to whole and back from whole to parts. [42]

This admirable recital serves two purposes: it reminds us of what we are talking about when we discuss the capitalist system; and, also, that the same notion of "totality" may be taken, by analogy, to a system of thought, and specifically to the mature thought of Marx. To trace a concept of alienation or (as in this case) a "myth of human self-identity" through from the immature writings to the mature, and systematic, thought of Marx, while failing at the same time to establish the meanings given to these concepts within the total context of historical materialism, is to embark upon too easy a philosophical refutation.

I find in all your writing a failure to give full weight to the concept of capitalism as system. This may perhaps be a consequence of suffering your formative intellectual years within a (supposedly) socialist system, whose manifest presence was neither socialist (in any way in which Marx or socialist utopians had given reason to expect) nor (unless as statist repression) systematic. In "The Myth of Human Self-Identity" you even offer at one point "a schema" of Marxist thought in which you are at pains to employ synonyms—"mediaeval European societies" for feudalism, and "industrial societies" for capitalism—which are, perhaps unintentionally, disintegrative of Marx's systematic constructions. Undoubtedly experience has made you sceptical as to the historical existence of any social system.

I cannot hope in a few pages to vindicate Marx's discovery of capitalism-as-system, with its concomitant discoveries of class struggle, of characteristic ideological and moral formations, and of innate contradiction. I can only say that in my own work, as an historian I have found nothing to challenge and very much to confirm this definition of capitalism-as-system. This does not mean that I have found capitalism to be always the same system, nor always exactly as Marx described it, nor (as I have sufficiently explained (p. 329)) that I can always accept Marx's own theoretical models which set out the "laws" or logic of capitalist process. But my own research and that of my colleagues within the Marxist tradition of historiography appears to confirm Marx's discovery of capitalism seen (in MacIntyre's terms) both as "a whole system of economic activity" and as human activities and intentions informed "by concepts which express the relationships characteristic of the system."

Nor do I find this only as a historian of capitalism in its 18th- and 19th-century evolution when (it may be argued) historical existence approximated most closely to Marx's own descriptions. Whatever may be said as to the failure of certain of Marx's forecasts to eventuate (when considered as predictive "laws") one has had abundant occasion, in the past twenty-five years, to observe the working-out of a *logic* of the system, which Marx first identified, in social experience.

I will take only one example. In the immediate post-war years the

British Labour Movement, in an unusually assertive mood, attempted to construct and to enlarge within the framework of the capitalist system alternative institutions with an alternative, socialist content. The mines and the railways were nationalized; a free Health Service was introduced; educational provision was expanded in ways which were intended to provide greater equality of opportunity to the children of the majority of citizens; some attempts were made to make taxation redistributive in function; and to develop social services and benefits according to criteria of need. In classical social-democratic theory these measures, taken together, could be seen as an "instalment" of socialism, a step upwards in a steady gradient leading from a capitalist to a socialist society, an ascent which might (after a due pause for breath and meditation) be resumed. I reject this view, but I also reject the view presented by certain Marxist doctrinaires which would see these reforms as excreted as part of the Machiavellian defence-mechanism of the capitalist organism itself. It can be shown (and Raymond Williams in his presentation of the alternative values generated within working-class experience itself has done much to show this) that the years 1944–6 were a high-water-mark in the morale and consciousness of British working people: miners and railwaymen wished to bring the mines and rails within "common ownership"; sixty years of socialist propaganda and organization, strengthened by the particular circumstances of wartime shortages and solidarities, had diffused very widely the criteria of need in social welfare and of "fairness" in the distribution of both products and opportunities. A very great number of working people aspired to place each particular reform within the totality of an egalitarian, socialist society.

In not many years it was clear enough that these aspirations would not, in the terms of "1945", be fulfilled. One may attempt to describe the reasons as a succession of events and contingencies: the bad faith of Labour leaders: balance-of-payments crises: the onset of the Cold War: the imposition of a statist and bureaucratic form of nationalism, etc. But each of these facts takes on new meaning when they are seen within the larger, controlling logic of capitalist *process*. I do not—and this is important in view of the dismissive, doctrinaire and ultimately "anti-working-class" attitude of some Marxist sectarians towards "reformism"—suppose that all reforms, without instant cataclysmic revolution, must be doomed to failure. Those reforms, if sustained and enlarged by an aggressive socialist strategy, might well have effected such a cancellation of the logic of capitalism that the system would have been brought to the point of crisis—a crisis not of despair and disintegration but a crisis in which the necessity for a peaceful revolutionary transition to an alternative socialist logic became daily more evident and more possible.

This is exactly what did not happen. The reforms of 1945 were assimilated and re-ordered within the system of economic activities, and also within the characteristic concepts, of the capitalist process. This entailed a translation of socialist meanings into capitalist ones. Socialized pits and railways became "utilities" providing subsidized coal and transport to private industry. Private practice, private beds in hospitals, private nursing-homes and private insurance impoverished the public health service. Equality of opportunity in education was, in part, transformed into an adaptive mechanism through which skilled labour was trained for private industry: the opportunity was not *for* the working class but for the scholarship boy to escape *from* this class. Accountants and company lawyers, first, and, later, Chancellors of the Exchequer, punched holes in the redistributive intent of taxation, and money quickly found new water-courses down which to run and amalgamate. Municipal housing forgot its first social function in a function that capitalism dictated as primal: that of servicing the moneylenders.

In short, what was defeated was not each "reform" (for around each of these—the schools, the future of the mines and their self-management, the sale of council houses—stubborn actions continue to be fought and should be fought) but the very meaning of reform as an alternative logic to that of private enterprise, profit, and the uncontrolled self-reproduction of money. The socialist meanings of each reform were surrendered (as they always must be if not sustained by a strong, conscious and aggressive socialist movement) because each took its place within an alien totality: capitalism. As each surrender took place, the socialist movement weakened in morale and direction, and the protagonists of capitalism gained in brashness and aggression. Today the organs of capitalism—such as the business supplements of the newspapers—celebrate acquisitive warfare and sheer monetary motivations with a blatancy and hedonism which would have been impossible, not only diplomatically but morally, in 1945.

I have taken this example, since I wish to emphasize capitalism as system and as logic of process, not in the safe territory surveyed by *Das Kapital*, but in a period in which in certain of its features it appears to have falsified certain of Marx's predictions. Whether these predictions were or were not falsified bothers me not one jot: Marx did not suppose that capitalism would endure so long, but, if he had, I doubt whether he would have supposed that it would endure as *exactly* the same kind of system, and if he did suppose so, then he was wrong. In any case one can show without difficulty that there were contemporaries of Marx, who shared his definition of capitalism-as-system, but who very clearly foresaw the possibility that capitalism, while not changing its innate "nature", would show very considerable capacities to prolong its existence and to adapt to working-class pressure: and among these,

William Morris, whom—despite the continuing neglect of his thought —I regard as a socialist thinker of stature.

This digression may help us to reconsider the question of *potentia* and that of self-identity. It can be seen that the reforms of "1945" embodied a socialist *potentia*, which was not only nourished by ideal influences (the thought of Marx, of Morris, and of socialist utopians: the strategies of British socialist and communist parties) but whose partial realization was fleshed by actually existent socialist values and practices within the working-class community, at variance with those individualist values and practices of the capitalist sytem within which, in the final analysis, these reforms were contained. Hence this socialist *potentia* may be seen simultaneously as immanent actuality and as aspiration; that is, it is not to be seen only as a theoretical aspiration, expressed in a passage of Marx's writings; it is an aspiration which requires *both* logical *and* historical examination. Moreover, the defeat of this aspiration, its failure to come to its full realization, may be dealt with not only in terms of its theoretical inadequacy (as, indeed, its characteristic "reformist" or social-democratic theoretical expression was sadly inadequate) but also in terms of the actual contradictions of social life—the cancellation of socialist meanings within a totality whose meaning and logic of process was capitalist.

This brief and simplified example will satisfy no-one. But, short of writing a long book, I can do no better.[43] And I am forced to offer this example, however inadequate, as a paradigm of the process of contradiction by which aspiration quarrels with actuality within class society. For, if feudalism and capitalism by no means take the same forms in all periods and places—and if we must give to both forms even greater flexibility than were given in the rather flexible typology of Marx—nevertheless we can describe them as systems because of (a) conformities in the ways in which the parts are related to the whole, giving a totality informed by characteristic concepts, and (b) because of an identity in the logic of social process. As systems each is also a matrix of possibilities for the actualization of human relations: hence, each system defines a possible in "human nature", and it is, simultaneously, a *denial* of alternative possibilities.

As we survey the fecundity and improvisations within the vast family of bourgeois societies, it seems that the possibilities opened by capitalism to "human nature" have been infinite. Nevertheless, these possibilities, while generically limitless, have been limited by the genus, capitalism. That is, while doubtless individuals within such societies may have been (at least in theory) capable of attempting to live any set of relations or imagine any social forms, the logic of capitalist process has set defined limits upon the possibility of their successful actualization. Communitarian experiments have been manifold within capitalist societies: but in each case the historian observes that their reality has been quickly eroded or disintegrated by capitalist process, or their meanings have been assimilated or strictly de-limited by capitalist meanings, whereas in feudal society certain kinds of communitarian association, in due institutional form, found their meanings endorsed and were actually given status and sustenance by the logic of feudal process.

Thus, I insist, the notion of "contradiction" must be seen not only as a theoretical category brought *to* history: it also has a large and identifiable empirical content. Aspiration can be shown as actual; and its defeat, by an alternative logic of process, can be shown to be actual also. When we say that the possibilities open to human nature are limited by the logic of capitalist process, and that they may be realized only by the transcendence of that logic (revolution) we are talking simultaneously in theoretical and in empirical terms. Moreover, the empirical investigation of the characteristic contradiction of capitalist process may quite properly give rise to the "predictive" conclusion that this contradiction can be transcended, not in any way that we choose, but only in certain ways: as that the atomized and predatory logic of capitalism (which persists even within statist forms) can only be displaced by the alternative intentions and aspirations of a social consciousness which can (as empirically-given historical fact) be shown to find partial and fragmented embodiment in the actual working-class movement. British history, over 150 years, has shown this alternative possibility to be waxing and waning and waxing again—not as *exactly the same* possibility, but as the same in terms of an alternative, socialist logic.

If we are considering the thought of the mature Marx, then the concepts of "alienation", civil versus political society, and *potentia* must be seen within this totality: and the contradiction of possibility is never presented as abstracted category, but as contradiction within the context of social system, with a consequent possibility of transcendence, not in *any* conceivable way, but in ways imposed by the prior contradiction and the alternative logic of process. There is, precisely, an empirical *potentia* which does actualize itself "in history" and which can be inferred from historical knowledge.

But to say this still does not—I agree—answer the problem which you pose as to the observer's attribution of valued significance. History has disclosed innumerable possibilities, but there are no grounds within empirical evidence (you may argue) for attributing valued priority to one over any other. And even if history has disclosed very many fewer systematized logics of social process than it has possibilities within each logic, why should we assume as empirically-given fact that later is in any sense more worthy of value than earlier? The logic of a primitive society may well (as Lévi-Strauss has reminded us) disclose a human *potentia* as worthy as that of 20th century Paris; and some observers of contemporary "socialist" states may and do say that they opt for the logic of capitalist process over any demonstrable alternative.

A short answer is that we *are* later rather than earlier. We cannot choose to be Nuer or Trobriand islanders. And if the Marxist notion of capitalist contradiction is well-founded, we cannot choose between capitalist logic (indefinitely prolonged) and socialist, but only between the ultimate breakdown of capitalism-as-system, in ways which may entail the destruction of civilization, and its transcendence. But I will not be content with a short answer, which appears as less comforting in 1973 than it might have appeared in 1873. A longer answer must encounter two major difficulties: (1) the philosophical difficulties entailed in attributing value to process, and (2) the theoretical and empirical difficulties presented by the notion of transcendence (or revolution) in the light of fifty years of "socialist" statism.

*   *   *

(1) What I have described in previous paragraphs may be seen as process but not as progress. Is there any reason why we should select from the possibilities disclosed by history one particular set and acclaim these as "truly human" *potentia?* For history has disclosed as bountifully possibilities of evil as of good (in the common usage of these terms), and we are, at this point in time, quite as aware of the former as of the latter.

Very well, I accept this. I accept also that if we select one set of possibilities among other sets as *potentia* this "project is a decision about the choice of values". But even here one might allow for a rational (and not eschatological) hope that the attribution of *potentia* is not a *post-facto* insertion by the observer only, but is simultaneously an empirically-given and demonstrable possibility within actual historical process. That is, one proposition does not invalidate the other: I may say as a matter of "faith" that I choose to identify with this *potentia* and not those others, and I may say as a historical investigator that the chosen *potentia* is one of the empirically-observable possibilities of choice, and I may then add that I am, in my choosing and valuing nature, an outcome of this *potentia*.

As a philosophical neophyte I fumble in my terms: and I fumble within the portico of one of the most exacting of philosophical problems—the segregated domains of the "is" and the "ought". All that I can hope to do is to signal to certain philosophers that certain historians are also aware of the problem. What the historian may offer to the discourse is the consideration that the idea of the human possible may equally have a naturalistic as an eschatological grounding. We may take this argument also in three steps:

(a) In the philosophical argument as to value and process I cannot offer original definitions. I can only borrow (perhaps in impermissible ways) arguments from philosophers, and I will choose these from yourself and from MacIntyre. It would appear that the mutually-exclusive epistemological integrities of "fact" and "value", once axiomatic within Anglo-Saxon analytic thought, may not, after all, be unbridgeable. You also have noted among the "common stock" of the Marxist tradition "the conviction that human cognitive activity should be always interpreted as an aspect of total historical praxis and that, for this reason, epistemological inquiry cannot be entirely divorced from genetic inquiry".[44] The same "common stock" assumes an analogous relation between human evaluative activity and genetic inquiry: as you argued in "History and Hope" (1957),

> 'Duty' is but the voice of a social need. In this sense the world of values is not an imaginary sky over the real world of existence, but also a part of it, a part that exists not only in the social consciousness, but that is rooted in the material conditions of life.[45]

This "genetic" relationship you appear to reaffirm, albeit in an overly passive way, in 1971 when you argue that "tradition is the only instrument that enables us to appropriate *values*"; that is, those values which men have affirmed in their past experience remain, in the present, as an arsenal from which we choose—although I would wish to add that the arts and the experiential present are also value-formative.[46] In any case, these values are genetically derivative from socially-experienced "fact".

This derivation from fact does not tell us how to choose between them. The historian or the sociologist may tell us something as to how we *do* choose between them; and in MacIntyre one detects the outlines of an epistemological bridge. Examining Hume he observes that "the transition from 'is' to 'ought' is made . . . by the notion of 'wanting'."

> And this is no accident . . . We could give a long list of the concepts which can form such bridge notions, between 'is' and 'ought': wanting, needing, desiring, pleasure, happiness, health—and these are only a few. I think there is a strong case for saying that moral notions are unintelligible apart from concepts such as these.[47]

But "wanting" is derivative from men in particular historical contexts, and from the possibilities given to their nature by these contexts. And MacIntyre has sketched a history of ethics which indicates not only ways in which men's moral wanting have changed, but the ways in which their own notions of valuing have themselves changed accordingly. Thus he has proposed that we may see "liberalism as a political and moral doctrine [which] depends on a picture of the individual as sovereign in his choice of values":

> The facts do not and cannot constrain such choice, but the free individual is determined by nothing but himself. For this to be so there must be discernible in the language that we speak a class of factual statements and a class of evaluative statements whose relationship is such that no set of factual statements can separately or jointly entail an evaluative statement. At the same time liberalism clearly is only at home in, its contentions are only intelligible against a background of certain types of historical and social setting. Thus a logical doctrine about fact and value might indeed be rooted in some more general moral and political doctrine which in turn presupposed the background of a certain type of society. [48]

The "certain types of historical and social setting" indicated in this passage MacIntyre (in earlier writings) identified more specifically with capitalist society, and with a historical disjunction between lived experience and the moral law, seen no longer as part of the natural order of things, nor as the dictates of "human nature", but as a set of (alternative) moral rules presented as "arbitrary fiats".[49] And in another passage of "the early MacIntyre" he sketches the possible view that the emergent socialist consciousness within capitalist society, by opposing itself to the "anarchistic individualist desires which a competitive society breeds" and by "a rediscovery of the deeper desire to share what is common in humanity", may carry us, across the bridge of "wanting" from fact to value: "moral rules and what we fundamentally want no longer stand in sharp contrast".[50]

I wish that MacIntyre could complete his own thought.[51] For it does indeed appear to connect historical and ethical inquiry in significant ways. This step, if I understand it rightly, might bridge the gap but at the same time deprive us of some of the liberal dignities of choosing. A socialist might properly be able to say that in his aspirations he fulfilled a *potentia* immanent (and empirically-discoverable) in history; but he would say this, not as an independent value-free extra-historical agent choosing one value among many alternatives, but as himself the value-conditioned product of exactly this *potentia*.

(b) As to the second step I will be brief, since it seems to me (in the present state of knowledge) hazardous and uncertain. It may be possible, with the advance of an infinitely-subtle, empirically-founded social psychology to translate certain notions of value, of good and evil behaviour, into diagnostic notions of psychic health or neurosis. This of course has been attempted (as in the work of Reich, Fromm, Foucault, Marcuse and many others). I find this approach hazardous because, while fragments of such historical analysis are convincing or promising (I have even attempted such an analysis myself in a rather notorious discussion of Methodism) I have not yet met with any work which appears to surmount difficulties intrinsic to this approach.

The deficiences arise most obviously in two forms: first, the unsatisfactory and questionable psychological categories (chiefly Freudian) which are brought to the investigation;[52] and, second, the inadequate proficiency of most of the practitioners within the historical disciplines. If this proves to be only a matter of an intellectual discipline in its infancy, then we would of course have the promise of an important step in our argument here. "History" has disclosed the possibilities of Athenian rational ardour and of the artistic ebullience of the *Quatrocento;* and it has equally disclosed the possibilities of Buchenwald and of the Soviet purges of the 1930s. If an empirically-grounded social psychology could show us that the morality or norms entailed in the first were an actual index of human health; and in the second may be diagnosed as sickness, then the notion of human *potentia* would acquire a rational justification independent of, or alongside, normative insertions.

The supposition has plausibility and has already occupied many scholars. One may often note when examining, for example, 19th century working-class history, ways in which men and women seem to be more "realized" as rational or moral agents, when acting collectively in conscious rebellion (or resistance) against capitalist process. And, equally, that the privatization of life which often ensues upon political or social defeats appears to bring with it a revenge into the most intimate personal relations, and the absence of an affirmative social context (even that of rebellion against the given context) appears to foster individual behaviour which psychiatrists would diagnose as neurotic. Hence it becomes plausible to offer the analogy between the neurotic or fulfilled individual personality, and the "personality" of a whole society. Just as psychotic illness may prevent a person from "being himself", from realizing his or her possibilities, so the analogy of "fully human" social *potentia* presses itself forward.

But there are still serious fissures in logic to be bridged. We know very well that notions of psychic health or sickness entail normative insertions; so that this method of analysis—important and fruitful as it may prove—may not offer a solution of the problem but simply a way of presenting it in a new form. And we must still jump the gap between the diagnosis of individual malaise and the diagnosis of process or of historical logic. It is my doubt as to whether this gap may legitimately be bridged which leaves me, as to this step, a sceptic.

(c) The third step may be offered, however, without the necessary intervention of the second. What is implied by Marx at some points as *potentia* is delineated more clearly at other points in the notion of the passage from the kingdom of necessity to the kingdom of freedom. And this notion, which is certainly located in mature Marx within systematized social contexts, is offered simultaneously as concept and as the consequence of empirical investigation.

Man's history is a story of human victim-hood, not because some men (or all men) have been irrational or immoral, but because the historical process has been the outcome, not of the sum of individual intentions, but of a collision of mutually-contradictory intentions:

> The subject of history is the human species and therefore is a whole, of which all the elements behave in a manner directed toward an end, but which as a whole does not behave in such a manner—

thus Kolakowski.[53] But—and this is crucial—in the thought of Marx the historical event is not merely the result of a collision of wills, or a collision of interest-groups. Hypothetically at least, such a collision might be mediated by institutions designed to reconcile opposing interests, so that the outcome—the historical process—could be seen as collective rationality, reconciled and adjusted intentions, or the "general will". The collision is always within a systematized context, within a social system conceived of as totality; for interest-groups we must replace the concept of class, and we must also see the collision as taking, not any haphazard form, but a form characterized by the logic of capitalist (or feudal) process which I have already discussed. In each age—

> the character of the rules is determined by the relationships between men which are involved in that particular mode of production, and these relationships are not between individuals but between groupings of men, who are united by their common economic and social role, and divided from other groupings by the antagonisms of economic and social interest. So—'all history is the history of class struggle'. This is not a generalization built up from instances, so much as a framework without which we should not be able to identify our instances; yet also a framework which could not be elaborated without detailed empirical study—

thus MacIntyre.[54]

The recognition of man's dual role, as victim and as agent, in the making of his own history is crucial to Marx's thought. Even in the *petit point* of piecemeal expedients we are also giving shape to the larger process of social change. But there is a critical difference in the degree of agency entailed in the two actions. In the detail of political life it appears that at least some men are free agents: they seem to choose between alternative policies, and the results of their actions may even bear some relation to their intentions. But the larger patterns of social process appear to design themselves. Although they arise as a consequence of individual actions, the way in which they arise and the forms which they take are inconsequential and unforeseen. Circumstances or events appear to will men, not men events, and men appear as victims of social forces which, in the final analysis, are the product of human will.

The increasing control which advances in knowledge and technique should give us is negatived by the partisan purposes and partisan consciousness of class society. Only in classless society will opposing and systematized interests and their derivative distortions of consciousness give way to a common human interest: this is where we appear to reach the threshold, in Marx's sense, of the kingdom of freedom. And this is also the threshold of the realization of immanent *potentia*. This "faith" of Marxism has been rehearsed in two related passages of MacIntyre:

> For Marx the emergence of human nature is something to be comprehended only in the terms of the history of class-struggle. Each age reveals a development of human potentiality which is specific to that form of social life and which is specifically limited by the class-structure of that society. The development of possibility reaches a crisis under capitalism. For men have up to that age lived at their best in a way that allowed them glimpses of their own nature as something far richer than what they themselves lived out. Under capitalism the growth of production makes it possible for man to re-appropriate his own nature, for actual human beings to realise the richness of human possibility. But not only the growth of production is necessary. The experience of human equality and unity that is bred in industrial working-class life is equally a precondition of overcoming men's alienation from this and from themselves. And only from the standpoint of that life and its possibilities can we see each previous stage of history as a particular form of approximation to a climax which it is now possible to approach directly.

And in the other passage, MacIntyre allows that Marx inherited from Hegel a conception of the "human essence".

> Human life at any given moment is not a realisation of this essence because human life is always limited in ways characteristic of the basis of a given form of society. In particular human freedom is always so limited. But in our age we have reached the point where this can change, where human possibility can be realised in a quite new way. But we cannot see the possibility of this realisation as the predictable outcome of laws governing human development independently of human wills and aspirations. For the next stage is to be characterised precisely as the age in which human wills and aspirations take charge and are no longer subservient to economic necessity and to the law-bound inevitability of the past. But Marxists surely say, not that this might happen, but that it will? If they say this, they are no longer predicting. They are re-affirming Marx's belief that human potentiality is such that men will take this new step, and this affirmation is of a different order from predicting. For the Marxist view of history can be written up in the end as the story of how the human ideal was after many vicissitudes translated into the human reality. [55]

To argue about *potentia* in this rather abstract way is to provoke, in 1973, instant scepticism. We have had enough glimpses, in this century, of human "possibility", and not all of them show man's nature as "rich". We are more preoccupied with the need to control certain propensities of human nature than to release a questionable *potentia*.

But the fact that the problem of *potentia* is of continuing significance will be told to us instantly by any thoughtful woman. For women are, at this moment, very concerned to examine their own culturally-transmitted nature. And they bring to this examination examples from history of what women have been in order to define what women might become. For if it is true that for large and enduring historical contexts women's nature has been conditioned within the categories and practices of male-dominated cultures, in which the role of women has been defined primarily in terms of sexual, maternal and familial functions and only secondarily in more general productive, social and cultural functions—then it seems important to investigate what might be the *potentia* of women's nature if liberated from these cultural definitions. One way of criticizing the fixity of traditional definitions is exactly by opposing to them the criticism of alternative possibilities revealed within alternative cultures, or even by opposing individual examples of women who, in exceptional circumstances, transcended the definitions of their own habitual culture. So evident is this critical need, at this moment, that one is tempted to exclude the case of feminine *potentia* from an important qualification within this general argument. If we cannot locate a "fully human" man in *potentia* within history, perhaps we may discover a "fully human" woman, potentially present but denied realization within dominative male cultures?

But one should resist this temptation. And first, because any history of "man" must also be, even if imperfectly, a history of woman. A male-dominative culture may turn out to be a culture which, in àttributing to women certain roles and functions and in depriving them of certain expressions, is a culture which is simultaneously itself deprived of certain components which it has defined or degraded as "feminine". But women do not have a history independent of that culture, or of that system and process which I have already discussed, even if historians have given inadequate attention to the parts of women within that history. The values of possessive individualism characteristic of a certain phase of capitalist process will manifest themselves in the attitudes of men to women, of women to men, and of both towards children: and so on.

But, second, what has been potential in history has not been one single "fully human" essence of womanliness, but precisely *the potential of feminine self-determination within changing historical contexts;* of freedom from being conditioned and limited by a masculine definition of her role and nature; or, perhaps, of freedom for men and women mutually to determine roles within a sexually egalitarian culture. The potential denied realization would, in each context, have been different; one cannot assume a hidden woman as the sum of glimpsed possibilities; the hidden woman is the woman who could "be herself", or of men and women who could, in sexual respects, be mutually "themselves"—and, moreover, be so not as abstracted essence but within the larger context of a given society.

This illustration may lead us back to *potentia* again, and may also show how your arguments in "Historical understanding and the intelligibility of history" may be reconciled with the notion of historically-emergent *potentia*. You argue that the attribution of intelligibility to history must always arise from an act of "faith" in the attributor; this intelligibility, as valued significance, cannot be derived from empirical evidence; "it is in relation to our *intention* that our historical heritage, which represents just so many preparatory acts for this intention, is organized". The fact that it is an act of faith does not invalidate this act; men *must* attribute significance, but they should be clear in doing so that they argue from the ground of ought rather than is.

But the example of feminine "nature" may help us to overcome the difficulty, which is that what one observer may glimpse as "rich" another may glimpse as "decadent", and that, in any selection from history of examples of the "possible", the observer is introducing normative principles of selection. For the example reminds us that the *potentia* is not of any one single "fully human" man; nor of some sum made up by adding Athenian philosophers to Renaissance sculptors, subtracting secret policemen and successful entrepreneurs, and multiplying the product by romantic lovers. The *potentia* is a concept coincident with that of the passage from the kingdom of necessity to that of freedom. And the *potentia* is exactly the human potential to act as rational and moral agents, to enter an age "in which human wills and aspirations take charge and are no longer subservient to economic necessity and to the law-bound inevitability of the past".

In Marxist utopianism, communism is the society in which things are thrown from the saddle and cease to ride mankind. Men struggle free from their own machinery and subdue it to human needs and definitions. Man ceases to live in a defensive posture, warding off the assault of "circumstances", his furthest triumph in social engineering a system of checks and balances and counter-vailing powers against his own evil will. He commences to live from his own resources of creative possibility, liberated from the determinism of "process" within class-divided societies. In empirical terms, the historian or sociologist may show that given societies at given technological levels and with given social systems simultaneously disclose and impose limits upon human possibilities. This is *potentia* as fact, or as denial.

And one may go on from this to restate (as E. J. Hobsbawm has recently done in a cogent study)[56] the traditional idea of "progress" as a "hierarchy of levels", of enlarged techniques and consonant socio-economic formations, each signifying "the growing emancipation of man from nature and his growing capacity to control it". This is to give at least some empirical substance to the notion of enlarging *potentia*, the growth and differentiation of human possibilities.

But we hesitate, at this moment of unfinished history, to accept too easily this "hierarchy of levels" as a progress. For we have seen the capacity to control nature as, simultaneously, the capacity to lay nature waste, bringing with it simultaneous opportunities for human emancipation and self-destruction. So that the critical point of *potentia* remains as a faith: that men can pass from process-determined "necessity" to the "freedom" of rational intentionality. As MacIntyre shows, there is no predictive historical "law" which entails the certainty that this will be so. But the faith required is not limitless or arbitrary. It is not a faith in any particular definition of *potentia*, as to which definition there might be many faiths. It is, very simply, a faith in the ultimate capacity of men to manifest themselves as rational and moral agents: "there is only the requirement that we shall recognize that it is in virtue of what they can be and not of what they always are that men are called rational animals".[57] And men would not have had a history at all, and certainly not one of scientific advance and of complex social organization, if they had not been capable, however imperfectly, of rational action and of submission to socially-cohesive values.

If we hold to the faith that men can effect the transition to the kingdom of freedom, it is true that we project this faith back upon history, and attempt by our own agency in the present to give *to* history that outcome. But in this projection we recognize ourselves in a million historical progenitors; and such an act of faith is not too large for a rational being to make. He is himself his own norm-giving reason.

(2) But should this kingdom of freedom be attained, the argument entails no guarantee whatsoever that men will choose wisely nor be good. And we encounter the second major difficulty (see p. 358), which will have been present in your mind and in the minds of all readers throughout the last passages, prompting in them impatience, scepticism or cynicism. "Show me this kingdom of freedom", you will say. "Does one enter it through the Berlin wall or at some point on the Czech frontier?"

You have already reassured the readers of *Encounter* that you disclaim belief "in the *final* elimination of *all* alienation and a *wholly* peaceful state of society without conflicts and contradictions." (See

p. 337). But if we disinfest this sentence of the terms of caricature it could read differently: as, for example, "the attainment towards the elimination of socially-determined forms of alienation and towards a state of society wherein conflicts and contradictions of interest are reconciled by rational democratic process". I do violence to your words in order to emphasize that what is at issue is a logic of process *towards* rather than the instantaneous fulfilment of some goal. And it is still relevant to enquire whether we can conceive of socialism-as-system in any way which makes it more likely for such a logic to operate within it than within capitalism-as-system.

You blockade the road to such an inquiry by assuming that, in the light of fifty years experience, the question has been already settled: "real communism appears only in the totalitarian shape, i.e. as the tendency to *replace* all crystallizations of the civil society by coercive organs of the state". (See p. 344.) This allows you to pursue two rather different lines of inquiry: (a) you suppose that Marxist concepts may themselves "engender" this consequence, this "cancerous growth of the quasi-omnipotent bureaucracy" (see p. 344); the "primordial intention" of Marx's "dream" was "not innocent": it could never "become real except in the cruel form of despotism" (p. 345); (b) you suppose simultaneously that there may be ulterior or intrinsic human tendencies or forces which were overlooked by Marx and which tend to the same outcome.

I will go as far as this along those roads with you. Anyone is a fool today who does not know that the critical questions in practical socialist theory are, first, the questions of the socialist state, its institutions, and the relation of state to people; and, second, the question of socialism-as-system, of socialist process. Insofar as Marx's cryptic expressions of faith as to the dramatic consequences of revolution disarmed socialist theory, led to a gross oversimplification of process, a very serious underestimation of the difficulties of socialist institution-making, a scepticism as to democratic values (which arose from a necessary critique of the democratic rhetoric of bourgeois politicians), an undue optimism as to the revolutionary transformation of human nature, and an inhibition of utopianism—insofar as this is true, and insofar as the contingent evolution of a dominant element in the Marxist tradition accentuated each of these omissions or inhibitions— then I will allow that the "dream" was "not innocent". But this is a small allowance. It does not allow that Marx's faith "engendered" these consequences: only that it failed to anticipate them and to warn against them.

The trouble (or one trouble) with your methods of inquiry is that they evade the critical problems of the socialist state and system. They do not even advance inquiry into the character of existent societies in Russia and East Europe (although they *assume* that this is understood, and that generalizations may be drawn from this basis). They simply capitulate before unexamined experience, and provide loosely-connected assertions at a level easily assimilated by those used to *Encounter's* customary fodder.

Let us follow through more closely one of these passages of argument, in "The Myth of Human Self-Identity". You assert that you can find no reasons for the belief that "once social classes . . . have been abolished, the struggle of private interests will stop":

> The class struggle in capitalist society is a historical form of the struggle for the distribution of surplus product. Why should we presume that the same struggle for surplus product will not go on within an economy based on public ownership . . .?

Such an assumption would suppose "a sudden restoration of the angelic nature of the human race". But now that we have got to "human nature" we are on very familiar and ancient pre-liberal territory: indeed, we are on the ground of human *anti-potentia*, man's innate evil will constrained by law, culture, and institutional devices. (You have even, I suspect, from some recent references to "the stock of instincts of the human species" and "the totality of the biologically inherited reflexes", been reading Lorenz, Desmond Morris, etc. with rapt attention.)[58] Marx had admitted to his thought "two very general false premises":

> . . . that all human evil is rooted in social (as distinct from biological) circumstances and that all important human conflicts are ultimately . . . reducible to class antagonisms. Thus he entirely overlooked the possibility that some sources of conflict and aggression may be inherent in the permanent characteristics of the species and are unlikely to be eradicated by institutional changes. In this sense he really remained a Rousseauist.[59]

In such passages as these I seem to see a fine and controlled method of philosophical analysis in a state of disintegration. In fact you are by no means examining the logic of Marx's own concepts but are opposing to these a set of unexamined counter-assertions which you are unprepared to expose to conceptual analysis in terms of the concepts you are criticizing. Like all bad arguments one may best advance backwards to faulty premises from the faulty conclusions. We may note that in your penultimate sentence you pass between two assertions of a very different order, the first of which by no means entails the second. One can scarcely disagree with the supposition that "some sources of conflict and aggression may be inherent in the permanent characteristics of the species". Indeed, one can see a score of academic Justice Shallows nodding their assent in a score of common rooms. "Good phrases are surely, and ever were, very commendable":

Certain, 'tis certain; very sure, very sure: death, as the Psalmist says, is certain to all; all shall die.—How a good yoke of bullocks at Stamford fair?

It would seem to a mere historian that *any* characteristics men have expressed at *any* point in their history must perforce belong to the possibilities of human nature and hence be "inherent" in the species. Reproduce the same conditions and the same culture and they are likely to reappear. It is rather unlikely that Marx would have admitted a premise that human evil was "rooted" in social as distinct from biological circumstances since he did not think of evil as a radish, nor of biological circumstances as a soil. Thus the entire weight of your assertion must fall on the second of the two "false premises": that "all important human conflicts are ultimately . . . reducible to class antagonisms." Once again, it appears that you are still thinking of evil and of conflicts as radishes, "unlikely to be eradicated by institutional changes". But what we are thinking about is not propensities (good or evil) arranged and controlled by institutions, but a total *expressive* human context, of culture (including socialization and education) and of institutions. And the equation "human conflicts" = "class antagonisms" is not one with which a Marxist should be happy. As you have noted elsewhere, Marxism has an "old antimechanistic orientation".[60] What Marx proposed (and I am thinking of the theses on Feuerbach) was that all human conflicts are observable only within specific social contexts. And the bare forked creature, naked biological man, is not a context which we can ever observe, because the very notion of man (as opposed to his anthropoid ancestor) is coincident with culture; man only is insofar as he is able to organize some parts of his experience and transmit it in specifically human ways. Thus to propose the investigation of "man" apart from his culture (or his lived history) is to propose an unreal abstraction, the investigation of non-man. And at least in recent history human conflicts have found expression within systematized social and cultural contexts, so that the conflict itself finds expression within the terms of that context: as, for example, we cannot understand certain kinds of aggression independently of the contextual concepts of the ownership of property or of nationhood.

That the history of all hitherto existing societies is the history of class struggle—an assertion which Marx made in a propagandist rather than a philosophical work—is true only in this sense. And it is a statement as to a way of interpreting the history of *societies*, not of "man" or of individual men. Hence, if we wish to propose (for analytical purposes) a category of instinctual drive (as aggression, sociability, etc.) and a category of realized phenomena (as war, mutual aid, etc.), we will still find that the second cannot be *reduced* to the first. For this is exactly as true and as untrue as to say that both rape and romantic love can be reduced to sex. We can only say that the drive (a) is realized in (b) certain expressive cultural forms and institutions. Human conflicts do not equal class antagonisms. Human conflicts, in class society, find expression and definition within the terms of, and work their way out according to, the logic of process of class.

Hence a classless society would certainly not "eradicate" these drives. The uncomfortable discovery that this is so is, of course, one of the ways in which the practical history of socialism of the past fifty years has been read. Disarmed by an overly utopian notion of "revolution", socialists have been astounded as every ancient Adam of history has walked onto the stages of the socialist state. If this is indeed the kingdom of freedom it appears to be the kingdom in which men are free to do evil.

But this very partial reading of fifty years of history is—even if salutary—a distraction from the critical point of analysis. And you have already, in the earlier stages of your argument, distracted us in this way. I don't know much about the nature of angels, although I imagine them to be much as Blake described them in *The Marriage of Heaven and Hell*. But Marx enjoyed the company of angels less frequently than did Blake; and he appears to propose, not an angelic nature, but men who within the context of certain institutions and culture can conceptualize in terms of "our" rather than "my" or "their". I was a participating witness, in 1947, in the euphoric aftermath of a revolutionary transition, of exactly such a transformation in attitudes. Young Yugoslav peasants, students, and workers, constructing with high morale their own railway, undoubtedly had this new affirmative concept of *nasha* ("our"), although this *nasha*—as may have proved fortunate for Yugoslavia—was in part the *nasha* of socialist consciousness, and in part the *nasha* of the nation.[61] The fact that this moment of euphoria proved to be evanescent—and that both the Soviet Union and "the West" did what they could to reverse the impulse—does not disallow the validity of the experience.

The class struggle in capitalist society, you say, is "a historical form of the struggle for the distribution of surplus product". And you ask why "the same struggle for surplus product" should not go on within an economy based on public ownership. A short answer is that if the struggle changed its historical form then it would not be the same struggle. And we cannot know of the struggle in a formless, decontextual way. But you are doing the same thing now with manifest and ulterior social impulses as you have done with innate evil and its actual social expression. You are proposing some underlying "conflict" which takes different "forms". Let us play with this sentence a little.

(1) We will leave aside "surplus product", although most economic historians would prefer to commence with the concept of scarcity rather than that of surplus; (2) We could try out various sentences, analogous in form, as thus: "the contest in the law-courts as to property-rights is . . ." or "negotiations between the Government and the T.U.C. are . . ." a historical form of the struggle for the distribution of surplus product. Or we could try such forms as: "football is a historical form of the expression of human aggression", or "brothels and monogamous marriage are historical forms for the satisfaction of male sexual drives". The first analogies reveal the utter lack of specificity of your definition, the second reveal its abject reductionism.

Capitalism is a historical form of class power, and it is also a particular structuring of productive relations with attendant concepts of property, etc. Your sentence is too generous in one sense, for capitalism distributes inequitably many other things than "surplus product", including cultural opportunities and power itself. It is not generous enough in another sense, since capitalism also involves a mode of producing that product rather more dynamic than any previously known. Class struggle in capitalist society is, in paramount terms, between those who own and those who do not own the means of production. It is utterly empty to propose a quantum "class struggle" without also proposing which classes are struggling. So that behind your seemingly-concrete proposal one can detect the hidden premise, which is simply that greed for the greatest possible share of the product underlies all "historical forms". So that the "two" premises which Marx "entirely overlooked" turn out to be, in character, only one; it is man's nature to be both greedy and aggressive (although perhaps moderated by a "religious consciousness"—the only other "irreplaceable" part of human culture as to which you are willing to pronounce) and he will continue to be so in any possible society.

It is surprising that Marx should have overlooked this rather ancient argument. Indeed, while I have deliberately set myself in this letter against any such exercises in quotation and counter-quotation, I think that one could show without difficulty that Marx did not overlook it at all. But we may now see why you preferred to make your point by employing the concept of "surplus product" rather than "scarcity". For since Marx argued that communism was possible only in a society that had attained a certain level of affluence, you would— if you had commenced with the second concept—have been forced to ask: "Why should we presume that the same struggle to distribute products in scarce supply will not go on within an affluent economy based on public ownership?" And this would instantly have brought the fallacy in your argument to your notice. For while such a struggle might go on, it would be likely to diminish in intensity, change its form, and lose priority before other motivations—unless, of course, one proposed an *insatiable* greed as one of the highest of human motivations: not an angelic but a truly diabolic human nature.

Capitalism is a system which not only sanctions the greed of the entrepreneur and the *rentier:* it cannot function without this. Its ideology and its orthodox modes of socialization actively foster competition and individualist values. In its latest, more affluent, stage it must actually stimulate new consumer "wants" or greed. What is at issue is whether you can show us that socialism as system will do the same, or whether you can show that socialist institutions must prove to be powerless to inhibit or divert man's innate greed and aggression from similar kinds of expression.

But you do not help us to see socialism either as system or as process, nor to explain the rationale of the particular kinds of statism under which you have suffered. You simply state: "I have lived there, I have suffered it, I know!" And you imply that from the experience of the past fifty years in Russia and East Europe it is legitimate to deduce conclusions about "real communism".

It is difficult to argue with this, and I do so with humility. I will touch only briefly on two substantial considerations. The first, which is in a sense insulting to living and suffering people, is simply that, to a historian, fifty years is too short a time in which to judge a new social system, if such a system is arising. The comparison of course is with the protracted and contradictory events which signalled the arrival of capitalism-as-system onto the historical scene. The second consideration is so familiar that I need not rehearse it; nor am I competent to do so with any authority. It lies in the host of limiting and constricting contingencies within which the first socialist revolutions came to realization. Any full account of this history leaves us with an extreme difficulty in extricating a logic of socialist process, or an innate logic of Marxism as ideology, from supremely powerful and immediate circumstances, contingencies, accidents, events, and from the logic of polarities within a divided world.

I would prefer to offer, very tentatively and with no more authority than the order in which one idea will follow another, a third line of inquiry. And first, what definitions and what evidence do we have of socialism as system and process? You offer us little here, although at one point, in "The Myth of Human Self-Identity", you refer to the proposition that "since public ownership must inevitably beget social layers endowed with privileges in controlling the means of production, the labour force and the instruments of coercion", one must suppose that "all devices will be employed to secure to these layers the stability of their position and the growth of their privileges".

This appears to offer the theory of the appropriation of the socialist state by a new bureaucratic caste, which by self-recruitment, educational and other privilege, will establish itself to futurity as a new ruling class. There will be an antagonism of interest between this class and the labour force more generally, but insofar as the former can provide a rising standard of material consumption, (and of certain cultural goods) such an antagonism need not—or need not for the foreseeable future—give rise to any social explosion. Moreover, the ruling class will control vast centralized means of influence, information, and repression, and hence of self-perpetuation.

We are by now familiar with this theory which is distinct at certain points from alternative theories, such as that of "state capitalism". Yugoslavia, having produced a generation of partisans of political freedom, is now producing partisans of intellectual freedom; and some of these have gone furthest in examining the implications of this theory. Among these Stoyanovic has offered the most lucid exposition of "oligarchic statism". His arguments against those theories which attempt to "excuse" Stalinism in terms of contingencies appear to me to be cogent:

> The understated formula about the 'crisis of socialism' lost its persuasiveness long ago, for we are talking about a system which normally and regularly generates such 'crises'. Nor can we speak any longer of 'socialism with severe deformations', since these deformations are so numerous and of such a nature that they have introduced a new quality—statism. A third commonly employed theoretical crutch has to do with 'abuses' in socialism. But there is a limit beyond which the character of the entity which is being abused changes. Thus it is high time that we resolve to speak no more of abuses, but rather of the *systematic* use of social means for the achievement of unsocialist goals. [62]

Historical experience, Stoyanovic argues, has shown "two possibilities and tendencies inherent in capitalism, i.e. statist and socialist". And he proposes various subsidiary categories of statism: primitive-politocratic, technocratic, oligarchic, etc.

But he fails to convince me that he has shown us statism as system or as process. And this may be too much to ask of any thinker. It took, after all, the best years of Marx's life to show capitalism in this way, and he could draw upon several hundred years of its manifestations as evidence. But we must still try to ask what logic or dynamic there may be in statism. In which direction does it appear to be evolving? What functions do the statist ruling-class perform, and is their power conditional upon the performance of these functions? Is this class itself intrinsically involved in the ownership or appropriation of the means of production; does it stand, through its representatives among the economic managers, in a unique relation to other social groups; or is it a powerful, highly-structured *parasitism* derivative from alternative productive relations?

Only the events will show which is true: and it is possible that both resolutions may still hang within the present balance. There is one empirical observation which might lead one to suppose that the alternative of a statist parasitism upon half-realized socialist relations of production might be a useful means of analysis, which is this. Whenever government appears in clearly predatory forms, and when the institutions of state are employed to secure private or sectional advantage, the political process can only be explained in terms of the rivalry of different interest-groups within the ruling caste itself. These may appear as rival nobles, as rival aristocratic "connections", or even (but this takes us at once to a deeper level of socio-economic analysis) as the rival interests of "land" and of great trading companies. We are familiar with the fact that observers of the political process in the Soviet Union describe it in exactly this way, as being moved by the rivalries of the Party (and Party regions), the Army, the managers of industry, the secret police, and so on.

But the sum of these rivalries does not add up to a single coherent process or rationale. If we try to trace back each interest to its ulterior function then both the theory of statism and that of parasitism appear as possibilities. Certain functions are disclosed which are simply those of holding and extending the power of the ruling groups. Other functions are disclosed which are not, in their character, "anti-socialist": as organizing and expanding the means of production, administering education and cultural facilities, or affording defence to the socialist state against external enemies: even if the forms and ideology within which these functions are performed are those of "oligarchic statism".

This is notably true of the forms and ideology of the ruling Communist Party. In Stoyanovic's words,

> *Permanently* based upon the principles of strict centralism, hierarchy and the absolute monopolization of social life, the party naturally aspired to fashion the entire social system in its own image. [63]

I am reminded of the words of our comrade, Alfred Dressler, who shortly before his death visited the Soviet Union. He remarked: "We always said that the new society would bear the birth-marks of the old; but we never supposed that these birth-marks would be, exactly, the C.P.S.U.(B.)." And he went on to stress his confidence in the socialist potential within contemporary Russia: only the restrictive, dominative forms and the repressive ideology of the Communist Party prevented the Russian people from realizing an alternative, democratic socialist potential.

His faith does not prove that it will be so. Or if it should prove so, the present forms of statism could endure and reinforce themselves for several generations before they give way. But if the forms are those of a parasitism, there are two grounds for guarded optimism in the ensuing logic of process. First, a political or statist parasitism can survive only so long as it does not actively oppose or seriously inhibit the larger social process upon which it is parasitic. If it does so, either the society is plunged into crisis, or the parasitism comes under such heavy challenge that it must either give way altogether or must "tame" itself, by performing its positive social functions more effectively.

Since this is an unduly organic metaphor, I will take an example from the history of England in the 18th century. Many features of 18th century political life, from at least the time of Walpole, can only be analysed at the level of parasitism. The family connections of the great Whigs were shamelessly predatory in their appropriation of the state; ministers milked the public revenues and appointed members of their "family" to sinecures; by a remorseless system of influence and interest, subordination was ensured and opposition was curbed; democratic institutions were restricted, or corrupted by purchase. But this parasitism performed vestigial functions (notably in opening ways to commercial imperialism), and it did not interfere with the self-reproduction of those social groups—the capitalist landed gentry and the commercial and financial adventurers—in whose interests it ruled (or for whom it "substituted") and whose political settlement of 1688 had established the basis for its power. When it did so threaten these interests (the South Sea Bubble, the loss of the American colonies) it came under heavy challenge, and the last decades of the century show some adaptation and resumption of function. Its ascendancy, throughout the middle decades of the century, did indeed bring a revival of the economic strength and general influence of an aristocracy which it had, in part, created. But this did not quite make up a new ruling-class or a new direction to the wider social process. And this parasitic formation was ultimately (just) peacefully (and partially) displaced in 1832.[64]

The example has little bearing on the contemporary Soviet Union. The Whig predators were vastly more predatory than (in my information) Soviet bureaucrats commonly are. But they did not have at their command an all-intrusive Party, and they were subject to some democratic criticism and legal control. Thus this is not proposed as a close analogy. The analogy may serve if it explains how a parasitism —and even a structured parasitism with substantial "real" social components—can be distinguished from a "new class". The parasitism which both exploits and substitutes for the social groups in whose name it rules must find its rationale, not in its own self-perpetuation, but in performing certain functions for those groups. The functions which the Soviet parasitism must perform, and must be seen to perform, include those of organizing production; of defending the state against external enemies, a function which is not and has not been in the past fifty years imaginary (even if Stalinism has had an unusual knack of imagining the wrong enemies), and which provides the parasitism with a major practical and ideological rationale; and of defending the integrity of socialism against internal enemies, a function which is wholly mystifying and wholly appropriated to protecting parasitism itself.

This last "function" might make it seem that even if the bureaucracy is a parasitism *upon* a socialist potential, there is very little chance of shaking it loose. But there is a second ground for guarded optimism within the process. This resides within the notion of a self-defensive ideology which masks the actuality of power and exploitation, which Wright Mills defined as "rhetoric" and which you define as "hypocrisy".[65] The rulers must not only perform certain functions but must *be seen to do so;* and if they do not, they must *seem* to do so. For long periods the rhetoric of a society—libertarian, moralistic, socialist—may seem to be so much at odds with reality that it is mere inert myth, mere hypocrisy. Indeed, to the observer who can penetrate to the reality this "smoke-screen" is merely nauseous. But then at some point of crisis this rhetoric suddenly becomes activated, and some members of the society act upon it as part of their internalized and deeply-held convictions. And this is not surprising, for the children have been socialized, and the adults have been indoctrinated and mystified, in precisely this set of assumed values. Hence from within the C.I.A. itself a James McCord turns up who will not follow the "games plan" and who, as a *real* "liberal" opposing the state, decides to follow "a course of his own". And hence those repeated experiences of courageous critics of the ruling Communist Parties emerging from within the Communist Parties themselves.

I don't know how matters now stand with the rhetoric of the Soviet Union, nor how far submersion to an empty and repressive rhetoric has generated mere cynicism or opportunism. But it might be so (some observers say it is so) that beneath the parasitism millions of Soviet citizens still think of their land and factories as *ours* rather than as *mine* or *theirs;* still hold a pride in the intentions of the October Revolution; are socialized in some socialist values; find something more than myth in Marxist texts; and hence already do and increasingly will criticize the practices of their own society in terms of its own rhetoric. Let us at least allow the possibility.

But there is a further and larger consideration. It might be possible, hideously inapposite as the metaphor appears, that the "socialist" countries have already shuffled across Marx's frontier into the "kingdom of freedom". That is, whereas in previous history social being appeared, in the last analysis, to determine social consciousness, because the logic of process supervened over human intentions; in socialist societies there may be no such determining logic of process, and social consciousness may determine social being. And, again, in the very last analysis, which analysis may work out through several centuries.

This thought is rather too metaphysical for a historian within a Marxist tradition to cope with. Its consequences, if it could be shown to have empirical validity, would be unsettling. Methods of historical analysis to which one had become habituated would cease to have the same validity in investigating socialist evolution. On the one hand, it opens up the perspective of a long protraction of tyranny. So long as any ruling group, perhaps fortuitously established in power at the moment of revolution, can reproduce itself and control or *manufacture* social consciousness there will be no inherent logic of process within the system which, as social being, will work powerfully enough to bring its overthrow. There will of course be plenty of conflicts of interest within "social being" to which the rulers (in order to control consciousness) must adjust; and the actual social experience of the majority of citizens will give rise incessantly to a critical social consciousness which it will always prove difficult for the rulers, even with the aid of terror and censorship, to control. The manipulation of social consciousness will be difficult; but I see no theoretical reason why it could not, over a considerable historical period, be done.

Of course if the ruling group failed altogether in its function of organizing and expanding production, then the old logic of process, of social being, would assert itself. But there is no necessary reason why the ruling group should fail. Nor is there any necessary reason why rising material standards and controlled cultural provision should set rationality free. As another Yugoslav theorist has argued:

A considerable improvement in the living conditions of individuals does not auto-matically entail the creation of a genuine human community, in which there is solidarity, and without which a radical emancipation of man is not possible. For it is possible to overcome poverty and still retain exploitation, to replace compulsory work with senseless and equally degrading amusements, to allow participation in insignificant issues within an essentially bureaucratic system, to let the citizens be virtually flooded by carefully selected and interpreted half-truths, to use prolonged education for a prolonged programming of human brains, to open all doors to the old culture and at the same time to put severe limits to the creation of the new one, to reduce morality to law, to protect certain rights without being able to create a universally human sense of duty and mutual solidarity. [66]

That is the dark side of the dialectic. But it has another side. For it suggests that over and above any challenge emerging from "social being" the ruling group has *most* to fear from the challenge of rational "social consciousness". It is exactly rationality and an open, evaluative moral process which "ought" to be the logic of socialist process, expressed in democratic forms of self-management and in democratic institutions. The dispersal of rational criticism is not one danger among many but the greatest danger of all to bureaucratic parasitism. This parasitism cannot survive without its mystificatory defensive ideology; nor could it survive the effective activization of the inert socialist rhetoric. And the activization of this rhetoric could be a swifter process than we imagine. This is why each contest over intellectual and cultural liberties in the Soviet Union is so stubbornly fought.

We may illustrate this by comparing the impact of Khrushchev's secret speech at the 20th Congress and the Watergate affair. I don't wish in any way to underestimate the importance of Watergate, both in the dangers of centralized authoritarian rule which it narrowly averted—or postponed—and in the large political realignments to which it may lead on. Both Watergate and Khrushchev's secret speech were dramatically de-mystificatory; and both reactivated a rhetoric which one might have thought was an empty hypocrisy. In the case of the United States, the rhetoric of constitutionalism and of personal liberty turned out to be somewhat tougher, more internalized, than one had come to suppose. But however far-reaching the political consequences, there is no sense at this time that this reactivation will in any way challenge capitalism-as-system.

Nor did Khrushchev's speech challenge socialism-as-system. But by de-mystifying orthodox ideology, by challenging the Party's legitimacy, by reactivating socialist rhetoric, it did challenge the ruling parasitism very seriously indeed. The dispersal of rationality took place with very great speed. Within six months or so both Poland and Hungary were brought to the point of insurrection; and I am not persuaded in these cases, any more than in the subsequent case of Czechoslovakia, that this process was leading necessarily to capitalist counter-revolution. Moreover, this process, if not interrupted, might have led very much further in the Soviet Union itself. And the interruption was not occasioned *only* by the self-protective measures of the bureaucracy.

We must remember that the failure of "1956" was in part a failure imposed by "the West". The West as anti-communist aggression; and the West as inadequate socialist response. Suez consolidated Soviet reaction; Kennedy's dance of death during the Cuban missile crisis precipitated the pragmatic Khrushchev's fall; the bombs falling in Vietnam were a background to the occupation of Prague. For the most manifest function of the statist oligarchies in the socialist countries is the organizing of defence against capitalist aggression. This function above all has provided a parasitism with a rationale.

This function has not been imaginary. And the hostility of Western social-democrats and liberals towards communism has not been always and in every case informed by principled opposition to its "deformities"; it has as often, and as forcibly, been directed against its achievements or promise. There is a complex polarity and mutual relationship between the "East" and the "West". At times when communism has shown a most human face, between 1917 and the early 1920s, and again from the battle of Stalingrad to 1946, the Western labour movement has been in good and assertive heart. But the reverse is also true. I have been an active socialist for thirty years, and through all that time (1944–1946 excluded) the greatest ideal obstacle has been the caricature of socialism presented by the fact of socialist states. But the failure of western socialist movements to effect a transition to a socialist system, with alternative and more democratic models of process, has of course helped to perpetuate that caricature.

I offer this hypothesis as to the inversion of social consciousness and social being without particular confidence. It is in any case a rather abstract notion, and the decisive part may be played by contingencies. It offers to restate Marx's notion of the passage from the kingdom of necessity to that of freedom in a diminuendo, shame-faced way. If he supposed that this passage could be instant and dramatic then he was wrong. The kingdom of necessity was never altogether so: the intentions of men can be seen imposing themselves within process, especially when we consider discrete histories (as for example of institutions); albeit these intentions are generally negated or transformed by "circumstances", or the larger logic of process, which logic is itself in part composed of intentions. The kingdom of freedom is not for instant proclamation. We may now observe, in the East, an in-between world, of attainment and approximation; social consciousness might begin to determine social being, but unless it does so through open democratic rational and moral process, it will not be the consciousness of all men but of a few, to whom the rest remain in bondage.

Beyond this—if such open process could be inserted—one might reassume the grounds for a guarded optimism. What we mean by the kingdom of freedom is that men will at last steal a march upon "circumstances". Since intentions will no longer be diverted from their outcome by an alternative logic of system it will become more possible to predict the outcome of some kinds of social choice. If the tide of affluence should ever come to lap the entire world so such choices might cease to be dictated by necessity and might arise from ideal considerations, disclosed in the democratic process. We shall cease to be obliged to produce as much as we can—or as much as the advertisers can induce us to consume—by the most expedient means. We can decide to produce in the way that we desire, with a new regard for individual self-fulfilment—for our working and living environment, our needs for variety and creative expression in work. The energies and anxieties of producing and consuming man may give way before more relaxed modes of existing and experiencing man, for whose goals we must look to Athenian or even "Indian" precedents.[67]

Moreover, men's choices will affect not only what things they produce but also the kinds of human nature which they produce. By this I do not mean the intolerable attempt to manipulate all men into a prescribed common mould, but that, in those areas in which the shaping of nature cannot but take place, the processes of socialization and of value-formation will become less involuntary and more fully disclosed. If man's culturally-endowed "nature" changes, these changes will increasingly appear as the product of open evaluative process.

What this does not entail is some faith that men will become naturally "good", or that opposing interests will disappear. There is no enchanter's wand which will banish propensities to greed or aggression. I accept your insistence that human conflicts will endure. Everything will depend upon men being able to create the institutional devices through which antagonisms of interest can be disclosed and rationally reconciled. The institutions, the culture, and the socially-endowed "nature" will not be identical in all parts of the socialist world. I would suppose that intellectual and moral controversy might become *more*, rather than less, strenuous in this new kingdom; since they will be free from the dictation of "circumstances", the ensuing choices will have more immediate social consequences. If the vast interest-groups of Army, Party, and secret police could be brought within control, lesser interest-groups (or alternative centres of commitment and identity) might assert themselves, as the commitment of men to particular institutions: the interest of this factory, this university, that city.

My own utopia, two hundred years ahead, would not be like Morris's "epoch of rest". It would be a world (as D. H. Lawrence would have it) where the "money values" give way before the "life values", or (as Blake would have it) "corporeal" will give way to "mental" war. With sources of power easily available, some men and women might choose to live in unified communities, sited, like Cistercian monasteries, in centres of great natural beauty, where agricultural, industrial and intellectual pursuits might be combined. Others might prefer the variety and pace of an urban life which rediscovers some of the qualities of the city-state. Others will prefer a life of seclusion, and many will pass between all three. Scholars would follow the disputes of different schools, in Paris, Jakarta or Bogota.

But one stirs uneasily within such dreams. The utopian imagination today has been diverted into the realm of space-fiction, whose authors examine, exactly, what societies might be created if social consciousness could impose itself upon social being. Their imaginings are not always comforting. Nothing will "happen" of its own accord, without conflict and without the assertion of choice.

Within such a perspective, we cannot immediately assume that statist socialist societies are more "advanced" than capitalist societies. It is impossible at any given moment of history to compare contemporary societies because what must be taken into account is not only the formal *status quo* but the potential; not only what they appear to be but what they are capable of becoming. We must select not only a comparative yardstick but also a datum-line. And in the case of contemporary pseudo-communist and late-capitalist societies, it is unlikely that future historians will find in 1973 their datum-line. And even if we judge from today's standpoint, and if we select as our yardstick the degree of approximation to a free and classless society, then it is possible to argue that Soviet society, which is in important respects more classless although it is certainly less free, is more advanced. This means, of course, that the attainment in Russia of effective political and intellectual liberties is more, not less, important, since it is only through the full democratic process that state ownership can become ownership in common and that planning will cease to be authoritarian manipulation and will become self-activity.

But by the same yardstick, one could also argue (and only the outcome will show) that a capitalist society with mature democratic traditions could be nearer to becoming a democratic classless society than a backward socialist country, with a corrupt and authoritarian ruling parasitism. Although constrained within capitalist forms, the socialist *potentia* could be greater. What we would be comparing would not be static *things* but processes of *becoming* whose outcome is uncertain since it depends upon what men choose to do.

To be a utopian, in 1973, is to be written off, in most "reputable" quarters, as a romantic and a fool. But perhaps to fall into a "realism" which is derivative from an obsession with men's evil propensities is only the symptom of an inverted or depressive romanticism. For to lose faith in man's reason and in his capacity to act as a moral agent is to disarm him in the face of "circumstances". And circumstances, mounted on man's evil will, have more than once in the past decades seemed likely to kill us all. It is the utopian nerve of failure, to which you were once a most eloquent witness, that we must still nourish.

In all this long foregoing argument I have offered you no effective reasons to refute despair. I do not announce, in new terms, the old millenium. I have offered only a refutation of your particular reasons for despair. At this moment of historical time, neither despair nor optimism appear to me to be founded upon rationally compelling arguments. It remains for men to act and to choose.

*   *   *

There might also be another logic at work on the "optimistic" side. Early in 1944 one young man whom you would perhaps describe as a Western Stalinist, but who was not, as it happens, particularly enthused by fantasies of splendid Asiatic hordes, wrote this:

> When a democrat dies—that is, a man who has shown, as they [the partisans of Yugoslavia] have, by word and action that he cares more than anything for democratic freedom—then one, or ten, or a hundred new ones are created by his example: one or ten or a hundred existing ones are strengthened in their resolve. When a fascist dies the effect on his confederates is the reverse. Only in the most confused and darkest periods of history does this not appear to be the case.[68]

The last two or three decades have been, exactly, such a confused and dark period of history. Even so, it is difficult to show that there are any men whose faith is sustained by the examples of Beria or of Rakosi. Whereas there are many hundreds of thousands who cherish the examples of the insurgents of Budapest in 1956 and of Prague in 1968. And the examples which a longer view of history provides are more numerous than that. It is possible that past culture can still provide reserves for "our" side.

You also have afforded to us an example, of intellectual integrity and moral courage. The price which you pay is that men watch you and judge you critically. I do not chide you for your despair. But I must and will chide you for hasty despair and for bad political judgment.

My criticisms are founded upon your *Encounter* interview (already discussed, pp. 335–36), your article in *Daedalus* on "Intellectuals against Intellect", and a recently-convened conference under the title "Is there anything wrong with the socialist idea?" held at the University of Reading. Since you came to "the West" you have made little attempt, it would seem, to enter a dialogue with those who thought themselves to be your friends. But you have been rather free with your intellectual favours elsewhere.

From your article in *Daedalus* I will select for criticism the following propositions or assertions. You argue that there have been historical examples of movements of "the oppressed and uneducated classes" which have been suspicious of rationality as an instrument of their oppressors: hence "they oppose their own spiritual poverty as a mark of superiority to the existing social order". "The great misfortune", however, of these classes has been "their inability to participate in the development of spiritual culture":

> It is incontestable that the position of intellectuals is a form of privilege, and that those who see their ideal in the absolute equality of mankind in every respect must demand the destruction of culture. If equality in every respect is the highest value, then the most important task of society is to press all people down to the level of its least enlightened parts.

You disclaim the view that Marx himself had any such intention: "his purpose was to provide access to culture for everybody. That is why the cult of, and the striving for, knowledge were characteristic traits of the labour movement at the time that it was under the strong influence of Marxian theory":

> Certain formulations of Marx suggest that he believed in the particular class character of the culture as a whole. It is certain, however, that Marxism, in its fundamental presuppositions, conceives of socialism as a continuation of the spiritual work of mankind, as the inheritor and not the destroyer of the existing bourgeois culture . . .

To the intellectuals of the Second International, with a few exceptions, being a socialist "did not mean being an advocate of an essentially different culture . . . which had different rules of thinking and different moral values". "There was no question of an essentially different 'proletarian culture' opposed as a whole to the 'bourgeois culture' and to bourgeois values."

Such a mistaken view you equate with the folly of Soviet "proletcult" which proposed to "create from nothing" an essentially different culture. This phenomenon is now only a "historical curiosity". But you also suggest that "social developments in this century" (a very large and unargued assumption) disallow the hope that "the idea of Marx that the industrial proletariat of highly developed countries should be the vehicles for socialist transformations" can be fulfilled. But certain Western intellectuals, who claim to be Marxists, continue ostentatiously to discard the values of Western bourgeois civilization (which, we must remember, you have more or less equated with "man's" spiritual culture) and "to humble themselves before the splendour of a second barbarism". They now find their vehicle in "masses of illiterate peasants from the most backward parts of the world":

> The contemporary enthusiasm of intellectuals for peasant and *lumpenproletarian* movements or for movements inspired by the ideology of national minorities is an enthusiasm for that which in these movements is reactionary and hostile to culture— for their contempt of knowledge, for the cult of violence, for the spirit of vengeance, for racism.

And from this you return to a defence of the universalist values of reason: "the idea that mankind should 'liberate' itself from its intellectual heritage and create a new 'qualitatively different' science or logic is a support for obscurantist despotism".

One could criticize this argument at several levels. For example, certain assertions are supported by mis-statements of historical fact. I would be interested to know how you could support your view that the intellectuals of the Second International did not advocate a socialist culture with different moral values, since several of the most interesting among them—including Bebel, Jaurès, and William Morris —were deeply and continuously concerned with the question of moral and cultural values in socialist society. And again—and this is relevant to my argument—one can demonstrate without difficulty that in British working-class history the "cult of, and striving for, knowledge" was by no means a consequence of "the strong influence of Marxian theory" but emerged out of the conditions of working-class life— its culture and its total conflict against its exploitation—many decades before the name of Marx had been heard of. Your formulation characteristically proposes culture and rationality as the perquisites of intellectuals, workers or "illiterate peasants" as inert and culture-less, as "vehicles" waiting in line for intellectuals to drive.

One could also assent to some parts of your argument. I know very well what you are pointing towards; I like no more than you do certain surrenders to irrationalism, certain dispositions to capitulate intellectually before the self-indulgences of a Western white guilt, certain tendencies to look for a new set of "vehicles" among the defeated, the merely violent, and the criminal, which flourished for a time in Marcusian and Sartreian circles. But at the same time I would chide you for taking as serious and permanent thought what are passing Western intellectual fashions, and also for taking the often ill-informed accounts offered by Western intellectuals of their own working classes, at their own pretentious self-valuation.

So I know what you are getting at, and why you are enraged. But your argument could more helpfully be criticized at other levels. And I would select two themes. First, there is the same sense of disintegrative unsystematic thought which I have noted before. Your thought is littered with unexamined, nightmarish assumptions about reality which are easily recognizable as the devalued currency of current bourgeois—not *thought*, but ideology. The world is made up of intellectual barbarians, romantic nostalgics, illiterate peasants, manic students, racist blacks, and mute consumerized workers like vehicles just off an assembly-line awaiting delivery to ideological drivers. And no doubt one may easily find in existence examples of all of these. But no examples are examined, no sense of system or process is involved. And the vitiating error is to suppose that intellectual culture and culture in its anthropological meanings are co-existent; that, for example, a theory of proletcult (which I agree was mainly folly) could offer to produce culture *ex nihilo*. So that even the challenge of *égalité* you must see as an abasement of culture to "the least enlightened parts" of the people: i.e. the destruction of "culture". The oppressed classes of history, in your view, have not even been allowed to participate "in the development of spiritual culture".

These assumptions—*so* familiar in the intellectual West—make me so angry, and this letter is already so long, that I cannot argue the matter through. I must content myself with counter-assertions. A good part of the lifetimes of intellectual work which I and many others in the Western Marxist tradition have given has been given precisely to disclosing, within history and within contemporary society, culture in its alternative anthropological meanings. I do not find in British working-class experience any *nihilo* but an active, value-formative cultural process. I do not find that the "spiritual culture" of the poor is always inferior to that of intellectuals; on the contrary, valid intellectuality can coexist with extreme spiritual poverty. I abhor intellectual games played with the values of violence, irrationalism and criminality; but I do not suppose for a moment that these games-players always offer a true account or a responsive understanding of the phenomena with which they play: thus intellectuals may exalt certain phenomena of "black power" movements for their own purposes and according to their own principles of selection, while entirely failing to respond to other, and very positive, qualities which these movements express.

In short, I affirm these propositions and negations. And I affirm them not only as arguments but as the fruit of experience. I have learned a great deal from working people in the past, and I hope to continue to do so. I have learned, from particular working people, about values, of solidarity, of mutuality, of scepticism before received ideological "truths", which I would have found it difficult to discover in any other ways, from the given intellectual culture. For the values of *égalité* are not ones which can be thought up, they must be learned through living them. And they teach that one may not bring to people some abstract intellectual meritocratic scale, which immediately supposes that equality entails the destruction of "culture" or its reduction to its "least enlightened parts".

For the worth of a human being—his capacity for loyalty, his qualities as a lover or parent, his creativity, his behaviour in the presence of death—is coincident in no way with his placing within a particular set of intellectual criteria. And it is the scandalous assumption that it is so—the product in this country of "public-school" élitism, seconded by decades of educational selectivity, within a system which rewards, not only in money and status but also in "worth", those who pass the intellectual tests—that is a vitiating error not only of intellectual life very generally but also of some socialist and "Marxist" groups, which, just like you, are inspecting the workers and the peasants as "vehicles", and (but you certainly don't share this unpleasant form of arrogance) propose themselves as the rationality which must direct an inert, pragmatic working-class movement and select for it its goals.

So that I am very much less alarmed than you are to observe the growing "romantic nostalgia for a pre-industrial society" and certain affirmations of "life values" against rationalized career values. Beneath some irrational forms, there is an affirmative and long-overdue impulse here: these are cultural antibodies generated by overlong exposure to mindless technological expansionism. Romanticism in this country offered a more radical criticism of the values of industrial capitalism than you seem to suppose; and Wordsworth attained in *The Prelude* to an insight into the *égalité* of human worth which one would gladly see appropriated to a socialist culture. You have no warrant to be so dismissive. We must be as patient as gardeners, pruning and training the impulses of revolt which arise within capitalist society, not turning away from each one—because it arises unbidden and in unexpected form—with abhorrence. If some young intellectuals in Western society turn their backs upon a cerebral, competitive and uncreative intellectual culture, and turn to what they think is Zen Buddhism, I will not run instantly to *Daedalus* in a state of shock. I will be happy to let them "Indianize" themselves, while arguing with them (and perhaps learning from them) along the way.

One tragedy of intellectuals in revolt within both Western and Eastern societies in the past two decades is that they have been, except for brief moments, isolated from larger popular movements, and they have sometimes perforce found these movements as their antagonists. Hence socialist aspiration, in its intellectual expression, walks gauntly along, picking at its own flesh. It learns no humility before experience, no mode of discourse with men of practice, because it sees always experience and practice as its enemy. And this very isolation breeds among intellectuals self-isolating attitudes, which make it more difficult to communicate with men who learn their ideas and live their values in more experiential ways. For a generation of American radical students, the entire white working-class of America was "written off".[69] There were real reasons for this: but the writing-off did damage to intellectual growth itself. And in such a situation both despair and rebellion can lead to the same terminus.

It is the pathetic fallacy of intellectuals that by their own thinking alone they can change the world. While at his own trade of thinking, the intellectual feels himself to be a free agent. But when he turns to act, in such a context as our own, this freedom appears to dissolve into illusion. His ideas break fruitlessly in mere foam against the cliffs of an insensate social reality. And this dilemma provokes two alternative reactive patterns. On the one hand, he attributes his ineffectiveness to the innate greed and aggressiveness of human nature, which may only be checked by an innate "religious consciousness". Or he accepts his despair, looks cautiously for the "levers" of power, and contents himself with the retreat into piecemeal, softly-softly social engineering. He finds in Sir Karl Popper "the greatest philosopher of the age", and he declares for the most modest empiricism. On the other hand, he swings to the opposite extreme of pure voluntarism. Only the impossible, utopian leap, the unplanned rebellion of the barricades, can break man's self-victimhood. The wheel swings around: a pusillanimous caution gives way to an irrationalist voluntarism. The young knit up their own exemplar from the twelve men of the *Granma*, or from Paris in May 1968. But Che Guevara's bones remind us that history is implacable. What is made by pure will is not a revolution but a myth.

Utter despair (or despair redefined as cautious empiricism) and absolute voluntarism, are two sides of the coin of social impotence. Both fail to connect with the actual potential of living men, both breed an intellectual self-isolationism. But there is a second theme in your argument which deserves attention. And this concerns the difference between intellectual culture as rationality and intellectual culture as ideology. This concerns a matter of definition, as to which you are more expert,[70] but as to which I must still offer disagreements. When you and I speak of ideology we appear to be speaking of different things. In "The Myth of Human Self-Identity" there is a curious passage of argument:

> It is plain, if not notorious, that an ideology is always weaker than the social forces which happen to be its vehicle and to try to carry its values. Consequently, since no real interests involved in social struggles are reducible to the simplicity of an ideological value system, we may be certain in advance that no political organism will be the perfect embodiment of its ideology. To state this of Marxism, as of any other ideology, we can dispense with historical knowledge.

Thus political organisms embody ideology imperfectly, and, once again, social forces are "vehicles" for values. Now I would argue in a manner quite contrary. Political organisms select from the available stock of ideas those which best serve their interests and justify (or mystify) their functions, and hence reduce ideas *to* ideology; and they often do this very perfectly. Social forces do not "happen" to be the "vehicle" for ideology and values; they shape ideas *into* ideology, they are idea-selective and value-selective. The ideology and the social forces are sometimes coincident in strength; sometimes forces select for themselves an inadequate ideology; and sometimes (I would hazard more often) an ideology proves stronger than the social forces which were its matrix, and outlives it. What has happened in the Soviet Union is that Marxism as rationality or idea has been transformed into ideology, a selective, closed justificatory and mystifying set of notions which clothes the actions of the ruling groups. To state this of Soviet Marxism is precisely to require the most careful historical analysis.

That this passage was not a casual slip of the pen can be shown if we look again at "Intellectuals against Intellect". "Certain formulations of Marx", you allow, "suggest that he believed in the particular class character of the culture as a whole". But these were, evidently, mistaken formulations and not the true Marx. For Marxism's "fundamental presuppositions" conceive of socialism "as a continuation of the spiritual work of mankind", and "as the inheritor and not the destroyer of the existing bourgeois culture". And the existing bourgeois culture becomes, very soon, a synonym for man's universal culture, indeed perhaps for rationality itself. "The idea that mankind should 'liberate' itself from its intellectual heritage and create a new 'qualitatively different' science or logic is a support for obscurantist despotism."

And so indeed it is. But we pass in that sentence between two different propositions. Science and logic are carefully-chosen words: and, I agree, liberation from these leads to obscuranticism. But man's "intellectual heritage" is not so simple a unified concept; "man" has many heritages, and the living do not inherit so much received property; they select, they use, they transform. And I see no necessary contradiction between Marx's formulations as to ideology, or as to bourgeois culture; and his presuppositions as to the universalist values of rationality.

One may see socialism as continuing the spiritual work of mankind, without also seeing socialism as inheriting this work as a received *quantum;* it continues it by reactivating it, by selecting from it, and by transforming it. Your method of caricature impedes rational argument. Such intellectuals as Marx and Morris did not advocate "an *essentially* different culture" which was "*opposed as a whole*" to bourgeois culture and bourgeois values. But they did, most emphatically, advocate the transformation of certain socially-critical concepts and values. It was not the "rules of thinking" which were at issue but, for example, the concepts of property as enshrined in capitalist economics, sociology and law. It was not the values of loyalty or mercy but the values of *nasha:* "ours" as against "yours" and "mine".

My notion of ideology is perhaps idiosyncratic. I have been told that it is not Marx's, although I remain unconvinced. I am not happy with the notion of "false consciousness", since while such ideological consciousness certainly falsifies universals and mystifies rationality, it can be a very forcible and "true" consciousness of the particular interests who espouse it, a necessary mask, a necessary set of concepts for their own systematized exploitation of other groups, and a powerful source of self-delusion and rhetoric which is, in its own right, a potent social force. "False consciousness" suggests a mask held up against reality, and a mask which can easily slip. But my notion proposes no theoretical difficulty in distinguishing between rationality and ideology, although in practice the difficulties are immense, since the most principled philosopher, however forewarned against the dangers, must work with concepts which arise genetically within a culture which has a distinct ideological colouring.

This disagreement as to ideology may make it evident why I do not find the idea of "a formidable revolution in men's minds" (p. 344) as absurd as you do. It remains, for me, a socialist possibility. But this disagreement recalls also to my mind another, and more practical disagreement. This is, in fact, the pain which originally occasioned this letter. I refer to your seeming innocence as to the existence, the resources, and the process of contemporary capitalist ideology.

*　　*　　*

In May, 1973, you convened a conference of selected scholars at the University of Reading. Your original proposal was to call it upon the theme: "What is wrong with the socialist idea?", although subsequent considerations of tact altered "what is?" to "is there anything?" The conference was convened under the auspices of Reading's "Graduate School of Contemporary European Studies", an institution with a known reputation. Let me content myself with saying that its very eminent advisory committee, which includes Sir John Wolfenden, the Hon. Michael Astor, the Hon. C. M. Woodhouse, and the Right Hon. K. G. Younger, does not include any men especially noted for divided allegiances or neutrality within the context of ideological cold war. The conference, I understand, was funded by Sir George Weidenfeld's publishing house.

The purposes of this conference were to be academic and not political. You therefore insisted that invitations be limited to persons who, while sharing "some basic socialist values", were not "committed to any well-established system of ideas". By these criteria you were able to exclude persons who combined a scholarly concern with socialism with practical, participatory experience of contemporary industrial conflict. This exclusion may have simplified discussion, since certain of the propositions which you placed before the conference could scarcely have survived the criticism of even British practice. Thus in your own contribution you proposed that:

> If the motives of private profit in production are eradicated, the organisational body of production—i.e. the state—becomes the only possible subject of economic activity and the only remaining source of economic initiative.

This is the kind of fallacy into which intellectuals commonly fall, when they know rather little about "industry", feel it to be alien, and are unwilling to bring into their strictly "academic" consultations co-operators and trade unionists, industrial workers and technicians. And you carry the thought further by gesturing towards "an undeniable tendency" in "different political systems" towards the growth of centralized power and the growth of bureaucracy. And among those tasks "which, as is widely acknowledged, should rest on the shoulders of central powers" you list "the welfare, health and educational systems; the control of wages, prices, investment and banking", etc.

> It is difficult to be self-consistent when one fulminates at the same time against the growth of the bureaucracy and against the uncontrolled wastefulness of the operation of private industry; more often than not the increasing control over private business means increasing the bureaucracy.

I can make my point neatly about the intrusion of ideological assumption into rationality by noting those give-away phrases: "as is widely acknowledged" (i.e. by people I have talked about it with at Oxford and at Berkeley), "the *control* of wages" (it is "widely acknowledged" that these must be controlled from above), "private industry" is to be brought under "increasing control" (from above), and so on. But any alert participant in the health and educational systems, and in some parts of the welfare system, would instantly repudiate the notion that his tasks "should rest on the shoulders of central powers". Practical experience, even in non-socialist Britain, shows a hundred ways in which devolution of powers are attempted, in which conflicts between central and local authorities are mediated, in which consumers assert (insufficiently) their own intentions, and in which local initiatives, including the powers to raise or to allocate moneys, are jealously safeguarded; and these ways range from elected bodies to bureaucratic committees to feudal self-governing communities of scholars (like All Souls') to incipient experiments in self-management and control.

Moreover, it is of course untrue that the social process in advanced capitalist countries shows a unified technologically-determined drive towards centralized power. Simultaneously with this drive towards centralization we have seen, in the last decades, a great increase in the impact upon the whole economy of the power of even quite small groups of organized workers and technicians when they withhold their labour. Power workers, transport workers, workers and technicians in the communications industries, and many others have a power undreamed-of by the founders of the socialist movement. And with this has grown the number and forms of localized resistance to centralization: sit-ins, work-ins, consumer and community organizations. Once again, this could have been introduced to the discussions by anyone with participatory experience of the contemporary socialist movement; but, alas, such persons might also have been disqualified by their commitment to a "well established system of ideas", i.e. socialism.

I also am concerned with the problem of how, within a capitalist society, the most searching and self-critical discussion of socialist theory can be promoted. I agree: it cannot be promoted by a comfortable meeting of the cosily committed, nor by an uncomfortable meeting of antagonistic sectarians. But I doubt whether it can be promoted in your way either, since your principles of selection exclude certain arguments and also relevant experience. In fact, some of those who attended your conference had excellent socialist credentials, some serious papers were exchanged, and Sir George Weidenfeld will make a passable book out of it all. And I don't wish to criticize any of those who, influenced by your reputation and integrity, did so attend.

Nor do I write this out of pique. As it happens I was not invited to attend, but if I had been so, I would have had to make the personal decision to refuse. For the organizing secretary for your conference (and deputy chairman of the Reading School of Contemporary European Studies) was Mr Robert Cecil, C.M.G. And consulting *Who's Who* I find that Mr Cecil was in His Majesty's Foreign Service from 1936 until 1968, when he joined the School at Reading. Among positions he has held have been those of First Secretary at the British Embassy in Washington (1945–8), a position at Bonn (1957–9), Director-General British Information Services, New York, at times between 1956 and 1961, and Head of the Cultural Relations Department of the Foreign Office (1962–7).

Mr Cecil is no doubt a cultivated and admirable man: he published a volume of poems in his youth, a book on Edwardian England in his maturity, and his club now is the Athenaeum. And no doubt he was discreet, in offering his services simply as an organizing aid. So that I am at a loss to explain to you why his presence as organizing secretary (together with certain other circumstances in the funding and auspices of the conference) would have imposed upon me a personal decision to be absent.

I would abstain for the same reasons that (if I were invited to write for it, which I am not) I would abstain from writing for *Encounter*.[71]

I would feel awkward in such company. I seek to impose my personal preferences upon no-one else. It is simply that I cannot overcome the habits of a lifetime. I have never attended a conference of socialists when I have not had to pay some part of the costs out of my own pocket. Sir George Weidenfeld did not fund the *New Reasoner* or the *May Day Manifesto;* we funded the initial launching of both publications from collective socialist donations. I would perhaps become bashful in Mr Cecil's presence and call him "sir". There is no virtue in any of these things, I know. They are confessions of a minority-minded self-isolation. If you are tolerant, you may consider me as a representative of a residual tradition, like Old Dissent, adhering meticulously to old forms whose significance daily diminishes. Like an 18th-century Quaker, who will not bare his head before authority nor take oaths, I will not take my holidays in Spain nor attend conferences in Rome funded by the Ford Foundation. I will be imprisoned in my own isolation rather than pay any tithes whatsoever to the Natopolitan Church.

I do not urge you to make the same abstentions. I simply say to you, as George Fox said to Penn when the latter was reluctant to discard his sword: "Wear it as long as thou canst!" You will have noticed, if you have followed my footnotes, that my criticisms of socialist reality have always been made in socialist journals. And at the time when I can no longer criticize socialism from such an unmistakable anti-capitalist standpoint, I will fall silent. For no matter how hideous the alternative may seem, no word of mine will wittingly be added to the comforts of that old bitch gone in the teeth, consumer capitalism. I know that bitch well in her very original nature; she has engendered world-wide wars, aggressive and racial imperialisms, and she is co-partner in the unhappy history of socialist degeneration. But this is "my" problem in a different way than it is "yours". "My" progenitors, and some of my contemporaries, have sown their lives into furrows, not to produce their own creative crops, but like a botanical prophylactic, to restrain the virulence of capitalist logic. And to the degree that they have succeeded, the apologists of capitalism appear with newly-soaped faces, and offer their beast as a beast of changed nature. But I know that that beast is not changed: it is held in the fragile but well-tempered chains of our own watchfulness and actions.

Your problem, as you see it, is a different one: it is to report your experience faithfully and without favour. Operating within a culture of universal rationality you cannot be bothered with the sectarian susceptibilities of another nation's Old Dissent. But I will offer to you two considerations. First, in the matter of capitalism as ideology. Your experience has been primarily of Stalinism as ideology: a new, brittle, uneasy, manifestly irrational institutional orthodoxy. This you can instantly identify. But perhaps you—and others like you who find refuge in the West—are thereby unprepared to identify the ideological expressions and forms of capitalism. You appear to have at hand the resources which you have lacked in socialist society most of all; freedom of expression, toleration of dissent, democratic institutions. The society appears, as contrasted with the East, as a society of unconstrained rational and moral process.

But capitalist ideology is neither new nor brittle. It expresses, and at the same time it is, a very ancient hegemony, and a hegemony so assured that it can dispense with many of the more vulgar institutional means of imposing orthodoxy. Its very form is to suggest that it is not a hegemony at all, that *its* way of life is very nature. It discloses itself today in certain fixities of concept: of property and the rights of money: of "innate" human nature: of political "realism": of academic "objectivity" (itself concealing such concepts): of dominative modes of communication, education and government: of utilitarian criteria in economic and social decisions: of negative "freedoms":—indeed, some of those very concepts which you have recently been assuming with too little examination. It is not of course without its active institutional mediations, within the communications industry, within the educational system, and through delicate institutional selectivities, reticencies, and resistencies which one must *live* through for some years before they can be understood. Mr Robert Cecil "finds" himself to be organizing your conference and Sir George Weidenfeld "finds" that he is publishing its results; but there has been no imposition of any kind—not the least discourtesy.

Oh, but one must be a dialectician to understand how this world goes! One substantial advantage of having been an organized communist is that one gains certain understandings of its institutional and ideological defences. But once that position is evacuated—why, the world is open as far as eye can see, every sin is forgiven. And a certain exhibition of intellectual revolt (but *not* practical revolt, such as vulgar strike-making) also has its subsidiary niche, as ornamentation to the ideological hegemony. So that the problem for a socialist intellectual is two-fold: (a) the near-impossibility of *not* selling himself, of not being "taken up" in certain secondary ways, and (b) the near-impossibility of communicating at all in primary and deeply-serious ways. And from this derives the seeming egotism of some passages in this letter. For one must, to survive as an unassimilated socialist in this infinitely assimilative culture, put oneself into a school of awkwardness. One must make one's sensibility all knobbly—all knees and elbows of susceptibility and refusal—if one is not to be pressed through the grid into the universal mish-mash of the received assumptions of the intellectual culture. One must strain at every turn in one's thought to resist the assumption that what one observes and what one is is in the very course of nature.

And even the role of the Jester, which is a role you chose for yourself in the East, is a role which must be played with discretion. For the jester, if he jests in all company and jests unwisely, may provide arguments which acquire a different meaning when employed by the subalterns of the Emperor. "What is truth? said jesting Pilate: but did not stay for an answer."

And this brings me to my second consideration. I will remind you that you remarked in *Encounter*:

> A Polish friend . . . recently wrote to me from Sweden saying that whenever he had dealings with the New Left he seemed to be watching a film of which he already knew the end. That is exactly how I feel.

But of course there are other films, whose endings are also known. And one of the oldest, on this side of the world, is that of revolutionary disenchantment. It is a film which was first made in about 1792, and it has been remade in different versions at repeated intervals. A powerful version was made in the 1930s and it has been running to packed houses ever since.[72]

The reactive pattern, by which disenchantment in revolutionary aspirations leads on, after creative difficulties and conflicts, to ultimate reconciliation with the pre-existent *status quo*—or even zealous ideological partisanship on behalf of the *status quo*—is deeply inscribed within western culture. And it has, within capitalist ideology today, a very important confirmatory and legitimating function. Confirmatory, because it can then be shown not only that capitalism works but that the alternative is unworkable. Legitimating, because it can be shown not only that capitalism conforms to human nature but that the alternative is dangerous, immoral and unnatural.

Hence the intellectual in refuge from the East has a role already pre-arranged for him in the West, with which he finds it difficult *not* to conform. And your predicament in this respect was anticipated by MacIntyre as early as 1958:

> The reassertion of moral standards by the individual voice has been one of the ferments of Eastern European revisionism. But, because of the way in which it is done, this reassertion too often leaves the gulf between morality and history, between value and fact as wide as ever. Kolakowski and others like him stress the amorality of the historical process on the one hand, and the moral responsibility of the individual in history on the other. And this leaves us with the moral critic as a spectator, the categorical imperatives which he proclaims having no genuine relationship to his view of history. One cannot revive the moral content within Marxism by simply taking a Stalinist view of historical development and adding liberal morality to it. But however one may disagree with Kolakowski's theoretical position, the kind of

integrity involved in reasserting moral principles in the Polish situation is entirely admirable . . . But to assert this position in the West is to flow with the stream. It is merely to conform. [73]

I think that MacIntyre does less than justice to your thought at that time. But in coming to the West and in conferring at Reading as you have done, you appear to fulfil a fifteen-year-old prediction.

But I can't believe that you have come to a point of rest. Established institutions will, of course, prepare various points of rest for you; they will beckon you on; the intellectual resolutions which they propose for you will be reputable and will entail no disgrace. But I believe that you will reject them all. I recognize your film, but I do not pretend to know how it will end. For you differ in one respect from those numerous actors who have performed the same transitory role of witness, within capitalist society, to the "failure" of socialism. In the pursuit of truth you have been implacable. You have wrestled with ideas without regard for your comfort or reputation. I believe you will continue so.

I ask you whether you cannot, even now, help us to break that logic of reactive process within a divided world, which, like a pair of moral scissors, repeatedly cuts through the universalist integument of socialist utopianism? To remake that universality of aspiration we need your skills. I ask you if you can show the same tenacity and resistance to assimilation within capitalist ideology that you have shown within the Stalinist.

This is to ask of you much. It is to require of you a higher morale than one has the right to expect. Not many of us in the West, whose experiences have been trivial beside your own, have been able to maintain this morale. I have, for ten years, suffered my own dejection consequent upon the sudden re-emergence throughout the West of the "closed" Marxisms (1) and (2), some of them in the most doctrinaire, didactic and thought-resistant forms. For a decade it has seemed that the possibilities for the redeployment and reintegration of thought within the tradition of Marxism (4) have been sealed off. One has been left talking, or merely thinking, to oneself.

I recalled, earlier in this letter, some lines of Yeats. I must now complete his thought:

> My mind, because the minds that I have loved,
> The sort of beauty that I have approved,
> Prosper but little, has dried up of late,
> Yet knows that to be choked with hate
> May well be of all evil chances chief.
> If there's no hatred in a mind
> Assault and battery of the wind
> Can never tear the linnet from the leaf.

"An intellectual hatred is the worst", and we cannot renew our morale unless we resist that kind of intellectual rancour. But this question is, as you would say, not one of "scientific procedure". It is a matter, in the end, of "faith", and advice in such matters is gratuitous.

We *can* not impose our will upon history in any way we choose. We *ought* not to surrender to its circumstantial logic. We can hope and act only as "gardeners of our circumstance".[74] In writing to you I have been, in one way, casting some thirty years of my own private accounts. I have been meditating not only on the meanings of "history" but on the meanings of people whom I have known and trusted. I have been encountering the paradox that many of those whom "reality" has proved to be wrong, still seem to me to have been better people than those who were, with a facile and conformist realism, right. I would still wish to justify the aspirations of those whom "history", at this point of time, appears to have refuted.

It is now eight years since I attempted any "historiosophical" flight. I don't know whether I shall wait for a further eight years before trying the air again—and after two or three such interludes I must certainly leave the resolution of the argument to "history". If I am silent it will not be because I have changed my opinions, although it might be because of a lessening of political or personal morale, or a lack of any sense of audience.

But of one thing, from the fixity of my present intellectual address, I can be certain. I will not be silenced by mere opposition. For the great bustard, by a law well-known to aeronautics, can only rise into the air against a strong head-wind. It is only by facing into opposition that I am able to define my thought at all.

In this way I have sometimes exaggerated differences and put friendships into jeopardy. I fear that you may think that I have been using your thought, as a medium of antagonism, in order to define my own.

And yet—I return to the first lines of this letter—I have some right to speak frankly, for I am (or was) some kind of kinsman of yours. There was a time when you, and the causes for which you stood, were present in our innermost thought. And in those days (only fifteen years distant!) whose meanings are now forgotten or falsified, when a "new left" was first projected, we shared another kinsman in our friend, C. Wright Mills.

It was Mills who defined this relationship, in words better than any of mine:

> I can no longer write seriously without feeling contempt for the indifferent pro-
> fessors and smug editors who so fearlessly fight the cold war, and for the cultural
> bureaucrats and hacks, the intellectual thugs of the official line who so readily have
> abdicated the intellect in the Soviet bloc. I can no longer write with moral surety

unless I know that Leszek Kolakowski will understand where I stand—and I think this means unless he knows I have feelings of equal contempt for both leading types of underdeveloped cultural workmen of the overdeveloped countries of the world. [75]

We knew, or thought we knew, what you were fighting—and against what precipitous odds—then and there. Did you give equal thought to the odds confronting Mills—or confronting any of us, in our small, disorderly contingents, over here? Did you understand Mills's "contempt" for capitalist ideology and its institutions, and the "cultural default" of which their intellectual servitors were accused?

If you also enter this "default", you threaten the "moral surety" of that common moment of utopian revolt. We understood you, and we came to your side, because you voiced, not particular or sectional, but universal socialist aspirations. Your claims upon the future could not be realized (or so we thought) without moving decisively outside both stalinist and capitalist strategies and remedies.

And now, as you fall back, so also half a world falls back with you. And today the most-publicized voices of Soviet or Eastern European dissidence are those of falling men—courageous but self-regarding, passionate only in their negatives, self-isolating, deeply-deluded about "the West"—voices which command only one's weary, defensive solidarity.

The solidarity which you once commanded was of a very different kind. You did not call upon our political charity: resolutions, petitions, letters to the *Times*, on behalf of liberalism's underprivileged, who sought only the benefits of the West's benign democracy. You called, or seemed to call, us into a common struggle, as arduous in practice as in intellect.

I do not think the time has gone by for such a struggle. I think it is with us, every day. In any case, can we meet one day and have a drink? I owe you more than one. And can we still drink to the fulfilment of that moment of common aspiration: "1956"?

Yours fraternally,

E. P. THOMPSON.

NOTES

Too little of Leszek Kolakowski's political and philisophical writing has been translated into English. There are however important collections: Leszek Kolakowski, *Marxism and Beyond* (London, 1969; Paladin paperback, 1971), with an introduction by Leopold Labedz; and "A Leszek Kolakowski Reader", *TriQuarterly*, Number 22, Fall 1971. The latter includes a useful selective bibliography.

In these notes I use the abbreviations L.K. for Leszek Kolakowski and E.P.T. for myself. At various points I indicate in my own writings a place where a point finds fuller development. In many cases better sources could have been indicated in the work of other writers, but the method which I have chosen defines more precisely the particular tradition from which I am arguing.

I am grateful to Ralph Miliband, John Saville, Dorothy Thompson and Martin Eve for reading this letter in manuscript and suggesting certain revisions. They are not, of course, in any way responsible for the outcome.

1. *Marxism and Beyond* (1969 edn.), pp. 105–177.
2. Ibid. p. 126.
3. E.P.T., "Agency and Choice", *New Reasoner* 5, Summer 1958.
4. In the sense which you defined in "The Concept of the Left", *Marxism and Beyond*, pp. 87–104.
5. *Marxism and Beyond*, p. 14.
6. Notably the major study, "Religious Consciousness and the Ties of the Church: Studies in the Non-Denominational Christianity of the Seventeenth Century" (Warsaw, 1965), translated (Paris, 1969) as *Chrétiens sans Église*, but not yet translated into English; and *The Alienation of Reason: a History of Positivist Thought* (Warsaw, 1966; New York, 1968; London, Penguin Books, 1972).
7. See especially "Historical understanding and the intelligibility of history" (discussed below) and "The epistemological significance of the aetiology of knowledge: a gloss on Mannheim", both in *TriQuarterly* 22.
8. One amusing index of the self-conscious rewriting of history entailed in this break was the appearance in *New Left Review* 60, March–April 1970 of "A Retrospect" of articles published in the first ten years of the review's existence; of 131 articles listed, only one was selected from the first 18 numbers of the review: and this one was by Ronald Laing. Not one article was listed by a founding member of the review's editorial board.
9. E.P.T., "The Peculiarities of the English", *Socialist Register*, 1965; Perry Anderson, "The Myths of Edward Thompson", *New Left Review*, 35, January–February 1966.
10. Raymond Williams, "In Memory of Goldman", *New Left Review*, 67, May–June 1971, and intro. to L. Goldmann, *Racine* (Cambridge, 1972).
11. George L. Kline, "Beyond revisionism: Leszek Kolakowski's recent philosophical development", *TriQuarterly* 22, p. 14.
12. L.K., "The Priest and the Jester", *Marxism and Beyond*, pp. 29–57.
13. I must apologize to ornithologists for my incorrect definitions of the great bustard, which obviously shares some attributes more proper to a dodo. But the dodo has been overworked, and the great bustard was, once, an English bird. The great bustard is indeed far from extinct, and inhabits the plains of Poland. It can fly a little better than I suggest, but is slow to get off the ground. It was therefore in England easy prey to foxes, and to the natives, who valued it for food. Indeed, in the village of Empirica Parva in Windsor Forest they once ate no other meat; and dead bustard was at that time a delicacy in great demand on collegiate high tables.
14. This and succeeding quotations are from L.K., "Permanent and Transitory Aspects of Marxism", *Marxism and Beyond*, pp. 193–207; and also in *The Broken Mirror*, ed. P. Mayewski (New York and London, 1958), pp. 157–174.
15. E.P.T., "Revolution Again", *New Left Review* 6, November–December, 1960.
16. L.K., "In Praise of Inconsistency", *Marxism and Beyond*, pp. 231–240.
17. See e.g. L.K., "Karl Marx and the Classical Definition of Truth", *Marxism and Beyond*, pp. 58–104.
18. See E.P.T., "The Peculiarities of the English", op. cit. pp. 351–2.

19. E.P.T., "The Long Revolution, II", *New Left Review*, 10, July–August 1961, pp. 28–29. Raymond Williams had of course indicated forcefully his criticism of the metaphor of basis-superstructure very much earlier: see e.g. *Culture and Society* (Pelican edn.), pp. 272–3. In his own account, it was his radical dissatisfaction with this "received formula", and his conviction that it was invalid as a methodology for cultural history and criticism (indeed, he describes it as "a bourgeois formula . . . a central position of utilitarian thought") which led him "to believe that I had to give up, or at least to leave aside, what I knew as the Marxist tradition". Thus both Williams and I share a central objection to this "received formula" of Marxism. His attempted solution, presented in *The Long Revolution*, was to offer an alternative, and original, theory "of relations between elements in a whole way of life"; while at the same time entering into an increasingly close dialogue with the Marxist tradition. (See R. Williams, in *New Left Review*, 67, May–June 1971 and intro. to Lucien Goldmann, *Racine* (Cambridge, 1972), pp. xiii–xiv). I was, and remain, dissatisfied with the solution which he then offered, for reasons argued in my review (cited above). My own attempts to explore the dialectical inter-relations of social being and social consciousness, or of culture and "not-culture", in relation to the Marxist tradition but without recourse to the formula, have been largely in historical practice: in *The Making of the English Working Class* and in subsequent (and forthcoming) historical work. Such historical analysis need not be—as some of my readers suppose—innocent of conceptualization, and of interest only as an account of "phenomenology".

20. My earlier borrowing from MacIntyre did not give his definition in full context: he writes—"As Marx depicts it the relation between basis and superstructure is fundamentally not only not mechanical, it is not even causal. What may be misleading here is Marx's Hegelian vocabulary. Marx certainly talks of the basis 'determining' the superstructure and of a 'correspondence' between them. But the reader of Hegel's *Logic* will realize that what Marx envisages is something to be understood in terms of the way in which the nature of the concept of a given class, for example, may determine the concept of membership of that class. What the economic basis, the mode of production, does is to provide a framework within which the superstructure arises, a set of relations around which the human relations can entwine themselves, a kernel of human relationship from which all else grows. The economic basis of a society is not its tools, but the people co-operating using these particular tools in the manner necessary to their use, and the superstructure consists of the social consciousness moulded by and the shape of this co-operation. To understand this is to repudiate the end-means morality; for there is no question of creating the economic base as a means to the socialist superstructure. Creating the basis, you create the superstructure. There are not two activities but one", Alasdair MacIntyre, "Notes from the Moral Wilderness, 1", *New Reasoner*, 7, Winter 1958–9. This very lucid gloss does not seem to me to get over the difficulties of a non-Hegelian use of "determination", nor those of the awkward metaphor. See also E.P.T., "The Communism of William Morris" (William Morris Society, 1965), pp. 17–18.

21. "Intellectuals, Hope and Heresy", *Encounter*, October 1971. The interview was not given in the first place to *Encounter* but comes from a West German source.

22. L.K., "Intellectuals against Intellect", *Daedalus*, Summer 1972.

23. L.K., "The epistemological significance of the aetiology of knowledge", *TriQuarterly*, 22.

24. As Harrington said of Hobbes.

25. L.K., "In Praise of Inconsistency", *Marxism and Beyond*, p. 231.

26. L.K., "Intellectuals against Intellect", op. cit. p. 13. One should recall that

William Morris also glimpsed this possibility, which he saw as arising from the *failure* of movements of revolutionary socialism: "If the present state of society merely breaks up without a conscious effort at transformation, the end, the fall of Europe, may be long in coming, but when it does, it will be far more terrible, far more confused and full of suffering than the period of the fall of Rome": E.P.T., *William Morris, Romantic to Revolutionary* (London, 1955), p. 838.

27. *Marxism and Beyond*, pp. 158–9.

28. *TriQuarterly* 22, pp. 103–117.

29. Ibid., p. 32.

30. Cyclostyled, for presentation at the University of Reading Conference (see above p. 389); and to be published shortly by Weidenfeld & Nicolson.

31. "Soteriological"—i.e. pertaining to salvation.

32. "Only when the real individual man will absorb back the abstract citizen of the state and—as individual man, in his empirical life, in his individual work, in his individual relationships—will become the species being, only when man will recognize and will organize his 'forces propres' as *social* forces and, consequently, will not separate from himself the social force in form of *political* force any more, only then the emancipation of man will be accomplished."

33. For this explanation as to why "we can dispense with historical knowledge" see p. 387.

34. Cf. Your insistence in "Determinism and Responsibility" that "the negation of a norm is a norm", *Marxism and Beyond*, p. 211; and your comments on "technocratic ideology" in L.K., *Positivist Philosophy* (Pelican, 1972), p. 235.

35. Quentin Lauer, introduction to E. Husserl, *Phenomenology and the Crisis of Philosophy* (New York, 1965), p. 4.

36. Husserl, op. cit. pp. 156–8.

37. Hegel, *Lectures on the Philosophy of History* (London, 1878), pp. 10–11. See also MacIntyre's comments on the differences in historical method of the *Phenomenology* and the *Logic* in his *Marcuse* (London 1970), pp. 32–33.

38. See Alasdair MacIntyre, *Marcuse*, passim.

39. L.K., "Althusser's Marx", *Socialist Register*, 1971, pp. 157–184.

40. The educator has been, for some twenty years, standing on his own head in the House of Commons, as a rather predictable Labour M.P.

41. See e.g. my comments in "Commitment in Politics", *Universities & Left Review*, 6, Spring 1959.

42. Alasdair MacIntyre, "Pascal and Marx: on Lucien Goldmann's *Hidden God*", *Against the Self-Images of the Age* (London, 1971), pp. 83–84; and compare M. Godelier on "Structure and Contradiction in *Capital*", *Socialist Register* 1967.

43. There is of course a very large amount of expert analysis by economists, social scientists and political theorists which tends towards the conclusions in the previous paragraphs: especially lucid analysis of certain phenomena have been made by Raymond Williams, Ralph Miliband, Bob Rowthorne, Dorothy Wedderburn, Michael Barratt Brown, notably *From Labourism to Socialism* (The Spokesman Press, 1972), Part I; and in certain sections of the *May Day Manifesto* (1967 & 1968).

44. L.K., "The Fate of Marxism in Eastern Europe", *Slavic Review*, 29, no. 2, June 1970, p. 181.

45. L.K., *Marxism and Beyond*, p. 164.

46. L.K., "On the Meaning of Tradition", *Evergreen Review*, 88, April 1971, p. 44. I find in this article an unduly passive presentation of value-formation. You argue, "tradition is the way in which values are preserved and transmitted". You do not discuss the ways in which in the course of changing life experience new values are formed, nor the operative function of the arts in changing men's values.

47. *Against the Self-Images of the Age*, p. 120.
48. MacIntyre, *Marcuse*, p. 20.
49. *Against the Self-Images of the Age*, pp. 123–4.
50. MacIntyre, "Notes from the Moral Wilderness, II", *New Reasoner*, 8, Spring 1959.
51. It would seem, from the fact that MacIntyre has not republished his "Notes from the Moral Wilderness" nor his "Breaking the Chains of Reason" in *Against the Self-Images of the Age* that he may have lost confidence in these arguments, or in the form in which they were expressed. One appreciates his difficulty: the problems confronted in these pieces were very large, and a thinker as exacting as MacIntyre may well have been dissatisfied with the solutions then proposed. To a historian, however, these essays, together with "Hume on 'is' and 'ought'" (*Against the Self-Images*, pp. 109–124) remain of the first importance, and one hopes that MacIntyre will return to these themes.
52. I find convincing on this L.K., "The Psychoanalytic Theory of Culture", *TriQuarterly*, 22, pp. 68–102; cf. MacIntyre, *Marcuse*, pp. 41–54.
53. L.K., *TriQuarterly*, 22, p. 109.
54. Alasdair MacIntyre, "Breaking the Chains of Reason", *Out of Apathy*, ed. E.P.T. (London, 1960), p. 218.
55. "Notes from the Moral Wilderness, II", *New Reasoner*, 8, Spring 1959, pp. 94–95; "Notes from the Moral Wilderness, I", *New Reasoner*, 7, Winter 1958–9, p. 100.'
56. E. J. Hobsbawm, "Karl Marx's contribution to historiography", *Diogenes* 64, Winter 1968, reprinted in *Ideology in Social Science*, ed. Robin Blackburn (London, 1972).
57. MacIntyre, *Against the Self-Images of the Age*, p. 210.
58. L.K., "On the Meaning of Tradition", *Evergreen Review*, April 1971, p. 43.
59. L.K., "The Myth of Human Self-Identity", passim.
60. L.K., "The Fate of Marxism in Eastern Europe", *Slavic Review*, June 1970, p. 181.
61. See *The Railway*, ed. E.P.T. (London, 1948), passim.
62. Svetozar Stojanovic, *Between Ideals and Reality* (Oxford, 1973), p. 60.
63. Ibid., p. 50.
64. I have argued this more fully in "Peculiarities of the English", *Socialist Register*, 1965; and hope to show the character of Walpole's parasitism in *Whigs and Hunters* (1975).
65. See e.g. C. Wright Mills, *Power, Politics and People*, ed. I. L. Horowitz, (Oxford, 1963), p. 190: "The leaders as well as the led, and even the mythmakers, are influenced by prevailing rhetorics of justification"; L.K., *Marxism and Beyond*, p. 172: "Generally speaking, the growth of hypocrisy is proof of moral progress, for it indicates that what used to be done openly and without fear of censure can no longer be done without incurring that risk."
66. Mihailo Markovic, "Human Nature and Present-day Possibilities of Social Development", *Tolerance and Revolution*, ed. Kurtz and Stojanovic (Beograd, 1970), p. 94.
67. See E.P.T., "Time, Work-Discipline and Industrial Capitalism", *Past and Present*, 38, December 1967.
68. *There is a Spirit in Europe: a Memoir of Frank Thompson* (London, 1947), pp. 20–21.
69. You appear to share this instant dismissal, writing in some preparatory notes for the Reading Conference: "Let us imagine what 'the dictatorship of the proletariat' would mean if the (real, not imaginary) working class took over exclusive political power now in the U.S." The absurdity of the question appears (in your view) to provide its own answer. But I doubt whether you have given to the question a moment of serious historical imagination: you have simply assumed a white working class, socialized by capitalist institutions as it is now, mystified by the mass media as it is now, structured into competitive organizations as it is now, without self-activity or its own forms of political expression:

i.e. a working class with all the attributes of subjection within capitalist structures which one then "imagines" to achieve power without changing either those structures or itself: which is, I fear, a typical example of the fixity of concept which characterizes much capitalist ideology.

70. See especially L.K., "The epistemological significance of the aetiology of knowledge", *TriQuarterly* 22.

71. I assume that you know the reasons for this. If you do not, you and every other prospective contributor to *Encounter* ought to. There is now no excuse for ignorance. Apart from the disclosures in the *New York Times* (27 April 1966) and in several issues of *Ramparts*, there is an outstanding study by Christopher Lasch, "The Cultural Cold War: a Short History of the Congress for Cultural Freedom", in *Towards a New Past*, ed. B. J. Bernstein (New York, 1968) which addresses itself especially to as much of the history of *Encounter* as can be discovered without the use of lie-detectors. See also Conor Cruise O'Brien, *Writers and Politics*, pp. 169–173. Of course, all this has now changed. The subsidy which used to come to *Encounter* from the C.I.A. via the Congress for Cultural Freedom (or via "laundry" Foundations) is now provided by the Ford Foundation: McGeorge Bundy, the President of the latter Foundation, wrote to the *New York Times*, in a letter dated 10 October 1972, confessing that the Ford grant was made in the context of "an interest which has led us also to give help for other notable magazines that also once had C.I.A. support" (e.g. *Survey, China Quarterly*). The grant of $50,000 to *Encounter* was "a good choice within our program purposes".

72. I have studied this pattern (for the 1790s) in E.P.T., "Disenchantment or Default?", *Power and Consciousness*, ed. C. C. O'Brien and W. D. Vanech (London, 1969); and (for the 1930s) in "Outside the Whale" in *Out of Apathy* (London, 1960).

73. Alasdair MacIntyre, "Notes from the Moral Wilderness, I", op. cit. p. 93.

74. From the poem of Thomas McGrath, "In a Season of War".

75. C. Wright Mills, *The Cause of World War Three*, (New York, 1958), pp. 128–9.

A Note on the Texts

The Poverty of Theory has been written for this book. I must thank Philip Corrigan, Alan Dawley, Martin Eve, Julian Harber, Harry Magdoff, Istvan Meszaros and Dorothy Thompson for comments, and Simon Clarke and Derek Sayer for the sight of unpublished essays. I also argued the case against Althusser at a MARHO meeting in New York, a *Radical America* meeting in Boston, and at lectures in New Delhi and Sussex, and thank the audiences for their critical support.

Outside the Whale was first published in *Out of Apathy* (1960), a collection of essays under my editorship by Raphael Samuel, Stuart Hall, Alasdair MacIntyre, Peter Worsley and Ken Alexander. The essay, as published, was severely cut for reasons of space. I have now replaced some passages from the original typescript, but I have also cut out some dated allusions and rhetoric from the final pages of the published version.

The Peculiarities of the English was published in *The Socialist Register*, 1965, edited by Ralph Miliband and John Saville. I have restored a few editorial cuts made in the original text. The essay called forth a lengthy reply from Perry Anderson, "Socialism and Pseudo-Empiricism", *New Left Review*, 35, January-February 1966, pp. 2-42. This essay fell into two parts: i) an impassioned refutation of every one of my criticisms, and ii) a counter-attack against the "vacuity" and "populism" of my own thought. Although this number of *New Left Review* ("Storm over the Left") announced a continuing discussion which "will extend to include many other contributors," this discussion proved to be still-born. 'No-one' came forward in support of my positions, and the Anderson/Nairn positions became the uncontested orthodoxy of the *New Left Review*.

I did not reply to Anderson, for these reasons. First, some of my own political friends made it clear that they regarded me as an aggressor in an unseemly and divisive polemic on the "Left." I don't think that this was so; if there was aggression, then this might equally be seen in the exclusion of many of the *Review's* founders from its pages, and in the tacit rejection of their political positions. But, in any case, theory cannot be developed or tested without *critique,* and critique must involve the direct identification of alternative positions in a polemical manner. If one cares about ideas, it is difficult to write about error (or imputed error) without a certain sharpness of tone. I hope that I have always argued *with reasons.*

I did not reply, in the second place, because I did not find that Anderson's article raised significant new questions; and he did not manage the tone of his polemic well. On the first page I was charged with "paranoia and bad faith". "Virulent travesty and abuse", and "reckless falsification", and such charges were stirred abundantly into the next forty pages, like fish into kedgeree. I am sure that the fish was appetising to many palates, but the rice of historical argument seemed to me to be pulpy re-hashed stuff. The tone was that of one who had been surrounded for too long by too deferential a circle of assent: to question his authority became a matter of scandal.

As to part (1) of Anderson's essay—his response to my criticisms—only three points of interest arise: a) I will agree that neither my theoretical characterisation nor his own of the seventeenth-century bourgeois revolution is adequate. This seems to me to be the weakest place in both our essays. b) It may be true (as he argued) that my account of Gramsci's usages of "hegemony" is inadequate. Undoubtedly he has authority greater than mine on this point. However, the problem to which I direct attention on those pages (pp. 282-4) remains, whichever reading one makes of Gramsci. c) In my own essay I employ the term "model" (as Anderson indicates in passing) in a way which I would now reject. Nevertheless, I think that such implicit "models" may be detected within Anderson, Nairn and much other "Marxist" writing.

As to part (2) of Anderson's essay—the counter-attack upon myself— I think it was best to leave it alone at that time. It was an impressionist's montage, made up of scraps of quotations wrested from their context (chiefly, the "Letter to Readers" column of *The New Reasoner*), in some cases mis-quoted, on other occasions single sentences from two different places run together as one. Within this rather malicious mélange, two significant questions were hidden: first, the question of any Marxist tradition in Britain prior to Anderson, its character and weaknesses, and, second, the question of "socialist populism" and the politics of the first New Left. I have touched on the first question in "The Poverty of Theory." The second question I will discuss in my introduction to the second volume of *Reasoning*.

An Open Letter to Leszek Kolakowski appeared in the *Socialist Register*, 1973. Leszek Kolakowski replied with "My Correct Views on Everything" in the *Socialist Register*, 1974. I can accept one point in his reply—his rejection of my notion of one "Marxist tradition." He asked: "Do you mean that all people who in one way or another call themselves Marxists form a family (never mind that they have been killing each other for half a century and still do) opposed as such to the rest of the world? And that this family is for you (and ought to be for me) a place of identification?" I have now stated this question very differently in "The Poverty of Theory." For the rest, Kolakowski's reply passed over most of my arguments, and was addressed, not to me, but to some German or Californian "New Leftist" of 1968. But I am deeply appreciative of the fact that he did reply; if any notion of Libertarian Communism is to survive the 20th century, it must submit itself to dialogue and exchanges as difficult as this, and even more difficult.